# Judicial Review
# A Practical Guide

## Second Edition

# Judicial Review
# A Practical Guide

Second Edition

Hugh Southey QC

Amanda Weston

Jude Bunting

JORDANS

Published by
Jordan Publishing Limited
21 St Thomas Street
Bristol BS1 6JS

British Library Cataloguing-in-Publication Data

A catalogue record for this book is available from the British Library.

ISBN 978 1 84661 295 4

Typeset by Letterpart Ltd, Reigate, Surrey

Printed in Great Britain by Hobbs the Printers Ltd, Totton, Hampshire

# FOREWORD

In the last half-century or so judicial review of governmental acts and omissions has come from almost nowhere – it didn't even feature in the Bar examinations in the 1960s – to centre-stage in both legal theory and legal practice.

There is a corresponding wealth of books on the doctrines of modern public law; but there remains surprisingly little in the way of practice books. Part of the reason is that this is a field in which practice and theory are almost inseparable. What kind of official or body, for example, is open to judicial review? Where is the interface between policy guidance and individual decision-making? Can a policy be attacked for stultifying decisions? Can a decision be attacked for conforming – or for not conforming – to a policy?

For public administrators and their lawyers the problems are migrainous. For their challengers the possibilities are numerous, but the constraints and obstacles are both real and necessary. Behind the rules and principles lies a network of legal controls, most but not all put in place by the judges. Time limits are very tight; disclosure is not merely a litigant's obligation but a public duty; remedies are discretionary.

There is in addition a unique relationship between the parties, one of which is always, in one guise or another, the state. It is a fundamental principle of the common law that the state comes before the courts on an equal footing with the individual. But this is not the whole story, for in public law litigation the state's object is not, or not necessarily, to win the particular case: it is to ensure that the law is correctly understood and developed. One of the striking features of my 25 years of public law litigation at the Bar was the preparedness of the successive Treasury Devils (from Nigel Bridge to John Laws) to forgo points which might win their case but would distort the law or retard its development. Another was their abstention from taking technical objections – for instance to the introduction of late arguments – unless these placed them in genuine difficulties: once again the object was to get the law straight, not necessarily to win the case.

One consequence of this forensic culture has been, I think, a more principled and less uneven development of modern public law than would otherwise have been the case. That is not to say that there are not anomalies and difficulties; but they tend to arise from the merits of individual cases less often than in some other fields of law. At the same time, public law has attempted – for example in developing the principles of legitimate expectation – to bring law more closely into line with justice. Thus fairness and proportionality tend now to be invoked where quasi-judicial decisions and rationality were once argued.

But it's no use having a good case if your tackle is not in order. The practicalities of judicial review may at times resemble an assault course, but they are logical and, in general, necessary. They are also interwoven with law. In *Judicial Review: A Practical Guide* practitioners on both sides of the fence (as well as the growing band of litigants in person) will find what they need to get their show on the road and to keep it running.

Stephen Sedley
*The Rt Hon Sir Stephen Sedley*
*March 2012*

# PREFACE

Judicial review is the cornerstone of the rule of law in our constitutional system. In particular, it ensures that a powerful executive acts lawfully. That may be more important now than it has ever been.

We are living through a period of extraordinary political conflict. Central government is seeking to introduce highly controversial policies such as reforms to welfare benefits, legal aid and the National Health Service. It is not necessarily unlawful to introduce those policies. However, they must be introduced in a manner that is consistent with the parameters set by Parliament. This is one area where judicial review plays such an important role.

Parts of the media present judicial review as the unelected judiciary undermining the political process. However, this misunderstands judicial review. Parliament has enacted legislation such as the Human Rights Act 1998 and the Equality Act 2010 that restrict the scope of the executive's powers. As a consequence, if the courts hold that government acted unlawfully by failing to comply with that legislation, they are simply enforcing the will of Parliament. The common law has developed to protect fundamental rights and freedoms from the Magna Carta onwards. These are the rights that judicial review upholds.

Judicial review is important because it ensures that controversial policies are genuinely the product of the democratic process and that decisions that affect the lives of individuals and groups are lawful. That is why we wrote this book. We hope that it will help to increase access to judicial review. Judicial review is not straightforward and even experienced lawyers can find it intimidating. This book is intended to act as a handbook for all. We hope that both experienced lawyers and litigants in person will be able to rely on this book to guide them through the process.

We would like to thank all of those who have provided us with support in writing this. Tony and his team at Jordans have worked tirelessly and shown us support and patience for which we are very grateful. Our wonderful colleagues at Tooks Chambers have provided us with ideas and inspiration. Sir Stephen Sedley generously prepared a characteristically eloquent foreword. Our families have put up with late nights and weekend working. Hugh would particularly like to thank Mum, Kate, Rebecca, Orla and Tommy. Amanda would like to thank Joby, Verity, Jojo and Millie for their insights about the importance of speaking truth to power and Catherine Oborne for her able assistance. Jude's work on this book is dedicated to the Great Franko. Finally but most importantly we owe an enormous debt to our partners. Thank you Jackie and Mohamed.

We have attempted to state the law as at 1 January 2012. We have, however, been able to include some subsequent developments.

There are some abbreviations used throughout the book. In particular:

CPR – Civil Procedure Rules 1998 (SI 1998/3132)

HRA – Human Rights Act 1998

Hugh Southey QC
Amanda Weston
Jude Bunting

*March 2012*

# CONTENTS

# TABLE OF CASES

References are to paragraph numbers.

R (Donnachie) v Cardiff Magistrates Court [2007] 1 WLR 3085                                2.3
R (Duka) v Secretary of State for the Home Department [2003] EWHC 1262
    (Admin)                                                                                          8.1
R (Duncan) v General Teaching Council for England [2010] EWHC 429
    (Admin)                                                                                          2.14.2
R (E) v JFS Governing Body [2009] 1 WLR 2353                                                10.2
R (Eastaway) v Secretary of State for Trade and Industry [2001] 1 WLR 2222,
    [2001] 1 All ER 27, [2001] CP Rep 67                              5.9.1, 5.9.2, 9.1.6
R (F) Mongolia v Secretary of State for the Home Department [2007] EWCA Civ
    769, [2007] 1 WLR 2523                                                                     3.3
R (F) v Secretary of State for the Home Department [2011] 1 AC 331                       2.16
R (Faithfull) v Ipswich Crown Court [2008] 1 WLR 1636                                      1.5.3
R (Farrakhan) v Secretary of State for the Home Department [2002] EWCA Civ
    606, [2002] QB 1391, [2002] 3 WLR 481, [2002] UKHRR 734, [2002] 4 All ER
    289, [2002] INLR 257, [2002] Imm AR 447, CA                                      2.14
R (Faulkner) v Secretary of State [2011] EWCA Civ 349                                      8.2.6
R (Ferguson) v Secretary of State for Justice [2011] EWHC 5 (Admin)                    2.8.6
R (Flenley) v Hammersmith and Fulham LBC [2008] EWHC 366 (Admin), [2008]
    JPL 1300                                                                                         2.14.2
R (G) v Barnet London Borough Council; R (W) v Lambeth London Borough
    Council; R (A) v Lambeth London Borough Council [2003] UKHL 57, [2004]
    2 AC 208, [2003] 3 WLR 1194, [2004] 1 FLR 454, [2004] 1 All ER 97, HL         2.11
R (G) v Immigration Appeal Tribunal [2004] EWCA Civ 1731, [2005] 1 WLR 1445       3.3
R (G) v X School Governors [2012] 1 AC 167                                                  2.8.8
R (GC) v Commissioner of the Police for the Metropolis [2011] 1 WLR 1230            1.1
R (Gentle) v Prime Minister [2008] 1 AC 1356                                                1.8
R (Girling) v Parole Board [2007] QB 783                                                     5.11
R (Goldsmith) v London Borough of Wandsworth (2004) CCL Rep 472                     2.11
R (Greenfield) v Secretary of State for the Home Department [2005] UKHL 14,
    [2005] 1 WLR 673, [2005] UKHRR 323                                      8.1.1, 8.2.6
R (Greenpeace Ltd) v Secretary of State for Trade and Industry [2007] Env LR
    623                                                                                              2.8.5
R (Grierson) v The Office of Communication [2005] EWHC 1899 (Admin)                5.8
R (Guardian News and Media Ltd) v City of Westminster Magistrates Court [2011]
    EWCA Civ 1188, [2011] 1 WLR 3253, [2011] 43 LS Gaz R 21, [2011] All ER
    (D) 207 (Oct)                                                                     3.4.3, 5.13.3
R (Gunn) v Secretary of State for the Home Department [2001] EWCA Civ 891,
    [2001] 1 WLR 1634, [2001] 3 All ER 481, [2001] CP Rep 107, CA                 10.4
R (H) v Ashworth Hospital Authority [2003] 1 WLR 127                                      7.4
R (Hardy) v Pembrokeshire County Council [2006] EWCA Civ 240, [2006] Env LR
    38                                                                                               3.1.1
R (Hasan) v Secretary of State for Trade and Industry [2008] EWCA Civ
    1311,[2009] 3 All ER 539                                                                    2.14
R (Hirst) v Secretary of State for the Home Department and Another [2002]
    EWHC 602 (Admin), [2002] 1 WLR 2929, [2002] UKHRR 758, QBD              2.16
R (Howard League for Penal Reform) v Secretary of State for the Home
    Department [2003] 1 FLR 484                                                              10.2
R (Hunt) v Criminal Cases Review Commission [2001] QB 1108, [2001] 2 WLR
    319, [2000] STC 1110, QBD                                                                 5.8
R (I-Cd Publishing Ltd) v Secretary of State & The Information Commissioner,
    Interested Party [2003] EWHC 1761 (Admin), [2003] ACD 98, [2003] All ER
    (D) 343 (Jul)                                                                                    3.1.1
R (Interbrew SA) v Competition Commission [2001] EWHC 367 (Admin)                 2.10
R (International Transport Roth Gmbh) v Secretary of State for the Home
    Department [2002] EWCA Civ 158, [2003] QB 728, [2002] 3 WLR 344, [2002]
    1 CMLR 52, CA                                                                               3.4.3
R (Jarrett) v Legal Services Commission [2001] EWHC 389 (Admin), [2002] ACD
    25                                                                                               2.8.8
R (K) v Secretary of State for the Home Department [2010] EWHC 3102
    (Admin)                                                                                          2.6.1

# TABLE OF STATUTES

References are to paragraph numbers.

# TABLE OF STATUTORY INSTRUMENTS

References are to paragraph numbers.

# TABLE OF EUROPEAN AND INTERNATIONAL MATERIAL

References are to paragraph numbers.

# PART I

## LAW AND PRACTICE

# CHAPTER 1

## THE SCOPE OF THE HIGH COURT'S JURISDICTION TO CONSIDER CLAIMS FOR JUDICIAL REVIEW

### 1.1 WHY IS JUDICIAL REVIEW IMPORTANT?

The United Kingdom's system of government confers upon the legislature, the executive and the courts different powers and responsibilities. That does not mean, however, that there is no overlap.[1] The court plays an important role in overseeing that the executive and, to a lesser extent, the legislature do not overstep their powers. Judicial review is usually the form of proceedings that enables the courts to intervene. It is, in the words of Mr Justice Sedley, intended 'to ensure that government is conducted within the law'.[2]

Over the last few years judicial review has been a growth area of litigation. There have been some indications that the growth has stalled as a consequence of steps taken to reduce the demands placed upon the Administrative Court.[3] However, the subjective view of most practitioners appears to be that judicial review will continue to grow.

One reason for that increase in judicial review claims is likely to be the increasing role of government in regulating many areas of life. Public bodies take a vast number of decisions that affect all our lives. Decisions vary in a number of ways. For example, decisions such as whether or not to develop new airports impact on huge numbers of people whilst other decisions such as a decision regarding benefit entitlement may affect a single individual. There are a large number of other variables.

Decisions regarding public expenditure are often highly political whilst those, for example, regarding the prosecution of an alleged criminal are not. We could continue to identify other factors that vary. However, one

---

[1] See Lord Hoffmann 'The Combar Lecture 2001: Separation of Powers' [2002] JR 137.
[2] *R v Secretary of State for Transport ex p London Borough of Richmond Upon Thames (No 3)* [1995] Env LR 409.
[3] A comparison of the Court Service annual reports for 2009–2010 and 2010–2011 shows a fall in the number of cases before the Administrative Court from 17,065 to about 12,000. That has, however, been explained in meetings of the Administrative Court users group as being the result of proceedings other than judicial review claims being transferred out of the Court's jurisdiction.

factor that is common to these decisions is that judicial review will normally be the correct procedure to challenge them.

The increase in government regulation means that all practitioners should be aware of the availability of judicial review proceedings. Although practitioners in areas such as immigration, planning and crime are experienced in judicial review, it can be relevant to every practitioner. For example, a personal injury lawyer may wish to challenge a decision to refuse exceptional public funding for his client. Judicial review would be the correct procedure.[4]

The increased role of human rights law has also contributed to an increase in the number of claims for judicial review. The HRA 1998 places the primary responsibility to respect rights under the European Convention on Human Rights on public authorities.[5] As a consequence, many of the most important cases regarding human rights have been judicial review cases. European Union law has also had an impact on the numbers of claims coming to the Administrative Court as has the introduction of public sector equality duties.[6]

In some ways it is not very helpful to provide examples of successful judicial review claims. Judicial review potentially permits challenges to such a wide range of decisions and contexts that it is more helpful to consider whether first principles mean that a decision may be challenged by way of judicial review. However, examples of successful claims do provide some idea of the scope of judicial review. Examples of recent claims that have been brought by way of judicial review and decided by the Supreme Court include:

(a)   a challenge to the police policy regarding the retention of DNA taken from persons arrested;[7]

(b)   a challenge to a refusal to pay compensation following a miscarriage of justice;[8]

(c)   a challenge to a policy adopted regarding the reclaiming of overpaid benefits;[9] and

(d)   a challenge arguing that the policy of preventing asylum seekers working was contrary to European Union law.[10]

---

4    Legal Services Commission decisions can be challenged by way of judicial review. See, for example, *R (Burrows (t/a David Burrows (a firm)) v Legal Services Commission* [2001] 2 FLR 998.
5    HRA 1998, s 6.
6    See, now, Equality Act 2010, s 149.
7    *R (GC) v Commissioner of the Police for the Metropolis* [2011] 1 WLR 1230.
8    *R (Adams) v Secretary of State* [2012] 1 AC 48.
9    *R (CPAG) v Secretary of State* [2011] 2 AC 15.
10   *R (ZO (Somalia)) v Secretary of State* [2010] 1 WLR 1948.

This limited list of examples shows that both a wide range of decision-makers may be challenged and also a wide range of individuals may wish to bring challenges. These matters are considered in greater detail later.

## 1.2 WHAT IS JUDICIAL REVIEW?

The High Court has a statutory jurisdiction to consider claims for judicial review.[11] The statutory provisions that give rise to the jurisdiction to consider claims for judicial review do not, however, define its scope. Instead, it is case law which has held that judicial review proceedings are public law proceedings that enable the High Court to control the decisions of public bodies and courts. It is not a jurisdiction that allows the High Court to intervene merely because it disagrees with the decision of the public body or court. Instead, it is 'a remedy invented by the judges to restrain the excess or abuse of power'[12] and 'secure that decisions are made by the executive or by a public body according to law'.[13] This means, for example, that the High Court is very reluctant to consider judicial review claims that require it to substitute its own findings of fact for those of the initial decision-maker.[14]

There are several important limitations on the scope of judicial review, which are considered later in this chapter. First, the court needs to be satisfied that a claimant has sufficient standing to bring a claim for judicial review. In addition, the court needs to be satisfied that the decision-maker is a person or body that can be subject to judicial review proceedings. Finally, the court needs to be satisfied that the decision is a public law decision.

## 1.3 IMPACT OF THE CIVIL JUSTICE REFORMS ON THE LANGUAGE OF JUDICIAL REVIEW

The Woolf reforms to civil justice have had a significant impact on judicial review. The resulting changes to this procedure will be considered later in this book. However, at this stage it is important to note the changes in language that have resulted because many of the reports cited will use language different from that used in this book. Important changes are set out below:

---

[11] Senior Courts Act 1981, ss 29 and 31.
[12] *R v Secretary of State for the Home Department ex p Brind* [1991] 1 AC 696, per Lord Templeman, at 751B.
[13] *Mercury Energy Ltd v Electricity Corporation of New Zealand Ltd* [1994] 1 WLR 521, per Lord Templeman, at 526A.
[14] See, for example, *R v Hillingdon London Borough Council ex p Puhlofer* [1986] AC 484, per Lord Brightman, at 518E, HL and *R v Secretary of State for the Home Department ex p Brind* [1991] 1 AC 696, per Lord Brightman, at 751B. This approach has relaxed to some extent (see, for example *R (Al Sweady) v Secretary of State* [2010] HRLR 2, at [18]. This matter will be considered in greater detail in Chapter 2.

| *Old language* | *New language* |
|---|---|
| Crown Office | Administrative Court[15] |
| Applicant | Claimant |
| Respondent | Defendant |
| Form 86a | Claim form |
| Ex parte hearing | Hearing without notice |
| Application for leave to move for judicial review | Application for permission to apply for judicial review |

The nomenclature of cases has also changed. In the past, judicial review proceedings were called *R v Respondent ex p Applicant*. Judicial review proceedings are now called *R (Claimant) v Defendant*.

## 1.4 WHO MAY APPLY FOR JUDICIAL REVIEW?

### 1.4.1 Challenges under domestic law

Claimants in claims for judicial review need to show that they have sufficient standing. In cases that do not raise issues under the HRA 1998, the limitation on standing is that contained in s 31(3) of the Senior Courts Act 1981, which provides:

> 'No application for judicial review shall be made unless the leave[16] of the High Court has been obtained in accordance with rules of court; and the court shall not grant leave to make such an application unless it considers that the applicant has a *sufficient interest* in the matter to which the application relates.' [emphasis added]

In many cases it will be obvious that a person has sufficient interest. For example, there can be no argument that a person convicted of a criminal offence has insufficient interest in challenging the decision of the magistrates' court to convict him. Similarly, there can be no argument that an asylum seeker has insufficient interest in challenging a decision to refuse his asylum claim. There are, however, more difficult cases that arise when a person wishes to challenge a decision that has no direct impact on him.

It is clear that the requirement that a person must have 'sufficient interest' is less restrictive than the requirement that a person must be 'aggrieved', which was the test previously used when considering applications for the prerogative orders, the form of proceedings from which judicial review developed.[17] This means that the courts have taken 'an increasingly liberal

---

[15] The Administrative Court is formally part of the High Court. However, it has its own offices and functions as a separate court that considers claims for judicial review.

[16] Note the use of the phrase 'leave'. As noted above, that is the old language.

[17] *Cook v Southend Borough Council* [1990] 2 QB 1, at 8B.

approach to standing'.[18] That is partly because the courts are keen to ensure that there is someone with sufficient standing to challenge an unlawful decision of a public body.[19]

The leading case on standing is probably *Inland Revenue Commissioners v National Federation of Self-Employed and Small Businesses Ltd.*[20] A group representing taxpayers sought to challenge an amnesty granted to other taxpayers. The House of Lords held that in most cases the issue of standing should not be determined as a preliminary issue because a court needs to consider the legal and factual background to the challenge when determining standing. The House applied that approach and concluded that the taxpayers lacked sufficient standing to challenge tax decisions regarding other taxpayers.

One theme that is clear from subsequent decisions is that the courts are concerned to prevent challenges by busybodies or others whose interest might be described as quixotic. Thus, the Divisional Court was unwilling to permit a client to challenge a decision by the Legal Aid Board regarding the assessment of a solicitor's fees.[21]

However, although a person applying for judicial review should not be a busybody, he does not need to be the most obvious challenger. For example, the courts have been willing to consider a challenge to restrictions on the broadcasting of statements made by representatives of Northern Irish groups brought by journalists instead of those whose statements could not be broadcast.[22]

The fact that a person need not be the most obvious challenger is also consistent with the fact that he need not have a financial or legal interest in the decision being challenged.[23] However, it is highly unlikely that a person with a financial or legal interest lacks sufficient interest.

The liberal approach to standing has resulted in the courts accepting that, in some circumstances, the public at large has sufficient standing. For example, Mr Justice Sedley held that:[24]

---

[18]  *R v Secretary of State for Foreign and Commonwealth Affairs ex p World Development Movement Ltd* [1995] 1 WLR 386, per Lord Justice Rose, at 395F.

[19]  *R (Bulger) v Secretary of State for the Home Department* [2001] 3 All ER 449, at [20].

[20]  [1982] AC 617.

[21]  See, for example, *R v Legal Aid Board ex p Bateman* [1992] 1 WLR 711, per Lord Justice Nolan, at 718C.

[22]  *R v Secretary of State for the Home Department ex p Brind* [1991] 1 AC 696.

[23]  See, for example, *R v Secretary of State for the Environment ex p Rose Theatre Trust Co* [1990] 1 QB 504, per Mr Justice Schiemann, at 520D.

[24]  *R v Somerset County Council and ARC Sourthern Ltd ex p Dixon* [1997] COD 323, at 328, in which Mr Justice Sedley held that a person who was, amongst other roles, a local resident, a parish councillor and a member of environmental group, had sufficient standing to bring a judicial review of a planning decision.

'[T]here will be, in public life, a certain number of cases of apparent abuse of power in which any individual, simply as a citizen, has a sufficient interest to bring the matter before the court.'

The approach of Mr Justice Sedley is consistent with the fact that the courts have been willing to permit challenges by pressure groups who claim only to represent the public interest. Indeed the judgments describe these litigants as 'public interest' claimants.[25] One reason why the courts have been willing to permit these public interest challenges is that they recognise that there are decisions that may not otherwise be challenged as a consequence of the likely absence of any alternative challenger.[26] Presumably, however, 'public interest' claimants can challenge only decisions that raise issues of general importance.[27] The courts will also be keen to ensure that claimants do not amalgamate to defeat arguments that the individual members of the group lack standing.[28]

Groups wishing to apply for judicial review should be aware that there has been some suggestion in the cases that an unincorporated association lacks the capacity to apply for judicial review.[29] Mr Justice Richards considered this issue and concluded that the objection to unincorporated associations was the risk that successful defendants could not recover their costs. He suggested that the solution to this problem was to ensure that a legal person is joined as a party when permission to apply for judicial review is granted.[30]

### 1.4.2 Considerations that arise in challenges under the Human Rights Act 1998

The HRA 1998 contains different restrictions on standing. Section 7 provides, so far as is relevant for this chapter:

'(1) A person who claims that a public authority has acted (or proposes to act) in a way which is made unlawful by ... may –
(a)   bring proceedings against the authority under this Act in the appropriate court or tribunal, or

---

[25]   *R v Secretary of State for Trade and Industry ex p Greenpeace Ltd* [2000] 2 CMLR 94, at [70].

[26]   *R v Secretary of State for Foreign and Commonwealth Affairs ex p World Development Movement Ltd* [1995] 1 WLR 386.

[27]   In *R v Lord Chancellor ex p Child Poverty Action Group* [1999] 1 WLR 347, Mr Justice Dyson appeared to suggest a link between the nature of a claim and the justification for a person bringing a claim despite the absence of any direct interest in the outcome.

[28]   *R v Secretary of State for the Environment ex p Rose Theatre Trust Co* [1990] 1 QB 504, at 521.

[29]   See, for example, *R v Darlington Borough Council ex p Association of Darlington Taxi Owners* [1994] COD 424.

[30]   *R v Ministry of Agriculture, Fisheries and Food ex p British Pig Industry Support Group* [2001] ACD 3.

(b)   rely on the Convention right or rights concerned in any legal proceedings, but only if he is (or would be) *a victim* of the unlawful act.

...

(3) If the proceedings are brought on an application for judicial review, the applicant is to be taken to have a sufficient interest in relation to the unlawful act only if he is, or would be, a victim of that act.

...

(7) For the purposes of this section, a person is a victim of an unlawful act only if he would be a victim for the purposes of Article 34 of the Convention if proceedings were brought in the European Court of Human Rights in respect of that act [emphasis added].'

Article 34 of the European Convention on Human Rights merely provides that it is only a 'victim' of a human rights violation who may bring proceedings in the European Court of Human Rights and so it provides little guidance on the meaning of s 7 of the HRA 1998. It is generally accepted that this test means that there will be people who have standing to bring claims for judicial review but who lack standing under the HRA 1998.[31]

To date, there has been little domestic case-law considering the correct approach to s 7 of the HRA 1998. Possibly the leading case is *Lancashire CC v Taylor*.[32] In that case the Court of Appeal concluded that a party to litigation was not a victim because they have 'not been and could not be personally adversely affected' by the relevant legislation.[33]

The lack of domestic law means that it is necessary to consider the decisions of the European Court of Human Rights. The European Court has expressly recognised that its own rules regarding standing are not necessarily the same as those governing domestic courts.[34]

Unsurprisingly, the decision of the Court of Appeal in *Lancashire CC v Taylor*[35] is consistent with the decisions of the European Court. Those decisions suggest that a person must be directly affected by an alleged violation of human rights. It is not sufficient for a person to argue in the abstract that a law violates the European Convention.[36] In practice this means that although bodies such as trade unions may claim to be victims

---

[31]   For example, a public authority cannot be a victim; *see R (Medway Council v Secretary of State for Transport)* [2003] JPL 583, at [20].
[32]   [2005] 1 WLR 2668.
[33]   Ibid, at 2679D.
[34]   *Norris v Ireland* (1991) 13 EHRR 186, at [31].
[35]   [2005] 1 WLR 2668.
[36]   *X v Austria* 7 DR 87.

if their rights have been interfered with,[37] they cannot claim to be victims because they represent individuals who have suffered an interference with their rights.[38] For example, in *Adams v Lord Advocate*,[39] a number of claimants sought to challenge legislation of the Scottish Parliament that sought to ban hunting by hounds. Lord Nimmo Smith held that pressure groups such as the Countryside Alliance, which did not consist exclusively of members who hunted in Scotland and had some members who merely supported hunting, lacked sufficient standing to bring a claim for judicial review because the groups could not show that all their members were victims. However, presumably the Countryside Alliance were able to claim that they would have been victims if legislation had been introduced restricting their activities. The particular conclusion reached in *Adams* may be questionable in light of *R (Countryside Alliance) v Attorney General*[40] in which there was no challenge in similar circumstances.

Companies have been held to be victims under Art 34 of the Convention even if they have been struck off the official register of companies.[41] However, there may be problems if the shareholders of a company seek to bring proceedings in relation to the company's rights.[42] Similarly, non-governmental organisations[43] and churches[44] have been held to be victims. In cases where bodies such as churches have been held to be victims, it is because their rights have been interfered with and not because the rights of their members have been interfered with.

Although a person must show that he is a victim, that does not necessarily mean that he needs to show that a law challenged has actually been enforced against him. For example, in *Norris v Ireland*,[45] the applicant to the European Court complained about Irish legislation criminalising certain homosexual activity. The respondent government argued that the applicant could not claim to be a victim as he had never been prosecuted under the legislation in question. The European Court held that the applicant was a victim as he could 'therefore be said to "run the risk of being directly affected" by the legislation in question'.[46]

As with the domestic courts, the European Court does appear to have been concerned on occasion that the requirement for a victim should not prevent cases being brought to its attention. Applications to the European

---

[37]   *Council of Civil Service Unions v United Kingdom* 50 DR 228.
[38]   *Purcell v Ireland* 70 DR 262.
[39]   [2002] UKHRR 1189.
[40]   [2007] QB 305, at 349D–349E.
[41]   *Pine Valley Developments Ltd and Others v Ireland* (1991) 14 EHRR 319.
[42]   In *Agrotexim v Greece* (1996) 21 EHRR 250 the European Court of Human Rights refused to consider a complaint by shareholders as the liquidators were able to assert the rights of the company.
[43]   *Open Door Counselling Ltd v Ireland* (1992) 15 EHRR 244.
[44]   *Canea Catholic Church Ltd v Greece* (1999) 27 EHRR 521.
[45]   (1991) 13 EHRR 186.
[46]   Ibid, at para 33.

Court cannot be made in the name of deceased victims. As a consequence, the European Court has been willing to consider cases brought by the next of kin of deceased victims.[47] Similarly, in cases involving secret security measures the European Court has recognised that it may be sufficient that a victim can point to the legislation permitting those measures.[48] The Court was concerned that a person might otherwise be denied remedies for a violation of his rights by reason of a lack of knowledge of a violation.[49]

One issue that appears to remain unclear is whether a person who has standing to apply for judicial review but is not a 'victim' can rely on the European Convention. Before the European Convention was incorporated into domestic law by the HRA 1998, it was possible to rely on the European Convention in judicial review proceedings. For example, there were dicta suggesting that the scope of the common law could be interpreted by reference to the European Convention.[50] It would appear that there can be no objection to a person who has brought judicial review proceedings but who is not a 'victim' seeking to rely on the European Convention as an aid to determining the scope of the common law if their challenge is that a decision is unlawful on the basis that it violates the common law. Similarly, there would appear to be no reason why common law rights (such as the right of access to a court[51]) cannot be relied upon by a person who is not a 'victim' for the purposes of the HRA 1998.

## 1.5 WHOSE DECISIONS MAY BE CHALLENGED?

### 1.5.1 Challenges under the common law

As noted above, judicial review is concerned with the decisions of public bodies (including individuals such as ministers of the state who have public law responsibilities and duties). The fact that a body is acting or has acted in an unlawful manner does not necessarily mean that it is possible to apply for judicial review. It must be shown that the body is public. Sometimes this will be obvious: for example, a government department or minister is plainly a public body. However, more difficult questions arise. For example, is an organisation a public body if it exercises regulatory functions in a particular field because those who operate in that field agree to be regulated?

Historically, the approach of the courts was to consider the source of a body's powers. Statutory bodies were generally regarded as being subject to judicial review. Other bodies were not. However, the approach of the

---

[47] See, for example, *Yasa v Turkey* (1999) 28 EHRR 408.
[48] *Klass v Germany* (1979–1980) 2 EHRR 214.
[49] Ibid, at [36].
[50] See, for example, *R v Mid Glamorgan Family Health Services ex p Martin* [1995] 1 WLR 110, per Lord Justice Evans, at 118H.
[51] See, for example, *R v Lord Chancellor ex p Witham* [1998] QB 575.

courts has developed so that they are now much more concerned with the nature of a body's functions. For example, Lord Oliver has held:[52]

> 'In my judgment, the susceptibility of a decision to the supervision of the courts must depend, in the ultimate analysis, upon the nature and consequences of the decision and not upon the personality or individual circumstances of the person called upon to make the decision.'

Authority has established that a body that has no statutory origin may be subject to judicial review if its functions are public in nature. This reflects the increasing use of non-statutory, private bodies to carry out public functions. For example, in *R v Panel on Takeovers and Mergers ex p Datafin plc*,[53] the Court of Appeal considered a challenge to a decision of an unincorporated association that derived its powers from the voluntary agreement of city financial institutions that they should be subject to self-regulation. The Court relied on matters such as the fact that the association was performing an important public duty, the fact that one motive for establishing the association was a concern that the absence of self-regulation could result in external government regulation and the inability of the claimants to obtain any private law remedy to hold that the Court had jurisdiction. In particular, Sir John Donaldson MR remarked:[54]

> '[The defendant's] source of power is only partly based upon moral persuasion and the assent of institutions and their members, the bottom line being the statutory powers exercised by the Department of Trade and Industry and the Bank of England. In this context I should be very disappointed if the courts could not recognise the realities of executive power and allowed their vision to be clouded by the subtlety and sometimes complexity of the way in which it can be exerted.'

The remarks of Sir John Donaldson MR have resulted in the courts subsequently placing significant weight on whether the absence of self-regulation would result in government regulation when determining whether a body is a public body for the purposes of judicial review. For example, advertising is something that the Director General of Fair Trading would wish to regulate if the Advertising Standards Authority did not exist. As a consequence, the Advertising Standards Authority is a public body.[55] In contrast, football is merely a form of public entertainment and so not an activity that the government would wish to regulate if the Football Association did not regulate it. As a consequence,

---

[52] *Leech v Deputy Governor of Parkhurst Prison* [1988] AC 533, at 583B–583C.
[53] [1987] QB 815.
[54] Ibid, at 838–839.
[55] *R v Advertising Standards Authority ex p Insurance Services* [1990] 2 Admin LR 77.

the Football Association is not subject to judicial review.[56] Similarly, Lloyd's of London is not subject to judicial review as the source of its powers is contractual.[57]

The fact that a body operates in a field in which government regulation would be inevitable were it not for self-regulation is closely related to another factor. It is of significance whether those subject to the decisions of a body submit voluntarily or under some form of compulsion. In cases in which self-regulation is accepted to avoid government regulation, there is in practice an element of compulsion to accept the self-regulation. However, in other circumstances there is no element of compulsion. If there is no element of compulsion, the decision-making body should not be regarded as a public body whose decisions are subject to judicial review jurisdiction. For example, decisions of the London Beth Din (the Court of the Chief Rabbi) are not subject to judicial review as there is no element of compulsion in its jurisdiction.[58]

There may be a limited exception to the requirement that there must be an element of compulsion in a body's jurisdiction before it can be subject to judicial review proceedings. It has been suggested that judicial review may be available if a body acts in breach of the terms of its royal charter or some similar document.[59] Presumably, it might be argued that the charter imposes public law restrictions upon a body that is subject to it.

The availability of private law remedies is a significant factor in determining whether a body is a public body for the purposes of judicial review. It is not the mere fact that private law remedies may be sought against a body that matters. Public bodies can be subject to private law actions. For example, a public body may act unlawfully towards an employee. If that happens then private law proceedings may normally be brought.[60] What will normally be determinative is whether private law remedies are available to correct illegal acts when a body is performing what might be regarded as public duties. De Smith, Woolf and Jowell comment that where a contract exists, a contractual claim will normally be an appropriate remedy that may bar judicial review.[61]

---

[56]   *R v Football Association Ltd ex p Football League Ltd* [1993] 2 All ER 833.
[57]   *R v Lloyd's of London ex p Briggs* [1993] 1 Lloyd's Rep 176, confirmed in *R (West) v Lloyd's of London* [2004] 3 All ER 251.
[58]   *R v London Beth Din ex p Bloom* [1998] COD 131.
[59]   *R v Disciplinary Committee of the Jockey Club ex p Aga Khan* [1993] 1 WLR 909, at 930E–930F, considered in *R v London Beth Din ex p Bloom* [1998] COD 131.
[60]   See, for example, *R v BBC ex p Lavelle* [1983] 1 WLR 23. See **1.6**, as not all employment decisions are private law matters.
[61]   De Smith, Woolf and Jowell *Judicial Review of Administrative Action* (Sweet & Maxwell, 6th revised edn, 2007), at [3-059].

Factors that are not relevant to whether a body is a public body are the fact that the decisions of the body have serious implications for those who are subject to them or the fact that the body might play an important role in public life.[62]

### 1.5.2 Where challenges raise the Human Rights Act 1998

Section 6 of the HRA 1998 provides, so far as is relevant for this chapter:

'(1) It is unlawful for a public authority to act in a way which is incompatible with a Convention right.

...

(3) In this section "public authority" includes –
(a) a court or tribunal, and
(b) any person certain of whose functions are functions of a public nature, but does not include either House of Parliament or a person exercising functions in connection with proceedings in Parliament.'

It is clear that s 6 of the HRA 1998 recognises that bodies may perform both public and private functions. This was acknowledged by the Government during debate upon the HRA 1998. It identified Railtrack as a body with both public and private functions: its role in ensuring the safe operation of the railway network is public in nature, while its role in acquiring property is private.[63] Essentially, there are core public authorities whose role is always public and other bodies who sometimes carry out public functions.

The fact that core public authorities are unable to bring proceedings under the HRA 1998 means that the courts should be reluctant to hold that bodies are core public authorities.[64]

The definition of a 'public authority' contained in s 6 raises issues that are similar to those that arise when the court considers whether a body is subject to judicial review. However, the issues are not identical. As the consequence, the case law regarding that issue is relevant but not determinative.[65]

The leading authority regarding s 6 is probably *L v Birmingham City Council*.[66] This makes it clear that s 6 should be interpreted purposively. As a consequence, the primary issue is whether a body is of such a nature that its actions would engage the responsibility of the United Kingdom

---

[62] See, for example, *R v Football Association Ltd ex p Football League Ltd* [1993] 2 All ER 833.
[63] Lord Williams in HL Deb, *Hansard*, col 1310 (3 November 1997).
[64] *Parochial Church Council of Aston Cantlow v Walbank* [2004] 1 AC 546, at 554D–554F.
[65] *YL v Birmingham City Council* [2008] 1 AC 95, at 126B.
[66] [2008] 1 AC 95.

before the European Court of Human Rights.[67] Factors identified by the court as relevant included the existence and source of any special powers,[68] democratic accountability, public funding in whole or in part, an obligation to act only in the public interest and a statutory constitution.[69]

Applying the principles identified in the paragraph above, a majority of the House of Lords concluded that a privately operated care home was not a public authority and was not carrying out functions of a public nature when providing places for persons whose places were public funded. Essentially, the majority concluded that the care home was in the same position when it was providing care to publicly and privately funded individuals.[70] As it was not a body carrying out public functions when it was providing services to privately funded residents, the same must apply in respect of its publicly funded residents.[71]

Although s 6 of the HRA 1998 provides that a court is a public authority, it cannot necessarily be relied on by a claimant to argue that the court is obliged to hold that a body which is not a 'public authority' within the terms of s 6 is liable for a violation of a person's rights.[72]

### 1.5.3 Considerations arising when a decision of a court is challenged

Some decisions of courts can be challenged by way of judicial review. However, not every court's decision is amenable to challenge. Essentially, the Administrative Court can consider only challenges to decisions of inferior courts. Thus, decisions of High Court judges when sitting as such are not open to challenge.[73] This is true even if the High Court judge is not actually sitting in court, provided that he is exercising his function as a High Court judge.[74] However, if acting in some other capacity, the High Court judge may be subject to challenge.[75]

---

[67]  Ibid, at 126B.
[68]  Ibid, at 132C–132D.
[69]  Ibid, at 132F–132G.
[70]  Ibid, at 138H–139C.
[71]  Ibid, at 139D–139F.
[72]  *Royal Society for the Prevention of Cruelty to Animals v Attorney General and others* [2002] 1 WLR 448, at 465D–465E.
[73]  *R v Secretary of State for the Home Department ex p Bulger* [2001] 3 All ER 449, at [13].
[74]  See, for example, *R v Manchester Crown Court ex p Williams and Simpson* (1990) 2 Admin LR 817, holding that a decision of a High Court judge to prefer a voluntary bill of indictment is not subject to judicial review as the statute that provides the power expressly confers the power on a High Court judge.
[75]  See, for example, *R v Secretary of State for the Home Department and the Parole Board ex p Norney* (1995) 7 Admin LR 861, in which a decision of a High Court judge sitting as Chairman of the Parole Board was challenged, and *R (Woolas) v Parliamentary Election Court* [2011] 2 WLR 1362, in which the Administrative Court held that a Parliamentary Election Court, presided over by two High Court judges, was amenable to judicial review.

County courts are clearly inferior courts. There is express recognition in ss 83–84 of the County Courts Act 1984 that county courts can be subject to judicial review proceedings.[76] In practice, however, it will often be inappropriate to apply for judicial review as a right of appeal will provide an alternative remedy.[77] An alternative remedy will often mean that the Administrative Court is unwilling to consider a claim for judicial review.[78]

Similarly, the Administrative Court has a statutory jurisdiction to consider judicial review challenges to decisions of a magistrates' court.[79] Although there is often a right of appeal from the magistrates' court to the Crown Court, that right of appeal does not necessarily mean that that the Administrative Court will reject a claim for judicial review.[80] The reasons why it is possible to challenge decisions of magistrates' courts but not the decisions of many other inferior courts or tribunals are considered in detail later.[81]

Particular considerations arise when a claimant wishes to challenge a decision of the Crown Court. In addition, the recent establishment of tribunals that have the status of being a court of record has also given rise to particular considerations. These matters are considered in detail below.

### Decisions of the Crown Court

The jurisdiction of the Administrative Court to consider applications for judicial review from decisions of the Crown Court is governed by s 29(3) of the Senior Courts Act 1981. It provides that judicial review can be used to challenge all decisions of the Crown Court other than 'matters relating to trial on indictment'. The Administrative Court has rejected arguments that it has an inherent jurisdiction to consider judicial reviews of decisions of the Crown Court that would otherwise be excluded from the scope of judicial review by s 29(3) of the Senior Courts Act 1981.[82]

Clearly, there are some matters that do not relate to a trial on indictment, because no indictment is involved in the proceedings. For example, judicial review may be used to challenge the decisions of the Crown Court while exercising its jurisdiction to consider appeals from the magistrates'

---

[76]   *R v Leeds County Court ex p Morris* [1990] 1 QB 523.
[77]   *R (Sivasubramaniam) v Wandsworth County Court* [2003] 1 WLR 475.
[78]   See **3.3**.
[79]   Senior Courts Act 1981, ss 29 and 31.
[80]   *R v Hereford Magistrates' Court ex p Rowlands and Ingram*; *R v Harrow Youth Court ex p Prussia* [1998] QB 110.
[81]   See **3.3**.
[82]   *R v Chelmsford Crown Court ex p Chief Constable of the Essex Police* [1994] 1 WLR 359 but compare with *R v Maidstone Crown Court ex p Harrow London Borough Council* [2000] QB 719 in which the court held that there might be a judicial review challenging a lack of jurisdiction in circumstances where the challenge might be said to relate to trial on indictment.

court.[83] Similarly, a decision to refuse legal help in an application to remove a disqualification from driving is also subject to challenge in the Administrative Court.[84] There are other matters that clearly cannot be challenged in the Administrative Court, such as conviction and sentence on a matter committed to the Crown Court for trial on indictment. In this context, the term 'trial' includes proceedings where a defendant pleads guilty to an indictment.[85] It also covers pre-trial hearings where no jury is sworn.[86]

When the Crown Court makes a decision that is ancillary to proceedings on indictment, it can be difficult to determine whether the Administrative Court has jurisdiction to consider the matter. For example, is it possible to challenge decisions made by the Crown Court that relate to legal aid in a case being tried on indictment?

The House of Lords has considered the scope of the Administrative Court's jurisdiction to review the Crown Court on a number of occasions. Their Lordships have declined to define the statutory phrases used to limit the jurisdiction of the Administrative Court.[87] They have, however, stated that if a decision of the Crown Court is one affecting the conduct of a trial on indictment given in the course of the trial or by way of pre-trial directions, it cannot be challenged by judicial review.[88] If such a decision occurs, an aggrieved defendant normally has the opportunity to appeal to the Court of Appeal under the Criminal Appeal Act 1968. For example, a decision to refuse to grant legal aid has been held to be a matter that relates to a trial on indictment.[89] This is not surprising, because the Court of Appeal has held that it is entitled to quash a defendant's conviction where it is rendered unsafe by a trial judge's decision regarding legal help.[90]

The absence of a right of appeal to the Court of Appeal does not necessarily mean that the Administrative Court will accept jurisdiction. For example, the Court has no jurisdiction to consider a challenge to a decision to refuse to order costs after acquittal.[91] This is because the statutory limit on the jurisdiction of the Court means that matters relating to a trial on indictment include orders made at the conclusion of a trial on indictment, if these orders are an integral part of the trial process.[92] Orders are an integral part of the trial process if they are based

---

[83]   *R v Bournemouth Crown Court ex p Weight* [1984] 1 WLR 980.

[84]   *R v Recorder of Liverpool ex p McCann* [1995] RTR 23.

[85]   *Re Smalley* [1985] AC 622.

[86]   *R v Harrow Crown Court ex p Perkins* (1998) *The Times*, April 28.

[87]   *Re Smalley* [1985] AC 622, per Lord Bridge, at 643H.

[88]   Ibid. See also *Re Ashton* [1994] 1 AC 9, at 15D–15F, 20C, and 21H–22A.

[89]   *R v Chichester Crown Court ex p Abodunrin* (1984) 79 Cr App R 293.

[90]   *R v Kirk* (1983) 76 Cr App R 194.

[91]   *Re Meredith* (1973) 57 Cr App R 451, *R v Harrow Crown Court ex p Perkins* (1998) 162 JP 527.

[92]   *Re Sampson* [1987] 1 WLR 194, per Lord Bridge, at 198G.

on what is learnt during the trial process.[93] Clearly, costs orders are based on what is learnt during the trial process.

The absence of a right of appeal does not necessarily result in the Administrative Court accepting jurisdiction, even if a person can claim to be a victim of a violation of the European Convention on Human Rights as a consequence of a Crown Court decision. The House of Lords' interpretation of s 29(3) of the 1981 Act is not incompatible with any Convention right since there is no Convention right to have all decisions reviewed, even though some decisions might breach Convention rights.[94] This is because the rights contained in the European Convention which are incorporated into domestic law by the HRA 1998 do not include a right to challenge a decision that is said to violate European Convention rights.[95] Article 13, which entitles a person to an effective remedy for a violation of the European Convention, has not been incorporated. The remedy for an alleged violation of Convention rights during the trial would, in any event, be in the Court of Appeal.[96]

If a claimant wrongly challenges a decision of the Crown Court by bringing judicial review proceedings when he is able to appeal, it is possible for the court to correct the problem by reconstituting itself as the Court of Appeal.[97]

Further assistance on the scope of the Administrative Court's jurisdiction is provided by Lord Browne-Wilkinson, who noted that decisions held to be open to challenge in the Administrative Court are those in which the order was made in a wholly different jurisdiction or where the order has been made against someone other than the accused.[98] The only possible exception to this is serious fraud cases, where the Administrative Court may be able to consider a decision to dismiss a case that has been

---

[93]  Ibid, at 197E.
[94]  *R (Regentford) Ltd v Canterbury Crown Court* [2001] HRLR 18.
[95]  *R (Shields) v Crown Court at Liverpool and the Lord Chancellor* [2001] UKHRR 610, at [58].
[96]  Ibid.
[97]  *R (Lichniak) v Secretary of State for the Home Department* [2002] QB 296.
[98]  *R v Manchester Crown Court ex p DPP* [1993] 1 WLR 1524, at 1530C.

transferred to the Crown Court under the special procedure provided by the Criminal Justice Act 1987.[99] Lord Browne-Wilkinson formulated the following guidance:[100]

> "'Is the decision sought to be reviewed one arising in the issue between the Crown and the defendant formulated by the indictment (including the costs of such issue)?' If the answer is "Yes", then to permit the decision to be challenged by judicial review may lead to delay in the trial: the matter is therefore probably excluded from review by the section. If the answer is "No", the decision of the Crown Court is truly collateral to the indictment of the defendant and judicial review of that decision will not delay his trial: therefore it may well not be excluded by the section.'

The decisions of the House of Lords have not prevented a degree of uncertainty about whether a matter is something that relates to a trial on indictment. Indeed, the lack of certainty has prompted Lord Justice Rose to call for legislation to clarify the scope of judicial review of Crown Court decisions.[101] There are, however, a number of precedents giving examples of matters that have been held to relate to a trial on indictment or matters that do not. These precedents can, at first glance, appear to be slightly arbitrary. For example, although a decision to remit a legal aid contribution at the end of a trial is not subject to judicial review,[102] a decision to make a contribution order is subject to review.[103] These precedents, however, are a useful guide as to whether the Court will accept that it has jurisdiction to consider a challenge to a particular decision.

Matters held to be those relating to a trial on indictment and therefore excluded from judicial review and appeal by way of case stated include the following:

(a)   an order discharging a jury;[104]

(b)   an order that an indictment lie on the file marked 'not to be proceeded with without leave of the court';[105]

---

[99]   In *R v Manchester Crown Court ex p DPP* [1993] 1 WLR 1524, at 1530G, Lord Browne-Wilkinson declined an opportunity to express a view on the correctness of *R v Central Criminal Court and Nadir ex p Director of the Serious Fraud Office* [1993] 1 WLR 949. Although his Lordship noted that the decision in *ex p Director of the Serious Fraud Office* relied on cases that he held had been wrongly decided, he went on to say that the wording of the Criminal Justice Act 1987 might give rise to special considerations. Since the decision in *ex p DPP*, the Administrative Court has continued to consider judicial reviews of decisions to dismiss proceedings following transfers under the provisions of the Criminal Justice Act 1987. See, for example, *R v Snaresbrook Crown Court ex p Director of the Serious Fraud Office* (1998) 142 SJLB 263.

[100]  *R v Manchester Crown Court ex p DPP* [1993] 1 WLR 1524, at 1530F.

[101]  *R v Manchester Crown Court ex p H* [2000] 1 WLR 760.

[102]  *R v Cardiff Crown Court ex p Jones* [1974] QB 113.

[103]  *Re Sampson* [1987] 1 WLR 194, per Lord Bridge, at 199F.

[104]  *Ex parte Marlowe* [1973] Crim LR 294.

[105]  *R v Central Criminal Court ex p Raymond* (1986) 83 Cr App R 94.

(c) the decision of a judge to order a defence solicitor to pay the costs occasioned by the granting of a defence application for an adjournment;[106]

(d) a decision as to whether the trial of one indictment should proceed before the trial of another indictment faced by the same defendant;[107]

(e) a refusal to stay an indictment as an abuse of process;[108]

(f) an order quashing an indictment because the Crown Court lacks jurisdiction;[109]

(g) an order that matters should be stayed as an abuse of process;[110]

(h) an order regarding costs after the prosecution announces its intent to offer no evidence at a pre-trial hearing;[111]

(i) an order preventing the naming of a witness under s 11 of the Contempt of Court Act 1981;[112] and

(k) a decision to decline to make a compensation order.[113]

Matters that have been held to be those not relating to a trial on indictment and which therefore may be challenged by judicial review or appeal by way of case stated include the following:

(a) forfeiture orders made against a person who was not a defendant in the trial;[114]

(b) an order committing an acquitted defendant to prison unless he agreed to be bound over;[115]

(c) a decision to extend a custody time-limit;[116]

(d) an order estreating the recognisance of a surety;[117] and

---

[106] *R v Smith (M)* [1975] QB 531, but note doubts expressed by Lord Bridge in *Re Smalley* [1985] AC 622, at 644F.
[107] *R v Southwark Crown Court ex p Ward* [1996] Crim LR 123.
[108] *R v Maidstone Crown Court ex p Shanks & McEwan (Southern) Ltd* [1993] Env LR 340.
[109] *R v Manchester Crown Court ex p DPP* [1993] 1 WLR 1524.
[110] *Re Ashton and others; R v Manchester Crown Court ex p DPP* [1994] 1 AC 9.
[111] *R v Harrow Crown Court ex p Perkins* (1998) 162 JP 527.
[112] *R v Central Criminal Court ex p Crook* (1984) *The Times*, November 8.
[113] *R (Faithfull) v Ipswich Crown Court* [2008] 1 WLR 1636.
[114] *R v Maidstone Crown Court ex p Gill* (1987) 84 Cr App R 96.
[115] *R v Inner London Crown Court ex p Benjamin* (1987) 85 Cr App R 267.
[116] *R v Norwich Crown Court ex p Cox* (1993) 5 Admin LR 689.
[117] *Re Smalley* [1985] AC 622.

(e)  an order lifting restrictions on the naming of juvenile defendants made under s 39(1) of the Children and Young Persons Act 1933.[118]

Ingenious arguments seeking to extend the Administrative Court's jurisdiction to consider decisions of the Crown Court have found little favour. For example, the Administrative Court has no jurisdiction to consider a challenge to a warrant of committal to prison, if that challenge is in reality a challenge to sentence.[119]

It used to be thought that decisions of the Crown Court regarding bail could not be challenged in judicial review proceedings. That was because there was an alternative remedy as the High Court had jurisdiction to consider bail decisions.[120] The abolition of that power means that it is now clear that judicial review proceedings can be brought to challenge Crown Court decisions regarding bail. That is true despite the fact that proceeding on indictment are pending.[121] The jurisdiction will, however, be exercised sparingly.[122]

## Decisions of the Upper Tribunal

Section 3(5) of the Tribunals, Courts and Enforcement Act 2007 provides that: 'The Upper Tribunal is to be a superior court of record'.

It was thought by some that this gave the Upper Tribunal a status equivalent to that of the High Court so that it could not be challenged in judicial review proceedings. The correctness of that analysis has now been determined authoritatively by the Supreme Court in *R (Cart) v Upper Tribunal*.[123]

The Supreme Court held that jurisdiction of the High Court to consider applications for judicial review could not be ousted in the absence of clear words.[124] However, the introduction of the new tribunal system required the adoption of a more restrained approach to judicial review.[125] The rational and proportionate approach was to restrict judicial review to those cases where the second-tier appeals criteria were made out.[126] Those criteria are that the claim raises some important point of principle or practice or that there is some other compelling reason to grant permission to appeal.[127]

---

[118]  *R v Manchester Crown Court ex p H* [2000] 1 WLR 760.
[119]  *R v Lewes Crown Court ex p Sinclair* (1993) 5 Admin LR 1.
[120]  Criminal Justice Act 1967, s 22(1).
[121]  *R (Mongan) v Isleworth Crown Court* [2007] EWHC 1087 (Admin).
[122]  Ibid.
[123]  [2011] 3 WLR 107.
[124]  Ibid, at 122C.
[125]  Ibid, at 124G and 128C–128F.
[126]  Ibid, at 128C–128F.
[127]  Tribunals, Courts and Enforcement Act 2007, s 13(6).

### Decisions of the Special Immigration Appeals Commission

Statute also provides that the Special Immigration Appeals Commission (SIAC) is a 'superior court of record'.[128] However, unlike the Upper Tribunal, it has first instance jurisdiction. That means that it has been held that judicial review is available.[129] There has been no suggestion that the criteria for a second-tier appeal should apply.

## 1.6 REQUIREMENT THAT DECISIONS MUST BE PUBLIC LAW DECISIONS

When considering whether a judicial review can be brought to challenge a decision of a public body, practitioners need to be aware of the divide between public law and private law. Judicial review is the normal route for claims alleging a breach of public law rights.[130] Judicial review is not the correct form of proceedings where there is an alleged breach of private law rights.

The distinction between public law and private law can be difficult to discern. One reason for this is that some decisions involve mixed issues of both public and private law that can be impossible to separate.[131] If a decision involves mixed issues the court should be reluctant to conclude that judicial review is an inappropriate form of proceedings. Lord Lowry has held:[132]

> '[U]nless the procedure adopted by the moving party is ill suited to dispose of the question at issue, there is much to be said in favour of the proposition that a court having jurisdiction ought to let a case be heard rather than entertain a debate concerning the form of the proceedings.'

Although the distinction between public and private law is hard to define, it is possible to identify some guiding principles. Where a decision that is to be challenged has been taken by a public body, this does not necessarily mean that the challenge relates to public law. For example, as noted earlier, public bodies have employees who may wish to challenge decisions that have been taken regarding their employment. As these decisions generally raise issues of private law, they are normally challenged through employment law proceedings rather than by judicial review.[133] However, even decisions that appear at first glance to be private law matters need to be considered carefully. Historically, some public officials have had no

---

[128] Special Immigration Appeals Commission Act 1997, s 1(3).

[129] *R (Cart) v Upper Tribunal* [2010] 2 WLR 1012.

[130] *O'Reilly v Mackman* [1983] 2 AC 237.

[131] *An Bord Bainne Coop Ltd v Milk Marketing Board* [1984] 2 CMLR 584.

[132] *Roy v Kensington, Chelsea and Westminster Family Practitioners Committee* [1992] 1 AC 624, at 655.

[133] See, for example, *R v BBC ex p Lavelle* [1983] 1 WLR 23, per Mr Justice Woolf, at 30C.

employment law rights and so a breach of the disciplinary code governing them may give rise to judicial review claims.[134]

Lord Justice Hobhouse considered the distinction between public and private law:[135]

> 'Where a statutory corporation purports to enter into a contract which it is not empowered by the relevant statute to enter into, the corporation lacks the capacity to make the supposed contract. This lack of capacity means that the document and the agreement it contains do not have effect as a legal contract ... The role of public law is to answer the question: what is the capacity of the local authority to contract? The role of private law is to answer the question: when one of the parties to a supposed contract lacks contractual capacity, does the supposed contract give rise to legal obligations?'

As this dictum clearly shows, public law determines the scope of a public body's decision-making powers and the procedure that should be adopted to exercise those powers. In contrast, private law obligations arise from the areas of civil law, such as tort and breach of contract, that govern the legal obligations of private individuals as well as public bodies.

The trend in recent judgments has been to suggest that one should commence judicial review proceedings in cases in which the correct form of proceedings is unclear.[136] There are good practical reasons why the advice of the courts makes sense. Although proceedings can be transferred into and out of the Administrative Court,[137] the tight time-limits that are applicable in judicial review proceedings mean that a judicial review claim is likely to be out of time if it is commenced as a private law claim. For example, the court has held that in a case concerning restitution of care home fees alleged to have been wrongly charged, by commencing proceedings as a private law action the claimant had deprived the defendant public authority of two important elements of protection as provided by the Civil Procedure Rules: the stringent time limit and the need to obtain the court's permission to proceed. As a consequence, the claim was an abuse.[138]

Despite the example in the paragraph above, the trend has been to suggest that the courts should adopt a flexible approach to their case management powers when dealing with cases that have been wrongly identified as public law proceedings when they are private law or vice versa.[139] This

---

[134]  *R v Secretary of State for the Home Department ex p Benwell* [1985] QB 554.

[135]  *Credit Suisse v Alderdale Borough Council* [1997] QB 306, at 350E.

[136]  See, for example, *Trustees of the Dennis Rye Pension Fund v Sheffield City Council* [1998] 1 WLR 840.

[137]  CPR 1998, r 30.5 – permitting transfer into the Administrative Court; and CPR, r 54.20 – permitting transfer out of the Administrative Court.

[138]  *Jones v Powys Local Health Board* (2009) 12 CCL Rep 68.

[139]  *Clark v University of Lincolnshire and Humberside* [2000] 1 WLR 1988, at 1997B.

means that proceedings should not be struck out unless a party has obtained some form of procedural advantage by commencing proceedings in the wrong forum.[140]

The fact that a decision relates to public law does not necessarily mean that judicial review is an appropriate form of proceedings. It is now recognised that both the magistrates' courts[141] and the county courts[142] often have jurisdiction to consider public law issues. That may mean that there are suitable alternative remedies.

## 1.7   STATUTORY EXCLUSIONS OF JUDICIAL REVIEW

Although, in theory, there is no bar to statutory provisions which exclude the jurisdiction of the Administrative Court to consider judicial review challenges to particular types of decisions or decisions of particular decision-makers, in practice, the courts have been extremely reluctant to find that a statutory provision excludes the jurisdiction of the Administrative Court. The courts rely on the following dictum of Lord Reid:[143]

> 'It is a well established principle that a provision ousting the ordinary jurisdiction of the court must be construed strictly – meaning, I think, that, if such a provision is reasonably capable of having two meanings, that meaning shall be taken which preserves the ordinary jurisdiction of the court.'

As a consequence, the courts have been willing to consider challenges to decisions where statute provides that the decision 'shall not be subject to appeal to, or review in, any court'.[144] The courts have also been willing to consider challenges to decisions of superior courts of record.[145]

Particular considerations may apply where a statute seeks to prevent challenges to decisions of courts of law or tribunals with a special statutory expertise. In those circumstances, courts may show a greater willingness to conclude that the statutory provision does exclude challenges.[146] However, even where a statute prohibits challenges to decisions of courts, the Administrative Court is reluctant to find that such provisions exclude challenges to decisions that courts lack jurisdiction to make. As a consequence, although statute excludes challenges to matters relating to trial on indictment,[147] a decision may be challenged on the

---

[140]   Ibid, at 1998B.
[141]   *Boddington v BTP* [1999] 2 AC 143.
[142]   *Manchester City Council v Pinnock* [2010] 3 WLR 1441.
[143]   *Anisminic Ltd v Foreign Compensation Commission* [1969] 2 AC 147, at 170.
[144]   *R v Secretary of State for the Home Department ex p Fayed (No 1)* [1998] 1 WLR 763.
[145]   *R (Cart) v Upper Tribunal* [2011] 3 WLR 1077. See **1.5.3**.
[146]   *Racal Communications Ltd, Re* [1981] AC 374, and *R (A) v Director of Establishments of the Security Services* [2010] 2 AC 1.
[147]   See **1.5.3**.

ground that the judge lacked jurisdiction to make it even if that decision is on a matter relating to trial on indictment.[148]

Provisions for alternative remedies do not normally exclude judicial review as the existence of an alternative remedy is a matter relevant to the court's discretion and not its jurisdiction. However, such provisions may mean that the Administrative Court is unwilling to consider judicial review proceedings.[149]

## 1.8    PARTICULAR TYPES OF DECISION THAT ARE NOT SUBJECT TO CHALLENGE

Historically, the courts have regarded some decisions as being exempt from challenge by judicial review despite the fact that they were public law decisions taken by public law bodies. The courts considered certain matters non-justiciable where the subject matter was regarded as being such that the courts should not intervene. The most important example of this limitation has been an unwillingness to consider challenges to a minister's exercise of certain prerogative powers. As Lord Roskill stated:[150]

> 'Prerogative powers such as those relating to the making of treaties, the defence of the realm, *the prerogative of mercy*, the grant of honours, the dissolution of Parliament and the appointment of ministers as well as others are not, I think, susceptible to judicial review because their nature and subject matter are such as not to be amenable to the judicial process.' [emphasis added]

However, one needs to be a little careful when considering old authorities regarding the scope of judicial review. The courts have shown an increasing willingness to consider challenges to decisions that were previously thought to be exempt from challenge. For example, despite the remarks of Lord Roskill above, the Administrative Court has considered a challenge to the exercise of the prerogative of mercy.[151] According to Lord Phillips MR, the approach of the courts has been that:[152]

> 'the issue of justiciability depends, not on general principle, but on subject matter and suitability in the particular case.'

---

[148]   *R v Maidstone Crown Court ex p Harrow London Borough Council* [2000] QB 719.
[149]   See **3.3**.
[150]   *Council of Civil Service Unions v Minister for the Civil Service* [1985] AC 374, at 418B.
[151]   *R v Secretary of State for the Home Department ex p Bentley* [1994] QB 349; compare with *Reckely v Minister of Public Safety and Immigration (No 2)* [1996] 1 AC, PC in which the Privy Council held that there could be no judicial review of the prerogative of mercy in a Bahamian case.
[152]   *R (Abbasi) v Secretary of State for Foreign and Commonwealth Affairs* (2002) 99 (47) LSG 29.

Areas in which the court remains highly reluctant to intervene absent exceptional circumstances include foreign policy[153] and defence.[154] The HRA 1998 has however enlarged the potential for review of matters previously considered non-justiciable.[155] In recent years, the approach of the courts has been to permit challenges to almost all public law decisions of public bodies but then to vary the standard of review depending upon the type of decision challenged. This is considered in detail below.

One matter that apparently cannot be raised in judicial review proceedings is the correct meaning of an international instrument operating purely on the plane of international law.[156] However, matters of international law can be considered if they are necessary to determine a matter of domestic law.[157]

## 1.9    EXTENT OF THE DISCRETION GIVEN TO PARTICULAR DECISION-MAKERS

It should be clear that there is a wide range of decisions that potentially may be subject to judicial review proceedings. Some of the decisions will concern matters that the courts have particular expertise in handling. For example, it is possible to challenge a decision of a magistrates' court regarding the admissibility of evidence.[158] Clearly, the courts ought to have the expertise to be able to determine whether evidence is admissible. However, other decisions may concern matters that are outside the scope of the courts' normal expertise. In particular, there are decisions that require a significant amount of political judgment. Examples of decisions that require political judgment include those related to foreign affairs and those that have resource implications. The courts do not regard themselves as being equipped with expertise in those areas.

The courts deal with their lack of expertise by showing a greater reluctance to permit challenges to decisions of public bodies in areas that involve political judgment. For example, Mr Justice Holman recently considered a challenge to the politically controversial to curtail the Building Schools for the Future programme.[159] Mr Justice Holman quoted dicta stating that:

---

[153]  *R (Gentle) v Prime Minister* [2008] 1 AC 1356, at 1363B (and, in the Court of Appeal, [2007] QB 689, at 712A–712D).

[154]  *R v Jones (Margaret)* [2007] 1 AC 136, at 162G.

[155]  *R (Gentle) v Prime Minister* [2008] 1 AC 1356. Although the challenge itself failed, the fact that it was considered is an indication of the increased willingness to consider challenges in sensitive areas.

[156]  *R (Campaign for Nuclear Disarmament) v The Prime Minister* [2003] ACD 36, at [36].

[157]  See, for example, *R v Secretary of State for the Home Department ex p Launder (No 2)* [1997] 1 WLR 839.

[158]  See, for example, *R v Manchester City Magistrates' Court ex p Birtles* (1994) The Times, January 25.

[159]  *R (Luton Borough Council) v Secretary of State for Education* [2011] EWHC 217 (Admin).

'the Secretary of State is exercising a broad discretionary power in a social, economic and ... political context. He has to balance a number of complex, and perhaps conflicting, social and economic variables in order to determine what he believes is the fair, effective and efficient solution to the central issue in question ... It is trite law that this court must be cautious in interfering with such an exercise of discretionary power, unless there are solid legal reasons for doing so, *and must not allow itself to become an umpire of a social and economic controversy that has been settled by due political process.'* [emphasis added by Mr Justice Holman]

He relied on this to conclude that the decision could not be challenged on irrationality grounds (although it could be challenged on other grounds).[160]

Similarly, Lord Nicholls held that the power contained in s 3 of the HRA 1998 to interpret a statute in a manner that accorded with the European Convention on Human Rights did not permit the courts to introduce a decision-making system that would have a 'material effect' on the 'allocation of scarce financial and other resources' as that was a matter for Parliament.[161]

It is not only the expertise of the courts in the dealing with the issues raised by a claim for judicial review that determines the level of scrutiny. The importance of the issues raised also determines, to an extent, the level of scrutiny. For example, Lord Justice Simon Brown has held that:[162]

'where fundamental human rights are being restricted, "the threshold of unreasonableness" is not lowered. On the other hand, the minister on judicial review will need to show that there is an important competing public interest which he could reasonably judge sufficient to justify the restriction and he must expect his reasons to be closely scrutinised. Even that approach, therefore, involves a more intensive review process and a greater readiness to intervene than would ordinarily characterise a judicial review challenge.'

The dictum of Lord Justice Simon Brown predates the entry into force of the HRA 1998. In cases where it is argued that a public body has acted in breach of its obligations contained in the HRA 1998 by violating the European Convention, an entirely different approach may be appropriate, which is considered later.[163] However, the dictum of Lord Justice Simon Brown remains relevant, as fundamental human rights are not necessarily restricted to those protected in the European Convention.

Although the European Convention is the United Kingdom's most important source of international human rights law, it is not the only source. The United Kingdom has ratified other human rights treaties that

---

[160] Ibid, at [47].
[161] *Re S (Children) (Care Order: Implementation of Care Plan), Re W (Children) (Care Order: Adequacy of Care Plan)* [2002] 2 AC 291, at 314E–315A.
[162] *R v Ministry of Defence ex p Smith* [1995] 4 All ER 427, at 445F.
[163] See **2.3**.

contain obligations. Although the other obligations are not given enhanced effect in domestic legislation such as the HRA 1998, they can still be relied on in arguments before domestic courts.

In general, the rights contained in these treaties are similar to those contained in the European Convention. These treaties can, however, be more specific about the scope of the rights. For example, the United Kingdom has ratified the United Nations Convention on the Rights of the Child.[164] This has provisions that can be more specific than the rights contained in the European Convention. For example, Art 37(c) of the United Nations Convention on the Rights of the Child provides that:

> 'Every child deprived of liberty shall be treated with humanity and respect for the inherent dignity of the human person, and in a manner which takes into account the needs of persons of his or her age. In particular, every child deprived of liberty shall be separated from adults unless it is considered in the child's best interest not to do so and shall have the right to maintain contact with his or her family through correspondence and visits, save in exceptional circumstances.'

The United Kingdom has also ratified the International Covenant on Civil and Political Rights.[165] It has particular value as a result of the case-law that has been developed by the United Nations Human Rights Committee about the scope of the provisions of the Covenant. For example, there is case-law considering the extent of the right to effective assistance from counsel.[166]

Finally, the Charter of Fundamental Rights of the European Union is increasingly important as it can be relied upon in circumstances in which European Union law is in issue.[167] This is a significant development. The Charter is no narrower than the European Convention on Human Rights, and in fact may be broader in its effect. As a consequence for example, proceedings before the Special Immigration Appeals Commission may be challenged as being contrary to the fair trial proceedings of the Charter even though Art 6 of the European Convention does not apply.[168]

A detailed consideration of these treaties is beyond the scope of this book. Full copies of these and other treaties, together with other relevant material, can be found on the website of the University of Minnesota Human Rights Library at http://www1.umn.edu/humanrts/.

---

[164] Adopted by the General Assembly on 20 November 1989, UN Doc A/44/49 (1989).

[165] Adopted by the General Assembly on 16 December 1966, 999 UNTS 171.

[166] See, for example, *Collins v Jamaica* (356/1989) holding that it is ineffective assistance for a counsel to withdraw an appeal without instructions.

[167] See Beal and Hickman 'Beano No More: The EU Charter of Rights After Lisbon' [2011] JR 113.

[168] *ZZ v Secretary of State* [2011] EWCA Civ 440.

# CHAPTER 2

## GROUNDS OF CHALLENGE IN JUDICIAL REVIEW CLAIMS

### 2.1 IMPORTANCE OF UNDERSTANDING THE CATEGORIES OF LEGAL CHALLENGE AVAILABLE

Judicial review claims are not unlimited appeals to the Administrative Court. Instead, parties applying to the Court by way of judicial review are restricted to raising certain limited grounds of challenge. This chapter sets out the categories of legal error that can be challenged in an application for judicial review. Understanding the scope of these categories and the ways in which they may overlap is extremely important. As Lord Irvine has said:[1]

> 'Categorisation of types of challenge assists in an orderly exposition of the principles underlying our developing public law. But these are not watertight compartments because the various grounds for judicial review run together.'

Lawyers acting for claimants in judicial review claims will be expected by judges in the Administrative Court to state which of the categories of legal error apply in their case. This is because it is provided in the CPR 1998 that a judicial review claim should state, inter alia, 'the legal basis for the claim to that remedy'.[2] A failure to set out the legal basis for a claim is likely to result in permission to apply for judicial review being refused.

In practice, the Administrative Court does not require the pleadings in judicial review proceedings to be as specific as in some other forms of civil litigation. It is also often willing to allow amendment of the grounds set out in an application for judicial review.[3] The Court will, however, expect to see a clear explanation of how the claim fits within the possible grounds for judicial review.

It is also important to ensure that the application identifies the grounds clearly and demonstrates a good understanding of the limits of the Court's powers in judicial review as it adds credibility to applications for judicial review if they are phrased in a way that shows an understanding

---

[1]  *Boddington v British Transport Police* [1998] 2 WLR 639, at 644E.
[2]  CPR, r 8.2(b)(ii) applied to judicial review proceedings by CPR, r 54.6(1).
[3]  See **5.7**.

of the grounds recognised by the Administrative Court. The judges sitting in the Court are concerned about the quality of applications for judicial review, so it is important that practitioners who are presenting applications show that they are familiar with the principles of judicial review. Judges have greater confidence in arguments raised by practitioners who can demonstrate their knowledge of those principles.

Lawyers for defendants also need to understand the categories of legal error that give rise to a potential claim for judicial review. Defendants are required to serve an acknowledgement of service if they wish to take part in any hearing regarding the grant of permission to apply for judicial review.[4] The acknowledgement of service must, 'where the person filing it intends to contest the claim, set out a summary of his grounds for doing so'.[5] In addition, defendants who wish to contest the claim for judicial review are required to serve 'detailed grounds for contesting the claim'.[6]

In practice, when filing the acknowledgement of service or the detailed grounds, defendants will wish, if possible, to argue that the case does not fall within any of the categories of grounds recognised by the Administrative Court.

While it is likely to be only in exceptional cases that the Administrative Court will be willing to recognise novel categories of legal error,[7] the grounds for judicial review are constantly evolving to ensure that judicial review of executive action remains an effective form of constitutional protection. The supervisory role of the courts in administrative law has increased significantly in recent decades, but judges are acutely aware of the limits to that role.[8] As a result, if it can be shown by a defendant that a claimant has failed to formulate a judicial review claim so that it identifies an error falling within previously recognised categories of legal error, the Court is likely to dismiss the claim.

## 2.2   CATEGORIES OF ERROR SUSCEPTIBLE TO CHALLENGE IN AN APPLICATION FOR JUDICIAL REVIEW

Although it is important to try to identify how an error falls within the scope of judicial review, this can be difficult to do in practice. Judicial review has been described as a 'highly acrobatic part of the law'[9] and

---

[4]   CPR, r 54.9(1)(a).

[5]   Ibid, r 54.8(4)(a)(i).

[6]   Ibid, r 54.14(1)(a).

[7]   *Council of Civil Service Unions v Minister for the Civil Service* [1985] AC 374, per Lord Diplock, at 410E.

[8]   See, for example, *R (Quintavalle) v Secretary of State for Health* [2003] 2 AC 687, per Lord Bingham, at 697H.

[9]   S A de Smith The Limits of Judicial Review: Statutory Discretions and the Doctrine of Ultra Vires *The Modern Law Review,* Vol 11, No 3 (Jul, 1948), pp 306–325.

there is considerable academic and judicial debate about the categories of legal error that allow a decision to be challenged in this way. Lord Diplock, however, gave what is often regarded as the definitive statement of the categories of error of law allowing the court to intervene by way of judicial review, when he stated:

'The first ground I would call "illegality", the second "irrationality" and the third "procedural impropriety". That is not to say that further development on a case by case basis may not in course of time add further grounds. I have in mind particularly the possible adoption in the future of the principle of "proportionality"[10] ...

By "illegality" as a ground for judicial review I mean that the decision-maker must understand correctly the law that regulates his decision-making power and must give effect to it. Whether he has or not is par excellence a justiciable question to be decided, in the event of dispute, by those persons, the judges, by whom the judicial power of the state is exercisable.

By "irrationality" I mean what can by now be succinctly referred to as "Wednesbury unreasonableness" ... It applies to a decision which is so outrageous in its defiance of logic or of accepted moral standards that no sensible person who had applied his mind to the question to be decided could have arrived at it. Whether a decision falls within this category is a question that judges by their training and experience should be well equipped to answer, or else there would be something badly wrong with our judicial system ...

I have described the third head as "procedural impropriety" rather than failure to observe basic rules of natural justice or failure to act with procedural fairness towards the person who will be affected by the decision. This is because susceptibility to judicial review under this head covers also failure by an administrative tribunal to observe procedural rules that are expressly laid down in the legislative instrument by which its jurisdiction is conferred, even where such failure does not involve any denial of natural justice.'[11]

Although Lord Diplock recognised 'illegality', 'irrationality' and 'procedural impropriety' as the three categories of legal error that allow the courts to intervene, these encompass other sub-categories of legal error, some of which have become so important that they are effectively recognised as separate errors of law. For example, the duty to give reasons and the concept of legitimate expectation are categories of legal error that are now recognised in their own right, although they are both essentially forms of procedural impropriety or irrationality. The meanings of the various categories are set out in more detail later.

---

[10] In practice, 'proportionality' has now become a ground which can be raised in an application for judicial review at least in certain circumstances.

[11] *Council of Civil Service Unions v Minister for the Civil Service* [1985] AC 374, at 410D.

The fact that matters such as legitimate expectation have become recognised as errors of law in their own right means that it can now be difficult to determine whether they are forms of procedural impropriety or irrationality. That has generated considerable academic debate.[12] From the practitioner's point of view, that debate is unlikely to be of primary assistance. As a consequence, we have not addressed it in this book.

### 2.2.1   Importance of the decision in *Anisminic*

Before the decision of the House of Lords in the *Anisminic* case,[13] it was thought that an error of law needed either to be jurisdictional or to appear on the face of the record if the courts were to have jurisdiction to consider an application for judicial review. It is now clear that in most circumstances, any error of law that comes within Lord Diplock's categories can lead to a decision being quashed. The error need not be apparent on the face of the record.

The Administrative Court may, however, be limited to considering errors of law that are either jurisdictional or on the face of the record when the Administrative Court considers judicial review of decisions of certain courts.[14] This is because it is presumed that Parliament intended that courts can determine issues of law and so courts are presumed not to make errors of law.[15] As a result, the Court may be able to intervene only if it is clear that the court had acted outside its jurisdiction or if there is a clear error on the face of the record. A similarly limited jurisdiction applies to challenges to visitors to academic institutions[16] and certain other examples such as the Charity Commissioners.[17]

In practice, however, any pre-*Anisminic* limitation on the scope of judicial review is unlikely to be a significant issue in most challenges to a decision of an inferior court. There are several reasons for this.

Firstly, the pre-*Anisminic* limitation on the scope of judicial review may apply only where there is a statutory provision making the decision of the court final and conclusive.

---

[12]   See, for example, David Pievsky '*Legitimate Expectation as a Relevancy*' [2003] JR 144.

[13]   *Anisminic Ltd v Foreign Compensation Commission* [1969] 2 AC 147.

[14]   See s 29(3) Senior Courts Act 1981 excluding matters relating to trial on indictment in the Crown Court.

[15]   *Re Racal Communications Ltd*, sub nom *Re A Company* [1981] AC 374, per Lord Diplock, at 382G.

[16]   *R v Hull University Visitor ex p Page* [1993] AC 682, at 704F.

[17]   *R v Charity Commissioners for England & Wales ex p Baldwin* [2001] HLR 538 (where the challenge was 'error of law').

'In the case of inferior courts where the decision of the court is made final and conclusive by the statute, this may involve the survival of those subtle distinctions formerly drawn between errors of law which go to jurisdiction and errors of law.'[18]

In addition, the Administrative Court has a clear jurisdiction to consider any errors of law made by certain inferior courts. For example, in the context of a judicial review of a decision of a magistrates' court, Lord Cooke of Thorndon has stated that:[19]

'[T]he authorities now establish that the Queen's Bench Division of the High Court has normally in judicial review proceedings jurisdiction to quash a decision of an inferior court, tribunal or other statutory body for error of law, even though the error is neither apparent on the face of the record nor so serious as to deprive the body of jurisdiction in the original and narrow sense of power to enter on the inquiry and to make against persons subject to its jurisdiction the kind of decision in question.'

There have been suggestions in some cases that different principles might apply when magistrates are committing a matter for trial. It is now clear, however, that the principle set out by Lord Cooke applies to magistrates when they are considering whether a matter should be committed for trial to the Crown Court,[20] as well as when they are trying matters and making other decisions such as withdrawing warrants for extradition.[21] The Administrative Court may, however, take account of the situation in which the legal error occurs when it decides whether to exercise its discretion to allow the application for judicial review.[22] As a result, the Administrative Court will consider any errors made by magistrates at committal, but may decide not to intervene and quash the committal. This might happen if the Crown Court will be able to cure any injustice suffered.

Similarly, there is clear authority that the pre-*Anisminic* approach does not apply to decisions of coroners' courts.[23] In reaching that conclusion Lord Justice Goff held that:[24]

'Lord Diplock did not intend to say that the *Anisminic* principle did not extend to inferior courts as well as tribunals.'

---

18  *Re Racal Communications Ltd*, sub nom *Re A Company* [1981] AC 374, per Lord Diplock, at 383.
19  *R v Bedwellty Justices ex p Williams* [1997] AC 225, at 232G.
20  Ibid, at 234D.
21  *R (Director of Serious Fraud Office) v Selby Magistrates Court* [2003] EWHC 2453 (Admin).
22  *R v Bedwellty Justices ex p Williams* [1997] AC 225; see also **7.1** regarding the discretionary nature of judicial review.
23  *R v Greater Manchester Coroner ex p Tal* [1985] QB 67.
24  Ibid, at 81.

It may not only be decisions of magistrates' and coroners' courts that are no longer subject to the pre-*Anisminic* approach. Apparently, it is only in the context of decisions of the Crown Court that there is any real authority that the Administrative Court is limited by the pre-*Anisminic* distinction. It is clear that the Administrative Court is increasingly unwilling to apply the pre-*Anisminic* distinction.[25] This means that it may be possible to use judicial review only to challenge errors of the Crown Court that are outside jurisdiction or on the face of the record. However, as the record includes oral reasons given by a Crown Court judge[26] and as there is a duty on professional judges to give reasons,[27] it is highly unlikely in practice that these pre-*Anisminic* distinctions will prevent an application for judicial review. This may be the reason why there have been no recent decisions considering the pre-*Anisminic* distinction in the context of decisions of the Crown Court.

A related issue which suggests a return to imposing restrictions on the grounds of judicial review in the context of challenges to courts is the approach taken to challenges to decisions of the Upper Tribunal. In that context unappealable decisions are subject to judicial review only where there is an important point of principle or practice or some other compelling reason for the case to be reviewed.[28] Essentially the Supreme Court has concluded that the enhanced tribunal set by the Tribunals, Courts and Enforcement Act 2007 requires a restrained approach to judicial review.

### 2.2.2    Factual disputes

As has already been noted, judicial review is a remedy that gives the Administrative Court jurisdiction to 'secure that decisions are made by the executive or by a public body according to law'.[29] The procedure in judicial review is generally inapt to resolve disputes of fact.[30] Accordingly the Administrative Court is generally concerned with the route by which a decision is reached and will not normally consider claims which dispute the defendant's view of the facts. There are some significant exceptions to this rule. It is possible to argue that the findings of fact made by a decision-maker are irrational.[31] In addition, it is possible to argue that the facts that trigger a decision-maker's power to act do not exist.[32] Finally, it

---

[25]  Eg ibid.

[26]  *R v Knightsbridge Crown Court ex p International Sporting Club Ltd* [1982] QB 304.

[27]  Ibid, at 314E.

[28]  *R (Cart) v Upper Tribunal* [2011] 3 WLR 107, replicating the 'second appeals' test set out in s 13(6) of the Tribunals Courts and Enforcement Act 2007.

[29]  *Mercury Energy Ltd v Electricity Corporation of New Zealand Ltd* [1994] 1 WLR 521, per Lord Templeman, at 526A.

[30]  *Anufrijeva v London Borough of Southwark* [2004] QB 1124, at 1153G; *R (St Helens Borough Council v Manchester Primary Care Trust* [2009] PTSR 105, at [13] referring to the 'paper' procedure in judicial review.

[31]  See **2.10**.

[32]  The 'precedent fact' jurisdiction of the court: see **2.5**.

is possible to argue that a decision-maker made a clear mistake of fact.[33] These exceptions exist to preserve the court's jurisdiction to make findings where errors of fact amount to an error of law or have resulted in an error of law.

The general position is that the Administrative court will not interfere in questions of 'fact and degree' absent strong justification such as perversity.[34] However, the House of Lords has recognised that if necessary, judicial review can be 'adjusted so as to enable issues of fact to be resolved'.[35] The key point is that determination of any factual issue must be essential to an error of law identified in the grounds of challenge. The Administrative Court has also recognised circumstances in which it must proceed on its own assessment of the facts in the context of challenges such as challenges to unlawful detention.[36]

The impact of the Human Rights Act 1998 has been to introduce further exceptions to the rule that the Administrative Court is unwilling to consider claims that a decision-maker has erred in its treatment of the facts. Section 6 of the Human Rights Act 1998 makes it unlawful for a public authority to act in violation of certain rights under the European Convention on Human Rights. Accordingly where for instance the issue is whether a public body has violated a Convention right, the court must reach its own assessment of the facts since the assessment of whether treatment violates a fundamental human right is one which the Court is required itself to make.[37] This may entail live evidence and cross-examination of witnesses in an appropriate case.[38] The Court of Appeal has subsequently held that cross-examination will be necessary only in circumstances in which any dispute about a violation of the Convention cannot be resolved on the basis of documentary evidence such as witness statements.[39] In *Al Sweady*, a case concerning alleged violations of Arts 2 and 3 of the Convention by British troops in Iraq, a full Divisional Court identified the need to determine '*hard-edged*' questions of fact 'where there is no legitimate room for disagreement' (as opposed to judgments that could only be challenged on irrationality

---

[33]   See **2.10.1**. It is important to recognise that this jurisdiction to consider mistake of fact does not permit the Administrative Court to make primary findings of fact. The correct facts must be clear and not in dispute.

[34]   *R v London Borough of Hillingdon ex p Pulhofer* [1986] AC 484, per Lord Brightman, at 518E.

[35]   *Doherty v Birmingham City Council* [2009] 1 AC 367, at 416 and 443D. See also, *Manchester City Council v Pinnock* [2010] 3 WLR 1441, at 1461B.

[36]   *R (A) v Secretary of State for the Home Department* [2007] EWCA Civ 804, at [62].

[37]   *R (Wilkinson) v Broadmoor Hospital* [2002] 1 WLR 419, followed in *R (N) v Secretary of State for Justice* [2009] EWHC 1921 (Admin).

[38]   See, for example, *R (Wilkinson) v Broadmoor Hospital* [2002] 1 WLR 419, at 431E–434B, in which the Court of Appeal concluded that witnesses should be called to determine whether treatment without consent violated a patient's rights under Arts 2, 3 and 8 of the European Convention.

[39]   *R (N) v Doctor M and others* [2003] 1 WLR 562.

grounds) as an exception to the general principle.[40] Noting the 'more far-reaching consequence' that, if the general principle were applied, a 'defendant would always succeed if sued for an infringement of human rights which was disputed', the court envisaged that such orders for cross-examination might occur with increasing regularity in cases where there are crucial factual disputes between the parties relating to jurisdiction of the Convention and the engagement of its Articles.[41]

In addition challenges to public authorities arising under the Equality Act 2010 including complaints regarding non-discrimination and breaches of the 'public sector equality duty' may also give rise to grounds for judicial review which necessitate determination of factual issues.[42]

The scope of the Administrative Court's jurisdiction to make findings of fact is particularly relevant when the Court is considering decisions taken by administrative decision-makers where Art 6 of the European Convention of Human Rights applies. Article 6 states that a person is entitled to a 'determination of his civil rights and obligations ... by an independent and impartial tribunal'. In practice, the civil rights of individuals are often determined by administrative decision-makers who lack the independence and impartiality required by Art 6. Absent an Art 6 compliant form of statutory review, the only tribunal that can comply with the requirements of Art 6 is the Administrative Court when it considers claims for judicial review challenging decisions taken by administrative decision-makers.

The domestic courts have generally concluded that the current scope of judicial review is adequate in circumstances in which the administrative decision-maker is required to exercise his judgment or discretion.[43] However, the European Court of Human Rights has held that the inability of the court on judicial review to rehear the evidence and take its own view of a claimant's credibility rendered it unable to cure a procedure before a housing benefit review board which was not 'independent and impartial'.[44] Where a decision is of the sort that it is properly entrusted to administrative decision-makers (such as regulatory functions or the administration of a scheme of social welfare) then the current scope of judicial review may be adequate (if there are adequate procedural safeguards).[45] Whether it will is an issue that continues to cause

---

[40]   *R (Al Sweady) v Secretary of State for Defence* [2010] HRLR 2, per Scott Baker LJ, at [18].

[41]   Ibid, at [19].

[42]   A full discussion of the impact of the Equality Act 2010 on judicial review is outside the scope of this work but see the useful summary in Mr Justice Sales 'The Public Sector Equality Duty' [2011] JR 1.

[43]   *R (Alconbury Developments Ltd and Others) v Secretary of State for the Environment, Transport and the Regions* [2003] 2 AC 295.

[44]   *Tsfayo v United Kingdom* (2009) 48 EHRR 18.

[45]   *Begum (Runa) v Tower Hamlets LBC* [2003] 2 AC 430. However, there will only be compliance with Art 6 if the administrative decision-maker acts in a manner that is fair.

considerable difficulties as there are arguments about whether a decision is truly administrative and whether there are sufficient safeguards.[46]

Unless it is possible to argue that conclusions of fact come within the exceptions set out above, it will be difficult to challenge the conclusions of fact in the Administrative Court.

Where there is a dispute about the factual background that led to the alleged error of law, for example, where it is alleged that the procedure adopted by the decision-maker or court was a breach of natural justice, an issue of fact may arise as to what procedure was in fact adopted. However, this is an issue that the Court is well placed to resolve on the basis of witness statement evidence.[47] The Administrative Court may however be reluctant to consider these disputes and may proceed on the basis that the defendant's version of events is presumed to be correct.[48] This is particularly true when the judicial review relates to alleged criminal conduct.[49] One consequence of this reluctance to consider disputes of fact is that the Divisional Court has held that it may be preferable to challenge the procedure adopted by a decision-maker such as a magistrates' court by exercising an alternative remedy such as an appeal to the Crown Court if it is impossible to determine by written evidence what procedure was actually adopted.[50] If a tribunal of fact exists which can find the relevant facts it will normally be good practice to postpone judicial review until after the fact-finding exercise has been conducted,[51] unless to do so would pre-empt or raise an obstacle to the judicial review claim.[52]

The Administrative Court's normal reluctance to resolve factual disputes does not mean that it is never appropriate to bring a judicial review in these circumstances. For example, the Divisional Court has accepted the version of events put forward by a claimant's solicitor, where a defendant magistrate could not back up his memory of events with any note.[53] A claimant bringing proceedings for judicial review should always put

---

See, for example, *R (Q and others) v Secretary of State for the Home Department* [2004] QB 36, in which the Court of Appeal held that the system for administrating asylum support was unfair and hence Art 6 could not be complied with. More generally, see *R (Wright) v Sercretary of State for Health* [2009] 1 AC 739, in which the House of Lords held that there must be safeguards to ensure an administrative decision maker is fair and impartial if judicial review is to ensure compliance with Art 6.

[46]  See, for example, *R (King) v Secretary of State for Justice* [2011] 1 WLR 2667, currently under appeal.

[47]  See, for example, *R (AM (Cameroon)) (No 2) v Asylum & Immigration Tribunal* [2008] 1 WLR 2062.

[48]  *R v Reigate Justices ex p Curl* [1991] COD 66; *R v Board of Visitors of Hull Prison ex p St Germain (No2)* [1979] 1 WLR 1401, at 1410H.

[49]  *R v Medicines Control Agency ex p Pharma Nord Ltd* [1997] COD 439.

[50]  *R v Haringey Justices ex p Branco* (1997) *The Independent*, December 1.

[51]  *R (Lower Mill Estate Ltd) v Revenue and Customs Commissioners* [2008] EWHC 2409 (Admin).

[52]  *R (Davies) v Revenue & Customs Commissioners* [2008] EWCA Civ 933.

[53]  See, for example, *R v Highbury Magistrate ex p Di Matteo* [1991] 1 WLR 1374.

forward the facts as the claimant believes them to be but must be aware that it may be difficult to persuade the court to accept this version of events if it becomes clear that the defendant does not. The burden will be on the claimant to prove his version of the facts.[54]

## 2.3   ILLEGALITY

In one sense, all decisions that are challenged by way of judicial review must be challenged on the basis that they are illegal because judicial review aims to 'secure that decisions are made by the executive or by a public body according to the law'.[55] Clearly, however, the term 'illegality' has a more restricted meaning in the context of Lord Diplock's categories. The restrictive meaning that was given to 'illegality' by Lord Diplock is the meaning that is usually used in judicial review pleadings.

Illegality is usually used to describe circumstances where decision-makers fail to direct themselves properly about the law. As Lord Scarman stated:[56]

> 'It is now settled law that an administrative or executive authority entrusted with the exercise of a discretion must direct itself properly in law.'

In practice, the Administrative Court regularly hears challenges that seek to argue that inferior courts and other decision-makers have misconstrued statutes that govern aspects of their work.

For example, in a criminal context, the Administrative Court can consider a challenge that seeks to argue that the statute that gives rise to an offence has been wrongly construed by an inferior court.[57] It can also consider a challenge relating to statutes that govern the admission of evidence[58] or whether a prosecution is time-barred.[59] Of course, not only courts may misdirect themselves regarding the law. For example a failure of a local authority to correctly direct itself regarding the meaning of a statute providing for the payment of grants to students was unlawful.[60]

The HRA 1998 has increased the scope for challenge on the basis that a decision-maker has acted unlawfully because s 6 of the Human Rights Act 1998 makes it unlawful for a public authority to act in a manner that violates the European Convention on Human Rights. Thus, the Administrative Court may be required to make findings of fact in order to

---

[54]  See, for example, *R (Mersey Care NHS Trust) v Mental Health Review Tribunal* [2003] EWHC 1182 (Admin).

[55]  *Mercury Energy Ltd v Electricity Corporation of New Zealand Ltd* [1994] 1 WLR 521, per Lord Templeman, at 526A.

[56]  *Akbarali v Brent London Borough Council and Other Cases* [1983] 2 AC 309, at 350D.

[57]  See, for example, *Vigon v DPP* [1998] Crim LR 289.

[58]  See, for example, *DPP v McKeown; DPP v Jones* [1997] 2 Cr App R 155.

[59]  *R (Donnachie) v Cardiff Magistrates Court* [2007] 1 WLR 3085.

[60]  *Akbarali v Brent London Borough Council and Other Cases* [1983] 2 AC 309.

determine whether the European Convention has been violated, despite the normal reluctance to make findings of fact.[61]

The scope of illegality has been increased further by the Equality Act 2010 and, in particular, by the public sector equality duty, which requires account to be taken of various matters intended to promote equality.[62]

A statute will not have been misconstrued if a decision-maker has reached findings of fact and then applied a statutory provision giving the words their normal meaning to determine whether the statute is engaged. In *Brutus v Cozens*,[63] Lord Reid held:[64]

> 'It is for the tribunal which decides the case to consider, not as law but as fact, whether in the whole circumstances the words of the statute do or do not as a matter of ordinary usage of the English language cover or apply to the facts which have been proved. If it is alleged that the tribunal has reached a wrong decision then there can be a question of law but only of a limited character. The question would normally be whether their decision was unreasonable in the sense that no tribunal acquainted with the ordinary use of language could reasonably reach that decision.'

This means that a magistrates' court does not misconstrue a statute if it reaches findings of fact regarding a person's behaviour and then concludes that the behaviour is insulting.[65] The conclusion that the facts found fit the statutory definition will not normally be an error of law. Similarly it is for the Monopolies and Mergers Commission to determine whether it has jurisdiction to consider a merger by determining whether the merger affects a substantial part of the United Kingdom.[66]

In practice, the dictum of Lord Reid is often relied on by defendants who seek to argue that there is no error of law. However, it clearly is an error of law to conclude that statutory words should be given a particular meaning when the statutory context shows that they should be given some other meaning.[67] Lord Reid was considering the application of findings of fact once the statute had been given its correct meaning. In addition, there will be circumstances in which it will be unreasonable and hence unlawful to conclude that a statute is engaged or not engaged.[68]

---

[61]   See **2.2.2**.
[62]   See, now, s 149 of the Equality Act 2010.
[63]   [1973] AC 854.
[64]   Ibid, at 861.
[65]   Ibid.
[66]   *R v Monopolies and Mergers Commission ex p South Yorkshire Transport* [1993] 1 WLR 23.
[67]   See, for example, *MacNiven (Inspector of Taxes) v Westmoreland Investments Ltd* [2003] 1 AC 311.
[68]   See **2.10**.

An important limitation on the scope of challenges to errors of law arises because judicial review is a discretionary remedy. This is considered later in more detail.[69] In practice, it means that the Administrative Court will not automatically intervene where a decision-maker has at some stage during proceedings misdirected himself regarding the law. Instead, the Court will want to be shown that the decision is 'a relevant error of law, ie an error in the actual making of the decision which affected the decision itself'.[70] The Court will not intervene if the error of law is not material to the decision. For example, a decision of magistrates that relied on a statutory provision that was not in force at the date of the decision was not quashed, because the court could have relied on an alternative provision that was almost identical and was in force,[71] or where the decision on the evidence would inevitably have been the same of the misdirection had not occurred.[72]

Lastly, the Court has recognised that a mistake of fact giving rise to unfairness is itself a separate head of challenge as an error of law.[73] The circumstances in which a mistake of fact may give rise to grounds for judicial review is dealt with in more detail below at **2.10.1**.

It is difficult to know whether a decision can be challenged on the grounds of illegality if no reasons are given for that decision. The circumstances where a duty to give reasons exists are discussed below.[74] Practitioners should be aware of this duty and attempt to obtain the reasons in order to consider whether there has been an error of law.

## 2.4   ULTRA VIRES

It is illegal for a body to act in a way that is either ultra vires or in excess of its jurisdiction. It can be extremely difficult to distinguish between a decision that is ultra vires and a decision in excess of jurisdiction. This is not surprising, as the terms are sometimes given very wide meanings. For example, it has been said that all illegal decisions are ultra vires including those that are in excess of jurisdiction.[75] The position is also confused because the term 'jurisdiction' is sometimes used by judges and practitioners when they are considering whether the Administrative Court is entitled to consider the application for judicial review. In practice,

---

[69]   See **7.1**.

[70]   *R v Hull University Visitor ex p Page* [1993] AC 682, per Lord Browne-Wilkinson, at 702C.

[71]   *R v Folkestone and Hythe Juvenile Court Justices ex p R (a Juvenile)* [1981] 1 WLR 1501, at 1508F.

[72]   *R (Warren) v Mental Health Review Tribunal London & North East Region* [2002] EWHC 811 (Admin), at [17].

[73]   *E v Secretary of State for the Home Department* [2004] QB 1044, at 1071D–1071E.

[74]   See **2.14**.

[75]   *R v Hull University Visitor ex p Page* [1993] AC 682, per Lord Browne-Wilkinson, at 701E; *Boddington v British Transport Police* [1999] 2 AC 143, per Lord Irvine, at 154B.

however, the terms 'ultra vires' and 'jurisdiction' should usually be used by claimants in judicial review proceedings to complain about particular errors of law.

In particular, it is normal to use a narrow definition of ultra vires when pleading it in the Administrative Court. A decision is said to be ultra vires where legislation has conferred powers on a decision-maker or court and the decision-maker or court ignores and exceeds the limitations on those powers imposed by the statute. The Administrative Court will apply the normal principles of statutory construction to decide the limits on a decision-maker imposed by a statute.

An example of an ultra vires decision is secondary legislation made by a public body when the primary legislation does not allow for the making of that secondary legislation. This means, for example, that it may be possible to challenge as being ultra vires the by-laws under which a person is being prosecuted. If that challenge is successful, it means that the person must be found not guilty.[76] An example of an ultra vires by-law was one that restricted access to common land. It was ultra vires because the statute that provided for the making of by-laws prevented the making of by-laws that 'prejudicially affect any right of common'. As a result, protestors at Greenham Common were able to challenge successfully their convictions under that by-law.[77]

The limitation on the power to make secondary legislation need not come from the particular primary legislation that enables the making of the secondary legislation. It can come from any primary legislation. Thus, in an immigration context, a statutory right of appeal could not be limited by benefits regulations that would have impeded the exercise of an appeal right.[78] The benefits regulations were held to be ultra vires. Similarly, secondary legislation or rules made under statute may be held to be ultra vires if they are so unclear as to offend the principle of legal certainty.[79]

It is not only restrictions in primary legislation that may result in a decision being ultra vires. Decisions can also be ultra vires if they violate restrictions on a decision-maker's powers contained in secondary legislation.[80]

An important limitation on the scope to make secondary legislation arises as a consequence of the principle of legality. The principle of legality means that a court will not interpret legislation as permitting a

---

[76] *DPP v Hutchinson* [1990] 2 AC 783.

[77] Ibid.

[78] *R v Secretary of State for Social Security ex p JCWI* [1997] 1 WLR 275, at 293E.

[79] *McEldowney v Forde* [1971] AC 632, at 643F.

[80] See, for example, *R v Oxford Regional Mental Health Review Tribunal ex p Secretary of State for the Home Department* [1988] AC 120, in which the House of Lords proceeded on the basis that a decision was unlawful as it was taken in violation of the Mental Health Review Tribunal Rules 1983 (SI 1983/942).

decision-maker to act in violation of fundamental rights unless the statute contains clear words permitting the violation.[81] This principle is reflected in the HRA 1998, which prohibits decision-makers from acting in violation of the European Convention on Human Rights unless there is an express provision requiring the decision-maker to act in that way.[82]

Another increasingly important limitation on the power to make legislation is European Union law. Legislation may be ultra vires if it is contrary to principles of EU law.[83] A full discussion of EU law is outside the scope of this book, but it is particularly important to be aware that legislation restricting trade or movement of people within Europe may be ultra vires.

## 2.5   ERRORS OF JURISDICTION

As noted above, the phrase 'in excess of jurisdiction' is capable of a wide meaning so that almost all decisions that can be challenged by way of judicial review may be said to be in excess of jurisdiction. However, it is helpful for the sake of clarity for practitioners to give the phrase a narrower meaning. It is suggested that a decision-maker or court should be said to have made an error of jurisdiction when it has misunderstood and acted outside the scope of its powers. This is consistent with the dictum of Lord Reid, who held that a decision should be regarded as being in excess of a decision-maker's jurisdiction if the decision-maker was not 'entitled to enter on the inquiry in question'.[84] Decisions that are said to be in excess of jurisdiction may include decisions that would not normally be described as ultra vires using the narrow definition considered at **2.4**, as well as those that are ultra vires, because a decision-maker's powers may arise from sources other than legislation.[85] The Administrative Court is not limited to considering judicial review of a decision where the power to take the decision arose from a statute. In principle, there is no reason why challenges to decisions in these circumstances could not be based on an alleged absence of jurisdiction.

An example of a decision that is both in excess of jurisdiction and ultra vires is a decision of the magistrates' court to allow a defendant to reopen his plea when the court had no power to make that decision. The Divisional Court held that the decision was in excess of jurisdiction.[86] However, although the court did not state that the decision was ultra vires, it is implicit that it was because the court relied on a limitation on the statutory power to allow the decision to be reopened.

---

[81]　See, for example, *R v Secretary of State for the Home Department ex p Simms* [2000] 2 AC 115.

[82]　HRA 1998, s 6.

[83]　*R v Secretary of State for Transport ex p Factortame Ltd (No 3)* [1992] QB 680.

[84]　*Anisminic Ltd v Foreign Compensation Commission* [1969] 2 AC 147, at 171C.

[85]　*R v Panel on Take-overs & Mergers ex p Datafin* [1987] 1 QB 815.

[86]　*R v Croydon Youth Court ex p DPP* [1997] 2 Cr App R 411.

Errors of jurisdiction that could arise include the decision-maker lacking the status required to make a particular type of decision. For example, some statutes require particular decisions to be taken by judges with a particular status. It is an error of jurisdiction for a judge without that status to take the decision.[87] It is also an error of jurisdiction for a decision to be taken when the public authority is *functus officio*.[88] Thus, once a court has made final orders, including costs orders, it normally cannot then reconsider and amend those orders.[89]

A public authority acts outside its jurisdiction when a condition precedent to the exercise of a power is not established. A condition precedent is a fact or event that triggers the power to act. There are many examples of circumstances in which a condition precedent must be established before a power can be exercised. In the criminal context, for example, the laying of an information is a condition precedent to a magistrates' court's jurisdiction to try a matter summarily on an information;[90] a committal to prison for non-payment of rates requires a means inquiry as a condition precedent;[91] and an extension of custody time-limits requires the court to find a good and sufficient cause as a condition precedent.[92] In another context, where a power to detain was contingent on an intention to deport, the Court concluded on enquiry that no such intention existed and accordingly that detention was unlawful.[93]

The absence of a condition precedent is closely linked to the Administrative Court's jurisdiction to consider precedent facts. When a precedent fact is required before a decision is taken, the Court may determine for itself whether that fact exists when it considers an application for judicial review.[94] This is an exception to the normal reluctance of the Court to make findings of fact when it considers applications for judicial review.

The Administrative Court has generally been reluctant to find that decisions require a precedent fact to be established. In general, the Court will conclude that a decision-maker has jurisdiction to make findings of fact that determine whether it should act and that those findings of fact should be respected.[95] Circumstances in which the Administrative Court

---

87    *R v Central Criminal Court ex p Francis & Francis* [1989] AC 346, at 368F.
88    *R v Parliamentary Commissioner for Administration ex p Dyer* [1994] 1 WLR 621, at 629F.
89    *R v Cripps ex p Muldoon* [1984] 1 QB 686. See also *R (Conservative and Unionist Party) v Election Commissioner* [2011] PTSR 416.
90    *R v Manchester Stipendiary Magistrate ex p Hill* [1983] 1 AC 328.
91    *R v Manchester City Magistrates' Court ex p Davies* [1989] QB 631.
92    *R v Governor of Winchester Prison ex p Roddie* [1991] 1 WLR 303.
93    *HXA v Home Office* [2010] EWHC 1177 (QB), where the court was applying public law principles.
94    See, for example, *R v Oldham Metropolitan Borough Council ex p Garlick* [1993] AC 509, at 520E.
95    *R v Secretary of State for Employment ex p National Association of Colliery Overmen, Deputies and Shotfirers* [1994] COD 218.

has been willing to find that a decision requires a precedent fact include where the decision relates to individual liberty,[96] where the Secretary of State for Education's is exercising a power to intervene in disciplinary proceedings concerning a teacher,[97] and where the Secretary of State's powers to intervene in the executive functions of a local education authority were contingent on unreasonable conduct by that authority and such unreasonable conduct was not established.[98] A recent example, of a precedent fact is the issue of whether a person is a child for the purposes of s 20 of the Children Act 1989.[99]

One example of the circumstances in which the Administrative Court requires a precedent fact to be established is where the Secretary of State asserts that a person is an illegal entrant.[100] The practice in this area demonstrates how a precedent fact is established. The Court will review the material presented to show that the person is an illegal entrant and determine whether this has been proved.

Errors of jurisdiction do not merely occur where a public authority acts when it lacks the power to do so. It is also an error of jurisdiction if a decision-maker wrongly declines to take a decision that it is required to take. For example, where magistrates wrongly conclude that they have no jurisdiction to consider an application to vary the conditions attached to a warrant of committal, they make an error of jurisdiction that enables the Administrative Court to intervene.[101]

## 2.6   BROAD STATUTORY DISCRETION AND ERRORS OF LAW

The statutory provision that empowers a decision-maker or court often gives it a wide discretion. For example, the statutory provision may state that a decision-maker may make a decision if it considers that it is 'just'. The decision-maker is unlikely to receive any explicit statutory guidance about the circumstances where making that decision will be just. The wide provisions of a discretionary statutory power do not mean, however, that all decisions that are based on a purported exercise of that power are legal.

First, the scope of that discretion needs to be determined by applying the normal principles of statutory construction to see whether there is any implicit statutory guidance as to how the power should be exercised. Thus, the discretion under s 142(2) of the Magistrates' Courts Act 1980 to

---

[96]   See, for example, *R v Secretary of State for the Home Department ex p Khawaja* [1984] AC 74.

[97]   *R (McNally) v Secretary of State for Education and Employment* [2002] ICR 15.

[98]   *Secretary of State for Education and Science v Tameside MBC* [1977] AC 1014.

[99]   *R (A) v Croydon LBC* [2009] 1 WLR 2557.

[100]  *R v Secretary of State for the Home Department ex p Khawaja* [1984] AC 74.

[101]  *In re Wilson* [1985] AC 750.

allow a case to be reheard where it is 'in the interests of justice' did not allow the court to rehear a defendant's case where the defendant had entered an unequivocal plea of guilty. A decision to allow a rehearing in these circumstances was one that the court had no jurisdiction to take as a result of the limitation on the statutory power. The implied purpose of the statutory power was to allow the magistrates' court to correct mistakes and so it can only be used in these circumstances.[102] The decision-maker is under a duty to understand the nature of the power being exercised for instance whether the power in question gives rise to a wide or narrow discretion, having regard to the statutory scheme.[103]

A statutory discretion may only be exercised consistently with the public purpose for which the powers were conferred. Accordingly where a Scottish licensing authority sought to use its statutory discretion for an 'ulterior object', however desirable, its decision to add a condition to the grant of a licence was unlawful.[104] However, a rule-making power granted by statute was, in the absence of express limitation, sufficiently wide to allow rule-making for collateral purposes in the public interest.[105]

### 2.6.1 The use of policy to guide the exercise of discretion

The exercise of a discretionary power may also be challenged in certain circumstances if the decision-maker has adopted a policy to assist him with the exercise of that power. There is nothing unlawful about the adoption of a policy, because it promotes 'consistency and certainty'.[106] However, any public authority that adopts a policy must be willing to consider whether the policy should not be applied in the circumstances of a particular case. If the public authority fails to do so, it risks unlawfully fettering its discretion. Lord Reid considered the correct approach to policy:[107]

> 'Bankes L.J. said, …
>
>> "There are on the one hand cases where a tribunal in the honest exercise of its discretion has adopted a policy, and, without refusing to hear an applicant, intimates to him what its policy is, and that after hearing him it will in accordance with its policy decide against him, unless there is something exceptional in his case. I think counsel for the applicants would admit that, if the policy has been adopted for

---

[102] *R v Croydon Youth Court ex p DPP* [1997] 2 Cr App R 411.
[103] See, for example, *R v Secretary of State for the Environment ex p Nottinghamshire County Council* [1986] AC 240, at 249C–249D, in which Lord Scarman categorised a mistake of law in misconstruing the limits imposed by statute as an abuse of power.
[104] *Stewart v Perth and Kinross Council* 2004 SLT 383.
[105] *R (Spath Holme Ltd) v Secretary of State for the Environment, Transport and the Regions* [2001] 2 AC 349.
[106] *R v Secretary of State for the Home Department ex p Venables* [1997] 2 WLR 67, per Lord Woolf, at 90B.
[107] *British Oxygen Company Limited v Minister of Technology* [1971] AC 610, at 625.

reasons which the tribunal may legitimately entertain, no objection could be taken to such a course. On the other hand there are cases where a tribunal has passed a rule, or come to a determination, not to hear any application of a particular character by whomsoever made. There is a wide distinction to be drawn between these two classes."

I see nothing wrong with that. But the circumstances in which discretions are exercised vary enormously and that passage cannot be applied literally in every case. The general rule is that anyone who has to exercise a statutory discretion must not "shut his ears to an application" (to adapt from Bankes L.J. ...). I do not think there is any great difference between a policy and a rule. There may be cases where an officer or authority ought to listen to a substantial argument reasonably presented urging a change of policy. What the authority must not do is to refuse to listen at all. But a Ministry or large authority may have had to deal already with a multitude of similar applications and then they will almost certainly have evolved a policy so precise that it could well be called a rule. There can be no objection to that, provided the authority is always willing to listen to anyone with something new to say – of course I do not mean to say that there need be an oral hearing.'

In practice, this means that the policy must not be so inflexible that it prevents the decision-maker from taking account of relevant factors.[108] Thus, for example, it is unlawful for a decision-maker to apply a policy in a manner that undermines the stated objective of the policy. In *R (P) v Secretary of State for the Home Department and another*,[109] the Court of Appeal held that the Prison Service policy regarding the separation of imprisoned women from their babies was unlawfully inflexible as it could operate in a manner that was contrary to the stated objective of promoting the welfare of children.

Similarly, the policy must not bind the decision-maker to acting in a certain way in the future as the factors relevant to the exercise of the discretion change.[110] A decision-maker must always consider the individual circumstances of a case. Thus, the Secretary of State for Education erred by applying a policy that stated that, as a consequence of a child's age, approval would not be granted for a child to attend a particular school without considering the individual circumstances of the case.[111]

When considering the degree of flexibility required from a particular policy, it is necessary to consider the context in which the policy operates. For example, when considering a policy that applies to prisoners, it is important that prisoners see that an adopted policy is clear, consistent

---

[108]   *R v Secretary of State for the Home Department ex p Venables* [1998] AC 407, at 497B.
[109]   [2001] 1 WLR 2002.
[110]   *R v Secretary of State for the Home Department ex p Venables* [1998] AC 407, at 496H.
[111]   *R v Secretary of State for Education and Employment, ex p P* [2000] ELR 300.

and practical.[112] This suggests that a greater degree of inflexibility may be acceptable in a prison context than in others because there is a particular need for consistency.

When a decision-maker has adopted a policy, it is clear that in principle a failure to follow the policy may be challenged unless sufficiently good reasons for departing from the policy have been given. Opinion has been divided as to whether the meaning of a policy is an issue for the court to be read objectively or for the policy-maker to determine. The Court of Appeal has held in the context of an ex gratia compensation scheme that the meaning of the policy adopted under the scheme was an issue for the court to decide.[113] This approach has subsequently been applied in other contexts.[114] Authority to the effect that courts will accept the interpretation of an immigration policy adopted by the decision-maker unless it can be shown that the interpretation is irrational[115] would appear to have been superseded at least in the context of published rather than purely internal policies.[116]

Where a policy has been adopted, sufficient of it must be published to enable a person to be informed and make meaningful representations before a decision is taken that affects them.[117]

One recent concern of the courts has been regarding policies that could be operated lawfully but that give rise to an unacceptable risk of illegality. The courts have accepted that such policies are unlawful.[118]

## 2.7  PROCEDURAL IMPROPRIETY

The most obvious form of procedural impropriety is a failure to comply with an express procedural requirement; this need not arise from primary legislation. For example, a failure to comply with procedural requirements contained in the Magistrates' Courts Rules 1981 is an error that enables the Administrative Court to intervene.[119]

Legislation may impose a wide range of procedural requirements on decision-makers and courts. A person may be given the right to be heard

---

[112]  *R (P) v Secretary of State for the Home Department and another* [2001] 1 WLR 2002.

[113]  *R (Raissi) v Secretary of State for the Home Department* [2008] QB 836.

[114]  See, for example, *R (Roberts) v The Welsh Ministers* [2011] EWHC 3416 (Admin) and *R (Kennedy) v Health and Safety Executive* [2009] EWCA Civ 25.

[115]  *R v Secretary of State for the Home Department ex p Gangadeen* [1998] INLR 206.

[116]  See *R (K) v Secretary of State for the Home Department* [2010] EWHC 3102 (Admin) and *R (Nori) v Secretary of State for the Home Department* [2011] EWHC 1604 (Admin).

[117]  *R (Lumba) v Secretary of State for the Home Department* [2011] 2 WLR 671, at [38].

[118]  *R (Suppiah) v Secretary of State for the Home Department* [2011] EWHC 2 (Admin), at [140].

[119]  *R v Dover Magistrates' Court ex p Kidner* [1983] 1 All ER 475.

or consulted about a decision.[120] There may also be an express right to be given notice of proceedings.[121] At the end of proceedings, there may be an express right to reasons for a decision.[122] Express procedural rules may benefit a third party who is affected by a decision, but who is not a party to proceedings. For example, a person has the right to be heard if they object to an occasional drinks licence.[123] The failure to comply with any of these express provisions will enable the court to intervene.

The historic approach to violations of express procedural rules was to consider the statutory provisions that impose the procedural requirements to determine whether they actually impose a mandatory procedure or whether they merely direct the decision-maker about the procedure that should normally be adopted. If the procedure was merely directory, the decision-maker or court was entitled to refuse to comply with the procedure in exceptional circumstances.[124] For example, the requirement contained in s 5(8) of the Children and Young Persons Act 1969 that a local authority should be informed of the prosecution of a young person is merely directory. Accordingly, a decision of a criminal court will not necessarily be quashed as a result of a failure to comply with this provision.[125]

If a procedural requirement is mandatory, a party complaining about a failure to comply with this procedure is not required to show prejudice.[126] One possible exception to this rule is where the failure to observe a mandatory procedural requirement was induced by the claimant's conduct.[127]

Clearly, if the procedural requirements are merely directory, the Administrative Court will still be able to consider a complaint alleging a failure to comply with those procedural requirements. However, because the procedure specified in a statute is directory, it is implicit that the decision-maker has a discretion to depart from that procedure.[128] As a result, the Court will quash a decision only if it is satisfied that the decision to depart from the directory procedural requirements was not taken in accordance with the principles of public law. For example, a decision taken following a failure to comply with a directory procedure will be quashed if it is unreasonable or taken for an improper motive.

---

[120] *R v Bromley Licensing Justices ex p Bromley Licensed Victuallers' Association* [1984] 1 WLR 585.

[121] *R v Seisdon Justices ex p Dougan* [1982] 1 WLR 1476.

[122] *R v Parole Board ex p Lodomez* [1994] COD 525.

[123] *R v Bromley Licensing Justices ex p Bromley Licensed Victuallers' Association* [1984] 1 WLR 585.

[124] *O'Reilly v Mackman* [1983] 2 AC 237, at 276A.

[125] *DPP v Cottier* [1996] 1 WLR 826; *R v Marsh* [1997] 1 WLR 649.

[126] *O'Reilly v Mackman* [1983] 2 AC 237, at 276A.

[127] *R v Secretary of State for the Home Department ex p Awais Karni Butt* [1994] Imm AR 11, at 13.

[128] *O'Reilly v Mackman* [1983] 2 AC 237, at 276A.

This conventional 'categorisation' approach was called into question by the decision of the Court of Appeal in *R v Immigration Appeal Tribunal ex p Jeyeanthan*.[129] In that case, Lord Woolf MR held:

> 'I suggest that the right approach is to regard the question of whether a requirement is directory or mandatory as only at most a first step. In the majority of cases there are other questions which have to be asked which are more likely to be of greater assistance than the application of the mandatory/directory test: The questions which are likely to arise are as follows:
>
> (a) Is the statutory requirement fulfilled if there has been substantial compliance with the requirement and, if so, has there been substantial compliance in the case in issue even though there has not been strict compliance? (The substantial compliance question.)
>
> (b) Is the non-compliance capable of being waived, and if so, has it, or can it and should it be waived in this particular case? (The discretionary question.) I treat the grant of an extension of time for compliance as a waiver.
>
> (c) If it is not capable of being waived or is not waived then what is the consequence of the non-compliance? (The consequences question.)
>
> Which questions arise will depend upon the facts of the case and the nature of the particular requirement. The advantage of focusing on these questions is that they should avoid the unjust and unintended consequences which can flow from an approach solely dependent on dividing requirements into mandatory ones, which oust jurisdiction, or directory, which do not. If the result of non-compliance goes to jurisdiction it will be said jurisdiction cannot be conferred where it does not otherwise exist by consent or waiver.'[130]

As a consequence, the Court of Appeal held that a failure by the Secretary of State to comply with an express procedural requirement had not made an application for leave to appeal to the Immigration Appeal Tribunal a nullity – the procedural requirement had been waived.[131]

Two members of the House of Lords subsequently endorsed the decision in *R v Immigration Appeal Tribunal ex p Jeyeanthan*.[132] The decision has also been distinguished in one Court of Appeal decision on the ground that the *Jeyeanthan* approach could not be applied where the procedural requirement in question is a condition precedent triggering the jurisdiction of a decision-maker because parties cannot consent to grant a decision-maker jurisdiction that it otherwise lacks.[133] However the *Jeyeanthan* approach has been followed widely in a range of other

---

[129] [2000] 1 WLR 354.

[130] Ibid, at 362.

[131] Ibid.

[132] *Attorney-General's Reference (No 3 of 1999)* [2001] 2 AC 91, per Lord Steyn and Lord Cooke.

[133] *Rydqvist v Secretary of State for Work and Pensions* [2002] 1 WLR 3343, at 3350B–3350H.

contexts.[134] In addition, it appears entirely consistent with the approach of the House of Lords in a criminal context.[135]

It is important to note that *Jeyeanthan* does not mean that there are no mandatory requirements. It merely means that one must start by considering whether Parliament intended that failure to comply with a provision should mean that subsequent steps are of no effect while recognising that it is unlikely that Parliament had such an intent. As Lord Rodger held:[136]

> '... any classification into mandatory or directory is the end of the relevant inquiry, not the beginning, and that the better test is to ask "whether it was a purpose of the legislation that an act done in breach of the provision should be invalid".'

One form of procedural requirement that is likely to be mandatory is a requirement to give notice of a decision. That is because it is an aspect of the right of access to justice that a person has notice of a decision that they may wish to challenge.[137]

## 2.8   NATURAL JUSTICE AND IMPARTIALITY

Judicial review claims in the Administrative Court based on procedural impropriety are more commonly expressed as a claimed breach of natural justice, rather than a failure to comply with express procedural requirements. Natural justice imposes two principle requirements on a decision-maker or court. The decision-maker or court must act impartially and must give a party a fair hearing.[138] The procedural requirements for a hearing to be regarded as fair are set out in detail below.[139] First, the text will focus on the issue of a lack of impartiality or bias.

A decision will be quashed for bias if a claimant for judicial review can show actual or apparent bias or that the decision-maker had a direct interest in the outcome.

Actual bias exists when a judicial decision-maker allows himself to be influenced by partiality or prejudice.[140] Actual bias is very rare and hard

---

[134]   See, for example, *Rochdale BC v Dixon* [2012] HLR 6; *R (McKay) v First Secretary of State* [2006] 1 P & CR 19; and *Fehily v Governor of Wandsworth Prison* [2003] 1 Cr App R 10.

[135]   *R v Soneji* [2006] 1 AC 340.

[136]   *R v Clarke* [2008] 1 WLR 338, at 351H.

[137]   *R (Anufrijeva) v Secretary of State for the Home Department* [2004] 1 AC 604, at 616G.

[138]   See, for example, *Kanda v Government of Malaya* [1962] AC 322, at 337, PC; *O'Reilly v Mackman* [1983] 2 AC 237, at 279G.

[139]   See **2.8.1–2.8.6**.

[140]   *Locabail v Bayfield Properties Ltd and another* [2000] QB 451, at 471.

to prove,[141] so it is rarely raised in the Administrative Court. If actual bias can be proved, a litigant has 'irresistible grounds' for objecting to his trial by that judicial decision-maker.[142] In practice, it is difficult to see why a claimant would wish to attempt to raise a claim of actual bias as it is considerably easier to prove apparent bias.[143]

If it can be shown that a judicial decision-maker has a direct interest in the outcome of litigation, it should result in automatic disqualification.[144] However, a direct interest is almost as difficult to prove as actual bias because the Administrative Court will not act if a judicial decision-maker had only a slight pecuniary interest in the outcome. For example, a member of the Law Society can sit as a justice in a case brought by the Society, as it is highly unlikely that the justice will become personally liable for any costs resulting from the proceedings.[145] What is necessary is a sufficiently significant interest that the outcome of the case could 'realistically' affect the interest of the judge.[146] If there is any doubt about whether the interest is sufficiently significant, that doubt must be resolved in favour of disqualification.[147]

The direct interest that gives rise to disqualification need not be a financial interest. It is clear that in a judicial review where a claimant is not seeking damages, a direct interest does not require a pecuniary interest in the outcome. It can arise where a judge or decision-maker has shown a direct interest in promoting the cause that is being considered in the judicial review.[148]

Despite the problems involved in proving actual bias and a direct interest in the outcome, the rules regarding bias provide significant protection for litigants because apparent bias is relatively straightforward to prove. Under the common law before the enactment of the HRA 1998, the test to be applied when considering whether the circumstances of a case indicated apparent bias on behalf of a decision-maker or court was identified by Lord Goff, when he held that:[149]

> '[H]aving ascertained the relevant circumstances, the court should ask itself whether, having regard to those circumstances, there was a real danger of

---

[141] *R v Gough* [1993] AC 646, at 661G.
[142] *Locabail v Bayfield Properties Ltd and another* [2000] QB 451, at 471.
[143] Ibid, at 472.
[144] Ibid.
[145] *R v Burton ex p Young* [1897] 2 QB 468.
[146] *Locabail v Bayfield Properties Ltd and another* [2000] QB 451, at 473.
[147] Ibid, at 473.
[148] *R v Bow Street Metropolitan Stipendiary Magistrate and others ex p Pinochet Ugarte (No 2)* [2000] 1 AC 119, in which the House of Lords held that there is no need for a pecuniary interest. The question is whether a judge is acting in his own cause. In this case, the House of Lords held that Lord Hoffmann was disqualified from considering the application to extradite General Pinochet as a result of his involvement with Amnesty International.
[149] *R v Gough* [1993] AC 646, at 670F.

bias on the part of the relevant member of the tribunal in question, in the sense that he might unfairly regard (or have unfairly regarded) with favour, or disfavour, the case of a party to the issue under consideration.'

The use of the phrase 'real danger' in Lord Goff's test required only the possibility of bias rather than the probability of bias.[150] In addition, the court considering claims of bias was not restricted to considering whether a reasonable man sitting in court would have decided that there was a real danger of bias.[151] This is because the court considering claims of bias may have information before it that would not have been available to an observer sitting in court.

Lord Goff's test did not require the court to investigate the decision-maker's state of mind to decide whether actual prejudice is established; the decision-maker may not even be conscious of any bias. Thus, in proceedings in the magistrates' court, an intervention from the chairman of the bench, stating that it was not the practice of the court to call police officers liars, allowed the Administrative Court to intervene. The intervention indicated a real danger of unconscious bias in favour of the evidence of police officers.[152]

Following the enactment of the HRA 1998 and the incorporation of Art 6 of the European Convention, the test initiated by Lord Goff has developed in a small but significant way.[153] In *Director General of Fair Trading v Proprietary Association of Great Britain*,[154] the Court of Appeal concluded that Art 6 of the European Convention required the following approach to bias:[155]

'(1)    If a judge is shown to have been influenced by actual bias, his decision must be set aside.

(2)    Where actual bias has not been established the personal impartiality of the judge is to be presumed.

(3)    The court then has to decide whether, on an objective appraisal, the material facts give rise to a legitimate fear that the judge might not have been impartial. If they do the decision of the judge must be set aside.

(4)    The material facts are not limited to those which were apparent to the applicant. They are those which are ascertained upon investigation by the court.

(5)    An important consideration in making an objective appraisal of the facts is the desirability that the public should remain confident in the administration of justice.'

---

[150]  Ibid, at 670E.
[151]  Ibid, at 670D.
[152]  *R v Highgate Magistrates' Court ex p Riley* [1996] COD 12.
[153]  *Porter v Magill* [2002] 2 AC 357, at 494G–494H.
[154]  [2001] 1 WLR 700.
[155]  Ibid, at 726F–726G.

The Court of Appeal then compared this approach to that of Lord Goff and concluded that:[156]

> 'The difference is that when the Strasbourg court considers whether the material circumstances give rise to a reasonable apprehension of bias, it makes it plain that it is applying an objective test to the circumstances, not passing judgment on the likelihood that the particular tribunal under review was in fact biased.'

Applying this approach, the Court of Appeal concluded that the Restrictive Practices Court erred when considering a complaint that one of the members of the court was biased as a consequence of applying for work with a consultancy, which was due to give evidence in proceedings before the Court. The Court of Appeal held that the Restrictive Practices Court should not have sought to determine the credibility of statements made by the member of the court about the circumstances of the application for work.[157] Instead, it should have considered whether objectively the circumstances of the application would have resulted in a fair-minded observer concluding that there was a real danger of bias.[158] The fair-minded observer should be taken to adopt a balanced approach that is 'neither complacent nor unduly sensitive or suspicious'.[159]

The approach of the Court of Appeal has subsequently been approved by the House of Lords.[160] The House of Lords did, however, make it clear that the 'real danger' test served no useful purpose. The issue was whether there was a 'real possibility' of bias.[161] This reflects the concept in Art 6 of access to an 'independent and impartial tribunal'. However, it does not in effect differ materially from the common law test.[162]

It is probably impossible to identify all the circumstances in which an allegation of apparent bias can be made. There are always likely to be novel circumstances in which a judicial review claimant will be able to argue that objectively the circumstances of the case give rise to an objective possibility of bias. An obvious example of apparent bias has been found where the decision-maker has made statements that suggest that he favours one of the parties. The decision-maker may be required to disqualify himself if the statements suggest unconscious bias in favour of one of the parties. For example, a Recorder who wrote a number of articles which were 'pro-claimant/anti-insurers' was disqualified from considering a case involving an insurance company.[163]

---

[156] Ibid, at 726H.
[157] Ibid, at 728E.
[158] Ibid, at 729D.
[159] *Lawal v Northen Spirit Ltd* [2003] ICR 856.
[160] *Porter v Magill* [2002] 2 AC 357, at 494C–494H.
[161] Ibid.
[162] *R v Abdroikov* [2007] 1 WLR 2679, at 2688F.
[163] *Locobail v Bayfield Properties Ltd and another* [2000] QB 451, at 496.

The case-law regarding Art 6 of the European Convention suggests that similar concerns arise if a judge has reached firm views regarding the merits of a case as a consequence of previous involvement in the case. For example, the European Court of Human Rights has held that Art 6 of the European Convention was violated in circumstances in which members of a court determining the constitutionality of legislation had previously advised on that matter.[164] Thus, the House of Lords held that Art 6 had been violated where a judge had previously been a government minister who had drafted or promoted legislation.[165] However, despite this case-law, the Court of Appeal has concluded that a decision by a judge to refuse permission to appeal following a consideration on the papers should not prevent that judge subsequently hearing the case.[166]

Apparent bias may also arise from information obtained by a judicial decision-maker outside the trial process. For example, where during pre-trial hearings in criminal proceedings magistrates have heard submissions or considered evidence without the defendant and his advisers being present, the magistrates may be obliged to order that the matter should be tried by another bench. If they do not do this, there is a danger of apparent bias.[167] However, not all relevant knowledge obtained outside court proceedings necessarily gives rise to an inference of apparent bias. For example, it is desirable that a magistrate considering licensing applications should have prior knowledge of licensing policy. As a result, a member of the licensing committee that refused an application for a licence could sit as a magistrate considering the same application.[168] However, where by the very fact of his presence when a search order was confirmed, a deputy prison governor had given the order his tacit assent and when, thereafter, the order was disobeyed and he ruled upon its lawfulness, a fair minded observer could think him biased towards finding the order lawful.[169]

Special considerations may apply where it is alleged that there is a real danger of bias by an adviser to a decision-maker such as a magistrates'

---

[164] *Procola v Luxembourg* (1995) 22 EHRR 193, at [43].
[165] *Davidson v Scottish Ministers (No 2)* [2005] 1 SC (HL) 7.
[166] *Sengupta v Holmes* [2002] EWCA Civ 1104, (2002) 99 (39) LSG 39.
[167] *R v South Worcestershire Magistrates' Court ex p Lilley* [1995] 4 All ER 186.
[168] *R v Bristol Crown Court ex p Cooper* [1990] 1 WLR 1031; see also *Johnson v Leicestershire Constabulary* (1998) *The Times*, October 7, in which it was held that where magistrates gained knowledge that a defendant had spent time in custody, as a result of one of their number being a prison visitor, the question was whether there was any real danger of bias. Lay magistrates are trained to put irrelevant matters out of their mind. These authorities need to be viewed with a degree of caution as they were decided before the HRA 1998 came into force and so they are not necessarily consistent with the decision in *Director General of Fair Trading v Proprietary Association of Great Britain* [2001] 1 WLR 700.
[169] *R (Carroll) v Secretary of State for the Home Department* [2005] 1 WLR 688.

clerk. The clerk may not actually have participated in the decision that is being challenged. Lord Goff stated that, in addition to bias, it must be shown that:[170]

> 'by reason of [the clerk's] participating in the decision-making process, there was a real likelihood that he ... would impose his influence on the justices or give them wrong legal advice.'

Where a judicial review application is brought complaining about bias, the Administrative Court has suggested that it is desirable that the Court be supplied with written evidence from the parties who were in court and from the decision-maker who is alleged to have shown bias. Thus, for example, in the Crown Court, the circuit judge hearing the appeal and counsel who appeared for the other side should sign witness statements.[171]

Although issues of bias are most commonly raised in the context of court proceedings, the common law rules of procedural fairness can mean that in principle there can be complaint of bias regarding an administrative decision-maker. If such a complaint is raised, the court will take account of the context of the decision being challenged but 'once proceedings have been successfully impugned for want of independence and impartiality on the part of the tribunal, the decision itself must necessarily be regarded as tainted by unfairness and so cannot be permitted to stand'.[172]

### 2.8.1 Fair hearing: an introduction

There are no universal standards that apply in every situation and determine whether the parties to a decision-making process have had a fair hearing. Instead, what fairness demands will depend on the circumstances of the case.[173] As a result, judges have been reluctant to lay down rigid rules defining the scope of natural justice.[174] It is clear, however, that a fair hearing does not require a decision-maker to adopt the highest possible standards of procedural fairness.[175] Instead, it requires the decision-maker to act fairly to do justice in the particular circumstances of the case.

Some authorities suggest that a person complaining about the absence of a fair hearing is not required to prove prejudice.[176] Even if it can be shown that a proper procedure would have made no difference, that will not

---

[170] *R v Gough* [1993] AC 646, at 664D.
[171] *R v Southwark Crown Court ex p Collman* (1998) *Archbold News*, August.
[172] *R (Carroll) v Secretary of State for the Home Department* [2005] 1 WLR 688, at 702F.
[173] See, for example, *Fairmount Investments Ltd v Secretary of State for the Environment* [1976] 1 WLR 1255, per Lord Russell, at 1265H.
[174] See, for example, *Wiseman v Borneman* [1971] AC 297, per Lord Morris, at 308H.
[175] See, for example, *R v Devon County Council ex p Baker & Johns* [1995] 1 All ER 73, per Dillon LJ, at 85C.
[176] See most recently *AF (No 3) v Secretary of State* [2010] 2 AC 269 holding that, although there are some cases where a court might be able to say inadequate disclosure made no

necessarily result in the Administrative Court declining to intervene. Authority suggests that the Court may be required to intervene despite the absence of prejudice. For example, Lord Wright held that:[177]

> 'If the principles of natural justice are violated in respect of any decision, it is, indeed, immaterial whether the same decision would have been arrived at in the absence of the departure from the essential principles of justice. The decision must be declared to be no decision.'

The matters above do not mean that prejudice is not a relevant consideration. If it can be shown that the 'outcome would have been the same whatever process was adopted', that finding may result in the Administrative Court deciding not to intervene (depending upon the context).[178] It is important to recognise that the Court will need to be satisfied that the outcome would have been bound to be the same. It would not be adequate for the Court to conclude that the decision was likely to be the same.[179] Once procedural unfairness has been established 'it would be enough to show that but for that procedural unfairness the outcome might have been different'.[180]

In practice, it may be that if it can be shown that the decision would have been the same in any event, that fact justifies a lower standard of procedural fairness. For example, it may be that where the correct decision is clear that justifies a 'process of consultation which might seem perfunctory or lacking in due process in a case where alternative solutions required to be carefully weighed'.[181]

To the extent that it is relevant to consider whether a procedural irregularity is material, there is some authority suggesting that the burden will be on the defendant to a judicial review claim to show that the procedural irregularity was not material. The Administrative Court may start by presuming that a procedural irregularity should lead to a decision being quashed. This approach was endorsed by Lord Donaldson when he held that:[182]

> 'Any unfairness, whether apparent or actual and however inadvertent, strikes at the roots of justice. I cannot be sure that the applicants were not prejudiced and accordingly I have no doubt that the justices' order should be quashed.'

---

difference, there were good policy reasons why sufficient disclosure was required to ensure a fair trial in control order proceedings.

[177] *General Medical Council v Spackman* [1943] AC 627, at 644–645.

[178] *R (Lichfield Securities Ltd) v Lichfield District Council* [2001] PLCR 32.

[179] Ibid, at [23].

[180] *R (Clegg) v Secretary of State for Trade and Industry* [2002] EWCA Civ 519, at [30].

[181] *R (Lichfield Securities Ltd) v Lichfield District Council* [2001] PLCR 32, at [23].

[182] *R v Leicester JJ ex p Barrow* [1991] 2 QB 260, at 290D.

Although the burden may be on the defendant to show that there is no prejudice, any actual prejudice or potential prejudice should always be pleaded and carefully evidenced by a claimant. Prejudice is significant, as it is a factor that tends to show that the procedure adopted was not fair in all the circumstances of the case. In most contexts, it is likely to be easy to show potential prejudice, because it will normally be possible to argue that the decision of a court or an administrative decision-maker might have been different if a different procedure had been adopted.[183] For example, potential prejudice was found when parties to proceedings were prevented from obtaining legal advice. Had the parties to the proceedings been able to obtain legal advice, they might have presented their case differently.[184]

### 2.8.2 Determining whether the right to a fair hearing arises in the circumstances of the case

The starting point for considering whether there is a right to a fair hearing is to look at the statutory framework under which the decision is taken. A statute may exclude the application of the rules of natural justice with a clear and express provision.[185] The Administrative Court is, however, likely to interpret such a statutory provision very narrowly. For example, a statutory provision excluding any duty to give reasons for a final decision did not exclude a duty to disclose concerns before the final decision, so that parties could respond to them.[186]

If there is no express statutory provision excluding the application of the rules of natural justice, one still needs to consider whether there are express procedural requirements imposed on the decision-maker. Express procedural requirements do not mean that the Administrative Court will not hold that the right to a fair hearing imposes additional procedural requirements on the decision-maker.[187] For example, the Court has held that the Magistrates' Courts Rules 1981 did not prevent the rules of natural justice imposing additional procedural requirements on magistrates.[188] Where the statutory procedure is, on its face, at odds with the principles of natural justice the Court may, absent any express statutory provision permitting a departure from the principles of natural justice, imply such principles into the procedure. Hence, where the statutory procedure under the Education Reform Act 1988 governing disciplinary proceedings provided for the representative of the local authority bringing the disciplinary proceedings to accompany the governors' panel in their deliberations in the absence of the parties, the Court of Appeal held that

---

[183] *John v Rees* [1970] CH 345, at 402.
[184] Ibid.
[185] *Wiseman v Borneman* [1971] AC 297, per Lord Wilberforce, at 318C.
[186] *R v Secretary of State for the Home Department ex p Fayed* [1997] 1 All ER 228.
[187] See, for example, *Lloyd v McMahon* [1987] AC 625, per Lord Bridge, at 702H.
[188] *R v Wareham Magistrates' Court ex p Seldon* [1988] 1 WLR 825.

the panel was entitled to require the local authority representative to leave and the outcome was not invalidated by the departure from the statutory procedure.[189]

In certain circumstances, however, a precise procedural code may exclude additional procedural requirements.[190] For example, there was no breach of natural justice where a case involving either-way offences was transferred to the Crown Court under s 53 of the Criminal Justice Act 1991 before the magistrates had been able to hold a hearing to determine the mode of trial. There was no reason why the terms of s 53 should not be given their normal meaning and that did not require magistrates to hold a mode of trial hearing.[191]

It is unlikely that a need for urgency alone will justify the exclusion of the principles of natural justice. Where, for example, the Secretary of State for Education's powers to direct that a person be appointed to replace the Director of Children's Services of a local authority were not subject to specific procedure and the power to direct needed to be exercised urgently, the consequential dismissal of the Director was unlawful. The procedure leading to the Secretary of State's decision had been intrinsically unfair. Although there had been urgency, it had not been such as to necessitate such a truncation of the requirements of fairness.[192]

One of the key factors that needs to be considered when deciding whether the right to a fair hearing imposes additional procedural requirements is the legislative purpose of the statute.[193]

In determining whether natural justice is excluded by express procedural requirements, the Administrative Court will also consider whether the express procedural rules provide for all parties affected by the decision to be heard. If the rules do not expressly provide for all persons to be heard when they are affected by a decision, it is likely that the Court will imply such a right. Thus, although magistrates were obliged to order the destruction of a dog under s 4 of the Dangerous Dogs Act 1991, natural justice still required that the owner of that dog should be heard.[194]

The rules of natural justice will apply to a case if they are not excluded by statutory provisions and if there are no express procedural requirements imposed by statute implicitly excluding natural justice.[195] The circumstances of the case will, however, determine which procedural requirements are imposed by these rules of natural justice. For example,

---

[189] *R (McNally) v Secretary of State for Education & Employment* [2002] ICR 15.

[190] *R v Secretary of State for the Environment ex p Hammersmith and Fulham London Borough Council* [1991] 1 AC 521.

[191] *R v Bakewell Magistrates' Court and Derbyshire CPS ex p Brewer* [1995] COD 98.

[192] *R (Shoesmith) v Ofsted* [2011] ICR 1195.

[193] For example, *Ridge v Baldwin* [1964] AC 40, at 141.

[194] *R v Trafford Magistrates' Court ex p Riley* [1995] COD 373.

[195] *Wiseman v Borneman* [1971] AC 297, per Lord Wilberforce, at 318C.

the rules of natural justice do not entitle everyone, including people who are not a party to the proceedings, to a fair hearing in all circumstances.

### 2.8.3  Who is entitled to a fair hearing?

A person is normally entitled to a fair hearing where that person will be directly affected by the decision that is to be made.

Lord Fraser has stated, in the context of judicial review of decisions of magistrates' courts that:[196]

> 'One of the principles of natural justice is that a person is entitled to adequate notice and opportunity to be heard before any judicial order is pronounced against him, so that he, or someone acting on his behalf, may make such representations, if any, as he sees fit ... [It] applies to all judicial proceedings, unless its application to a particular class of proceedings has been excluded by Parliament expressly or by necessary implication.'

The right to be heard may arise in circumstances where a person is not a party to proceedings, but is affected by a decision. Lord Diplock has stated that:[197]

> 'Where an Act of Parliament confers upon an administrative body functions which involve its making decisions which affect to their detriment the rights of other persons or curtail their liberty to do as they please, there is a presumption that Parliament intended that the administrative body should act fairly towards those persons who will be affected by their decision.'

Thus, the owner of a dog is entitled to be heard before a destruction order is made under the Dangerous Dogs Act 1991, even if proceedings have been discontinued against the owner.[198]

A person's right to a fair hearing can be expressly or implicitly excluded by statute. Thus, the terms of the Police and Criminal Evidence Act 1984 were held to exclude the right of a suspect to be heard when the police applied for the disclosure of special procedure material relating to the suspect under the provisions of that Act[199] because the statutory provisions were intended to protect the person holding the documents that were the subject of the application for disclosure and not the suspect.

A party may even have a right to be heard where he will not be directly affected by the outcome; a sufficient interest in the outcome is enough. Thus, the prosecution had the right to be heard regarding a warrant of

---

[196]  *Re Hamilton; Re Forrest* [1981] AC 1038, at 1045B.
[197]  *Hillingdon London Borough Council v Commission for Racial Equality* [1982] AC 779, at 787F.
[198]  *R v Walton Street Justices ex p Crothers* [1992] COD 473.
[199]  *R v Manchester Crown Court ex p Taylor* [1988] 1 WLR 705.

commitment for the non-payment of a confiscation order, when it was the prosecution who had originally sought the confiscation order.[200]

In limited circumstances, a judicial review claimant may be able to rely on a failure to hear from a third party. Thus, a decision of a local authority to implement a decision regarding contact with a child without consulting with the guardian ad litem was held to be unlawful.[201] A criminal defendant, however, cannot complain about a failure to hear the prosecution.[202] The distinction is presumably that a criminal defendant will not be prejudiced by the failure to consult the prosecution.

### 2.8.4　Scope of the right to a fair hearing: the right to be heard

A number of basic rights have been identified as the elements of a fair hearing. It has been held repeatedly that a right to a fair hearing gives a person a right to be heard and a right to receive sufficient information to enable him to make informed representations.[203] The principle was clearly stated by Lord Mustill:[204]

> 'Fairness will very often require that a person who may be adversely affected by the decision will have an opportunity to make representations on his own behalf either before the decision is taken with a view to producing a favourable result; or after it is taken, with a view to procuring its modification; or both.'

In addition, there may be further rights depending on the circumstances of the case.

The right to be heard is the most fundamental right. For example, in the context of proceedings in the magistrates' court, it has been held repeatedly that the court is required to provide persons affected by a decision with an opportunity to be heard. Magistrates are obliged to provide a person accused of contempt of court with an opportunity to apologise.[205] Magistrates are required to ensure that a community charge defaulter has actually received notice informing him of a hearing to show why he is in default.[206] Magistrates are required to ensure that a person is

---

[200]　*R v Harrow Justices ex p DPP* [1991] 1 WLR 395.

[201]　*R v North Yorkshire County Council ex p M* [1989] QB 411.

[202]　*R v Liverpool Magistrates' Court ex p Ansen* [1998] 1 All ER 692.

[203]　*Kanda v Government of the Federation of Malaya* [1962] AC 322, at 337.

[204]　*R v Secretary of State for the Home Department ex p Doody* [1994] 1 AC 531, at 560D–560G.

[205]　*R v Pateley Bridge Magistrates' Court ex p Percy* [1994] COD 453; see also *R v Tamworth Magistrates' Court ex p Walsh* [1994] COD 277, DC, where it was held that a person facing an allegation of contempt should have the opportunity to reflect on his conduct and seek advice.

[206]　*R v Newcastle upon Tyne Justices ex p Devine* [1998] COD 420.

given adequate notice of proceedings during which the court is considering issuing a warrant of commitment.[207]

One circumstance in which there is no duty to give a person an opportunity to be heard is where the court is proposing to make a bind over because there has been a disturbance in the face of the court and a breach of the peace is imminent.[208] The Administrative Court justified this exception to the basic right to a fair hearing on the basis that it was obvious when there was a disturbance in the face of the court. The finding of the Court may, however, also suggest that a failure to give a party a fair hearing will not result in a decision being quashed if the failure was the result of the conduct of the claimant for judicial review. This is consistent with other case-law in which it has been held that a failure to comply with an express procedural requirement cannot be challenged if the failure was induced by the conduct of the person prejudiced.[209]

The entitlement to a fair hearing implies that the decision-maker or court will take account of the representations made by a party. Thus, it is an error for a magistrate to appear to be engaged in another activity instead of listening to the proceedings before him.[210]

The right to be heard is not limited to court hearings and may include, for example, providing a reasonable opportunity for a detained mother to make representations before separating her from her baby[211] and providing a housing applicant with an opportunity to know the reasons why an authority has disbelieved them and with an opportunity to respond to the authority's concerns.[212]

### 2.8.5 The duty to consult

In circumstances in which the decision-maker is not a court, the requirement that a person should be heard is often interpreted as meaning that a person should be consulted about a decision. This may occur in an individual case or in the context of a decision that has implications for many. Obviously, a consultation exercise will not normally involve the sort of procedure associated with a court hearing. The Court of Appeal encapsulated the essential ingredients as follows:[213]

---

[207] *Re Hamilton; Re Forrest* [1981] AC 1038.

[208] *R v North London Metropolitan Magistrate ex p Haywood* [1973] 1 WLR 965. See, however, *Practice Direction (Magistrates' Court Contempt)* [2001] 2 Cr App R 17, in which it was suggested that any contempt trial should take place in front of a different bench.

[209] *R v Secretary of State for the Home Department ex p Awais Karni Butt* [1994] Imm AR 11, at 13.

[210] *R v Worcester Justices ex p Daniels* (1997) 161 JP 121.

[211] *R (CD) v Secretary of State for the Home Department* [2003] 1 FLR 979, at [28].

[212] *R v London Borough of Hackney ex p Decordova* [1995] HLR 108, at [113].

[213] *R v North and East Devon Health Authority ex p Coughlan* [2001] QB 213, at 258C–258D.

> 'To be proper, consultation must be undertaken at a time when proposals are still at a formative stage; it must include sufficient reasons for particular proposals to allow those consulted to give intelligent consideration and an intelligent response; adequate time must be given for this purpose; and the product of consultation must be conscientiously taken into account when the ultimate decision is taken.'

These requirements are said to apply whether a decision-maker is obliged to consult as a matter of law or agrees to consult as a matter of discretion.[214]

Circumstances in which the court has found that the procedure fell short of the essential requirements of a proper consultation include where the consultation document contained insufficient information[215] and where inadequate time was allowed for a response.[216]

The trigger for the duty to consult may be a legitimate expectation of consultation arising from an unequivocal promise of prior consultation or an exceptional circumstance giving rise to a duty to consult such as:[217]

> 'where a decision-maker's proposed action would otherwise be so unfair as to amount to an abuse of power, by reason of the way in which it has earlier conducted itself. In the paradigm case of procedural expectations it will generally be unfair and abusive for the decision-maker to break its express promise or established practice of notice or consultation.'

The court's assessment of the essential features of adequate consultation is reflected in the consultation criteria set out in the HM Government Code of Practice on Consultation.[218]

The Code states that it 'does not have legal force, and cannot prevail over statutory or mandatory requirements', but that it, 'sets out the Government's general policy on formal, public, written consultation exercises'.[219] The Code no longer states that it is binding on government departments which undertake consultation exercises. However, the Code states that although deviations from the Code may be unavoidable, departments are recommended to be 'open' about such deviations.[220]

The Code identifies seven criteria that should be applied (unless an explanation is given for their departure) when a government department elects to hold a formal consultation exercise:

---

[214]　Ibid.

[215]　*R (Greenpeace Ltd) v Secretary of State for Trade and Industry* [2007] Env LR 623.

[216]　*R (Amvac Chemical UK Ltd) v Secretary of State for Environment, Food and Rural Affairs* [2001] EWHC 1011 (Admin).

[217]　*R (Bhatt Murphy) v Independent Assessor* [2008] EWCA Civ 755, per Laws LJ, at [42].

[218]　Published by the Cabinet Office dated July 2008 and available online at http://www.bis.gov.uk/files/file47158.pdf.

[219]　HM Government Code of Practice on Consultation, p 5.

[220]　Ibid, p 6.

1. Formal consultation should take place at a stage when there is scope to influence the policy outcome.

2. Consultations should normally last for at least 12 weeks with consideration given to longer timescales where feasible and sensible.

3. Consultation documents should be clear about the consultation process, what is being proposed, the scope to influence and the expected costs and benefits of the proposals.

4. Consultation exercises should be designed to be accessible to, and clearly targeted at, those people the exercise is intended to reach.

5. Keeping the burden of consultation to a minimum is essential if consultations are to be effective and if consultees' buy-in to the process is to be obtained.

6. Consultation responses should be analysed carefully and clear feedback should be provided to participants following the consultation.

7. Officials running consultations should seek guidance in how to run an effective consultation exercise and share what they have learned from the experience.[221]

The Code does not apply to non-departmental public authorities unless they have adopted it.[222]

## 2.8.6 Scope of the common law right to a fair hearing: the right to receive information

The right to a fair hearing is closely linked to the right to receive sufficient information to make adequate representations. As Lord Morris stated:[223]

'It is well established that the essential requirements of natural justice at least include that before someone is condemned he is to have an opportunity of defending himself, and in order that he may do so that he is to be made aware of the charges or allegations or suggestions which he has to meet ... My Lords, here is something which is basic to our system; the importance of upholding it far transcends the significance of any particular case.'

Similarly, Lord Mustill stated:[224]

---

[221] Ibid, p 4.
[222] A list of the organisations that have adopted the Code is available at http://www.berr.gov.uk/policies/bre/consultation-guidance.
[223] *Ridge v Baldwin* [1964] AC 40, at 113.
[224] *In Re D (Minors) (Adoption Reports: Confidentiality)* [1996] AC 593.

'it is a first principle of fairness that each party to a judicial process shall
have an opportunity to answer by evidence and argument any adverse
material which the tribunal may take into account when forming its
opinion.'

As the dicta above suggest, much of the case law considering the right to
receive information has focused on the entitlement to be informed of
allegations against a party. However, the right to receive information can
be wider than that. The case law indicates that there can be a right not to
be taken by surprise.[225] Thus, it is a violation of the right to a fair hearing
for a planning inspector to base his decision on a matter that the parties
had no opportunity to comment on;[226] for a university to remove a
student from the Register of Graduate Students without giving her an
opportunity to respond to the grounds for removal;[227] or for the Secretary
of State for the Home Department to refuse an individual naturalisation
as a British citizen without affording him an opportunity to rebut an
allegation of bad character or deception.[228]

The right to be informed is not limited to court hearings. For example, the
courts have held that a prisoner convicted of murder is entitled to be
informed of a judge's reasons for making a recommendation regarding
tariff, so that the prisoner can then make representations to the Secretary
of State before he sets the tariff,[229] and that a person subject to an
extradition request is entitled to disclosure of the material held by the
Secretary of State relevant to whether he could obtain a fair trial if
extradited.[230]

The extent to which disclosure is required by the right to a fair trial may
be limited. For example, in a court of law, there is no need for a
decision-maker to inform the parties what he is minded to decide if the
parties have been given a fair hearing at which they could present their
rival cases.[231] Disclosure may also be unnecessary if it would frustrate the
purpose of the court proceedings. Thus, there is no absolute obligation on
the police to disclose in advance the evidence that they seek to rely on
when making an application for disclosure of special procedure material
under the Police and Criminal Evidence Act 1984. Disclosure in these
circumstances might frustrate the purpose of the application.[232]

---

[225] *R (Anufrijeva) v Secretary of State for the Home Department* [2004] 1 AC 604, per
Lord Steyn, at 622C: 'In our system of law surprise is regarded as the enemy of justice'.
[226] *Fairmount Investments Ltd v Secretary of State for the Environment* [1976] 1 WLR 1255.
[227] *R (Persaud) v University of Cambridge* [2001] ELR 480, at [38]–[39].
[228] *R (Thamby) v Secretary of State for the Home Department* [2011] EWHC 1763
(Admin).
[229] *R v Secretary of State for the Home Department ex p Doody* [1994] 1 AC 531.
[230] *R (Ramda) v Secretary of State for the Home Department* [2002] EWHC 1278 (Admin),
at [25].
[231] See *F Hoffman-La Roche & Co AG v Secretary of State for Trade and Industry* [1975] AC
295.
[232] *R v Inner London Crown Court ex p Baines & Baines* [1988] 1 QB 579.

More recently the Supreme Court has held that there is no absolute right to disclosure where disclosure might harm national security.[233] However, there are circumstances in which the importance of the issues means that a person is entitled to the gist of the allegations that they face.[234] For example, the House of Lords has held that there is a 'core irreducible minimum' entitlement to know sufficient information 'about the allegations forming the sole or decisive grounds of suspicion against him' to enable a person to give effective instructions to a special advocate in a statutory closed-material procedure regarding control orders.[235] In addition, an entitlement to a 'gist' of the case against an individual may be derived from European Union law as a consequence of the right to an effective remedy, at least in cases raising a European Union law element.[236]

In practice, administrative decision-makers may adopt a procedure by which they provide people affected by a decision with reasons why they are 'minded' to take the decision before the decision is actually taken; thus providing those people with an opportunity to respond to the proposed decision. There may be an obligation to provide a further reasoned decision if, for example, further representations received raise matters which have not previously been considered or if the decision is, on its face, at odds with published policy.

The right to receive information can require a decision-maker to disclose documents that he is considering.[237] However, this will not always be the case. The disclosure requirements depend upon the circumstances of the decision. In some circumstances, it will be sufficient to disclose the gist of the documents placed before the decision-maker. Thus, for example, the Prison Service is required to disclose only the gist of documents being placed before the committee that determines whether prisoners should remain in category A conditions.[238]

Claimants are no longer required to rely solely on common law rights to a fair hearing to obtain documentation relied on by a decision-maker. The Data Protection Act 1998 and the Freedom of Information Act 2000 may be used to obtain documentation from a public authority.[239]

---

[233] *Tariq v Home Office* [2011] 3 WLR 322.

[234] *AF (No 3) v Secretary of State for the Home Department* [2010] 2 AC 269.

[235] *Secretary of State for the Home Department v AF (No 3)* [2010] 2 AC 269, applying the decision of the European Court of Human Rights in *A v United Kingdom* (2009) 49 EHRR 29.

[236] See, for example, *Kadi (No 2) v European Commission (T-85/09)* [2011] 1 CMLR 24, and *ZZ v Secretary of State for the Home Department* [2011] EWCA Civ 440, in which the Court of Appeal referred the issue to the Court of Justice of the European Union.

[237] *R v Camden LBC ex p Paddock* [1996] CLY 3961.

[238] *R v Secretary of State for the Home Department ex p Duggan* [1994] 3 All ER 277, applied in *R (Ferguson) v Secretary of State for Justice* [2011] EWHC 5 (Admin).

[239] See *R (Lord) v Secretary of State for the Home Department* [2003] EWHC 2073

In criminal proceedings in the magistrates' court and in the Crown Court, where the investigation of the offence began on or after 1 April 1997, the disclosure of material held by the prosecution is governed by the Criminal Procedure and Investigations Act 1996 and the associated codes of conduct. The 1996 Act excludes the common law rules regarding disclosure that existed before 1 April 1997.[240]

Although the previous common law rules regarding disclosure have now been abolished, the Administrative Court has concluded that the provisions of the Criminal Procedure and Investigations Act 1996 do not exclude the jurisdiction of the courts to impose fresh duties of disclosure on the prosecution. In particular, it has held that there can be a duty on a prosecutor to make disclosure before committal although the provisions of the 1996 Act do not apply.[241]

In addition, there are still circumstances in criminal cases where a person is entitled to be informed of the case against him by a person other than the prosecution. In particular, there are occasions where the court will be obliged to inform a person of matters that he needs to know. For example, where a surety is unrepresented and attends a hearing to consider whether he should forfeit the recognisance, the court should assist the surety by explaining the principles involved in ordinary language.[242]

The extent to which procedural guarantees provided by the European Convention on Human Rights require a decision-maker to disclose material on which the decision was based or permit a decision-maker to rely on undisclosed material when defending judicial review proceedings has received particular judicial scrutiny in the context of decisions to withhold material on national security or other public interest grounds.[243] The Supreme Court judgment in *Al Rawi v Security Service,*[244] in which the Court held that a civil court could not embark on a closed material procedure without statutory authority,[245] has been applied by the Administrative Court in reviewing a decision by a judge in the Crown Court, when deciding whether to issue a production order, to admit

---

(Admin) for an example of a case in which the Data Protection Act 1998 was used to obtain documents in circumstances in which the common law would only have required production of a gist.

[240] Criminal Procedure and Investigations Act 1996, s 21.

[241] *R v DPP ex p Lee* [1999] 1 WLR 1950.

[242] *R v Uxbridge Justices ex p Heward-Mills* [1983] 1 WLR 56.

[243] See for example, *R (AHK) v Secretary of State* [2009] 1 WLR 2049.

[244] [2011] 3 WLR 388.

[245] There was some apparent disagreement between the members of the court as to whether a closed material procedure could be embarked upon by consent absent statutory authority. Lord Brown JSC took the view that such a procedure could not be embarked upon in the absence of statutory authority. Lord Hope DPSC and Lord Kerr JSC doubted whether such a procedure was possible. In contrast, Baroness Hale and Lord Mance JJSC held that the court could adopt some form of closed material procedure, if the claimant consents, to avoid denying the claimant any form of access to the court because the case has become untriable.

'closed' evidence of an officer which could not be challenged by cross-examination.[246] How *Al Rawi* should be applied in the context of judicial review proceedings is, at the time of writing, an issue pending before the Administrative Court.[247]

### 2.8.7 Scope of the right to a fair hearing: other rights

Depending on the circumstances of the case, the right to a fair hearing may also entitle parties to sufficient time to prepare,[248] the right to representation,[249] the right to an oral hearing,[250] and the right to cross-examine a witness.[251] For example, it is the right to a fair hearing that normally requires magistrates to offer legal representation to a person accused of contempt of court.[252]

Consideration of the right to a fair trial begins by noting that there are no universal rules determining the scope of the right to a fair hearing. Instead, the requirements of a fair hearing depend on the circumstances of the case. This principle is particularly important when considering the rights in the paragraph above. The fact that a court has identified that there are occasions when fairness requires matters such as legal representation does not necessarily mean that there is always a right to legal representation.[253] It has to be shown that fairness requires legal representation in the circumstances of the case. But where there is a discretion to allow legal representation, that discretion must be exercised reasonably.[254]

If a decision-maker is not obliged to ensure that certain standards of procedural fairness are adopted, the decision-maker may have a discretion to adopt those standards. If a decision-maker has that discretion, he must consider exercising it. For example, an immigration officer conducting an interview with a person seeking admission to the United Kingdom may not be obliged to allow legal representatives to attend. However, he has to consider whether allowing legal representation in the circumstances of the

---

[246] *R (British Sky Broadcasting Ltd) v Central Criminal Court* [2011] EWHC 3451 (Admin).
[247] In *R (AHK & others) v Secretary of State for the Home Department* (CO/1076/2008).
[248] *R v Tamworth Magistrates' Court ex p Walsh* [1994] COD 277.
[249] *R v Board of Visitors of HM Prison The Maze ex p Hone* [1988] AC 379; see also *R v Leicester JJ ex p Barrow* [1991] 2 QB 260, suggesting that in certain circumstances the right to a fair hearing extends to other forms of legal assistance, such as a McKenzie friend advising a litigant in person.
[250] *R v Department of Health ex p Gandhi* [1991] 1 WLR 1053.
[251] *R v Wellingborough Magistrates' Court ex p François* [1994] COD 462; *R v Birmingham City Juvenile Court ex p Birmingham City Council* [1988] 1 WLR 337.
[252] *R v Pateley Bridge Justices ex p Percy* [1994] COD 453.
[253] *Enderby Town Football Club v Football Association* [1971] Ch 591.
[254] *R v Board of Visitors of Albany Prison ex p Tarrant* [1985] QB 251.

case is appropriate.[255] A failure to consider allowing legal representation when a request is made could give rise to grounds for applying for judicial review.

Where a decision-maker, particularly in a case which involves a fundamental right such as the right to liberty, adopts a procedure which impedes or obstructs access to legal advice and representation, this may give rise to a challenge of grounds of procedural unfairness. This is because, 'Access to legal advice is one of the fundamental rights enjoyed by every citizen under the common law.'[256]

### 2.8.8    European Convention on Human Rights, Article 6

Article 6 of the European Convention on Human Rights provides:

> '1   In the determination of his civil rights and obligations or of any criminal charge against him, everyone is entitled to a fair and public hearing within a reasonable time by an independent and impartial tribunal established by law. Judgment shall be pronounced publicly but the press and public may be excluded from all or part of the trial in the interests of morals, public order or national security in a democratic society, where the interests of juveniles or the protection of the private life of the parties so require, or to the extent strictly necessary in the opinion of the court in special circumstances where publicity would prejudice the interests of justice.
>
> 2   Everyone charged with a criminal offence shall be presumed innocent until proved guilty according to law.
>
> 3   Everyone charged with a criminal offence has the following minimum rights:
> (a)    to be informed promptly, in a language which he understands and in detail, of the nature and cause of the accusation against him;
> (b)    to have adequate time and facilities for the preparation of his defence;
> (c)    to defend himself in person or through legal assistance of his own choosing or, if he has not sufficient means to pay for legal assistance, to be given it free when the interests of justice so require;
> (d)    to examine or have examined witnesses against him and to obtain the attendance and examination of witnesses on his behalf under the same conditions as witnesses against him;
> (e)    to have the free assistance of an interpreter if he cannot understand or speak the language used in court.'

---

[255]   *R v Secretary of State for the Home Department ex p Vera Lawson* [1994] Imm AR 58; see also *R v Guildford Crown Court ex p Siderfin* [1990] 2 QB 683, in which it was held that, although a person was not entitled to legal representation on an appeal against a refusal to excuse a person from jury service for reasons of conscience, it would be rare that a request for an adjournment to allow legal representation should be refused.

[256]   *R v Shayler* [2003] 1 AC 247. See also the useful summary of the authorities on the right to unimpeded and confidential access to legal advice by Munby J in *R (Karas & Milandinovic) v Secretary of State for the Home Department* [2006] EWHC 747 (Admin), (2006) 150 SJLB 540.

Article 6 overlaps with the common law right to a fair hearing considered above. Article 6 does not fundamentally change the common law right but it does in certain circumstances alter the scope of the right. For example, as demonstrated above, Art 6 has made the bias test slightly more objective.[257]

Article 6 is relevant in the context of judicial review for two reasons. First, a decision may be challenged on the basis that it violates Art 6. Hence, for example, a decision may be quashed because it was taken by a biased judicial decision-maker.[258] In addition, Art 6 may be relevant because the Administrative Court may be bound by the requirements of Art 6 when considering a claim for judicial review. Hence, Art 6 may require the Court to resolve disputes of fact.[259]

When considering the potential relevance of Art 6 in an individual case the first issue is whether proceedings determine a 'criminal charge' or a person's 'civil rights and obligations' or neither of these matters. It is important to recognise that matters that can be raised in judicial review proceedings are not necessarily matters that engage Art 6. For example, proceedings regarding the expulsion of a foreign national do not engage Art 6 because procedural rights in this context are contained in another European Convention provision (which is not incorporated into domestic law in the HRA 1998).[260]

## (1) Definition of a criminal charge

From a claimant's point of view, there will often be benefits if it can be shown that proceedings determine a 'criminal charge' because Art 6(2) and (3) of the European Convention on Human Rights include greater rights for a claimant facing proceedings that determine a 'criminal charge'.

The term 'criminal charge' has an autonomous meaning under Art 6 to prevent States from depriving a person of the benefits of the Article by classifying an offence as disciplinary rather than criminal.[261] In *Engel v Netherlands*,[262] the European Court of Human Rights identified the three factors that need to be considered when determining whether a matter is a criminal charge for the purposes of Art 6.

The first issue is the domestic classification of the matter. That, however, is far from decisive since the European Convention is intended to achieve

---

[257] See **2.8**.
[258] Ibid.
[259] See **2.2.2**.
[260] *Maaouia v France* (2001) 33 EHRR 42.
[261] *Engel v Netherlands* (1976) 1 EHRR 647, at [81].
[262] (1976) 1 EHRR 647.

uniform standards across Europe and that aim could be defeated if domestic rules were decisive.[263] It is the second and third criteria that, in practice, are of greater significance.

The second issue is the nature of the offence. It is particularly important to consider whether the offence is one that is applicable to the community at large or merely applicable to part of the community. For example, offences against military discipline may not be criminal as they do not apply to the whole community.[264] When considering this issue, courts may be influenced by the fact that an offence has a 'colouring' that is not entirely consistent with it being disciplinary.[265] Hence, it is relevant that prison disciplinary offences . – which obviously do not apply to the community at large – are in identical terms to criminal offences that do apply to the community at large.[266] In some cases, the serious nature of the disciplinary offence may be sufficient to mean that the criminal limb of Art 6 is engaged.[267]

The final issue is the penalty at risk and the penalty actually imposed. Loss of liberty is almost always sufficient to mean that disciplinary proceedings are criminal unless it can be shown that it is not appreciably detrimental.[268] However, other less significant penalties can be criminal. In particular, proceedings that result in financial penalties may be criminal.[269]

### *(2) Disciplinary proceedings that are not criminal*

It is important to recognise that, even where proceedings are not criminal, disciplinary proceedings may still entitle a person to some of the rights that are normally regarded as being the entitlement of a defendant in criminal proceedings but not that of a party to civil proceedings.[270] In addition, some of the rights that are express in the context of criminal proceedings may be implicit in civil proceedings.[271]

### *(3) The significance of proceedings being criminal*

The fact that proceedings are criminal is significant: a person will be entitled to additional procedural rights contained in Art 6(2) and (3) of the European Convention on Human Rights.[272] In practice, it is probable that the three most significant additional rights are that: Article 6(2)

---

[263] *R v H* [2003] 1 WLR 411, at 419B.
[264] *Engel v Netherlands* (1976) 1 EHRR 647.
[265] *Ezeh and Connors v United Kingdom* (2002) 35 EHRR 28, at [70].
[266] Ibid.
[267] *R (Smith) v Governor of Belmarsh Prison* [2009] EWHC 109 (Admin).
[268] *Ezeh and Connors v United Kingdom* (2002) 35 EHRR 28, at [95].
[269] *Öztürk v Germany* (1984) 6 EHRR 409; *Lauko v Slovakia* (2001) 33 EHRR 40.
[270] *Re Westminster Property Management Ltd (No 1)* [2000] 1 WLR 2230.
[271] See the consideration of the right to legal aid at **2.8.7(1)**.
[272] See **2.8.7** for the text of Art 6.

provides that there is a presumption of innocence; Art 6(3) includes a right to legal representation; and Art 6(3) protects against the use of hearsay and anonymous evidence.

The presumption of innocence has generated a significant amount of litigation following the entry into force of the HRA 1998. Criminal defendants have sought to argue that provisions reversing the burden of proof violate the presumption of innocence. The decisions of the domestic courts make it clear that in principle a reverse burden of proof may be acceptable. It is necessary to consider matters such as the purpose of the legislation, what the defendant must prove and whether the reverse burden is a legal or evidential burden.[273]

Article 6 may entitle a person to legal aid in civil proceedings.[274] In *Steel & Morris v United Kingdom*[275] the European Court of Human rights held that:[276]

> 'The question whether the provision of legal aid is necessary for a fair hearing must be determined on the basis of the particular facts and circumstances of each case and will depend *inter alia* upon the importance of what is at stake for the applicant in the proceedings, the complexity of the relevant law and procedure and the applicant's capacity to represent him or herself effectively.'

The Strasbourg court considered that the denial of legal aid to the applicants who had sought to defend libel proceedings had deprived them of the opportunity to present their case effectively before the court and contributed to an unacceptable inequality of arms in breach of Art 6.[277]

However, in criminal proceedings there is an automatic right to legal aid where the means of the defendant require it and it is in the interests of justice that legal aid is provided.[278] Where a defendant is at risk of losing his liberty, the interests of justice will almost inevitably require the provision of legal aid.[279]

Article 6 protects a person against the use of hearsay and anonymous evidence but the right to this protection is not absolute. Instead, Art 6 requires a consideration of the circumstances of the use of hearsay and anonymous evidence, including the importance of that evidence in the

---

[273]   *R v Lambert* [2002] 2 AC 545; *R v S* [2003] 1 Cr App R 35; *Barnfather v Islington Education Authority* [2003] 1 WLR 2318.

[274]   *Airey v Ireland* (1979–1980) 2 EHRR 305, holding that legal aid may be required where it is essential for effective access to the courts. See also *R (Jarrett) v Legal Services Commission* [2002] ACD 25 and *R (Viggers) v Legal Services Commission* [2011] EWHC 2221 (Admin).

[275]   (2005) 41 EHRR 22.

[276]   Ibid, at [61].

[277]   Ibid, at [72].

[278]   *Granger v United Kingdom* (1990) 12 EHRR 469.

[279]   *Benham v United Kingdom* (1996) 22 EHRR 293.

criminal proceedings. Thus, where the hearsay evidence was central to the conviction, there may be a violation of Art 6.[280]

## (4) Definition of civil proceedings

*James v United Kingdom*[281] considered the circumstances in which Art 6 of the European Convention on Human Rights is engaged by civil proceedings. The European Court of Human Rights held:[282]

> 'Article 6(1) extends only to "contestations" (disputes) over (civil) "rights and obligations" which can be said, at least on arguable grounds, to be recognised under domestic law: it does not in itself guarantee any particular content for (civil) "rights and obligations" in the substantive law of the Contracting States.'

This judgment indicates that one matter which must be determined is whether there is a dispute regarding civil rights. As with the determination of whether a matter is a criminal charge, the domestic classification of proceedings is far from decisive.[283]

In practice, the distinction that is usually drawn is between disputes regarding civil rights as opposed to public law rights. As a consequence of this there is little doubt that disputes between private individuals are civil proceedings for the purposes of Art 6. In *König v Germany*,[284] the Court held that where the dispute involves the government, it is necessary to consider: '[t]he character of the legislation which governs how the matter is to be determined'.[285] Thus, in *Feldbrugge v Netherlands*,[286] the European Court of Human Rights considered whether a complaint by an individual that she had been denied statutory sickness benefit engaged Art 6, and concluded that it did. In reaching that conclusion, the Court considered that a number of features of public law were present: the character of the legislation;[287] the compulsory nature of the legislation regarding insurance against sickness;[288] and the assumption by the state of responsibility for social protection.[289] The Court also considered that a number of features of private law were present: the personal and

---

[280] *Al-Khawaja v United Kingdom* (2011) *The Times*, December 22.
[281] (1986) 8 EHRR 123.
[282] *James v United Kingdom* (1986) 8 EHRR 123, at [81].
[283] *König v Germany* (1978) 2 EHRR 170.
[284] Ibid.
[285] Ibid, at [90].
[286] (1986) 8 EHRR 425.
[287] *Feldbrugge v Netherlands* (1986) 8 EHRR 425, at [32].
[288] Ibid, at [33].
[289] Ibid, at [34].

economic nature of the asserted right;[290] the connection with a contract of employment;[291] and the affinities with insurance under ordinary law.[292] The Court concluded that:[293]

> 'Having thus evaluated the relative cogency of the features of public law and private law present in the instant case, the Court finds the latter to be predominant. None of these various features of private law is decisive on its own, but taken together and cumulatively they confer on the asserted entitlement the character of a civil right within the meaning of Article 6(1) of the Convention.'

The trend has been towards an increased expansion of the scope of civil rights into the public law area. This was explained by the European Court of Human Rights in the following terms:[294]

> '... the state's increasing intervention in the individual's day-to-day life, in terms of welfare protection for example, has required the court to evaluate features of public law and private law before concluding that the asserted right could be classified as "civil".'

If it can be shown that there is a dispute regarding civil rights, it must still be shown that the dispute is directly decisive of those civil rights before Art 6 is engaged.[295] Hence, the placing of a person on a register of people deemed unsuitable to work with children or vulnerable adults can engage Art 6 if the register has the effect of preventing that person from applying for employment or being employed.[296]

It is important to recognise that the distinction between civil rights and public law rights means that there will be some proceedings in the Administrative Court that do not attract the protection of Art 6, as they will be regarded as public law proceedings. Perhaps the most obvious example of this is that many immigration proceedings will not attract the protection of Art 6.[297] In addition, decisions in respect of tax,[298] an entitlement to ex gratia payments,[299] or a person's designation as a person believed to be associated with Al-Qaida, Usama bin Laden or the Taliban

---

[290]  Ibid, at [37].

[291]  Ibid, at [38].

[292]  Ibid, at [39].

[293]  Ibid, at [40].

[294]  *Ferrazzini v Italy* (2001) 34 EHRR 1068, at [27].

[295]  See, for example, *Fayed v United Kingdom* (1994) 18 EHRR 393 and *Secretary of State for the Home Department v BC and another* [2010] 1 WLR 1542.

[296]  *R v Secretary of State for Health ex p C* [2000] 1 FLR 627 and *R (Wright) v Secretary of State for Health* [2009] 1 AC 739. See also, in the context of an internal disciplinary hearing involving a teaching assistant, *R (G) v X School Governors* [2012] 1 AC 167.

[297]  *Maaouia v France* (2001) 33 EHRR 42 and *RB (Algeria) v Secretary of State for the Home Department* [2010] 2 AC 110. It is worth noting that Art 1 of Protocol No 7 of the European Convention on Human Rights contains procedural protections in immigration matters. Protocol No 7 is still to be ratified by the United Kingdom.

[298]  *Ferrazzini v Italy* (2001) 34 EHRR 1068.

[299]  *Nordh v Sweden* Application No 14225/88, 3 December 1990.

pursuant to the Terrorism (United Nations Measures) Order 2006 or Council Regulation (EC) No 881/2002 are not civil rights.[300] Similarly, he Supreme Court has held that a decision by a local housing authority under s 193(5) Housing Act 1996 that it had discharged its duty to secure that accommodation was available for occupation by a homeless applicant was not a determination of that person's '*civil rights*' within the meaning of Art 6.[301] However, a decision to impose a control order does engage a person's '*civil rights*', even if its obligations are comparatively light.[302]

Although Art 6 does not necessarily apply to all proceedings before the Administrative Court, there is some suggestion that common law fair trial rights have extended to provide equivalent rights in circumstances in which Art 6 does not apply.[303] It should not be assumed that the standard of fairness set by the common law for the determination of issues arising in civil litigation is in any respect less robust than that set by Art 6 of the Convention.[304]

### (5) Rights contained in the European Convention on Human Rights, Article 6(1)

There are three aspects to Art 6(1) of the European Convention on Human Rights: the right to a fair trial; the right to have that trial take place before an independent and impartial tribunal; and the right to have the trial take place within a reasonable time period.[305] The significance of the three aspects of Art 6 is that each aspect of Art 6 must be considered separately. It is no answer to a complaint regarding independence and impartiality to say that a trial was fair.[306] It would appear that none of the three aspects of Art 6 can be compromised in the public interest.[307]

There are a number of rights that expressly or implicitly form part of the right to a fair trial, eg the right to equality of arms or the right to legal representation.[308] The domestic courts have concluded that although the right to a fair trial inherent in Art 6 is an absolute right in the sense that the fairness of the trial cannot be qualified, compromised or restricted in any way, the constituent rights may be compromised providing that any

---

[300] *R (Maftah) v Secretary of State for Foreign and Commonwealth Affairs* [2012] 2 WLR 251.

[301] *Ali v Birmingham City Council* [2010] 2 AC 39.

[302] *Secretary of State for the Home Department v BC and another* [2010] 1 WLR 1542. This decision is likely to apply with equal force to orders made under the Terrorism Prevention and Investigation Measures Act 2011.

[303] *R v Secretary of State for the Home Department ex p Saleem* [2001] 1 WLR 443; *Lawal v Northern Spirit Ltd* [2003] ICR 856, at 862B.

[304] *R (Maftah) v Secretary of State for Foreign and Commonwealth Affiiars* [2012] 2 WLR 251, at 255C and 261A–261C.

[305] *Porter v Magill* [2002] 2 AC 357, per Lord Hope, at 489A.

[306] Ibid.

[307] *Mills v HM Advocate (No 2)* [2004] 1 AC 441, per Lord Steyn, at 448F.

[308] See **2.8**.

qualification of those rights is directed towards a clear and proper public objective, and is proportionate to that objective.[309]

*The right to an independent tribunal*

The right to an independent tribunal entitles a person to a trial before a tribunal that is independent of the executive. In *Starrs v Ruxton*[310] the High Court of Justiciary concluded that the appointment of temporary sheriffs to sit as judges violated Art 6. The Court considered matters such as the method of appointment of the temporary sheriffs and security of their tenure to determine whether there were sufficient objective guarantees of independence. In *R (Anderson) v Secretary of State for the Home Department,*[311] the House of Lords held that the Secretary of State for the Home Department's power to fix sentencing tariffs was incompatible with the right to a fair trial guaranteed under Art 6. The court had a duty to seek to give effect to the jurisprudence of the European Court of Human Rights which had made it clear that the fixing of a tariff was considered to be a sentencing exercise rather than the administrative implementation of a life sentence that had already been passed.

The right to a hearing before an independent tribunal is closely linked to the right to an impartial tribunal. Hence the European Court of Human Rights often considers both issues together.[312] The requirements of impartiality are considered above.[313]

*The right to a trial within a reasonable period*

The right to a trial within a reasonable period of time is a right that has generally been of greater significance in some other European jurisdictions where there has been a culture of excessive delay. Fortunately, that culture does not exist in the United Kingdom. In determining whether there has been unreasonable delay it is necessary to consider the complexity of the case, the conduct of the parties and the State, and the nature of what is at stake.[314] It is, however, not necessary for a defendant to show that he has been prejudiced.[315]

In a criminal case, time runs from the date of charge. Although the concept of a charge for Art 6 purposes is not necessarily the same as the concept of a charge as a matter of domestic law, in most cases time will

---

[309]    *Brown v Stott* [2003] 1 AC 681.
[310]    [2000] UKHRR 78.
[311]    [2003] 1 AC 837.
[312]    See, for example, *Findlay v United Kingdom* (1997) 24 EHRR 221, at [73].
[313]    See **2.8**.
[314]    *Zimmermann and Steiner v Switzerland* (1983) 6 EHRR 17, at [24].
[315]    *Attorney-General's Reference (No 2 of 2001)* [2004] 2 AC 72.

run from the date a defendant was charged as a matter of domestic law.[316] Time will then run until the exhaustion of all ordinary appeal rights.[317]

It is important to recognise that a violation of the right of a criminal defendant to trial within a reasonable period will not necessarily result in those proceedings being stayed if the defendant is unable to show that he has been prejudiced. Some other remedy such as a reduction in sentence may be appropriate.[318]

In a civil case, time runs from the date that proceedings are commenced unless it is necessary to exhaust some form of alternative remedy before commencing proceedings. If it is necessary to exhaust an alternative remedy, time will start to run from the date that steps were first taken to exhaust that form of alternative remedy.[319] Time will then run until the exhaustion of all ordinary appeal rights.[320] As in the criminal context, delay in the hearing of a civil matter will not necessarily render the hearing itself unfair. Thus the court has found that even where there is finding of a breach of Art 6 by reason of excessive delay in a hearing, in the absence of a finding that the hearing could not take place fairly, the proceedings would not be dismissed for unfair delay.[321]

*The right to a public hearing*

The right to a public hearing has been considered on several occasions since the HRA 1998 entered into force. The starting point is that there is a presumption that proceedings should take place in public.[322] However, there are circumstances in which proceedings may take place in private.[323] First, there are express provisions in Art 6(1) that permit hearings to take place in private in certain circumstances.[324] Secondly, proceedings may take place in private where there are exceptionally good reasons.[325] Finally, a party to proceedings may waive his right to a public hearing, provided that the waiver is unequivocal and does run counter to an important public interest.[326]

---

[316]  Ibid.
[317]  *Eckle v Germany* (1982) 5 EHRR 1, at [7]. See also *O'Neill (Charles Bernard) v HM Advocate* 2010 SCCR 357.
[318]  *Attorney-General's Reference (No 2 of 2001)* [2004] 2 AC 72.
[319]  *König v Germany* (1978) 2 EHRR 170, at [98].
[320]  Ibid.
[321]  *Eastaway v Secretary of State for Trade and Industry* [2007] BCC 550.
[322]  *Clibbery v Allan* [2002] Fam 261. See also *Scott v Scott* [1913] AC 417, for the position under the common law.
[323]  *R (Pelling) v Bow County Court* [2001] UKHRR 165.
[324]  See text of Art 6 set out in **2.8.7**.
[325]  Such as security concerns, as in *Campbell and Fell v United Kingdom* (1984) 7 EHRR 165, at [88].
[326]  *Pauger v Austria* (1997) 25 EHRR 105, at [58].

*Equality of arms*

Equality of arms is one of the most important rights inherent in Art 6. The principle of equality of arms means that each party to proceedings is entitled to present his case under conditions that do not place him at a substantial disadvantage vis-à-vis his opponent.[327] The central importance of the principle featured prominently in the Strasbourg court's conclusion, in *A v United Kingdom*,[328] that a detainee had to be given the opportunity effectively to challenge the basis of the allegations against him. That could require the court to hear witnesses whose testimony on its face appeared to have a material bearing on the continuing lawfulness of the detention as well as requiring that the detainee or his representative be given access to documents in the case file which formed the basis of the case against him.[329] However, there may be restrictions on the right to a fully adversarial procedure where strictly necessary in the light of a strong countervailing public interest.[330]

## 2.9 DELEGATION OF DECISION-MAKING POWERS

The power that enables a decision-maker or court to make a decision may not allow for the delegation of that power to a third party. For example, magistrates must be careful to ensure that it does not appear that they have passed certain decision-making powers to other persons working in the magistrates' court. It is for magistrates to make findings of fact in criminal trials, so the clerk should not retire with the magistrates when the only question before the magistrates is one of fact.[331] Magistrates should not delegate to police officers their power to decide whether a bail applicant should appear in handcuffs.[332] It is not only courts that may be prevented from delegating their powers. Where a statute permitted a local council to delegate decision-making to a committee, it was not permissible to delegate the decision-making to a committee chair. The use of the word 'committee' suggested that more than one person should be involved in decision-making.[333]

Where it is claimed that a power has been wrongly delegated, the Administrative Court considers the provisions of the relevant legislation and the nature of the decision to be taken. The nature of the legislation is relevant as delegation of powers may be expressly or implicitly prohibited by the statute. For example, the Administrative Court has held that the

---

[327] *Kaufman v Belgium* 50 DR 98.
[328] (2009) 49 EHRR 29, at [204].
[329] Ibid, at [204].
[330] Ibid, at [205].
[331] *R v Barry (Glamorgan) Justices ex p Kashim* [1953] 2 All ER 1005.
[332] *R v Cambridge Justices ex p Peacock* [1993] COD 19.
[333] *R v Secretary of State for the Environment ex p Hillingdon LBC* [1986] 1 WLR 807.

statute allowing the Crown Prosecution Service to review criminal prosecutions did not allow for that review to be delegated to people who were not lawyers.[334]

The nature of a power is relevant when considering implicit limitations on that power. For example, it is particularly likely that the Administrative Court will find that the presumption against the delegation of a statutory power prevents delegation where the power is a judicial power.[335] However, there are other statutory powers that require decisions to be taken so frequently that the nominated decision-maker (who is often a government minister) cannot be expected personally to take the decision. An example of this is that the powers of the Secretary for the Home Department regarding immigration may be delegated.[336] In addition, authorities suggest that a power to delegate must be exercised reasonably.[337]

When the Administrative Court considers the nature of a power, it will consider the impact of the exercise of the power on others. As a result, it is not surprising that only magistrates or their clerks may issue summonses, although magistrates may delegate the receipt of informa- tions to administrative staff.[338] The rationale appears to be that the consequence of an error in the receipt of an information is likely to be less serious than an error in the issue of a summons as the issue of a summons will restrict the rights of a third party.

## 2.10  IRRATIONALITY

Irrationality that amounts to error of law is often described as *Wednesbury* unreasonableness. This comes from the statement of Lord Greene in the *Wednesbury* case that:[339]

> '[I]f a decision on a competent matter is so unreasonable that no reasonable authority could ever have come to it, then the courts can interfere.'

Clearly, it is not every mistaken exercise of judgment that can be properly categorised as unreasonable.[340] If the Administrative Court were to intervene by way of judicial review and quash every mistaken exercise of

---

[334]  *R v DPP ex p First Division Civil Servants* (1988) *The Times*, May 24.
[335]  See, for example, *R v Manchester Stipendiary Magistrate ex p Hill* [1983] 1 AC 328, per Lord Roskill, at 343D.
[336]  *R v Secretary of State for the Home Department ex p Oladehinde* [1991] 1 AC 254.
[337]  *R v Institute of Chartered Accountants in England and Wales ex p Nawaz* [1997] CLY 1. See also *R v Secretary of State for the Home Department ex p Doody* [1994] 1 AC 531, at 566F–566G.
[338]  *R v Manchester Stipendiary Magistrate ex p Hill* [1983] 1 AC 328, at 342G.
[339]  *Associated Provincial Picture Houses Ltd v Wednesbury Corporation* [1948] 1 KB 223, at 230.
[340]  *Secretary of State for Education and Science v Tameside Metropolitan Borough Council* [1977] AC 1014, at 1070H.

judgment, there would be no distinction between judicial review and appellate jurisdictions.[341] As Lord Hailsham LC has stated:[342]

> 'Two reasonable [persons] can perfectly reasonably come to opposite conclusions on the same set of facts without forfeiting their title to be regarded as reasonable ... Not every reasonable exercise of judgment is right, and not every mistaken exercise of judgment is unreasonable.'

The Administrative Court sometimes imposes a heavy burden on persons claiming that a decision is irrational. It has been said that a decision is unreasonable if it is 'devoid of any plausible justification',[343] or so 'outrageous in its defiance of logic or of accepted moral standards that no sensible person who had applied his mind to the question to be decided could have arrived at it'.[344] The proof required to show unreasonableness must be 'overwhelming'.[345] The courts have used a range of expressions to describe irrationality in practice such as 'a decision which does not add up – in which, in other words, there is an error of reasoning which robs the decision of its logic',[346] where 'the reasons make no sense and are without foundation';[347] or where the decision is 'oppressive'.[348] However a plain disagreement as to the conclusion reached will be insufficient to found any challenge and claimants must be careful to ensure that grounds do not descend into an argument with the decision reached rather than an objective demonstration of its irrationality. In practice therefore, the high burden on claimants for judicial review who seek to claim irrationality means that relying on perversity as the only ground for challenge is rare. Instead, it is normally pleaded with other linked complaints such as a failure to take account of relevant factors.[349]

Although there is often a heavy burden placed on a claimant seeking to argue that a decision is irrational, it is not an unrealistic threshold and the court will vary the intensity with which the reasonableness of a decision is scrutinised in accordance with the subject matter. For example, in the context of criminal proceedings, the Administrative Court has quashed the decision of a magistrates' court to accept jurisdiction as being irrational because the case-law showed that the sentence for the offence

---

[341] *R v Secretary of State for the Home Department ex p Brind* [1991] 1 AC 696, per Lord Ackner, at 757F.

[342] *Re W (An Infant)* [1971] AC 682, at 700D.

[343] *Bromley London Borough Council v Greater London Council* [1983] 1 AC 768, per Lord Diplock, at 821B.

[344] *Council for Civil Service Unions v Minister for the Civil Service* [1985] AC 374, per Lord Diplock, at 410G.

[345] *Associated Provincial Picture Houses Ltd v Wednesbury Corporation* [1948] 1 KB 223, at 230.

[346] *R v Parliamentary Commissioner for Administration ex p Balchin* [1998] 1 PLR 1, per Sedley J, at 3E–3F.

[347] *R (Interbrew SA) v Competition Commission* [2001] EWHC 367 (Admin), per Moses J, at [31].

[348] *R (Khatun) v London Borough of Newham* [2005] QB 37, per Laws LJ, at [41].

[349] See **2.11**.

was frequently greater than that which the magistrates could impose.[350] The Court has also quashed a decision to dismiss informations as unreasonable where the prosecution had failed to attend because the failure was the result of misinformation supplied by the court and the prosecutor was attempting to attend court.[351] In the context of immigration proceedings, the Court has quashed the decision of an immigration officer to exclude an interpreter on the basis of her father's political activity because the decision was irrational as there was no evidence that the interpreter had engaged in political activity.[352]

There is some suggestion that reliance on irrationality as a ground for applying for judicial review will decrease as a consequence of the increasing importance of the principle of proportionality.[353] However, although it is clear that proportionality is a basis for applying for judicial review in a case that involves the European Convention on Human Rights or European Union law, in cases that purely raise issues of domestic law the courts have been reluctant to abandon reasonableness as the test to be applied. Instead, it has been held that a change of approach is a matter for the House of Lords.[354]

Although unreasonableness remains a ground for applying for judicial review, the courts have been willing to lower the threshold for unreasonableness and increase the intensity of review in cases in which fundamental rights are under consideration. In such circumstances, the intensity of review is greater than was previously applied, and greater even than the 'heightened scrutiny test' that had been adopted by the Court of Appeal in some cases prior to the Human Rights Act 1998.[355] The domestic court must now make a value judgment or an evaluation, by reference to the circumstances prevailing at the relevant time and judge objectively the proportionality of the decision for itself.[356] In practice, therefore, the requirement to subject a decision to anxious scrutiny may mean that the Administrative Court is required to go beyond determining whether a decision is irrational.

---

[350] *R v Northampton Magistrates' Court ex p Commissioners of Customs and Excise* [1994] COD 382.

[351] *R v Hendon Justices ex p DPP* [1994] QB 167.

[352] *R v Secretary of State for the Home Department ex p Bostanci* [1999] Imm AR 411.

[353] See **2.16**.

[354] *R (Association of British Civilian Internees (Far East Region)) v Secretary of State for Defence* [2003] QB 1397.

[355] See, for example, *R v Ministry of Defence, Ex p Smith* [1996] QB 517, per Sir Thomas Bingham MR, at 554.

[356] *R (SB) v Governors of Denbigh High School* [2007] 1 AC 100, per Lord Bingham, at 116D. See also *E (A Child), Re* [2009] 1 AC 536, per Lord Carswell, at 559; and see further on proportionality as a domestic principle below at **2.16**.

## 2.10.1 Mistake of fact

It is now clear that judicial review is available where a decision-maker makes a fundamental mistake of fact. This may also be categorised as an irrational failure to have regard to a material fact or irrationally taking into account an irrelevancy. In *R (Alconbury Developments Ltd) v Secretary of State for the Environment, Transport and the Regions,*[357] Lord Slynn stated:

> 'In *R v. Criminal Injuries Compensation Board, ex p. A* [1999] 2 A.C. 330, 344 I accepted that the court had jurisdiction to quash for a misunderstanding or ignorance of an established and relevant fact. I remain of that view which finds support in Wade & Forsyth Administrative Law (7th edn, 1994), pp 316–318. I said:

>> "Your Lordships have been asked to say that there is jurisdiction to quash the board's decision because that decision was reached on a material error of fact. Reference has been made to Wade & Forsyth, Administrative Law (7th edn, 1994), pp. 316–318 in which it is said:

>>> 'Mere factual mistake has become a ground of judicial review, described as "misunderstanding or ignorance of an established and relevant fact', [*Secretary of State for Education and Science v. Tameside MBC* [1977] A.C. 1014, 1030], or acting 'upon an incorrect basis of fact" ... This ground of review has long been familiar in French law and it has been adopted by statute in Australia. It is no less needed in this country, since decisions based upon wrong facts are a cause of injustice which the courts should be able to remedy. If a "wrong factual basis" doctrine should become established, it would apparently be a new branch of the ultra vires doctrine, analogous to finding facts based upon no evidence or acting upon a misapprehension of law.'

>> de Smith, Woolf and Jowell, Judicial Review of Administrative Action (5th edn, 1995), p. 288:

>>> 'The taking into account of a mistaken fact can just as easily be absorbed into a traditional legal ground of review by referring to the taking into account of an irrelevant consideration, or the failure to provide reasons that are adequate or intelligible, or the failure to base the decision on any evidence. In this limited context material error of fact has always been a recognised ground for judicial intervention.'"[358]

In *E v Secretary of State for the Home Department,*[359] the Court of Appeal considered the circumstances in which an error of fact would give

---

[357] [2003] 2 AC 295.
[358] Ibid, at 321D–321H.
[359] [2004] QB 1044.

rise to a freestanding ground of appeal in a statutory appeal on a point of law. Without 'laying down a precise code' the court identified the following factors:[360]

> 'First, there must have been a mistake as to an existing fact, including a mistake as to the availability of evidence on a particular matter. Secondly, the fact or evidence must have been "established", in the sense that it was uncontentious and objectively verifiable. Thirdly, the appellant (or his advisers) must not been have been responsible for the mistake. Fourthly, the mistake must have played a material (not necessarily decisive) part in the tribunal's reasoning.'

The Court further held that there was no practical difference between an appeal on 'error of law' grounds and grounds for judicial review.[361]

Examples of decisions that have been quashed owing to errors of fact include a decision of police officers to caution an offender, which was quashed in circumstances where the police officers accepted that they would not have taken that decision had they realised the correct facts,[362] and a decision of the Secretary of State for the Home Department to reject an application for registration as a British citizen owing to a mistaken belief that an application for settlement had not been made.[363]

The critical point about mistake of fact is that it may be difficult in most circumstances to establish that there was a demonstrable mistake of fact. Claimants will need objectively verifiable evidence of the true factual picture. In many cases, the normal discretion of a public authority to decide the facts will mean that the Administrative Court will not wish to take on a fact-finding role.[364] There will need to be clear evidence that the decision-maker got a material fact wrong.

## 2.11   RELEVANT FACTORS AND IMPROPER MOTIVE

A failure to take account of relevant factors or taking account of irrelevant factors is a ground of challenge that is closely linked to or a species of irrationality. Clearly, a decision that ignores a relevant factor might be said to lack logic. As Lord Carswell has held:[365]

> 'the [decision maker] was bound to have regard to the proper factors and not to have regard to any other improper factor in reaching his decision.'

---

[360]   Ibid, at 1071D–1071E.
[361]   Ibid, at 1063D–1063F.
[362]   *R (Omar) v Chief Constable of Bedfordshire* [2003] ACD 5.
[363]   *R (Ali) v Secretary of State for the Home Department* [2007] EWHC 1983 (Admin).
[364]   Subject to exceptions identified above at **2.2.2**.
[365]   *In Re Duffy* [2008] NI 152, at [53].

Or as Lord Slynn put it:[366]

> '... if the Secretary of State ... takes into account matters irrelevant to his decision or refuses or fails to take account of matters relevant to his decision ... the court may set his decision aside.'

When deciding what factors are relevant to a decision, and what factors are irrelevant to a decision, the Administrative Court will look first at the terms of the legislation providing for the decision-making power. The Court will seek to determine whether the statute provides any indication of the relevant factors to be taken into account by the decision-maker.[367] Such an indication may be express. For example, where a statutory provision required magistrates to consider the value of the property before making an order depriving an offender of the property,[368] a failure to take account of the value of a car to be forfeited led to that order being quashed.[369]

It is not only express provisions that can be relied upon in support of arguments about a failure to have regard to relevant factors. By applying normal principles of statutory construction, the Administrative Court may hold that it is implied that a range of factors is to be taken into account by a decision-maker. For example, when magistrates are asked to consider whether they will rehear a case, they are not restricted to considering merely whether the delay in applying for a rehearing means that the case should not be reheard. Parliament had repealed a previous statutory provision imposing a strict time-limit on the time for applications for rehearing, which implied that the delay was not the only factor that could be taken into account by magistrates when deciding whether to allow a rehearing.[370]

Administrative decision-makers as well as courts have to ensure that they take account of relevant factors and ignore irrelevant factors. For example, in deciding whether to make a stopping order under s 209 of the Town and Country Planning Act 1971, the Secretary of State was required to take account of the impact of the order on a business adjacent to the highway.[371] Particular decision-makers may be required to take into account resources,[372] disability equality issues,[373] or specific policy guidance.[374] However, a discretionary decision is not vitiated by a failure to take into account a consideration which the decision-maker is not

---

[366] *R (Alconbury Developments Ltd) v Secretary of State for the Environment, Transport and the Regions* [2003] 2 AC 295, at 320E.

[367] *Re Findlay* [1985] AC 318, per Lord Scarman, at 333H.

[368] Powers of Criminal Courts Act 1973, s 43(1A)(a).

[369] *R v Highbury Magistrate ex p Di Matteo* [1991] 1 WLR 1374.

[370] *R v Ealing Magistrates' Court ex p Sahota* [1998] COD 167.

[371] *Vasiliou v Secretary of State for Transport* [1991] 2 All ER 77.

[372] *R (G) v Barnet London Borough Council* [2004] 2 AC 208, at 225B.

[373] *R (Chavda) v Harrow London Borough Council* [2008] LGR 657.

[374] *R (Rashid) v Secretary of State for the Home Department* [2005] INLR 550.

obliged by the law or the facts to take into account, even if the decision-maker may properly do so.[375] In addition, a decision maker is not required to take account of the HRA 1998 providing that their decision is in fact consistent with the European Convention.[376]

If a decision is to be quashed as a result of a failure to approach the issue of relevant and irrelevant factors correctly, it must also be shown that the mistake was material. Thus, the court must be persuaded that the decision might have been different if the irrelevant factor had been ignored or the relevant factor had been taken into account.[377] Thus, a decision of the Crown Court regarding the destruction of a dog should not be quashed as a result of a failure to take account of the dog's disposition, when that factor would have made no difference to the final decision of the Crown Court.[378]

If the statute which provides for the power to make the decision does not require, either expressly or by implication, particular factors to be taken into account, a decision about the matters to be taken into account in the circumstances of a particular case can be impugned only on limited grounds. The Administrative Court will need to be persuaded that the decision that a particular factor should or should not be taken into account is irrational or otherwise contrary to the principles of public law.[379]

The decision about the factors that are to be taken into account must be distinguished from the decision about the weight to be given to the various factors. Public authorities are entitled to give relevant factors whatever weight they regard as appropriate in all the circumstances of the case; and the court will intervene only if that decision is irrational.[380]

Closely linked to the concept of relevant and irrelevant factors are the concepts of improper motive and abuse of power. A decision can be quashed if it can be shown that the decision-maker was motivated by an improper motive. For example, a decision to arraign a defendant in the Crown Court can be quashed if it was motivated by a desire to avoid the defendant being bailed, as a result of the operation of custody time-limits. The purpose of arraignment is trial management and so a decision to arraign should not be motivated by other concerns.[381] Improper motive

---

[375] *R (Corner House Research) v Director of the Serious Fraud Offfice* [2009] 1 AC 756, per Lord Bingham, at 844G.

[376] *Belfast City Council v Miss Behavin' Ltd* [2007] 1 AC 1420.

[377] *R v Thurrock Borough Council ex p Tesco Stores Ltd* [1993] 3 PLR 114, at 124D.

[378] *R v Teeside Crown Court ex p Bullock* [1996] COD 6.

[379] *R v Secretary of State for Transport ex p Richmond-upon-Thames London Borough Council* [1994] 1 WLR 74, per Laws J, at 95C.

[380] *Tesco Stores Ltd v Secretary of State for the Environment* [1995] 1 WLR 759, per Lord Keith, at 764G. See also *R (Staff Side of the Police Negotiating Board) v Secretary of State for the Home Department* [2008] EWHC 1173 (Admin), at [66].

[381] *R v Maidstone Crown Court ex p Clark* [1995] 1 WLR 831.

may border on abuse of power or oppressive conduct, such as the 'spiriting away of the claimants from the jurisdiction before there was likely to be time for them to obtain and act upon legal advice or apply to the court.'[382]

## 2.12 LEGITIMATE EXPECTATION

An application for judicial review can be based on a claim that a decision-maker has failed to fulfill a legitimate expectation. Claimants for judicial review must be careful to identify clearly how their cases fall within the categories of circumstances which, it has been held, give rise to legitimate expectation. A legitimate expectation, however, arises only in certain very limited circumstances and so practitioners acting for claimants should specify precisely how the legitimate expectation arises. Lord Justice Simon Brown identified three sets of circumstances where a legitimate expectation may arise:[383]

(1)  where the decision-maker has made a clear and unambiguous representation regarding a substantive right which it was reasonable for the claimant to rely on, the claimant may be entitled to that benefit. This, however, cannot give rise to a legitimate expectation if the granting of the substantive right is inconsistent with the decision-maker's statutory duty;[384]

(2)  where the claimant has an interest in some ultimate benefit that he hopes to retain (or possibly attain), fairness may require the claimant to be given an opportunity to make representations about the withdrawal of that benefit;[385] and

(3)  where the decision-maker has promised that he will adopt some form of procedure that he would not otherwise be required to adopt, the claimant may be entitled to require the decision-maker to adopt that procedure.[386]

Lord Justice Simon Brown also recognised that the term 'legitimate expectation' is sometimes said to encompass the right to a fair procedure generally, but he described this use of the concept as 'superfluous and unhelpful'.[387] The right to a fair hearing is really a separate category of legal error considered earlier in this chapter.[388]

---

[382]  *R (Karas & Milandinovic) v Secretary of State for the Home Department* [2006] EWHC 747 (Admin), at [84].

[383]  *R v Devon County Council ex p Baker* [1995] 1 All ER 73.

[384]  Ibid, at 88E.

[385]  Ibid, at 88J.

[386]  Ibid, at 89E. See also a useful discussion of the third category in *R (Niazi) v Independent Assessor* [2008] EWCA Civ 755.

[387]  *R v Devon County Council ex p Baker* [1995] 1 All ER 73, at 89B.

[388]  See **2.8**.

It is important to establish which category a claim falls within because this may determine the role of the Administrative Court. If it can be established that a case falls within the first category, the role of the Court is to decide whether the decision-maker has identified some sufficiently important reason for departing from its previous promise.[389] If it has not, then the Court will intervene if the conduct of the decision-maker amounts to a 'misuse of the authority's power'.[390] When the case comes within the other categories, the court's role will be to decide whether a fair procedure has been adopted.[391]

The best indication of which category a claim falls within is the number of people that can rely on the expectation. In practice, it is unlikely that a case will fall within the first category and bring substantive benefits unless only a few people can rely on the expectation.[392] This is presumably why it has been held in a criminal context that legitimate expectation gives rise to substantive rights. In a criminal context, it will normally only be the defendant who can rely on the expectation.

In the context of criminal proceedings, the concept of legitimate expectation has been applied so that a decision by one bench of magistrates that a matter would be dealt with in a particular way gave rise to a legitimate expectation that a second bench would deal with the case in the same way in the absence of new information.[393]

However, it is not only in a criminal context that a promise has been held to give rise to a substantive benefit. A promise that accommodation would be provided to people as a home for life may be sufficient to give rise to a substantive legitimate expectation.[394]

The mere fact that a decision-maker has adopted a policy does not necessarily give rise to a legitimate expectation that the policy will be applied in the circumstances in any particular case. Depending upon the circumstances in which the policy was adopted, it may be possible for a decision-maker to depart from the policy, provided that it takes account of the previous policy.[395]

The circumstances in which a legitimate expectation arises were considered by Lord Justice Stuart-Smith in *R v Jockey Club ex p RAM Racecourses*.[396] He held that the claimant must prove:[397]

---

[389]  *R v North and East Devon Health Authority ex p Coughlan* [2001] QB 213, at 242E.
[390]  Ibid, at 251E.
[391]  Ibid, at 242E.
[392]  Ibid, at 242H.
[393]  *R v Nottingham Magistrates' Court ex p Davidson* [2000] Crim LR 118.
[394]  *R v North and East Devon Health Authority ex p Coughlan* [2001] QB 213.
[395]  Ibid, at 242C.
[396]  [1993] 2 All ER 225.
[397]  Ibid, at 236H.

'(1)   A clear and unambiguous representation ...

(2)   That since the applicant was not a person to whom any representation was directly made it was within the class of persons who are entitled to rely upon it; or at any rate that it was reasonable for the applicant to rely upon it without more ...

(3)   That it did so rely upon it.

(4)   That it did so to its detriment. While in some cases it is not altogether clear that this is a necessary ingredient, since a public body is entitled to change its policy if it is acting in good faith, it is a necessary ingredient where, as here, an applicant is saying, "You cannot alter your policy now in my case; it is too late".

(5)   That there is no overriding interest arising from [the defendant's] duties and responsibilities ... which entitled [them] to change their policy to the detriment of the applicant.

The burden of proving the first four points is, in my judgement, upon the applicant . . . As to the fifth requirement, it seems to me that that is a matter for the [defendant] to establish.'

It is important to recognise it is not always necessary for the claimant to show that he relied on the legitimate expectation to his detriment.[398] For example, in the criminal cases cited above it is difficult to identify any reliance by the defendant on the promise by the magistrates. In some cases communication or knowledge of a policy giving rise to a legitimate expectation is not even necessary.[399] That is because legitimate expectation is essentially the most common example of unfairness amounting to an abuse of power.[400] As a consequence, there is inherent flexibility in the concept.

The analysis of Lord Justice Stuart-Smith needs to be viewed in the light of the guidance offered by Lord Justice Schiemann,[401] who held that:[402]

'In all legitimate expectation cases, whether substantive or procedural, three practical questions arise. The first question is to what has the public authority, whether by practice or by promise, committed itself; the second is whether the authority has acted or proposes to act unlawfully in relation to its commitment; the third is what the court should do.'

Two particular matters require consideration when a claim is based on a legitimate expectation. First, it would appear to be clear that a legitimate

---

[398]  *Francisco Javier Jaramillo-Silva v Secretary of State for the Home Department* [1994] Imm AR 352, per Lord Justice Stuart-Smith, at 357.

[399]  *R (Rashid) v Secretary of State for the Home Department* [2005] INLR 550, at [25].

[400]  Ibid, at [34].

[401]  *R (Bibi) v London Borough of Newham* [2002] 1 WLR 237.

[402]  Ibid, at 244B.

expectation cannot require a decision-maker to act unlawfully.[403] Secondly, a promise can usually only bind a decision-maker if it is made by that decision-maker.[404]

Legitimate expectation is a concept that applies in the context of European Convention and European Union law.[405] It may well be difficult to argue that a decision that is contrary to a promise is proportionate.

## 2.13   INCONSISTENCY

Inconsistency has long been recognised as an error that allows the court to intervene because good public administration requires consistent decision-making.[406] It is also linked to the concept of irrationality, as an inconsistent decision may be said to lack logic. In *Kruse v Johnson*,[407] Lord Russell CJ held:[408]

> 'I do not mean to say that there may not be cases in which it would be the duty of the Court to condemn by-laws, made under such authority as these were made, as invalid because unreasonable. But unreasonable in what sense? If, for instance, they were found to be partial and unequal in their operation as between different classes; if they were manifestly unjust; if they disclosed bad faith; if they involved such oppressive or gratuitous interference with the rights of those subject to them as could find no justification in the minds of reasonable men, the Court might well say, "Parliament never intended to give authority to make such rules; they are unreasonable and ultra vires".'

The House of Lords has emphasised the desirability of consistency in administrative decision-making on more than one occasion.[409] The principle has been applied in the context of immigration to allow the courts to quash an immigration rule made pursuant to primary legislation, because the rule discriminated between two classes of apparently similar people.[410]

Although it is clear that consistency is a matter that can be raised in an application for judicial review, the Administrative Court will be reluctant to find that a decision should be quashed simply because it is inconsistent

---

[403]   *R v Secretary of State for Education and Employment ex p Begbie* [2000] 1 WLR 1115.
[404]   *R (Bloggs 61) v Secretary of State for the Home Department* [2003] 1 WLR 2725, holding that the police cannot bind the Prison Service. But see *R (BAPIO Action Ltd) v Secretary of State for the Home Department* [2008] 1 AC 1003, at 1026D, in which one government department was bound by rules issued by another government department.
[405]   *R (Nadarajah) v Secretary of State* [2005] EWCA Civ 1363, at [68].
[406]   *R v Hertfordshire County Council ex p Cheung* (1986) *The Times*, April 4.
[407]   [1898] 2 QBD 91.
[408]   *Kruse v Johnson* [1898] 2 QBD 91, at 99.
[409]   *R (O'Brien) v Independent Assessor* [2007] 2 AC 312, at 328H, and *N v Secretary of State for the Home Department* [2005] 2 AC 296, at 302F.
[410]   *R v Immigration Appeal Tribunal ex p Begum* [1986] Imm AR 385, at 394.

with a decision in an apparently similar case.[411] The Administrative Court is aware that two cases will never be precisely the same.[412] In practice, it is therefore very difficult to argue that a decision should be quashed because it is inconsistent with another decision. Indeed it has been suggested that it would only be possible to challenge a decision on the basis of inconsistency in circumstances in which there were inconsistent policies or policies that produce inconsistent results and not in circumstances in which individual cases have been considered in an inconsistent manner.[413] Alternatively inconsistency in decision-making may be better expressed as unfairness[414] or arbitrariness.[415]

## 2.14 CIRCUMSTANCES IN WHICH THERE IS A DUTY TO GIVE REASONS

The giving of reasons is 'one of the fundamentals of good administration'.[416] Reasons are often important from the perspective of a potential claimant because they are likely to provide the information necessary to bring a claim for judicial review. For example, reasons may indicate that a decision-maker has made an error of law or failed to take a relevant factor into account. In addition, a requirement to give reasons ensures that a decision-maker focuses on the relevant factors that it is required by law to consider. However, some decision-makers refuse to provide reason. Although the conventional view is that there is no general common law duty to give reasons for administrative decisions,[417] the courts are increasingly willing to imply a duty to give reasons in a wide variety of contexts.

In judicial review proceedings it may be possible to argue that an administrative or court decision is flawed by a failure to give reasons if the claimant can show that the decision-maker was under a duty to give reasons. In some circumstances, the legislation governing the decision will require the decision-maker to give reasons. For example, where a defendant is appealing by way of case stated from a decision of a magistrates' court or Crown Court, the court will be required to state a case (which will include reasons). It can refuse to state a case only if it

---

[411]   *R v Special Adjudicator ex p Kandasamy* [1994] Imm AR 333.
[412]   *R v Secretary of State for the Home Department ex p Mohammed Yasin* [1995] Imm AR 118.
[413]   *R (Potter) v Secretary of State for the Home Department* [2002] ACD 27, at [64].
[414]   *R v Immigration Appeal Tribunal ex p Kandasamy* [1994] Imm AR 333, per Hidden J.
[415]   *R (S) v Secretary of State for the Home Department* [2007] ACD 94.
[416]   *Breen v Amalgamated Engineering Union* [1971] 2 QB 175, at 191C.
[417]   *Stefan v General Medical Council* [1999] 1 WLR 1293; *R (Hasan) v Secretary of State for Trade and Industry* [2009] 3 All ER 539.

views the appeal as frivolous.[418] If the reasons are inadequate, the Administrative Court can send the stated case back to the magistrates' court for amendment.[419]

In some ways, the obligation imposed on criminal courts to state a case is an unusual example of the obligation to provide reasons because the requirement to state a case does not require reasons at the time that a decision is taken. An express duty to give reasons is more normally found in a procedural rule that requires reasons at the time of decision, such as where the Parole Board rules provided that the Parole Board gave reasons.[420]

In the absence of a statutory or policy requirement to give reasons, as there is no general duty implied by the common law requiring reasons for all administrative and court decisions, the issue of whether there is a duty to give reasons depends on the circumstances of the case.[421]

The courts will also consider whether fairness demands reasons when it decides whether there is a duty to give reasons in a particular case.[422] Attempts to define exhaustively the circumstances in which fairness results in a common law duty to give reasons may be of limited assistance. However, Mr Justice Sedley has provided the following useful summary:[423]

> '(1) [T]here is no general duty to give reasons for a decision, but there are classes of case where there is such a duty. (2) One such class is where the subject matter is an interest so highly regarded by the law (for example, personal liberty), that fairness requires that reasons, at least for particular decisions, be given as of right. (3)(a) Another such class is where the decision appears aberrant. Here fairness may require reasons so that the recipient may know whether the aberration is in the legal sense real (and so challengeable) or apparent; (b) it follows that this class does not include decisions which are themselves challengeable by reference only to the reasons for them. A pure exercise of academic judgement is such a decision. And (c) Procedurally, the grant of leave in such cases will depend upon prima facie evidence that something has gone wrong.'

---

[418] Crown Court Rules 1982 (SI 1982/1109), r 26(6); Magistrates' Courts Act 1980, s 111(5).

[419] Senior Courts Act 1981, s 28A(2).

[420] *R v Parole Board ex p Lodomez* [1994] COD 525.

[421] *R v Secretary of State for the Home Department ex p Doody* [1994] 1 AC 531, at 564E–564F.

[422] *R v Civil Service Appeal Board ex p Cunningham* [1991] 4 All ER 310, per Lord Donaldson MR, at 319B; De Smith, Woolf and Jowell, *Judicial Review of Administrative Action* (Sweet & Maxwell, 6th edn, 2007), para 7.091.

[423] *R v Higher Education Funding Council ex p Institute of Dental Surgery* [1994] 1 WLR 242, at 263A, approved by the Court of Appeal in *R (Wooder) v Feggetter and Another* [2003] QB 219.

That approach is relevant not only to the duty to give reasons at all but the quality or detail of the reasons to be given.[424] In practice, the Administrative Court will look at a wide range of factors when it decides whether fairness implies a duty to give reasons. These may include the need for justice to be seen to be done.[425]

In general, there is a duty on professional judges to give reasons for their decisions.[426] However the existence of a right of appeal may mean that there is no duty to give reasons[427] because they are unnecessary if a person can restate his case on an appeal on both facts and law. However, Art 6 of the European Convention on Human Rights may impose a requirement for reasons to enable a potential appellant to determine the merits of his appeal.[428] Whether the reasons given by the court are sufficient will depend on the facts and circumstances of the case.[429]

In many cases administrative decisions attract no right of appeal. Where there is no appeal, judicial review will often be the only way of challenging a decision. The difficulties faced by the Administrative Court in seeking to identify whether grounds for judicial review exist when there are no or insufficient reasons is also a factor that is taken into account when deciding whether there is a duty to give reasons and the scope of that duty.[430]

The difficulties faced by the Administrative Court may partially explain why there is a clear trend towards requiring greater openness from decision-makers.[431] Greater openness means that reasons are required in an increasing variety of circumstances. In addition, the impact of the Human Rights Act 1998 has been to focus the minds of decision-makers on the need to give reasons, and practitioners have noticed that bodies such as magistrates' courts are increasingly willing to give reasons. In addition, the higher courts have noted that Art 6 of the European Convention on Human Rights can require a decision-maker to give reasons.[432]

---

[424] *R (Asha Foundation) v Millennium Commission* [2003] ACD 50.

[425] *Save Britain's Heritage v Number 1 Poultry Ltd* [1991] 1 WLR 153.

[426] *R v Knightsbridge Crown Court ex p International Sporting Club Ltd* [1982] QB 304, at 314H; *Flannery v Halifax Estate Agencies Ltd* [2000] 1 WLR 377.

[427] *R v Civil Service Appeal Board ex p Cunningham* [1991] 4 All ER 310, per Lord Donaldson MR, at 318A. See also *R v Burton-upon-Trent Justices ex p Hussain* (1997) 9 Admin LR 233, in which a duty was said to arise when magistrates were acting as an appellate authority.

[428] *Hadjianastassiou v Greece* (1993) 16 EHRR 219, at [33]. See also *English v Emery Reimbold & Strick Ltd* [2002] 1 WLR 2409.

[429] *Cook v Consolidated Finance Ltd* [2010] BPIR 1331, at [23].

[430] *R v Secretary of the State for the Home Department ex p Doody* [1994] 1 AC 531, per Lord Mustill, at 565F.

[431] *R v Secretary of State for the Home Department ex p Doody* [1994] 1 AC 531, at 561E.

[432] *English v Emery Reimbold & Strick Ltd* [2002] 1 WLR 2409.

The Administrative Court's willingness to consider a failure to give reasons in a case where the decision appears to be 'aberrant' is also important. Where the circumstances of a case indicate that a particular decision should have been taken if it was to accord with the legislative purpose of the decision-maker's power but another decision has been taken, an absence of reasons may lead the Court to draw the inference that the decision-maker had no good reason for the decision.[433] Lord Reid stated:[434]

> 'If it is the Minister's duty not to act so as to frustrate the policy and objects of the Act, and if it were to appear from all the circumstances of the case that that has been the effect of the Minister's refusal, then it appears to me that the court must be entitled to act.'

However, the Court of Appeal has been unwilling to find that 'under established principles of judicial review, the absence of reasons gives rise to the view that none exists.'[435]

### 2.14.1   The importance of requesting reasons

Asking for reasons is always important, because it may be very difficult to challenge a failure to give reasons if there has been no application for reasons.[436] In addition, even if there is no duty to give reasons, the decision-maker will still have a discretion to give reasons.[437] The exercise of that discretion is governed by the same principles as the exercise of any other discretion, which means that a failure to give reasons could be challenged if it were shown that the exercise of the discretion was unlawful. For example, a failure to give reasons where there is a discretion to give reasons could be challenged if it can be shown that the failure to give reasons is irrational or unfair.

### 2.14.2   The scope of the duty to give reasons

Lord Brown set out the correct standard of reasoning where a duty to give reasons arises as follows:[438]

> 'The reasons for a decision must be intelligible and they must be adequate. They must enable the reader to understand why the matter was decided as it was and what conclusions were reached on the "principal important controversial issues", disclosing how any issue of law or fact was resolved. Reasons can be briefly stated, the degree of particularity required depending

---

[433]   *Padfield v Minister of Agriculture Fisheries and Food* [1968] AC 997, at 1032G.
[434]   Ibid.
[435]   *R (Farrakhan) v Secretary of State for the Home Department* [2002] QB 1391, per Lord Phillips, at 1400G.
[436]   *R v The Crown Court of Southwark ex p Samuel* [1995] COD 249.
[437]   *R v Secretary of State for the Home Department ex p Fayed* [1997] 1 All ER 228.
[438]   *South Bucks District Council v Porter (No 2)* [2004] 1 WLR 1953, per Lord Brown, at 1964D–1964G.

entirely on the nature of the issues falling for decision. The reasoning must not give rise to a substantial doubt as to whether the decision-maker erred in law, for example by misunderstanding some relevant policy or some other important matter or by failing to reach a rational decision on relevant grounds. But such adverse inference will not readily be drawn. The reasons need refer only to the main issues in the dispute, not to every material consideration.'

As Lord Bridge held in another case, reasons have to be 'proper, intelligible and adequate'.[439] The Court of Appeal made similar remarks when it considered the scope of reasons required from a judge:[440]

'[I]f the appellate process is to work satisfactorily, the judgment must enable the appellate court to understand why the Judge reached his decision. This does not mean that every factor which weighed with the Judge in his appraisal of the evidence has to be identified and explained. But the issues the resolution of which were vital to the Judge's conclusion should be identified and the manner in which he resolved them explained. It is not possible to provide a template for this process. It need not involve a lengthy judgment. It does require the Judge to identify and record those matters which were critical to his decision. If the critical issue was one of fact, in may be enough to say that one witness was preferred to another because the one manifestly had a clearer recollection of the material facts or the other gave answers which demonstrated that his recollection could not be relied upon.'[441]

These two passages indicate that the critical matter to consider when deciding whether reasons are adequate is to determine whether reasons have been given that address the key issues raised by the parties. If they address those issues and in particular explain how the decision-maker reached a conclusion regarding those key issues, that is likely to mean that adequate reasons have been given.

The two passages also indicate that the reasons required need not be very extensive.[442] At least, in certain circumstances, a sentence or two giving some indication of the court's reasoning may be all that is required.[443] For example, where the Crown Court is acting in an appellate capacity, the presiding judge must demonstrate merely that the court has identified the main contentious issues in the case and explain how it has resolved them.[444] In the context of disciplinary proceedings, 'what is required by way of reasons is an outline of the story which has given rise to the complaint, a summary of the basic factual conclusions and a statement of the reasons which have led the committee to reach their conclusion on

---

[439]  *Save Britain's Heritage v Number 1 Poultry Limited* [1991] 1 WLR 153, at 166H.
[440]  *English v Emery Reimbold & Strick Ltd* [2002] 1 WLR 2409.
[441]  Ibid, at 2418D–2418E.
[442]  See also *Stefan v General Medical Council* [1999] 1 WLR 1293, at 1304B.
[443]  *R v Southwark Crown Court ex p Brooke* [1997] COD 81.
[444]  *R v Harrow Crown Court ex p Dave* (1994) 99 Cr App R 114.

those basic facts' but 'it is not necessary for every factor to be dealt with explicitly in order for the reasoning to be legally adequate'.[445]

Where there is a breach of a statutory duty to give reasons, the normal remedy should be an order to quash and retake the decision.[446] This is because where the duty to give reasons is an important statutory protection, a failure to give reasons will normally be grounds to set aside the decision.[447] But where a non-statutory duty to give reasons arises, the absence of reasons will not necessarily result in the Administrative Court quashing the decision. The Court will not act if there is obviously no injustice in the failure to give reasons.[448] If the Court does act, it may not in its discretion quash the decision that is the subject of the judicial review. Instead, it may merely act to require the decision-maker to provide adequate reasons. Thus, reasons given during the course of a judicial review may result in the Court refusing to grant relief.[449]

In most circumstances, however, the Administrative Court will be reluctant to permit a decision-maker to give additional reasons as the Court will be concerned to ensure that those given are not an *ex post facto* rationalisation and not the real reasons relied on at the time of the decision.[450] For example, the Court of Appeal has suggested that a court should 'at the very least be circumspect about allowing material gaps to be filled by affidavit evidence or otherwise',[451] and has held that, 'In principle a decision-maker who gives one set of reasons cannot, when challenged, come up with another set.'[452]

To determine whether the Administrative Court will accept supplementary reasons, it is necessary to consider the origin of the duty to give reasons. Stanley Burnton J identified the following principles:

(a)   if there is a statutory duty to provide reasons when a decision is notified, the Court will not accept supplementary reasons except in exceptional circumstances;[453]

---

[445]   *R (Duncan) v General Teaching Council for England* [2010] EWHC 429 (Admin), per Ouseley J, at [6].

[446]   *Hall v Wandsworth LBC* [2005] 2 All ER 192.

[447]   *R v Macdonald (Inspector of Taxes) ex p Hutchinson & Co Ltd* [1998] STC 680 per Carnwath J: 'Given the strength of the powers under section 20, the limited procedural safeguards provided by Parliament are of great importance'.

[448]   *Cedeno v Logan* [2001] 1 WLR 86.

[449]   *R v Legal Aid Area No 8 (Northern) Committee ex p Angell* (1991) 3 Admin LR 189, at 207D.

[450]   *S v Special Educational Needs Tribunal* [1995] 1 WLR 1627, at 1637B.

[451]   *R Westminster City Council ex p Ermakov* (1996) 28 HLR 819, at 829. The Court of Appeal was concerned that the supplementary reasons advanced in that case were not 'merely amplification and explanation' but wholly different.

[452]   *R (Bancoult) v Secretary of State for Foreign & Commonwealth Affairs* [2008] QB 365, at 407A (judgment over-turned by the House of Lords, [2009] 1 AC 453).

[453]   *R (Nash) v Chelsea College of Art and Design* (2001) *The Times,* July 25, at [34].

(b)   in other cases, the Court should be cautious about accepting supplementary reasons;[454]

(c)   in deciding whether to accept reasons, the Court will consider a number of matters including: the subject matter of the decision (as the less important the subject matter, the more willing the Court will be to accept supplementary reasons);[455] the qualifications of the decision-maker (as a higher standard of reasoning can be expected from lawyers);[456] and the timing of the reasons (as the Court should be particularly reluctant to accept reasons given after litigation has been commenced).[457]

The *Nash* principles may not apply with as much force in the context of challenges to decisions of courts. The Court of Appeal in *English v Emery Reimbold & Strick Ltd*[458] identified policy concerns which suggest that courts and tribunals should be able to supplement their reasons to avoid unnecessary litigation.[459] However *English* was concerned with appeals (rather than judicial review). It has been applied by the Administrative Court, in a judicial review of the Mental Health Review Tribunal.[460] However, in other cases, the Court has declined to take this approach.[461] The Court of Appeal has also cautioned against adopting the *English* approach where the inadequacy of reasoning is on its face so fundamental that there is a real risk that supplementary reasons will be reconstructions of proper reasons; nor will it be appropriate where there have been allegations of bias.[462]

## 2.15   BAD FAITH

Bad faith is a free-standing ground of judicial review which overlaps with the concepts of abuse of power and improper motive. In practice, however, it is extremely unusual for an application for judicial review to be based on bad faith because of the need to provide particularly clear and

---

[454]   Ibid, at [34].

[455]   Ibid, at [35].

[456]   Ibid, at [36].

[457]   Ibid, at [34].

[458]   [2002] 1 WLR 2409. See also 'English v Emery Reimbold in the Administrative Court: a second bite of the cherry or a sensible way forward in a reasons challenge?' [2007] JR 82.

[459]   *English v Emery Reimbold & Strick Ltd* [2002] 1 WLR 2409, at 2419C.

[460]   *R (Mersey Care NHS Trust) v Mental Health Review Tribunal* [2003] EWHC 1182. It is important to note that special considerations may have permitted Sullivan J to rely on *English v Emery Reimbold & Strick Ltd* [2002] 1 WLR 2409 in the context of this case. The claimant was seeking to challenge a decision of the Mental Health Review Tribunal to release a patient. It clearly is undesirable for a person to be denied their liberty as a consequence of a technical failure to provide adequate reasons.

[461]   *VK v Norfolk County Council* [2005] ELR 342, at [79]; *R (Flenley) v Hammersmith and Fulham LBC* [2008] JPL 1300, at [42]; a planning decision in which the supplementary reasons sought to be relied upon had been absent from the response to the pre-action protocol letter.

[462]   *Barke v SEETEC Business Technology Centre Ltd* [2005] ICR 1373, at 1389B–1389C.

cogent evidence when making an allegation of bad faith against a public authority. Indeed, a claimant is essentially required to adduce evidence of the state of mind of the decision-maker. It is likely to be more straightforward to prove bias or one of the other grounds of challenge.[463] Practitioners should also be aware of the requirements of the Bar Code of Conduct that barristers should not plead fraud unless there is 'reasonably credible material' that establishes a prima facie case.[464] This may limit a barrister's scope to plead bad faith.

## 2.16 PROPORTIONALITY

Judges considering judicial review applications have anticipated for some time that the concept of proportionality might become part of English law.[465] Indeed, Lord Cooke suggested that proportionality might replace irrationality as a ground for applying for judicial review.[466] More recently, Lord Hope left open the question of whether proportionality gave rise to a free-standing ground for judicial review, describing the issue as being one of 'considerable importance and difficulty'.[467] However, at present, it is clear that proportionality may be relied upon as a ground of challenge only in cases in which the European Convention on Human Rights or European Union law is engaged,[468] unless it can be shown that a decision under challenge is so disproportionate as to be irrational.[469]

The European Court of Human Rights has applied the principle of proportionality in a range of cases including, for example, alleged interferences with the right to private life and family life under Art 8, in which the Court will determine whether the interference was proportionate to the legitimate aim pursued.[470] Thus, a decision to deport a person as a result of his criminal offending will be a breach of Art 8 of the European Convention if the interference with his private and family life is not proportionate to the aim of maintaining public order.[471]

It is important to be aware that proportionality is not necessarily relevant to all alleged breaches of the European Convention. In general, it is relevant only to articles that expressly state that breaches of the rights that they protect can be justified on the grounds set out in the article. For example, Art 8 allows for interferences with rights to private and family

---

463  See **2.8**.

464  See para 704(c) of the Code of Conduct of the Bar of England and Wales.

465  See, for example, *Council of Civil Service Unions v Minister for the Civil Service* [1985] AC 374, per Lord Diplock, at 410E.

466  *R (Daly) v S ecretary of State for the Home Department* [2001] 2 AC 532, at 549C.

467  *Somerville v Scottish Ministers* [2007] 1 WLR 2734, at 2755G.

468  See **2.10** and *R (Association of British Civilian Internees (Far East Region)) v Secretary of State for Defence* [2003] QB 139.

469  See, for example, the 'sledgehammer to crack a nut' analogy in *R v Secretary of State for the Home Department ex p Brind* [1991] 1 AC 696, at 759D.

470  See, for example, *Z v Finland* (1997) 25 EHRR 371, at [96].

471  *Moustaquim v Belgium* (1991) 13 EHRR 802.

life as Article 8(2) provides specific grounds for justifying such interferences. As a consequence it is necessary to consider whether any interference with Art 8 rights is proportionate.

Article 3 of the European Convention provides no grounds for justifying inhuman and degrading treatment. As a consequence, it is generally the case that a state can provide no justification for acting in a manner that exposes an individual to ill-treatment contrary to Art 3. For example, in the context of immigration law, a State cannot balance the risk that a person will be ill-treated if removed from the United Kingdom against the reasons for that removal.[472] The absence of any consideration of the justification for an interference with Art 3 rights means that in general it will be unnecessary to consider proportionality.

Similarly, the right to a fair trial inherent in Art 6 of the European Convention is an absolute right in the sense that the fairness of the trial cannot be qualified, compromised or restricted in any way.[473] As a consequence a state can provide no justification for the denial of a fair trial and in general it will be unnecessary to consider proportionality.

However proportionality may be relevant in certain circumstances to the Articles of the European Convention that contain absolute rights. For example, although the Art 6 right to a fair trial is an absolute right, the constituent rights may be compromised providing that the qualification of those rights is directed towards a clear and proper public objective and that it represents no greater qualification than the situation calls for.[474] As a consequence, it may be necessary to consider whether a qualification of the constituent rights is proportionate. For example, a constituent right within Art 6 is the right to protection against self-incrimination.[475] However, legislation providing that a motorist must answer questions was not a violation of Art 6 as it was a proportionate response to the problems of road safety.[476]

Proportionality may even be relevant to Art 3 of the European Convention in certain limited circumstances. For example, it has been suggested that a disproportionate prison sentence may be a violation of Art 3.[477]

Proportionality is also regarded as a fundamental principle of European Union law. In *Fromançais SA v Fonds d'Orientation et de Regularisation des Marches Agricoles*,[478] the European Court of Justice held that:[479]

---

[472]  *Chahal v United Kingdom* (1996) 23 EHRR 413; *Ahmed v Austria* (1996) 24 EHRR 278 recently confirmed in *Sufi v United Kingdom* (2012) 54 EHRR 9.
[473]  *Brown v Stott* [2003] 1 AC 681.
[474]  Ibid.
[475]  *Funke v France* (1993) 16 EHRR 297.
[476]  *Brown v Stott* [2003] 1 AC 681.
[477]  *Weeks v United Kingdom* (1987) 10 EHRR 293.
[478]  [1983] ECR 395.

'In order to establish whether a provision of Community law is consonant with the principle of proportionality it is necessary to establish, in the first place, whether the means it employs to achieve its aim correspond to the importance of the aim and, in the second place, whether they are necessary for its achievement.'

This principle has been applied by the European Court to conclude that regulations that provide for a penalty for a failure to comply with contractual obligations must ensure that the penalty is commensurate with the seriousness of the failure to comply with the contract.[480]

The issues to be considered when determining whether a decision is proportionate are clear. In *R (Daly) v Secretary of State for the Home Department*,[481] Lord Steyn approved the dictum of the Privy Council in *de Freitas v Permanent Secretary of Ministry of Agriculture, Fisheries, Lands and Housing*,[482] holding that the issues to be considered are:[483]

'whether: (i) the legislative objective is sufficiently important to justify limiting a fundamental right; (ii) the measures designed to meet the legislative objective are rationally connected to it; and (iii) the means used to impair the right or freedom are no more than is necessary to accomplish the objective.'

This dictum has been applied by the courts on a number of occasions and is supplemented by an additional factor; 'the need to balance the interests of society with those of individuals and groups',[484] which is 'an aspect which should never be overlooked or discounted.'[485]

The burden is upon the state to demonstrate proportionality.[486]

Circumstances in which the courts have been willing to quash decisions as disproportionate include where an adjudication by the Advertising Standards Authority constituted a disproportionate interference with the right to freedom of expression under Art 10,[487] or where regulations aimed at preventing sham marriages went beyond the mischief aimed at and prevented genuine marriages.[488] By contrast, where a regulator of social housing landlords was deciding which landlord should be the

---

479 *Fromançais SA v Fonds d'Orientation et de Regularisation des Marches Agricoles* [1983] ECR 395, at [8].
480 *Atalanta Amsterdam BV v Produktschap voor Vee en Vlees* [1979] ECR 2137.
481 [2001] 2 AC 532.
482 [1999] 1 AC 69.
483 *R (Daly) v Secretary of State for the Home Department* [2001] 2 AC 532, at 547A–547C.
484 *R (Razgar) v Secretary of State for the Home Department* [2004] 2 AC 368, at 390B.
485 *Huang v Secretary of State for the Home Department* [2007] 2 AC 167, at 187E.
486 *R (Quila) v Secretary of State for the Home Department* [2012] 3 WLR 836, at [44].
487 *Re Kirk Session of Sandown Free Presbyterian Church's Application for Judicial Review* [2011] NIQB 26.
488 *R (Baiai and another) v Secretary of State for the Home Department (Nos 1 and 2)* [2009] 1 AC 287.

transferee of certain land, the appropriate test of proportionality was a balancing exercise and a decision which was justified on the basis of a compelling case in the public interest and as being reasonably necessary, but did not have to be the least intrusive of human rights.[489]

It is also clear that the courts are often reluctant to find that a policy that provides for no flexibility is proportionate, as it fails to permit consideration of whether an interference with rights is necessary in the circumstances of a particular case. For example, the Court of Appeal has held that it is necessary to consider the circumstances of a case involving the failure to pay excise duty when importing goods to determine whether the forfeiture of a person's vehicle used in the importation was a proportionate response.[490] Similarly, the Court of Appeal has held that an immigration policy that required a person to leave to the United Kingdom to apply for entry to be with his spouse is disproportionate if it prevented consideration of the impact of Home Office delay in a particular case.[491] More recently, the sex offender registration scheme was held to be disproportionate as it did not permit an individual to apply for exemption from it.[492] However, the Administrative Court does not limit its criticism of a lack of proportionality to cases in which a policy fails to permit consideration of the circumstances of a particular case.

As to the standard of review that the Court should undertake in considering proportionality, in *Daly* Lord Steyn commented that:

> '... the intensity of review is somewhat greater under the proportionality approach. Making due allowance for important structural differences between various convention rights, which I do not propose to discuss, a few generalisations are perhaps permissible. I would mention three concrete differences without suggesting that my statement is exhaustive. First, the doctrine of proportionality may require the reviewing court to assess the balance which the decision maker has struck, not merely whether it is within the range of rational or reasonable decisions. Secondly, the proportionality test may go further than the traditional grounds of review inasmuch as it may require attention to be directed to the relative weight accorded to interests and considerations. Thirdly, even the heightened scrutiny test developed in *R v Ministry of Defence ex p Smith* [1996] QB 517, 554 [493] is not necessarily appropriate to the protection of human rights.'[494]

The consideration of the standard of review has developed further. In particular, the Court of Appeal suggested in *R (Samaroo) v Secretary of*

---

[489]  *R (Clays Lane Housing Cooperative Ltd) v Housing Corporation* [2005] 1 WLR 2229.
[490]  *Lindsay v Customs and Excise Commissioners* [2002] 1 WLR 1766.
[491]  *Shala v Secretary of State for the Home Department* [2003] INLR 349.
[492]  *R (F) v Secretary of State for the Home Department* [2011] 1 AC 331.
[493]  See consideration of anxious scrutiny at **2.10**.
[494]  *R (Daly) v Secretary of State for the Home Department* [2001] 2 AC 532, at 547E–547G.

*State for the Home Department*[495] that it is necessary to consider two stages when considering proportionality:[496]

> 'At the first stage, the question is: can the objective of the measure be achieved by means which are less interfering of an individual's rights? ... At the second stage, it is assumed that the means employed to achieve the legitimate aim are necessary in the sense that they are the least intrusive of Convention rights that can be devised in order to achieve the aim.'

*Samaroo* was a case in which the Secretary of State for the Home Department was seeking to deport a foreign national who was a drugs offender. The Court applied the criteria identified in de Freitas to consider the first stage and concluded that it could not be said that there was a less restrictive alternative to deportation that could achieve the same objective. However, it then went on to consider whether deportation had a disproportionate effect on the claimant.[497]

In the view of the court in *Samaroo* the 'second stage' raised a 'discretionary area of judgment' within which it may be necessary for the Administrative Court to show a degree of deference to an administrative decision-maker.[498] However in Huang v Secretary of State for the Home Department[499] Lord Bingham held:[500]

> 'The giving of weight to factors such as these is not, in our opinion, aptly described as deference: it is performance of the ordinary judicial task of weighing up the competing considerations on each side and according appropriate weight to the judgment of a person with responsibility for a given subject matter and access to special sources of knowledge and advice. That is how any rational judicial decision-maker is likely to proceed.'

The Divisional Court recently preferred the 'appropriate weight' analysis in a challenge to the Secretary of State to allow access to a detainee for the purposes of interview.[501]

In addition, the Court should be less willing to defer to the executive when it is considering the first stage:[502]

> 'The aim of the relevant policy here is not deliberately to deprive the prisoner of his Convention right; it is to recognise that right and only to interfere with it so far as is necessary to achieve a specific objective or

---

[495] [2001] UKHRR 1150.
[496] Ibid, at [19] and [20].
[497] Ibid, at [20].
[498] Ibid, at [35].
[499] [2007] 2 AC 167.
[500] Ibid, at 185F.
[501] *R (British Broadcasting Corporation) v Secretary of State for Justice* [2012] EWHC 13 (Admin).
[502] *R (Hirst) v Secretary of State for the Home Department* [2002] 1 WLR 2929, at 2943D–2943E.

objectives. The courts can with more confidence exercise a tighter review of the restriction to ensure that it does not unnecessarily interfere with Convention rights. There is not simply a general striking of a balance between individual rights and the public interest with deference being shown to the views of the state authorities; the starting point is the Convention right, which it is accepted in principle remains in play. The authority must demonstrate a proper basis for interfering with it, and show that nothing short of the particular interference will achieve the avowed objective.'

It should, however, be noted that a less intensive approach to the issue of proportionality should be applied when considering property rights, as set out in Art 1 of the First Protocol to the Convention, than when considering the 'core' rights set out in Arts 8 to 11 of the Convention. Such property rights can be overridden unless a decision is manifestly unreasonable.[503]

In the context of Art 14, the approach to proportionality depends upon the reason for discrimination. For example, discrimination on the basis of race or gender is unlikely to be proportionate.[504] Some other grounds for discrimination may be easier to justify.

A less intrusive approach is taken to proportionality when considering some aspects of European Union law, particularly where the issue concerns domestic law-making. In *R (Sinclair Collis Ltd) v Secretary of State for Health*,[505] the Court of Appeal considered the correct approach to the issue of proportionality in a challenge to a ban on cigarette vending machines that was said to be in breach of an EU Treaty prohibition on 'quantitative restrictions on imports and all measures having equivalent effect.' However, the relevant EU treaty permitted prohibitions or restrictions that were based upon public health. The Court of Appeal upheld the ban as proportionate, but all three members of the Court took a different approach to the issue of proportionality. Laws LJ, in a minority judgment, considered that public health was of such importance that it required the courts to confer a broad margin of appreciation on the decision-maker:[506]

'...the court leaves a wider space for the decision-maker's own judgment as to the application of the standards. The question the standards represent must still be asked and answered, first by the decision-maker himself; but the broader the margin of appreciation, the less inclined the court will be to strike an autonomous balance of the material factors.'[507]

Arden LJ disagreed, holding that a proportionality challenge in the case of public health measures could only succeed only when the measure was

---

[503] *AXA General Insurance Ltd, Petitioners* [2011] 3 WLR 871.
[504] *R (Carson) v Secretary of State for Work and Pensions* [2006] 1 AC 173, at 182F–183A.
[505] [2012] 2 WLR 304.
[506] Ibid, at 326G.
[507] Ibid, at 326G.

'manifestly inappropriate' having regard to the objective which the decision-maker was seeking to pursue:[508]

> 'The effect of the level of intensity of review denoted by the expression "manifestly inappropriate" is that the Court of Justice does not apply the "least intrusive means" requirement ... or, if it does, it applies it with the lower level of intensity of scrutiny consistent with the "manifestly inappropriate" level ...
>
> ... Not all member states will seek to protect public health in the same way. European Union law allows for that choice to be made by the national legislature, not free from EU control but with a much less intensive level of scrutiny than under a strict test of proportionality.'

As a result, the role of the courts in reviewing EU proportionality challenges in the public health sphere should be one of taking, '... a spirit level or chisel to the task, rather than the heavy-handed hammer of the strict test of proportionality'.[509]

Lord Neuberger MR's position was closer to that of Arden LJ than that of Laws LJ. He held that a failure to opt for the 'less restrictive alternative' may constitute a breach of the proportionality principle, but:[510]

> '... where there is an alternative possible measure, there may be a difference in view as to which measure would be less onerous, and, unless the view of the Member State's government that its measure is the more appropriate is manifestly wrong, the court should not substitute its own view for that of the government.'

It follows that the courts are likely to adopt a much more permissive approach when considering EU law proportionality challenges than challenges under the 'core rights' set out in the European Convention of Human Rights. It should be remembered, however, that there are circumstances where 'core rights' are in issue despite EU law being engaged.[511] That will result in the same approach being taken to proportionality as is taken in other cases when the European Convention is in issue.

---

[508]  Ibid, at 351D–351F.
[509]  Ibid, at 353H.
[510]  Ibid, at 353H.
[511]  For example, Art 8 of the European Convention can apply to decisions regarding free movement (*Dereci v Bundesministerium für Inneres*, C-256/11).

# CHAPTER 3

# MATTERS TO BE CONSIDERED BEFORE APPLYING FOR JUDICIAL REVIEW

## 3.1 DELAY IN APPLYING FOR JUDICIAL REVIEW

### 3.1.1 Determining whether there has been delay in judicial review proceedings

The timing of an application for judicial review can be crucial. The Administrative Court can reject an application if it is either premature or too late. In practical terms, the Administrative Court's increasing workload means that the Court is more often willing to find that a claim is out of time. As a consequence, it is important to know whether a claim is at risk of being judged out of time so that arguments and any relevant evidence can be presented addressing that issue.

The key provision determining whether an application is late is CPR 1998, r 54.5. This provides:

> '(1) The claim form must be filed –
> (a)   promptly; and
> (b)   in any event not later than 3 months after the grounds to make the claim first arose.
> (2) The time limit in this rule may not be extended by agreement between the parties.
> (3) This rule does not apply when any other enactment specifies a shorter time limit for making the claim for judicial review.'

The above provision raises a number of important points. Firstly, it should be noted that a judicial review claim will not necessarily be regarded as being in time, merely because it is made within the 3-month period. Practitioners often wrongly assume that an application will be regarded as being in time merely because it is made within 3 months of the date on which the grounds arose. The key requirement is that the application is made promptly. As a result, in the past it has been held that an application for judicial review may be rejected as being out of time if there has been delay <u>within</u> the 3-month period.[1]

---

[1]   There are numerous examples of this, including *R v Independent Television Commission ex p TV NI Ltd* (1991) *The Times*, December 30; *R v Brighton and Hove Magistrates' Court ex p Clarke* (1997) *Archbold News*, June.

In some areas where there is a particular need for claimants to move speedily, the courts have adopted an approach that appeared almost to amount to an amendment of the rule contained in Part 54. In particular, in the context of planning law (where developers and other commercial organisations need to be able to make rapid decisions in reliance on planning decisions) there developed a practice of expecting claimants to apply within 6 weeks of the decision challenged.[2] However, the House of Lords rejected this approach, holding that judicial policy-making cannot change the clear provisions of Part 54.[3]

Although it is now clear that there can be no rigid rule applied by the Administrative Court changing the time-limit contained in Part 54 in particular areas of the law, it is still relevant to consider the context in which a claim is brought when deciding whether a claim is brought promptly. Thus, for example, it would appear to be particularly important that a claimant should act promptly to challenge regulations made at a national level[4] – presumably as a consequence of the large number of people entitled to rely on the regulations. In particular, the courts have recognised that it is important for claimants to act promptly when it is clear that the judicial review claim may have implications for the interests of third parties.[5]

The doubt expressed by the House of Lords[6] as to whether the requirement that a claimant apply for judicial review 'promptly' is sufficiently certain to be compatible with Art 6 of the European Convention on Human Rights has since been resolved by the Court of Appeal[7] in light of a decision of the European Court of Human Rights holding as manifestly unfounded a complaint that Art 6 of the European Convention was violated when a judicial review claim was dismissed as not having been brought promptly, despite being brought within 3 months.[8] The Strasbourg court held that the promptness requirement did not offend the principle of legal certainty as it was a 'proportionate measure taken in pursuit of a legitimate aim'. As a consequence, claims brought within 3 months may be dismissed as not having been brought promptly where, for example, prejudice to third parties has arisen consequent on the failure to bring a speedy challenge.

---

[2]  *R v London Borough of Hammersmith and Fulham and others ex p Burkett and another* [2002] 1 WLR 1593, per Lord Steyn, at 1610H, commenting on the misunderstanding of the observations of Laws J in *R v Ceredigion County Council ex p McKeown* [1998] 2 PLR 1.

[3]  *R v London Borough of Hammersmith and Fulham and others ex p Burkett and another* [2002] 1 WLR 1593.

[4]  *R (I-Cd Publishing Ltd) v Secretary of State & The Information Commissioner (Interested Party)* [2003] ACD 98.

[5]  See, for example, *R v Secretary of State for Trade and Industry ex p Greenpeace Ltd* [1998] Env LR 415, pers Laws J, at 438.

[6]  *R v London Borough of Hammersmith and Fulham and others ex p Burkett and another* [2002] 1 WLR 1593.

[7]  *R (Hardy) v Pembrokeshire County Council* [2006] Env LR 38, at 664–667.

[8]  *Lam v United Kingdom*, Application No 41671/98.

The position in the context of judicial review challenges raising points of EU law is however different. In *Uniplex (UK) Ltd v NHS Business Services Authority*[9] the Court of Justice of the European Union accepted that the requirement to act promptly and 'without delay' was too uncertain. Accordingly the only question arising in considering whether a claim raising issues of EU law is in time is whether proceedings were brought within 3 months.[10]

The determination of whether an application has been brought promptly does not merely involve a consideration of whether a claimant acted promptly.[11] Thus, a lack of knowledge that grounds for judicial review exist does not mean that time does not start to run. It may, however, be a good reason for extending time.[12] Note also that the House of Lords has held that notice of a decision is required before it can have the character of legal effect such as to affect adversely an individual's rights.[13]

In the case of an application for a quashing order[14] in respect of a judgment, order, conviction or proceeding, the grounds for the application will be taken to have arisen on the 'date of that judgment, order, conviction or proceeding'.[15] Although there are no provisions determining when time begins in other judicial review claims, it is likely the time will be taken as beginning on an equivalent date (ie the date of the court order) when the judicial review relates to the decision of a court or tribunal.

The Administrative Court is reluctant to allow judicial review of interim decisions taken during the course of court proceedings.[16] A decision to wait until a final determination of the proceedings will not, however, normally lead to the Court regarding a judicial review application as being delayed; the judicial review will be a challenge to the final decision of the court. It will be said that the final decision is flawed as a result of the interim decision. Time will, as a result, run only from the date of the

---

9    [2010] 2 CMLR 47, at [41]–[43].
10   See, for example, *R (U & Partners (East Anglia) Ltd) v Broads Authority & Environment Agency* [2012] Env LR 5. However, the Administrative Court has subsequently confirmed that the promptness requirement still applies in cases that do not raise issues of EU law, see *R (Macrae) v Herefordshire DC* [2012] 1 CMLR 28, at [64].
11   *R v Cotswold DC ex p Barrington Parish Council* (1998) 75 P & CR 515.
12   See, for example, *R v Secretary of State for the Home Department ex p Ruddock* [1987] 1 WLR 1482, per Mr Justice Taylor, at 1485F. See also **3.1.1** for details of the court's approach to extending time.
13   *R (Anufrijeva) v Secretary of State for the Home Department* [2004] 1 AC 604.
14   See **8.2.1** for a description of the orders that can be sought during an application for judicial review.
15   Practice Direction 54A, para 4.1.
16   *Streames v Copping* [1985] QB 920, at 929, holding that the Administrative Court should be reluctant to consider challenges to interim decisions in criminal proceedings save '[i]n a very special instance'. There is no reason to believe that a different approach applies to interim decisions in other jurisdictions. Where proceedings are pending, a potential claimant should be expected to wait until those proceedings are completed, as any complaint about an interim decision may become immaterial if the potential claimant obtains the desired result at the end of the proceedings.

final decision. Interim decisions to refuse to adjourn or stay proceedings may however be appropriately challenged by way of judicial review in order to prevent a serious breach of natural justice.[17]

In cases challenging executive decisions, it may be more difficult to determine when time commences.[18] However, the House of Lords has rejected suggestions that time should run from an occurrence of an act that gives rise to the real substance of the challenge if that decision is taken before a final decision that has legal effect.[19] In reaching this conclusion, Lord Steyn (who delivered the leading judgment) placed weight on the fact that a claimant should not be put to the effort of applying for judicial review unless and until it is clear that a decision will have legal effect.[20]

It is also important to be aware that, in certain circumstances, it may be possible to argue that there is a continuing breach of a decision-maker's legal duties.[21] The effect of this may be that it is possible to argue that time for bringing an application for judicial review has never started to run. However, the fact that there is a continuing breach does not necessarily mean that it is irrelevant to consider the date at which the breach began.[22] The court will be anxious to see that there is a prompt application for judicial review and will be unsympathetic to a claimant who has delayed.

Similar considerations may apply when a decision-maker has adopted an unlawful policy. The mere fact that a policy has been in force for in excess of 3 months should not necessarily mean that the policy should not be challenged.[23] The continuing application of an unlawful policy might be said to be a continuing unlawful act. In addition, it may be significant that there would be nobody with any interest in challenging the policy within the 3-month period.

Occasionally, claimants have requested a decision-maker to review a decision that has already been taken. If the decision-maker agrees to this request, it can then be argued that the result of the review is a fresh decision attracting its own time-limits.[24] In practice, however, the Administrative Court will be reluctant to regard a decision as a fresh

---

[17]  *R (AM Cameroon) v Asylum & Immigration Tribunal* [2008] 1 WLR 2062.

[18]  This is dealt with in more detail at **3.2** where premature applications are considered.

[19]  *R v London Borough of Hammersmith and Fulham and others ex p Burkett and another* [2002] 1 WLR 1593.

[20]  Ibid, at 1610D–1610E. This approach is consistent with the approach to challenges to interim decisions in criminal proceedings, as it suggests that potential claimants should have to wait until it is clear whether any errors are material.

[21]  See discussion in *Somerville v Scottish Ministers* [2007] 1 WLR 2734, at 2753G–2753H, 2763C–2763F, 2778C–2778E, and 2794C–2794E.

[22]  See, for example, *R v Essex County Council ex p C* [1993] COD 398, per Jowitt J.

[23]  See, for example, *R v Warwickshire County Council ex p Collymore* [1995] ELR 217, at 228B–229E.

[24]  See, for example, *R v Richmond-upon-Thames London Borough Council ex p McCarthy &*

decision merely because it is a response to representations containing matters already raised.[25] The Court will often need to be convinced that the decision has developed in some material way.

Where a claimant is seeking to raise arguments that a review of any original decision amounts to a fresh decision, it may also be possible to argue that, in any event, the time for bringing an application for judicial review should be extended so that the original decision that was reviewed can be challenged. This is because the application for a review of the decision might be said to be a reasonable attempt to resolve the matter without bringing an application for judicial review.[26]

The concepts of continuing breach and fresh decisions are unlikely to be relevant in the context of judicial review of final decisions of courts. This is because the court will probably be *functus officio* after it has taken a decision and so unable to review that earlier decision. However, there have been suggestions in the context of courts that it may be worth seeking a review by the court so that it can consider whether to oppose the claim for judicial review.[27]

The time-limit contained in CPR, Part 54 refers to the lodging of the claim form rather than the decision on the application for permission or the substantive application. As a result, for time to cease to run, it is crucial that the application is lodged in the correct form with the Administrative Court.[28] If it is not lodged in the correct form, it may be rejected and time may continue to run.

Although time ceases to run when the application for permission is lodged, it is also important to put a potential defendant on notice of a potential judicial review as soon as possible and to supply them with all the information that they reasonably request about the application because the Administrative Court may take account of this when it decides what action should be taken as a result of any delay.[29] A defendant who has been prejudiced by not being warned of potential judicial review proceedings may have a stronger argument that a claim should be held to be out of time.

---

Stone *(Developments) Ltd* [1992] 2 AC 48, where the challenge was to a decision to refuse to revoke a policy that had been affecting the claimant for several years.

[25]  *R v Commissioner for Local Administration ex p Field* [2000] COD 58.

[26]  See, for example, *R ( Young) v Oxford City Council* [2002] EWCA Civ 990 in which it was held that the claimant had acted reasonably in seeking 'further information before commencing proceedings. See *R v Commissioner for Local Administration ex p Croydon London Borough Council* [1989] 1 All ER 1033, in which Woolf LJ held, at 1046G, that the courts will not deprive a sensible and reasonable litigant of a remedy to which he is otherwise entitled.

[27]  See **4.1** for a consideration of pre-action protocol letters.

[28]  See Chapter 5 for details of the procedural requirements that must be complied with if an application for judicial review is to be properly lodged.

[29]  *R v Cotswold DC ex p Barrington Parish Council* (1998) 75 P&CR 515. See also **4.1** for a consideration of the need for a clear and sufficiently detailed letter before action.

### 3.1.2   Defendant's consent to delay

Before seeking to justify the delay in an application for judicial review, claimants may wish to consider whether they can obtain the defendant's consent to proceedings being brought out of time. CPR, r 54.5 expressly provides that the agreement of the parties cannot bind the Administrative Court. Nevertheless, before amendment of the CPR 1998 to contain rules regarding judicial review the Administrative Court did, however, appear to consider that the consent of the defendant was relevant to the issue of delay, by enabling confirmation of the consent to be submitted with the application.[30] As noted below, the existence and extent of any prejudice to the defendant is a matter that the Administrative Court should take account of when deciding whether to extend time. The consent of the defendant suggests that there has not been any prejudice.

### 3.1.3   Effect of delay – extending the time-limit

Where there has been delay, the Administrative Court has a power to extend time for bringing the claim if it is satisfied that there is a good reason for extending the time period, as CPR, r 3.1(2)(a) provides that:

> '(2) Except where these Rules provide otherwise, the court may –
>   (a)   extend or shorten the time for compliance with any rule, practice direction or court order (even if an application for extension is made after the time for compliance has expired).'

The decision as to whether time should be extended should be made when the application for permission to apply for judicial review is determined.[31] It is for the claimant for judicial review to show that there is a good reason for extending time.[32] Matters that can amount to a good reason for extending time are considered below; as noted, none of these matters automatically results in time being extended. As a consequence, legal advisers should generally seek to avoid claims being delayed so that they are out of time and should rarely be satisfied that they have a good reason for seeking an extension of time.

One good reason for extending time can be an explanation for the delay in applying for judicial review, such as problems obtaining public funding.[33] Practitioners will need to evidence that the application for public funding was made promptly and the Legal Services Commission chased where

---

[30]   *Practice Direction (Uncontested Proceedings: Crown Office List (Applications Outside London): Judicial Review)* [1983] 1 WLR 925.

[31]   *R v Criminal Injuries Compensation Board ex p A* [1999] 2 AC 330.

[32]   *R v Warwickshire County Council ex p Collymore* [1995] ELR 217, per Judge J, at 228F.

[33]   *R v Stratford on Avon District Council ex p Jackson* [1985] 3 All ER 769; but see *R v Metropolitan Borough of Sandwell ex p Cashmore* (1993) 25 HLR 544, in which it was held that it is not automatic that time will be extended as a result of problems obtaining legal aid. It appears that the critical issue for a claimant seeking to rely on delay in obtaining legal aid as an explanation is the need to show that efforts were made to chase the application and that the application was not merely allowed to meander. For

necessary. Similarly, mistakes made by legal advisers[34] and an attempt by the claimant to seek other legitimate remedies[35] may be good reason for extending the time for bringing a judicial review. However, it is important to recognise that, as the footnotes show, none of these matters automatically results in time being extended.

It is unlikely that delay caused by writing a letter before bringing a claim will be an adequate explanation of delay in applying for judicial review.[36] As the pre-action protocol in judicial review states: 'Compliance with the protocol alone is unlikely to be sufficient to persuade the court to allow a late claim.'[37] Where any delay is attributable to correspondence which has been aimed at clarifying the prospective defendant's position, seeking further relevant information on a laconic decision, or reasonable attempts to resolve the issue without litigation, the courts are unlikely to penalise a late claimant[38] but the need for and purpose of such correspondence must be carefully evidenced.

A good reason for extending time is not restricted to matters that are an explanation for delay. In particular, the importance of the substantive issues raised may in themselves be good reason for an extension of time. For example, Mr Justice Taylor held that:[39]

> 'I have concluded that since the matters raised are of general importance, it would be a wrong exercise of my discretion to reject the application on grounds of delay, thereby leaving the substantive issues unresolved. I therefore extend time to allow the claimant to proceed.'

Although the importance of the matters raised is a matter of significance,[40] even very grave matters will not automatically result in time being extended. Even when the important common law right to liberty is in issue[41], the importance of the issues does not necessarily mean that a

---

example, in *R v University of Portsmouth ex p Lakareber* [1999] ELR 135, at 140, Simon Brown LJ relied on the failure of the claimant to adduce any evidence regarding the efforts made to obtain legal aid.

[34]  *R v Secretary of State for the Home Department ex p Oyeleye* [1994] Imm AR 268; but see *R v Tavistock General Commissioners ex p Worth* [1985] STC 564, in which it was held that reliance on an adviser who was not legally qualified was no good reason for delay.

[35]  *R v University College London ex p Ursula Riniker* [1995] ELR 213, at 215. It is important to note that pursuit of alternative remedies will not automatically be a good reason for the extension of time. For example, in *R v Essex County Council ex p Jackson Projects Ltd* [1995] COD 155, delay caused by a decision to pursue a compensation claim resulted in the rejection of an application for judicial review.

[36]  See **4.1** for a consideration of letters before claim.

[37]  Footnote 1 to Judicial Review Pre-action Protocol.

[38]  See, for example, *R v Hammersmith & Fulham London Borough Council, ex p Burkett* [2001] Env LR 39, at 693 (judgment subsequently over-turned by the House of Lords).

[39]  *R v Secretary of State for the Home Department ex p Ruddock* [1987] 1 WLR 1482, at 1485G.

[40]  *PJG v Child Support Agency* [2006] EWHC 423 (Fam).

[41]  see, for example, *Hinds v The Queen* [1977] AC 195, at 226D.

claim for judicial review cannot be out of time if it seeks to challenge a decision to detain an individual.[42] Challenges to unlawful detention may be brought by way of habeas corpus in which delay acts as no bar provided the claimant remains detained. Remedies for historic periods of unlawful detention may be better sought by civil claims for false imprisonment.

In determining whether to extend time for the bringing of an application for judicial review, the Administrative Court will be concerned about the strength of the claim for judicial review.[43] If the grounds for judicial review are particularly strong, the court will be reluctant to hold that delay is a sufficient reason for refusing to consider the application.[44]

The Administrative Court is also likely to be concerned about the nature of the decision that is being challenged because, as noted above, challenges to certain decisions such as planning decisions can potentially have significant financial consequences for third parties. For example, a challenge to a planning decision may harm the commercial interests of a developer. In contrast, challenges to other decisions may have no significant consequences for third parties – in an immigration context the claimant is likely to be the only person affected, as he will be the person at threat of removal. The Administrative Court has been particularly keen to ensure that planning judicial review challenges are brought promptly.[45] It is not merely potential financial consequences that may mean there is a need to act speedily. An education challenge may need to be brought promptly because it will potentially result in a large education system being kept in suspense.[46]

The fact that the Administrative Court is likely to be concerned about the nature of the decision that is being challenged means that defendants should consider raising arguments regarding the consequences of delay in their acknowledgement of service.[47]

Where the challenge is to a decision in proceedings before an inferior court, the Administrative Court is also likely to be concerned about the stage those proceedings have reached. For example, the Administrative Court will be reluctant to extend the time for bringing an application for judicial review to challenge an interim decision taken in criminal proceedings, as that will result in the substantive criminal proceedings being delayed.[48]

---

[42]   *R (Sheikh) v Secretary of State for the Home Department* [2001] INLR 98.

[43]   *R v Warwickshire County Council ex p Collymore* [1995] ELR 217, per Judge J, at 228G.

[44]   The court may still take account of the delay when it decides what form of relief to order. See, for example, the decision of Roch J in *R v Rochdale Metropolitan Borough Council ex p Schemet* [1994] ELR 89.

[45]   See **3.1.1**.

[46]   See, for example, *R v Leeds City Council ex p N* [1999] ELR 324.

[47]   See **5.4** regarding acknowledgements of service.

[48]   Per Lord Browne-Wilkinson, *R v Manchester Crown Court ex p DPP* [1993] 1 WLR

If the Administrative Court finds that there is good reason why time should be extended despite delay in the case, that does not mean that delay becomes irrelevant. The court can still refuse relief at the substantive hearing. The Administrative Court will need to be satisfied that the provisions of s 31(6) of the Senior Courts Act 1981 (SCA 1981[49]) mean that the relief sought by the claimants for judicial review should not be granted.[50] Section 31(6) of the SCA 1981 provides:

> 'Where the High Court considers that there has been undue delay in making an application for judicial review, the court may refuse to grant –
> (a)     leave for the making of the application; or
> (b)     any relief sought on the application,
> if it considers that the granting of the relief sought would be likely to cause substantial hardship to, or substantially prejudice the rights of, any person or would be detrimental to good administration.'

The consideration of the issues relevant to s 31(6) of the SCA 1981 should generally take place at the substantive hearing rather than the permission hearing as the question concerns the relief stage and the Administrative Court may not have the information that it requires to determine this issue at the permission stage.[51] Although the Administrative Court should not review the decision to extend time at the substantive hearing, that limitation on its powers does not mean that any findings reached at the permission stage regarding delay are irrelevant.

First, if it has been found at the permission stage that a claim for judicial review has been brought promptly, a defendant should only in limited circumstances be permitted to argue that there has been delay. These circumstances were identified by the Court of Appeal in *R (Lichfield Securities Ltd) v Lichfield DC*,[52] as follows:[53]

> '(i)     if the judge hearing the initial application has expressly so indicated;
> (ii)    if new and relevant material is introduced on the substantive hearing;
> (iii)   if, exceptionally, the issues as they have developed at the full hearing put a different aspect on the question of promptness; or
> (iv)    if the first judge has plainly overlooked some relevant matter or otherwise reached a decision per incuriam.'

In addition, the factors taken into account when deciding to extend time are not irrelevant to the exercise of discretion under s 31(6) of the SCA 1981. For example, the reasons for the delay, as well as any failure to make

---

1524, at 1529F, HL, holding that delay was one reason why judicial review was not available to challenge decisions taken by a Crown Court in relation to matters being tried on indictment.

49     Previously the Supreme Court Act 1981, renamed under the Constitutional Reform Act 2005.

50     *R v Stratford on Avon District Council ex p Jackson* [1985] 3 All ER 769.

51     *R v Dairy Produce Quota Tribunal ex p Caswell* [1990] 2 AC 738, per Lord Goff, at 747D.

52     (2001) 3 LGLR 35.

53     *R (Lichfield Securities Ltd) v Lichfield DC* (2001) 3 LGLR 35, at [34].

full and frank disclosure, are considered when the Administrative Court decides whether to exercise its discretion to refuse relief under s 31(6) of the SCA 1981.[54]

It is likely to be obvious when delay has caused hardship or prejudice to the rights of any person. For example, the interests of a developer may mean that delay in challenging a planning permission should result in relief being denied.[55] The circumstances in which relief should be refused because it would be detrimental to good administration are perhaps less obvious and have rarely been identified by the Administrative Court because it can rarely be in the interests of good public administration for an abuse of power to go uncorrected.[56]

It is important to recognise that s 31(6) of the SCA 1981 provides the Administrative Court with a discretion to refuse relief (as should be clear from the use of the word 'may' in that provision). Delay in the circumstances covered by s 31(6) will not automatically result in the denial of relief.

### 3.1.4  The need for disclosure of delay

One of the basic principles that govern judicial review is that claimants are subject to a duty of full and frank disclosure. They are obliged to disclose any matters that are adverse to their case. A failure to disclose such matters can result in permission to bring an application being refused or it can affect orders made for costs.[57] Delay is one of the matters that claimants for judicial review are required to disclose. Practice Direction 54A requires that: 'The claim form must include or be accompanied by ... any application to extend the time limit for filing the claim form.'[58] It is implicit in this passage of the Practice Direction that delay must be addressed if there is a need to extend time. As a claim for judicial review can be held to be out of time even if brought within 3 months,[59] this means that the issue of delay may need to be addressed if a claim is brought within 3 months. It is good practice to address in the claim form any issues of delay within the 3-month period if there is a period of unexplained delay that might lead a judge to question whether the claim has been brought sufficiently promptly.

---

[54]   *R v Criminal Injuries Compensation Board ex p A* [1999] 2 AC 330 in the Court of Appeal. The application of s 31(6) of the SCA 1981 was not subsequently considered by the House of Lords.
[55]   See, for example, *R v North West Leicestershire ex p Moses (No 2)* [2000] Env LR 443, at 450.
[56]   *R (Lichfield Securities Ltd) v Lichfield DC* (2001) 3 LGLR 35, at [39].
[57]   See **5.3**.
[58]   Practice Direction 54A, para 5.6.
[59]   See **3.1.1**.

## 3.2 PREMATURE APPLICATIONS FOR JUDICIAL REVIEW

It was noted above that the House of Lords has held that a claim for judicial review can be left until the final decision that has legal effect.[60] In the course of reaching that conclusion, Lord Steyn (who delivered the leading judgment) suggested that a challenge to a decision that might still change would be premature.[61] That is, of course, consistent with the approach of the House of Lords to delay. If, as the House of Lords found, there are good reasons why claimants should not be expected to commence judicial review claims until a decision has been taken that has legal effect, presumably there are good reasons why defendants should not be required to respond to a judicial review claim until they have committed themselves to a decision that will have legal effect.

Although, in general, a claimant will be expected to wait until a final decision has been taken, the Administrative Court may be willing to consider an interim challenge if it can be shown that there is a particularly good reason why the claim should not be delayed. For example, it has already been noted that in general interim decisions in criminal proceedings should not be challenged.[62] However, although that is generally true, the Administrative Court has shown itself willing to consider such challenges where there is prejudice to the claimant eg where a decision taken during criminal proceedings has resulted in a person being unlawfully detained.[63] In addition, a decision of a magistrates' court to decline jurisdiction where the matter could only be tried summarily has been challenged by judicial review before there had been a final conclusion of the matter.[64] Presumably, that is because it is not in the public interest for a court to expend resources on the consideration of a matter that it has no jurisdiction to consider.

## 3.3 EXISTENCE OF AN ALTERNATIVE REMEDY

Judicial review is a remedy of 'last resort',[65] a 'long stop',[66] and a claimant should exhaust any proper alternative remedy available to him. However, as noted above,[67] the Administrative Court is extremely reluctant to hold that a statutory provision excludes its jurisdiction to consider an application for judicial review. The effect of an alternative statutory

---

[60] *R v London Borough of Hammersmith and Fulham and others ex p Burkett and another* [2002] 1 WLR 1593.

[61] Ibid, at 1610H.

[62] *Streames v Copping* [1985] QB 920, at 929.

[63] See, for example, *R v Maidstone Crown Court ex p Clark* [1995] 1 WLR 831, allowing a challenge to an arraignment to defeat custody time-limits.

[64] *R v Hatfield Justices ex p Castle* [1981] 1 WLR 217.

[65] *R(G) v Immigration Appeal Tribunal* [2005] 1 WLR 1445, at 1457D.

[66] *R v Serumaga* [2005] EWCA Crim 370.

[67] See **1.7**.

procedure is better categorised as a matter going to the court's discretion to refuse a remedy.[68] As a result, in practice it is unlikely that the mere existence of an alternative remedy will be held to exclude judicial review.

The Administrative Court will take account of any alternative remedy when it decides whether to exercise its discretion to grant the remedies sought. For example, Lord Justice Watkins held that:[69]

> '[J]udicial review is a remedy of last resort in the sense that where a claimant invokes this jurisdiction without having sought to deploy another remedy which is available to him, he is likely to find that, in the exercise of the court's discretion, he will be refused relief here ... But, as has often been acknowledged, it is a matter of discretion; and it follows that the court is entitled to take into account the convenience of the other remedy and the common sense of the situation.'

The Judicial Review Pre-action Protocol[70] places an onus on both claimant and defendant to ensure that all alternatives to pursuing a remedy by way of judicial review are diligently pursued thus:[71]

> 'Both the Claimant and Defendant may be required by the Court to provide evidence that alternative means of resolving their dispute were considered. The Courts take the view that litigation should be a last resort, and that claims should not be issued prematurely when a settlement is still actively being explored.'

An alternative remedy is most likely to result in the Administrative Court denying relief where the alternative is statutory.[72] Indeed, it has sometimes been said that judicial review applications should be brought only in exceptional circumstances if there is an alternative statutory remedy available.[73] In practice, however, the Administrative Court will sometimes allow judicial review despite the existence of an alternative remedy in circumstances that are not exceptional. The Administrative Court will consider whether the alternative remedy is suitable and effective.[74]

Non-statutory forms of alternatives to judicial review include internal complaints procedures and some ombudsmen. Many internal complaints procedures may be lengthy and lack independence. Should a

---

[68]  *Leech v Deputy Governor of Parkhurst Prison* [1988] AC 533, at 580C–580D.

[69]  *R v Metropolitan Stipendiary Magistrate ex p London Waste Regulation Authority* [1993] 3 All ER 113 at 120B, rejecting the right to apply for a voluntary bill as an alternative remedy.

[70]  See    http://www.justice.gov.uk/guidance/courts-and-tribunals/courts/procedure-rules/civil/contents/protocols/prot_jrv.htm.

[71]  Judicial Review Pre-action Protocol, para 3.1.

[72]  See, for example, *R (F) Mongolia v Secretary of State for the Home Department* [2007] 1 WLR 2523.

[73]  See, for example, *Harley Development Inc v Commissioner of Inland Revenue* [1996] 1 WLR 727, per Lord Jauncey, at 736C.

[74]  *Ex p Waldron* [1986] QB 824, at 852F–853A.

decision-maker – for instance a local authority refuse to stay the implementation of a decision pending the outcome of such a procedure a claimant may be justified in seeking judicial review and in an appropriate case – interim relief. In community care cases the courts are likely to consider whether the remedy sought should have been pursued by way of complaint to the relevant ombudsman. Judicial review will in any event be inapt to resolve any disputes of fact arising.[75]

There are a number of circumstances in which the Administrative Court will consider judicial review claims despite the existence of an alternative remedy. For example, in a criminal context, the right to appeal against a conviction to the Crown Court does not mean that the Administrative Court will not consider an application for judicial review.[76] Parliament clearly intended that defendants in the magistrates' court be entitled to two fair trials, as it provided a right to a rehearing in the Crown Court. The right of appeal to the Crown Court is not an adequate remedy, as it may result in a person receiving only one fair trial.

The idea that a right of appeal should not exclude judicial review, as Parliament intended that a person should have two fair hearings, would appear to be limited to criminal cases. In an education context, a right of appeal to an independent appeal panel should normally be exercised, even if earlier decisions were taken in an unfair manner, as the panel will provide a fair hearing.[77] If the earlier decisions resulted in the panel's proceedings being unfair then that can be cured by judicial review proceedings challenging the decision of the Panel.[78]

Another example of a situation in which a remedy has been found to be inadequate occurs in an immigration context. The courts have accepted that an appeal right that can only be exercised outside the United Kingdom does not exclude judicial review if the person is claiming that removal will violate their rights under the European Convention on Human Rights.[79] An appeal right cannot be regarded as adequate if a person can exercise it only by exposing themselves to a violation of their human rights.

One circumstance in which an alternative remedy is likely to be regarded as inadequate is where it is clear that the Administrative Court's guidance is needed[80] or its supervisory jurisdiction is in play.[81] The Court recognises

---

[75]   See eg Collins J in *Gunter v South Western Staffordshire PCT* [2005] EWHC 1984 (Admin), [2006] 9 CCLR 121, at [9].

[76]   *R v Hereford Magistrates' Court ex p Rowlands and Ingram; R v Harrow Youth Court ex p Prussia* [1998] QB 110, applied in *Balogun v DPP* [2010] 1 WLR 1915.

[77]   *R (A) v Kingsmead School Governors* [2003] ELR 104.

[78]   Ibid.

[79]   *R (L) v Secretary of State for the Home Department* [2003] 1 WLR 1230. See also, in the Art 8 context, *R (Majera) v Secretary of State for the Home Department* [2009] EWHC 825 (Admin), at [19].

[80]   *R (A) v Kingsmead School Governors* [2003] ELR 104, at [45].

that it can give definitive guidance on important legal issues, which inferior courts and administrative decision-makers will then follow. Such guidance may not be obtained from exercising an alternative remedy.

Finally in circumstances where the decision under challenge concerns an unappealable decision of the Upper Tribunal, the Supreme Court has held that such challenges should be the exception notwithstanding the absence of any statutory alternative remedy or ouster to the court's jurisdiction.[82]

### 3.3.1　Appeal by way of case stated

The Administrative Court has a statutory power to consider appeals by way of case stated from a decision of a magistrates' court[83] or the Crown Court.[84] The scope of that power means that the issues considered are very similar to those in a claim for judicial review.

The Administrative Court has held that judicial review is the only appropriate method for applying to quash a conviction imposed by the magistrates' court or the Crown Court where an appeal by case stated was inapposite or inappropriate. For example, Mr Justice Brooke criticised applicants for judicial review of a conviction in the magistrates' court when he stated:[85]

> 'Our task in this case was made unnecessarily difficult because the applicants did not adopt the procedure prescribed by Parliament for referring a point of law which has arisen in a magistrates' court to the High Court for decision. If the justices had stated a case for our opinion, we would have known what their findings of fact had been and their reasons for the decisions they took and they would have identified the relevant points of law for our decision in the familiar way.'

In practice, the availability of an appeal by way of case stated does not prevent a significant number of judicial reviews of convictions in the magistrates' courts or the Crown Court, because the Administrative Court often does not need a record of the findings of fact and law when it considers a challenge to the conviction. Instead, it needs evidence about things that happened during the trial of the matter and this evidence cannot normally be presented during an appeal by way of case stated. The procedure that the Court adopts when considering applications for judicial review is usually the only appropriate way of presenting the Court with the evidence that it needs in these circumstances.

---

[81]　*R (AM) Cameroon v Asylum & Immigration Tribunal (No 2)* [2008] 1 WLR 2062.

[82]　*R (Cart) v Upper Tribunal* [2011] 3 WLR 107 in which the court specified the need to raise important points of principle or other compelling reasons.

[83]　Magistrates' Courts Act 1980, s 111(1).

[84]　Senior Courts Act 1981, s 28(1).

[85]　*R v Morpeth Ward JJ ex p Ward* (1992) 95 Cr App R 215, at 221. It is significant to note, however, that, despite these comments, the Administrative Court did consider the substantive merits of the judicial review application.

For example, complaints about matters such as bias, a failure to adopt a procedure that satisfies the requirements of natural justice or a decision that is contrary to the applicant's legitimate expectation do not require a record of the court's findings of fact or law. Instead, they require written evidence from persons present in court explaining the procedure adopted by the court.

Even where case stated is considered the appropriate route of challenge, the courts are reluctant to defeat a claim 'unless prejudice is caused to a party, or there is some other good reason'.[86]

### 3.3.2   Alternative dispute resolution

Increasingly, the courts and the Ministry of Justice have been encouraging would-be litigants in judicial review to take advantage of the methods of alternative dispute resolution (ADR) such as mediation.[87] That trend has had an effect on the Administrative Court, which should perhaps not be surprising as ADR is in one sense a form of alternative remedy.

The clearest guidance on the need to consider ADR was given by the Court of Appeal in *R (Cowl and others) v Plymouth City Council*[88] in which the Court held that:[89]

'The courts should ... make appropriate use of their ample powers under the CPR to ensure that the parties try to resolve the dispute with the minimum involvement of the courts.'

The Court of Appeal went on to state that:[90]

'[T]he court may have to hold, on its own initiative, an inter partes hearing at which the parties can explain what steps they have taken to resolve the dispute without the involvement of the courts. In particular the parties should be asked why a complaints procedure or some other form of ADR has not been used or adapted to resolve or reduce the issues which are in dispute.'

The Court of Appeal also encouraged the Legal Services Commission to co-operate with ADR.[91] The authors are aware of at least one case in which this dictum has encouraged the Commission to fund representation during an extensive mediation procedure which, it was anticipated, would resolve a judicial review claim.

---

[86]   *R (Brighton & Hove City Council) v Brighton & Hove Justices* [2004] EWHC 1800 (Admin), at [25].
[87]   Pre action Protocol. See **3.3**.
[88]   [2002] 1 WLR 803.
[89]   *R (Cowl and others) v Plymouth City Council* [2002] 1 WLR 803, at 803H.
[90]   *R (Cowl and others) v Plymouth City Council* [2002] 1 WLR 803, at 803H–804A.
[91]   Ibid, at 803H.

In practice, despite the guidance of the Court of Appeal, it appears that ADR is rarely used (or at least rarely ordered by the courts). There are probably a number of reasons for this. First, it can be more expensive than judicial review as it can be wider ranging. In addition, because it may be wider ranging, it may be harder for one of the parties to justify their position. For example, a defendant's decision may be one that they were legally entitled to take. However, it also may be difficult for a defendant to prevent a mediator concluding that it was not the best decision they could have taken. Finally, in many judicial reviews, there is little room for compromise. For example, in an immigration context, a person will either be removed from the United Kingdom or they will not. It might also be argued that ADR is not appropriate in some cases, as it is in the public interest for the Administrative Court to deliver a judgment that will provide important guidance to decision-makers.

## 3.4  WHETHER THE ISSUE IS A CRIMINAL CAUSE OR MATTER

### 3.4.1  Importance of the distinction

Although a judicial review application may arise out of a practitioner's criminal practice, it will not necessarily be regarded as a criminal cause or matter by the Administrative Court. For example, a judicial review that relates to an alleged offence under the prison rules is not regarded as a criminal cause or matter by the Administrative Court.[92] The distinction between a criminal cause or matter and other cases is significant, as the procedure adopted when bringing proceedings in the Administrative Court depends on whether a matter is a criminal cause. In particular, there is no right of appeal to the Court of Appeal from any judgment of the Administrative Court in any criminal cause or matter, except in very limited circumstances.[93] In addition, although in principle it is possible for a single High Court judge to consider a criminal judicial review, the practice is that a criminal judicial review will normally be heard by a Divisional Court.[94]

As a result of the procedural distinctions, practitioners will need to know whether each case relates to a criminal cause or matter, so that they follow the correct procedure if they act for a claimant. If practitioners act for a defendant, they may wish to argue that the wrong procedure has been adopted, so that a particular court has no jurisdiction.

---

[92]  *R v Board of Visitors of Hull Prison ex p St Germain* [1979] QB 425.
[93]  Senior Courts Act 1981, s 18(1)(a).
[94]  In addition, matters relating to criminal justice that are not technically criminal will often be heard by a Divisional Court (eg *R (McFetrich) v Secretary of State for the Home Department* (2003) *The Times*, July 28).

### 3.4.2   Decision determining whether an issue is a criminal cause or matter

As noted above, the most significant difference between a criminal cause or matter and other proceedings is that there is no right of appeal to the Court of Appeal. In determining whether there is a right of appeal to the Court of Appeal, the court will not be concerned with the nature of the order made by the Administrative Court. Indeed, the orders that might be sought when applying for a judicial review in a criminal cause or matter are the same as those sought in other matters. Instead, the court will consider whether the decision challenged in the Administrative Court was a criminal cause or matter.[95]

### 3.4.3   Definition of a criminal cause or matter

The appeal courts have generally given a wide definition to the phrase 'criminal cause or matter'. For example, Lord Esher has held that the phrase:[96]

> '[A]pplies to a decision by way of judicial determination of any question raised in or with regard to proceedings, the subject-matter of which is criminal, at whatever stage of the proceedings the question arises.'

Similarly, Lord Wright held that:[97]

> '[I]f the cause or matter is one which, if carried to its conclusion, might result in the conviction of the person charged and in a sentence of some punishment, such as imprisonment or fine, it is a "criminal cause or matter" ... Every order made in such a cause or matter by an English court, is an order in a criminal cause or matter, even though the order, taken by itself, is neutral in character and might equally have been made in a cause or matter which is not criminal. The order may not involve punishment by the law of this country, but if the effect of the order is to subject by means of the operation of English law the persons charged to the criminal jurisdiction of a foreign country, the order is, in the eyes of English law for the purposes being considered, an order in a criminal cause or matter.

There has, however, been some recent recognition that there is a degree of incoherence in this area so that a narrower approach following some of the more recent authorities may be appropriate.[98] In particular, there has been a recognition that that some matters have been so collateral that they are not criminal (see below).

---

[95]   *Carr v Atkins* [1987] QB 963, at 967B.
[96]   *Ex parte Alice Woodhall* (1888) 20 QBD 832, at 836.
[97]   *Amand v Home Secretary* [1943] AC 147, at 162.
[98]   *R (Guardian News and Media Ltd) v City of Westminster Magistrates' Court* [2011] 1 WLR 3253.

Although the judgments cited above appear to suggest that the phrase 'criminal cause or matter' relates to a decision of a court, other authorities show that there is no need for the decision-maker to be a court. A decision whether or not to refer a matter to the criminal courts can be a criminal cause or matter. For example, under the legislative scheme that existed before the establishment of the Criminal Cases Review Commission, a refusal by the Secretary of State to refer a matter to the Court of Appeal was a criminal matter.[99] The courts have taken the same approach to cases concerning the Criminal Cases Review Commission.[100]

The impugned decision also need not be a final decision of a criminal court for it to be a criminal cause or matter. For example, a decision relating to evidence that may be used in criminal proceedings is a criminal cause or matter, even if the proceedings have not commenced. Thus, an order of a Crown Court judge in relation to the production of special procedure material under Sch 1 to the Police and Criminal Evidence Act 1984 is a criminal cause or matter, even if proceedings have not commenced.[101]

Once the criminal courts have imposed a sentence, a decision about the effect of the penalty imposed by the criminal court has also been treated as a criminal cause or matter. Thus, the calculation of the number of days to be served as a result of the imposition of a sentence of imprisonment has been treated as a criminal cause or matter.[102]

There are, however, circumstances where the effect of the sentence that has been imposed is determined by the exercise of a discretionary power by the Home Secretary. A challenge to the exercise of that executive discretion is not treated as a criminal cause or matter. Thus, a challenge to the tariff to be served by a mandatory life prisoner when set up by the Home Secretary was not a criminal cause or matter.[103] Similarly, a deportation order made following a recommendation by a criminal court is not a criminal cause or matter, although the actual recommendation is a criminal cause or matter.[104]

Although the decision that is being challenged need not be a decision of a criminal court if the case is to be a criminal cause or matter, it must, however, relate in some way to a possible trial by a criminal court.[105]

---

[99] *R v Secretary of State for the Home Department ex p Garner* [1990] COD 457.

[100] *R (Kevin Davis) v (1) Secretary of State for the Home Department and (2) Criminal Cases Review Commission* [2011] EWHC 1509 (Admin).

[101] *Carr v Atkins* [1987] QB 963.

[102] *R v Secretary of State for the Home Department ex p François* [1999] 1 AC 43.

[103] See, for example, *R v Secretary of State for the Home Department ex p Pierson* [1998] AC 539.

[104] *R v Secretary of State for the Home Department ex p Dannenberg* [1984] QB 766.

[105] *R v Board of Visitors of Hull Prison ex p St Germain* [1979] QB 425, per Lord Justice Shaw, at 453C.

Thus, a general challenge to a police policy is clearly not a criminal cause or matter.[106] In addition, the proceedings must relate in some way to the 'enforcement and preservation of public law and order' rather than being merely domestic disciplinary proceedings.[107] Thus, proceedings relating to an alleged breach of prison rules are not a criminal cause or matter.[108] Similarly, disciplinary proceedings against a solicitor are not a criminal cause or matter.[109]

Not every decision by a criminal court in relation to criminal proceedings is a criminal cause or matter. Some decisions of the criminal courts are so collateral to the criminal proceedings that gave rise to the decision that it cannot be regarded as a criminal cause or matter.[110] The Court of Appeal recently held that a refusal of a District Judge to allow a newspaper to have access to various articles was not a criminal cause or matter.[111] Similarly, the Court of Appeal has held that a decision to estreat a recognisance is not a criminal cause or matter as '[a] recognisance is in the nature of a bond. A failure to fulfil it gives rise to a civil debt'.[112] The issue of a witness summons is, however, not so collateral that it is not a criminal cause or matter.[113]

Challenges to the decisions of criminal courts may also not be a criminal cause or matter if the decision challenged relates to civil proceedings. For example, there are forms of civil proceedings that are brought in the magistrates' court. Thus, a decision to commit a person to jail for non-payment of non-domestic rates is not a criminal cause or matter.[114]

As noted earlier, the definition of a criminal charge for the purposes of the European Convention on Human Rights is different from the domestic law definition.[115] It would appear that a finding that proceedings are criminal for the purposes of Art 6 makes no difference to the determination of whether a judicial review is a criminal cause or matter

---

[106] See, for example, *R v Chief Constable of North Wales and others ex p Thorpe* [1998] 3 WLR 57.

[107] *R v Board of Visitors of Hull Prison ex p St Germain* [1979] QB 425, per Lord Justice Shaw, at 452B.

[108] *R v Board of Visitors of Hull Prison ex p St Germain* [1979] QB 425.

[109] In *Re EF Hardwick* (1883) 12 QB 148.

[110] *Carr v Atkins* [1987] 1 QB 963, per Sir John Donaldson MR, at 970F.

[111] *R (Guardian News and Media Ltd) v City of Westminster Magistrates' Court* [2011] 1 WLR 3253.

[112] *R v Southampton Justices ex p Green* [1976] QB 11, per Lord Denning MR, at 15H. Care must be taken when considering this case as it is clear that the full scope of the judgment of the Court of Appeal is regarded as unreliable. See, for example, *Carr v Atkins* [1987] 1 QB 963, per Sir John Donaldson MR, at 969E onwards. However, it was recently endorsed in this context in *R (Guardian News and Media Ltd) v City of Westminster Magistrates' Court* [2011] 1 WLR 3253.

[113] *Day v Grant* [1987] QB 972.

[114] *R v Thanet Justices ex p Dass* [1996] COD 77.

[115] See **2.8.7(1)**.

for procedural purposes.[116] That is perhaps not surprising as Art 6 does not entitle a person to any particular form of appeal proceedings (which is essentially what judicial review often is in a criminal context).

## 3.5    SHOULD AN ORDER BE SOUGHT LIMITING THE REPORTING OF THE MATTER?

### 3.5.1    Approach in the case of adults

There is no inherent power to restrict reporting of court proceedings.[117] Section 11 of the Contempt of Court Act 1981, however, provides that:

> 'In any case where a court (having power to do so) allows a name or other matter to be withheld from the public in proceedings before the court, the court may give such directions prohibiting the publication of that name or matter in connection with the proceedings as appear to the court to be necessary for the purpose for which it was so withheld.'

Section 11 is the power that is relied on by the Administrative Court when it gives directions restricting the reporting of a matter involving adults. It is the provision that is relied on whenever an adult who is a party to proceedings seeks to limit or prevent reporting of the matter. Thus, for example, it is the provision used where the Court wishes to avoid news reporting of the name of a person who has provided assistance to the police.[118]

In general, it is a rule of the English legal system that the administration of justice should be done in public. This means that, in general, nothing should prevent the 'publication to a wider public of fair and accurate reports of proceedings'.[119] As a result, the Administrative Court will approach any application for an order restricting reporting of proceedings on a presumption that no order should be made. The general rule will be departed from only in the following situation:[120]

> '[W]here the nature or circumstances of the particular proceeding are such that the application of the general rule in its entirety would frustrate or render impracticable the administration of justice or would damage some other public interest for whose protection Parliament has made some statutory derogation from the rule.'

---

[116]  *R (International Transport Roth Gmbh) v Secretary of State for the Home Department* [2003] QB 728, in which the Court of Appeal concluded that the decisions challenged were criminal for the purposes of Art 6.

[117]  *R v Newtonabbey Magistrates' Court ex p Belfast Telegraph Newspapers Ltd* [1997] NI 309.

[118]  See, for example, *R v Secretary of State ex p G* (1990) *The Times*, June 26 for an example of a case where such an order was made.

[119]  *Attorney-General v Leveller Magazine* [1979] AC 440, per Lord Diplock, at 450B.

[120]  Ibid, at 450C.

An example of circumstances where an order under s 11 of the Contempt of Court Act 1981 should be made arises when there is a real risk that a person 'will suffer real significant physical or mental harm' as a result of publication.[121] It is unnecessary in these circumstances for the court to consider whether a claimant for judicial review would withdraw proceedings if there was no order preventing publication.

The risk of serious physical and mental harm is presumably why it has become almost automatic for the Administrative Court to make orders restricting the reporting of the name of mentally ill claimants.[122] Similarly, the Administrative Court has shown a willingness to restrict the reporting of claims involving asylum seekers whose cases have not been determined,[123] presumably in order to avoid the harm that might result should their persecutors discover that they are in the United Kingdom.[124]

The matters above were the sort of matters that appeared to result in a greater willingness on the part of the courts to order reporting restrictions in judicial review proceedings. That trend may have been reversed by the decision of the Supreme Court in *Re Guardian News and Media Ltd.*[125] This judgment reemphasised the general rule that proceedings are held in public and that the names of parties are reported.

Mr Justice Brooke considered the procedure that should be adopted when applying for an order under s 11 of the Contempt of Court Act 1981 in proceedings in the Administrative Court. First, the claimant should contact the Administrative Court before lodging papers if there is any concern that the papers lodged may reveal details that will give rise to adverse publicity. That will enable the claimant to ensure that the application can be considered immediately. In any event, it may be appropriate to hold any hearing to determine whether the order should be made in camera. Alternatively, it may be appropriate to make an interim order pending a full consideration of the merits of the application. Such an order might be made if it would enable the claimant to obtain further evidence to show that a final order would be justified.[126]

The guidance offered by Mr Justice Brooke was delivered before Administrative Court procedures were updated and, in particular, before

---

[121] See, for example, *Re D* (unreported) 17 November 1997, CO/3369/97, per Mr Justice Dyson.

[122] See, for example, *R (D) v Secretary of State for the Home Department* [2003] 1 WLR 1315; *R (B) v Ashworth Hospital* [2003] 1 WLR 1886.

[123] See, for example, *R (Q) v Secretary of State for the Home Department* [2004] QB 36.

[124] See also *Practice Note (Anonymisation in asylum & immigration cases in the Court of Appeal* [2006] 4 All ER 928. This note provides for automatic anonymisation in the Court of Appeal, a practice which appears to be followed in the Administrative Court. See, for example, *R (AO) v Secretary of State for the Home Department* [2010] EWHC 764 (Admin), at [2], in which the court declined to make the order but the judgment was anonymised anyway.

[125] [2010] 2 AC 697.

[126] *R v Somerset Health Authority ex p S* [1996] COD 244.

the procedure for seeking urgent consideration of a case was introduced. However, the guidance would appear to remain valid. The application for an anonymity order should be made at section 7 of the N461 dealing with 'other applications'. Should the need be urgent an N463 urgent consideration form should be submitted with the claim seeking appropriate orders, such as an order under s 11 of the Contempt of Court Act 1981 or an order that an in camera hearing be heard urgently.

Linked to the provision allowing the reporting of proceedings to be restricted is the inherent power of the High Court to hold the hearing of a matter in camera. As noted above, this may well be appropriate where there is an application for an order under s 11 of the Contempt of Court Act 1981, during which the claimant will seek to rely on sensitive material. The application should be heard in camera if the disclosure of the material relied on in support of the application for an order will frustrate the purpose of the order.[127]

Article 6 of the European Convention on Human Rights has express provisions that normally require a hearing to take place in public.[128] In addition, Art 10 of the Convention may entitle the media to report court proceedings. There is little to suggest that either Convention provision has significantly changed the approach of the domestic courts.[129] However, there have been some developments. For example, as regards media access to 'closed' courts such as the Court of Protection, stressing the importance of the principle of 'open justice' the court recently acceded to a media application to attend and report on proceedings, where there was in the circumstances of the case no conflict with the protected person's best interests.[130] This case demonstrates the balance inherent in many applications for reporting restrictions between the interests of the public in reporting and the interests of the individual.

When an order is sought restricting the reporting matters, it is important to ensure that it is sufficiently precise. An order that is not sufficiently precise may be impossible to enforce.[131]

### 3.5.2   Approach in the case of young people

Special considerations arise in relation to reporting restrictions in cases regarding young people. The reporting of cases in these circumstances is governed by s 39(1) of the Children and Young Persons Act 1933 (CYPA 1933), which provides that the court may direct that:

> '(1) In relation to any proceedings in any court ... the court may direct that –

---

[127]  *R v Tower Bridge Magistrates' Court ex p Osbourne* [1988] Crim LR 382.
[128]  See **2.8.7** and **2.8.7(4)**.
[129]  See e g *Clibbery v Allan* [2002] Fam 261.
[130]  *London Borough of Hillingdon v (1) Steven Neary (2) Mark Neary* [2011] CP Rep 32.
[131]  *Briffett v Crown Prosecution Service* [2002] EMLR 12.

(a)  no newspaper report of the proceedings shall reveal the name, address or school, or include any particulars calculated to lead to the identification, of any child or young person concerned in the proceedings, either as being the person [by or against] or in respect of whom the proceedings are taken, or as being a witness therein:

(b)  no picture shall be published in any newspaper as being or including a picture of any child or young person so concerned in the proceedings as aforesaid; except in so far (if at all) as may be permitted by the direction of the court.'

Before the HRA 1998 entered into force, the courts were, in general, willing to exercise their powers under s 39 of the CYPA 1933. For example, the Court of Appeal has held that, although the public normally has a legitimate interest in receiving reports of criminal proceedings, the mere fact that a person appearing before the courts is a child or young person can be sufficient to justify the making of an order under s 39 of the CYPA 1933.[132] In deciding whether to make an order under s 39 of the CYPA 1933, the court would take account of the nature of that provision, as it is clearly a child welfare provision, and the stage that any proceedings had reached.[133]

The Court of Appeal has, in considering the approach to the reporting of court proceedings in cases involving children in the light of the European Convention on Human Rights recognised[134] that reporting may amount to an interference with a child's right to private life under Art 8.[135] As a consequence, there is a need to balance the interference with private life against the right of the media to freedom of expression.[136]

In practice, it would appear that there should be a reluctance to reveal the identity of a child involved in litigation. In many cases, any reporting will reveal matters that are sufficiently sensitive for there to be a real risk that the reporting will cause harm to any children identified. The importance attached to the best interests of children[137] means that, in practice, that risk will often be sufficient to justify reporting restrictions.

---

[132]  Per Watkins LJ, *R v Leicester Crown Court ex p S* [1993] 1 WLR 111, at 114D. Note, however, that it is now clear that it is not only in 'rare and exceptional cases' that an order should not be made. See *R v Central Criminal Court ex p Simpkins* (1998) *The Times*, October 26; *R v Anthony Lee* (1993) 96 Cr App R 188, CA.

[133]  *R v Manchester Crown Court ex p H* [2000] 1 WLR 760.

[134]  *Re S (Identification: Restrictions on Publication)* [2003] 2 FLR 1253.

[135]  Ibid, at [49].

[136]  Ibid, at [60].

[137]  *Re F (Adult Patient)* [2000] UKHRR 712, at 732D.

# CHAPTER 4

# STEPS TO BE TAKEN BEFORE APPLYING FOR JUDICIAL REVIEW

## 4.1 PRE-ACTION PROTOCOL

### 4.1.1 Claimant's obligations

Before the advent of the pre-action protocol, it was accepted practice that most claimants should write to the proposed defendants explaining the basis of the challenge. The letter would give the decision-maker an opportunity to address the complaint before proceedings started.[1] The importance of this process is recognised in the Judicial Review Pre-action Protocol.[2] The Protocol expressly states that, normally, a claimant should write a letter before claim and that proceedings should not be commenced until the time for response has passed.[3]

The Protocol might be read as not being obligatory, as it is described as a code of good practice.[4] It would however be a brave claimant who decided to ignore it without good reason. The Protocol warns that a failure to comply may have costs implications or may be taken account of during case management by the court.[5] The Court of Appeal has also stressed the importance of the Protocol.[6]

The Protocol identifies the matters to be raised in a letter before claim. A precedent letter before claim is included in Part III.[7] As should be clear from this precedent, it is good practice to divide the letter with subheadings so that it is clear that all the material required by the

---

[1]  *R v Horsham District Council ex p Wenman* [1995] 1 WLR 680, in which legal advisers were fortunate to avoid a wasted costs order for failing to conduct a judicial review properly. Mr Justice Brooke held, inter alia, that claimants should write a letter before claim except in exceptional circumstances as litigation should normally be regarded as a weapon of last resort (at 709F).

[2]  See Part IV.

[3]  Judicial Review Pre-action Protocol, paras 8 and 12.

[4]  Ibid, para 5.

[5]  Ibid, para 7.

[6]  *R (Bahta) v Secretary of State for the Home Department* [2011] EWCA Civ 895, [2011] CP Rep 43, at [64].

[7]  See Precedent 1.

Protocol has been included – this enables judges and anyone else involved in the case to see immediately that all relevant matters have been addressed in the letter before claim.

An effective, Protocol-compliant letter must address several matters. Firstly, the letter must identify the decision under challenge and set out clearly the claimant's reasons for challenging the decision. The letter should give the defendant a clear opportunity to avoid litigation but should also be written mindful of the need to make it quite clear to the judge considering costs orders that the claimant's complaint was spelt out to the defendant prior to litigation. In practice, it appears that the reasons need not be set out in as much detail as any subsequent grounds, partly because, in many cases, the defendant will have greater knowledge of the background to the decision than a judge reading the claim form. However, the defendant must be left in no doubt about the basis of the proposed challenge. In addition, it is important to make it clear whether interim relief is being sought so that the proposed defendant can consider that separate issue.[8]

In general, the letter before claim should be sent to the decision-maker. There are public bodies, however, that have set up specific departments to receive letters before claim. These are listed in the Protocol.[9]

The letter should not merely be sent to a proposed defendant. Proposed interested parties[10] should also receive a copy for information.[11]

The letter before claim should normally give a proposed defendant 14 days to respond.[12] As a consequence, it is important that it is sent promptly and well within the 3-month time-limit for applying for judicial review.[13] The Protocol states that 'compliance with the protocol alone is unlikely to be sufficient to persuade the court to allow a late claim.'[14] If no letter before claim has been written until shortly before the expiry of the 3-month time-limit for applying for judicial review, it may well be better to lodge the claim rather than write a letter before claim giving the defendant 14 days to respond. However, it is also likely that the Administrative Court will need to be persuaded that there was a very good reason why the letter was not written earlier. If the court is not satisfied that there is a good reason then it could potentially determine that the claim has not been brought promptly.[15]

---

8    Judicial Review Pre-action Protocol, paras 7 and 16.
9    Judicial Review Pre-action Protocol, section 2. This list has been changed from time to time but the up-to-date version can be checked at http://www.justice.gov.uk/guidance/courts-and-tribunals/courts/procedure-rules/civil/contents/protocols/prot_jrv.htm.
10   See **5.2.1** for a consideration of who should be made an interested party to proceedings.
11   Judicial Review Pre-action Protocol, para 11.
12   Ibid, at Appendix A, section 1, para 12.
13   See **3.1**.
14   Footnote 1 to Judicial Review Pre-action Protocol.
15   See **3.1**.

Problems in obtaining Community Legal Service funding may be unlikely to justify delay in writing a letter before claim because funding for the letter before claim can sometimes be obtained sometimes under the Legal Help scheme.[16]

One exception to the need for a letter before claim arises where the decision being challenged has been taken by a court or tribunal, because the decision challenged will normally be a final decision. As a result, the court will often be *functus officio* and so unable to reverse the decision challenged. The Protocol recognises that in these circumstances there is no need to write a letter before claim.[17] It is still, however, good practice to inform the court that an application is being brought for judicial review. Indeed, one High Court judge has suggested that it may still be good practice to write a letter before claim in these circumstances so that the court challenged can consider whether its order should be remitted by consent.[18]

Where the judicial review seeks to challenge an interim decision of a court that is not *functus officio*, the court should be put on notice that a judicial review will be sought. The claimant should apply for an adjournment of the proceedings before the court so that the claim for judicial review may be brought.[19] If the application for an adjournment is refused, a stay of proceedings in the lower court may be sought from the Administrative Court as a form of interim relief.[20]

There will also be cases where the urgency of the application means that it is not practical for a detailed letter before claim to be written. The urgency may also mean that it is impossible to give the decision-maker an opportunity to reverse his decision. Urgency is likely to be particularly relevant where interim relief is required. An example is where a claimant is about to be made homeless, to be removed from the United Kingdom or denied urgent community care services. The Protocol acknowledges that, in these circumstances, it is acceptable that no letter before claim has been written.[21] It is still regarded as good practice to inform the defendant that a claim is being brought for judicial review.[22] The Protocol suggests that a defendant should be supplied with a draft copy of the claim form which the claimant intends to issue.[23]

---

[16] See **4.2.1**.

[17] Judicial Review Pre-action Protocol, para 6.

[18] Scott Baker J 'A View from the Bench: Pre-Action Protocol in Judicial Review' [2002] JR 69.

[19] See, for example, in a criminal context, *Streames v Copping* [1985] QB 920, at 929.

[20] See **7.4**.

[21] Judicial Review Pre-action Protocol, para 6.

[22] See *R v Cotswold District Council ex p Barrington Parish Council* (1998) 75 P&CR 515, for an example of the importance attached to informing parties who may be affected by a judicial review that an application has been made.

[23] Judicial Review Pre-action Protocol, para 7.

There are some cases where the urgency of the application will not be so great that there is no opportunity to give a defendant an opportunity to respond to the letter before claim but the urgency is still such that the Administrative Court will need to rule on the matter rapidly. For example, a decision may have been taken that means that a person will be homeless in weeks. In those circumstances, the time for response to the letter before claim should be abridged. When deciding to what extent the time for response should be abridged the urgency of the case, is important as is the need to ensure that the Administrative Court is given a sensible opportunity to consider the case. Judges are unlikely to be impressed if the letter before claim gives a defendant seven days to respond and the Administrative Court is then asked to rule on the permission application within one day.

If the claim is going to need urgent consideration, it is also important that it is brought particularly promptly. Again, judges are unlikely to be impressed if the letter before claim gives a defendant two days to respond when the claimant has taken seven days to write it.

If the Protocol has not been completely complied with, the failure to comply should be explained in the claim form.[24]

### 4.1.2   Defendant's obligations

The Judicial Review Pre-action Protocol[25] contains obligations for a potential defendant who receives a letter before claim. A defendant should normally respond within 14 days.[26] The Protocol warns that a failure to comply may have costs implications or the defendant may be penalised.[27] The Court of Appeal has also underlined the importance that a failure to respond to a Pre-action Protocol will have when the Court considers costs.[28] One further sanction that could be imposed is that the Administrative Court might decline to hear a defendant at the permission stage. As a defendant who fails to file an acknowledgement of service can be prevented from being heard at the permission stage,[29] there would appear to be no reason why the same approach should not apply when a defendant fails to respond to a letter before claim. Indeed, the authors are aware of one case where that has occurred.

In practice, it is likely to be in the interests of a defendant to write a detailed and careful response to a letter before claim, as it may avoid

---

24   See Precedent 3 in Part III.
25   See Part IV.
26   Judicial Review Pre-action Protocol, para 13.
27   Ibid.
28   *R (Bahta) v Secretary of State for the Home Department* [2011] EWCA Civ 895, [2011] CP Rep 43.
29   CPR, r 54.9.

litigation. A detailed response may persuade a claimant that he has no grounds for applying for judicial review.

A defendant might ask for additional time to respond to a letter before claim. He needs, however, to be aware that the parties cannot extend time for applying for judicial review by consent.[30] As a consequence, a claimant might legitimately refuse to agree to extend time if the consequences of extending time are that he will be out of time. If, in other circumstances, consent to extend time to respond is unreasonably withheld, that failure to consent may have consequences for a claimant who then commences his claim.[31] In particular, there is a risk that a claimant will be unable to recover his costs.

The Protocol identifies the matters to be addressed in a letter in response to a letter before claim. A precedent letter in response is included in Part III.[32] As should be clear from the precedent that has been included, it is good practice to divide the letter with subheadings so that it is clear that all the material required by the Protocol has been included. This practice enables judges and anyone else involved in the case to see immediately that all relevant matters have been addressed.

The defendant's letter should clearly state whether the proposed claim is opposed in whole or in part.[33] It should also state whether any application for interim relief is opposed.[34] The letter may also contain additional reasons justifying the decision taken. Proposed defendants will, however, need to be aware of the limitations on a defendant's ability to supplement reasons.[35]

The Protocol provides that claimants can request information and documentation. However, the Protocol also states that it does not impose a greater obligation on a public body to disclose documents or give reasons for its decision than that already provided for in statute or common law.[36]

When defendants receive a request for documents they ought to bear in mind the Data Protection Act 1998 and the Freedom of Information Act 2000 which impose significant disclosure obligations upon data holders and public bodies. A detailed consideration of this legislation is beyond the scope of this book. However, it should be sufficient to say that it does mean that public authorities require a good reason for refusing to

---

[30]   See **3.1.2**.
[31]   Judicial Review Pre-action Protocol, para 14.
[32]   See Precedent 2.
[33]   Judicial Review Pre-action Protocol, paras 15 and 16.
[34]   Ibid, para 16.
[35]   See **2.14.2**.
[36]   Judicial Review Pre-action Protocol, para 6. See also *R v Lancashire County Council ex p Huddleston* [1986] 2 All ER 941, in which the Court stressed, at 945G, that there should be a '*cards face up on the table*' approach to judicial review.

disclose documentation that relates to an individual. As a consequence, a defendant needs to think carefully before refusing to disclose documentation that relates to the proposed claimant, whether in judicial review proceedings or by means of a formal request under the Data Protection Act 1998 or Freedom of Information Act 2000.

In addition, defendants should be aware of the fact that they are subject to a duty of candour once the judicial review claim commences.[37] If that duty applies once a judicial review claim has commenced, there are arguments that it should apply earlier. A claimant would be entitled to complain and seek costs if he is put to the expense of commencing a claim which is then undermined by the disclosure of material by the defendant which could and should have been disclosed earlier.

## 4.2  PUBLIC FUNDING

Much of the guidance cited in this section can be found on the website of the Legal Services Commission at www.legalservices.gov.uk. It is also contained in the Legal Services Commission Manual, to which both solicitors and barristers who provide publicly funded services should have access. The guidance and the legislation made under it should be kept under review in light of proposed changes contained in the Legal Aid, Sentencing and Punishment of Offenders Bill currently before Parliament.

Public funding is normally provided to enable claimants to bring judicial reviews. Hence the focus on this section of the book is on claimants. However, there is, in principle, no reason why public funding cannot be provided for an interested party. This will occasionally be appropriate. For example, if a hospital challenges the decision of a Mental Health Review Tribunal to release a patient, the patient may well wish to participate as an interested party. The same considerations apply as when public funding is provided to a claimant.

### 4.2.1  Forms of public funding available

Legal Help is available to provide initial assistance. This can include writing a letter before claim. It will often be unclear what the merits of the claim are at that stage and investigative help in order to assess the merits may be appropriate. As should be clear below, full legal representation normally requires an assessment of the merits of the claim.

Legal Help can be used to provide funding to obtain counsel's opinion regarding the merits of a judicial review claim, provided that is reasonably necessary.[38] An advice can assist the Legal Services Commission to grant full representation. However, the fees will be taken from a fixed fee if one

---

[37]  See **5.5**.
[38]  LSC General Civil Contract, para 3.75.

is applicable.[39] In addition, the Commission may need to be convinced that this is a valid use of Legal Help funding as it may believe that a solicitor ought to be able to determine the merits of the claim.[40] One alternative to a formal advice may be that counsel is willing to provide informal advice.

The drafting of a claim for judicial review and all subsequent steps must be funded by a certificate for legal representation. There are several reasons for this. First, Legal Help cannot be used for issuing or conducting proceedings.[41] As a consequence, the Commission will not fund the work unless a certificate is issued. In addition, the fact that the Commission will not fund the work means that the claimant will not receive the normal protection against costs that is available to publicly funded claimants. In simple terms, a publicly funded claimant will not normally be required to pay the defendant's costs if he loses.[42] As a consequence, a failure to obtain a certificate for legal representation may leave a claimant at risk of costs that he would not normally be liable for.

Legal representation cannot be provided for a judicial review claim which arises out of the claimant's business unless the proceedings concern the serious wrongdoing, abuse of position or power or significant breach of human rights by a public authority.[43]

Solicitors need to be aware that there may be restrictions on the work that they can obtain public funding for. For example, in general, a certificate for legal representation cannot be obtained for immigration work by a firm of solicitors that has no immigration or public law contract. In addition, a certificate for legal representation cannot be obtained for criminal work by a firm of solicitors that has no criminal or public law contract.

### 4.2.2   Merits test for providing legal representation

Legal representation is subject to both a merits test and a means test. It is unnecessary for the purposes of this book to consider in detail the means test as it varies from time to time and is generally assessed by the Legal Services Commission, provided that the correct form is completed. Practitioners do, however, require a detailed knowledge of the merits test.

The merits test involves the consideration of two matters. First, the prospects of success must be sufficient to justify the claim proceedings. In addition, in general, the benefit to the proposed claimant must be sufficient to justify public funding.

---

[39]   LSC General Civil Contract, para 3.76.
[40]   LSC General Civil Contract, para 3.77.
[41]   LSC Funding Code: Criteria, para 2.1.
[42]   Access to Justice Act 1999, s 11; and see also **10.4**.
[43]   LSC Funding Code: Decision Making Guidance, para 3.3.

The LSC Funding Code requires the prospects of success to be measured against a number of categories:[44]

- 'Very good', which means that the prospects of success are 80% or more;

- 'Good', which means that the prospects of success are 60–80%;

- 'Moderate', which means that the prospects of success are 50–60%;

- 'Borderline', which means that the prospects of success are not poor, but, because there are difficult disputes of fact, law or expert evidence, it is not possible to say that prospects of success are better than 50%;

- 'Poor', which means that the prospects of success are clearly less than 50%, so that the claim is likely to fail; and

- 'Unclear', which means that the case cannot be put into any of the above categories because further investigation is required.

The Funding Code stipulates that a certificate providing for full representation to commence proceedings will be refused if the prospects of success are unclear (which can presumably be addressed by work funded by Legal Help[45] or investigative help[46]) or poor. Full representation will also be refused if the prospects of success are borderline and the case does not appear to have significant wider public interest, to be of overwhelming importance to the client or to raise significant human rights issues.[47]

In practice, very few judicial review claims can be said to have 'very good' or 'good' prospects of success, as judicial review is an inherently high-risk form of litigation. There will often be a dispute regarding the law that will not be clear. In addition, at the stage one is applying for judicial review, the defendant's case may be unclear.

In addition, few judicial review claims are, in practice, funded on the basis that the prospects of success are 'borderline' because, although there will often be a dispute regarding the law, experienced counsel or solicitors ought to determine with some degree of accuracy whether the prospects of success are greater than 50% (in which case they are moderate) or less than 50% (in which case they are poor).

---

[44]    LSC Funding Code: Criteria, para 2.3.
[45]    See **4.2.1**.
[46]    See below.
[47]    LSC Funding Code: Criteria, para 7.4.5.

If a claim is 'borderline', it is necessary to show that the claim has one of three additional factors present: there is significant wider public interest; it is of overwhelming importance to the client; or, it raises significant human rights issues. A case that is of significant wider public interest is one that will produce real benefits to individuals other than the client.[48] Cases that will determine a point of legal principle that will have consequences for a large number of people will come within this category. A case that is of overwhelming importance to the client is one that affects his life, liberty, physical safety or a roof over the heads of the client or his family.[49] Asylum cases are generally regarded as coming within this category of case. It should be relatively clear whether a case raises significant human rights issues.

Even if the prospects of success are sufficiently strong, funding will generally be refused if there are administrative appeals or other procedures that should be pursued.[50] For example, the Legal Services Commission will normally expect a prisoner to appeal against a disciplinary adjudication through the internal appeals procedure before it will fund the case.

If the prospects of success are unclear, it may be possible to obtain investigative help funding. This can be obtained when the prospects of success are uncertain and substantial investigative work is required, provided that there are reasonable grounds for believing that the funding criteria will be met once the investigations are complete.[51]

If the prospects of success are sufficiently high, it is necessary to consider the benefits to the client. It must be shown that the likely benefits justify the proceedings.[52] This requires consideration of whether a reasonable private paying client would be prepared to litigate.[53] It may also be possible to justify funding on the basis that the case has a wider public benefit.[54] Before the Legal Services Commission will be willing to provide funding on this basis, it may require the matter to be referred to its public interest panel, who will need to be satisfied that genuinely there are a significant number of people who will benefit from the litigation.

It is important to be aware that funding will generally initially not extend past the permission stage and the service of any evidence by the defendant. As a consequence, it will be necessary to review the merits at that stage, which is considered later in this book.[55]

---

[48]   Ibid, para 2.4.
[49]   Ibid.
[50]   LSC Funding Code: Criteria, para 7.4.3.
[51]   Ibid, paras 5.6.2, 5.6.4 and 7.2.1.
[52]   Ibid, para 7.4.6.
[53]   Ibid, para 5.7.4.
[54]   Ibid, para 5.7.5.
[55]   See **5.10.7**.

### 4.2.3   Continuing obligation to review the merits of public funding

Practitioners involved in proceedings in which their clients are in receipt of public funding should be aware of the professional obligations that they owe to the Legal Services Commission. These obligations mean that a practitioner is obliged to review the merits of his client's case and ensure that the Commission is informed if it is no longer reasonable for his client to be in receipt of public funding.[56] The Commission is likely to withdraw public funding in these circumstances. In addition, practitioners are required to report any matter that may be relevant to the continuation of funding.[57] That is likely to include relevant developments in the case, such as a decision to refuse permission on the papers.

A failure to review the merits of a claim is clearly a breach of professional obligations. It may also result in problems obtaining payment. If, at the conclusion of the application for permission or any other hearing, the Administrative Court believes that proceedings should not have been brought, it cannot refuse an order for assessment of a party's Legal Services Commission costs. It can, however, make the Costs Judge aware of its views on the merits of the application and this will be taken into account when the assessment takes place.[58] If this happens, the legal representatives will have significant difficulties in obtaining the payment of costs.

### 4.2.4   Procedure for applying for public funding

A detailed explanation of the procedure is beyond the scope of this book, primarily because the procedures change on a relatively regular basis. There are, however, several important points to be noted.

First, it is generally impossible to obtain retrospective funding. However, it is possible to obtain emergency funding at relatively short notice. Firms of solicitors with devolved powers that entitle them to grant emergency funding can grant themselves funding. Other firms can make faxed applications to the Legal Services Commission.

An application for emergency funding should obviously be made if a matter is urgent. However, the Legal Services Commission is unlikely to regard a matter as urgent merely because there has been earlier delay in preparing the judicial review claim. Solicitors should not assume that they can make an emergency application shortly before the 3-month time-limit for judicial review expires and that it will be granted.

---

[56] Civil Legal Aid (General) Regulations 1989 (SI 1989/339), regs 67 and 70.
[57] Ibid, reg 70(1)(c).
[58] See, for example, *R v Secretary of State for the Home Department ex p Shahina Begum* [1995] COD 176.

If an application is made for emergency funding, the Legal Services Commission will expect the substantive application to be submitted within a time that the Commission will specify.[59] If that does not happen, funding will be cancelled.[60] If work is done under an emergency certificate and the funding is cancelled, the Commission will proceed as though emergency funding was never granted.[61] This means that no fees will be paid by the Commission.

One important piece of advice that must be given to a proposed claimant when applying for public funding is about the potential consequences of the statutory charge. Essentially, the statutory charge means that any damages must be first used to pay the cost of the litigation. In most judicial review claims this is not relevant as damages will not be sought. However, damages can be sought in judicial review[62] and, if they are, then the client must be advised regarding the statutory charge.

## 4.3  APPOINTMENT OF A LITIGATION FRIEND

CPR, r 21 sets out the special procedure to be followed in cases concerning children and protected parties. It has been comprehensively revised to bring it into line with the Mental Capacity Act 2005, which sets out the statutory test for determining when a vulnerable adult lacks capacity.

### 4.3.1  Litigation friends in cases involving children

CPR, r 21 provides that 'a child must have a litigation friend to conduct proceedings on his behalf unless the court makes an order'. A child is defined as being a person aged under 18.[63] The terms of this rule appear wide and include judicial review proceedings in the Administrative Court.[64] In practice, in cases of urgency or where a young person is able to give instructions directly, it appears that claims are sometimes issued without the intervention of a litigation friend. That, however, cannot be regarded as good practice. An appropriate litigation friend should be appointed to act at the commencement of litigation in the Administrative Court, unless an order is sought dispensing with the need for a litigation friend. Where the case is urgent but a suitable litigation friend has not yet been identified, this should be explained in the claim form and where

---

59   LSC Funding Code: Procedures, para C11.7. At present, this is within 5 working days.

60   Ibid, para C11.8.

61   Ibid, para C11.9.

62   Senior Courts Act 1981, s 31(4), CPR, r 54.3(2) and Practice Direction 16, para 15. Monetary remedies are available under three broad heads: where damages would be recoverable in an equivalent private law action; damages for breaches of European Community law and '*just satisfaction*' under the Human Rights Act 1998.

63   CPR, r 21.1(2)(a).

64   Indeed, CPR, r 2.1 states that the CPR apply to all proceedings in the High Court save for certain exceptions. These exceptions do not include judicial review.

possible a statement given by the solicitor confirming that a claim has been commenced mindful of the best interests of the child.

Practice Direction 21 states that a person can become a litigation friend either without a court order under CPR, r 21.5 or by a court order on application under CPR, r 21.6.[65] Paragraph 2.2 to the Practice Direction sets out both the procedure for becoming a litigation friend without a court order. It provides that a person who wishes to become a litigation friend without a court order must file a certificate of suitability in Practice Form N235, which makes the following points:

'(a)   stating that he consents to act,

(b)   stating that he knows or believes that the relevant party either is a child or lacks capacity to conduct the proceedings,

(c)   in the case of a protected party, stating the grounds of his belief and, if his belief is based upon medical opinion or the opinion of another suitably qualified expert, attaching any relevant document to the certificate,

(d)   stating that he can fairly and competently conduct proceedings on behalf of the child or protected party and has no interest adverse to that of the child or protected party, and

(e)   where the child or protected party is a claimant, undertaking to pay any costs which the child or protected party may be ordered to pay in relation to the proceedings, subject to any right he may have to be repaid from the assets of the child or protected party.'

These criteria also provide a useful summary of the necessary qualities and duties of a litigation friend. The rules provide a standard form certificate of suitability, which is included in Part III.[66]

In practice, a parent is usually appointed to act as litigation friend, as they are most likely to be able to take on the obligations set out above. Alternatively, social workers may be persuaded to act as a litigation friend in a case in which there is no parent available to act as a litigation friend. However, before a social worker is appointed, care must be taken to ensure that they have no conflict of interest which would prevent them from taking on the role of litigation friend. For example, many claims regarding children will be about matters such as education or community care. As the defendant will often be the local authority that employs the social worker, this might well be regarded as meaning that the social worker has an adverse interest in the proceedings.

As noted above, if nobody can be identified as a suitable person to act as a litigation friend, an order can be sought dispensing with that requirement.[67]

---

[65]   Practice Direction 21, para 2.1.

[66]   See Precedent 21.

[67]   CPR, r 21.2(3).

The court may make an order appointing a person to act as litigation friend.[68] An application for such an order should be made in accordance with the procedure set out in CPR, r 23 and must be supported by evidence to satisfy the court that he or she:

(a) consents to act;

(b) can fairly and competently conduct proceedings on behalf of the child or protected party;

(c) has no interest adverse to that of the child or protected party; and

(d) where the child or protected party is a claimant, undertakes to pay any costs which the child or protected party may be ordered to pay in relation to the proceedings, subject to any right he may have to be repaid from the assets of the child or protected party.

The title of the case in any pleadings concerning a child should be in the following form:

'A.B (a minor, by his litigation friend D.E.)'[69]

Alternatively, if there is no litigation friend, the heading should be in the following form:

'A.B. (a minor)'[70]

Clearly, the rules regarding litigation friends do not merely govern cases brought by children as claimants. For example, a child may be the interested party in a judicial review claim brought by the prosecution if the child is the defendant in criminal proceedings which are the subject of the judicial review claim. In those circumstances, a litigation friend should be appointed to act on the child's behalf, unless an order is obtained dispensing with the need for a litigation friend. That is because the permission of the court is needed to take any steps in proceedings, save for issuing and serving a claim form, or making an application for the appointment of a litigation friend, unless the child has a litigation friend.[71] It might well be cumbersome to seek the permission of court for bringing each stage. As a result, it is sensible to ensure either that a litigation friend is appointed or that an order is sought dispensing with the need for a litigation friend.

---

[68]   Ibid, r 21.6(1).
[69]   Practice Direction 21, para 1.2(1).
[70]   Ibid, para 1.2(2).
[71]   CPR, r 21.3(2).

Any order that is sought in relation to litigation friends should be handled in the same way as other interim orders in proceedings in the Administrative Office.[72]

### 4.3.2    Litigation friends in cases involving protected parties

A 'protected party' defined as 'a party, or an intended party, who lacks capacity to conduct the proceedings'.[73] The test for determining capacity is set out in s 2 of the Mental Capacity Act 2005 which provides that:

> '… a person lacks capacity in relation to a matter if at the material time he is unable to make a decision for himself in relation to the matter because of an impairment of, or a disturbance in the functioning of, the mind or brain.'

It is important to note that:

(a)    it does not matter whether the impairment or disturbance is permanent or temporary;[74]

(b)    a lack of capacity cannot be established merely by reference to:

(i)     a person's age or appearance; or

(ii)    a condition of his, or an aspect of his behaviour, which might lead others to make unjustified assumptions about his capacity;[75]

(c)    any question whether a person lacks capacity within the meaning of the Mental Capacity Act 2005 must be decided on the balance of probabilities.[76]

The question of inability to make decisions is defined at s 3 Mental Capacity Act 2005, which provides that a person is unable to make a decision for himself if he is unable:

(a)    to understand the information relevant to the decision. A person is not to be regarded as unable to understand the information relevant to a decision if he is able to understand an explanation of it given to him in a way that is appropriate to his circumstances (using simple language, visual aids or any other means);

---

[72]    See **5.10.4(1)**.

[73]    CPR, r 21.1(2).

[74]    Section 2(2) Mental Capacity Act 2005. See also the Code of Practice to the Mental Capacity Act 2005.

[75]    Section 2(3) Mental Capacity Act 2005.

[76]    Section 2(4) Mental Capacity Act 2005.

(b)    to retain that information. The fact that a person is able to retain the information relevant to a decision for a short period only does not prevent him from being regarded as able to make the decision;

(c)    to use or weigh that information as part of the process of making the decision; or

(d)    to communicate his decision (whether by talking, using sign language or any other means).

The information relevant to a decision includes information about the reasonably foreseeable consequences of deciding one way or another, or failing to make the decision.[77]

It is important to note that the test for mental capacity is not the same as that for detaining a patient under the Mental Health Act 1983 or the 'fitness to plead' test in criminal law[78]. Capacity is 'task specific'. Hence, a person detained under the Mental Health Act 1983 will not require a litigation friend unless they lack capacity under the Mental Capacity Act 2005. Similarly, a person need not be detained under the Mental Health Act 1983 in order to need a litigation friend.

When a person is a protected party, the court has no power to make an order dispensing with the need for a litigation friend.[79]

Since the repeal of Part VII of the Mental Health Act 1983 on 1 October 2007, the principles governing capacity to conduct litigation and the appointment and role of a litigation friend are those set out in the Mental Capacity Act 2005 and Code of Practice. While neither CPR, r 21 nor the Mental Capacity Act 2005 explicitly sets out the role and duties of litigation friends appointed to act on behalf of protected parties, the authors consider that a litigation friend must act consistently with the duty, set out in s 1(5) of the Mental Capacity Act 2005, to act in act in accordance with the 'best interests' of a person who lacks capacity and the detailed process set out in s 4 of the Mental Capacity Act 2005 by which such 'best interests' must be determined.

The Official Solicitor may also act as litigation friend of last resort for protected parties in judicial review in appropriate cases.[80]

It is possible that a person may become a protected person after an action has been commenced. If that happens, no steps may be taken in the

---

[77]    Section 3(4) Mental Capacity Act 2005.
[78]    *R v Pritchard* (1836) 7 C&P 303.
[79]    CPR, r 21.2(1).
[80]    See *Practice Note (Official Solicitor: Declaratory Proceedings: Medical and Welfare Decisions for Adults who Lack Capacity)* [2006] 2 FLR 373.

proceedings without the permission of the court until the protected person has a litigation friend to act on his behalf.[81]

---

[81]  CPR, r 21.3(3).

# CHAPTER 5

## PROCEDURE FOR BRINGING A CLAIM FOR JUDICIAL REVIEW IN THE HIGH COURT[1]

### 5.1 URGENT APPLICATIONS

Normally, an application for judicial review is commenced by lodging an application in the form set out below and then allowing the defendant to respond. There are, however, cases where the delay will defeat the purpose of the application. These cases are often cases in which interim relief is sought. For example, in a case where the judicial review application relates to a decision to refuse a person welfare benefits, it may be important that benefits continue until the judicial review claim is heard as a denial of benefits may result in a person becoming homeless.[2] The Administrative Court has procedures that enable it to make rapid decisions in this type of urgent situation. The procedure to be followed depends upon whether it is necessary to apply to a duty judge at night and during the weekend or whether it is possible to apply during court hours.

It is important to be aware that there is no procedure for producing instant decisions. It takes several hours to contact the duty judge out of hours. During court hours the Administrative Court will expect papers to be lodged with it and it will then take time for the Court to consider the papers. As a consequence, practitioners acting for claimants must apply for interim relief in sufficient time to ensure that an order has value. For example, in an immigration matter, interim relief must be sought hours before proposed removal so that the UK Border Agency can be notified of any order in good time to ensure that removal does not take place.

#### 5.1.1 Out-of-hours applications for judicial review

As soon it becomes clear that there is a need to apply to the duty judge, the duty judge's clerk should be contacted on the main telephone number for the Royal Courts of Justice (at the time of writing, 020 7947 6000). He will then make arrangements for the duty judge to hear the application, which will be heard either by telephone or in person, depending on the location of the duty judge and the urgency of the application. If

---

[1]   Readers should also make reference to the Procedural Guide contained in Part II.
[2]   See Chapter 7 for a consideration of interim relief.

necessary, additional documents can be sent to the duty clerk by email (at the time of writing, qbdutyclerk@hmcts.gsi.gov.uk).

Although the application is likely to focus on whether the interim relief sought should be ordered, there would appear to be no reason in principle why the duty judge should not grant permission to apply for judicial review.

The duty judge will be aware that he lacks the depth of information that he normally has when considering an application for permission to apply for judicial review. As a result, he will want to know why the application cannot wait until the next day in which the court sits, and why it could not have been brought on the last date in which the court sat. For example, in a case where the urgency results from the claimant being in custody, it may be unlikely that the court will be satisfied that this is a good reason for the matter to be considered out of hours because it is unlikely that an inmate will be released until the start of the next working day, as the prison will require official notification from the court of any order releasing the claimant; and so the matter can be considered on the following day.

The text later comments on the duty of disclosure that arises when a person applies for judicial review.[3] When an application is made to the duty judge, it is particularly important to ensure that he is made aware of all material facts and law. The duty judge may well not be as experienced in judicial review matters as the judges who normally sit in the Administrative Court because the duty judge may be any High Court judge of the Queen's Bench division. A judge may not have any of the relevant papers in front of him and may know nothing at all about the case. The duty judge is also unlikely to be assisted by representations on behalf of the defendant (although there have been times when defendants have also made telephone representations). Accordingly, in telephone hearings, the duty to make proper disclosure requires more than merely including relevant documents in the court bundle. Proper disclosure for this purpose means specifically identifying all relevant documents for the judge, taking the judge to the particular passages in the documents which are material and taking appropriate steps to ensure that the judge correctly appreciates the significance of what he is being asked to read. Submissions should include reference to arguments likely to be made by the defendant in any substantive hearing. A failure to make proper disclosure is likely to be regarded as a serious matter by the Administrative Court.[4]

The fact that a defendant is not normally heard by a duty judge has prompted some defendants to write to the Administrative Court office when they anticipate an application to the duty judge. The letter will

---

3    See **5.3**.
4    *R (Lawer) v Restormel Borough Council* [2007] EWHC 2299 (Admin), at [69].

identify the reasons why relief should not be granted and will include a request that it be put before the duty judge. This tactic has been adopted by the UK Border Agency when it is seeking to remove a large number of people by charter flight.

Where an application is made to the duty judge out of hours, thr judge may require the claimant to lodge the papers required to commence an application with the Administrative Court at the start of business on the next working day. As a result, it is important that the claimant's solicitor works on those papers while counsel is making the application. It is also important that the claimant's solicitor keeps in contact with counsel, as the solicitor is likely to be required to inform parties affected of the terms of any orders for interim relief. It is also essential that a full note is kept of the documents placed before the judge and the submissions made and that a copy of this note is made available to the defendant whether requested or not.[5]

Although applications to a duty judge are often made by counsel, there is no reason in principle why an application cannot be made by a solicitor. As the application is not being made in open court, solicitors have sufficient rights of audience.

### 5.1.2   Urgent applications for judicial review during court hours

During court hours, it is necessary to follow the practice statement on urgent applications to the Administrative Court.[6] This requires a claimant to serve the claim form and grounds on the defendant and any interested parties as well as the application for urgent consideration.[7]

The application for urgent consideration must include details of the timescale for consideration of the case and the reason why the case is urgent.[8] Great care must be taken when selecting the timescale as the Administrative Court has warned that wasted costs orders will be made where this procedure is abused.[9]

Once the urgent consideration application is served on the other parties and then lodged with the Administrative Court, it is good practice to call an Administrative Court lawyer to alert him to the urgency of the matter. (They can be contacted on 020 7947 6000.) This will help to ensure that the urgent application is not overlooked.

---

[5]   *Interoute Telecommunications (UK) Ltd v Fashion Gossip Ltd, The Times*, November 10, 1999.

[6]   *Practice Statement (Administrative Court: Listing and Urgent Cases)* [2002] 1 WLR 810. See Part IV.

[7]   Ibid.

[8]   See Form N463, reproduced as Precedent 5 in Part III.

[9]   See Practice Statement in Part IV.

If the application for urgent consideration is refused in whole or interim relief is refused, there is a right to renew it orally to the High Court. This procedure should be used instead of appealing.[10] If necessary, the application can be made by telephone to the duty judge.[11]

Although this urgent consideration procedure is often used where there is a need for almost immediate interim relief, it can be used in other circumstances.

First, there are cases where there is no extreme urgency but where the normal procedure will be too slow. For example, there may be a challenge to an interim decision of an inferior court or tribunal and a stay is required of the proceedings in those courts. In those circumstances, an urgent consideration application may be necessary to ensure that the application for a stay is considered before the next hearing. Obviously, the urgent consideration form should not require the judge to consider the claim within hours; it is merely necessary for the form to ensure that the stay is considered before the next hearing.

Further, there are cases where the claim is not urgent but some ancillary order is sought as a matter of urgency. For example, an order may need to be sought restricting the reporting of the claim.[12] In those circumstances, the limited nature of the urgent consideration sought should be made clear on the urgent consideration form.

## 5.2 DOCUMENTS TO BE LODGED WITH THE ADMINISTRATIVE COURT

It is crucial that applications for judicial review are properly lodged with the Administrative Court. A failure to comply with the procedural requirements may result in the papers being returned. That return may result in delay, with consequent problems for the claimant. In particular, it might result in an application being brought outside the 3-month time-limit if the defective papers were lodged only shortly before the expiry of the 3-month time-limit.[13]

Except in urgent cases, judicial review applications are commenced by lodging a claim form and other documents in the Administrative Court.

---

[10]   *R (MD (Afghanistan) v Secretary of State for the Home Department* [2012] EWCA Civ 194, at [21].
[11]   Ibid, and see **5.1.1**
[12]   See **3.5.1**.
[13]   See **3.1** for a consideration of delay. It is important to note that the Notes for Guidance produced by the Administrative Court expressly state that, although incomplete bundles can be accepted in cases of urgency, the Court will not regard a matter as being urgent merely because a time-limit is expiring.

## 5.2.1   Claim form

Practice Direction 54A, para 5.6 provides:

'The claim form must include or be accompanied by –
(1)   a detailed statement of the claimant's grounds for bringing the claim for judicial review;
(2)   a statement of the facts relied on;
(3)   any application to extend the time limit for filing the claim form;
(4)   any application for directions.'

A precedent for the claim form and the accompanying grounds are set out in Part III.[14] It should be clear from the precedent that it is usual to attach a detailed statement of the facts and grounds to the claim form. Although there is no one correct method of drafting this statement of facts and grounds, it appears that the key principle to be followed when drafting is to ensure that the statement is sufficiently clear that the judge will fully understand the claim without referring to any other material.

If there has been delay, an application to extend time can be included in the grounds and claim form.

A claimant may consider seeking to include in the claim form a direction restricting reporting,[15] a direction dispensing with the need for a litigation friend[16] or an order making provision for interim relief.[17]

The claim form must identify any interested party. CPR, r 54.1(2)(f) provides: '"interested party" means any person (other than the claimant and defendant) who is directly affected by the claim'. There is very little case-law on the meaning of the phrase 'all persons directly affected', although it is clear that a person will only be directly affected if they will be affected without the intervention of another agency.[18] Thus, for example, in a criminal context, any prosecuting authority must clearly be served as well as any defendant court. In addition, in an education context, an excluded child will be an interested party in a judicial review brought by a victim of the excluded child who seeks to challenge a decision to reinstate that child.

The role of an interested party is limited to making submissions in relation to the main claim but only to the extent that he or she is not merely affected by it but is 'directly affected' by it. This means that any

---

[14]   See Precedents 3, 4 and 18.
[15]   See **3.5**.
[16]   See **4.3**.
[17]   See Chapter 7.
[18]   *R v Rent Officer Service ex p Muldoon* [1996] 1 WLR 1103. In this case, the Department of Social Security was not directly affected by a judicial review of a local authority's housing benefit payments, even though it was responsible for meeting a significant proportion of the costs of those benefit payments.

claim by an interested party must arise out of the relief sought by the claimant at the outset of a substantive hearing. The Court does not have jurisdiction to consider a discrete claim for relief by an interested party, unless permission is separately sought. Where an interested party seeks to advance a different claim to a claimant in a judicial review claim, the divergence of relief sought is likely to mean that the interested party is not directly affected by the claimant's claim.[19]

### 5.2.2  Other documents to be lodged

Practice Direction 54A, para 5.7 provides that the claim form needs to be accompanied by the following documentation:

> '(1)  any written evidence in support of the claim or application to extend time;
> (2)  a copy of any order that the claimant seeks to have quashed;
> (3)  where the claim for judicial review relates to a decision of a court or tribunal, an approved copy of the reasons for reaching that decision;
> (4)  copies of any documents on which the claimant proposes to rely;
> (5)  copies of any relevant statutory material; and
> (6)  a list of essential documents for advance reading by the court (with page references to the passages relied on).'

Until the claim form was amended to include a statement of truth, it was necessary for claimants to submit an affidavit or witness statement containing evidence regarding the facts relied on and also exhibiting documentation. In most cases this is now unnecessary as the claim form requires someone to confirm the truth of the facts set out in the grounds, which means that there will often be no additional need for evidence. In addition, the claim form and Practice Direction 54A make it clear that relevant documents can be supplied to the Administrative Court without being exhibited to a witness statement.

Occasionally, a witness statement or affidavit will be necessary. In general, this is where the claimant or his solicitor wishes to give evidence in greater detail than can normally be set out in the grounds. For example, in a prison case, it may be necessary to put forward in evidence full details of the regime that a prisoner is subjected to if that is relevant to his case. However, it will not necessarily be relevant to plead the full details of the regime in the grounds. Similarly, where there is a complex history that explains the delay in commencing the claim, it may be worth setting out the full history in a witness statement.

The CPR make it clear that evidence at a hearing other than the trial should normally be given by witness statement, but a claimant may swear an affidavit.[20] In practice, we can envisage no circumstances in which it is

---

[19]  *R (McVey) v Secretary of State for Health* [2010] EWHC 437 (Admin).
[20]  Practice Direction 32, paras 1.2–1.4.

necessary to swear an affidavit rather than sign a witness statement. This is important as, in some circumstances, it will be considerably easier to obtain a witness statement. For example, clearly it will be considerably easier to have a witness statement signed where the claimant is in custody. A precedent for a witness statement is set out in Part III.[21]

Relevant documents can be exhibited to a witness statement. Where a bundle of correspondence is exhibited to a witness statement, this should be a separate exhibit and the front sheet should make it clear that a bundle of correspondence is being exhibited.[22] The correspondence should be included in chronological order, with the earliest at the top.[23]

Where an exhibit contains more than one document, it should not be stapled but should be secured in a manner that does not hinder reading.[24] The documents should be paginated consecutively at bottom centre of the page.[25] Where an original document is illegible (because, for example, it is handwritten notes), a typed copy should follow in the bundle and be paginated with the same page number followed by an 'a' (ie an illegible p 5 should be followed by a typed version at p 5a).[26]

If no witness statement is submitted but documents are submitted in support of the claim, the guidance in the two paragraphs above should be followed when bundles of documents are prepared.

Claimants should be selective about the documents that they submit. They have a duty of disclosure[27] and hence must supply material documents. However, there is no reason to supply irrelevant documents just because they were involved at some stage in the decision-making process challenged.[28]

A bundle of statutory material containing complete copies of all the statutory provisions that are relevant should also be supplied to the Administrative Court. The statutory provisions can be photocopied from any reputable textbook or obtained from one of the online services that supply updated versions of statutory provisions. In practice, it assists the Administrative Court if this bundle includes copies of any reports or transcripts of judgments relied on that have not been published in law reports that are readily available.[29]

---

21   See Precedent 7.
22   Practice Direction 32, para 12.2.
23   Ibid, para 12.1.
24   Ibid, para 15.1(1).
25   Ibid, para 15.1(2).
26   Ibid, para 15.2.
27   See **5.3**.
28   Mr Justice Collins 'A View From The Bench: The New Procedures in the Administrative Court' [2002] JR 1.
29   Mr Justice Collins op cit. If unreported authorities are cited, it is important to be aware of Practice Direction on Citation of Authorities (see Part IV). This limits the use of

A list of the pages of essential reading for the judge should also be provided with the bundles. This should identify only the key documents: one of the easiest ways of annoying a judge is to include all documents in the list of essential reading. The list may be provided as a separate document or by annotating the index to the bundle. It should be made clear if only part of a document is essential reading; if only part of the page is essential reading, this should be shown by sidelines or in some other way, but not by highlighting.[30]

A copy of any public funding certificate should be lodged with the Administrative Court. This is necessary as the Court will normally refuse to make an order for the assessment of the claimant's costs if a certificate is not supplied.[31] The public funding certificate is one document that need not be supplied to the other parties. Instead, a notice of issue of the funding certificate should be served.[32]

Two copies of all the documents must be submitted to the court in indexed and paginated bundles.[33] In practice, many solicitors submit the originals in one bundle and two copy bundles. The Administrative Court will normally accept this, although it is not required. If the original documents are submitted in a bundle, the claimant must make it clear to the Court which bundle contains the original documents.

Additional copies of the bundle can be submitted to the Administrative Court if required. Additional copies will be returned by the Court, sealed. If only two copies are submitted then only one copy will be returned sealed. There is, however, no need to have additional copies of the bundle sealed.

A fee must be paid before the papers in support of the application can be lodged with the Administrative Court. The fee is at present £60, but this should be checked against an up-to-date list of court fees. Alternatively, the Administrative Court can be contacted on 020 7947 6000 to check the court fees; that number should also be used for any other general enquiries regarding lodging claims for judicial review.

The papers must be lodged at one of High Court's district registries. Claims may be issued at the District Registry of the High Court at

---

certain unreported authorities. When relying on transcripts, practitioners should be aware of *Practice Statement (Supreme Court: Judgments)* [1998] 1 WLR 825, *Practice Statement (Supreme Court: Judgments) (No 2)* [1999] 1 WLR 1, and *A City Council v T and others (W intervening)* [2011] 1 WLR 819, which limit the use of transcripts to circumstances in which there is no official report.

[30] Notes for Guidance produced by the Administrative Court, available at http://www. justice.gov.uk/downloads/guidance/courts-and-tribunals/courts/administrative-court/ judicial-review.pdf .

[31] See **10.11** for an explanation of the importance of obtaining an order for assessment.

[32] See Precedent 8 in Part III.

[33] Practice Direction 54A, para 5.9.

Birmingham, Cardiff, Leeds or Manchester as well as at the Royal Courts of Justice in London. The general expectation is that proceedings will be issued and determined in the region with which the claimant has the closest connection, subject to the following considerations as applicable:

(a)   any reason expressed by any party for preferring a particular venue;

(b)   the region in which the defendant, or any relevant office or department of the defendant, is based;

(c)   the region in which the claimant's legal representatives are based;

(d)   the ease and cost of travel to a hearing;

(e)   the availability and suitability of alternative means of attending a hearing (for example, by videolink);

(f)   the extent and nature of media interest in the proceedings in any particular locality;

(g)   the time within which it is appropriate for the proceedings to be determined;

(h)   whether it is desirable to administer or determine the claim in another region in the light of the volume of claims issued at, and the capacity, resources and workload of, the court at which it is issued;

(i)   whether the claim raises issues sufficiently similar to those in another outstanding claim to make it desirable that it should be determined together with, or immediately following, that other claim; and

(j)   whether the claim raises devolution issues and for that reason whether it should more appropriately be determined in London or Cardiff.[34]

The claimant's decision as to where to lodge the claim does not decide where the claim will be heard. The court may on an application by a party or of its own initiative direct that the claim be determined in a region other than that of the venue in which the claim is currently assigned.[35]

Papers can be lodged in person or via the Document Exchange or postal system. If a firm is outside London and the matter is urgent, an agent can be used to lodge the papers.

---

[34]   Practice Direction 54D, para 5.2 and Notes for Guidance produced by the Administrative Court, at para 4.3.
[35]   Practice Direction 54D, para 5.3.

The Administrative Court may not accept applications that fail to comply with requirements of Practice Directions and procedure rules, even where an undertaking is offered to correct errors, except in exceptional circumstances such as urgency. The Administrative Court has stated that an application will not be regarded as exceptional except where a decision is required from the Administrative Court within 14 days of lodging the application.[36] As a consequence, the fact that time for bringing the claim is about to expire will not mean the claim is urgent or exceptional.

### 5.2.3   Service on the defendant and any interested parties

As noted above, the Administrative Court will return one copy of the bundle (unless additional copies are served on the Court). A copy of the claim form should then be served on the defendant and (unless the Court orders otherwise) any interested party within 7 days.[37] In practice, the full bundle is always served rather than just the claim form; and the authors have had experience of a judge criticising a claimant who failed to do this. A certificate of service must then be lodged within 7 days of serving the documents. The certificate of service should be in form N215.

### 5.2.4   Applications for Permission in Immigration and Asylum Cases Challenging the Removal of an Individual from the United Kingdom

Where a person who has been served with a copy of directions for his removal from the United Kingdom by the UK Border Agency makes an application for permission to apply for judicial review before his removal takes effect, he is subject to further requirements in addition to those set out above.

Such a person must file a claim form and a copy at Court.[38] The claim form must indicate on its face that Part II of the Practice Direction to CPR 54 applies;[39] and must be accompanied by:

(a)   a copy of the removal directions and the decision to which the application relates; and

(b)   any document served with the removal directions including any document which contains the UK Border Agency's factual summary of the case;[40] and

---

[36]   Ibid, para7.9.
[37]   CPR, r 54.7.
[38]   PD 54A, para 18.2(1).
[39]   Ibid, para 18.2(1)(a).
[40]   Ibid, para 18.2(1)(b).

(c) the detailed statement of the claimant's grounds for bringing the claim for judicial review.[41]

If the claimant is unable to provide these documents, the claim form must contain or be accompanied by a statement of the reasons why.[42]

Upon the issue of the claim, the claimant must send copies of the issued claim form and accompanying documents immediately to the Treasury Solicitor.[43]

The Administrative Court will then refer the claim to a Judge for consideration as soon as practicable.[44] It will notify the parties that it has done so. If the Court considers that the application is clearly without merit, it will include an indication to that effect in the order refusing permission.[45]

## 5.3 DUTY OF DISCLOSURE APPLYING TO CLAIMANTS

### 5.3.1 Application of the duty when papers are lodged

The grounds in support of the claim and any evidence filed in support must comply with the duty of disclosure imposed on claimants. The Administrative Court expects claimants to disclose all material facts in the notice of application and the written evidence. A fact is material if it 'might affect the judge's decision whether to grant relief or what relief to grant'.[46] It is for the Court and not for a claimant to decide whether a fact is material.[47] The duty of disclosure relates to facts[48] and law.[49] Disclosure

---

[41] Ibid, para 18.2(1)(c).

[42] Ibid, para 18.2(1)(d).

[43] Ibid, para 18.2(2). CPR, r 54.7 also requires the defendant to be served with the claim form within 7 days of the date of issue. CPR, r 6.10 provides that service on a Government Department must be effected on the solicitor acting for that Department, which in the case of the UK Border Agency is the Treasury Solicitor.

[44] PD 54A, para 18.3.

[45] Ibid, para 18.4.

[46] *Fitzgerald v Williams* [1996] QB 657, per Sir Thomas Bingham MR, at 667H.

[47] *Brink's Mat Ltd v Elcombe* [1988] 1 WLR 1350, at 1356H, applied in the context of judicial review in *R v Jockey Club Licensing Committee ex p Wright* [1991] COD 306.

[48] See, for example, *R v Secretary of State for the Home Department ex p Begum* [1995] COD 176, in which a wasted costs order was made against the claimant's legal advisers for failing to put a letter from the defendant before the court despite a request to do so.

[49] See, for example, *R v Secretary of State for the Home Department ex p Li Bin Shi* [1995] COD 135, in which permission was set aside as a result of a failure to disclose a number of relevant legal authorities. See also para 708(c) of the Bar Code of Conduct, which provides that a barrister conducting proceedings at court: 'must ensure that the Court is informed of all relevant decisions and legislative provisions of which he is aware whether the effect is favourable or unfavourable towards the contention for which he argues'.

is particularly relevant when there has been delay[50] or where there is an alternative remedy available to the claimant.[51]

The duty of disclosure was developed in part as a consequence of the difficulties that the High Court would experience when it was required to consider an application without the defendant being represented. Amendments to the judicial review procedure mean that a judge is now likely to have access to submissions for a defendant when he rules on any aspect of the case. However, that does not appear to have changed the attitude of the Administrative Court to disclosure.[52] This is consistent with the fact that, before the judicial review procedure was amended, the duty of disclosure was never limited to circumstances in which a defendant did not make representations.[53]

The duty is not limited to matters known to the claimant and his advisers. It has been held that claimants are under a duty to carry out proper enquiries, so they are obliged to disclose facts that could have been discovered if they had carried out proper enquiries.[54] This is consistent with a judgment of Sir Thomas Bingham MR, who held that it is no answer to say that any failure to disclose material facts was made in good faith.[55] However, good faith is a relevant factor for the Administrative Court to consider when it determines what action to take as a result of a failure to make full disclosure.[56] The Court has discretion whether to take any action as a result of non-disclosure;[57] in particular, whether to refuse the relief sought.[58] Alternatively, the Court has discretion to take account of a failure to make disclosure when it makes orders for costs;[59] in

---

[50] See **3.1** for a consideration of delay.
[51] See **3.3** for a consideration of alternative remedies.
[52] See, for example, *R (Tshikangu) v Newham London Borough Council* [2001] EWHC 92 (Admin), (2001) *The Times*, April 27, and *R (Done Brothers (Cash Betting) Limited) v The Crown Court at Cardiff* [2003] EWHC 3516 (Admin).
[53] See, for example, *R v Secretary of State for the Home Department ex p Gashi* [1999] Imm AR 415 in which the defendant was criticised for failure to disclose the true position.
[54] *Brink's Mat Ltd v Elcombe* [1988] 1 WLR 1350, at 1356H, applied in the context of judicial review in *R v Jockey Club Licensing Committee ex p Wright* [1991] COD 306. See also, *R (Konodyba) v The Royal Borough of Kensington and Chelsea* [2011] EWHC 2653 (Admin), at [27].
[55] *Fitzgerald v Williams* [1996] QB 657, at 668A.
[56] *Brink's Mat Ltd v Elcombe* [1988] 1 WLR 1350, at 1357D, applied in the context of judicial review in *R v Jockey Club Licensing Committee ex p Wright* [1991] COD 306.
[57] In *Fitzgerald v Williams* [1996] QB 657, at 668B, Sir Thomas Bingham MR emphasised that non-disclosure will not always result in permission being set aside.
[58] See, for example, *R v Jockey Club Licensing Committee ex p Wright* [1991] COD 306, for an example of a case where permission was set aside as a result of material non-disclosure. Note, however, that there are now limitations on the circumstances in which it is possible to apply to set aside a grant of permission. See **5.10.3**.
[59] The discretion with respect to costs is not limited to wasted costs being ordered against lawyers acting for claimants. In *R v Liverpool City Council ex p Filla* [1996] COD 24, claimants were refused an order for inter-partes costs as a result of material non-disclosure. See also CPR, r 44.3(4)(a), which provides that when considering costs orders, the Administrative Court will take account of the conduct of the parties.

exercising that discretion, the Court will seek to ensure that a claimant is deprived of any advantage that may have been gained through a failure to make full disclosure.[60]

Although an adverse matter must be disclosed, it does not necessarily need to be highlighted. It is enough that it is not hidden.[61] Tactically, however, it may be better to highlight the problem in the grounds and then explain the claimant's answer to the problem. If the claimant's advisers do not do that, they run the risk that the defendant will identify the problem and plead it in his acknowledgement of service or that the judge will identify the problem and dismiss the application as a result.

### 5.3.2   Continuing duty of disclosure

Although the duty of disclosure is most relevant when pleadings are drafted at the start of the claim, the duty does not cease once papers have been lodged. Claimants have a duty to keep the Administrative Court and the defendants informed of relevant developments.[62] Hence, if there are developments meaning that a claimant no longer needs to seek judicial review, the Administrative Court should be informed of that fact, even if the claimant wishes to continue pursuing the claim as a test claim.[63]

In practical terms, it is not uncommon for the claimant and defendant to correspond regarding a judicial review claim after the claim has commenced. This correspondence can significantly change the nature of the claim; the claim may become academic; or the grounds may change. If this sort of correspondence is occurring, the Administrative Court should be informed of this development as soon as possible, even if the claimant is not in a position to update his grounds to address the developments because the correspondence is continuing. In these circumstances, the Administrative Court will usually wait to see how matters develop before taking further steps.

### 5.4   ACKNOWLEDGEMENT OF SERVICE

Any party served with the claim form must file an acknowledgement of service on a form N462 if wishing to participate in the proceedings.[64] The acknowledgement of service must be filed on the Court within 21 days of

---

[60]   *Brink's Mat Ltd v Elcombe* [1988] 1 WLR 1350, at 1357C, applied in the context of judicial review in *R v Jockey Club Licensing Committee ex p Wright* [1991] COD 306.

[61]   *R v Warwickshire County Council ex p Collymore* [1995] ELR 217, at 229F, relying on the fact that adverse material was expressly referred to in the grounds of application.

[62]   *R (Tshikangu) v Newham London Borough Council* [2001] EWHC 92 (Admin), [2001] NPC 33.

[63]   *R (Tshikangu) v Newham London Borough Council* (2001) *The Times*, April 27 and *R (Done Brothers (Cash Betting) Limited) v The Crown Court at Cardiff* [2003] EWHC 3516 (Admin).

[64]   CPR, r 54.8(1). See Precedent 9 in Part III.

service of the claim form.[65] It must then be served as soon as practicable and, in any event, in not more than 7 days on all parties named in the claim form unless the Administrative Court has ordered that an interested party need not be served.[66]

The CPR again provide that the time-limits for filing the acknowledgement of service may not be extended by agreement.[67] However, in practice, if all the parties agree upon an extension of time, the Administrative Court will normally agree to it. From a defendant's point of view, the critical issue is to seek an order extending time before it expires. Otherwise, the defendant risks a judge granting permission before the acknowledgement of service has been submitted.

The defendant (and any interested party) is not obliged to file an acknowledgement of service. However, such failure will prevent a defendant appearing at a permission hearing unless the permission of the Administrative Court is obtained.[68] A defendant who fails to file an acknowledgement of service will still be able to attend the substantive hearing if he serves detailed grounds and any written evidence.[69] Failure to serve an acknowledgement of service may also have costs implications.[70] In practical terms, it is difficult to see why a defendant would decide not to serve an acknowledgement of service. This is particularly true as the defendant will normally be able to obtain the costs of drafting the acknowledgement of service if they successfully defend the claim.[71]

The first matter that the acknowledgement of service requires a defendant (or interested party) to consider is whether he intends to oppose the claim for judicial review. In general, it will be obvious whether a defendant should oppose the claim. However, special considerations arise where the defendant is a court or tribunal.

Where the defendant is a court or tribunal, it will often take a neutral position. For example, it has been held that where there is a challenge to a decision of a magistrates' court, the magistrates should not be represented by counsel unless there is some special factor such as an allegation of misconduct on the part of the magistrates.[72] However, the Administrative Court will wish to have the views of the defendant when it determines the

---

[65]　Ibid, r 54.8(2).
[66]　Ibid, r 54.8(2).
[67]　Ibid, r 54.8(3).
[68]　Ibid, r 54.9(1)(a).
[69]　Ibid, r 54.9(1)(b).
[70]　Ibid, r 54.9(2).
[71]　See **9.3**.
[72]　*R v Camborne Justices ex p Pearce* [1954] 2 All ER 850, at 856A. But note the remarks of Lord Justice Simon Brown asking Treasury Solicitors to instruct counsel to review the merits of a large number of judicial reviews of warrants of commitment in the light of

application,[73] particularly where a claim raises issues of general principle as to jurisdiction and procedure[74] or the court or tribunal exercises a highly specialist jurisdiction.[75] As a result, in most cases the defendant should serve an acknowledgement of service that at least comments on the factual background to the judicial review claim. In particular, it should highlight any factual matters in the claimant's claim that are not agreed, or any other matters that the Court will find relevant. This is particularly true where there is an allegation of bias or other misconduct on behalf of a judicial figure.[76]

If a defendant is a court that is taking a neutral position, there will normally be an interested party who is the claimant's opponent in litigation before the defendant court. It will be the interested party who will take on the role of opposing the claim for judicial review if the claim is to be opposed. As a consequence, it is particularly important that an interested party considers his position carefully in a judicial review challenge to a decision of a court.

The acknowledgement of service requires a defendant to identify any person or body whom he believes should be served as an interested party.[77] The meaning of interested party is considered above.[78]

The acknowledgement of service also requires a defendant or interested party to provide summary grounds if contesting the claim; these may include a factual and/or legal response. Although described as summary grounds, in practice they can be relatively detailed. Indeed, it is in the interests of a defendant to ensure that they are detailed, as this may persuade a judge to refuse permission to apply for judicial review. The level of the detail will depend on the extent of the dispute between the

---

his judgment in *R v Oldham Justices ex p Cawley* [1996] 1 All ER 464, at 481G, which suggests that the court increasingly finds that it is assisted by defendants being represented.

[73] For example, in *R v Gloucester Crown Court ex p Chester* [1998] COD 365 it was held that, even where a claimant erred by bringing judicial review proceedings instead of an appeal by case stated, the defendant should at least write a letter stating whether he opposed the application.

[74] *S (A Minor) v Special Educational Needs Tribunal* [1995] 1 WLR 1627, at 1632A–1632B.

[75] See the cases summarised in *R (Davies) v Birmingham Deputy Coroner* [2004] 1 WLR 2739, at 2747D–2747F.

[76] *R v Southwark Crown Court ex p Collman* (1998) *Archbold News*, August. See also *R (Mersey Care NHS Trust) v Mental Health Review Tribunal* [2003] EWHC 1182 (Admin), where Sullivan J, as he then was, implicitly recognised that it was legitimate for the Mental Health Review Tribunal to defend a claim as a consequence of the nature of the claim.

[77] See Precedent 9 in Part III.

[78] See **5.2.1**.

parties and the complexity of the issues. There is no one correct style of drafting the summary grounds. However, a precedent is included in Part III.[79]

The acknowledgement of service permits a defendant or interested party to identify orders that may be sought, the most obvious being orders for costs.[80] It is normal for defendants to seek the costs of completing an Acknowledgment of Service. The discretion that now exists to conduct proceedings out of London may mean that transfer to another court centre may be sought.[81] Urgent consideration of the matter may also be sought, if there is some particularly good reason why the case must be heard by a particular date.

Relevant documents should be supplied with the acknowledgement of service.[82] Guidance on the manner in which these documents should be presented is dealt with above.[83]

## 5.5   DUTY OF DISCLOSURE APPLYING TO DEFENDANTS

When drafting an acknowledgement of service on behalf of a defendant, it is important to be aware that there is a 'very high duty' on defendants to assist the Court with a full and accurate explanation of all the facts relevant to the issue the Court must decide.[84] For example, Lord Woolf MR, as he then was, held that: 'it is the obligation of the respondent public body in its evidence to make frank disclosure to the court of the decision-making process'.[85] That is because the defendant to a judicial review is expected to assist the court and also because citizens seeking to investigate or challenge governmental decision-making start off at a serious disadvantage in that frequently they are left to speculate as to how a decision was reached.[86] Accordingly, Sir John Donaldson has held that the relationship between the courts and defendants should be one of 'partnership'.[87] The duty of disclosure applies not only to all relevant facts and documents. As a consequence, there is no requirement to disclose material merely because it relates in some way to the decision challenged. Where a public authority relies on a document as significant

---

[79]   See Precedents 9 and 10.
[80]   See Chapter 10 for a consideration of costs.
[81]   See **5.2.2**.
[82]   See **5.5** regarding the duty of disclosure, which contains details of the documents that should be served.
[83]   See **5.2.2**.
[84]   *R (Quark Fishing Limited) v Secretary of State for Foreign & Commonwealth Affairs* [2002] EWCA Civ 1409, at [50].
[85]   *R v Secretary of State for the Home Department ex p Fayed* [1997] 1 All ER 228, at 239D.
[86]   *Re Brenda Downes* [2006] NIQB 77, at [35].
[87]   *R v Lancashire County Council ex p Huddleston* [1986] 2 All ER 941, at 945C.

to its decision, it is ordinarily good practice to exhibit it as the primary evidence. Any summary, however conscientiously and skilfully made, may distort.[88]

It is not acceptable to fail to disclose evidence merely because it may give rise to other grounds for judicial review. Indeed, disclosure by a defendant often gives rise to additional grounds of challenge.

Increasingly defendants may seek to avoid disclosure on the grounds of national security or other public interest. The Supreme Court has held that a closed material procedure (such as that adopted by the High Court in 'control order' proceedings) cannot be read across to contexts in which there is no statutory provision for such an approach, such as civil actions.[89] Litigation is pending on the extent to which closed proceedings may be imposed in judicial review claims.[90] Pending this litigation, it seems that it is for the defendant (whether under CPR, r 31.19 or by the issue of a public interest immunity certificate) to make its case for non-disclosure to the court

## 5.6 CLAIMANT'S RESPONSE TO ACKNOWLEDGEMENT OF SERVICE

There is nothing in the CPR that provides for a claimant to respond to an acknowledgement of service. In practice, however, there appears to be nothing to prevent a claimant filing relevant observations. Such observations should not merely repeat the original grounds; they should focus on any fresh points raised by the defendant or interested party and the claimant's response to those observations.

The claimant's response should be filed quickly as there will be nothing to prevent the Administrative Court ruling on the permission application once the acknowledgement of service has been received. It may be worth contacting the Court and asking it to delay consideration of the permission application if a claimant intends to file a response.

## 5.7 AMENDMENT OF THE GROUNDS AND SERVICE OF ADDITIONAL EVIDENCE

Under old procedure rules, permission was required to amend grounds lodged with the Administrative Court before permission had been granted to apply for judicial review.[91] There is now no provision regarding amendment before the grant of permission. However, in practice it

---

[88]  *Tweed v Parades Commission for Northern Ireland* [2007] 1 AC 650, at 655G.
[89]  *Al-Rawi v Security Service* [2011] 3 WLR 388.
[90]  See *R (AHK and others) v Secretary of State for the Home Department* (CO/1076/2008, CO/8598/2008, CO/4391/2007, CO/8559/2010).
[91]  RSC Ord 53, r 3(6).

appears to be assumed that permission is required to amend the claim. In one sense it might be argued that it is sensible that permission is required, to prevent abuse should grounds be substantially amended to include a challenge that would be out of time if commenced afresh. However, such abuse could be addressed by judges exercising their discretion to refuse permission.

Whether or not permission is formally required, the practice of the Administrative Court appears to be that, generally, it is willing to allow amendments of the grounds before the permission stage. However, one circumstance where there may be a reluctance to permit amendment is where the new grounds raise a completely new issue and a claim for judicial review seeking to raise that issue alone would be out of time. A copy of the proposed amended grounds should be supplied to the court (and all the parties) as soon as possible. This should, if possible, be before the hearing of the application for permission.

The Administrative Court also has a discretion to allow the amendment of grounds and the submission of additional evidence on behalf of the claimant after the granting of permission to apply for judicial review.[92] However, all parties must be given notice and served with copies of the proposed amendments or additional written evidence. In particular, any amendments to the grounds must be served at least 7 clear days before a hearing date (or warned list date).[93]

In practice, the Administrative Court is likely to be willing to allow amendment of grounds and service of evidence by both parties, provided that there is no prejudice caused by late service. The Court will be aware that grounds often change as a result of evidence served by the defendant after the grant of permission.[94] The Court will also wish to be satisfied that any additional grounds meet the test for the grant of permission.

## 5.8 DETERMINING WHETHER PERMISSION TO APPLY FOR JUDICIAL REVIEW SHOULD BE GRANTED

Judicial review is a two-stage process, as no application for judicial review may be brought without the permission of the Administrative Court.[95] As a result, the Administrative Court will first determine whether permission should be granted. Until the introduction of the CPR 1998, applying for permission was known as applying for leave. When reading old judgments, it is important to be aware of this.

---

[92] CPR, rr 54.15 and 54.16.
[93] Practice Direction 54A, para 11.1.
[94] For example, in *R v Barnsley Metropolitan Borough Council ex p Hook* [1976] 1 WLR 1052, at 1058C, Lord Denning noted that grounds 'should not be treated as rigidly as a pleading in an ordinary civil action'.
[95] CPR, r 54.4.

In determining whether to grant permission, the court takes account of the purpose of the requirement that claimants obtain permission. Lord Diplock has held that the permission stage is intended to:[96]

> '[P]revent the time of the court being wasted by busybodies with misguided or trivial complaints of administrative error, and to remove the uncertainty in which public officers and authorities might be left as to whether they could safely proceed with administrative action while proceedings for judicial review of it were actually pending even though misconceived.'

Thus, the Court of Appeal has held that the judge considering an application for permission should consider whether the case is suitable for full investigation at a hearing of which all parties have been given notice.[97] This approach has led the courts to hold on numerous occasions that permission should not be granted if the application for judicial review is unarguable.[98]

The Administrative Court is not restricted to considering whether a case is arguable when it decides whether to grant permission. It will also consider delay[99] and the availability of an alternative remedy, and may refuse permission as a consequence of these matters.[100]

Lord Diplock stated that the permission stage should involve only a 'quick perusal of the material then available'.[101] However, that statement does not accurately reflect the current practice of the Administrative Court.[102] Many applications for permission involve a far more detailed consideration of the case than a quick perusal and judges often seem to want to be satisfied that there is clear merit. There have even been cases where the court has received a considerable volume of material and heard extensive argument from both the claimant and the defendant.[103]

---

[96]   *R v Inland Revenue Commissioners ex p National Federation of Self-Employed and Small Businesses Ltd* [1982] AC 617, at 643A.

[97]   *R v Secretary of State for the Home Department ex p Begum* [1990] COD 107. Obviously, in practice, the defendant will now often attend the oral hearing of a judicial review claim. However, the approach will not change if that happens. The Administrative Court will be aware when considering the permission application that it has not heard full argument. As a consequence, one fact that it will take account of is whether the application for permission relates to a matter that ought to be resolved after full argument.

[98]   See, for example, *R v Secretary of State for the Home Department ex p Begum* [1990] COD 107, in which permission was refused as the case was unarguable; *R v Legal Aid Board ex p Hughes* (1993) 5 Admin LR 623, at 628D, in which Lord Donaldson MR held that permission should be granted if an application is prima facie arguable.

[99]   See **3.1**.

[100]   See **3.3**.

[101]   *R v Inland Revenue Commissioners ex p National Federation of Self-Employed and Small Businesses* Ltd [1982] AC 617, at 644A.

[102]   In *R v Legal Aid Board ex p Hughes* (1993) 5 Admin LR 623, Lord Donaldson MR held that things had moved on from Lord Diplock's dictum.

[103]   See, for example, *Mass Energy Ltd v Birmingham City Council* [1994] Env LR 298.

In a case in which there has been a considerable volume of material presented to the Administrative Court and the Court has heard extensive argument, it is possible that the Court will apply a higher threshold than merely considering whether the claim is arguable. The Court may wish to be satisfied that the judicial review claim is 'likely to succeed'.[104] Indeed, the Administrative Court can apply a flexible test to the question of permission, one that takes account of such factors as the financial consequences of the grant of permission to an innocent third party.[105]

All applications for permission are now considered first on the papers. In practice, this means that there are four possible outcomes:

— permission may be granted;

— permission may be refused;

— permission may be granted in respect of some only of the grounds;[106]

— a permission hearing may be ordered so that the judge will have the advantage of hearing oral submissions.

If the last is the case, the judge may order that the permission hearing be heard in open court after notice has been given. If the judge decides that he may be assisted by oral submissions, he can also order that the substantive hearing of the matter should follow immediately upon any grant of permission. Although this is unusual, it has the advantage that it avoids the need for two fully argued hearings.

Where a judge decides to grant permission in relation to some but not all grounds, the claimant can seek a review of the decision to refuse some grounds within 7 days.[107] However, Lord Woolf MR suggested that claimants need merely inform the other parties that they will seek to rely on the additional grounds and then seek the permission of the Administrative Court to rely on them at the substantive hearing.[108]

When the court decides to grant permission, it can also decide whether to make directions. The directions will often relate to the interim relief that should be ordered.[109] If interim relief is sought, this should be specified on the claim form and on any application for urgent consideration. Other

---

[104]  Ibid.

[105]  *R (Grierson) v The Office of Communication* [2005] EWHC 1899 (Admin), at [27].

[106]  CPR, r 54.12. The requirement in this rule that permission must be obtained before the claimant can raise arguments regarding grounds in relation to which they have been refused permission is considered later in this chapter.

[107]  CPR, r 54.12. See **5.9** for consideration of the procedure for renewing an application for permission.

[108]  *R (Hunt) v Criminal Cases Review Commission* [2001] QB 1108, at 1114C–1114D.

[109]  See Chapter 7 for details of the interim relief that is available.

directions that might be sought include case management directions, such as specific directions regarding the filing of evidence or the listing of the matter, which are intended to ensure that the issue is heard promptly. There will normally be no specific case management hearings, unlike some other forms of litigation.

## 5.9   FURTHER STEPS FOLLOWING A REFUSAL OF PERMISSION

When an application for permission to apply for judicial review is refused on the papers, the application may always be renewed orally in court.[110] In practice, in a criminal cause or matter,[111] the renewed application is usually made to a Divisional Court. In any other case, the renewed application is usually made to a single High Court judge sitting in open court. The defendant and/or any interested party will normally attend any renewed hearing.

When permission to apply for judicial review is refused, the claimant will be supplied with the written reasons of the judge who has refused permission and these should be considered carefully when deciding whether the application should be renewed. Indeed, in most publicly funded cases, there will be a limitation placed on the claimant's funding certificate, requiring the claimant to obtain an extension of the certificate before the claim is renewed. The certificate will not be extended unless the claimant can satisfy the Legal Services Commission that the merits test is met.[112] In practice, that normally requires counsel to advise on the merits of renewing.

The application for permission should be renewed within 7 days of service of the judge's reasons for refusing permission.[113] An application for permission should be made by filing a form that is supplied by the Administrative Court with the judge's reasons. The form requests a statement of the grounds for renewing. Normally it would appear that these grounds need not be particularly specific, provided that the initial grounds are specific. A precedent is included in Part III.[114] There is no fee for renewing an application for judicial review in the Administrative Court.

Permission hearings are listed for 30 minutes although the parties may provide a written estimate of the time required for the hearing and request a special fixture.[115] In practice, the guidance regarding 30 minutes provides an indication for the parties on the time that it is expected a

---

[110]   CPR, r 54.12(3).
[111]   See **3.4** for consideration of the definition of a criminal cause or matter.
[112]   See **4.2.2** for consideration of the merits test.
[113]   CPR, r 54.12(4).
[114]   See Precedent 11.
[115]   Notes for Guidance produced by the Administrative Court, para 11.4.

normal application for permission will take. If there is some good reason for believing that a claim is particularly complex and will take longer, the Administrative Court should be informed of that. The listing of the permission application is likely to take no account of the views of the parties.[116]

There is no requirement to provide a skeleton argument for the permission hearing. However, where detailed reasons have been provided refusing permission, it is good practice to provide a skeleton. This should be provided well in advance of the permission hearing so that the judge has an adequate opportunity to read it.

One matter that it is particularly important for the parties to address at any permission hearing is the issue of costs.[117] Where the Court makes an order granting permission to apply for judicial review and its order does not mention costs, it will be deemed to include an order for the claimant's costs in the case.[118]

It is now normal for the defendant or another interested party to be represented at a hearing to determine whether permission should be granted. The procedural rules governing judicial review claims therefore expressly include provisions to enable a defendant to participate in the permission process.

Although parties other than the claimant are encouraged to attend permission hearings, they are not obliged to attend unless the Administrative Court so orders.[119] If they do attend the Court will not generally grant them the costs of attending.[120] However, it may well be in the interests of a defendant to attend as it may allow them to avoid the need to defend a substantive claim for judicial review. Many claimants are in receipt of public funding and so a defendant may be unlikely to seek its costs in any event. Persuading the Court to reject the permission application may limit its costs.

When an application for permission is refused following an oral hearing, it is possible to renew the application in the Court of Appeal, provided that the matter is not a criminal cause or matter.

### 5.9.1   Appeal against refusal: criminal cases

In a criminal cause or matter, there appears to be no way of renewing the claim unless the Administrative Court is at least willing to grant a

---

[116]   Letter from Ouseley J dated 4 July 2011.
[117]   See **10.3** for a further consideration of costs at permission.
[118]   CPR, r 44.13(1A)(b).
[119]   Practice Direction 54A, para 8.5.
[120]   Ibid, para 8.6.

certificate of general public importance.[121] It is clear that the Court of Appeal has no jurisdiction to consider criminal matters.[122] As a consequence, a criminal claim can only be renewed in a criminal case if the Supreme Court has jurisdiction. In a civil case, the Supreme Court has no jurisdiction to consider refusals of permission to apply for judicial review unless permission to appeal against that decision has been granted.[123] This suggests that the Supreme Court has no jurisdiction to consider a refusal to grant permission to apply for judicial review in a criminal matter unless the normal preconditions for an appeal to the Supreme Court exist. The most important precondition is that a certificate of general public importance has to have been issued by the Divisional Court. In practical terms, it is thus extremely unlikely that a person will be able to appeal against a refusal of permission following an oral hearing in a criminal cause or matter as it is highly unlikely that a certificate of general public importance will be issued. As the whole issue of renewal in the Supreme Court is uncertain, if a claimant has good reason to appeal to the Supreme Court, the safest thing would be to ask a Divisional Court to grant permission and immediately refuse the substantive claim so that there is no doubt that the claimant can appeal to the Supreme Court.

### 5.9.2   Appeal against refusal: civil cases

In any case that is not criminal, the renewed application is made to the Court of Appeal.[124] The judgment of the single judge should be considered when deciding whether to renew. The Court of Appeal will be particularly alert to renewed applications that lack merit.[125] The procedure to be followed is that which applies to other appeals,[126] save that an application must be made within 7 days.[127] In addition, the documents to be filed are slightly different and are governed by para 15.4 of Practice Direction 52.[128]

When the Court of Appeal considers the application for permission to apply for judicial review, it is technically required to consider whether to grant permission to appeal (although it can grant permission to apply for judicial review when considering whether to grant permission[129]). This is of significance as it is only possible to appeal to the Supreme Court if

---

[121] See **9.3** for appeals in criminal matters.

[122] Senior Courts Act 1981, s 18(1)(a).

[123] *R (Eastaway) v Secretary of State for Trade and Industry* [2001] 1 WLR 2222.

[124] CPR, r 52.15.

[125] See, for example, *R v Secretary of State for the Home Department ex p Panther* (1996) 8 Admin LR 154, at 162F, in which Lady Justice Butler-Sloss held that the costs assessment should consider the fact that an application to the Court of Appeal lacked merit when legal aid costs were determined.

[126] See Chapter 9 for consideration of appeal procedure.

[127] CPR, r 52.15(2).

[128] See **9.1.3**.

[129] CPR, r 52.15(3).

leave to appeal has been granted.[130] That means that the Court of Appeal might be persuaded to grant permission even if it subsequently dismisses the claim if there is some good reason why the Supreme Court might wish to consider the case[131]. One example would be where there is an authority binding on the Court of Appeal that is not binding on the Supreme Court.

The test that the Court of Appeal will apply when deciding whether to grant permission to appeal in an appeal against a decision to refuse permission to apply for judicial review is whether there is a realistic (as opposed to merely fanciful) prospect of the appellant showing that the refusal to grant permission to apply for judicial review was wrong.[132] If the Court concludes that there is, it will normally grant permission to apply for judicial review.[133] However, applications for permission to appeal are considered first on the papers and so, if the Court is merely persuaded that there is a realistic prospect that the claimant would be able to persuade the Court that he should be granted permission to appeal after an oral hearing, an oral hearing should be ordered but with the substantive hearing to follow immediately after the permission hearing to avoid the need for two hearings.[134]

If the Court of Appeal grants permission to apply for judicial review, it will normally remit the matter to the Administrative Court for hearing. However, the Court can decide to consider the judicial review claim itself.

## 5.10  CONDUCT OF THE JUDICIAL REVIEW APPLICATION AFTER OBTAINING PERMISSION

### 5.10.1  Payment of the claimant's fee

After the grant of permission a claimant must pay a fee (at the time of writing of £215) within 7 days if he wishes to pursue the claim.[135] If that is not done, the Administrative Court may close the file on the matter. If the Administrative Court does close the file, it can often be persuaded to reopen it, provided that there is some good reason for the delay.[136]

---

[130]  *R (Eastaway) v Secretary of State for Trade and Industry* [2001] 1 WLR 2222, and *R (Burkett) v London Borough of Hammersmith and Fulham and others* [2002] 1 WLR 1593.

[131]  *R (LO Jordan) v Secretary of State* [2011] EWCA Civ 164.

[132]  *R (Werner) v The Commissioners of Inland Revenue* [2002] EWCA Civ 979, [2002] STC 1213, at [31].

[133]  Ibid, at [31].

[134]  Ibid, at [32].

[135]  Notes for Guidance produced by the Administrative Court.

[136]  By way of an application for relief from a sanction imposed by the Court, pursuant to CPR, r 3.9.

## 5.10.2 Grounds and additional evidence relied on by a defendant or interested party

The CPR provide that if a defendant or an interested party wishes to be heard at the substantive hearing of the judicial review claim, he must serve detailed grounds of resistance and any evidence that he seeks to rely on 35 days after the order granting permission.[137] In addition, where he seeks to rely on any documents that have not already been filed, a file of documents must be lodged.[138]

In principle, there appears to be no discretion regarding the requirement to file detailed grounds. However, in practice, it appears that defendants often fail to file detailed grounds. This is not necessarily surprising as summary grounds often contain a significant amount of detail and so it would appear that there is often little extra that can be added. However, even if there is little or no additional material to be added, it would appear that it is good practice to file detailed grounds. A precedent is included in Part III.[139]

When documents are drafted on behalf of a defendant or interested party, practitioners should be aware of the duty of disclosure imposed on defendants.[140] They should also be aware that, unlike summary grounds, detailed grounds are not verified by any statement of truth, which probably means that any facts included in the detailed grounds which are not contained in evidence elsewhere should be confirmed by witness statement evidence.[141] Witness statements will also be needed if the defendant wishes to establish facts that are not established in the evidence elsewhere or if the defendant believes that it is necessary to supply the Administrative Court with the background to the decision challenged.

## 5.10.3 Application to set aside a grant of permission

Until the introduction of the CPR, defendants were able to apply to have a grant of permission set aside. The CPR provide that a defendant or other person served with the claim form is unable to apply to set aside a grant of permission,[142] presumably because he would have had opportunities to make any relevant representations at the time permission was granted.

In practice, it will rarely be appropriate for a person to seek to have a grant of permission set aside, even if he was not served with the claim form. A blatant failure to make adequate and proper disclosure would

---

[137] CPR, r 54.14.
[138] Practice Direction 54A, para 10.1.
[139] See Precedent 12.
[140] See **5.5**.
[141] See **5.2.2** for consideration of how witness statements should be drafted.
[142] CPR, r 54.13.

probably need to be shown before the Administrative Court would be willing to set aside a grant of permission.

## 5.10.4   Interim applications

Once permission has been granted, all the parties should consider whether there is a need for any specific orders governing the conduct of the matter that have not already been made at the time when permission was granted. In particular, there is in principle no reason why any of the case management orders provided for in the CPR cannot be sought. Orders sought might include orders requiring the disclosure of documents and cross-examination and other interlocutory applications.

The reluctance of the Administrative Court to consider factual disputes during an application for judicial review means that orders for matters such as cross-examination. are rarely made during judicial review proceedings.[143] For example, the Administrative Court will be reluctant to consider a dispute about facts that are said to give rise to an allegation of bias on the part of magistrates.[144] As a result, the Administrative Court is extremely unlikely to hear oral evidence and cross-examination of witnesses to determine whether there was bias.

The usual procedure in judicial review cases is, first, for there to be no oral evidence and, second, in so far as there are factual disputes between the parties, the Court is ordinarily obliged to resolve them in favour of the defendant[145] However, where there is a 'hard-edged' question of fact relating to the applicability of the European Convention on Human Rights, the Administrative Court may consider cross-examination to be necessary.[146] For example, in *R (Wilkinson) v Broadmoor Hospital*[147] the Court of Appeal concluded that witnesses should be called to determine whether treatment without consent violated a patient's rights under Arts 2, 3 and 8 of the European Convention. Although the Court of Appeal has commented that *Wilkinson* should not be regarded as authority for routine applications for oral evidence,[148] the Administrative Court has suggested that cross-examination might occur with increasing regularity in cases where there are crucial factual disputes between the parties relating to jurisdiction of the European Convention of Human

---

[143]   See, for example, *R v Inland Revenue Commissioners ex p Rossminster* [1980] AC 952, at 1027B, in which Lord Scarman stated that these powers should be used 'sparingly'.

[144]   In *R v Haringey Justices ex p Branco* (1997) *The Independent*, December 1, it was held that a defendant should normally appeal to the Crown Court in these circumstances.

[145]   See, for example, *R v Board of Visitors of Hull Prison ex p St Germain (No2)* [1979] 1 WLR 1401, at 1410H; *R (McVey and others) v Secretary of State for Health* [2010] EWHC 437 (Admin), at [35].

[146]   See, for example, *R (Al-Sweady) v Secretary of State for Defence* [2009] EWHC 2387 (Admin), [2010] HRLR 2, at [15]-[21].

[147]   [2002] 1 WLR 419.

[148]   *R (N) v Dr M* [2003] 1 WLR 562, at 575.

Rights.[149] Whether there needs to be oral evidence and cross-examination will depend upon the alleged breach of the Convention.[150] It should also be noted that the Administrative Court has considered oral evidence even in cases that do not raise issues under the Convention.[151]

The Administrative Court will also be reluctant to make interlocutory orders for matters such as the supply of further information or the disclosure of documents, as it will expect the defendant to provide it with all the information that it requires.[152] In practice, the Court will want to be satisfied that there is a particularly good reason why an order for the supply of further information or the disclosure of documents should be made. One good reason may be that a case raises crucial issues of fact relating to the application of the European Convention of Human Rights. Such cases tend to be very fact-specific and any judgment on the proportionality of a public authority's interference with a protected European Convention right is likely to call for a careful and accurate evaluation of the facts. However, Lord Bingham has stressed that, even in these cases, disclosure should not be automatic. The test will be whether, in the given case, disclosure appears to be necessary in order to resolve the matter fairly and accurately.[153] Full disclosure may also be vital where there is to be cross-examination of witnesses. In such cases, the approach to disclosure should be similar to that in an ordinary Queen's Bench action.[154]

One order that may need to be sought is that permitting the claimant to serve evidence in response to evidence served by the defendant or any interested party. There is no procedural rule permitting a claimant to do this. As a result, the CPR require a claimant to seek permission to serve such evidence.[155] In practice, it appears that the Administrative Court is highly unlikely to prevent a claimant relying on additional evidence, provided that it is served in good time before any substantive hearing. Indeed, it is the practice of many High Court judges to make express orders for the service of evidence by a claimant in response if they set a timetable for expedition when permission is granted.

---

[149]   *R (Al-Sweady) v Secretary of State for Defence* [2010] HRLR 2, at [19].

[150]   *R (N) v Dr M* [2003] 1 WLR 562, at 575.

[151]   See, for example, *R (Aru) v Chief Constable of Merseyside Police* [2004] 1 WLR 1697, and, in Northern Ireland, *Re Brenda Downes* [2006] NIQB 77, at [16].

[152]   See **5.3** and **5.5** for details of the duty of disclosure imposed on the parties to judicial review proceedings. In *R v Arts Council of England ex p Women's Playhouse Trust* [1998] COD 175, it was held that interlocutory orders for discovery would not be made unless there was something to suggest that prima facie there had been a failure to comply with the duty of disclosure.

[153]   *Tweed v Parades Commission for Northern Ireland* [2007] 1 AC 650, at 655G.

[154]   See, for example, *R (Al-Sweady) v Secretary of State for Defence* [2010] HRLR 2, at [27].

[155]   CPR, r 52.16.

### *Procedure for seeking interim orders*

Interim applications are usually made by filing an application notice (N244) with the Administrative Court.[156] Precedents are included in Part III.[157] There is also a fee, which is currently £80. The application notice must state the order that is being sought and why it is being sought.[158] It must also state the title of the case, the reference number of the claim, the full name of the applicant for the order, the address for service (including a postcode) if the applicant for the order is not a party to the proceedings, and a request for a hearing or a request that the matter is considered without a hearing.[159] If there is a request that the matter is considered without a hearing, the Court may still order that a hearing must take place.[160]

Except in cases where the order sought is very simple, the applicant for an order should produce a draft of the order sought.[161] In cases where the order sought is very complex, the draft should be supplied on computer disk.[162]

When a party seeks an interim order, the consent of the other parties should normally be sought. If all parties consent, they should sign the draft order, which should also include a statement of the reasons why it should be made. (A precedent consent order is included in Part III.[163]) That order should then be filed with the Administrative Court so that a judge can consider whether the order should be made.

In any event, notice of the interim application should be given to the other parties unless there is some good reason why this cannot happen. A copy of the application notice, together with any evidence in support, should normally be served on the other parties at least 3 days before the proposed date for hearing the application.[164]

### 5.10.5   Transfer of proceedings

One particular form of interim order that might be obtained is an order transferring the proceedings out of the Administrative Court so that they continue as normal civil proceedings.[165] As already noted, there can be some uncertainty as to whether proceedings relate to a public law issue.[166]

---

[156]   Ibid, r 23.3(1).
[157]   See Precedents 14, 15, 19 and 20.
[158]   CPR, r 23.6.
[159]   Practice Direction 23A, para 2.1.
[160]   Ibid, para 2.5.
[161]   Ibid, para 12.1.
[162]   Ibid.
[163]   See Precedent 13.
[164]   CPR, r 23.7(1).
[165]   CPR, r 54.20.
[166]   See **1.6**.

If it becomes clear that proceedings should have been commenced as a private law matter, an application can be made for transfer.

The terms of the CPR make it clear that the power to transfer is a discretionary power. Historically, the Administrative Court has not necessarily been particularly willing to transfer matters, especially if the proceedings have come near to resolution.[167]

The introduction of the CPR and the overriding objective of ensuring that cases are dealt with justly[168] has resulted in a more flexible approach to transfer.[169]

### 5.10.6   Reference to the European Court

Another form of interim order that might be sought is a reference to the Court of Justice of the European Union. Article 19(3) of the Treaty on European Union provides that:

> 'The Court of Justice of the European Union shall ... give preliminary rulings, at the request of courts or tribunals of the Member States, on the interpretation of Union law or the validity of acts adopted by the institutions ...'

It is important to recognise that, because there is a right of appeal from the Administrative Court, the power to refer to the European Court is discretionary. In practical terms, factors that are likely to be relevant are the degree of uncertainty and the extent to which the issue of European law is relevant to the determination of the matter.

Part 68 of the CPR provides the procedure for making a reference. It provides that an order making a reference may be made by the Administrative Court of its own initiative or following an application by one of the parties.[170] In practice, it is highly unlikely that a reference will be made until permission has been granted.

### 5.10.7   Extending public funding

Public funding certificates will generally be limited to steps up until the service of any evidence by the defendant and any interested party. At that stage it will normally be necessary to have the certificate extended so that it covers all work up to and including the trial of the case.

---

[167]   *R v Reading Justices ex p South West Meat Ltd* (1992) 4 Admin LR 401.
[168]   CPR, r 1.1(1).
[169]   *R (Oxford Study Centre Ltd) v British Council* [2001] ELR 803, in which Collins J dismissed a claim for judicial review but then proceeded as though it had been a claim for breach of contract. See also, *Clark v University of Lincolnshire and Humberside* [2000] 1 WLR 1988, at 1997B–1997C.
[170]   CPR, r 68.2.

### 5.10.8 Solicitor ceasing to act

Where a solicitor is acting for a party under the terms of a public funding certificate and that certificate is revoked or discharged, the solicitor should send the notice revoking or discharging public funding to the Administrative Court so that he ceases to be the solicitor on the record.[171] He must give notice to the other parties and to counsel instructed.[172] If the party who was receiving public funding wishes to continue the action he must serve notice of change of representation on all the parties.

Otherwise, where a solicitor ceases to act for a party in proceedings in the Administrative Court, the party is obliged to give notice of that change of representation.[173] The form to be used is a form N434, which can be found on the website of the Ministry of Justice.[174]

If the party fails to give notice of the change of representation, the former solicitor may apply to the Administrative Court for an order that he has ceased to act.[175] Without an order, the Court will continue to regard the previous solicitor as acting. As a result, the previous solicitor will be responsible for compliance with the CPR and practice directions.

The application for an order that a solicitor has ceased to act is made in the same manner as an application for other interim orders.[176] Notice of the application must be given to the party for whom the solicitor formerly acted[177] and must be supported by evidence explaining the basis of the application.[178] If an order is obtained, it must be served on all parties to the proceedings.[179] Once the order is served, a certificate of service must be filed with the Administrative Court.[180]

### 5.11 ACTING FOR A POTENTIAL PARTY WHO HAS NOT BEEN SERVED WITH THE CLAIM FORM

If a party is aware of judicial review proceedings but has not been served with the claim form, an application can be made to the court that he should be heard. Such an application should be made promptly. The court has a discretion to order that any person may be heard on a judicial review claim or file evidence.[181] The scope of this provision is wide and it

---

[171] Civil Legal Aid (General) Regulations 1989 (SI 1989/339), reg 82.
[172] Ibid.
[173] CPR, r 42.2(2) requires the notice to be filed and served on all parties.
[174] See www.justice.gov.uk/about/hmcts/index.htm.
[175] CPR, r 42.3.
[176] See **5.10.4**.
[177] CPR, r 42.3(2)(a). Proof of service will be required if the party does not attend a hearing regarding this matter.
[178] Ibid, r 42.3(2)(b).
[179] Ibid, r 42.3(3)(a).
[180] Ibid, r 42.3(3)(b).
[181] CPR, r 54.17.

does not restrict the Administrative Court to considering submissions made by parties who should have been served with the claim form.

In practice, the Administrative Court is willing on occasion to allow third parties to appear. For example, courts considering judicial review applications regularly hear amici curiae instructed by the Attorney General when the court feels it will be assisted by submissions.[182] Indeed, if a judicial review raises important issues that will affect many cases and that will not be fully considered if only the parties make submissions, it may be worth claimants considering whether the Treasury Solicitors should be approached to see whether they wish to instruct an amicus curiae.

## 5.12 SETTLING THE CLAIM OR OTHERWISE DISPOSING OF IT WITHOUT A HEARING

The CPR provide for a claim to be disposed of without a hearing where all the parties agree.[183] This permits the parties to enter a consent order where all the parties agree how the matter may be resolved. A consent order (together with two copies) should be sent to the Administrative Court, signed by all the parties agreeing on the disposal of the case.[184] A precedent is included in Part III.[185]

In principle, the Administrative Court will not necessarily make an agreed consent order. As a consequence, a statement of reasons for the order should be included with the order. However, normally this need not be extensive as it is highly unlikely that the Court will refuse to make an agreed order.

The fact that a defendant consents to provide the claimant with what they are seeking does not necessarily mean that the claim should not be continued. First, it may be the case that providing the claimant with what he seeks reveals further errors. For example, a challenge seeking reasons may reveal reasons that show that a defendant acted unlawfully. In addition, it may be possible to argue that the claim has not become academic if the claim raises important issues of principle.[186]

In principle, a claimant can often withdraw a claim for judicial review without the consent of other parties in accordance with the CPR, Part 38. The only times that claimants need either the consent of the Court or the consent of another party are: when the Court has granted an injunction

---

[182] See, for example, *R v Governor of Brockhill Prison ex p Evans* [2001] 2 AC 19 for an example of a case in which the House of Lords sought the assistance of an amicus regarding a difficult issue. See also *R (Girling) v Parole Board* [2007] QB 783.

[183] Ibid, r 54.18.

[184] Notes for Guidance produced by the Administrative Court.

[185] See Precedent 16.

[186] See **8.1.1** for consideration of academic challenges.

or an undertaking has been given to the Court;[187] where there has been an interim payment;[188] and, where there is more than one claimant.[189] If the claim is withdrawn without consent, a notice of withdrawal must be filed at Court and served on the parties.[190]

In practice, withdrawal is normally done by consent as the consequence of withdrawing without consent is that the claimant becomes liable for all the costs unless an order is obtained making some other provision for costs.[191] In practice, a claimant is likely to be able to persuade a defendant that there should be no order for costs as a consequence of the Administrative Court's reluctance to penalise those who withdraw (particularly if they are publicly funded).[192] In addition, a publicly funded claimant will need an order that his costs should be assessed. As a consequence, a consent order should be agreed, permitting the claimant to withdraw and making appropriate provision for costs.

## 5.13  SUBSTANTIVE HEARING

### 5.13.1  Listing arrangements

In cases where there is particular urgency, a judge may make specific directions requiring a case to be heard on or by a particular date. Alternatively, if there is urgency, a judge may order that a matter is to be expedited. This may not result in the matter being heard very quickly but will mean that it is at least given priority when the normal listing arrangements operate. There are standard listing arrangements where no direction regarding listing has been made.

When the case is ready for listing, it will be placed with others in the warned list.[193] These cases will then be listed, with priority given to those that have been expedited.[194] As a consequence, parties should seek an order for expedition if there is some reason why the matter needs to be heard promptly. This will also reduce the possibility of the Administrative Court vacating the hearing.

The hearing will be fixed in the following manner. Where counsel are on record (which they will normally be, as their details are required on the

---

[187]  CPR, r 38.2(2)(a), requiring the Court to grant permission.

[188]  Ibid, r 38.2(2)(b), requiring either the defendant to consent or the Court to grant permission.

[189]  Ibid, r 38.2(2)(c), requiring either the other claimants to consent or the Court to grant permission.

[190]  Ibid, r 38.3.

[191]  Ibid, r 38.6.

[192]  See Chapter 10.

[193]  The case will be ready when either the defendant and interested party have served the detailed grounds and any evidence or the time for the service of those documents has expired.

[194]  *Practice Statement (Administrative Court: Listing and Urgent Cases)* [2002] 1 WLR 810.

claim form), their chambers will be contacted by the Administrative Court and supplied with a list of dates to agree.[195] In practice, the Court will also seek a time estimate from the parties at this stage. If the parties do not contact the Court within 48 hours to agree a date, the matter will be fixed by the Court.[196] If a date is fixed in this manner, an adjournment must either be agreed by all the parties or obtained following an application to the Court on notice to all the parties.[197]

A small number of cases are placed in a short warned list,[198] which means that a case can be called on at less than 24 hours' notice.[199] If a case does not come on during the warned list period, it will be fixed following the procedure that normally applies.[200] In principle, it is possible to request that a matter should be taken out of the warned list. However, in practice, the Administrative Court will be reluctant to agree to this.

## 5.13.2   Preparation

The first (and possibly most important) thing that needs to be done in preparation for the judicial review claim is the submission of a skeleton argument on behalf of each party attending. The claimant's skeleton argument needs to be submitted 21 *working* days before the date of the substantive hearing of the matter or the date when the matter enters the warned list.[201] Although the requirement that it be served 21 working days is almost certainly a mistake (as the requirement must have been intended to be that the skeleton should be served 3 weeks in advance), the Administrative Court does seek to enforce that time-limit. If there is some good reason why the 21-working-day time-limit cannot be complied with, the consent of the other parties to late service should be sought and a letter should be sent to the Administrative Court seeking the Court's agreement to an extension of time.

The defendant and any other party who wishes to be heard should submit their respective skeleton arguments 14 *working* days before the date of the substantive hearing in the matter.[202] The defendant and other parties should take a similar approach to the claimant regarding the time-limits.

Practice Direction 54A[203] provides that the skeleton arguments must contain:

---

[195]   *Practice Statement (Administrative Court: Listing and Urgent Cases)* [2002] 1 WLR 810.
[196]   Ibid.
[197]   Ibid.
[198]   Ibid.
[199]   Ibid.
[200]   Ibid.
[201]   Practice Direction 54A, para 15.1.
[202]   Ibid, para 15.2.
[203]   Ibid, para 15.3.

(1) a time estimate for the complete hearing, including delivery of judgment;[204]

(2) a list of issues;

(3) a list of the legal points to be taken (together with any relevant authorities, with page references to the passages relied on);   .

(4) a chronology of events (with page references to the bundle of documents[205]);

(5) a list of essential documents for the advance reading of the court (with page references to the passages of the bundle relied on) (if different from that filed with the claim form) and a time estimate for that advanced reading; and

(6) a list of persons referred to.

In practice, skeleton arguments also normally contain a summary of the relevant facts.

A precedent skeleton argument has been included in Part III.[206] There is no one correct style for drafting a skeleton argument. The critical concern when drafting the skeleton argument is that the judge hearing the case should be left in no doubt as to that party's arguments when reading into the case in advance of the hearing.

The Administrative Court can consider extracts from *Hansard* when it determines questions of law.[207] If *Hansard* is to be cited, a copy of the citation together with a summary of the argument relating to the parliamentary material must be served on all parties and two copies must be lodged with the Administrative Court. This must happen at least 5 days

---

[204] This requirement applies despite the fact that a time estimate will normally have been supplied when the matter was listed.

[205] The reference to the bundle of documents is a reference to the trial bundle. See below.

[206] See Precedent 17.

[207] *Pepper (Inspector of Taxes) v Hart and Related Appeals* [1993] AC 593, in which the House of Lords held that extracts from *Hansard* may be relied on when a statute is ambiguous and the statements to be relied on are clear and were made by the legislation's promoter. This may not be the only circumstance in which *Hansard* is referred to. Lord Browne-Wilkinson stated, at 638H–639A that: '[T]he Attorney General's contentions are inconsistent with the practice which has now continued over a number of years in cases of judicial review. In such cases, *Hansard* has frequently been referred to with a view to ascertaining whether a statutory power has been improperly exercised for an alien purpose or in a wholly unreasonable manner'. The Human Rights Act 1998 extended the circumstances in which it is appropriate to refer to *Hansard*: reference is appropriate when considering the purpose of legislation in order to determine whether it is compatible with the European Convention (*Wilson v First County Trust Ltd (No 2)* [2004] 1 AC 816).

before the date of the hearing.[208] In practice, this should normally be done by including the argument regarding *Hansard* in the skeleton.

Having drafted their skeleton arguments, counsel will normally agree a bundle of authorities (containing law reports, legislation and other materials to be cited in argument) to be submitted to the Administrative Court. There is normally no formal requirement for this but it is regarded as good practice as it enables all authorities to be made available in a usable form. The bundle should be supplied a few days in advance of the hearing so that judges have an opportunity to use the reports while they prepare.

Despite the fact that a bundle will have been lodged in support of the application for permission, the claimant's solicitors will need to supply a trial bundle.[209] In practice, this ought to be supplied a few days in advance of the date when the skeleton argument is due so that the skeleton argument can include page references to the bundle. The bundle must include all documents that will be relied on by any party proposing to attend the hearing. For simple judicial reviews it is often sensible to include every document that has been submitted to the Administrative Court and all the Court orders made in the claim. However, in a more complex claim where very substantial documentation has been lodged, it may be preferable to agree a trial bundle with the defendant that will include only relevant documents.

The bundle should be paginated and indexed. The documents in the bundle must be secured together, arranged in chronological order beginning with the earliest documents at the front of the bundle,[210] indexed and paginated consecutively with the numbers at centre bottom. The bundle is usually secured by placing it in a lever arch file. If the bundle contains more than 100 pages, numbered dividers should be placed at intervals between groups of documents. The documents contained in the bundles must be legible.

Only one copy of the skeleton and the bundles need be lodged with the Administrative Court unless the case is to be heard by a Divisional Court, in which case there needs to be one copy of the skeleton and the bundles for each judge.[211]

---

[208] *Practice Direction (Hansard extracts)* [1995] 1 WLR 192.

[209] Practice Direction 54A, para 16.1.

[210] In practice, documents of the same type are usually grouped together so that the pleadings are normally placed at the front of the bundle, orders made by the Administrative Court follow, and the evidence is then included in chronological order.

[211] Notes for Guidance produced by the Administrative Court.

### 5.13.3   The conduct of the substantive hearing

Substantive civil judicial review claims are normally heard by a single judge, although they can occasionally be heard by a Divisional Court consisting of two or three judges. In a criminal cause or matter, the case will normally be heard by a Divisional Court, although it can be heard by a single judge.

The claimant will make his submissions to the court first. The defendant will then be able to respond, followed by any interested party. The claimant will be able to make final submissions in response.

In considering the submissions of the parties, the Administrative Court or the Divisional Court will normally regard itself as being bound by an earlier decision of the same court unless it can be shown that the earlier decision is clearly wrong.[212] One exception to this may be where the HRA 1998 entitles the Court to review earlier decisions which were reached before that Act entered into force and which failed to take account of the European Convention on Human Rights.[213]

The orders that the Administrative Court may make are considered in more detail later.[214] There are two important matters to consider at the stage when the Court delivers its judgment.

First, it is essential that an order for assessment for the purposes of the Community Legal Service is sought if the claimant is in receipt of public funding.[215]

In addition, it is important to consider whether permission to appeal should be sought. In a criminal cause or matter, any appeal can only be heard by the Supreme Court. This requires leave to appeal and a certificate under s 1 of the Administration of Justice Act 1960 that the case involves a point of law of general public importance. Where the matter is not a criminal cause or matter,[216] it is possible to appeal to the Court of Appeal. Leave to appeal is still necessary. Appeals are considered in more detail in Chapter 9.

---

[212]  *R v HM Coroner for Greater Manchester ex p Tal* [1985] QB 67.
[213]  See, for example, *R (D) v Secretary of State for the Home Department* [2003] 1 WLR 1315, at 1327D–1327F.
[214]  See Chapter 8.
[215]  See **10.11**.
[216]  Or is merely collateral to a criminal cause or matter, see, for example, *R (Guardian News and Media Ltd) v City of Westminster Magistrates Court* [2011] EWCA Civ 1188.

## 5.14 MATTERS THAT APPLY AT ALL STAGES OF THE PROCEDURE

### 5.14.1 Service of documents

The CPR govern the service of all documents once proceedings have begun in the Administrative Court. Documents may be served by:

(a) personal service;[217]

(b) first class post, document exchange or other service which provides for delivery on the next business day, in accordance with the relevant Practice Direction ;[218]

(c) leaving the document at an address for service;[219]

(d) fax or other means of electronic communication in accordance with the relevant Practice Direction;[220] or

(e) any method authorised by the Court.[221]

The place for service is also defined by the rules.[222] Individuals may be served at their usual or last known residence. A company can be served at the principal office or any place of business that has a real connection with the proceedings. In practice, the address for service is unlikely to be a significant issue as it will have been identified in correspondence in accordance with the Judicial Review Pre-Action Protocol.[223]

The rules provide for the deemed day of service.[224] Documents are deemed to have been served on the second business day after they have been sent.

### 5.14.2 Time-limits

Time-limits are determined by reference to the CPR: the day on which a time period starts is not included in that period, or, if the period is defined

---

[217] CPR, r 6.3(1)(a). If a party has been notified that a solicitor is authorised to be served with documents, a document may not be served personally: the solicitor must be served (CPR, r 6.7(1)). Where a company is to be served, service may be on a person holding a senior position (CPR, r 6.5(3)(b)). Where a partnership is to be served, service may be on a partner or a person with control of the business (CPR, r 6.5(3)(c)).

[218] CPR, r 6.3(1)(b).

[219] Ibid, r 6.3(1)(c).

[220] Ibid, r 6.3(1)(d).

[221] Ibid, r 6.3(1)(e) and 6.15.

[222] Ibid, rr 6.6 and 6.9.

[223] See **4.1**.

[224] CPR, r 6.14.

by an end event, that date is not included.[225] Hence, for example, the claimant's skeleton argument is due 21 working days before the substantive hearing.[226] When calculating the date on which the skeleton is due, the 21-day period does not include the date of the substantive hearing. Where a period in the Rules or Practice Directions is 5 days or less, Saturdays, Sundays, bank holidays, Good Friday and Christmas Day do not count.[227]

---

[225] Ibid, r 2.8(3).
[226] See **5.3.2**.
[227] CPR, r 2.8(4).

# CHAPTER 6

# JURISDICTION OF THE UPPER TRIBUNAL
# TO CONSIDER JUDICIAL REVIEW

## 6.1 INTRODUCTION

The Tribunals, Courts and Enforcement Act 2007 is a genuinely historic piece of legislation as it created a jurisdiction for a body other than the High Court to consider judicial review claims. It did this by granting the Upper Tribunal power to grant the following forms of relief:

(a)   a mandatory order;

(b)   a prohibiting order;

(c)   a quashing order;

(d)   a declaration; and

(e)   an injunction.[1]

In addition, damages can be awarded by the Tribunal where the claim includes a claim for damages arising from a matter to which the claim relates and the Tribunal is satisfied that damages would have been awarded in proceedings commenced in the High Court.[2]

It should be noted that the relief that can be granted does to include a declaration of incompatibility under s 4 of the Human Rights Act 1998. That is not surprising as s 4 expressly limits the courts that can make a declaration of incompatibility and its provisions do not permit the Upper Tribunal to make a declaration.

In deciding whether to grant relief, the High Court must apply the principles that it would apply when considering an application for judicial

---

[1]   Tribunals, Courts and Enforcement Act 2007, s 15(1). See Chapter 8 for a consideration of the various forms of relief.

[2]   Tribunals, Courts and Enforcement Act 2007, s 16(6). See **8.2.6** for a consideration of the circumstances in which damages may be awarded.

review.[3] Where relief is granted, it can be enforced as if it were relief granted by the High Court in judicial review proceedings.[4]

The jurisdiction of the Upper Tribunal is limited. The 2007 Act provides the jurisdiction summarised above can only be exercised if either certain conditions are met or the Tribunal is authorised to proceed even if the conditions are not met.[5]

The conditions that must be met are:

(a)   the claim does not seek anything other than the relief available that is described above, interest, or costs;[6]

(b)   the application does not question anything done by the Crown Court;[7]

(c)   the case falls within a class specified in a direction given in accordance with the Constitutional Reform Act 2005;[8]

(d)   the person hearing the case is a judge of the Court of Appeal or High Court or they have been authorised by the Lord Chief Justice and the Senior President of the Tribunals.[9]

Directions have been given under the Constitutional Reform Act 2005 that provide that the Upper Tribunal has jurisdiction in relation to:

(a)   Decisions of the First-Tier Tribunal regarding the Criminal Injuries Compensation Scheme.[10]

(b)   Decisions of the First-Tier Tribunal regarding procedural matters or whether to review a decision under s 9 of the Tribunals, Courts and Enforcement Act 2007 where there is no right of appeal.[11]

(c)   Decisions that further representations are not a fresh claim for asylum or protection under the Human Rights Act 1998 on the basis that the material is not sufficiently different.[12] It is expressly said that this does not extend to applications that seek declarations of

---

3    Tribunals, Courts and Enforcement Act 2007, s 15(5)(a).
4    Tribunals, Courts and Enforcement Act 2007, s 15(3)(b).
5    Tribunals, Courts and Enforcement Act 2007, s 15(2).
6    Tribunals, Courts and Enforcement Act 2007, s 18(4).
7    Tribunals, Courts and Enforcement Act 2007, s 18(5).
8    Tribunals, Courts and Enforcement Act 2007, s 18(6).
9    Tribunals, Courts and Enforcement Act 2007, s 18(8).
10   *Practice Direction (Upper Tribunal: Judicial Review Jurisdiction)* [2009] 1 WLR 327.
11   Ibid.
12   Fresh claim judicial review: Direction – class of cases specified for the purposes of s 18(6) of the Tribunals Courts and Enforcement Act 2007 (http://www.judiciary.gov.uk/ Resources/JCO/Documents/Practice%20Directions/Administrative/class-cases-specified-for-purposes-section-18(6)-07102011.pdf).

incompatibility under s 4 of the Human Rights Act 1998 or that challenge detention.[13] These claims are known as challenges to immigration fresh claim decisions.

The circumstances in which the Tribunal is authorised to hear a claim without the conditions being met are essentially when a case is transferred to the Tribunal by the High Court.[14] In those circumstances the judicial review is essentially treated as though proceedings had been commenced in the Tribunal.[15] In practice this jurisdiction to transfer proceedings has been used where there is a need for substantial fact finding. In particular, it has been used in the context of challenges to decisions regarding the age of unaccompanied asylum seekers.

## 6.2    PROCEDURE IN UPPER TRIBUNAL

The procedure when applying for judicial review in the Upper Tribunal is broadly similar to that when applying for judicial review in the High Court. In particular, judicial review remains a two-stage process in which permission has to be sought to apply for judicial review.[16] However, the rules that govern judicial review in the Tribunal are different and that results in some differences in the procedure.[17] It should be noted that the rules differentiate between judicial reviews of immigration 'fresh claim' decisions and other judicial review in the Tribunal. The procedure adopted in immigration fresh claims is particularly similar to that adopted in the High Court.

## 6.3    COMMENCING A CLAIM FOR JUDICIAL REVIEW IN UPPER TRIBUNAL

An application for permission to apply for judicial review must be made in writing to the Tribunal.[18] There are three forms that are to be used when making an application for permission to apply for judicial review: one for immigration fresh claims;[19] one for criminal injuries compensation cases;[20] and, one for other judicial review claims.[21] There are significant differences between the three forms. However, all are self-explanatory. There are also guidance notes regarding completion. The only complex

---

[13]   Ibid.
[14]   Tribunals, Courts and Enforcement Act 2007, s 19(3), 19(4).
[15]   Ibid.
[16]   Tribunals, Courts and Enforcement Act 2007, s 16(2).
[17]   Tribunal Procedure (Upper Tribunal) Rules 2008 (SI 2008/2698).
[18]   Tribunal Procedure (Upper Tribunal) Rules 2008 (SI 2008/2698), r 28(1).
[19]   http://www.justice.gov.uk/downloads/global/forms/tribunals/immigration-asylum/upper/fresh-claim-judicial-review-claim-form.pdf.
[20]   http://www.justice.gov.uk/downloads/global/forms/tribunals/aa/jrc1-form.pdf.
[21]   http://www.justice.gov.uk/downloads/global/forms/tribunals/aa/jr1-form.pdf.

part of each form is the section or sections that require statements of the grounds and facts. These sections should be completed in the same way as they are for the High Court.[22]

The time limit for applying for judicial review is normally the same as that applied in the High Court in that an application must be made promptly and within three months of the date of the decision.[23] That rule is qualified in two respects in the Upper Tribunal. Firstly, the relevant rules provide that another enactment may specify a shorter time limit. In addition , they provide that a claim may be commenced outside the time specified in the basic rule if it is a challenge to a decision of the First-Tier Tribunal and it is made within one month of written reasons having been sent or notification that an application to set aside those written reasons has been refused.[24]

The procedure rules provide that the application must include:

(a)    the name and address of the applicant, the respondent and any interested party;

(b)    the name and address of any solicitor who acted;

(c)    the address for service on the applicant;

(d)    details of the decision challenged (including the date, the full reference and the identity of the decision maker);

(e)    it must state that an application is made for permission to apply for judicial review;

(f)    the outcome that the applicant is seeking; and

(g)    the facts and grounds on which the applicant relies.[25]

These details will be provided if the standard application notice is properly completed.

The application must be accompanied by any written record of the decision challenged that is in the possession of the applicant together with any documents to be relied upon.[26] It must also include any application to extend time.[27]

---

22   See **5.2**.
23   Tribunal Procedure (Upper Tribunal) Rules 2008 (SI 2008/2698), r 28(2). See **3.1** for consideration of the effect of the equivalent rule in the High Court.
24   Tribunal Procedure (Upper Tribunal) Rules 2008 (SI 2008/2698), r 28(3).
25   Tribunal Procedure (Upper Tribunal) Rules 2008 (SI 2008/2698), r 28(4).
26   Tribunal Procedure (Upper Tribunal) Rules 2008 (SI 2008/2698), r 28(6).
27   Tribunal Procedure (Upper Tribunal) Rules 2008 (SI 2008/2698), r 28(7).

There is a slight difference between the procedure which applies to fresh claim immigration judicial reviews and other judicial reviews in the Tribunal.

In an immigration fresh claim case the application must be accompanied by either any required fee or an undertaking to provide the fee.[28] The fee is currently £60.[29] It must also be accompanied by a copy of any relevant statutory provisions and a list of essential reading.[30] The applicant must serve the application and accompanying documents upon any respondent and interested party.[31] The applicant must also serve a written statement on the Tribunal explaining when and how this was done.[32] This must all be done within nine days.[33]

Further obligations apply where the claim for judicial review challenges an individual's removal. In those circumstances, the application must:

(a)   state on its face that Part 5 of the Practice Directions: Fresh Claim Judicial Review in the Immigration and Asylum Chamber of the Upper Tribunal applies;

(b)   be accompanied by a copy of the removal directions and any document served with the removal directions including any factual summary of the case; and

(c)   be accompanied by a detailed statement of the grounds for making the application.[34]

Where the matters set out in (b) or (c) cannot be complied with, the application must include a statement including the reasons for non-compliance.[35]

It should be noted that the procedure described above in immigration cases is broadly similar to that adopted in the High Court.

---

[28]   Tribunal Procedure (Upper Tribunal) Rules 2008 (SI 2008/2698), r 28A(1).
[29]   The Upper Tribunal (Immigration and Asylum Chamber) (Judicial Review) (England and Wales) Fees Order 2011 (SI 2011/2344).
[30]   Practice Direction: Fresh Claim Judicial Review in the Immigration and Asylum Chamber of the Upper Tribunal, para 4.
[31]   Tribunal Procedure (Upper Tribunal) Rules 2008 (SI 2008/2698), r 28A(2).
[32]   Tribunal Procedure (Upper Tribunal) Rules 2008 (SI 2008/2698), r 28A(2).
[33]   Tribunal Procedure (Upper Tribunal) Rules 2008 (SI 2008/2698), r 28A(2).
[34]   Practice Direction: Fresh Claim Judicial Review in the Immigration and Asylum Chamber of the Upper Tribunal, para 15.1.
[35]   Practice Direction: Fresh Claim Judicial Review in the Immigration and Asylum Chamber of the Upper Tribunal, para 15.2.

In any other case, there is no requirement to serve the additional documents. In addition, it is the Tribunal that serves the application upon the respondent and any interested party.[36]

## 6.4   URGENT APPLICATIONS

The nature of the claims that can currently be brought in the Upper Tribunal means that it is likely that urgency will only arise in immigration fresh claim judicial reviews. As a consequence, it is not surprising that the only guidance on urgent applications is in this context.

In an immigration fresh claim case, an application for urgent consideration must be made using the 'Request for Urgent Consideration' form[37] which is displayed upon the Tribunal website.[38] The form used is essentially identical to that used in applications for urgent consideration in the High Court.[39] The application must include:

(a)    an explanation of the need for urgency;

(b)    the timescale sought for consideration of the application;

(c)    the date by which the substantive hearing should take place;

(d)    a copy of the draft order sought; and

(e)    the grounds for an injunction.[40]

## 6.5   OBLIGATIONS OF A RESPONDENT OR INTERESTED PARTY SERVED WITH AN APPLICATION

A person served with an application for permission must provide a response within 21 days of the date when the application was sent if he wishes to take part in the proceedings.[41] Service should be acknowledged by using a standard form. There is one form that is used in the context of

---

[36]   Tribunal Procedure (Upper Tribunal) Rules 2008 (SI 2008/2698), r 28(8).
[37]   http://www.justice.gov.uk/downloads/global/forms/tribunals/immigration-asylum/upper/fesh-claim-judicial-review-app-urgent.pdf.
[38]   Practice Direction: Fresh Claim Judicial Review in the Immigration and Asylum Chamber of the Upper Tribunal, para 11.1.
[39]   See **5.1.2**.
[40]   Practice Direction: Fresh Claim Judicial Review in the Immigration and Asylum Chamber of the Upper Tribunal, para 11.
[41]   Tribunal Procedure (Upper Tribunal) Rules 2008 (SI 2008/2698), r 29(1).

immigration fresh claim judicial reviews[42] and a second form for other forms of judicial review.[43] The acknowledgment of service should indicate:

(a)   whether the person supports or opposes the application for permission;

(b)   the grounds for supporting or opposing permission; and

(c)   the name and address of anyone who has not been named but who is thought to be an interested party.[44]

The penalty for not providing an acknowledgment of service is that a person who does not provide an acknowledgement of service may not take further part in the determination of whether permission should be granted unless allowed to do so by the Tribunal.[45] The tactical considerations that should govern the approach of a respondent are the same that apply in the High Court.[46]

A person who files an acknowledgement of service must serve it on the applicant in an immigration fresh claim matter.[47] There is no obligation to serve the acknowledgment of service in other contexts. An applicant who has been served will want to consider serving a response in the same way that they will in the High Court.[48]

## 6.6   DETERMINATION OF THE APPLICATION FOR PERMISSION

The procedure rules do not specify the test to be applied by the Upper Tribunal when deciding whether to grant permission to apply for judicial review. However, there is no reason why the Tribunal would apply a different approach to the High Court.[49] That is clear from the fact that the legislative scheme is intended to ensure that the Tribunal's jurisdiction is normally equivalent to that of the High Court.[50] In particular, the legislation provides that permission may be refused if the applicant does not have a sufficient interest in the claim.[51] It also provides that permission and relief can be refused where there has been undue delay in

---

[42]   http://www.justice.gov.uk/downloads/global/forms/tribunals/immigration-asylum/upper/
fresh-claim-judicial-review-ack-form.pdf.

[43]   http://www.justice.gov.uk/downloads/global/forms/tribunals/aa/jr2-form.pdf.

[44]   Tribunal Procedure (Upper Tribunal) Rules 2008 (SI 2008/2698), r 29(2).

[45]   Tribunal Procedure (Upper Tribunal) Rules 2008 (SI 2008/2698), r 29(3).

[46]   See **5.4**.

[47]   Tribunal Procedure (Upper Tribunal) Rules 2008 (SI 2008/2698), r 29(2A).

[48]   See **5.6**.

[49]   See **5.8** for a consideration of that approach.

[50]   Tribunals, Courts and Enforcement Act 2007, ss 15 and 16.

[51]   Tribunals, Courts and Enforcement Act 2007, s 16(3). See **1.4.1** for a consideration of this test in the context of the High Court.

making an application and granting relief would cause substantial hardship, or where the grant of permission would prejudice the rights of another person or would be detrimental to good administration.[52] These provisions replicate provisions applied by the High Court.

The decision on permission must be sent to the applicant, each respondent and any other person who provided an acknowledgment of service.[53] If permission is refused, reasons must be provided for the decision.[54]

The implication appears to be that permission will initially be determined on the papers. That is clear from the fact that where permission is refused without a hearing or is granted on limited grounds, permission can be reconsidered at an oral hearing if the applicant makes an application.[55] Such an application must be made within 14 days of the Tribunal sending its decision unless the claim is one that relates to an immigration fresh claim.[56] In an immigration case it must be made within 9 days.[57] The same sort of considerations arise in the Upper Tribunal as arise in the High Court when deciding whether to renew an application for permission.[58]

Where there has been a hearing, it is clear that an applicant can seek to appeal to the Court of Appeal.[59] The procedure would to be the same as that adopted following the final determination of a claim for judicial review by the Upper Tribunal.[60]

## 6.7 PROCEDURE FOLLOWING A GRANT OF PERMISSION

Where permission is granted, a person who wishes to contest the claim or support it with additional grounds must provide detailed grounds supporting their position within 35 days.[61] Presumably, additional evidence must also be served in this period although the procedural rules make no specific provision for this while generally permitting parties to submit evidence save that evidence may not be submitted at the hearing of an application for permission.[62]

---

[52]   Tribunals, Courts and Enforcement Act 2007, s 16(4). See **3.1.3** for a consideration of this test in the context of the High Court.
[53]   Tribunal Procedure (Upper Tribunal) Rules 2008 (SI 2008/2698), r 30(1)(a).
[54]   Tribunal Procedure (Upper Tribunal) Rules 2008 (SI 2008/2698), r 30(1)(b).
[55]   Tribunal Procedure (Upper Tribunal) Rules 2008 (SI 2008/2698), r 30(4).
[56]   Tribunal Procedure (Upper Tribunal) Rules 2008 (SI 2008/2698), r 30(5).
[57]   Tribunal Procedure (Upper Tribunal) Rules 2008 (SI 2008/2698), r 30(5).
[58]   See **5.9** for consideration of the approach in the High Court.
[59]   Tribunals, Courts and Enforcement Act 2007, s 16(8).
[60]   See **6.9**.
[61]   Tribunal Procedure (Upper Tribunal) Rules 2008 (SI 2008/2698), r 31.
[62]   Tribunal Procedure (Upper Tribunal) Rules 2008 (SI 2008/2698), r 33(a).

If the applicant seeks to rely on additional grounds after the grant of permission, they must seek permission to do that. Where an application for judicial review relates to an immigration fresh claim decision and there is to be an application to rely on additional grounds, written notice must be given to the Tribunal and any other person served with the application at least seven days before the substantive hearing.[63]

The Tribunal is permitted to consider amendments to the grounds that raise issues that require it to transfer the proceedings to the High Court on the basis that they fall outside of its jurisdiction.[64] However, if permission is granted to raise such an issue, the Tribunal must transfer the case back to the High Court.[65] The Tribunal may also transfer proceedings to the High Court where it appears just and convenient.[66]

The procedure rules provided that any party, and with the permission of the Upper Tribunal, any other person may:

(a)   submit evidence;

(b)   make representations at any hearing that they are entitled to attend; and

(c)   make written representations in relation to a decision without a hearing.[67]

In an immigration fresh claim judicial review, the applicant must serve a skeleton argument at least 21 days before the substantive hearing.[68] It should be noted that that this rule contrasts with the practice direction in the High Court, which provides that a skeleton argument must be served 21 *working* days before a hearing.[69] Any other party must serve a skeleton argument at least 14 days before the substantive hearing.[70] The skeleton argument must include:

(a)   a time estimate for the hearing including the time needed to deliver judgment;

(b)   a list of issues;

---

[63]   Practice Direction: Fresh Claim Judicial Review in the Immigration and Asylum Chamber of the Upper Tribunal, para 7.1

[64]   Tribunal Procedure (Upper Tribunal) Rules 2008 (SI 2008/2698), r 33A(2).

[65]   Tribunal Procedure (Upper Tribunal) Rules 2008 (SI 2008/2698), r 33A(3)(a).

[66]   Tribunal Procedure (Upper Tribunal) Rules 2008 (SI 2008/2698), r 33A(3)(b).

[67]   Tribunal Procedure (Upper Tribunal) Rules 2008 (SI 2008/2698), r 33A.

[68]   Practice Direction: Fresh Claim Judicial Review in the Immigration and Asylum Chamber of the Upper Tribunal, para 8.1.

[69]   See **5.13.2**.

[70]   Practice Direction: Fresh Claim Judicial Review in the Immigration and Asylum Chamber of the Upper Tribunal, para 8.2.

(c) a list of legal points to be taken (together with any relevant authorities with page references to the passages relied upon);

(d) a chronology (with references to the bundle of documents);

(e) a list of essential documents; and

(f) a list of persons referred to.[71]

Essentially it would seem that the skeleton argument must be in a similar form to that required in the High Court.

At the same time that the skeleton argument is served, a bundle must be served by the applicant containing all documents that they intend to rely on at the hearing.[72] It must also include any documents that the respondent or anyone else expected to make representations wishes to have included.[73]

The summary of the procedure above makes it clear that the procedure in immigration fresh claims is very similar to that adopted in the High Court. However, in other claims there is more informality. In part that is presumably because it is envisaged that those claims will be relatively simple. For example, it is clear that the Upper Tribunal has jurisdiction to consider challenges regarding the Criminal Injuries Compensation Scheme because there is no right of appeal. However, there is no reason why challenges should be any more complex than appeals from the First-Tier Tribunal.

If a claim is complex, the parties may want to agree directions to ensure that the claim is progressed effectively. These will probably reflect those in immigration fresh claims.

## 6.8   JUDGMENT OF THE UPPER TRIBUNAL

There is no reason in principle why the Upper Tribunal should not deliver a judgment immediately following the hearing of a claim for judicial review. However, the Tribunal will often reserve its judgment and deliver its reasons in writing. Even if it delivers an oral decision, it must normally deliver a decision in writing.[74]

---

[71]   Practice Direction: Fresh Claim Judicial Review in the Immigration and Asylum Chamber of the Upper Tribunal, para 8.3.

[72]   Practice Direction: Fresh Claim Judicial Review in the Immigration and Asylum Chamber of the Upper Tribunal, para 9.1.

[73]   Practice Direction: Fresh Claim Judicial Review in the Immigration and Asylum Chamber of the Upper Tribunal, para 9.2.

[74]   Tribunal Procedure (Upper Tribunal) Rules 2008 (SI 2008/2698), r 40(2). A decision should include written reasons, unless the parties have consented to the decision or that no written reasons need be given, r 40(3).

If the claim is partially or completely successful, as noted above, the Upper Tribunal has jurisdiction to grant most forms of relief that are available in judicial review proceedings in the High Court.[75] The Tribunal is required to apply the principles that the High Court would apply.[76] These are considered elsewhere in this book.[77]

In immigration fresh claim challenges, the presumption appears to be that the parties should seek to agree an order in light of the judgment.[78] If agreement can be reached, the order should be lodged with a short statement explaining the matters relied upon to justify the order.[79] Relevant authorities or statutory provisions should be provided.[80] A hearing will be arranged if the Tribunal is unwilling to make the order agreed.[81] This procedure would also appear to be good practice in claims that do not relate to immigration fresh claims.

The Tribunal may make an order for costs.[82] There is no guidance in the relevant procedure rules as to how this discretion should be exercised save that it is said that account should be taken of an party's resources where the paying party is an individual.[83] There has been some suggestion that the Tribunal should adopt a different approach to that taken by the High Court. In particular, it has been suggested that the Tribunal could implement proposals for one-way costs shifting so that an individual rarely pays costs.[84] That would be consistent with the requirement of a party's resources. An individual is likely to have far less resources than a state authority. It is too early to know whether these suggestions will be acted upon.

## 6.9   APPEALS

The procedure rules provide that a person may apply to the Upper Tribunal within 1 month of the decision challenged.[85] Separate time limits are said to apply in immigration cases. These rules are complex and set different time limits depending upon whether a person is detained, at liberty in the United Kingdom or overseas.[86] However, those time limits

---

[75] See Chapter 8.
[76] Tribunals, Courts and Enforcement Act 2007, s 15(4).
[77] See Chapter 8.
[78] Practice Direction: Fresh Claim Judicial Review in the Immigration and Asylum Chamber of the Upper Tribunal, para 10.1.
[79] Ibid.
[80] Ibid.
[81] Practice Direction: Fresh Claim Judicial Review in the Immigration and Asylum Chamber of the Upper Tribunal, para 10.3.
[82] Tribunal Procedure (Upper Tribunal) Rules 2008 (SI 2008/2698), r 10(3).
[83] Tribunal Procedure (Upper Tribunal) Rules 2008 (SI 2008/2698), r 10(7)(b).
[84] Gareth Mitchell *Judicial Review, But Not As we Know It: Judicial Review in the Upper Tribunal* [2010] JR 112.
[85] Tribunal Procedure (Upper Tribunal) Rules 2008 (SI 2008/2698), r 44(4).
[86] Tribunal Procedure (Upper Tribunal) Rules 2008 (SI 2008/2698), r 44(3B).

would not appear to apply in any judicial reviews as they depend upon there being an appeal to the First-Tier Tribunal.[87] An application can be made to extend time to appeal.[88] The application for permission to appeal must identify:

(a)   the decision challenged;

(b)   the error or errors of law that are said to have been made; and

(c)   the result that the party seeking to appeal is seeking.[89]

Where an application is made for permission to appeal, the Upper Tribunal may review its own decision where it overlooked a binding provision or decision or where binding authority has been delivered since the Tribunal determined the claim.[90] If the Tribunal decides not to review its decision, it must decide whether or not to grant permission to appeal.

If permission to appeal is refused, an application for permission to appeal may be made to the Court of Appeal.[91]

The procedure in the Court of Appeal (whether or not permission has been granted by the Tribunal) would appear to be the same as adopted when appealing from the High Court.[92]

---

[87]   Ibid.
[88]   Tribunal Procedure (Upper Tribunal) Rules 2008 (SI 2008/2698), r 44(6).
[89]   Tribunal Procedure (Upper Tribunal) Rules 2008 (SI 2008/2698), r 44(7).
[90]   Tribunal Procedure (Upper Tribunal) Rules 2008 (SI 2008/2698), r 45(1).
[91]   Tribunals, Courts and Enforcement Act 2007, s 11(4).
[92]   See Chapter 9 for a consideration of that procedure.

# CHAPTER 7

## ORDERS FOR INTERIM RELIEF AVAILABLE FROM THE ADMINISTRATIVE COURT DURING A JUDICIAL REVIEW CLAIM

### 7.1 PROCEDURE FOR INTERIM RELIEF APPLICATIONS

The Administrative Court has a wide discretion to take the course which seems most likely to produce a just result.[1] This means that the Court may exercise a range of flexible powers to make orders to secure a position pending resolution of judicial review claims. These include the power to direct that proceedings be stayed,[2] interim declarations and both mandatory and prohibitory injunctions.

Where any form of interim relief is sought, this should be made clear on the claim form.[3] This means, in practice, that the section of the claim form permitting interim applications to be made should be completed so that it is clear that there is such an application. A High Court judge will then normally consider whether to grant interim relief at the same time as the application for permission to apply for judicial review or, if urgent consideration of the application for relief is sought, prior to the permission decision.

In practice, the normal procedure for considering applications for permission may mean that there is a delay in the permission application being considered. If interim relief is needed before a decision on permission, the procedure for seeking urgent consideration should be followed.[4] The need for interim relief can be used to justify an application for urgent consideration of permission, or, in an appropriate case, an application for interim relief may be considered prior to permission. In addition, injunctive relief may be sought and granted in a very urgent case prior to the issue of a claim.

If the need for interim relief arises after the claim for judicial review has been commenced, it may be sought by adopting the procedure that is used to make any other interim application.[5] It is important to file evidence in

---

[1] *Belize Alliance of Conservation Non-Governmental Organisations v Department of the Environment of Belize* [2003] 1 WLR 2839, 2850 per Lord Walker, at [39].
[2] CPR, r 54.10(2).
[3] CPR, r 54.6(1)(c).
[4] See **5.1**.
[5] See **5.10.4**.

support of the application for interim relief because the Administrative Court may be concerned as to why the application was not made when the claim was commenced and will wish to see justification for seeking interim relief.

The Administrative Court will expect the application to be made after the other parties to the proceedings have been put on notice, unless there is a particularly good reason why this has not happened.[6] In practice it would be extremely difficult to persuade the Administrative Court to accept an application for interim relief if notice has not been given. A pre-action protocol letter should indicate whether any interim measures are requested and whether, in the event that such interim measures (such as a stay) are refused, interim relief will be sought.[7]

Defendants should consider whether to contest an application for interim relief. The mere fact that a defendant wishes to contest the substantive judicial review claim does not necessarily mean that he should contest the application for interim relief if that application has merit. If a decision is taken to contest the application, the defendant should file and serve evidence in support of its objection. An order for interim relief will normally provide that a defendant may apply to the court to have any order varied or discharged on notice to the other party. If the defendant does apply for an order to be varied or discharged, the defendant will need to file and serve evidence in support of the application and provide the other parties with a reasonable opportunity to do likewise.

## 7.2    RIGHT TO APPLY FOR BAIL WHILE JUDICIAL REVIEW PROCEEDINGS ARE PENDING IN THE ADMINISTRATIVE COURT

The first matter that needs to be considered when a claimant is detained is whether he wishes to apply for bail. This may not be as straightforward an issue as it might appear to be. If a claimant is serving a criminal sentence, applying for bail in the course of an unsuccessful judicial review claim may require a return to prison without any reduction in the time served;[8] release from prison will be later than it would have been had bail not been granted. In practice, therefore, it may be in the interests of the claimant to seek an expedited hearing of the claim for judicial review rather than bail.

When a person has sought permission to bring judicial review proceedings for a quashing order challenging proceedings in the Crown Court, that person is entitled to apply to the Crown Court for bail.[9] The application

---

[6]    Per Lord Justice Parker, in *R v Kensington and Chelsea Borough Council ex p Hammell* [1989] QB 518, at 539B. See also *Practice Statement (Administrative Court: Listing and Urgent Cases)* [2002] 1 WLR 810, at 812A.

[7]    See **4.1.1**.

[8]    *R (Akhtar) v Governor of Newhall Prison* [2001] ACD 69.

[9]    Senior Courts Act 1981, s 81(1)(e).

to the Crown Court must be on at least 24 hours' notice.[10] The procedure for making an application is the same as when a defendant in proceedings in the magistrates' court seeks bail in the Crown Court.[11] If the Crown Court does grant bail, and an application of judicial review is determined or withdrawn, magistrates may issue a process enforcing the decision that is the subject of the judicial review.[12] There is no equivalent power allowing the magistrates' court to grant bail.[13]

Where detention under the Immigration Acts is challenged the First Tier Tribunal (Immigration and Asylum Chamber) has jurisdiction to grant bail in most cases,[14] including where there is no appeal before it. However, in practice, the Tribunal will often decline to grant bail where it is contended that detention is unlawful or has become so, for instance by reason of its length. This is because the First Tier Tribunal (Immigration and Asylum Chamber) often takes the view that the exercise of its statutory discretion to grant bail is premised on a lawful detention. As a consequence, it has no jurisdiction to determine the legality of detention.[15]

The power of an inferior court or tribunal to consider a bail application does not necessarily mean that the Administrative Court cannot also do so. Where a defendant applies for permission to seek an order quashing a conviction or sentence in the magistrates' court or challenging proceedings in the Crown Court, there is a statutory right to apply to the Administrative Court for bail.[16] The Administrative Court also has an inherent power to grant bail in the course of applications for judicial review.[17] The inherent power to grant bail applies whether the case is a criminal cause or matter or some other form of proceedings.[18]

There has been some suggestion that a judicial review claimant should only apply for bail to the Administrative Court after taking advantage of any alternative jurisdiction permitting an application for bail to an

---

[10]  Crown Court Rules 1982 (SI 1982/1109), r 19(2).

[11]  Ibid.

[12]  CPR, Sch 1, RSC Ord 79, r 9(11).

[13]  *Ex parte Blyth* [1944] KB 532, holding that an express statutory provision is required if a person is to be bailed after conviction. This, however, contrasts with decisions of the High Court that it has an inherent power to grant bail during a judicial review.

[14]  Immigration Act 1971, Sch 2, para 22, Immigration and Asylum Act 1999, s 54, Nationality Immigration and Asylum Act 2002, s 62(3).

[15]  *R (Konan) v Secretary of State* [2004] EWHC 22 (Admin).

[16]  Criminal Justice Act 1948, s 37(1)(b)(ii) and (d).

[17]  *R v Secretary of State for the Home Department ex p Turkoglu* [1988] QB 398, at 399H and 401G.

[18]  See e g *Amand v Home Secretary* [1943] AC 147 for a case where, in the context of a criminal habeas corpus application, it was assumed that there was an inherent power to grant bail. That inherent power may be limited following conviction: *ex p Blyth* [1944] KB 532. See e g *R v Secretary of State for the Home Department ex p Turkoglu* [1988] QB 398, where the Court determined that it had an inherent power to grant bail in a civil context.

inferior court or tribunal.[19] In practice, the Administrative Court will generally hear bail applications despite the existence of an alternative right of application.[20] This is perhaps not surprising as the Administrative Court will be better able to judge the merits of the judicial review challenge, which is clearly a factor that will be relevant to the grant of bail. Also the critical importance of judicial oversight of the legality of administrative detention means that the right to apply for discretionary bail in an alternative jurisdiction is not a relevant factor either to the merits of any substantive challenge to detention or to the Administrative court's discretion to grant bail.[21]

There are no explicit procedural rules governing applications for bail in cases that are not a criminal cause or matter. The procedure specified for applications that are criminal causes or matters is set out below. However, this procedure is generally not followed precisely, even in a criminal cause or matter as it appears to have been primarily designed for High Court bail applications in chambers where there were not proceedings pending in the Administrative Court. As a consequence, the procedure is normally adapted to reflect the normal procedure for making interim applications.

In criminal causes or matters, the procedure rules provide that bail applications should be made by claim form using Form 97.[22] However, in practice, an application for bail is normally made by so indicating on the claim form or, alternatively, by filing an application notice seeking bail and filing and serving a bail summons or draft order setting out the proposed conditions for the grant of bail, sureties' names, dates of birth, nationality and addresses.[23] The defendant should be given adequate time to consider proposed sureties, bail addresses and any proposed reporting conditions. Where bail is applied for at the time of issuing the claim it is good practice for the claimant to seek an order for abridgment of time for service of the defendant's acknowledgment of service and the listing of a prompt bail hearing thereafter. This will ensure that the Administrative Court is in the best position to reach an informed decision on bail.

In a criminal case, the bail application must be served on the prosecutor and on the Director of Public Prosecutions, if the prosecution is being brought by him.[24] In any other case, it should be served on the parties to

---

[19]  *R v Secretary of State for the Home Department ex p Kelso* [1998] INLR 603.

[20]  For example, *R (Sezek) v Secretary of State for the Home Department* [2001] INLR 675. The Court of Appeal has the same bail jurisdiction as the court appealed: Senior Courts Act 1981, s 15(3).

[21]  *R (Lumba) v Secretary of State for the Home Department* [2011] 2 WLR 671, at 706C. For the same reasons a refusal of discretionary bail in an alternative jurisdiction is not of itself relevant to the legality of detention.

[22]  CPR, Sch 1, RSC Ord 79, r 9(2). Form 97 is not a standard court form, which supports the practice of not submitting it.

[23]  See Precedents 14 and 15 in Part III.

[24]  CPR, Sch 1, RSC Ord 79, r 9(2)(a).

the judicial review and those responsible for the decision to detain the claimant in the highly unlikely event that they are not a party to the judicial review proceedings.

Service of a bail application in a criminal cause or matter must take place at least 24 hours before the date set for the hearing.[25] The rules state that the application must be supported by a witness statement or affidavit.[26] In practice, this is usually unnecessary in the context of a claim for judicial review as the evidence in support of the judicial review claim can normally stand as the evidence in support of the bail application. Clearly, in that case, the evidence in support of the judicial review claim must include all matters relevant to the grant of bail.

There is no reason, in principle, why bail should not be granted before permission to apply for judicial review has been ordered, as the inherent and statutory jurisdiction to grant bail extends to applications for permission.[27] In practice, however, the application for bail is normally considered at the same hearing as the application for permission, partly because a High Court judge is unlikely to be willing to grant bail unless satisfied that the application for judicial review is arguable and will wish to have the benefit of the defendant's acknowledgment of service in reaching a decision on the merits of the challenge.

In principle, bail can be considered by the High Court judge who rules on the paper application for permission. In practice, however, the judge is more likely to list an application for bail for hearing on notice whether or not permission is granted on the papers. If bail and permission are refused, it will be possible to make a renewed application for permission in the Administrative Court.[28] It would appear, however, that in a criminal cause or matter bail cannot be sought from a High Court judge when an application for bail, has previously been refused.[29] Thus, it may be worth asking the judge not to rule on bail when he considers a paper application if he is minded to refuse permission.

Clearly, if a High Court judge refuses permission to apply for judicial review following an oral hearing, the Administrative Court is *functus officio* and so is unable to consider a bail application. In a claim that is not a criminal cause or matter, the claimant may, however, renew the application for permission to apply for judicial review in the Court of Appeal.[30] If the application is renewed, the claimant may apply for bail in the Court of Appeal.[31]

---

[25]  Ibid, r 9(2).
[26]  Ibid, r 9(3).
[27]  *R v Secretary of State for the Home Department ex p Turkoglu* [1988] QB 398.
[28]  See **5.9**.
[29]  CPR, Sch 1, RSC Ord 79, r 9(12).
[30]  See **5.9**.
[31]  *R v Secretary of State for the Home Department ex p Turkoglu* [1988] QB 398 and *R (Sezek) v Secretary of State for the Home Department* [2001] INLR 675.

The fact that there is a need for bail is highly likely to justify a request for the judicial review claim to be given urgent consideration as the court will prioritise applications where the liberty of the subject is at stake.[32]

The right to bail under s 4 of the Bail Act 1976 does not apply to bail applications during judicial review proceedings in the Administrative Court.[33] However, this does not mean that the Administrative Court will not grant bail, but merely that there is no presumption that bail should be granted.

When the Administrative Court considers an application for bail, it is not limited to a review jurisdiction but will consider for itself whether continued detention is justified as lawful and proportionate, having regard to all relevant factors including those advanced on behalf of the detaining authority as justifying detention.[34]

Prosecutors or others can make an application to the Administrative Court for an order varying the conditions imposed on bail by the High Court. At least 24 hours' notice of the application should be given to the person who has been granted bail.[35] It should be made in the same manner as an application for bail. This application should be supported by an affidavit or witness statement.[36]

## 7.3   STAYS OF THE ENFORCEMENT OF CRIMINAL PENALTIES

Bail can effectively act as a stay of an order imprisoning a claimant. However, as judicial review proceedings are often used to challenge the decisions of the magistrates' courts, convicted defendants will often not be imprisoned but instead be subject to other penalties.

As far as the authors are aware, there are no specific statutory provisions providing for the stay of penalties other than imprisonment imposed by criminal courts while post-conviction judicial review proceedings are pending in the Administrative Court. A direction for a stay may be sought as interim relief where permission is granted (see below). Despite the lack of specific statutory provision, the Administrative Court has, on at least one occasion, ordered the suspension of a criminal penalty pending judicial review proceedings.[37]

---

[32]   See **5.1**.

[33]   Bail Act 1976, s 4(2).

[34]   *R (Sezek) v Secretary of State for the Home Department* [2001] INLR 675.

[35]   CPR, Sch 1, RSC Ord 79, r 9(2)(b).

[36]   Ibid, r 9(3).

[37]   In *Martin v Harrow Crown Court* [2007] EWHC 3193 (Admin), the Court suspended a driving disqualification pending judicial review.

Alternatively, if there is a real risk that a person who has been convicted will experience significant hardship as a result of the enforcement of any criminal penalty while proceedings are pending in the Administrative Court, an application may be made for urgent consideration.[38] The need to have the penalty quashed should be given as justification for the urgent application.

## 7.4  STAYS OF PROCEEDINGS PENDING A JUDICIAL REVIEW CHALLENGE

Normally, when a judicial review is to be sought of an interim decision of a court or tribunal, the court or tribunal that took the decision should be asked to stay the proceedings in that court pending the judicial review claim. If that is refused, a stay may be obtained as interim relief during the judicial review claim. Where permission is granted, the Administrative Court may direct that the proceedings which are the subject of judicial review should be stayed.[39] The Court interprets this power to include the power to stay the implementation of administrative decisions pending judicial review proceedings[40] and to suspend administrative decisions that have already been implemented.[41] The Court gives a wide interpretation to the power to stay proceedings in order to 'enhance the effectiveness of the judicial review jurisdiction'.[42]

A claimant in judicial review proceedings may be concerned that a stay is essential to preserve the status quo by preventing the executive acting on a decision under challenge. For example, a claimant who seeks to challenge a decision to prosecute may also seek a stay to prevent the prosecution commencing or a claimant seeking to challenge a decision to close a care home may also seek a stay on further implementation of that decision, pending, for example, consultation.

In most cases in which a stay is sought, the judicial review claim will need to be considered as a matter of urgency as a stay can only be directed once permission to apply for judicial review has been granted. As a result, it will be necessary to make an application for urgent consideration.[43] The application for a stay can be used as justification for the need for urgent consideration and the urgent consideration form should ask for the stay to be considered at this stage.

If the application is not made at the permission stage, it can be made as an interim application, provided that permission has been granted.[44]

---

[38]  See **5.1**.
[39]  CPR, r 54.10(2).
[40]  *R v Secretary of State for Education and Science ex p Avon CC (No.2)* [1991] 1 QB 558.
[41]  *R (H) v Ashworth Hospital Authority* [2003] 1 WLR 127, at 140D.
[42]  Ibid, at 138H.
[43]  See **5.1**.
[44]  See **5.10.4**.

As soon as a stay is granted, it should be served on all the other parties to the judicial review claim so that any unnecessary expense on the matters stayed can be avoided.

## 7.5    OTHER FORMS OF INTERIM RELIEF AVAILABLE DURING APPLICATIONS FOR JUDICIAL REVIEW

There would appear to be no reason in principle why the Administrative Court cannot grant any interim relief that is available to the court under Part 25 of the CPR.[45] The forms of interim relief that are most likely to be relevant and sought are an interim injunction and an interim declaration.

There would also appear to be no reason in principle why the Administrative Court cannot grant interim relief before permission is granted or even before the claim is issued.[46] In practice, this regularly happens when a claimant makes an urgent application by telephone.[47] For example, the duty High Court judge will often be required to grant interim relief to prevent a claimant being made homeless or removed from the United Kingdom. However, the judge will not normally grant permission when the application is made by telephone, in the absence of an acknowledgment of service or submissions from the defendant.

### 7.5.1    Interim injunctions

The High Court may grant injunctions when it is 'just and convenient' to do so.[48] Injunctions are a very important form of interim relief in judicial review, as it is now well established that an injunction can be issued against the Crown.[49] Thus, a claimant for judicial review may seek an injunction to prevent a government department from acting in accordance with a decision that is being challenged by way of judicial review or to require a government department to take steps notwithstanding the decision under challenge.

The jurisdiction to grant interim injunctions overlaps with the jurisdiction to grant stays.[50] However, in practice, that does not mean that injunctions are of limited significance as injunctive relief, unlike a stay, is not contingent on a grant of permission and may be mandatory as well as prohibitory. A mandatory injunction may be used positively to compel a

---

[45]    CPR, r 25.1.
[46]    CPR, r 25.2(1).
[47]    See **5.1.1**.
[48]    Senior Courts Act 1981, s 37(1).
[49]    In *Re M* [1994] 1 AC 377.
[50]    Se **7.4**.

decision-maker to do something, such as to continue to provide benefits[51] or, in an extreme case, to grant entry clearance to enable an individual to come to the United Kingdom.[52]

When the Administrative Court hears an application for an interim injunction, it will consider whether there is a serious issue to be tried and whether the claimant or the defendant will suffer greater inconvenience as a result of the decision regarding interim relief. It will compare the position of the claimant if he is successful at the conclusion of the action but has been refused interim relief, with the position of the defendant if interim relief is granted, but the claimant is eventually unsuccessful.[53]

In private law actions, the court will take account of the adequacy of damages as a remedy for the claimant and compare this with the value of an undertaking from the claimant for damages suffered by the defendant as a result of the injunction.[54] In some judicial review claims, the court may be able to take a similar approach. In most claims for judicial review however, damages are not likely to be an issue of significance. As a result, the Administrative Court tends to be more concerned about minimising the risk of injustice when it considers an application for an injunction during judicial review proceedings.[55] However, although damages are less significant, the Administrative Court may still be reluctant to grant an interlocutory injunction without an undertaking from the claimant for damages suffered by the defendant as a result of the injunction.[56] The court will not normally require an undertaking where the claimant is in receipt of public funding.

In practice, undertakings for damages are regarded as most significant where a claimant is challenging a decision that will have commercial significance for both the claimant and other parties. The Administrative Court will be unlikely to impose a requirement to give an undertaking for damages where the claimant is an individual who is at risk of significant irreversible harm – for example, where the claimant is about to be

---

[51]  See, for example, *R v Servite Homes ex p Goldsmith* (2000) 3 CCLR 354.

[52]  See, for example, *R (Moyo) v Entry Clearance Officer*, unreported, (CO/6257/2009).

[53]  *American Cyanamid Co v Ethicon Ltd* [1975] AC 396, applied in a public law context in cases such as *R v Ministry of Agriculture, Fisheries and Food ex p Monsanto Plc (No 2)* [1999] QB 1161, at 1166, and *R v Secretary of State for Transport ex p Factortame (No 2)* [1991] 1 AC 603, at 672D. See also the useful discussion of these principles in the more recent judgment of *R (Leeds Unique Education Ltd t/a Leeds Professional College) v Secretary of State for the Home Department* [2010] EWHC 1030 (Admin), at [26]–[30].

[54]  Indeed, Practice Direction 25A, para 5.1(1) provides that, unless the Administrative Court orders otherwise, an interim injunction must include: 'an undertaking by the applicant to the court to pay any damages which the respondent sustains which the court considers the applicant should pay'.

[55]  Per Lord Bridge, *R v Secretary of State for Transport ex p Factortame (No 2)* [1991] 1 AC 603, at 659F.

[56]  *R v Secretary of State for the Environment ex p Rose Theatre Trust Company (No 1)* [1990] COD 47.

removed from the United Kingdom, made homeless or denied welfare benefits for a significant period of time.[57]

Other factors that are clearly relevant when deciding whether an injunction should be granted include the strength of the claim[58] and the public interest.[59] It is also necessary to consider the scope of the proposed injunction. For example, the Administrative Court is likely to be particularly reluctant to grant an injunction that disapplies existing legislation.[60] Where the injunction relates not to primary legislation but to implementation of government policy, the balance of convenience may lay in favour of the party seeking a stay, depending on the facts of the case.[61]

In judicial review, where the defendant is a public authority with a duty to act in the public interest, the Court will consider the balance of convenience more widely and will take into account the interests of the public in general to whom the duties are owed.[62] This may assist a claimant, for instance when no cross-undertaking in damages can be given, but it can also benefit a defendant.[63]

Where the judicial review claim includes a claim under the Human Rights Act 1998, it is important to remember that it is not necessarily unlawful for a public body to act in a manner that is inconsistent with the European Convention on Human Rights where for instance that conduct is consistent with primary legislation.[64] In other circumstances, it appears that the normal balance of convenience test applies, although, in applying the balance of convenience, appropriate weight should be given to the human rights in issue.[65]

In the context of mandatory injunctions, where an order is being sought in the interim to compel a public authority to undertake action rather

---

[57]　See, for example, *R (Q) v Secretary of State for the Home Department* [2003] EWHC Admin 195, (2003) *The Times*, February 20, in which large numbers of injunctions were granted to prevent people becoming destitute without the need for undertakings for damages.

[58]　See, for example, *R v Servite Homes ex p Goldsmith* (2000) 3 CCLR 354, in which the Court of Appeal held that, although it was not appropriate to express a view about the prospects of success, it was significant that the judge had encouraged an appeal; and *R v National Trust ex p Scott* [1998] 1 WLR 226, in which Tucker J suggested that the fact that a claimant had an arguable claim did not necessarily mean that an injunction should be granted.

[59]　See, for example, *R v Servite Homes ex p Goldsmith* (2000) 3 CCLR 354.

[60]　*R v HM Treasury ex p British Telecommunications Plc* [1994] 1 CMLR 621.

[61]　See, for example, *R (Medical Justice) v Secretary of State for the Home Department* [2010] EWHC 1425 (Admin).

[62]　*Smith v Inner London Education Authority* [1978] 1 All ER 411, at 422H.

[63]　See, for example, *Belize Alliance of non-Governmental Organisations v Department of the Environment (Practice Note)* [2003] 1 WLR 2839.

[64]　See **8.2.5(1)** for consideration of declarations of incompatibility. See also *R (Aggregate Industries Ltd) v English Nature* [2001] EWHC 934 (Admin).

[65]　*Douglas v Hello! Ltd* [2001] QB 967.

than to restrain it, a 'strong prima facie case'[66] must be shown and the court should feel a 'high degree of assurance' that at the trial it will appear that the injunction was rightly granted.[67] The test for establishing a strong prima facie case is higher than the threshold for the grant of permission to apply for judicial review. Thus it is possible to be granted permission to apply for judicial review but be refused interim relief.[68] However, even where the court is unable to feel any high degree of assurance that the claimant will succeed in his claim, there may still be circumstances in which it is appropriate to grant a mandatory injunction at an interlocutory stage. Those circumstances will exist where the risk of injustice if the injunction is refused sufficiently outweigh the risk of injustice if it is granted,[69] for example where a mandatory injunction is sought to prevent a breach of human rights.

Where injunctions are sought to disapply domestic law that is said to be inconsistent with the law of the European Union it appears that a different approach is applied. In particular, the domestic court must normally decide that there are serious doubts as to the validity of the Community measure and, should the question of the validity of the contested measure not already have been brought before the Court of Justice of the European Union, it must refer the question to the Court. It must also decide whether there is urgency and a threat of serious and irreparable damage to the applicant and it must take due account of the Community's interests as well as any decisions of the Court of Justice.[70]

## 7.5.2   Interim declarations

Although the CPR now make it clear that the power to make an interim declaration is available to the courts, the courts were previously concerned that there might not be such a power.[71] As a result, there is little case-law considering the approach of the Administrative Court to applications for an interim declaration.[72]

---

[66]   *De Falco v Crawley Borough Council* [1980] QB 460, *Francis v Kensington and Chelsea Royal London Borough Council* [2003] 1 WLR 2248, at 2253F.

[67]   *Shepherd Homes Ltd v Sandham* [1971] Ch 340, at 351.

[68]   *R (Omatoyo) v City of Westminster* [2006] EWHC 2572 (Admin), at [15].

[69]   *Nottingham Building Society v Eurodynamics Systems* [1993] FSR 468, at 474.

[70]   *R (ABNA Ltd) v Secretary of State for Health* [2003] EWHC 2420 (Admin), [2004] 2 CMLR 39.

[71]   See, for example, Lord Woolf, *In Re M* [1994] 1 AC 377, at 423A, who stated that he could see 'advantages' in the court having jurisdiction to make interim declarations; and Mr Justice Jacob, holding that an interim declaration would be 'juridical nonsense', in *Newport Association Football Club Ltd v Football Association of Wales Ltd* [1995] 2 All ER 87, at 92A.

[72]   Indeed, in *Amalgamated Metal Trading Ltd v City of London Police Financial Investigation Unit* [2003] 1 WLR 2711, at 2717B, Mr Justice Tomlinson suggested that it remains to be worked out what are the circumstances in which it might be appropriate to resort to in applications for an interim declaration.

An interim declaration in judicial review proceedings may operate in a manner that is equivalent to an injunction because a public body ought to be expected to act in accordance with the law and hence respect the terms of an interim declaration. The courts do appear to be influenced by the similarity between injunctions and declarations when considering applications for interim declarations. First, it appears clear that the Administrative Court will be keen to prevent the making of interim declarations that act as injunctions, but which defeat the requirement for undertakings regarding damages.[73] In addition, the Administrative Court is likely to apply the balance of convenience test when considering an application for an interim declaration.[74] Circumstances in which the court has made interim declarations include the 'best interests' jurisdiction of the High Court to protect vulnerable adults.[75]

In practice, the Administrative Court is likely to be reluctant to make an interim declaration defining the rights and obligations of parties when it has not heard the full argument. A more informal approach may often be appropriate. For some time it has been the practice of High Court judges to make appropriate informal remarks on the position of the parties. These remarks are clearly not binding, but parties must take them seriously when considering the merits of the case. A failure to take the remarks seriously, or a decision to press ahead with a decision in the face of a strong challenge, may result in strong judicial criticism[76] or costs penalties.[77]

---

[73]  *R v Secretary of State for the Environment ex p Royal Society for the Protection of Birds* (1995) 7 Admin LR 434, at 443.

[74]  *R (Mayer Parry Recycling Ltd) v Environmental Agency* [2001] Env LR 35.

[75]  See, for example, *NHS Trust v T (Adult Patient: Refusal of Medical Treatment)* [2005] 1 All ER 387.

[76]  See, for example, *R v Secretary of State for Education and Science ex p Hardy* [1989] LG Rev 592.

[77]  See, for example, *R v Metropolitan Stipendiary Magistrate ex p Ali* [1997] Env LR D15.

# CHAPTER 8

## RELIEF AVAILABLE AT THE END OF JUDICIAL REVIEW PROCEEDINGS

### 8.1 DISCRETION AND JUDICIAL REVIEW

Judicial review is a discretionary remedy.[1] Thus, the fact that a claimant establishes that a public body erred in law does not necessarily mean that the Administrative Court will make the order that the claimant seeks or indeed provide any relief. Lord Justice Hobhouse considered the scope of the Court's discretion when deciding whether to grant a remedy and if so, what. He held that:

> 'The discretion of the court in deciding whether to grant any remedy is a wide one. It can take into account many considerations, including the needs of good administration, delay,[2] the effect on third parties, the utility of granting the relevant remedy. The discretion can be exercised so as partially to uphold and partially quash the relevant administrative decision or act.'[3]

However, despite the discretionary nature of judicial review, in practice the Administrative Court is likely to grant the remedy sought unless there is some particularly good reason why relief should be refused[4] because the Court is likely to be concerned about reaching a conclusion that permits a public body to continue to act in an unlawful manner.

An exercise of discretion may result in relief being refused as a result of any of the factors identified by Lord Justice Hobhouse. However, his list is not exhaustive. Factors that are relevant to the exercise of discretion in the context of judicial review include a failure by the applicant to make proper disclosure,[5] the existence of an alternative remedy[6] and the fact that the application has become academic.[7]

Possibly the most significant factor that is relevant to the issue of discretion is the materiality of the error identified. It has been noted

---

[1]  *R v Panel on Take-overs and Mergers ex p Guinness Plc* [1990] 1 QB 146, per Lord Donaldson MR, at 177E.
[2]  See **3.1**.
[3]  *Credit Suisse v Allerdale Borough Council* [1997] QB 306, at 355D.
[4]  See, for example, *R v General Medical Council ex p Toth* [2000] 1 WLR 2209.
[5]  See **5.3**.
[6]  See **3.3**.
[7]  See **8.1.1**.

earlier that there are circumstances in which materiality is relevant. For example, an error of law would result in a claim for judicial review succeeding only if it could be shown that the error was material.[8] Furthermore, prejudice may be relevant to the issue of whether procedural unfairness should result in a decision being quashed.[9] In principle, there is no reason why this approach should not be applied in other contexts. In particular, if it can be shown that the error made no difference then that provides a strong argument that a claimant should be denied relief.

Materiality means that, in an immigration case, the Administrative Court may consider whether the Secretary of State could properly deny a claimant an appeal using his statutory powers when it is properly argued that a claimant has been wrongly denied a right of appeal as a consequence of the Secretary of State's misdirection regarding the scope of the right of appeal.[10] The scope of the right of appeal will be immaterial if the right of appeal can be denied in any event.

Materiality may also mean that relief will be denied where a claimant will receive no benefit from a grant of relief because the decision-maker has already changed his practice so that the legal error highlighted in the claim will not happen in future.[11]

Materiality is important in part because of the practice of some decision-makers of giving alternative reasons for a decision. Some decision-makers will say 'even if I am wrong' before giving alternative reasons for the decision. This approach permits the decision-maker to argue that any error is not material unless all the alternative reasons can also be shown to be flawed.

Linked to materiality is the Court's discretion to refuse relief on the basis that a claim has become academic.[12] It might be said that an error is not material if the judicial review challenge has become academic.

It was noted earlier that the Administrative Court is likely to be concerned about the subject matter of the decision that is being challenged when determining whether time should be extended to enable a judicial review claim to be brought.[13] A similar approach is likely to apply to the Court's exercise of discretion. For example, it is highly unlikely that the Court would deny relief if that would result in a claimant remaining unlawfully detained.

---

[8]   See **2.3**.

[9]   See **2.8.1**.

[10]  *R (Duka) v Secretary of State for the Home Department* [2003] EWHC 1262 (Admin).

[11]  *R v Secretary of State for the Home Department ex p Harry* [1998] 1 WLR 1737.

[12]  See **8.1.1**.

[13]  See **3.1.2**.

The discretionary nature of judicial review is not merely relevant to the issue of whether it is appropriate to grant any relief; the Court also has discretion to consider the form of relief that is ordered. Thus, the form of relief may be affected by matters such as delay.[14] The Administrative Court could determine that a decision is unlawful, but decide merely to make a declaration rather than quash the decision that is being challenged.[15]

The Administrative Court can consider the exercise of its discretion both when the applicant for judicial review asks for permission and when final relief is considered at the substantive hearing. As noted earlier, permission will be refused if it appears that the judicial review application is unarguable.[16] Clearly, if discretionary factors mean that the Administrative Court will be bound to refuse relief when it considers the substantive hearing, permission will be refused.

### 8.1.1 Judicial review and academic challenges

The concept of discretion is linked to the Administrative Court's reluctance to consider judicial review claims that raise theoretical or academic issues. In circumstances where the applicant will not benefit from a clarification of the law, the Administrative Court may well be reluctant to determine a question of law – for example, on a number of occasions the courts have expressed a reluctance to consider a case as a 'test case' that will enable the courts to determine hypothetical issues.[17]

Although the Administrative Court has shown a reluctance to consider theoretical issues, that does not mean that the courts never consider such issues. The courts increasingly recognise that there is a public interest in resolving issues that will affect the public at large. The Administrative Court can give guidance that will assist public decision-makers to exercise their powers lawfully. Thus, in particular cases, the courts have recognised that there is a role for them to give guidance in circumstances where that guidance will not produce an immediate benefit for the particular claimant.[18] Historically, this has often been done by making obiter remarks.

---

[14]   *R v Rochdale Metropolitan Borough Council ex p Schemet* [1994] ELR 89.
[15]   See *R v Dairy Produce Quota Tribunal ex p Caswell* [1990] 2 AC 738 for an example of a case where the court made a declaration to govern future conduct, but refused an order giving the applicant relief in relation to previous conduct.
[16]   See **5.8**.
[17]   See, for example, *R v Secretary of State for the Home Department ex p Wynne* [1993] 1 WLR 115.
[18]   For example, *R v Lewes Justices ex p Secretary of State for the Home Department* [1973] AC 388, at 410H, is an example of a case where the House of Lords decided to give guidance on a legal issue that was not decisive to the case in issue in response to a request by one party.

In the last few years the courts have shown a greater willingness to go beyond merely making obiter remarks about matters that might appear academic from the perspective of an individual claimant and have granted relief. For example, the Court of Appeal was willing to grant a declaration that the listing practice of the Mental Health Review Tribunal was unlawful, despite the fact that the claimant was no longer detained under the Mental Health Act 1983.[19] The Court relied on the fact that the claim raised issues of general public importance and that the claimant suffered from a mental disorder which meant that he might be detained in similar circumstances in future.[20]

One matter that is plainly relevant to whether the courts should consider an academic claim is whether the subject matter of the claim means that it is only ever likely to arise in academic claims.[21]

There may be stronger arguments that claims regarding the HRA 1998 should be determined despite the fact that they are academic. The European Court of Human Rights has indicated that people remain victims with standing before it unless the domestic system acknowledges the fact that they have suffered breaches.[22] The domestic courts have also acknowledged the value of a finding that human rights have been violated.[23] Despite this the Court of Appeal was recently unwilling to consider a human rights claim that it concluded would bring no benefit to anyone.[24]

If developments mean that it might be argued that a judicial review claim has become academic, it is important that the parties keep the Administrative Court informed of those developments.[25] It is for the Court (and not the parties) to decide whether there is sufficient public interest in a claim being resolved that it should be heard despite an argument that it is academic.

In practice, lawyers acting for individual applicants will normally wish to settle an application by consent if there is no benefit for the applicant. Privately funded clients are unlikely to wish to resolve issues of law that have no relevance to their case. In addition, the duty owed by lawyers acting for a publicly funded client to the Legal Services Commission may mean that it will be difficult to justify a judicial review application that

---

[19]   *R (C) v Mental Health Review Tribunal* [2002] 1 WLR 176.
[20]   Ibid, at 179E.
[21]   See, for example, *R v Horseferry Road Magistrates' Court ex p Bennett* (1994) 99 Cr App R 123, at 130.
[22]   *Scordino v Italy* (2007) 45 EHRR 7, at [170].
[23]   *R (Greenfield) v Secretary of State for the Home Department* [2005] 1 WLR 673, at 684B.
[24]   *R (MD (China)) v Secretary of State for the Home Department* [2011] EWCA Civ 453, at [13].
[25]   *R (Tshikangu) v Newham London Borough Council* [2001] NPC 33.

has no benefit to the client.[26] However, lawyers acting for public bodies may well wish to have the court determine an issue that will be relevant to other cases: they will need to be aware that they may have to show a good reason why the court should resolve the issue, if the court is not to refuse to decide the issue; and will need to consider the issue of costs and possibly whether they wish to fund their opponent so that the matter can be heard.

The procedure for settling a claim that has become academic has already been considered.[27]

## 8.2 JUDICIAL REVIEW ORDERS

The Administrative Court has exclusive jurisdiction to make a quashing order, a mandatory order or a prohibiting order at the conclusion of an application for judicial review.[28] It may also grant an injunction or make a declaration or award damages.[29]

It is important to be aware of the effect of a judicial review judgment (and any remedy granted): it determines how the law always has been. Thus, a decision-maker who acts in good faith may be liable for acting unlawfully, even if he acted in accordance with the law as it was generally understood prior to the judicial review judgment.[30] There is some suggestion that the courts should be able to limit the effect of judgments so that they only have future effect. So far, however, the courts have been unwilling to adopt that approach.[31] The fact that judgments do not change the law means that the Supreme Court was recently unwilling to stay orders that it made holding that secondary legislation was ultra vires.[32] That is because a stay of the order would obfuscate the position. Ultra vires secondary legislation will always have been unlawful whether or not an order has been made.

Where the Administrative Court considers a judicial review claim, it is possible that the Court will consider that it is appropriate to grant relief in relation to part (but not the whole) of the decision challenged.[33] Whether the Court will do this is likely to depend in part on the extent to which

---

26  See **4.2.2** for a consideration of the merits test that applies in the context of judicial review. It is important to be aware that this does now permit a claim to be funded on the basis of public interest.
27  See **5.12**.
28  Senior Courts Act 1981, s 31(1) and CPR, r 54.2.
29  SCA 1981, s 31(2) and CPR, r 54.3.
30  *R v Governor of Brockhill Prison ex p Evans (No 2)* [2001] 2 AC 19.
31  Ibid.
32  *A v HM Treasury* [2010] 2 AC 534.
33  See, for example, *R v Belmarsh Magistrates' Court ex p Gilligan* [1998] 1 Cr App R 14, in which the committal of some but not all criminal charges was quashed.

aspects of the decision challenged may be severed. If aspects of the decision cannot be severed then the Court may well grant relief in relation to the whole decision.

### 8.2.1 Quashing order

A quashing order is the order most usually sought in judicial review proceedings because it is the remedy by which the Administrative Court quashes a decision that has been challenged. For example, this is the form of order that the Administrative Court makes when it quashes either a criminal conviction or a sentence. It is not merely used to quash decisions of the courts; executive decisions are also often quashed. For example, a planning decision that is flawed will normally be quashed. When the court makes a quashing order, it can also remit the decision for reconsideration. Hence, a successful judicial review claim challenging a decision of a lower court will normally result in the decision being quashed and the matter being remitted for reconsideration.

The CPR make it clear that where a quashing order is made, the Administrative Court is not obliged to remit the matter. The Court may, 'in so far as any enactment permits, substitute its own decision for the decision to which the claim relates'.[34] Section 31(5A) of the Senior Courts Act 1981 provides that this power can only be used where the decision challenged was taken by a court and there is no other decision that the court could take.

In practice, it appears that the power of the Administrative Court to take a fresh decision is rarely (if ever) exercised, probably because the Court will be reluctant to substitute its own judgment for that of a decision-maker who has statutory responsibility for deciding upon the matter. Before exercising the power the Court may wish to be satisfied that there is only one decision that could be taken lawfully.

One area where the Administrative Court may be likely to substitute its own decision is where it quashes a sentence imposed by a lower court. In those circumstances, it has a specific statutory power to substitute a sentence. This is considered in detail below.[35]

### 8.2.2 Mandatory order

A mandatory order is an order requiring a court or public body to carry out its duty. For example, it is the order sought when a claimant seeks to force a court to state a case.[36] Similarly, such an order can be sought to

---

[34] CPR, r 54.19(2)(b).
[35] See **8.3**.
[36] Senior Courts Act 1981, s 29(3), where the Crown Court refuses to state a case; and Magistrates' Courts Act 1980, s 111(6), where the magistrates' court refuses to state a case.

force a court to consider a matter when it has wrongly held that it has no jurisdiction.[37] It is not only courts that can be subject to mandatory orders. For example, a mandatory order would be sought where an administrative decision-maker such as a local council has refused to take a decision that it is legally obliged to take.

In practice, there is a degree of judicial reluctance to make mandatory orders. The Administrative Court will often regard its judgment as giving sufficient guidance as to what a public body should do in future if it is to act lawfully.

### 8.2.3   Prohibiting order

A prohibiting order is an order preventing an inferior court or public body from acting outside its jurisdiction in the future. As a result, it is sometimes sought in addition to a quashing order. If a decision-maker has already made a decision that is in excess of jurisdiction, a quashing order and
a prohibiting order can be sought. A quashing order can be sought to quash that decision and a prohibiting order can be sought to prevent the decision-maker continuing to act in excess of jurisdiction. The quashing order addresses past decisions and the prohibiting order addresses the future.

A prohibiting order may be sought preventing a decision in excess of jurisdiction, even where there is a right of appeal against that decision.[38]

### 8.2.4   Injunctions

An injunction is an order that is 'indistinguishable' in its effect from a mandatory or prohibiting order[39] because it is an order that requires a party either to act or to refrain from acting. As a result, injunctions are rarely granted as relief following the substantive hearing.[40] Instead, the Administrative Court will normally make a mandatory or prohibiting order in preference to an injunction. Injunctions are more commonly sought as a form of interim relief.[41]

---

[37]   See, for example, *R v Oxford Justices ex p D* [1987] QB 199.
[38]   *Turner v Kingsbury Collieries Ltd* [1921] 3 KB 169, at 174.
[39]   *In Re M* [1994] 1 AC 377, per Lord Woolf, at 415E.
[40]   There are, however, examples of injunctions being granted at the conclusion of judicial review proceedings: see, for example, *R v North Yorkshire County Council ex p M* [1989] QB 411.
[41]   See **7.5.1**.

## 8.2.5 Declarations

Declarations enable a High Court judge to clarify the law by stating the law in an order.[42] As one of the roles of judicial review proceedings is to ensure that public decision-makers act according to the law, declarations are obviously important as they help decision-makers to act in accordance with the law. Thus, although the Administrative Court may not be satisfied that a particular decision should be quashed, it may grant a declaration. This will benefit decision-makers with similar decisions yet to be taken. For example, although a decision to refuse public funding might not be quashed, the Administrative Court may make a declaration about the scope of the jurisdiction to grant legal aid.[43] Declarations may also be made regarding matters personal to a claimant, such as his age,[44] or as to the period for which detention had been unlawful.[45] In practice, obtaining a declaration may be almost as beneficial to a claimant as obtaining any other order because public decision-makers should regard themselves as being bound by the terms of the declaration.

The circumstances in which a declaration may be granted are provided for by s 31(2) of the Senior Courts Act 1981:

> 'A declaration may be made or an injunction granted under this subsection in any case where an application for judicial review, seeking that relief, has been made and the High Court considers that, having regard to –
> (a)　the nature of the matters in respect of which relief may be granted by mandatory, prohibiting or quashing orders;
> (b)　the nature of the persons and bodies against whom relief may be granted by such orders; and
> (c)　all the circumstances of the case,
>
> it would be just and convenient for the declaration to be made or the injunction to be granted, as the case may be.'

In practice, the Administrative Court may be reluctant to make declarations where it believes that the terms of a judgment ought to provide sufficient guidance as to how a public authority ought to act in future.[46]

### Declaration of incompatibility

The HRA 1998 has now provided the Administrative Court with the power to make a declaration of incompatibility. A declaration of

---

[42]　See, for example, *Vine v National Dock Labour Board* [1957] AC 488, per Lord Morton, at 504.

[43]　*R v Recorder of Liverpool ex p McCann* [1995] RTR 23.

[44]　See, for example *R (Y) v London Borough of Hillingdon* [2011] EWHC 1477 (Admin).

[45]　*R (MI (Iraq)) (AO (Iraq)) v Secretary of State for the Home Department* [2011] ACD 15.

[46]　See, for example, *R (Betteridge) v Parole Board* [2009] EWHC 1638 (Admin), at [29].

incompatibility can be made only after the Court has attempted to construe primary legislation in a manner that is compatible with the European Convention on Human Rights but failed.[47] As s 3 of the HRA 1998 requires the Court to read legislation in a manner that is compatible with the Convention 'so far as it is possible to do so', it will be unusual for the Court to conclude that a statute cannot be construed in such a manner.

The most obvious circumstances in which a declaration of incompatibility could be made is where a statute provides that a particular decision-maker (such as an administrative decision-maker) is required to take a decision but the Convention requires another decision-maker (such as a court or tribunal) to take it.[48] This reflects a wider concern that the Courts should not use their powers in s 3 of the HRA 1998 to legislate.[49]

The fact that primary legislation cannot be construed in a manner that is compatible with the European Convention on Human Rights does not necessarily mean that a declaration of incompatibility should be made. The Court has a discretion to refuse to make a declaration of incompatibility. However, in practice, it is difficult to imagine circumstances in which a provision was found to be incompatible but a declaration would be refused. For example, the House of Lords has been willing to issue a declaration despite the fact that the Government had acknowledged and accepted that legislation was incompatible with the Convention.[50] One situation in which a declaration has been refused is where a declaration had already been made in Scotland.[51]

### 8.2.6 Power to award damages at conclusion of claim

The Administrative Court has power to award damages at the conclusion of a judicial review claim, as s 31(4) of the Senior Courts Act 1981 provides:

'(4) On an application for judicial review the High Court may award to the applicant damages, restitution or the recovery of a sum due if
(a) the application includes a claim for such an award arising from any matter to which the application relates; and
(b) the court is satisfied that such an award would have been made if the claim had been made in an action begun by the applicant at the time of making the application.'

---

[47] *Wilson v First Country Trust Ltd (No 2)* [2004] 1 AC 816.
[48] *Re S (Children) (Care Order: Implementation of Care Plan), Re W (Children) (Care Order: Adequacy of Care Plan)* [2002] 2 AC 291, applied in *R (Anderson) v Secretary of State for the Home Department* [2003] 1 AC 837 and *R (D) v Secretary of State for the Home Department* [2002] 1 WLR 1315.
[49] *Re S (Minors)* [2002] 2 AC 291, at 313E.
[50] *Bellinger v Bellinger* [2003] 2 AC 467.
[51] *R (Chester) v Secretary of State for Justice* [2011] 1 WLR 1436.

The terms of the statute and the CPR make it clear that damages can be sought only if some other form of judicial review remedy is being sought.[52] This may not be a problem, in practice, as a claimant is likely to seek a declaration that the behaviour giving rise to the claim for damages is unlawful.

There is no general right to damages for a breach of public law.[53] However there are three circumstances in which damages may be claimed: (i) where the remedy of damages would have been available if the claim had been brought as a private law action (for example negligence or false imprisonment); (ii) where 'just satisfaction' is sought for a breach of the HRA 1998; and (iii) where it is successfully claimed that a public body has infringed an individual right in European Union law.

Turning first to judicial review claims which also sound in private law, it is clear that, in order for damages to be claimed, it needs to be established that the facts of the claim show some recognised form of private law action that gives rise to damages. A consideration of the full range of circumstances in which it is possible to claim damages is well beyond the scope of this book. There are, however, some brief points that are worth making.

A claim for damages for breach of statutory duty might at first glance appear to be the most obvious head of tort that could be relied on. However, for a claim for breach of statutory duty to be established, it must be shown that Parliament intended that individuals should be able to claim damages for a breach of the statute's provisions.[54] The Courts have generally been unwilling to conclude that breach of a statute gives rise to a claim for damages unless there is some express provision addressing the issue of damages.

A more promising basis for claiming damages might appear to be to allege that there is misfeasance in public office. However, again it appears that such a claim may be difficult to establish as misfeasance in public office requires proof of the following matters:[55]

(1)    the defendant is a public officer;

(2)    the defendant was exercising his power as a public officer;

---

[52]    CPR, r 54.3(2).

[53]    *R v Secretary of State for Transport ex p Factortame Ltd (No 2)* [1991] 1 AC 603, per Lord Goff, at 672H.

[54]    *R v Deputy Governor of Parkhurst Prison ex p Hague* [1992] 1 AC 58.

[55]    *Three Rivers District Council v Bank of England (No 3)* [2003] 2 AC 1.

(3)   the defendant had a particular frame of mind (either he must have intended to injure the claimant or he must have known that he had no power to act and that his actions were likely to injure the claimant);

(4)   causation of loss;[56]

(5)   knowledge on the part of the defendant that loss would be probable.

Given that judicial review rarely involves fact finding, it is unlikely that the required mental elements will be established in the context of a judicial review claim.

In principle, any other head of tort might give rise to a claim for damages. However, in practice, the limitation on fact finding in judicial review means that it is difficult to establish most of these torts. Perhaps the area where there has been the greatest number of claims for damages in the context of judicial review is in the context of unlawful detention or the tort of false imprisonment.[57] In particular, there have been a large number of claims for damages for immigration detention.[58]

The practice of the Administrative Court is that it usually considers the merits of the judicial review claim that is said to give rise to damages first. If the claim is successful, it will normally adjourn the hearing for the resolution of the claim for damages and transfer to the Queens Bench Division if appropriate.

## Damages under the Human Rights Act 1998

The circumstances in which it is possible to obtain damages have been extended by the HRA 1998. Sections 8 and 9 of the HRA 1998 permit damages to be awarded in circumstances in which the European Court of Human Rights would award damages.[59]

In *Anufrijeva v Southwark LBC*[60] the Court of Appeal considered the correct approach to damages claimed for a violation of Art 8 of the Convention caused by maladministration. The Court encouraged the use of alternative dispute mechanisms such as a complaint to the Local Government Ombudsman rather than litigation as a way of avoiding disproportionate costs being incurred in litigation. The Court even suggested that where judicial review claims are commenced, the damages

---

[56]   Material loss is a requirement of the tort, *Watkins v Secretary of State for the Home Department* [2006] 2 AC 395.

[57]   See, for example, *R v Governor of Brockhill Prison ex p Evans (No 2)* [2001] 2 AC 19.

[58]   See, for example, *R (Lumba) v Secretary of State for the Home Department* [2011] 2 WLR 671.

[59]   HRA 1998, s 8(4).

[60]   [2004] QB 1124.

aspect of the claim should be stayed until alternative dispute mechanisms have been used. In practice, the courts have generally been willing to consider claims for human rights damages without considering whether there are alternative dispute mechanisms. In part that that may be because a person remains a victim of a breach of the European Convention on Human Rights able to bring proceedings in the European Court unless appropriate damages are awarded.[61]

Subsequently, in *R (Greenfield) v Secretary of State*[62] the House of Lords emphasised that the courts should not follow the approach to the award of damages in tort. There are two reasons for this. Firstly, the HRA 1998 is not a tort statute.[63] In addition, the purpose of the HRA 1998 is not to award persons greater damages than that they can achieve through apply to the European Court of Human Rights.[64]

The problem with applying the approach in *Greenfield* is that it is difficult to determine what damages would be awarded by the European Court. That is because there are essentially no articulated principle that govern the award of damages by the European Court.[65]

### Damages under European Union Law

The scope for individuals to claim damages against public bodies for infringements of EU law rights was first acknowledged in *Francovich and Bonifaci v Italian Republic.*[66] The conditions defining when such relief is available were clarified in *Brasserie du Pecheur and Factortame.*[67] Damages are available to a successful claimant where:

(a)   the rule of European law infringed is one intended to confer rights on individuals;

(b)   the breach of that rule is 'sufficiently serious'; and

(c)   there is a 'direct causal link' between the breach and the damage sustained by the claimant.[68]

---

61   *Ciorap v Moldova (No 3)*, Application No 7481/06, at [24]–[26].
62   [2005] 1 WLR 673.
63   *R (Greenfield) v Secretary of State for the Home Department* [2005] 1 WLR 673, at 684A.
64   Ibid, at 684C.
65   *R (Faulkner) v Secretary of State* [2011] EWCA Civ 349, at [6].
66   [1993] 2 CMLR 66.
67   *Brasserie du Pecheur S.A. v Federal Republic of Germany, R v Secretary of State for Transport, ex p Factortame (No 4)* [1996] QB 404.
68   Ibid, at 499C. Where the breach concerns a field giving rise to a wide discretion on the part of the state, it must be shown the state has 'manifestly and gravely disregarded the limits on the exercise of its powers' (at 498D–498E).

It is also important to note that the principle of 'state liability' in damages for breaches of EU law extends beyond the administrative and legislative context and includes domestic courts.[69] In certain circumstances, where a domestic court of last instance itself fails to apply EU law correctly, the state may also be liable to individuals in damages for such a failure.[70] However such failures must be 'manifest'.[71] In order for the domestic court to decide whether such an error by a court gives rise to liability in damages, the court should take into account a range of relevant circumstances, including, in particular, the degree of clarity and precision of the rule infringed, whether the infringement was intentional, whether the error of law was excusable or inexcusable, the position taken, where applicable, by a Community institution, and non-compliance by the court in question with its obligation to make a reference for a preliminary ruling.[72]

Examples of the approach taken by the Administrative Court to damages for breaches of EU law include an award for a breach of the prohibition of discrimination on nationality grounds,[73] and a decision that the threshold for state liability in damages was not met where, as a consequence of a failure to implement EU Directive 2003/9 and in breach of Art 11 of the Directive, an asylum seeker had been denied permission to work.[74]

## 8.3 POWER TO VARY A SENTENCE FOLLOWING JUDICIAL REVIEW

Section 43(1) of the Senior Courts Act 1981 provides the Administrative Court with a specific statutory power to vary a sentence imposed by a magistrates' court or the Crown Court following a committal for sentence or an appeal against sentence if there has been a successful application for a quashing order. Before exercising the power, the Administrative Court must be satisfied that the sentence was one that the magistrates' court or Crown Court had no power to impose. When the Administrative Court exercises the power, it can impose any sentence that the court that passed sentence could have imposed.

Although s 43(1) requires the High Court to be satisfied that the sentence was not one that the magistrates' court or Crown Court had the power to impose, that does not mean that the power can only be exercised where the sentence imposed was in excess of the maximum prescribed by law. For example, a sentence imposed in breach of natural justice can be

---

69 *Köbler v Republik Österreich* (Case C-224/01) [2004] QB 848.
70 Ibid, at 905D–905E.
71 Ibid. at 904F.
72 Ibid, at 904G. For an application of this principle, see *Cooper v Attorney General* [2011] QB 976, at 1015B.
73 *R v Secretary of State for Transport ex p Factortame Ltd (No 5)* [1998] 3 CMLR 192.
74 *R (Negassi) v Secretary of State for the Home Department* [2011] 2 CMLR 36.

quashed and a fresh sentence imposed after the Administrative Court has heard the representations that magistrates would have heard had they not acted in breach of natural justice.[75]

---

[75]   *R v Pateley Bridge Justices ex p Percy* [1994] COD 453.

# CHAPTER 9

## APPEAL PROCEDURE

### 9.1 CIVIL APPEALS TO THE COURT OF APPEAL

The procedure for appealing depends upon whether or not an issue is a criminal cause or matter. As a consequence, when deciding the appeal procedure to be followed, it is necessary to review whether the issue is a criminal cause or matter.[1]

#### 9.1.1 Public funding

Whether a party to a judicial review in the Administrative Court is successful or unsuccessful, that person's public funding certificate will not normally cover the costs of an appeal to the Court of Appeal. An extension of the certificate will be necessary to obtain public funding for the appeal. This will involve an assessment of the merits of the appeal, applying the same merits test as applies when funding is initially granted.[2]

#### 9.1.2 Permission to appeal

Unsuccessful parties in civil judicial review proceedings may appeal to the Court of Appeal (Civil Division) against a decision of the Administrative Court on the grounds that the decision was: (a) wrong; or (b) unjust because of a serious procedural or other irregularity in the proceedings in the lower court.[3] Grounds of appeal should specify why (a) or (b) is said to apply and should state in respect of each ground whether the ground raises an appeal on a point of law or is an appeal against a finding of fact.[4] Permission to appeal is required before such an appeal can be heard.[5]

According to the CPR:[6]

---

[1]   See **3.4**.
[2]   See **4.2.2**.
[3]   CPR, r 52.11(3).
[4]   Practice Direction 52, para 3.2.
[5]   CPR, r 52.3(1).
[6]   CPR, r 52.3(6).

'(6) Permission to appeal will only be given where
    (a)   the court considers that the appeal would have a real prospect of success; or
    (b)   there is some other compelling reason why the appeal should be heard.'

This rule clearly envisages that there are two reasons why permission to appeal may be granted: the merits of an appeal are sufficient; and the issues raised are sufficiently important.

In one sense, it might be thought that permission to appeal should be granted in all unsuccessful judicial review claims as a High Court judge has already decided that the claim is arguable. However, the correct answer to a claim for a judicial review may become clear after careful consideration during a substantive judicial review hearing, even if it is not clear after the relatively brief review that takes place when permission is considered. As a consequence, the fact that permission has been granted to apply for judicial review is not an indication that permission to appeal will be granted.

The relevant Practice Direction provides that an application for permission should be made orally at the hearing at which the decision to be appealed against is made,[7] although in practice such applications are also made in writing following the circulation of a draft judgment. When a claim for judicial review is refused following a substantive hearing, there should be no problem making an application for permission after the judgment is delivered. In practice, however, an application for permission to appeal is not normally made at a hearing where permission to apply for judicial review is refused. This is because there is such similarity between the test for granting permission to apply for judicial review and the test for granting permission to appeal that it would only be in exceptional circumstances that a judge would refuse permission to apply for judicial review but then grant permission to appeal.

If permission to appeal is refused by the Administrative Court (or no application is made), an application for permission to appeal can be made to the Court of Appeal.[8] Essentially, this is commenced by lodging the same papers as an appeal where permission to appeal has been granted. However, the application notice must state that permission to appeal is being sought.[9] This is unlikely to cause problems as the relevant court form includes tick boxes dealing with the issue of permission to appeal.

In practice, an application for permission to appeal is first considered in the Court of Appeal on the papers by a single judge.[10] Essentially, there are four ways in which the judge can dispose of the case:

---

[7]    Practice Direction 52, para 4.6.
[8]    CPR, r 52.3(2)(b).
[9]    Ibid, r 52.4(1).
[10]   Ibid, r 52.3(4) implicitly recognises that an application for permission to appeal can be

– grant permission to appeal on all grounds or on certain grounds only;

– refuse permission to appeal;

– refuse permission to appeal and make an order that the person seeking permission may not request the decision to be reconsidered at a hearing;[11] or

– order that there should be an oral hearing of the application for permission to appeal.

If the last order is made, the order will also provide whether notice should be given to the other parties in the Administrative Court.

If permission is granted, the Court of Appeal may order that other parties have liberty to apply to have it set aside. This is particularly likely if the appellant has successfully sought some form of interim relief. The Court will be conscious that it has not heard submissions on behalf of other parties.

If a single judge refuses permission to appeal following a review of the papers, an appellant can make a request for permission to appeal to be reconsidered at an oral hearing, unless the Court of Appeal considers that the application is totally without merit. A request for permission to be reconsidered at an oral hearing must be made within 7 days of the initial refusal.[12] The request for renewal should be served on the other parties to the Administrative Court proceedings.[13]

The application for permission will be considered at an oral hearing if it is renewed. Notice of the hearing will be given to the respondent but he is not required to attend unless the Court of Appeal requests him to do so.[14] If the Court requests a party's attendance at the hearing, the appellant must supply copies of the appeal bundle to other parties within 7 days of the direction that notice is to be given.[15] If attendance is not requested by the Court, it is unusual for respondents to attend (unlike applications for permission to apply for judicial review).

---

considered on the papers as it provides that a person can request a review if permission is refused without a hearing (unless the Court of Appeal considers that the application is totally without merit).

[11] Ibid, r 52.3(4A) provides that the Court of Appeal can make such an order if it considers, on the papers, that the application is totally without merit.

[12] CPR, r 52.3(5) and Practice Direction 52, para 4.14.

[13] Practice Direction 52, para 4.14.

[14] Practice Direction 52, para 4.15.

[15] Ibid, para 4.16.

### 9.1.3   Procedure – commencing the appeal

An application for permission to appeal or an appeal is commenced by lodging an appellant's notice (form N161). The notice must be lodged in the Court of Appeal within 21 days unless the lower court orders otherwise.[16] An important exception to that rule is that an appeal against a refusal to grant permission to apply for judicial review must be lodged within 7 days.[17] An appellant can seek an order from the Court of Appeal extending time for filing of the appellant's notice (whether or not time for filing the notice has expired).[18] However, the parties to the appeal cannot extend time by consent.[19] In practice however it is helpful to seek the prior agreement of the other party before making an application to extend time.

The grounds of appeal that are submitted in support of the appeal are often relatively skeletal, containing bullet points identifying instances where it is said that the judge erred. This is because the appellant's notice must be accompanied by a skeleton argument,[20] unless the appellant is not represented,[21] or it is impracticable for the appellant's skeleton argument to accompany the appellant's notice (in which case it must be filed and served on all respondents within 14 days of filing the notice).[22] The skeleton argument can and should be far more detailed.

The format of the skeleton argument can be similar to that used in the Administrative Court.[23] The major difference is that it should specifically address the reasons given by the judge in the Administrative Court for refusing the judicial review claim. In addition, if permission to appeal has not been granted, it may be worth addressing the issues to be considered when deciding whether permission to appeal should be granted.[24] Matters such as the importance of the issues raised should be identified if they may persuade the Court of Appeal to grant permission to appeal.

The skeleton argument should address the reasons given by the judge in the Administrative Court, so it may be sensible to wait until the transcript of the judgment is available before completing a skeleton argument. This may not be within 14 days of the submission of the appellant's notice, and, if so, an extension of time for submission of the notice can be requested by the advocate writing to the Court of Appeal. However, where an official transcript or other suitable record of the Administrative Court's decision is not available within the time within which the

---

[16]   CPR, r 52.4(2).
[17]   Ibid, r 52.15(2).
[18]   Ibid, r 52.6(1).
[19]   Ibid, r 52.6(2).
[20]   Practice Direction 52, para 5.9(1).
[21]   Ibid, para 5.9(3).
[22]   Ibid, para 5.9(2).
[23]   Ibid, paras 5.10 and 5.11 contain the formal requirements for the contents of the skeleton argument.
[24]   See **9.1.2**.

appellant's notice must be filed, the appellant's notice must still be completed to the best of the appellant's ability on the basis of the documentation available. However it may be amended subsequently with the permission of the appeal court.[25]

The appellant's notice should include details of any applications being made by the appellant, the most obvious being an application for a stay. The mere fact of an appeal does not operate as a stay.[26]

In addition to the appellant's notice and the skeleton argument, the appellant should also file the following documents with the Court of Appeal:

(a)    two additional copies of the appellant's notice for the Court of Appeal and one additional copy for each of the other parties to the appeal;[27]

(b)    one copy of the skeleton argument for each copy of the appellant's notice that is filed;[28]

(c)    the sealed order made at the conclusion of the judicial review claim together with the sealed order refusing or granting permission to appeal (if this was considered separately);[29]

(c)    the reasons given for the decision to refuse or grant permission to appeal;[30]

(d)    any witness statements or affidavits in support of any application contained in the appellant's notice[31] (in practice, this is most likely to be necessary where an appeal is out of time and a witness statement is needed to explain why an extension of time is necessary);

(e)    an appeal bundle – this will contain all the documents listed above, together with 'any other documents which the appellant reasonably considers necessary to enable the appeal court to reach its decision on the hearing of the application or appeal' and 'such other documents as the court may direct'.[32]

---

[25]    Practice Direction 52, para 5.13.
[26]    CPR, r 52.7.
[27]    Practice Direction 52, para 5.6(2)(a) and (b).
[28]    Ibid, para 5.6(2)(c).
[29]    Ibid, para 5.6(2)(d) and (e).
[30]    Ibid, para 5.6(2)(e).
[31]    Ibid, para 5.6(2)(f).
[32]    Ibid, para 5.6A(1)(l) and (m).

The Court of Appeal will also require a fee to be paid. At present this is £235 unless permission to appeal was granted by the Administrative Court, in which case the fee is £465.[33]

It is important to note that the bundle should not contain every document that was in the bundle in the Administrative Court – it is necessary to be more selective. In general, the bundle should include:

(a) the transcript of the judgment of the judge in the Administrative Court.[34] In the unlikely event that a transcript is not available or the urgency of the case means that it is not possible to wait for a transcript to be prepared, a copy of the judgment in writing, endorsed with the judge's signature, or an agreed note prepared by the advocates can be provided;[35]

(b) the claim form and grounds, together with any detailed grounds submitted by other parties (or if detailed grounds were not submitted by a party, summary grounds);[36] and

(c) the original decision that was the subject of judicial review proceedings.[37]

In addition, the bundle may include:

(d) any evidence directly relevant to the subject matter of the appeal[38] – in practice, this is unlikely in an appeal from a judicial review decision (although evidence might be necessary if it was alleged that the judge had behaved in some inappropriate manner);

(e) any other documents that the appellant reasonably considers necessary to enable the appeal court to reach its decision on the hearing of the application or appeal[39] (eg evidence that was part of the Administrative Court trial bundle or the skeleton arguments relied on before the Administrative Court may be particularly relevant); and

(f) such other documents as the court may direct.[40]

Paragraph 5.6A(2) of the relevant Practice Direction provides that all documents that are extraneous to the issues to be considered on the

---

33 Civil Proceedings Fees (Amendment) Order 2011 (SI 2011/586), Sch 1.
34 Practice Direction 52, paras 5.6A(1)(f) and 5.12.
35 Ibid, para 5.12.
36 Ibid, para 5.6(A(1)(g).
37 Ibid, para 5.6A(1)(j).
38 Ibid, para 5.6A(2).
39 Ibid, para 5.6A(1)(l).
40 Ibid, para 5.6A(1)(m).

application or the appeal must be excluded from the bundle.[41] Where the appellant is represented, the appeal bundle must contain a certificate signed by his solicitor, counsel or other representative to the effect that he has read and understood para 5.6A(2), and that the composition of the appeal bundle complies with it.[42] Copies of the filed bundle should be retained as it may need to be served on the other parties and the Court of Appeal may require further copies.

If any document cannot be filed with the Court of Appeal, this should be made clear on the appellant's notice. An explanation should be provided on the notice for the failure to file documentation, together with a reasonable estimate of when the missing documentation can be filed. Any missing documentation must be filed as soon as reasonably practicable.[43]

The appellant's notice must be served on the other parties as soon as possible and, in any event, within 7 days of the appellant's notice being filed.[44] The skeleton argument must also be included, unless it is impracticable to do so, in which case it must be served within 14 days, or as soon as it is filed.[45]

If permission to appeal is granted by the Court of Appeal, the Court will serve on all the parties notice of the decision giving permission to appeal, notification of the 'listing window' for the appeal, and any other directions made by the Court.[46] It will also serve on the appellant an Appeal Questionnaire.[47]

The Appeal Questionnaire must be returned to the Court of Appeal within 14 days.[48] It must contain the time estimate for the hearing of the appeal provided by the advocate instructed in the case, if the appellant is legally represented.[49] It must also contain confirmation that copies of the Appeal Questionnaire and the appeal bundle have been served on respondents (including the date of that service).[50] Finally, it must contain confirmation that additional bundles have been prepared and will be supplied on request.[51] This is because the Court of Appeal will need additional copies of the bundle for the hearing as there will be more than a single judge considering the matter.

---

[41] Ibid, para 5.6A(2).
[42] Ibid, para 5.6A(3).
[43] Ibid, para 5.7.
[44] CPR, r 52.4(3).
[45] Practice Direction 52, paras 5.9(2) and 5.21.
[46] Ibid, para 6.3.
[47] Ibid, para 6.4.
[48] Ibid, para 6.5.
[49] Ibid, para 6.5(1). Unlike in the Administrative Court, where the parties must provide a time estimate for the hearing, including delivery of judgment (see Practice Direction 54A, para 15.1), there is no requirement in the Court of Appeal to provide an estimate of the time needed to give judgment (see Practice Direction 52, para 6.6).
[50] Practice Direction 52, para 6.5(4).
[51] Ibid, para 6.5(3).

Once permission is granted (by either the lower court or the Court of Appeal), copies of all documents filed in the Court of Appeal must be served on all the other parties within 7 days of receiving the order giving permission to appeal.[52]

When the questionnaire is filed a fee (which is currently £465) must be paid unless the full appeal fee has already been paid because the appellant was granted permission to appeal by the Administrative Court.[53]

### 9.1.4 Procedure – respondents' response

The response of the respondents to an appeal depends upon whether the appellant has been granted permission to appeal.

If permission to appeal has not been granted then the respondents need not do anything while the application for permission on the papers is pending unless the Court of Appeal orders otherwise.[54] However, in practice, the Court appears to be willing to consider any observations by a respondent regarding the application for permission that a respondent may wish to volunteer. Any observations should be served on an appellant. The costs of such observations are unlikely to be obtained from the appellant.[55] Where the court does request submissions from, or attendance by, a respondent, the Court will normally allow the respondent his costs if permission is refused.[56]

The respondent is first required to act once the Court has considered an application for permission to appeal. If permission is granted by the Court then the procedure is essentially the same as that applying when permission is granted by the lower court. If permission is not granted but the judge directs that there should be a hearing with notice given to the respondents, the procedure to be followed will normally depend on the directions given by the judge, as he will normally make specific provision for matters such as skeleton arguments. If permission is not granted and the judge makes no directions, the respondent will still be required to do nothing.

If permission to appeal is granted, the first matter that a respondent must consider is whether he wishes to oppose the appeal. If he does not, the respondent can seek to dispose of the matter by consent.[57]

Assuming that a respondent does wish to oppose the appeal, the first matter that he must consider is whether to apply to set aside a grant of

---

[52] Ibid, para 6.2.
[53] Civil Proceedings Fees (Amendment) Order 2011 (SI 2011/586), Sch 1.
[54] Practice Direction 52, paras 4.22 and 5.22.
[55] Ibid, para 4.23.
[56] Ibid, para 4.24.
[57] See **9.1.5**.

permission to appeal or to impose conditions on the grant of permission. However, the CPR make it clear that the Court of Appeal will be reluctant to set aside permission or impose conditions as the Court must be satisfied that there are compelling reasons for acting in this manner.[58] In practice, the most obvious reason for applying to the Court will be where it is argued that the Court was misled. Alternatively, an order for security for costs might be sought.[59] A respondent who was present at the hearing at which permission was given may not apply to set aside a grant of permission to appeal or for the imposition of conditions on the grant of permission.[60]

In addition, a respondent must consider whether he wishes to cross-appeal. The parties to a judicial review can cross-appeal if either they wish to challenge a ruling of the Administrative Court or they wish to have the decision of the Administrative Court upheld on a different basis.[61] If the respondent wishes to cross-appeal, he should complete a respondent's notice, which must be filed within 14 days of service of the appellant's notice (if permission to appeal was granted by the Administrative Court), within 14 days of the date on which the respondent is served with notification that the appeal court has given the appellant permission to appeal, or within 14 days of the date on which the respondent is served with notification that there will be a combined hearing of the application for permission to appeal and the appeal.[62] The respondent must file the following documents with his respondent's notice – two copies of respondent's notice plus one additional copy for each party must be filed and a copy of his skeleton argument (where it is filed along with his respondent's notice).[63] If a skeleton argument is not included with the respondent's notice, the respondent must file and serve his skeleton argument within 14 days of filing his notice.[64] The respondent's notice must be served on the other parties as soon as possible and, in any event, within 7 days of the respondent's notice being filed.[65] A fee must be paid when the respondent's notice is filed, which is currently £235, unless the respondent is also appealing and the Administrative Court has granted permission to appeal, in which case the respondent must pay the full fee of £465.[66]

Form N162 is used as the respondent's notice and it must contain the grounds for the cross-appeal. It must also contain an application for permission to appeal if this is required. If the cross-appeal seeks to vary

---

[58]   CPR, r 52.9(2).
[59]   Ibid, r 25.15.
[60]   CPR, r 52.9(3).
[61]   Ibid, r 52.5(2).
[62]   Ibid, r 52.5.
[63]   Practice Direction 52, para 7.10.
[64]   Ibid, para 7.7(1).
[65]   CPR, r 52.5(6).
[66]   Civil Proceedings Fees (Amendment) Order 2011 (SI 2011/586), Sch 1.

the orders of the lower court (which is unlikely in a judicial review context), the respondent will need permission to appeal.[67] Otherwise, this will be unnecessary.

If the respondent does not serve a respondent's notice, he will be prevented from relying on any argument that he did not rely on in the Administrative Court (unless the Court of Appeal grants the respondent permission to do so).[68]

If the respondent wishes to rely on any documents which he reasonably considers as necessary to enable the appeal court to reach its decision on the appeal and which are not in the bundle lodged by the appellant, he must make every effort to agree amendments to the appeal bundle with the appellant. If the parties are unable to reach such an agreement, the respondent can prepare a supplementary bundle, which must be filed with the respondent's notice, or within 21 days of service of the appeal bundle (where a respondent's notice is not filed).[69]

The respondent must consider the time estimate supplied by the appellant. If the respondent's advocate disagrees with the appellant's time estimate, he must inform the Court of Appeal of his time estimate within 7 days of receipt of the Appeal Questionnaire.[70]

A respondent must file two copies of the skeleton argument,[71] which can be done with any respondent's notice.[72] If no respondent's notice has been served then the skeleton argument must be filed at least 7 days before the appeal hearing.[73] Essentially, the skeleton should reflect the format of the skeleton argument in the Administrative Court, and should answer the arguments set out in the appellant's skeleton argument.[74]

### 9.1.5   Settling the appeal or otherwise disposing of it without a hearing

An appellant (unless a child or a protected party) can notify the Court of Appeal that he no longer wishes to pursue his appeal and seeks an order dismissing the appeal.[75] The notice should state that the appellant is not a child or protected party and that the appeal or application is not from a decision of the Court of Protection.[76]

---

[67]   Practice Direction 52, para 7.1.
[68]   Ibid, para 7.3(2).
[69]   Ibid, para 7.11 and 7.12.
[70]   Ibid, para 6.6.
[71]   Ibid, para 7.10.
[72]   Ibid, para 7.6.
[73]   Ibid, para 7.7.
[74]   Ibid, paras 5.10, 5.11 and 7.8 contain the formal requirements for the contents of the skeleton argument.
[75]   Ibid, paras 12.1 and 12.2.
[76]   Ibid, para 12.2.

In practice, an appellant should normally seek the consent of the respondents to the withdrawal of the appeal because, if consent is not sought, the appellant is likely to be ordered to be liable for costs of the respondents.[77]

The Court of Appeal will not normally allow an appeal unless it is satisfied that the decision of the lower court is wrong.[78] If it is agreed to dispose of an appeal by consent, the Court should be supplied with a copy of the proposed consent order, a statement that none of the parties is a child or a protected party and that the appeal or application is not from a decision of the Court of Protection, an explanation of the relevant history and of any matters that are said to justify the making of the order sought.[79] The statement should be sufficiently detailed to persuade the Court of Appeal that the decision of the lower court was wrong or that there are good and sufficient reasons for allowing the appeal.

### 9.1.6 The appeal hearing

The Court of Appeal requires that advocates agree and submit a bundle of no more than 10 authorities for pre-reading by the Court (unless the scale of the appeal warrants more extensive citation). This should be lodged at least 7 days before the hearing date or immediately if less than 7 days' notice of the hearing is given.[80] If this is done, a supplementary bundle of authorities can be filed at the hearing. In practice, this is infrequently done and, instead, a complete bundle of the relevant authorities is lodged with the Court often a few days before the hearing. Although the normal practice is to lodge copies of all relevant authorities, careful consideration must be given to whether each authority is necessary as the Court has expressed concerns about the large number of authorities that have been lodged.[81] Sufficient copies of the bundle of authorities should be supplied for each judge.

Similarly, if the appeal bundles exceed 500 pages, a core bundle consisting of no more than 150 pages must be lodged with the Court of Appeal within 28 days of receipt of the order giving permission to appeal or, where permission to appeal was granted by the Administrative Court, within 28 days of the date of service of the appellant's notice on the respondent.[82]

Some appeals are placed in the 'short-warned list', which means that they can be listed at only a half day's notice. Cases are placed in this list because the Court of Appeal regards them as those which an advocate

---

[77]   Practice Direction 52, paras 12.2 and 12.3.
[78]   Ibid, para 13.1.
[79]   Ibid.
[80]   Ibid, para 15.11.
[81]   *R (C) v Secretary of State* [2009] QB 657, at 664E.
[82]   Practice Direction 52, paras 15.2 and 15.3.

can prepare with limited notice and so they do not need to be conducted by the advocate initially instructed.[83] The appellant may apply in writing for the appeal to be removed from the 'short-warned list' within 14 days of notification of its assignment, but such an application will only be granted for the most compelling reasons.[84]

The appeal hearing will normally take place before three judges (although it can take place before two judges). The Court of Appeal will have all the powers that the Administrative Court had.[85] As a consequence, it can make the same orders for costs as the Administrative Court.[86] It is therefore important that an order for assessment for the purposes of the Community Legal Service is sought if a party to the appeal is in receipt of public funding.[87] In addition, the same orders for relief can be sought at the conclusion of the appeal.

The Court of Appeal will often deliver a reserved judgment. If that happens, copies of it will be supplied to legal advisers in advance, on condition that the contents are kept confidential.[88] Where this procedure is adopted, the parties should attempt to agree consequential orders so as to avoid the need for attendance.[89] They should also consider whether any application for permission to appeal can be considered on the basis of written submissions.[90]

The only route of appeal from the Court of Appeal is to the Supreme Court. Such an appeal is possible only if permission to appeal has been granted.[91] If an appellant wishes to appeal to the Supreme Court, the Court of Appeal must be asked for permission to appeal.[92] It is, however, unlikely to grant it and permission to appeal can then be sought from the Supreme Court.

## 9.2 CIVIL APPEALS TO THE SUPREME COURT

If an appellant is in receipt of public funding, he will need to obtain specific public funding to appeal to the Supreme Court. This will again

---

[83] Ibid, paras 15.8 and 15.9.
[84] Ibid, para 15.9(3).
[85] CPR, r 52.10(1).
[86] See Chapter 10.
[87] See **10.11**.
[88] Practice Direction 52, para 15.12 and Practice Direction 40E.
[89] *Practice Note (CA: Civil Division: Handing Down of Reserved Judgments)* [2002] 1 WLR 344, and Practice Direction 40E, para 4.1.
[90] *Practice Note (CA: Civil Division: Handing Down of Reserved Judgments)* [2002] 1 WLR 344, and Practice Direction 40E, paras 4.3 and 4.4.
[91] See, for example, *R (Eastaway) v Secretary of State for Trade and Industry* [2001] 1 WLR 2222.
[92] Supreme Court Rules 2009 (SI 2009/1603), r 10(2).

involve an assessment of the merits of the appeal, applying the same merits test as applies when funding is initially granted.[93]

Where an appellant is seeking public funding he should notify the Registrar of the Supreme Court within the time period for lodging an application for permission to appeal.[94] This will extend the time for lodging a petition for leave to appeal until 28 days after the final determination of the funding application.[95]

A application for permission to appeal can be submitted to the Supreme Court within 28 days of the decision appealed against.[96] It is important to note that this period runs from the date of the substantive order appealed from, not from the date on which the order is sealed or the date of any subsequent order refusing permission to appeal.[97] The Supreme Court may accept an application for permission to appeal which is out of time if the application sets out the reason(s) why it was not filed within the time limit and is in order in all other respects.[98] The Justices or the Registrar of the Supreme Court can extend any time limit set out in the Supreme Court Rules 2009 on application, and such an application may be granted even after the time limit has expired.[99]

An application for permission to appeal must be signed, and produced on Form 1 on A4 paper, securely bound on the left, using both sides of the paper.[100] The application should set out briefly the facts and points of law and include a brief summary of the reasons why permission should be granted. The grounds of appeal should not normally exceed 10 pages of A4 size. Brevity is of the utmost importance, as the Registrar will reject any application where the grounds appear without adequate explanation to be excessive in length.[101] The application for permission to appeal must clearly set out (and provide reasons for) any application for the Supreme Court to:

(a) depart from one of its own decisions or from one made by the House of Lords;

(b) make a declaration of incompatibility under the Human Rights Act 1998;

---

[93] See **4.2.2**.
[94] Supreme Court Practice Direction 2, para 2.1.12(c).
[95] Ibid.
[96] Supreme Court Rules 2009 (SI 2009/1603), r 11, and Supreme Court Practice Direction 1, para 1.2.9.
[97] Supreme Court Practice Direction 2, para 2.1.12(a).
[98] Ibid, para 2.1.13.
[99] Ibid, para 2.1.14.
[100] Supreme Court Practice Direction 3, paras 3.1.2 and 3.1.4, Form 1 is available as Annex 1 to Supreme Court Practice Direction 7.
[101] Supreme Court Practice Direction 3, paras 3.1.2.

(c)    make a reference to the Court of Justice of the European Union.[102]

A copy of the application for permission to appeal must be served on the respondents or their solicitors, and on any person who was an intervener in the court below, before it is filed.[103] A certificate of service, giving the full name and address of the respondents or their solicitors, must be included in the original application and signed.[104]

It will only be possible to obtain payment for junior counsel's fees for drafting an application for leave to appeal or attending an oral hearing in a permission application.[105]

Along with the original application for permission to appeal, an appellant must file the following at the Supreme Court Registry:

(a)    three further copies of the application;[106]

(b)    one copy of the order appealed from;[107]

(c)    if separate, one copy of the order of the court below refusing leave to appeal to the Supreme Court;[108] and

(d)    a fee of £1,000.[109]

If the substantive order appealed against is not immediately available, the application should be filed within the required time limit and the order filed as soon as it is available.[110]

Within one week of the application for permission to appeal being lodged, the following documents should be lodged:[111]

(a)    four copies of the application;

(b)    four copies of the order appealed from;

(c)    if separate, four copies of the order of the Court of Appeal refusing permission to appeal to the Supreme Court;

---

[102]   Ibid, para 3.1.3.
[103]   Supreme Court Rules 2009 (SI 2009/1603), r 12.
[104]   Supreme Court Practice Direction 3, para 3.1.6.
[105]   Ibid, para 3.3.14 and para 3.4.8.
[106]   Supreme Court Practice Direction 3, para 3.1.7.
[107]   Supreme Court Rules 2009 (SI 2009/1603), r 14(1)(a).
[108]   Ibid, r 14(1)(b).
[109]   Updated fees can be accessed at Sch 1 of the Supreme Court Fees Order 2009 (SI 2009/2131).
[110]   Supreme Court Practice Direction 3, para 3.1.7.
[111]   Supreme Court Rules 2009 (SI 2009/1603), r 14, and Supreme Court Practice Direction 3, para 3.2.1.

(d)   four copies of the official transcript of the judgment of the Court of Appeal (certified by the court if marked 'in draft');

(e)   four copies of the final order of the court of first instance;

(f)   four copies of the official transcript of the judgment of the court of first instance;

(g)   four copies of any unreported judgment cited in the petition or judgment of a court below;

(h)   four copies of a document which sets out the history of the proceedings.

An appellant who wishes to provide documents other than those listed above must give a detailed explanation of why they are needed.

The Appeal Panel decides first whether an application for permission to appeal is admissible. If the Appeal Panel decides that an application is admissible, the Panel may then: (a) refuse permission; (b) give permission; (c) invite the parties to file written submissions as to the grant of permission on terms whether as to costs or otherwise; or (d) direct an oral hearing.[112] Permission to appeal is granted for applications that, in the opinion of the Appeal Panel, raise an arguable point of law of general public importance which ought to be considered by the Supreme Court at that time, bearing in mind that the matter will already have been the subject of judicial decision and may have already been reviewed on appeal.[113]

Where permission to appeal is granted by the Supreme Court, the application for permission to appeal will stand as the notice of appeal and the grounds of appeal are limited to those on which permission has been granted. The appellant must, within 14 days of the grant by the Supreme Court of permission to appeal, file notice under that he wishes to proceed with his appeal.[114] When the notice is filed, the application for permission to appeal will be re-sealed and the appellant must then serve a copy on each respondent, on any recognised intervener, and on any person who was an intervener in the court below. The appellant must also file seven copies together with a certificate of service.[115]

Where a respondent is served with an application for permission to appeal, he must file notice of objection by sending five copies (including

---

[112]   Supreme Court Rules 2009 (SI 2009/1603), r 16 and Supreme Court Practice Direction 3, para 3.3.2.

[113]   Supreme Court Practice Direction 3, para 3.3.3.

[114]   Supreme Court Rules 2009 (SI 2009/1603), r 18(1) and Supreme Court Practice Direction 3, para 3.4.1.

[115]   Supreme Court Rules 2009 (SI 2009/1603), r. 18(2).

the original) of Form 3 together with a certificate of service and a fee of £160 within 14 days.[116] A respondent who does not file such a notice will not be permitted to participate in the application for permission and will not be given notice of its progress. An order for costs will not be made in favour of a respondent who has not given notice.[117] Where the Appeal Panel refers an application for permission to appeal for an oral hearing, a respondent may seek to file more fully reasoned objections within 14 days of being informed that the application has been referred for a hearing.[118]

Once permission is granted, the procedure in the Supreme Court is governed by the detailed Practice Directions of the Supreme Court. All parties should read this carefully to ensure that they understand the procedure. Copies can be found on the internet.[119]

## 9.3   CRIMINAL APPEALS TO THE SUPREME COURT

If an appellant is in receipt of public funding, he will need to obtain specific public funding to appeal to the Supreme Court. Again, this will involve an assessment of the merits of the appeal, applying the same merits test as applies when funding is initially granted.[120]

A party to a judicial review in a criminal cause or matter can appeal only to the Supreme Court.[121] The Administrative Court can grant leave to appeal.[122] However, that is extremely unlikely. In practice, it is likely to be necessary to obtain leave to appeal from the Supreme Court.[123] However, for reasons that are considered below, the Supreme Court may lack jurisdiction to consider an application for leave to appeal.

An application for permission to appeal should be made to the Administrative Court within 28 days of the date that the Court dismisses the claim for judicial review or provides reasons for its decision.[124] If permission is refused, an appellant must apply for permission to appeal to the Supreme Court within 28 days of the decision of the Administrative Court refusing permission.[125] These time-limits can be extended only where the party seeking permission to appeal was a defendant in the

---

[116] Supreme Court Rules 2009 (SI 2009/1603), r 13(1) and Supreme Court Practice Direction 3, para 3.3.7. Form 3 is available at Annex 1 to Supreme Court Practice Direction 7. Updated fees can be accessed at Sch 1 of the Supreme Court Fees Order 2009 (SI 2009/2131).
[117] Supreme Court Practice Direction 3, para 3.1.10.
[118] Ibid, para 3.3.13.
[119] http://www.supremecourt.gov.uk/procedures/practice-directions.html.
[120] See **4.2.2**.
[121] Administration of Justice Act 1960, s 1.
[122] Ibid.
[123] Ibid.
[124] Ibid, s 2(1)
[125] Ibid.

criminal proceedings.[126] An application by an appellant for legal aid suspends these time limits until 28 days after the determination of the application for legal aid, so long as the Registrar of the Supreme Court is notified in writing of the application for public funding.[127]

Before an application for permission to appeal can be made to the Supreme Court, the Administrative Court must issue a certificate that there is a point of law of general public importance.[128]

Technically, it would appear that an application for a certificate of public importance is not subject to the same time-limits as an application for leave to appeal.[129] In practice, however, the application to the Administrative Court for it to certify a point of law of general public importance is made at the same time as the application for permission to appeal. This is primarily because the Administrative Court must certify a point of law of general public importance at the same time as it grants permission to appeal, if such permission is granted.

Great care must be taken to draft a question that both reflects the issues raised in the case and raises a point that is of significant general importance. The Administrative Court is unlikely to permit a prospective appellant to have more than one attempt to formulate a question and so it is important that the question is properly formulated the first time.

If the Administrative Court either grants permission to appeal and/or certifies that there is a point of law of general public importance, an application for permission to appeal to the Supreme Court should be drafted. It will only be possible to obtain payment for junior counsel's fees for drafting an application for permission to appeal.[130] The Supreme Court Practice Directions can be accessed on the internet and contain a detailed description of the form that an application for permission to appeal should take.[131] The Supreme Court Practice Directions suggest that the provisions of Practice Direction 3 govern the form of applications for permission to appeal in criminal matters.

It follows that, where permission to appeal is being sought, the appellant should apply for permission using Form 1. Practice Direction 3 suggests that appellants should lodge the following documents at the Supreme Court Registry:[132]

---

[126] Administration of Justice Act 1960, s 2; and *R v Weir* [2001] 1 WLR 421, holding that time could not be extended for a prosecutor to appeal.

[127] Supreme Court Practice Direction 12, para 12.3.7.

[128] Administration of Justice Act 1960, s 1, and Supreme Court Practice Direction 12, paras 12.2.1 and 12.1.4.

[129] *Westley v Hertfordshire County Council* (unreported) 22 October 1998.

[130] Supreme Court Practice Direction 3, para 3.4.8.

[131] http://www.supremecourt.gov.uk/procedures/practice-directions.html.

[132] Supreme Court Practice Direction 12, at para 12.4.1 and Supreme Court Practice Direction 3, at para 3.1.2.

(a)    the original application, plus three further copies of the application;[133]

(b)    one copy of the order appealed from;[134]

(c)    if separate (and if permission has been refused), one copy of the order of the court below refusing leave to appeal to the Supreme Court;[135]

(d)    a copy of the Administrative Court's certificate of public importance.[136]

No fee is payable in respect of criminal proceedings, other than the fee payable on submitting a claim for costs.[137]

A copy of the application must have been served on the other parties before it can be filed in the Registry of the Supreme Court.[138]

Practice Direction 3 suggests that the following documents should be lodged within one week of the application for permission to appeal being lodged:[139]

(a)    four copies of the application;

(b)    four copies of the order appealed from;

(c)    four copies of the order of the Administrative Court refusing permission to appeal to the Supreme Court (if separate and if permission has been refused);

(d)    four copies of the transcript of the judgment of the Administrative Court.

(e)    four copies of any unreported judgment cited in the petition or judgment of the Administrative Court;

(f)    four copies of a document which sets out the history of the proceedings, and

---

133  Supreme Court Practice Direction 12, at para 12.4.1 and Supreme Court Practice Direction 3, at para 3.1.7.
134  Supreme Court Rules 2009 (SI 2009/1603), r 14(1)(a).
135  Ibid, r 14(1)(b).
136  Supreme Court Practice Direction 12, para 12.4.3.
137  Supreme Court Fees Order 2009 (SI 2009/2131), art 2(2) and Sch 1.
138  Supreme Court Practice Direction 12, at para 12.4.1 and Supreme Court Practice Direction 3, at para 3.1.6.
139  Supreme Court Rules 2009 (SI 2009/1603), r 14, Supreme Court Practice Direction 12, at para 12.4.1 and Supreme Court Practice Direction 3, at para 3,2,1 and, by analogy, para 3.6.10.

(g)  four additional copies of the Administrative Court's certificate, if not contained in the order.

Where a respondent is served with an application for permission to appeal, he must file notice of objection by sending five copies (including the original) of Form 3.[140] A respondent who does not file such a notice will not be permitted to participate in the application for permission and will not be given notice of its progress. An order for costs will not be made in favour of a respondent who has not given notice.[141] Where the Appeal Panel refers an application for permission to appeal for an oral hearing, a respondent may seek to file more fully reasoned objections within 14 days of being informed that the application has been referred for a hearing.[142]

Once the application is lodged, the procedure in the Supreme Court is governed by the detailed Practice Directions of the Supreme Court. All parties should read this carefully to ensure that they understand the procedure. Copies can be found on the internet.[143]

---

[140] Supreme Court Rules 2009 (SI 2009/1603), r.13(1) and Supreme Court Practice Direction 3, at para 3.3.7. Form 3 is available at Annex 1 to Supreme Court Practice Direction 7.

[141] Supreme Court Practice Direction 3, para 3.1.10.

[142] Ibid, para 3.3.13.

[143] http://www.supremecourt.gov.uk/procedures/practice-directions.htmlhttp://www.publications.parliament.uk/pa/ld199697/ldinfo/ld08judg/bluebook/bluebk-1.htm#.

# CHAPTER 10

## COSTS

### 10.1 INTRODUCTION

This chapter considers the orders for costs that can be made during and at the end of proceedings; it should be read together with **4.2**, which considers the tests that the Legal Services Commission apply when deciding whether a party to judicial review proceedings should be granted public funding.

### 10.2 RULES GOVERNING COSTS BETWEEN THE PARTIES

The CPR govern the award of costs in the Administrative Court. In particular, Part 44 governs orders for costs against parties and provides that the court has a very broad discretion when it considers applications for costs orders against parties to proceedings. It can determine whether costs are payable by one party to another, the level of those costs and the time for payment.[1] However, Part 44 also provides that the general rule is that the unsuccessful party will pay the costs of the successful party,[2] and that consideration of the parties' conduct will be a material factor, particularly the extent to which the parties followed the relevant pre-action protocol.[3] It is important to note that special considerations apply in certain circumstances, such as when the unsuccessful party is in receipt of public funding[4] or when a court or tribunal that tried the matter is a party.[5] These are considered later.

In deciding whether to award costs in favour of a successful party, the fact that a successful party is in receipt of public funding should normally make no difference.[6] Despite some historical reluctance on the part of judges to award costs against one public authority that go straight to

---

[1]  CPR, r 44.3(1).
[2]  Ibid, r 44.3(2).
[3]  Ibid, r 44.3(4)(a) and 44.3(5).
[4]  See **10.4**.
[5]  See **10.5**.
[6]  Access to Justice Act 1999, s 22, considered in *R (Boxall) v Waltham Forest London Borough Council* (2001) 4 CCL Rep 258, at [10].

another public authority (the Legal Services Commission), the Court of
Appeal has now made it clear that a culture of making no order for costs
where one party is publicly funded and the other is a public body is no
longer acceptable.[7] Although the mere fact that some consider that
publicly funded lawyers are inadequately remunerated is not an acceptable
reason to make an order for costs in favour of a claimant, the Courts have
warned of the serious consequences of a failure to make an order for
costs in favour of a publicly funded party.[8]

An issue that often arises in judicial review is whether a party has actually
been successful. For example, a party to judicial review proceedings may
succeed on some, but not all, of the grounds. Alternatively, he may obtain
some, but not all, of the relief sought.

In practice, if a claimant is only partially successful the Administrative
Court is likely to attempt to assess the proportion of the costs that were
unnecessarily incurred as a consequence of the unsuccessful matters
raised. The Court will then seek to reflect the fact that unnecessary costs
were incurred in the final order.[9] Of course, it is important to recognise
that the additional costs that result from unnecessary grounds may, in
many cases, be minimal as much of the preparation would have been
necessary in any event.

In determining whether or not a party is successful, it is important to be
aware that special considerations may arise as a result of the discretionary
nature of judicial review proceedings. It may be proper for a party to
bring proceedings to clarify the law in circumstances where the relief
sought is not obtained. Thus, a prosecutor was able to obtain costs from
central funds[10] in a case where it was proper for him to appeal, although
delay in determining the matter meant that the appeal should not be
allowed.[11]

One of the most significant matters that the Administrative Court will
take account of when deciding what costs orders to make and whether the
general rule should be departed from is the conduct of the parties during
the litigation.[12] When considering the conduct of the parties, the
Administrative Court has the power to take account of the manner in

7   *R (Bahta) v Secretary of State for the Home Department* [2011] CP Rep 43, at [59]–[62] and [64]–[65].
8   Ibid. See also, *R (Boxall) v Waltham Forest London Borough Council* (2001) 4 CCL Rep 258, at [12], *R (Scott) v Hackney London Borough Council* [2009] EWCA Civ 217, at [50], and *R (E) v JFS Governing Body* [2009] 1 WLR 2353, at 2363D–2364A.
9   For example, in *R (Howard League for Penal Reform) v Secretary of State for the Home Department* [2003] 1 FLR 484, Munby J awarded the claimant only 50% of its costs to reflect the fact that a significant amount of unnecessary work had been undertaken in relation to unsuccessful grounds.
10  See **10.7** for a consideration of the power to award costs from central funds.
11  *Griffith v Jenkins* [1992] 2 AC 76, at 84G.
12  CPR, r 44.3(4)(a).

which the litigation was pursued.[13] It is clear from this that the Administrative Court will use costs orders as a way of discouraging unreasonable conduct during litigation.[14]

The CPR state that the overriding objective of the Administrative Court is to deal with cases justly.[15] This objective includes, as far as practicable, saving expense and allotting to the case an appropriate share of the court's resources, while taking into account the need to allot resources to other cases.[16] Parties have a duty to help the court to further the overriding objective.[17] Clearly, unreasonable conduct by a party is likely to be in breach of this duty; and the court will take account of such breach when it determines costs issues.[18] Unreasonable conduct may even result in wasted costs being ordered against a party's advisers.[19]

The requirement to behave reasonably means that, where the claim has become academic, it is important that either the claim is withdrawn or the Administrative Court is informed that it is being pursued as a test case.[20] Allowing the case may incur disproportionate costs, which will be reflected in the final disposal.[21]

The approach of the Administrative Court means that practitioners must be particularly careful to review the merits of their case at all stages. A party to proceedings who concludes that he is very unlikely to succeed should consider settling the matter to save costs. Proceeding with a case that has little merit is likely to result in an order being made for costs including the costs of the substantive hearing. Settling the case promptly may avoid any order for costs.

The Administrative Court will not necessarily award costs against a defendant merely because he has withdrawn the decision that is being challenged, or consented to a settlement that gives the claimant the relief that he has been seeking. The Administrative Court recognises that it is legitimate for a respondent to avoid the cost and uncertainty of pending proceedings by settling those proceedings. In *R (Boxall) v Waltham Forest*

---

13    Ibid, r 44.3(5)(c).
14    See, for example, *R (Soylemez) v Secretary of State for the Home Department* [2003] EWHC 1056 (Admin), in which the costs order reflected the late service of the claimant's evidence that resulted in the claim succeeding. Similarly, in *R (Kemp) v Denbighshire Local Health Board* [2006] EWHC 181 (Admin), the claimant effectively succeeded in obtaining funding of his nursing home costs. However, because he had failed to comply with the pre-action protocol, and there was no evidence that the defendant would not have offered a review had a protocol letter been written, no order for costs was made.
15    CPR, r 1.1(1).
16    Ibid, r 1.1(2).
17    Ibid, r 1.3.
18    Ibid, r 1.2.
19    See **10.9**.
20    See **8.1.1** for a consideration of when a claim can be pursued despite being academic.
21    *R (Tshikangu) v Newham London Borough Council* [2001] NPC 33.

*London Borough Council*,[22] Mr Justice Scott Baker considered the principles that should be applied when deciding whether a defendant should pay costs after a decision is withdrawn. He held:[23]

> '(i)   the court has power to make a costs order when the substantive proceedings have been resolved without a trial but the parties have not agreed about costs;
>
> (ii)   it will ordinarily be irrelevant that the Claimant is legally aided;
>
> (iii)   the overriding objective is to do justice between the parties without incurring unnecessary court time and consequently additional cost;
>
> (iv)   at each end of the spectrum there will be cases where it is obvious which side would have won had the substantive issues been fought to a conclusion. In between, the position will, in differing degrees, be less clear. How far the court will be prepared to look into the previously unresolved substantive issues will depend on the circumstances of the particular case, not least the amount of costs at stake and the conduct of the parties;
>
> (v)   in the absence of a good reason to make any other order the fall back is to make no order as to costs;
>
> (vi)   the court should take care to ensure that it does not discourage parties from settling judicial review proceedings for example by a local authority making a concession at an early stage.'

The Court of Appeal has recently stressed that these principles should be read in the context of the importance of the pre-action protocol procedure for judicial review. In *R (Bahta) v Secretary of State for the Home Department*,[24] the Court of Appeal emphasised that the pre-action protocol for judicial review is intended to prevent litigation and facilitate and encourage parties to settle the dispute at an early stage, if at all possible.

Thus, if a respondent is considering making a concession, the appropriate time to make such a concession is at the pre-action protocol stage. An extension of time for responding can be sought, if necessary. In the absence of an adequate response to a letter before claim, a claimant is entitled to proceed to institute proceedings. If the claimant then obtains the relief sought, or substantially similar relief, the claimant can expect to be awarded costs against the respondent. When relief is granted, the respondent bears the burden of justifying a departure from the general rule that the unsuccessful party will be ordered to pay the costs of the successful party. This burden is likely to be a heavy one if the claimant has, and the respondent has not, complied with the pre-action protocol.[25]

---

[22]   (2001) 4 CCL Rep 258.
[23]   *R (Boxall) v Waltham Forest London Borough Council* (2001) 4 CCL Rep 258, at [22].
[24]   [2011] CP Rep 43.
[25]   Ibid, at [59], [64], [65], [72], [75] and [76].

## 10.3 COSTS FOR THE PERIOD BEFORE THE PERMISSION DECISION

Permission hearings[26] were considered earlier, with discussion regarding the general rule that defendants will be unable to obtain the costs of attending a permission hearing. Although those comments reflected the normal approach to costs, it is important to recognise that it is possible to obtain costs for the period before permission is granted.

First, the CPR require a defendant to take the step of filing an acknowledgement of service before permission is determined.[27] As a consequence, it has been held that a defendant can recover these costs even if he is unable to obtain the costs of a permission hearing.[28]

In addition, although the rule is that, generally, there will be no order for costs for a defendant attending a permission hearing, it is only a general rule and can be departed from in exceptional circumstances.[29]

In *R (Mount Cook) v Westminster City Council*[30] the Court of Appeal considered the factors to be considered when determining whether there are exceptional circumstances. These include the hopelessness of the claim, the persistence of the claimant despite having been alerted to the hopelessness, whether the claim has sought to abuse the process of judicial review for collateral ends and whether the claimant has essentially had the advantage of an early substantive hearing. The resources of the claimant may also be a relevant factor when the Court decides whether to order costs.

If a defendant does require costs for attending a permission hearing or some other aspect of the pre-permission costs, this should be made clear on the acknowledgement of service.[31]

Historically, claimants also found it difficult to obtain their costs for the period before the grant of permission. The old rule was that claimants could only obtain their costs if they could show that there were exceptional circumstances.[32] However, this approach should now be read in the context of the importance of the pre-action protocol procedure for judicial review claims. The approach set out above, in *Bahta*, should also apply at the pre-permission stage.[33]

---

[26] See **5.9**.

[27] See **5.4**.

[28] *R (Leach) v Commissioner for Local Administration* [2001] CP Rep 97 endorsed in *R (Mount Cook) v Westminster City Council* [2004] CP Rep 12.

[29] *R (Mount Cook) v Westminster City Council* [2004] CP Rep 12.

[30] [2004] CP Rep 12.

[31] *R (Leach) v Commissioner for Local Administration* [2001] CP Rep 97.

[32] *R v Royal Borough of Kensington & Chelsea ex p Ghebregiogis* (1995) 27 HLR 602.

[33] *R (Bahta) v Secretary of State for the Home Department* [2011] CP Rep 43, considered at **10.2**.

If a person wishes to obtain his costs of attending the permission hearing at which permission is granted, he should seek an order reserving costs.[34]

## 10.4 SPECIAL CONSIDERATIONS WHEN THE UNSUCCESSFUL PARTY IS IN RECEIPT OF PUBLIC FUNDING

When the unsuccessful party is in receipt of public funding, the Administrative Court shall not order him to pay any costs that would exceed what is reasonable having regard to all the circumstances of the case, including the resources of the parties and their conduct during the matter.[35] In determining the resources available to the unsuccessful party, the Administrative Court shall discount that person's clothes, household furniture and the tools and implements of his trade.[36] The first £100,000 of the value of the publicly funded party's interest in the main or only home is disregarded when assessing his or her financial resources and cannot be the subject of any enforcement process by the receiving party.[37] In practice, this means that the Administrative Court should make an order that the unsuccessful party pay the reasonable costs of the successful party subject to s 11 of the Access to Justice Act 1999. This means that a costs judge will determine what costs should be paid[38]. Often they will make an order that costs may be enforced only with the leave of the court.[39] However, this is not automatic. In particular, in cases in which the unsuccessful party is required to pay a contribution towards his public funding, the Administrative Court may be willing to require him to make payments towards his opponent's costs by instalments.

The limitation on the recovery of costs against a person in receipt of public funding extends only to those proceedings covered by the public funding certificate for the period during which the certificate provides funding for the party's representation.[40] As a result, it is potentially negligent for practitioners to fail to ensure that a public funding certificate actually covers all steps taken on behalf of a party.[41] This is particularly important in judicial review proceedings, as the certificate issued at the start of the claim is unlikely to cover all steps of the proceedings. Instead, it is likely to cover all steps up to the service of the defendant's evidence

---

[34] See **5.9**.

[35] Access to Justice Act 1999, s 11(1).

[36] Ibid, s 11(2).

[37] Costs Practice Direction, para 21.12.

[38] Community Legal Service (Costs) Regulations 2000 (SI 2000/441).

[39] These orders are often called 'football pools orders' as they are intended to allow a successful party to enforce costs if the unsuccessful party wins the pools. It is not automatic that such an order will be made. Judges can sometimes be persuaded to make no order if there is no sensible prospect of the unsuccessful party obtaining money to pay costs (see, for example, *R (B) v Ashworth Hospital Authority* [2002] EWHC 1142 (Admin)).

[40] Civil Legal Aid (General) Regulations 1989 (SI 1989/339), reg 124(1).

[41] *Turner v Plasplugs Ltd* [1996] 2 All ER 939.

and obtaining counsel's advice on that evidence. It may also not cover an oral permission hearing after permission has been refused on the papers. Practitioners will need to ensure that the certificate is amended, as the case proceeds, to cover all steps, provided the merits justify this.

After a Court has decided upon the liability for costs of the unsuccessful party in receipt of public funding, it can make an order for payment of the successful party's costs by the Legal Services Commission, if an order for costs would have been made but for the provisions of the Access to Justice Act 1999.[42] Such an order is highly unlikely in judicial review proceedings in the Administrative Court as an order can only be made at first instance where the successful party is an individual.[43] The limitations on the scope of judicial review proceedings mean that it is unlikely that the successful party will be an individual if the unsuccessful party is in receipt of public funding because a public body must be involved in the proceedings.

The restriction that a successful party must be an individual does not apply on an appeal.[44] Before making an order that the Legal Services Commission should pay the costs of the successful party on an appeal, the Court must be satisfied that making an order is just and equitable.[45] Generally, the prohibition on the successful party obtaining his costs means that it will be just and equitable to make a costs order against the Legal Services Commission.[46] An application for costs against the Legal Services Commission should be made to a costs judge rather than to the Court of Appeal.[47]

## 10.5 SPECIAL CONSIDERATIONS WHEN A MAGISTRATES' COURT OR OTHER COURT OR TRIBUNAL IS THE DEFENDANT

In general, magistrates' courts, and other inferior tribunals, should not be represented in cases where their decision is being challenged.[48] If magistrates do attend at a hearing when they should not have attended, the Administrative Court will be required to take account of the reasonableness of their conduct before ordering costs.[49] This means that if the magistrates attend and are unsuccessful, they increase the risk that

---

[42] Access to Justice Act 1999, s 11(4) and Community Legal Service (Cost Protection) Regulations 2000 (SI 2000/824) (as amended).

[43] Community Legal Service (Cost Protection) Regulations 2000 (SI 2000/824) (as amended), reg 5(3)(c).

[44] Ibid.

[45] Ibid, reg 5(3)(d).

[46] *R (Gunn) v Secretary of State for the Home Department* [2001] 1 WLR 1634.

[47] Ibid.

[48] See **5.4** for a consideration of when a court or tribunal should attend as a party in judicial review proceedings.

[49] CPR, r 44.3(4)(a).

costs will be awarded against them.[50] If they are successful, the Administrative Court may be unwilling to order costs in their favour unless they can show that there were particularly good reasons why they should have attended.

When courts or other inferior tribunals are involved in proceedings in the Administrative Court as the defendant, the Administrative Court will be reluctant to order costs against them. Lord Justice Brooke summarised the established practice of the courts as follows:

'(i)    The established practice of the courts was to make no order for costs against an inferior court or tribunal which did not appear before it except when there was a flagrant instance of improper behaviour or when the inferior court or tribunal unreasonably declined or neglected to sign a consent order disposing of the proceedings;

(ii)    The established practice of the courts was to treat an inferior court or tribunal which resisted an application actively by way of argument in such a way that it made itself an active party to the litigation, as if it was such a party, so that in the normal course of things costs would follow the event;

(iii)   If, however, an inferior court or tribunal appeared in the proceedings in order to assist the court neutrally on questions of jurisdiction, procedure, specialist case-law and such like, the established practice of the courts was to treat it as a neutral party, so that it would not make an order for costs in its favour or an order for costs against it whatever the outcome of the application;

(iv)    There are, however, a number of important considerations which might tend to make the courts exercise their discretion in a different way today in cases in category (iii) above, so that a successful applicant ... who has to finance his own litigation without external funding, may be fairly compensated out of a source of public funds and not be put to irrecoverable expense in asserting his rights after a coroner (or other inferior tribunal) has gone wrong in law, and there is no other very obvious candidate available to pay his costs.'

Thus, the Administrative Court has awarded costs against magistrates in a case where they took a perverse decision in flagrant disregard of elementary principles.[51] Costs have also been awarded in cases where there was failure to take a grant of permission sufficiently seriously in a case challenging a refusal to state a case,[52] and where magistrates caused an

---

[50]   *R (Touche) v Inner London North Coroner* [2001] QB 1206, at 1221, suggesting that different considerations apply if a judicial figure attends court.

[51]   See, for example, *R v Lincoln Justices ex p Count* (1996) 8 Admin LR 233, in which magistrates refused to adjourn a case as there was no specific statutory power enabling them to adjourn.

[52]   *R v Huntingdon Magistrates' Court ex p Percy* [1994] COD 323; see also *R v Metropolitan Stipendiary Magistrate ex p Ali* [1997] Env LR D15, where costs were awarded against a magistrate for continuing to refuse to state a case when the judge who had granted permission had said that it would be impossible to know if the magistrate had erred if he did not state a case.

unnecessary substantive hearing by failing to sign a consent order.[53] However, the Administrative Court will be particularly reluctant to award costs against magistrates in cases when they have not appeared.[54]

In cases where costs are awarded against magistrates, they can obtain costs from the Lord Chancellor in most circumstances. In a criminal case, costs must be awarded from local funds unless it is proved that the magistrates acted in bad faith.[55] In other cases, the magistrates are required to be indemnified if they acted reasonably and in good faith in the matter that gave rise to proceedings in the Administrative Court, and may be indemnified in other circumstances.[56] Decisions regarding indemnification are taken by the Lord Chancellor.[57]

The fact that a court may not be ordered to pay the costs of a judicial review claim will not necessarily prejudice a successful claimant because it may be possible to obtain costs from a third party who opposes the claim. This issue is considered in the next section.

## 10.6 SPECIAL CONSIDERATIONS AS TO THE COSTS OF THIRD PARTIES AND NON-PARTIES

In judicial review proceedings, it is common for third parties to be the claimant's effective opponent. For example, although magistrates may be the named defendant, it is likely to be the prosecution who actively oppose a judicial review. In principle, costs can be awarded against a third party for maintaining the proceedings.[58] When determining whether to make an order for costs, the Administrative Court will take account of the general rules regarding costs that are set out above.[59]

Third parties who are successful in defending a claim may have problems obtaining their costs, at least where they are not the only party to have defended the claim. In principle, there is no reason why they should not obtain costs. However, in practice, the Administrative Court will be reluctant to make more than one order of costs, unless there is some good reason why it was appropriate for more than one party to be represented.[60] In particular, the Court will not merely award a party costs simply because it has been served with the proceedings.[61]

---

[53] *R v Newcastle Under Lyme Justices ex p Massey* [1994] 1 WLR 1684, at 1692F.
[54] Ibid, at 1692A.
[55] Courts Act 2003, s 35(3).
[56] Ibid, s 35(4).
[57] Ibid, s 35(5).
[58] See, for example, *R v Hastings Licensing Justices ex p John Lovibond & Sons Ltd* [1968] 1 WLR 735.
[59] See **10.2**.
[60] See, for example, *R v Secretary of State for the Environment ex p Kirkstall Valley Campaign Ltd* [1996] 3 All ER 304, at 342J.
[61] *R v Industrial Disputes Tribunal ex p American Express Co Inc* [1954] 1 WLR 1118.

One set of circumstances in which it is clear that a third party will have good reason to attend and participate in judicial review proceedings is where his liberty is at stake. Hence, a patient who seeks to uphold a challenged decision of the Mental Health Review Tribunal is entitled to his costs despite the fact that the Tribunal was also opposing the judicial review claim.[62]

The Administrative Court has the power to make costs orders in favour of or against non-parties.[63] Before doing this, those persons must be added as a party and given an opportunity to be heard.[64] In practice, costs orders are rarely made against non-parties. Circumstances in which such orders have been made include cases where costs orders have been made against
non-parties who have funded unsuccessful litigation,[65] and cases where non-parties have caused unnecessary costs to be incurred as a result of their unreasonable conduct.[66] Similarly, in general, costs orders are not made in favour of a non-party such as an amicus curiae.[67]

## 10.7   COSTS FROM CENTRAL FUNDS

A Divisional Court has the power to award costs to a defendant from central funds in any criminal cause or matter that it determines.[68] Similarly, the Supreme Court may make such an order in an appeal from a Divisional Court.[69] A similar power exists to award costs to a prosecutor who is not a 'public authority' or a person acting on its behalf or in his capacity as an official appointed by such an authority.[70]

There is no provision for costs from central funds in civil cases or indeed in any case where there is not a statutory power to make such an order.[71] Criminal causes are sometimes considered by a single High Court judge rather than by a Divisional Court. At present, it appears that costs from central funds cannot be awarded by a single High Court judge because they are not a Divisional Court, although the recent Practice Direction on

---

[62]   *R (Secretary of State for the Home Department) v Mental Health Review Tribunal* [2002] EWCA Civ 1868, (2003) 6 CCL Rep 319.

[63]   Senior Courts Act 1981, s 51.

[64]   CPR, r 48.2(1).

[65]   *R v Darlington Borough Council ex p Association of Darlington Taxi Owners (No 2)* [1995] COD 128.

[66]   *R v Lambeth Borough Council ex p Wilson* (1996) 8 Admin LR 376; although this was set aside on appeal: *R v Lambeth Borough Council ex p Wilson* [1997] 3 FCR 437.

[67]   See, however, *B v Croydon Health Authority (No 2)* [1996] 1 FLR 253, in which an amicus curiae obtained part of his costs from the successful party as a result of the considerable assistance provided to the court.

[68]   Prosecution of Offences Act 1985, s 16(5)(a); see **3.4** for a definition of the scope of a 'criminal cause or matter'.

[69]   Ibid, s 16(5)(b).

[70]   Ibid, s 17.

[71]   *Steele Ford and Newton v Crown Prosecution Service (No 2)* [1994] 1 AC 22.

costs in criminal proceedings suggests that the 'High Court' may make a defendant's costs order on determining proceedings in a criminal cause or matter.[72]

Costs from central funds can be of relevance in cases in which a claimant is in receipt of public funds. A claimant may be unable to obtain costs from the defendant court.[73] However, if the claimant does not obtain a costs order in his favour, he may be required to pay a contribution towards his public funding. In addition, the limited funds of the Legal Services Commission will be required to pay for a successful claim. Finally, a claimant's representatives may receive lower rates of remuneration if they do not obtain a costs order in favour of their client. All these matters mean that costs should be sought from central funds in cases in which a party is in receipt of public funds. It is important to be aware that the fact that the claimant is in receipt of public funding should make no difference to costs orders, which suggests that there is no reason why costs should not be ordered from central funds.[74]

## 10.8   ADVANCE ORDERS FOR COSTS

The Administrative Court has the power to make a final order regarding costs before the final determination of proceedings. This is an important power because a party may seek to raise arguments that are of public importance, but which he will not be able to afford to proceed with if at risk of a costs order. In these circumstances, it may be open to the Administrative Court to make an order preventing or restricting the defendant from recovering costs in any event. These pre-emptive orders are known as 'protective costs orders' [PCOs] and 'costs capping orders'.

Mr Justice Dyson held that the test to be applied in applications for a PCO was:[75]

'[T]he necessary conditions for the making of a pre-emptive costs order in public interest challenge cases are that the court is satisfied that the issues raised are truly ones of general public importance, and that it has a sufficient appreciation of the merits of the claim that it can conclude that it is in the public interest to make the order. Unless the court can be so satisfied by short argument, it is unlikely to make the order in any event ... These necessary conditions are not, however, sufficient for the making of an order. The court must also have regard to the financial resources of the applicant and respondent, and the amount of costs likely to be in issue.'

---

[72]   *Practice Direction (Criminal Proceedings: Costs)* [2010] 1 WLR 2351, at para 2.3.1.

[73]   See **10.5**.

[74]   Access to Justice Act 1999, s 22, considered in *R (Boxall) v Waltham Forest London Borough Council* (2001) 4 CCL Rep 258, at [10].

[75]   *R v Lord Chancellor ex p Child Poverty Action Group; R v DPP ex p Bull and another* [1999] 1 WLR 347, at 358D.

He also held that:[76]

> 'The essential characteristics of a public law challenge are that it raises
> public law issues which are of general importance, where the applicant has
> no private interest in the outcome of the case.'

In *R (Corner House Research) v Secretary of State for Trade and
Industry*[77] the Court of Appeal reviewed the jurisdiction and procedure of
PCOs and re-stated the relevant principles as follows:[78]

> '(1) A protective costs order may be made at any stage of the proceedings,
> on such conditions as the court thinks fit, provided that the court is satisfied
> that: (i) the issues raised are of general public importance; (ii) the public
> interest requires that those issues should be resolved; (iii) the applicant has
> no private interest in the outcome of the case; (iv) having regard to the
> financial resources of the applicant and the respondent(s) and to the
> amount of costs that are likely to be involved, it is fair and just to make the
> order; and (v) if the order is not made the applicant will probably
> discontinue the proceedings and will be acting reasonably in so doing.
>
> (2) If those acting for the applicant are doing so pro bono this will be likely
> to enhance the merits of the application for a PCO.
>
> (3) It is for the court, in its discretion, to decide whether it is fair and just to
> make the order in the light of the considerations set out above.'

The Court of Appeal also modified Mr Justice Dyson's second
guideline:[79]

> 'no PCO should be granted unless the judge considers that the application
> for judicial review has a real prospect of success ...'

Although PCOs will not be routinely granted, there is no additional
criterion that a case be exceptional.[80] The nature and extent of an
applicant's 'private interest' in the decision under challenge and its weight
or importance in the overall context should be treated as a flexible
element in the court's consideration of the question whether it is fair and
just to make a PCO.[81]

---

[76]   Ibid, at 353G.

[77]   [2005] 1 WLR 2600.

[78]   Ibid, at 2625F–2625G.

[79]   Ibid, at 2625D.

[80]   *R (Compton) v Wiltshire Primary Care Trust* [2009] 1 WLR 1436, at 1446G and 1458A.

[81]   *Wilkinson v Kitzinger* [2006] 2 FLR 397, at [54] and *R (Bullmore) v West Hertfordshire
       Hospitals NHS Trust* [2007] EWHC 1350 (Admin), per Lloyd Jones J (as approved by
       the Master of the Rolls in *R (Buglife) v Thurrock Gateway Development Corp* [2008]
       EWCA Civ 1209, [2009] CP Rep 8, at [18]). In *R (Public Interest Lawyers Ltd) v Legal
       Services Commission* [2010] EWHC 3259 (Admin), the Administrative Court held that
       the applicants' strong private interest in the decision under challenge was not a major
       factor in the balance, given that the applicants were prominent players in advancing
       public interest matters.

Where a court makes a PCO in favour of a claimant, it might also be appropriate to cap the liability of the defendant should the claimant win. There should be no automatic assumption that the claimant's and defendant's costs should be capped at the same amount: the amount of any cap depends on the circumstances.[82]

A PCO should be sought on the face of the claim form, supported by the requisite evidence, which should include a schedule of the claimant's future costs of and incidental to the full judicial review application. If the defendant wishes to resist the PCO, or the sums set out in the claimant's schedule, it should set out its reasons in the Acknowledgment of Service. The application will then be considered by the judge on the papers. If the judge refuses to grant a PCO and the Claimant requests that the decision is reconsidered at a hearing, the hearing should be limited to one hour.[83]

There is no reason in principle why a protective costs order should not in an appropriate case extend to protect the position of a defendant. However, such an order would be 'unusual and no doubt exceedingly rare'.[84]

An application for a costs capping order is now subject to the CPR. The court will make a costs capping order only in exceptional circumstances.[85] This means that the Court will only grant such an order if:

(a)   it is in the interests of justice to do so;

(b)   there is a substantial risk that without such an order costs will be disproportionately incurred; and

(c)   the Court is not satisfied that the risk in sub-paragraph (b) can be adequately controlled by case management directions or orders and detailed assessment of costs.[86]

A costs capping order can be made in respect of the whole litigation or any issues which are ordered to be tried separately.[87] A costs capping order, once made, will limit the costs recoverable by the party subject to the order unless that party successfully applies to vary the order.

---

[82]   *R (Buglife) v Thurrock Gateway Development Corp* [2008] EWCA Civ 1209, [2009] CP Rep 8.

[83]   *R (Corner House Research) v Secretary of State for Trade and Industry* [2005] 1 WLR 2600, at 2626H–2627E.

[84]   *R (Ministry of Defence) v Wiltshire & Swindon Coroner* [2006] 1 WLR 134, at 142G–143A.

[85]   Costs Practice Direction, para 23A.1.

[86]   CPR, r 44.18(5).

[87]   Ibid, r 44.18(4).

Although a costs capping order can be made at any stage of the proceedings,[88] an application for a costs capping order must be made as soon as possible,[89] and on notice in accordance with CPR Part 23.[90] The application notice must:

(a)   set out whether the costs capping order is in respect of the whole of the litigation or a particular issue which is ordered to be tried separately;

(b)   provide the reasons why a costs capping order should be made; and

(c)   be accompanied by an estimate of costs setting out (i) the costs (and disbursements) incurred by the applicant to date; and (ii) the costs (and disbursements) which the applicant is likely to incur in the future conduct of the proceedings.[91]

The court may give such directions as it sees fit for the determination of the application, including an order requiring a party to file written submissions on all or any part of the issues arising. If necessary, the Court will fix a date and time estimate for a hearing of the application.[92]

An application to vary a costs capping order must also be made on notice in accordance with CPR Part 23.[93] A variation will only be made if (a) there has been a material and substantial change of circumstances since the date when the order was made; or (b) there is some other compelling reason.[94]

## 10.9   WASTED COSTS AGAINST LEGAL ADVISERS

The Administrative Court has a statutory power to make an order for wasted costs against a legal adviser.[95] There was authority before the CPR 1998 to suggest that this statutory power does not enable a proposed respondent to obtain costs from the applicant's legal adviser at the permission stage of proceedings as the proposed respondent is not a party.[96] However, this is unlikely to prevent an order for wasted costs in an appropriate case as a consequence of the Court's inherent jurisdiction.[97]

Before making an order for wasted costs, the Administrative Court must be satisfied that the legal adviser has acted in an improper, unreasonable

---

[88]   Ibid, r 44.18(5).
[89]   Costs Practice Direction, para 23A.2.
[90]   CPR, r 44.19(1).
[91]   Ibid, r 44.19(2).
[92]   Ibid, r 44.19(3).
[93]   Ibid, r 44.20.
[94]   Ibid, r 44.18(7).
[95]   Senior Courts Act 1981, s 51(6).
[96]   *R v Camden London Borough Council ex p Martin* [1997] 1 All ER 307.
[97]   *R v Immigration Appeal Tribunal ex p Gulbamer Gulsen* [1997] COD 430.

or negligent manner, that those acts have caused unnecessary costs, and that, in all the circumstances, it is reasonable to order payment of some or all of the costs.[98] The court must give the legal adviser an opportunity to give reasons why an order should not be made.[99]

One matter that the Administrative Court must take into account when deciding whether to make a wasted costs order is the fact that a lawyer's client may not have waived privilege, which may prevent the lawyer putting forward arguments in response to the application for wasted costs.[100] An order for wasted costs can be made only if the Court is satisfied that the lawyer would have had no answer to the application if he had been able to put all matters before the Court.[101]

## 10.10 ASSESSMENT OF COSTS

The are two methods of assessment. The Administrative Court can order summary assessment and should normally do so if a hearing has taken less than one day.[102] In the Court of Appeal there are slightly different rules governing the circumstances in which a summary assessment should take place. Essentially, summary assessment should normally take place following interlocutory hearings or appeal hearings of less than one day.[103] There is always a discretion as to whether summary assessment should be ordered.

Summary assessment must not be ordered when costs are obtained by a party in receipt of public funding.[104] In practice, this means that there is rarely summary assessment in a case in which a party is in receipt of public funding.

Where solicitors are acting for parties who may be seeking costs at the conclusion of a substantive hearing of less than one day, they are under a duty to assist the Court in the summary assessment of costs.[105] They should therefore consider filing statements of costs in accordance with the relevant Practice Direction.[106] The statement of costs should follow as closely as possible the form N260.[107]

---

[98] *Ridehalgh v Horsefield* [1994] Ch 205, endorsed by the House of Lords in *Medcalf v Mardell* [2003] 1 AC 120. See also the Costs Practice Direction, para 53.4.

[99] CPR, r 48.7(2).

[100] See, for example, *Persaud v Persaud* [2003] PNLR 26.

[101] *Medcalf v Mardell* [2003] 1 AC 120.

[102] Costs Practice Direction, para 13.2(2).

[103] CPR PD 52, para 14.1.

[104] Costs Practice Direction, para 13.9.

[105] Ibid, para 13.5(1).

[106] Ibid, para 13.5(2).

[107] Ibid, para 13.5(3). Form N260 is available on the Ministry of Justice website, at http://www.justice.gov.uk/guidance/courts-and-tribunals/courts/procedure-rules/civil/menus/forms.htm.

The procedure for a detailed assessment is complex and requires both the payer and payee to serve notices within time-limits. In practice, it will almost certainly be essential to rely on the advice of a costs draftsperson.

Where a costs order is made, the Administrative Court can order that assessment will take place on a standard basis or an indemnity basis.[108] If the order does not state the basis of assessment, it is assumed that it is the standard basis.[109] Generally, the Court will only make an order for indemnity costs if it can be shown that a party acted unreasonably to a high degree and was not merely misguided with the benefit of hindsight.[110] In either case, costs that are unreasonably incurred or unreasonable in amount will not be allowed.[111] In addition, if the costs are awarded on a standard basis, the court will allow only costs that were proportionate and will also resolve any doubt about the reasonableness of any costs in favour of the paying party.[112]

Where a costs order is made against a party, that party's solicitor must notify his client of the order in writing within 7 days of its receipt if the client was not present when the order was made.[113] The solicitor must also inform the client of the reasons for the order.[114] For these purposes, the client includes any person liable for the costs, such as a trade union or the Legal Services Commission.[115]

## 10.11　PRACTICAL CONSIDERATIONS WHEN A CLIENT IS IN RECEIPT OF PUBLIC FUNDING

A solicitor who receives a public funding certificate should send it by post to the Administrative Court as soon as it is received (if proceedings have begun) or it should be lodged with the Court at the commencement of proceedings (if proceedings have not begun).[116] In addition, a notice in a form approved by the Legal Services Commission must be served on all other parties to the proceedings.[117] A precedent for this notice is included in Part III.[118]

At the conclusion of proceedings in the Administrative Court, an order should be sought for the assessment of Commission costs,[119] ie the costs payable by the Commission are assessed by the Court. Unless the costs

---

[108] CPR, r 44.4(1).
[109] Ibid, r 44.4(4).
[110] *Kiam v MGN Ltd (costs)* [2002] 1 WLR 2810.
[111] CPR, r 44.4(1).
[112] Ibid, r 44.4(2).
[113] Ibid, r 44.2.
[114] Costs Practice Direction, para 7.2.
[115] Ibid, para 7.1.
[116] Civil Legal Aid (General) Regulations 1989 (SI 1989/339), reg 50(4).
[117] Ibid, reg 50(1)(a).
[118] See Precedent 8.
[119] Civil Legal Aid (General) Regulations 1989 (SI 1989/339), reg 107.

are less than £2500, a failure to seek an order is likely to mean that there is no basis for payment of the costs. The only exception arises when the costs can be assessed under the legal aid regulations.[120] The Court has no discretion as to whether to make an order but can draw attention of the costs judge to matters that might be disallowed.[121]

If proceedings have not been commenced, costs will be assessed by the Commission.[122] Although persons applying for judicial review must apply for permission to bring the application, the application for permission is not normally regarded, for legal aid purposes, as being a step before the proceedings have commenced. As a result, the normal practice is to seek an order for assessment of Commission costs at the conclusion of the application for permission, although the Administrative Court may decline to make an order if permission is granted because an assessment can be ordered later in the proceedings.

---

[120] Civil Legal Aid (General) Regulations 1989 (SI 1989/339), reg 105.
[121] *R v Secretary of State ex p Shahina Begum* [1995] COD 176.
[122] Civil Legal Aid (General) Regulations 1989 (SI 1989/339), reg 105.

# PART II

## PROCEDURAL CHECKLIST

**P2**   This checklist has been drafted on the assumption that judicial review proceeds according to the normal timetable. As this book makes clear, it is possible that time periods may be shortened if there is particular urgency.

| | | |
|---|---|---|
| Is the claim one that must be commenced in the Upper Tribunal? | If it is one related to the Criminal Injuries Compensation Scheme, it relates to a procedural decision of the First Tier Tribunal where there is no appeal or it relates to an immigration fresh claim, it should be commenced in the Upper Tribunal. | See **6.1**, **6.3** |
| Requirements for a person to bring a claim for judicial review. | A person must have a sufficient interest. In addition, in a human rights claim, a person must be a victim. | Senior Courts Act 1981, s 31(3); Tribunal, Courts and Enforcement Act 2007, s 16(3); Human Rights Act 1998, s 7 See **1.4**, **6.6** |
| | Decision challenged must be a decision of a public body or an inferior court. | See **1.5** |
| | Decision challenged must be a public law decision. | See para **1.6** |
| | The decision is not of a type that means that judicial review is not available. | See **1.7** and **1.8** |
| When must claim be commenced. | Promptly and, in any event, within 3 months. Special considerations apply in cases that raise issues of European Union law. | CPR 1998, r 54.5; Tribunal Procedure (Upper Tribunal) Rules 2008 (SI 2008/2698), r 28(2), 28(3) |

|  | The rule is qualified in the Upper Tribunal. Firstly, statute can specify a shorter time limit. In addition, an application may be made outside the time limit if it is a challenge to a First-Tier Tribunal decision and made within one month of written reasons having been sent or notification that an application to set aside has been refused. | See **3.1, 6.3** |
|---|---|---|
|  | Time to apply for judicial review can be extended. | CPR 1998, r 3.1(2)(a). See **3.1, 6.3** |
| Steps to be taken by the claimant before the claim is commenced. | Claimant writes a letter before claim. This must be written promptly and in sufficient time to lodge the claim. Other parties should be given 14 days to respond. | Judicial Review Pre-action Protocol See **4.1** See Precedent **1** |
|  | Before drafting and lodging the claim, the claimant should obtain public funding if this is required. | See **4.2** |
|  | In the High Court, if claimant is a child or mentally ill, consideration needs to be given to the appointment of a litigation friend. | See **4.3** |
| Steps to be taken by other parties before the claim is commenced. | Within 14 days of letter before claim, the other parties should respond to the letter before claim. | Judicial Review Pre-action Protocol See **4.1** See Precedent **2** |
|  | In the High Court, if party is a child or mentally ill, consideration needs to be given to the appointment of a litigation friend. | See **4.3** |

| | | |
|---|---|---|
| How is claim commenced? | The claimant must obtain permission to bring the claim. | CPR 1998, r 54.4; Tribunal, Courts and Enforcement Act 2007, s 16.2<br>See **5.8, 6.3** |
| | The application for permission is commenced by lodging the papers set out below, unless an urgent out-of-hours application is made. | See **5.1.1** for details of out-of-hours applications |
| Papers to be lodged in High Court when seeking permission to apply for judicial review. | The claim form. | Practice Direction 54A, para 5.6<br>See **5.2.1**<br>See Precedents **3**, **4** and **18** |
| | Any written evidence. | Practice Direction 54A, para 5.7<br>See **5.2.2**<br>See Precedent **7** |
| | A copy of any order that the claimant wishes to have quashed. | Practice Direction 54A, para 5.7<br>See **5.2.2** |
| | Where the claim relates to a decision of a court or tribunal, an approved copy of the reasons for the decision. | Practice Direction 54A, para 5.7<br>See **5.2.2** |
| | Copies of any documents on which the claimant wishes to rely. | Practice Direction 54A, para 5.7<br>See **5.2.2** |
| | Copies of any relevant statutory material. | Practice Direction 54A, para 5.7<br>See **5.2.2** |
| | A list of essential reading. | Practice Direction 54A, para 5.7<br>See **5.2.2** |
| | A notice of issue of the public funding certificate. | See **5.2.2**<br>See Precedent **8** |
| | Two copies of all the documents submitted in indexed and paginated bundles. | Practice Direction 54A, para 5.9<br>See **5.2.2** |
| | A copy of any certificate granting public funding. | See **5.2.2** |
| | Court fee. | See **5.2.2** |

| | | |
|---|---|---|
| Papers to be lodged in Upper Tribunal when seeking permission to apply for judicial review. | Papers to be lodged depend upon the nature of the decision challenged. | See **6.3** |
| If claim commenced in High Court, decision will need to be taken as to whether to lodge in London or regions. | Normally commenced in region that Claimant has closest connection to subject to other factors suggesting listing elsewhere. | See **5.2.2** |
| Requirements to be considered when drafting and filing. | Claimants are subject to a duty of disclosure. | See **5.3** |
| | The written evidence must comply with the requirements of Practice Directions. | Practice Direction 32 See **5.2.2** |
| Other issues to be considered when applying for permission. | Decide whether there is a need for urgent consideration. | See **5.1.2, 6.4** |
| | Decide whether claimant seeks interim relief. | See **5.2.1, 6.1** |
| | Decide whether there is a need for an order restricting the reporting of the matter. | See **3.5** |
| Can grounds be amended or additional evidence submitted? | It would appear the Administrative Court and the Upper Tribunal have a discretion to permit amendment or service of evidence. | See **5.7, 6.7** |
| When should an application be made to submit amended grounds or additional evidence? | In the High Court, the amended grounds or additional evidence must be submitted at least 7 clear days before the hearing date or warned list date. | Practice Direction 54A, para 11.1 See **5.7** |
| | Different rules apply in the Upper Tribunal depending upon the nature of the claim | See **6.7** |
| Steps to be taken by the claimant after papers have been lodged. | In the High Court, the bundle must be served within 7 days on other parties. | CPR 1998, r 54.7 See **5.2.3** |

| | A certificate of service must be lodged with the Administrative Court within 7 days of service. | See **5.2.3** |
|---|---|---|
| | Different rules apply in the Upper Tribunal depending upon the nature of the claim | See **6.3** |
| Steps to be taken by parties served by the claimant. | Before drafting and lodging any pleadings, a party should obtain public funding if this is required. | See **4.2** |
| | If proceedings are being brought in the High Court, acknowledgment of service must be filed with the Administrative Court within 21 days. | CPR 1998, r 54.8 See **5.4** See Precedent **9** |
| | This must be served on all parties named in claim form within 7 days unless the Court orders otherwise. | CPR 1998, r 54.8(2) See **5.4** See Precedents **9** and **10** |
| | In the Upper Tribunal, different rules apply. | See **6.5** |
| Requirements to be considered when drafting and filing. | Defendants are subject to a duty of disclosure. | See **5.5** |
| Steps to be taken by the claimant after he has been served with the acknowledgment of service. | Claimant can file relevant observations. | See **5.6, 6.5** |
| How is the application for permission to apply for judicial review determined? | It will be determined initially on the papers. | See **5.8, 6.6** |
| | Permission is normally granted if the application is arguable. | Eg *R v Secretary of State for the Home Department ex parte Begum* [1990] COD 107 See **5.8** |
| Steps to be taken by the claimant if permission is refused. | The application for permission can be renewed, provided that there is still merit. | See **5.9, 6.6** |

| | | |
|---|---|---|
| How is application renewed? | In the High Court, form is filed with Administrative Court within 7 days of receipt of judge's reasons. | CPR 1998, r 54.12(4) See **5.9** |
| | In the Upper Tribunal, different rules apply. | See **6.6** |
| How is renewed application for permission considered? | In the High Court, the application is considered following an oral application in open court. Other parties to the judicial review claim may attend this hearing. | CPR 1998, r 54.12(3) See **5.9** |
| | The hearing will be listed for 30 minutes unless the parties indicate that a longer hearing is required. | Notes for Guidance produced by the Administrative Court See **5.9** |
| Steps to be taken by the claimant if permission is refused at the oral hearing? | In a civil cause or matter, it is possible to appeal to the Court of Appeal. | See **5.9, 6.6** |
| | Application for permission to appeal must be made within 7 days. Different time limits apply in the Upper Tribunal. | CPR 1998, r 52.15(2) See **5.9, 6.6** |
| | In a criminal cause or matter, it is probably impossible to take the matter further. | See **5.9** |
| Steps to be taken by the claimant if permission is granted. | In the High Court, the court fee must be paid within 7 days. | Notes for Guidance produced by the Administrative Court See **5.10.1** |
| | Consideration should be given to whether it is necessary to apply for any interim case management orders. | See **5.10.4** |
| | Public funding will need to be extended to cover trial. | See **5.10.7** |

| | | |
|---|---|---|
| | A trial bundle must be filed and served at least 21 working days before the hearing. In practice, this should be done in sufficient time to permit the skeleton argument to refer to it. The bundle must be paginated and indexed. | Practice Direction 54A, para 16.1 See **5.13.2** |
| | At least 21 working days before the hearing, a skeleton argument must be filed and served on all the other parties. | Practice Direction 54A, para 15.1 See **5.13.2** |
| | In a case where the hearing may take less than 1 day and no party is in receipt of public funding, a statement of costs should be filed. | See **9.10** |
| | In the Upper Tribunal, different rules apply. | See **6.7** |
| Steps to be taken by the other parties if permission is granted. | Consideration should be given to settling the claim by consent. | See **5.12** |
| | Detailed grounds of resistance and any evidence must be served within 35 days of the grant of permission. | CPR 1998, r 54.14 See **5.10.2** |
| | Consideration should be given to whether it is necessary to apply for any interim case management orders. | See **5.10.4** |
| | Public funding will need to be extended to cover trial. | See **5.10.7** |
| | At least 14 working days before the hearing, a skeleton argument must be filed and served on all the other parties. | Practice Direction 54, para 15.2 See **5.13.2** |

| | In a case where the hearing may take less than 1 day and no party is in receipt of public funding, a statement of costs should be filed. | See **9.10** |
| --- | --- | --- |
| | In the Upper Tribunal, different rules apply. | See **6.7** |
| How will the matter be listed? | In the Administrative Court, in accordance with standard listing arrangements. | *Practice Statement (Administrative Court: Listing and Urgent Cases)* [2002] 1 WLR 810 <br> See **5.13.1** |
| Matters to be considered at the conclusion of the hearing. | The Administrative Court and the Upper Tribunal have a discretion as to whether to grant relief. | See **6.8**, **7.1** |
| | The Administrative Court and the Upper Tribunal can make a quashing order, a mandatory order or a prohibiting order. | Senior Courts Act 1981, s 31(1), Tribunal, Courts and Enforcement Act 2007, s 15(1) and CPR 1998, r 54.2 <br> See **6.1**, **7.2** |
| | The Administrative Court and the Upper Tribunal can also grant an injunction, make a declaration or award damages. | Senior Courts Act 1981, s 31(2), Tribunal, Courts and Enforcement Act 2007, s 15(1) and 16(6) and CPR 1998, r 54.3 <br> See **6.1**, **7.2** |
| | Only the Administrative Court can make a declaration of incompatibility under the Human Rights Act 1998. | Human Rights Act 1998, section 4. <br> See **7.2.5** |
| | The Administrative Court can vary a sentence. | Supreme Court Act 1981, s 43(1) <br> See **7.3** |
| | The Administrative Court and the Upper Tribunal can issue an order for costs. | See **6.8** and Chapter 9 |

| | The Administrative Court and the Upper Tribunal can order the assessment of Legal Services Commission costs. | See **9.11** |
|---|---|---|
| | The Administrative Court and the Upper Tribunal can grant permission to appeal. In addition, in a criminal cause or matter, it can certify a point of law of general public importance. | See **6.9** and Chapter 8 for a consideration of appeal procedure |
| The approach of the Administrative Court to the award of costs. | In general the principle is that the unsuccessful party should pay the costs of the successful party. | CPR 1998, r 44.3(2) See **9.2** |
| | Special considerations apply when the unsuccessful party is in receipt of public funding. | See **9.4** |
| | Special considerations apply when a court is a party. | See **9.5** |
| | In a criminal cause or matter, it may be possible to apply for costs from central funds. | Prosecution of Offences Act 1985, ss 16 and 17 See **9.7** |
| The approach of the Upper Tribunal to the award of costs. | The Upper Tribunal can issue an order for costs, and will take account of a party's resources where the paying party is an individual. | Tribunal Procedure (Upper Tribunal) Rules 2008 (SI 2008/2968), rr 10(3) and 10(7) See **6.8** |
| Matters to be considered by the unsuccessful party. | Whether to appeal. | |
| | The procedure to be adopted depends on whether the matter is a criminal cause or matter. | See **3.4** for a consideration of what matters are a criminal cause or matter. See Chapter 9 for a consideration of appeal procedure. |

| | |
|---|---|
| The procedure to be adopted depends on whether the claim was determined by the Upper Tribunal | See **6.9** for a consideration of the procedure in the Upper Tribunal |

# PART III

## FORMS AND PRECEDENTS

Most of the precedents in this part relate to a fictional criminal judicial review. They are included to illustrate the format of the documents. The format would be identical if the challenge was to a civil executive decision. This can be seen by comparing Precedent 18 (grounds in a civil case) with Precedent 4 (grounds in the fictional criminal case). The format is the same despite the fact that the issues are very different.

## P3.1   LETTER BEFORE CLAIM[1]

We act for the above named in relation to the Prison Service's failure to provide adequate medical treatment.

This matter may give rise to judicial review proceedings. Accordingly we are writing this letter to provide you with an opportunity to respond to the relevant issues in the hope that litigation might be avoided. Please accept this letter as a formal letter before claim as required by the pre-action protocol governing claims for judicial review.

### Our client

We act on behalf of the above named of [          ].[2]

### Proposed defendant

Should proceedings become necessary, the proposed defendant is the Secretary of State for Justice.

### Interested parties

Should proceedings become necessary there are no proposed interested parties.[3]

### Previous correspondence and your reference details[4]

The most recent letter from the Prison Service is dated 1 May 2011. The reference on that letter is [          ].[5]

### Relevant issues

As you will no doubt be aware, our client suffers from a long-standing problem with back pain. Our client has been told that he requires an operation to treat the causes of that pain.

Our client was seen at Birmingham General Hospital on 1 April 2009. During that appointment our client was told that he required surgery. A letter was subsequently sent to our client informing him that he had been placed on the waiting list for day surgery.

---

1   The Judicial Review Pre-action Protocol provides that this letter must be addressed to certain specified addresses.
2   Insert claimant's address.
3   See **5.2.1** for details of the circumstances in which an interested party should be named.
4   Section 3 of the Judicial Review Pre-action Protocol expressly requires that particular types of references are used for specific decision-makers. For example, it provides that in many immigration cases, a Home Office reference should be provided.
5   Insert the reference on the letter if there is one.

It appears from the notes obtained from Birmingham General Hospital that our client was offered appointments on 1 April 2010, 13 May 2010, 8 July 2010, 21 September 2010 and 1 February 2011. It appears that the Prison Service cancelled all these appointments as they were inconvenient.

It appears to us that the repeated cancellation of medical appointments has essentially resulted in a violation of the Prison Service Standard regarding medical care that entitles our client to care equivalent to that provided by the National Health Service. Had our client been a patient of the NHS in the community then he would have been able to attend his appointments at Birmingham General Hospital. It was only his status as a prisoner that prevented our client attending those appointments.

We submit that the failure to provide our client with care equivalent to that provided by the NHS is also a violation of Art 3 of the European Convention on Human Rights ('the ECHR'). It has resulted in our client suffering significant unnecessary pain.

Finally, we submit that the failure to provide our client with care equivalent to that provided by the NHS is a violation of Art 8 of the ECHR. We recognise that Art 8 is not an absolute right. However, no justification has been provided for the failure to provide our client with the treatment he requires.

## Action required

We request confirmation that you will now contact Birmingham General Hospital and make arrangements for the cancelled appointments to be re-arranged for our client as soon as possible.

In the event that you intend to oppose this claim, we request confirmation that you will not oppose an interim order requiring that no further appointments are cancelled without leave of the court.[6]

## Details of information sought

We would appreciate it if you would confirm that you accept that the notes that we have obtained from Birmingham General Hospital correctly record the history of this matter.

## Details of documents sought

We would appreciate it if you would supply us with a copy of our client's prison medical records.

## Address for reply and service of documents

[                ][7] at the address on this letter.

---

6   The letter before claim should expressly state if interim relief will be sought.
7   Insert the name of the potential claimant's representative.

**Proposed reply date**

We look forward to hearing from you within 14 days[8] of the date of this letter failing which we reserve the right to commence Judicial Review Proceedings without further recourse to you.

---

[8]    14 days is the period that it is normally expected that a claimant will give a defendant to respond. However, if the matter is a matter of urgency the time for response can be reduced. See **4.1.1**.

## P3.2   LETTER IN RESPONSE TO THE LETTER BEFORE CLAIM

We act for the Secretary of State for Justice in relation to your client's proposed judicial review claim. Please accept this letter as a formal response to a letter before claim as required by the pre-action protocol governing claims for judicial review.

### Proposed claimant

We note that you act for [          ]⁹ who is the proposed claimant.

### Proposed defendant

We note that you suggest that should proceedings become necessary, the proposed defendant is the Secretary of State for Justice. We confirm that we agree the Secretary of State is legally responsible for the decision that you propose to challenge.

### Interested parties

Should proceedings become necessary we agree that there are no interested parties.¹⁰

### Previous correspondence and reference details

Our reference in relation to this matter is [          ].¹¹ We confirm that all correspondence regarding this matter should now be addressed to this office. Earlier decisions were the responsibility of the Governor of HMP Birmingham.

We note that your reference is [          ].¹²

### Response to the proposed claim

In simple terms we do not accept that the factual basis of this claim is as described. Attached to this letter are your client's prison medical records. They do not record that appointments were offered as described. As far as our client is concerned, your client is still awaiting an appointment from Birmingham General Hospital. Any delay in your client receiving treatment is the responsibility of the hospital.

Our client does not oppose the interim relief that you seek as our client does not intend to cancel any appointment offered to your client. However, we do not

---

⁹    Insert the name of the proposed claimant.
¹⁰   See **5.2.1** for details of the circumstances in which an interested party should be named.
¹¹   The reference on the letter should be included if there is one.
¹²   Ibid.

accept that there is any basis for applying for judicial review in the light of our understanding of the correct facts in this matter.

## Address for reply and service of documents

[          ]¹³ at the address on this letter.

---

¹³     Insert the name of the potential defendant's representative.

## P3.3   CLAIM FORM

This Precedent should be read with **Precedent 4**, which is the grounds to be attached to the claim form. Numbers in brackets refer to notes at the end of the Precedent.

# Judicial Review
## Claim Form

| In the High Court of Justice |
| --- |
| Administrative Court |

**Notes for guidance are available which explain how to complete the judicial review claim form. Please read them carefully before you complete the form.**

Seal

| For Court use only | |
| --- | --- |
| Administrative Court Reference No. | |
| Date filed | |

**SECTION 1   Details of the claimant(s) and defendant(s)**

Claimant(s) name and address(es)

name
John Smith

address
1 The Crescent
London
EC3A 1PP

Telephone no.
020 7111 1111

Fax no.

E-mail address

Claimant's or claimant's solicitors' address to which documents should be sent.

name
Smith & Co

address
2 The Crescent
London
EC3A 1PP

Telephone no.
020 7111 2222

Fax no.
020 852 7708

E-mail address

Claimant's Counsel's details

name
Hugh Southey QC

address
Tooks Chambers
81 Farringdon Street
London EC4A 4BL

Telephone no.
020 7842 7575

Fax no.
020 7842 7576

E-mail address
clerks@tooks.co.uk

1st Defendant

name
The London Magistrates' Court

Defendant's or (where known) Defendant's solicitors' address to which documents should be sent.

name

address
1 High Street
London
EC3A 1QQ

Telephone no.
020 7111 4444

Fax no.
020 7111 5555

E-mail address

2nd Defendant

name

Defendant's or (where known) Defendant's solicitors' address to which documents should be sent.

name

address

Telephone no.

Fax no.

E-mail address

**SECTION 2  Details of other interested parties**

Include name and address and, if appropriate, details of DX, telephone or fax numbers and e-mail

| name | name |
|---|---|
| The Crown Prosecution Service (1) | |

| address | address |
|---|---|
| 2 High Street | |
| London | |
| EC3A 1QQ | |

| Telephone no. | Fax no. | Telephone no. | Fax no. |
|---|---|---|---|
| 020 7111 6666 | | | |

| E-mail address | E-mail address |
|---|---|
| | |

**SECTION 3  Details of the decision to be judicially reviewed**

Decision:
Decision to commit the Claimant to the Crown Court (2)

Date of decision:
19 July 2011

Name and address of the court, tribunal, person or body who made the decision to be reviewed.

| name | address |
|---|---|
| The London Magistrates' Court | 1 High Street |
| | London |
| | EC3A 1QQ |

**SECTION 4  Permission to proceed with a claim for judicial review**

I am seeking permission to proceed with my claim for Judicial Review.

| | | |
|---|---|---|
| Is this application being made under the terms of Section 18 Practice Direction 54 (Challenging removal)? | ☐ Yes | ☒ No |
| Are you making any other applications? If Yes, complete Section 7. | ☒ Yes | ☐ No |
| Is the claimant in receipt of a Community Legal Service Fund (CLSF) certificate? | ☒ Yes | ☐ No |
| Are you claiming exceptional urgency, or do you need this application determined within a certain time scale? If Yes, complete Form N463 and file this with your application. | ☐ Yes | ☒ No |
| Have you complied with the pre-action protocol? If No, give reasons for non-compliance in the space below. | ☐ Yes | ☒ No |

The Defendant is a court and is functus officio having ruled on this matter.

| | | |
|---|---|---|
| Have you issued this claim in the region with which you have the closest connection? (Give any additional reasons for wanting it to be dealt with in this region in the box below). If No, give reasons in the box below. | ☒ Yes | ☐ No |

(3)

Does the claim include any issues arising from the Human Rights Act 1998?

If Yes, state the articles which you contend have been breached in the space below.  ☐ Yes  ☒ No

(4)

**SECTION 5  Detailed statement of grounds**

☐ set out below    ☒ attached

**SECTION 6  Details of remedy (including any interim remedy) being sought**

1. A quashing order quashing the decision challenged

2. An order remitting the Claimant's case to the London Magistrates' Court.

3. A declaration that the Claimant's committal to the Crown Court is unlawful. (5)

4. Costs

5. Further or other relief. (6)

**SECTION 7  Other applications**

I wish to make an application for:-

For the reasons set out in the attached grounds, the Claimant seeks an extension of the time for bringing this claim for judicial review. (7)

**SECTION 8  Statement of facts relied on**

See attached

**Statement of Truth**

I believe (The claimant believes) that the facts stated in this claim form are true.

Full name   E Jones

Name of claimant's solicitor's firm    Smith & Co

Signed _____   Position or office held    Solicitor

Claimant ('s solicitor)                              (if signing on behalf of firm or company)

**SECTION 9  Supporting documents**

If you do not have a document that you intend to use to support your claim, identify it, give the date when you expect it to be available and give reasons why it is not currently available in the box below.

Please tick the papers you are filing with this claim form and any you will be filing later.

☒ Statement of grounds        ☐ included     ☒ attached

☒ Statement of the facts relied on        ☐ included     ☒ attached

☒ Application to extend the time limit for filing the claim form        ☒ included     ☒ attached

☐ Application for directions        ☐ included     ☐ attached

☐ Any written evidence in support of the claim or
application to extend time

☒ Where the claim for judicial review relates to a decision of
a court or tribunal, an approved copy of the reasons for
reaching that decision

☒ Copies of any documents on which the claimant
proposes to rely

☐ A copy of the legal aid or CSLF certificate *(if legally represented)*

☒ Copies of any relevant statutory material

☒ A list of essential documents for advance reading by
the court *(with page references to the passages relied upon)*

If Section 18 Practice Direction 54 applies, please tick the relevant box(es) below to indicate which papers you are filing with this claim form:

☐ a copy of the removal directions and the decision to which
the application relates        ☐ included     ☐ attached

☐ a copy of the documents served with the removal directions
including any documents which contains the Immigration and
Nationality Directorate's factual summary of the case        ☐ included     ☐ attached

☐ a detailed statement of the grounds        ☐ included     ☐ attached

---

Reasons why you have not supplied a document and date when you expect it to be available:-

Public funding was granted on an emergency basis. No certificate has been received. The certificate will be lodged once it has been received.

Signed _____ Claimant ('s Solicitor) _____

6 of 6

(1)    See **5.2.1** for consideration of who should be named as an interested party

(2)    The decision challenged should be described in simple language

(3)    If the claim is not issued in the court with which the Claimant has the closest connections, an explanation should be included here. See **5.2.2**

(4)    Any articles of the European Convention on Human Rights that are said to have been violated should be listed here

(5)    Where a declaration is sought, the terms of the declaration should be specified

(6)    All relief sought should be listed

(7)    Any application for directions should be sought in this section of the form

## P3.4    GROUNDS IN SUPPORT OF THE CLAIM

This precedent relates to a fictional criminal judicial review. It is included to illustrate the format of grounds. The format would be identical if the challenge was to a civil executive decision. This can hopefully be seen by comparing Precedent **18** (grounds in a civil case) with this precedent.

### 1    The issues[14]

1.1    Whether the Magistrates' Court acted unlawfully by committing the Claimant to the Crown Court for sentencing contrary to a legitimate expectation that had arisen that the Magistrates' Court would pass sentence.

### 2    Factual background

2.1    On 1 June 2011 the Claimant was charged with one count of possessing a false passport. On 3 June 2011 the Claimant was charged with two further counts of using a false instrument.

2.2    On 1 July 2011 the Claimant appeared before the Magistrates' Court and entered a guilty plea in relation to all three matters. A full plea in mitigation followed during which the court was invited to either pass sentence immediately or adjourn the matter for a pre-sentence report. The court decided to adjourn the matter and gave an indication that it would deal with the matter. The court ordered a pre-sentence report.

2.3    The matter returned to the Magistrates' Court on 19 July 2011. On that date a pre-sentence report was available. It concluded that:

> Mr Smith is suitable for a Community Service Order, understands what is involved and work is available. However, because I have been unable to verify any of the information he has given me about his recent circumstances, and there is a doubt about whether or not he is truly resident in London, sentencing to a community disposal may [sic] cause problems for ongoing contact, if he does not remain in the area.[15]

2.4    The District Judge considering the matter on 19 July 2011 decided to commit the matter to the Crown Court for sentencing. Before this happened her attention was drawn to the decision in *R v Nottingham Magistrates Court ex p Davidson* [2000] 1 Cr App R (S) 167. The Judge distinguished that case on the basis that there was no record of the indication given by the Magistrates' Court on 1 July 2011 endorsed on the court file.

---

[14]    It is helpful for the judge or judges to have some basic guide to reason for the judicial review claim before they consider the grounds. It means that they can read matters such as the factual background in context.

[15]    There is a duty of disclosure imposed on judicial review claimants. See **5.3** for full details. In practice that means that claimants should give details of significant matters that are adverse to their interests. A failure to do this may result in the Administrative Court concluding that there has been a failure to comply with the duty of disclosure. The claim is also likely to be regarded as lacking credibility. Adverse matters that should be addressed include legal matters as well as factual matters.

## 3   Legal framework[16]

3.1   The maximum sentences for the offences in relation to which the Claimant has entered guilty pleas are 6 months if imposed by a Magistrates' Court but 10 years if imposed by the Crown Court (Forgery and Counterfeiting Act 1981, s 6). The Magistrates' Court would have been entitled to impose consecutive sentences for the three offences, provided that they did not exceed a total of 12 months (Magistrates' Court Act 1980, s 133).

3.2   Section 3(2) of the Powers of Criminal Courts (Sentencing) Act 2000 provides that:

> If the court is of the opinion –
> (a)    that the offence or the combination of the offence and one or more offences associated with it was so serious that greater punishment should be inflicted for the offence than the court has power to impose, or
> (b)    in the case of a violent or sexual offence, that a custodial sentence for a term longer than the court has power to impose is necessary to protect the public from serious harm from him,
>
> the court may commit the offender in custody or on bail to the Crown Court for sentence ...[17]

3.3   In *R v Jockey Club ex parte RAM Racecourses* [1993] 2 All ER 225, Stuart-Smith LJ analysed the elements of a claim based on legitimate expectation. He held that the Claimant must prove:

> (1)    A clear and unambiguous representation ...
> (2)    That since the applicant was not a person to whom any representation was directly made it was within the class of persons who are entitled to rely upon it; or at any rate that it was reasonable for the applicant to rely upon it without more ...
> (3)    That it did so rely upon it.
> (4)    That it did so to its detriment. While in some cases it is not altogether clear that this is a necessary ingredient, since a public body is entitled to change its policy if it is acting in good faith, it is a necessary ingredient where, as here, an applicant is saying, "You cannot alter your policy now in my case; it is too late".
> (5)    That there is no overriding interest arising from [the defendant's] duties and responsibilities ... which entitled [them] to change their policy to the detriment of the applicant.[18]

3.4   Although in *ex p RAM Racecourses*, Stuart-Smith LJ held that there was a need for the Claimant to show that he relied on the legitimate expectation to his detriment, it may not be necessary for the claimant to prove this in all cases. For example, in *Francisco Javier Jaramillo-Silva v Secretary of State for the Home*

---

[16]   When considering whether to cite authorities it is important to be aware of the Practice Direction on Citation of Authorities [2001] 1 WLR 1001. See Part IV. Good practice suggests that any unreported authorities should be included in the legislative bundle.

[17]   Although it is normal practice to cite relevant passages of statutory authorities, the citation of relevant authorities does not mean that these authorities should not be included in the bundle of statutory authorities. See **5.2.2**.

[18]   It is normal practice to cite relevant passages of judgments that support the claim for judicial review. Many of the passages the practitioners will require are set out earlier in this book.

*Department* [1994] Imm AR 352 Simon Brown LJ held that reliance on a legitimate expectation is not a necessary requirement.[19]

3.5 It is clear that the concept of legitimate expectation can be applied to sentencing decisions. In *ex p Davidson* Lord Bingham CJ held that:

> If a court at a preliminary stage of the sentencing process gives to a defendant any indication as to the sentence which will or will not be thereafter passed upon him, in terms sufficiently unqualified to found a legitimate expectation in the mind of the defendant that any court which later passes sentence upon him will act in accordance with the indication given, and if on a later occasion a court, without reasons which justify departure from the earlier indication, and whether or not it is aware of that indication, passes a sentence inconsistent with, and more severe than, the sentence indicated, the court will ordinarily feel obliged, however reluctantly, to adjust the sentence passed so as to bring it into line with that indicated. (at p 169)

Applying these principles the Court quashed a decision of a Magistrates' Court to commit a matter for sentence under s 38(2) of the Magistrates' Court Act 1980 after the Magistrates' Court had previously accepted jurisdiction to pass sentence and adjourned the matter for a pre-sentence report. The Court based its decision on affidavit evidence from the Claimant's solicitor stating that no indication was given that committal for sentence was still an option.

3.6 Similarly, in *R v Warley Magistrates' Court ex p DPP and other cases* [1999] 1 WLR 216 Kennedy LJ held that:

> [I]f [a Magistrates' Court] says that it is satisfied that the case is not one in which it will be necessary for it to commit to the Crown Court for sentence, and then adjourns for the pre-sentence report, when the matter comes back before a differently constituted bench that second bench is likely to consider that so far as committal for sentence is concerned its hands are tied. (at p 223)

## 4   The Claimant's submissions

4.1   It is the Claimant's respectful submission that the proceedings before the Magistrates' Court on 1 July 2002 gave rise to a legitimate expectation that he would not subsequently be committed for sentence to the Crown Court. In support of this submission the Claimant relies on the indication given by the Magistrates' Court that it would deal with the matter and the order that pre-sentence reports should be prepared which were sufficient to give rise to a legitimate expectation (*ex p Davidson* and *ex p DPP*).

4.2   Further, it is the Claimant's submission that nothing in the pre-sentence report could justify departure from the earlier legitimate expectation. In particular any difficulties enforcing a Community Service Order could not justify committal for sentence as they were not matters that could have justified a longer custodial sentence. It is the Claimant's submission that the District Judge appeared to recognise this as she did not seek to justify her departure from the earlier legitimate expectation but instead sought to distinguish *ex p Davidson*.

---

[19]   Although one can cite passages of judgments, it is equally acceptable to state the ratio of the case.

4.3    Further, it is the Claimant's submission that the reason given by the District Judge for distinguishing *ex p Davidson* is not a satisfactory reason. The absence of a note on the court file does not determine whether a legitimate expectation has arisen. Instead the issue is whether the statements and orders made by the Magistrates' Court on 26 May 2000 gave rise to a legitimate expectation.

4.4    Further, in the light of all the matters above the Magistrates' Court erred by committing the Claimant to the Crown Court for sentence.

HUGH SOUTHEY QC[20]
TOOKS CHAMBERS

**In a case in which there had been delay, it might be necessary to include the following passages:**

## Under '2. Factual background'

2.5    The Claimant sought public funding for this claim on 21 July 2002. Unfortunately public funding was initially refused on 24 July 2002. It was only following repeated requests for a review that it was granted on 10 September 2002.

## Under '3. Legal framework'

3.7    Problems obtaining Legal Aid can be a good reason for extending time to bring a claim for judicial review (R v Stratford on Avon District Council ex parte Jackson [1985] 3 All ER 769).

3.8    In R v Secretary of State for the Home Department ex parte Ruddock [1997] 1 WLR 1482 at 1485G Taylor J held that:

> I have concluded that since the matters raised are of general importance, it would be a wrong exercise of my discretion to reject the application on grounds of delay, thereby leaving the substantive issues unresolved. I therefore extend time to allow the applicant to proceed.

## Under '4. The Claimant's submissions'

4.5    The Claimant acknowledges that a claim can be held to be out of time if it is not brought promptly. The Claimant submits that this claim should not be held to be out of time:

4.5.1    Any delay is explained by problems obtaining Legal Aid (*R v Stratford on Avon District Council ex parte Jackson*, supra); and

4.5.2    The issues raised are of importance to the Claimant as they potentially relate to liberty (*R v Secretary of State for the Home Department ex parte Ruddock*, supra).

---

[20]    The pleadings should always be signed by the counsel who were responsible for drafting them, if they were drafted by counsel.

# P3.5 APPLICATION FOR URGENT CONSIDERATION

This Precedent should be read with Precedent **6**, which is the draft order to be supplied with this application. Numbers in brackets refer to notes at the end of the Precedent.

## Judicial Review
### Application for urgent consideration

This form must be completed by the Claimant or the Claimant's advocate if exceptional urgency is being claimed and the application needs to be determined within a certain time scale.

The claimant, or the claimant's solicitors must serve this form on the defendant(s) and any interested parties with the N461 Judicial review claim form.

**To the Defendant(s) and interested party(ies) Representations as to the urgency of the claim may be made by defendants or interested parties to the Administrative Court Office by fax - 020 7947 6802**

| In the High Court of Justice Administrative Court | |
|---|---|
| Claim No. | |
| Claimant(s) *(including ref.)* | John Smith |
| Defendant(s) | The London Magistrates' Court |
| Interested Parties | The Crown Prosecution Service |

**SECTION 1  Reasons for urgency**

The Claimant's sentencing hearing is due to take place in the Crown Court on 1 August 2002. The Claimant argues in this claim that he should not have been committed to the Crown Court. Clearly the merits of this claim should be considered before the hearing on 1 August 2002 so that a stay can be ordered if appropriate. (1)

**SECTION 2  Proposed timetable** *(tick the boxes and complete the following statements that apply)*

☑ a) The N461 application for permission should be considered within 2 (2) _____ hours/days

☑ b) Abridgement of time is sought for the lodging of acknowledgements of service

☐ c) If permission for judicial review is granted, a substantive hearing is sought by (3) _____ (date)

**SECTION 3  Interim relief** *(state what interim relief is sought and why in the box below)*

A draft order must be attached.

A stay of proceedings in the Crown Court is sought to enable the merits of this claim to be considered before the Crown Court sentence the Claimant. (4)

**SECTION 4  Service**

A copy of this form of application was served on the defendant(s) and interested parties as follows:

**Defendant**

☐ by fax machine to          time sent
Fax no.                       time

(5)

☐ by handing it to or leaving it with
name

☐ by e-mail to
e-mail address

Date served
Date

**Interested party**

☐ by fax machine to          time sent
Fax no.                       time

☐ by handing it to or leaving it with
name

☐ by e-mail to
e-mail address

Date served
Date

Name of claimant's advocate
name

Claimant (claimant's advocate)
Signed

(1)     The need for urgent consideration should be described in simple language.

(2)     The time scale for urgent consideration should be considered carefully so that the Administrative Court is not put under unnecessary pressure but does make a decision in time to provide any interim relief sought. Always make it clear whether the suggested time scale is hours or days.

(3)     In generally it may be difficult to say that the claim should be considered by any particular date if interim relief is being sought as the interim relief will protect the position.

(4)     Details of any case management orders sought should be included in this section. For example, an order reducing the time for the service of the defendant's evidence may be sought. This will be important if the claimant requires a substantive hearing by a particular date.

(5)    Details of the service of this form (and the claim form and grounds) should be entered here before this form is filed. Note that, despite the reference to the Claimant's advocate, the signature on this section of the form should be the Claimant's solicitor if (as is almost certainly the case) they served claim form.

## P3.6 ORDER ON APPLICATION FOR URGENT CONSIDERATION

This Order would be provided in draft with the Urgent Consideration form.

IN THE HIGH COURT OF JUSTICE

QUEEN'S BENCH DIVISION

ADMINISTRATIVE COURT

IN THE MATTER OF A CLAIM FOR JUDICIAL REVIEW

THE QUEEN (on the application of JOHN SMITH) -v- LONDON MAGISTRATES' COURT

The Honourable Mr/Mrs Justice

Upon reading the claim form and the application for urgent consideration

It is ordered that:

1. The proceedings in the Crown Court in the Claimant's case be stayed.

## P3.7   WITNESS STATEMENT

This precedent relates to a fictional criminal judicial review. It is included to illustrate the format of grounds. The format would be identical if the challenge was to a civil executive decision.

*Witness statements should be produced on A4 paper with 3.5cm margins.[21] They must be legible and on a single side of the paper.[22] They must be bound securely in a manner that will not hamper filing, or otherwise each page should be endorsed with the case number and should bear the initials of the witness.[23] It should be paginated consecutively.[24]*

Witness statement No 1 of E JONES

Exhibits:                          EJ1

Signed:                        [      [2011][25]

On behalf of the Claimant[26]

IN THE HIGH COURT OF JUSTICE                COURT REF:

QUEEN'S BENCH DIVISION

ADMINISTRATIVE COURT

IN THE MATTER OF AN APPLICATION FOR PERMISSION TO APPLY FOR JUDICIAL REVIEW

BETWEEN

R (on the application of JOHN SMITH)

– v –

LONDON MAGISTRATES' COURT

_____

WITNESS STATEMENT OF ELAINE JONES

_____

I, ELAINE JONES, of 350 Chancery Lane, London, EC4, a solicitor of the Supreme Court of England[27] and Wales STATE as follows:-

---

[21]   CPR PD 32, para 19.1(1).

[22]   Ibid, para 19.1(2).

[23]   Ibid, para 19.1(3).

[24]   Ibid, para 19.1(4).

[25]   The full date should be inserted here.

[26]   This heading must be included on the front page of the Witness Statement as well as on the backsheet and the exhibit sheet (PD 32, paras 3.2, 11.3, 17.2 and 18.5).

[27]   The witness statement should always state the witness's, name, address, occupation or description. It should also state whether they are a party to proceedings (Practice Direction 32, para 18.1).

1.[28] I am an assistant solicitor in the employ of [name of the firm] and I have conduct of the above matter on behalf of the Claimant.[29]

2. Save as set out herein, the matters set out in this witness statement are within my knowledge.[30]

3. I refer[31] to the notes of a hearing that took place on 1 July 2011[32] at London Magistrates' Court and which are marked '**EJ 1**'.[33]

[*The body of the evidence should then be set out*]

I believe that the facts stated in this statement are true.[34]

Signed .......................................................

Elaine Jones

---

28   The witness statement should be divided into numbered paragraphs (PD 32, para 19.1(5)). Each paragraph should be confined to a distinct, chronological portion of the subject (PD 32, para 19.2).

29   Where a witness statement is made by a witness in their professional or business capacity, the affidavit should clearly state what that capacity is (PD 32, para 18.1(2)).

30   Witness statements must make it clear which statements are made from the personal knowledge of a witness. If a statement is not made from a witnesses own knowledge, it must be made clear what the source of knowledge is (PD 32, para 18.2).

31   This is the form of wording used when documents are to be exhibited to a witness statement (PD 32, para 18.4).

32   All numbers and dates must be expressed in figures (PD 32, para 19.1(6)).

33   Exhibits should be numbered consecutively with those in prior witness statements signed by the same person (PD 32, paragraph 18.6). References to documents should either be in the margin or in bold (PD 32, para 19.1 (7)).

34   A statement of truth must be included (PD 32, para 20).

Witness statement No 1 of E JONES

Exhibits: EJ1

Signed: [2011][35]

On behalf of the Claimant[36]

COURT REF

IN THE HIGH COURT OF JUSTICE

QUEEN'S BENCH DIVISION

ADMINISTRATIVE COURT

IN THE MATTER OF AN APPLICATION FOR PERMISSION TO APPLY FOR JUDICIAL REVIEW

BETWEEN

R (on the application of JOHN SMITH)

- v -

LONDON MAGISTRATES' COURT

---

WITNESS STATEMENT OF ELAINE JONES

---

DATE: 2011

Exhibits: 1

[        ][37]

Ref:

Solicitors for the Claimant

---

[35] The full date should be inserted here.
[36] This heading must be included on the front page of the Witness Statement as well as on the backsheet and the exhibit sheet (PD 32, paras 3.2, 11.3, 17.2 and 18.5).
[37] The name and address of the solicitors for the claimant should be included here.

*A sheet like the one below needs to be in front of all documentary exhibits.
Documentary exhibits should be exhibited in the manner described in Practice
Direction 32.*[38]

Witness statement No 1 of E JONES

Exhibits:          EJ1

Signed:            [2011]

On behalf of the Claimant

IN THE HIGH COURT OF JUSTICE                    COURT REF:

QUEEN'S BENCH DIVISION

ADMINISTRATIVE COURT

IN THE MATTER OF AN APPLICATION FOR PERMISSION TO APPLY
FOR JUDICIAL REVIEW

BETWEEN

R (on the application of JOHN
SMITH)

– v –

LONDON MAGISTRATES'
COURT

———————————————

EJ1

———————————————

This is the exhibit marked 'EJ1' referred to in my witness statement.

Signed ....................................................

Elaine Jones

---

[38]    See **5.2.2**.

## P3.8   NOTICE OF CLS FUNDING

Legal Services Commission

Access to Justice Act 1999

Notice of Issue of CLS Funding Certificate

IN THE HIGH COURT OF JUSTICE                    COURT REF:

QUEEN'S BENCH DIVISION

ADMINISTRATIVE COURT

IN THE MATTER OF AN APPLICATION FOR PERMISSION TO APPLY FOR
JUDICIAL REVIEW

BETWEEN

R (on the application of JOHN SMITH)

– v –

LONDON MAGISTRATES' COURT

TAKE notice that a CLS Funding Certificate No. [      ][39] dated the 10 September
2011 has been issued by the Legal Services Commission to John Smith[40] to bring
an application for judicial review against the Defendant.[41]

The certificate is: emergency[42]/substantive.[43]

The level of service covered by the certificate is full representation.[44]

The description/scope of the certificate is:

[      ][45]

[The emergency certificate [has][has not] been granted for a specified period. [It
will expire on;[            ]]][46]

Dated 10 September 2011

---

[39]   Insert the certificate number.
[40]   Insert the claimant's name.
[41]   Insert the details of what the funding is for.
[42]   If an emergency certificate has been issued, the notice should state whether the certificate has been
       granted for a specific period (as it normally will be) and when it will expire (if it has been granted for
       a specific period).
[43]   Delete as appropriate.
[44]   The level of service provided for a judicial review will normally be full representation. See **4.2**.
[45]   This should be copied from the certificate.
[46]   This is required if an emergency certificate has been issued.

Signed ....................................................

Elaine Jones of Smith & Co

Solicitor for the Claimant

**To the Defendant**

**And to the Judge**

## P3.9 ACKNOWLEDGEMENT OF SERVICE

This Precedent should be read with **Precedent 10**, which is the grounds to be attached to the Acknowledgement of Service. Numbers in brackets refer to notes at the end of the Precedent.

| Judicial Review<br>Acknowledgment of Service | In the High Court of Justice<br>Administrative Court | |
|---|---|---|
| **Name and address of person to be served** | **Claim No.** | |
| name<br>The London Magistrates' Court | **Claimant(s)**<br>*(including ref.)* | John Smith |
| address<br>1 High Street<br>London<br>EC3A 1QQ | **Defendant(s)** | The London Magistrates' Court |
| | **Interested Parties** | The Crown Prosecution Service |

**SECTION A**

Tick the appropriate box

1. I intend to contest all of the claim   ☐ ⎫
2. I intend to contest part of the claim   ☐ ⎬ complete sections B, C, D and E
                                        ⎭
3. I do not intend to contest the claim   ☐ complete section E
4. The defendant (interested party) is a court or tribunal and **intends** to make a submission.   ☑ complete sections B, C and E
5. The defendant (interested party) is a court or tribunal and **does not intend** to make a submission.   ☐ complete sections B and E

**Note:** If the application seeks to judicially review the decision of a court or tribunal, the court or tribunal need only provide the Administrative Court with as much evidence as it can about the decision to help the Administrative Court perform its judicial function.

**SECTION B**

Insert the name and address of any person you consider should be added as an interested party.

| name<br>None (1) | name |
|---|---|
| address | address |
| Telephone no.    Fax no. | Telephone no.    Fax no. |
| E-mail address | E-mail address |

**SECTION C**

Summary of grounds for contesting the claim. If you are contesting only part of the claim, set out which part before you give your grounds for contesting it. If you are a court or tribunal filing a submission, please indicate that this is the case.

See attached

**SECTION D**

Give details of any directions you will be asking the court to make, or tick the box to indicate that a separate application notice is attached.

(2)

**SECTION E**

| | | |
|---|---|---|
| *delete as appropriate | *(I believe)(The defendant believes) that the facts stated in this form are true. | (if signing on behalf of firm or company, court or tribunal) |
| | *I am duly authorised by the defendant to sign this statement. | **Position or office held** — Cerk to the Magistrates |

(To be signed by you or by your solicitor or litigation friend)

**Signed**

**Date**

Give an address to which notices about this case can be sent to you

**name**
The Chief Clerk

**address**
The London Magistrates' Court
1 High Street
London
EC3A 1QQ

**Telephone no.** 020 7111 4444   **Fax no.** 020 7111 5555

**E-mail address** clerks@londonmags.gov.uk

If you have instructed counsel, please give their name address and contact details below.

**name**

**address**

**Telephone no.**   **Fax no.**

**E-mail address**

**Completed forms,** together with a copy, should be lodged with the Administrative Court Office, Room C315, Royal Courts of Justice, Strand, London, WC2A 2LL, within 21 days of service of the claim upon you, and further copies should be served on the Claimant(s), any other Defendant(s) and any interested parties within 7 days of lodgement with the Court.

3 of 3

(1)   See **5.2.1** for consideration of who should be named as an interested party.

(2)   Directions that a defendant might seek include an order for costs (See Chapter 9) and case management orders requiring the case to be heard by a particular date. Note that it is normal for a defendant to seek the costs of preparing an acknowledgment of service.

## P3.10   SUMMARY GROUNDS OF DEFENCE[47],[48]

This Precedent relates to a fictional criminal judicial review. It is included to illustrate the format of grounds. The format would be identical if the challenge was to a civil executive decision.

### 1   Factual background

1.1   The Defendant accepts that the factual background is as set out in the Claimant's grounds save for the single matter set below.[49]

1.2   The Defendant does not accept that on 1 July 2011 any indication was given that the magistrates' court would deal with the matter. The Defendant has contacted Frank Thomas and sought his views on the claim. Mr Thomas was the chair of the bench of magistrates who considered the Claimant's case on 1 July 2011. Attached to these grounds is a witness statement from Mr Thomas.[50] It is clear from this witness statement that although Mr Thomas has no notes of the hearing, he is confident that he would not have given any indication that the magistrates' court would deal with the matter.

### 2   Legal framework

2.1   The Defendant accepts that the legal framework is as described in the Claimant's grounds.[51]

### 3   Submissions on behalf of the Defendant

3.1   The Defendant does not accept that anything was said or done on 1 July 2011 that gave rise to any legitimate expectation. In particular nothing was said or done that could properly be interpreted as amounting to an agreement that the magistrates' court would deal with this case.

HUGH SOUTHEY QC[52]
TOOKS CHAMBERS

---

[47]   These grounds have been drafted for a defendant. However, there is no reason why the same format should not be used for an interested party.

[48]   This precedent relates to a claim in which there is a simple factual dispute. Obviously the grounds would be far more detailed and complex if there was a more complex legal dispute.

[49]   It is unnecessary to set out the factual background unless there is a dispute.

[50]   It is not technically necessary to include a separate witness statement as the accuracy of the grounds is confirmed by a statement of truth. However, in a case like this it may be worth including a witness statement with full details of the witness's recollection of what happened so that the grounds can summarise the key points from the witness statement.

[51]   There is no need to set out the legal framework if this is not in dispute.

[52]   The pleadings should always be signed by the counsel who were responsible for drafting them if they were drafted by counsel.

# P3.11   REASONS FOR RENEWING A CLAIM

1.   The Claimant submits that the Defendant erred in law when taking the decision challenged for the reasons set out in the grounds in support of this claim.

2.   As a consequence the Claimant submits that the learned judge erred by refusing the Claimant permission to apply for judicial review.

3.   In particular the Claimant submits that ...[53]

---

[53]   In many cases the first two paragraphs will be adequate. If, however, there are particular grounds for arguing that the decision of the High Court judge refusing permission is flawed, that is a matter that might be expressly addressed. That will often be done in a skeleton argument submitted in good time before the hearing. It is done in that way as public funding may not be available when the claim is renewed.

## P3.12   DETAILED GROUNDS OF RESISTANCE[54]

IN THE HIGH COURT OF JUSTICE                    COURT REF:

QUEEN'S BENCH DIVISION

ADMINISTRATIVE COURT

IN THE MATTER OF A CLAIM FOR JUDICIAL REVIEW

BETWEEN

R (on the application of
JOHN SMITH)

– v –

LONDON MAGISTRATES'
COURT

---

DEFENDANT'S DETAILED
GROUNDS OF RESISTANCE

---

**1. Factual background**

1.1   The Defendant accepts that the factual background is as set out in the Claimant's claim save for the single matter set below.[55]

1.2   The Defendant does not accept that on 1 July 2002 any indication was given that the magistrates' court would deal with the matter. The Defendant has contacted Frank Thomas and sought his views on the claim. Mr Thomas was the chair of the bench of magistrates who considered the Claimant's case on 1 July 2002. The court has previously been supplied with a witness statement from Mr Thomas. It is clear from this witness statement that although Mr Thomas has no notes of the hearing, he is confident that he would not have given any indication that the magistrates' court would deal with the matter.

1.3   Since drafting the summary grounds, the Defendant has seen the witness statement of Timothy Phillips, the CPS solicitor who attended the hearing on 1 July 2002. The Defendant submits that Mr Phillips' evidence is essentially neutral. Although he states that 'I can only say that it is my purely personal impression, in view of my outline of the case to the Court, that they intended to retain the case for sentence', he has not identified any conduct by the Defendant that can actually be said to give rise to a legitimate expectation.

**2.   Legal framework**

2.1   The Defendant accepts that the legal framework is as described in the Claimant's grounds.[56]

---

[54]   This precedent relates to a claim in which there is a simple factual dispute. Obviously the grounds would be far more detailed and complex if there was a more complex legal dispute.

[55]   It is unnecessary to set out the factual background unless there is a dispute.

[56]   There is no need to set out the legal framework if this is in dispute.

2.2    The Defendant wishes to point out that it is for a Claimant in judicial review proceedings to establish the factual basis of the claim (eg *R (Mersey Care NHS Trust) v Mental Health Review Tribunal* [2003] EWHC 1182 (Admin)).

## 3.    Submissions on behalf of the Defendant

3.1    The Defendant does not accept that anything was said or done on 1 July 2002 that gave rise to any legitimate expectation. In particular nothing was said or done that could properly be interpreted as amounting to an agreement that the magistrates' court would deal with this case.

3.3    Further, the Defendant submits that the Claimant has failed to meet the evidential burden of establishing that anything was said or done at the hearing on 1 July 2003 that gave rise to a legitimate expectation.

HUGH SOUTHEY QC[57]
TOOKS CHAMBERS

---

[57]    The pleadings should always be signed by the counsel who were responsible for drafting them, if they were drafted by counsel.

## P3.13 CONSENT ORDER

[Insert court reference number]

IN THE HIGH COURT OF JUSTICE

QUEEN'S BENCH DIVISION

ADMINISTRATIVE COURT

IN THE MATTER OF A CLAIM FOR JUDICIAL REVIEW

THE QUEEN (on the application of JOHN SMITH) -v- LONDON MAGISTRATES' COURT

The Claimant and the Defendant do hereby consent to the matter to being adjourned to be listed not before 14 days.

The costs of this application to be reserved.

Dated this          day of August 2011

....................................................

[*insert name*]

Signed on behalf of the Claimant

....................................................

[*insert name*]

Signed on behalf of the Defendant

Statement of reasons

The Defendant needs additional time to review this matter with a view to resolving the matter by consent.

## P3.14 APPLICATION FOR BAIL

This precedent relates to an application for bail. However, the same format would be used whenever an interim application is made. This can hopefully be seen by comparing Precedents **19** and **20** (grounds in a civil case) with this precedent. This precedent should be read with Precedent **15**, which is the draft order to be supplied with this application.

### Application notice

For help in completing this form please read the notes for guidance form N244Notes.

| | |
|---|---|
| Name of court: High Court, Queen's Bench Division, Administrative Court | |
| Claim no. | C/100/2011 |
| Warrant no. (if applicable) | |
| Claimant's name (including ref.) | John Smith |
| Defendant's name (including ref.) | The London Magistrates' Court |
| Date | 1 August 2011 |

1. What is your name or, if you are a solicitor, the name of your firm?

   Elaine Jones

2. Are you a ☐ Claimant ☐ Defendant ☒ Solicitor

   ☐ Other *(please specify)*

   If you are a solicitor whom do you represent? Claimant

3. What order are you asking the court to make and why?

   The Claimant be granted bail.

4. Have you attached a draft of the order you are applying for? ☒ Yes ☐ No

5. How do you want to have this application dealt with? ☒ at a hearing ☐ without a hearing

   ☐ at a telephone hearing

6. How long do you think the hearing will last? 1 Hours ☐ Minutes

   Is this time estimate agreed by all parties? ☐ Yes ☒ No

7. Give details of any fixed trial date or period

8. What level of Judge does your hearing need? High Court Judge

9. Who should be served with this application? Defendant and Interested Party

10.  What information will you be relying on, in support of your application?

        ☒ the attached witness statement

        ☐ the statement of case

        ☐ the evidence set out in the box below

> If necessary, please continue on a separate sheet.
>
>
>
>
>
>
>
>
> _____
>
> **Statement of Truth**
>
> (I believe) (The applicant believes) that the facts stated in this section (and any continuation sheets) are true.
>
> Signed     _____    Dated     _____
>            Applicant('s Solicitor)('s litigation friend)
>
> Full name     _____
>
> Name of applicant's solicitor's firm     _____
>
> Position or office held     _____
> (if signing on behalf of firm or company)

11.  Signature and address details

Signed     _____    Dated     _____
           Applicant('s Solicitor)('s litigation friend)

Position or office held    Solicitor _____
(if signing on behalf of firm or company)

Applicant's address to which documents about this application should be sent

| Smith & Co<br>1 The Crescent<br>London | | | | | | | If applicable | |
|---|---|---|---|---|---|---|---|---|
| | | | | | | | Phone no. | 020 7777 1111 |
| | | | | | | | Fax no. | |
| Postcode | | | | | | | DX no. | |
| E | C | 1 | A | 1 | P | P | Ref no. | JS/2 |

| E-mail address | |
|---|---|

# Application Notice (Form N244) – Notes for Guidance

Court Staff cannot give legal advice. If you need information or advice on a legal problem you can contact Community Legal Service Direct on 0845 345 4 345 or www.clsdirect.org.uk, or a Citizens Advice Bureau. Details of your local offices and contact numbers are available via their website www.citizensadvice.org.uk

### Paying the court fee
A court fee is payable depending on the type of application you are making. For example:

- To apply for judgment to be set aside
- To apply to vary a judgment or suspend enforcement
- To apply for a summons or order for a witness to attend
- To apply by consent, or without service of the application notice, for a judgment or order.

No fee is payable for an application by consent for an adjournment of a hearing if it is received by the court at least 14 days before the date of the hearing.

### What if I cannot afford the fee?
If you show that a payment of a court fee would involve undue hardship to you, you may be eligible for a fee concession.

For further information, or to apply for a fee concession, ask court staff for a copy of the combined booklet and form EX160A - Court fees - Do I have to pay them? This is also available from any county court office, or a copy of the leaflet can be downloaded from our website www.hmcourts-service.gov.uk

## Completing the form

### Question 3
Set out what order you are applying for and why; e.g. to adjourn the hearing because..., to set aside a judgment against me because... etc.

### Question 5
Most applications will require a hearing and you will be expected to attend. The court will allocate a hearing date and time for the application. Please indicate in a covering letter any dates that you are unavailable within the next six weeks.
The court will only deal with the application 'without a hearing' in the following circumstances.

- Where all the parties agree to the terms of the order being asked for;
- Where all the parties agree that the court should deal with the application without a hearing, or
- Where the court does not consider that a hearing would be appropriate.

Telephone hearings are only available in applications where at least one of parties involved in the case is legally represented. Not all applications will be suitable for a telephone hearing and the court may refuse your request.

### Question 6
If you do not know how long the hearing will take do not guess but leave these boxes blank.

### Question 7
If your case has already been allocated a hearing date or trial period please insert details of those dates in the box.

### Question 8
If your case is being heard in the High Court or a District Registry please indicate whether it is to be dealt with by a Master, District Judge or Judge.

### Question 9
Please indicate in the box provided who you want the court to sent a copy of the application to.

### Question 10
In this section please set out the information you want the court to take account of in support of the application you are making.
If you wish to rely on:

- **a witness statement,** tick the first box and attach the statement to the application notice. A witness statement form is available on request from the court office.
- **a statement of case,** tick the second box if you intend to rely on your particluars of claim or defence in support of your application.
- **written evidence** on this form, tick the third box and enter details in the space provided. You must also complete the statement of truth. Proceedings for contempt of court may be brought against a person who signs a statement of truth without an honest belief in its truth.

### Question 11
The application must be signed and include your current address and contact details. If you agree that the court and the other parties may communicate with you by Document Exchange, telephone, facsimile or email, complete the details

## Before returning your form to the court
Have you:
- signed the form on page 2,
- enclosed the correct fee or an application for fee remission,
- made sufficient copies of your application and supporting documentation. You will need to submit one copy for each party to be served and one copy for the court.

## P3.15   PRECEDENT DRAFT ORDER GRANTING BAIL

This Precedent relates to a fictional criminal judicial review. It is included to illustrate the format of a draft order to be supplied with an interim application. The format would be identical if the interim application challenged a civil executive decision.

C/100/2002

IN THE HIGH COURT OF JUSTICE

QUEEN'S BENCH DIVISION

ADMINISTRATIVE COURT

IN THE MATTER OF A CLAIM FOR JUDICIAL REVIEW

THE QUEEN (on the application of JOHN SMITH) -v- LONDON MAGISTRATES' COURT

Whereas John Smith was previously detained pursuant to a warrant of committal issued by London Magistrates' Court on 10 December 2011.

And whereas John Smith has applied for judicial review and pursuant to that application has applied for bail.

And upon hearing counsel for the said John Smith.

It is ordered that the said John Smith, after complying with the condition(s) specified in Schedule 1 hereto, shall be released on bail, subject to the condition(s) specified in Schedule 2 hereto, and with a duty to surrender to this court on a time and a date to be notified.

**Schedule 1**

Conditions to be complied with before release on bail

The Claimant will provide one surety of £500.[58]

**Schedule 2**

Conditions to be complied with after release on bail

The Claimant will reside at [*insert address*][59]

---

[58]   Insert here details of any other conditions that are being offered and that should be complied with prior to release.

[59]   Insert here details of any other conditions that are being offered and that should be complied with after release.

## P3.16 CONSENT ORDER DISPOSING OF THE CASE

IN THE HIGH COURT OF JUSTICE

QUEEN'S BENCH DIVISION

ADMINISTRATIVE COURT

BEFORE THE HONOURABLE MR JUSTICE

IN THE MATTER OF A CLAIM FOR JUDICIAL REVIEW

THE QUEEN (on the application of JOHN SMITH) -v- LONDON MAGISTRATES' COURT

Whereas the Claimant was to be committed to the Crown Court for trial.

The Claimant and the Defendant do hereby consent to an order of the court being issued in the terms of the attached order.

Dated this            day of August 2011

......................................................

[*insert name*]

Signed on behalf of the Claimant

......................................................

[*insert name*]

Signed on behalf of the Defendant

Statement of reasons

The Defendant now accepts that it appears that remarks were made at the hearing on 1 July 2011 that gave rise to a legitimate expectation that the Magistrates' Court would deal with the matter.[60]

[*Insert court reference number*]

DATED the            day of            2011[61]

---

[60]   A statement of reasons must be included.
[61]   Leave the precise date blank for the Administrative Court to complete.

IN THE HIGH COURT OF JUSTICE

QUEEN'S BENCH DIVISION

ADMINISTRATIVE COURT

BEFORE THE HONOURABLE MR JUSTICE

IN THE MATTER OF A CLAIM FOR JUDICIAL REVIEW

THE QUEEN (on the application of JOHN SMITH) -v- LONDON MAGISTRATES' COURT

UPON READING the Claim Form in this matter.

AND UPON READING the form of consent together with the particulars and statement of reasons signed by all parties to these proceedings.

AND the Court being satisfied that the Consent Order hereinafter set out should be made.

AND pronouncing the said Order in Open Court without the requirement of the parties' attendance.

AND no order for costs having been sought or made save as is hereinafter provided.

BY CONSENT

IT IS ORDERED that the order made by the Defendant committing the Claimant for trial in the Crown Court be quashed.

IT IS FURTHER ORDERED that there be no order for costs save that the costs of the Claimant be subject to a detailed Community Legal Services funding assessment.[62]

BY THE COURT

**In a case in which the claim is being withdrawn by consent, the following wording should be used:**

**IT IS ORDERED** that the Claimant be allowed to withdraw her claim for judicial review.

---

[62]    It is important to address the issue of costs in any consent order.

# P3.17  PRECEDENT SKELETON ARGUMENT

This precedent relates to a fictional criminal judicial review. It is included to illustrate the format of a skeleton argument. The format would be identical if the challenge was to a civil executive decision.

*This document should be paginated.*

| | |
|---|---|
| **In the High Court** | **CO/**[63] |
| **Queen's Bench Division** | **1 August 2011** |
| **Divisional Court** | |
| **Administrative Court** | |

IN THE MATTER OF AN APPLICATION FOR PERMISSION TO APPLY FOR JUDICIAL REVIEW

BETWEEN

**R (on the application of
JOHN SMITH)**

– v –

**LONDON MAGISTRATES'
COURT**

---

**SKELETON ARGUMENT**

---

*Page references are to the trial bundle*[64]

## 1  Time estimate

Hearing:        1 hour (including judgment)

Reading:        ½ hour

List of essential reading:

Para 7 of the first witness statement of Elaine Jones, p 9

Exhibit EJ1, p 13

Exhibit EJ2, p 15

Para 4 of the witness statement of Timothy Phillips, p 15

---

[63]   It is important to include the court reference and the hearing date at the front of the skeleton argument.

[64]   Practice Direction 54A, para 15.3 requires that there should be page references to any documents in the trial bundle.

Paras 8 to 10 of the witness statement of Frank Thomas, p 19

Exhibit SED 1 of the witness statement of Sheila Duck, p 33

## 2 The issues[65]

2.1    Whether the Magistrates' Court acted unlawfully by committing the Claimant to the Crown Court for sentencing contrary to a legitimate expectation that had arisen that the Magistrates' Court would pass sentence.

## 3 Propositions to be advanced

### *Factual background*[66]

3.1    The Claimant submits that the factual background is as set out in the claim form. The Claimant recognises that there is a dispute of evidence regarding this issue. That matter is considered later.

### *Submissions*

3.2    It is clear that a Magistrates' Court may fetter its discretion to commit a defendant to the Crown Court for sentence if it acts in a way that gives rise to a legitimate expectation on behalf of the defendant.

3.3    In this context it is accepted by the Claimant that merely adjourning a matter for pre-sentence reports is not sufficient to give rise to a legitimate expectation. However, a statement by magistrates that they are of the opinion that their sentencing powers are sufficient to deal with a matter together with a failure to warn the defendant that a subsequent bench will not be bound is sufficient to give rise to a legitimate expectation. It is the unqualified statement that is significant. If justices wish to retain the discretion to commit to the Crown Court they should say so.

   *R v Nottingham Magistrates' Court ex p Davidson* [2000] 1 Cr App R (S) 167 at 173

   *R v Norwich Magistrates' Court ex p Elliot* [2000] 1 Cr App R (S) 152 at 159[67]

---

[65]    This should be a summary of the matters for the Administrative Court to decide (PD 54A, para 15.3(2))

[66]    Although there is no formal need to detail the factual background, it will often be helpful to include a summary. This is particularly the case if there have been significant developments since the grounds were lodged. If a factual summary is included, it will help the Court to include page references to the documents that establish particular facts.

[67]    Practice Direction 54A, para 15.3 provides that the skeleton argument must make reference to any pages in the authority that are relied on. In addition, the *Practice Direction (Citation of Authorities)* [2001] 1 WLR 1001 means that it must be made clear what proposition the authority is being cited to support. When citing this authority, it is important to be aware of this Practice Direction, which requires an explanation for the use of certain types of authority, including overseas authority. This Practice Direction is included in Part III.

(Both authorities are cited as ex p Davidson is the most recent authority on point but ex p Elliot is cited for other reasons[68]).

3.4   In considering whether a legitimate expectation arose in the mind of a defendant, it is important to consider the perceptions of the professional representatives of the prosecution and the defence. If they believed that the justices had accepted jurisdiction then that is a strong indication that a legitimate expectation had arisen.

> *R v Norwich Magistrates' Court ex p Elliot* [2000] 1 Cr App R (S) 152 at 159 onwards (the South East Northumberland Justices Case)

3.5   In this particular case it is clear that after the Claimant had entered his guilty pleas, the Crown Prosecution Service outlined the offences and matters relevant to sentence [see para 3 of the witness statement of Timothy Phillips]. The defence then made a plea in mitigation [see para 7 of the first witness statement of Elaine Jones, bundle p 9]. After these submissions the matter was adjourned for pre-sentence reports. The hearing was clearly a lengthy hearing [see EJ1 exhibiting a file note showing a 42 minute hearing, bundle p 13].

3.6   There is a conflict in the evidence regarding the adjournment:

3.6.1   The Claimant's solicitor is clear that the justices adjourned the case and stated that this was a case that they would deal with [see para 7 of the first witness statement of Elaine Jones, p 9]. The Claimant's solicitor is also clear that no statement was made that the matter might be committed to the Crown Court;

3.6.2   The Crown Prosecution Service's solicitor states that 'I can only say that it is my purely personal impression, in view of my outline of the case to the Court, that they intended to retain the case for sentence' [see para 4 of the witness statement of Timothy Phillips, p 15];

3.6.3   The Chairman of the Court disputes the evidence in para 3.6.1 and states that he would remember saying that the justices were accepting jurisdiction had that happened as it would have been so unusual for him to do such a thing [see paras 8 to 10 of the witness statement of Frank Thomas, p 19]; and

3.6.4   There is a copy of the court record that appears to merely record court orders [see exhibit SED 1 of the witness statement of Sheila Duck, p 33].

3.7   From the above evidence it should be clear that the impression of both professional representatives was that justices had agreed to retain the case when they adjourned it for pre-sentence reports. The Claimant submits that is conclusive that whatever was said or done gave rise to a legitimate expectation. If both solicitors present conclude that the justices have agreed to deal with the matter, one cannot expect a defendant to come to a different conclusion.

---

[68]   The *Practice Direction (Citation of Authorities)* [2001] 1 WLR 1001 requires an explanation to be provided where two authorities are cited for the same proposition.

3.8  Further, to the extent that it is necessary to consider the evidence in greater detail, the Claimant would submit that it is appropriate for the Court to accept the evidence of Elaine Jones. In support of this submission the Claimant relies on the following matters:

3.8.1  Ms Jones is a solicitor of twenty-three years experience and a partner and the head of criminal litigation with Jones & Smith, a highly reputable firm and one of the largest Legal Aid practices in the United Kingdom [see para 1 of the first witness statement of Elaine Jones, p 9];

3.8.2  Ms Jones has a clear file note stating 'Mags agree to deal' [see exhibit EJ1, p 13] and Ms Jones also wrote to the client on 3 July 2002 saying that the magistrates have agreed to deal with the matter [see exhibit MW2, p 15]. These are clear records that were made while the matter was fresh in the mind of Ms Jones. As an experienced solicitor Ms Jones would not have acted in this way if the magistrates had not said that they were willing to deal with the matter;

3.8.3  It is true that the letter does say 'the risk of you being Committed to the Crown Court for Sentence looks to have subsided' and does not say that the defendant could not be committed to the Crown Court. That, however, is no more than a correct statement of the law in circumstances in which a legitimate expectation has arisen. It is clear in these circumstances that committal can still take place providing that there is something to justify the committal;

> *R v Nottingham Magistrates' Court ex p Davidson* [2000] 1 Cr App R (S) 167 at 172

3.8.4  The evidence accords with the impression of the solicitor representing the Crown Prosecution Service;

3.8.5  Mr Thomas does not say that he can remember what he said. He merely relies on his normal practice;

3.8.6  Mr Thomas has no notes or other record to support his evidence. The only record is the court file which clearly only records formal decisions of the court; and

3.8.7  In light of the matters above, this claim is one of those rare claims where the Claimant's version of the evidence can and should be accepted.

> *R v Highbury Magistrate ex p Di Matteo* [1991] 1 WLR 1374 at 1378 as an example of the circumstances in which a Claimant's version of events was accepted.

3.9  It is clear that when the matter returned to the Magistrates' Court the District Judge did not identify any reason for departing from the legitimate expectation [see para 4 of the witness statement of Sheila Duck, p 26].

# 4 Chronology of events

| | |
|---|---|
| 1 June 2002 | Claimant's arrest [p 3] |
| 1 June 2002 | Claimant charged with a single count of possessing forged passport [p 3] |
| 2 June 2002 | Claimant remanded in custody [p 8] |
| 3 June 2002 | Claimant charged with two further charges and remanded in custody [p 8] |
| 1 July 2002 | Matter adjourned for pre-sentence reports [p 9] |
| 19 July 2002 | Claimant committed to the Crown Court [p 9] |

# 5 Persons referred to

| | |
|---|---|
| Sheila Duck | District Judge who considered the matter on 19 July 2002 |
| Elaine Jones | Claimant's solicitor |
| Timothy Phillips | Crown Prosecution solicitor who appeared at hearings in the Claimant's case |
| John Smith | Claimant |
| Frank Thomas | Chair of the Bench that considered the Claimant's case on 1 July 2002 |

HUGH SOUTHEY QC[69]
TOOKS CHAMBERS

---

[69] The pleadings should always be signed by the counsel who were responsible for drafting them.

## P3.18   GROUNDS FOR A NON-CRIMINAL CASE

*Set out below are grounds in a case that relates to a decision of a local authority regarding community care. It illustrates that although the decision is very different from that challenged in the first precedent, the format of the grounds should be the same.*

## GROUNDS IN SUPPORT OF THE CLAIM

### 1   The issue that arises in this claim

1.1   Whether the Claimant is entitled to support under s 21 of the National Assistance Act 1948 ('the 1948 Act').

### 2   Factual background

2.1   The Claimant is a national of Pakistan. The Claimant speaks little or no English.

2.2   On 1 July 2010 the Claimant was granted leave to enter the United Kingdom to join her husband who is a United Kingdom national. She then resided with her husband at 1 Smith Street, Cambridge.

2.3   The Claimant's marriage has now broken down as a consequence of domestic violence. In March 2011 the Claimant's husband attempted to strangle the Claimant and attacked her with a knife. In May 2011 the Claimant was again attacked. Following that attack a friend of the Claimant took her from Cambridge to London. That incident was reported to the police in Wandsworth.

2.4   The Claimant returned to Cambridge following the attack in May 2011 because the Claimant's husband promised not to harm her. However, on 17 May 2011 the Claimant was taken by her husband and his family to Stockport and locked in a family home. In that home she was violently attacked by her husband and her sister-in-law.

2.5   The Claimant was able to escape from the home in Stockport and travel to Cambridge. On arrival in Cambridge she attended Cambridge Police Station. The police contacted Cambridgeshire County Council. The County Council then accommodated the Claimant at the Cambridge Guest House, 1 Brown Road, Cambridge.

2.6   On 1 June 2011 the Claimant's solicitors requested support under s 21 of the 1948 Act. On 10 June 2011 Cambridgeshire County Council responded seeking additional information. In a letter dated 20 June 2011 the County Council wrote stating, inter alia, that:

> It is clear from the information known to Social Services that you have no significant needs either mentally or physically which would qualify you for support.

Unfortunately, the Social Services Department is therefore unable to provide you with any further support and we have notified your landlord.

The letter also provided a copy of the assessment undertaken by the County Council. The assessment indicated that the Claimant had needs for 'safe and secure accommodation', 'access to money' and 'legal advice'. The assessment stated that the matter should be passed to a service manager for a decision under s 21 of the 1948 Act.

2.7 The letter from Cambridgeshire County Council crossed with a letter from the Claimant's solicitors dated 20 June 2011. That letter pointed that the Claimant was not an asylum seeker and so was not entitled to support from the National Asylum Support Service. The County Council responded on 21 June 2003 stating that:

> [Y]ou will be aware that our obligations are to consider your client's needs under section 21 of the National Assistance Act and the criteria for support in accordance with the case law is to consider whether your client has a material need over and above lack of funds and accommodation.

The letter also supplied the County Council's criteria for assessments conducted under s 47 of the National Health Service And Community Care Act 1990 ('the 1990 Act'). These criteria indicate that there is a high need for service where, inter alia, there is:

> Imminent significant risk of physical harm to self or others by person(s) or their environment.

2.8 It is now understood that the Claimant was taken from Cambridge to Stockport by her husband's family towards the end of June 2011. The police in Stockport intervened and charges of kidnapping and false imprisonment were considered. The police arranged for the Claimant to be placed in a women's refuge. However, the Claimant obtained the assistance of a friend to travel to London.

2.9 On 5 July 2011 the Claimant's solicitors obtained an undertaking from Cambridgeshire County Council that it would support the Claimant for 7 days pending an assessment. On 16 July 2011 that support was extended for a further 7 days.

2.10 On 30 July 2011 the Claimant's solicitors faxed Cambridgeshire County Council expressing their concern that the Claimant's landlord had threatened to evict her as a consequence of rent arrears and that it appeared that no assessment had been conducted.

2.11 Cambridgeshire County Council wrote to the Claimant's solicitors on 30 July 2011 informing them that an assessment had been undertaken. The assessment was supplied. The assessment noted that the Claimant had been the subject of abuse from her husband since being resident in the United Kingdom. The assessment noted that she had been found by her husband and taken to Stockport. The Claimant was said to believe that the landlord of the bed and breakfast where she was staying had informed her husband of her whereabouts.

The assessment noted that the Claimant's problems with English meant that she was isolated and unable to find employment. It also noted that the Claimant was low in mood. The report concluded by noting that the Claimant needed:

Financial assistance to cover rent and basic living costs.

To register with a local GP if staying in a area where she is now.

To register for English classes and to make contact with the local community.

2.12   The Claimant was initially informed on 30 July 2011 that her support would terminate on 6 August 2011. That decision was confirmed in a letter to the Claimant's solicitors dated 30 July 2011, which stated, inter alia, that:

As regards section 2 Local Government Act 2000 we consider that the effect of section 21(1A) of the National Assistance Act 1948 is a restriction or limitation on the powers within the meaning of section 3 and given the Council consider that it has no obligation to your client under section 21 support cannot be provided under section 2.

2.13   In response to a letter from the Claimant's solicitors dated 31 July 2011 Cambridgeshire County Council agreed to review its decision to terminate support as there were no reasons given for it.

2.14   In a letter dated 1 August 2011 Cambridgeshire County Council wrote to the Claimant's solicitors stating that:

We note you rely on the case of *R v Wandsworth LBC ex parte O* (2000) but you indicate that your client's need for care and attention arises out of the threat of violence from her husband. We do not think that this is a correct interpretation of the case law. It is evident from the judgement of Simon Brown LJ that the circumstances envisaged which would trigger support under section 21 of the National Assistance Act 1948 would be those related to age, illness or disability.

2.15   On 6 August 2011 Cambridgeshire County Council concluded its review and maintained its decision to terminate the Claimant's support. In support of that decision the County Council served a statement from Carol Frost, which stated inter alia, that:

I am aware that Mrs Khan's Solicitors ... have raised the issue of the possibility of physical violence from her husband and suggest that if services are not provided she would be at risk of physical harm. I consider that Mrs Khan can take steps to prevent any violence from her husband by informing the police or taking out an appropriate injunction. ...

The test of eligibility under [the National Assistance Act 1948] is whether Mrs Khan's need for care and attention is to any extent made more acute by circumstances other than lack of accommodation and funds. It is clear to me from the assessment, that whilst Mrs Khan does lack accommodation and funds, there is nothing within the assessment which leads me to believe that there is some other circumstances that makes her need more acute.

2.16   The Claimant has sought leave to remain in the United Kingdom on the basis of the Secretary of State for the Home Department's policy on victims of domestic violence.

# 3   Legal framework

3.1   Section 21 of the 1948 Act provides, inter alia, that:

> (1) Subject to and in accordance with the provisions of this Part of this Act, a local authority may with the approval of the Secretary of State, and to such extent as he may direct shall, make arrangements for providing –
> (a)   residential accommodation for persons who by reason of age, illness, disability or any other circumstances are in need of care and attention which is not otherwise available to them; and . . .
>
> (1A) A person to whom section 115 of the Immigration and Asylum Act 1999 (exclusion from benefits) applies may not be provided with residential accommodation under subsection (1)(a) if his need for care and attention has arisen solely –
> (a)   because he is destitute; or
> (b)   because of the physical effects, or anticipated physical effects, of his being destitute.
>
> (1B) Subsections (3) and (5) to (8) of section 95 of the Immigration and Asylum Act 1999, and paragraph 2 of Schedule 8 to that Act, apply for the purposes of subsection (1A) as they apply for the purposes of that section, but for the references in subsections (5) and (7) of that section and in that paragraph to the Secretary of State substitute references to a local authority.

The Claimant is a person to whom section 115 of the Immigration and Asylum Act 1999 ('the 1999 Act') applies.

3.2   Subsection 95(3) of the 1999 Act provides:

> For the purposes of this section, a person is destitute if –
> (a)   he does not have adequate accommodation or any means of obtaining it (whether or not his other essential living needs are met); or
> (b)   he has adequate accommodation or the means of obtaining it, but cannot meet his other essential living needs.

3.3   It is not necessary to wait until care and attention is actually required before providing assistance under s 21 of the 1948 Act. In *R v Hammersmith and Fulham LBC ex parte M* (1997) 30 HLR 10 Lord Woolf MR held that:

> . . . the authorities can anticipate the deterioration which would otherwise take place in the asylum seeker's condition by providing assistance under the section. They do not need to wait until the health of the asylum seeker has been damaged.

The Court applied this principle to hold that the destitution to which asylum seekers could be reduced over time could satisfy the criteria laid down in s 21 of the 1948 Act so that assistance would be available.

3.4   The restrictions on the provision on assistance contained in s 21(1A) of the 1948 Act were considered by the Court of Appeal in *R v Wandsworth LBC ex parte O* [2000] 1 WLR 2539. Simon Brown LJ (with whose judgement the other members of the Court agreed) held that:

> The applicants contend for an altogether different approach. They submit that if an applicant's need of care and attention is to any material extent made more acute by some circumstance other than mere lack of accommodation and funds, then, despite being subject to immigration control, he qualifies for assistance. Other relevant circumstances include, of course, old age, illness and disability, all of which are expressly mentioned in section 21 itself. If, for example, an immigrant as well as being destitute is old, ill or disabled, he is likely to be yet more vulnerable and less able to survive than if he were merely destitute.
>
> Given that both constructions are tenable, I have not the least hesitation in preferring the latter. The word 'solely' in the new section is a strong one and its purpose there seems to me evident. Assistance under the Act of 1948 is, it need hardly be emphasised, the last refuge for the destitute. If there are to be immigrant beggars in the streets, then let them at least not be the old, ill or disabled.

This judgment was considered by Elias J in *R (on the application of J) v Enfield LBC* [2002] 2 FLR 1 who held:

> The Court accepted [in ex p O], there could be such an entitlement even if only ordinary accommodation were needed provided the need for that accommodation did not simply result from the fact of being homeless but also as a consequence of some other circumstance falling within the terms of the section.

3.5   Section 47(1) of the 1990 Act provides:

> Subject to subsections (5) and (6) below, where it appears to a local authority that any person for whom they may provide or arrange for the provision of community care services may be in need of any such services, the authority –
> (a)   shall carry out an assessment of his needs for those services; and
> (b)   having regard to the results of that assessment, shall then decide whether his needs call for the provision by them of any such services.

3.6   Article 3 of the European Convention on Human Rights ('the ECHR') provides that:

> No one shall be subjected to torture or to inhuman or degrading treatment or punishment.

3.7   It is clear that Art 3 of the ECHR requires States to protect people within their jurisdiction from treatment that amounts to torture or inhuman or degrading treatment, including treatment administered by private individuals (see eg *A v United Kingdom* (1998) 27 EHRR 611).

3.8   In *R (Wilkinson) v Broadmoor Hospital* [2002] 1 WLR 419 the Court of Appeal agreed to hear evidence so that it could make findings of fact to determine whether treatment given under a compulsion to a patient under the Mental Health Act 1983 amounted to a violation of Arts 2, 3 and 8 of the ECHR.

## 4 Submissions on behalf of the Claimant

4.1 The Claimant submits that it is unlawful for Cambridgeshire County Council to conclude that she is not entitled to support under s 21 of the 1948 Act as that conclusion was clearly unreasonable. In support of this submission the Claimant relies on the following matters:

4.1.1 The assessment conducted by Cambridgeshire County Council recognised that the Claimant had been victim of severe domestic violence. It identified no reason to doubt the Claimant's claim that the most recent incident of domestic violence was caused by a previous landlord's actions in contacting her husband's family. That showed that the Claimant needed accommodation that would provide her with security from her former husband;

4.1.2 The submission in the sub-paragraph above is consistent with the fact that the first assessment in the Claimant's case indicated that she had needs for 'safe and secure accommodation';

4.1.3 The submissions in the two sub-paragraphs above are supported by Cambridgeshire County Council's own criteria for assessments conducted under s 47 of the 1990 Act. That recognizes that the need to provide protection against physical harm may give rise to particularly acute needs;

4.1.4 The availability of the police and injunctions do not undermine the Claimant's submissions that she needs secure accommodation. The Claimant's husband has already shown that he is willing to break the law. As a consequence legal mechanisms such as the police and injunctions are unlikely to provide adequate protection if the Claimant is left without secure accommodation in a society where she knows few people other than her husband's family;

4.1.5 The Claimant submits that s 21 of the 1948 Act permits the provision of accommodation and support in a wide range of circumstances. It is not limited to the provision of accommodation where needs arise as a consequence of age, illness, disability as suggested by Cambridgeshire County Council in their letter dated 1 August 2003. It is clear that the needs of a victim of domestic violence such as a Claimant for secure accommodation are 'other circumstances' that enable a council to provide accommodation;

4.1.6 Further, in the light of the matters above, the Claimant's need for secure accommodation means that her needs are more acute than those of a person who is merely homeless. She has an additional need for security. As a consequence the restrictions on the provision on assistance contained in s 21(1A) of the 1948 Act do not apply; and

4.1.7 Further or alternatively, the Claimant also has additional needs as a consequence of her lack of English and her low mood. The restrictions on the provision on assistance contained in s 21(1A) of the 1948 Act do not apply to those needs.

4.2 The submissions in the paragraph above are supported by the ECHR. The Claimant submits that the United Kingdom will be in breach of its obligations under the ECHR if she is not provided with support under s 21 of the 1948 Act. Firstly, the Claimant will not have been provided with adequate protection against ill-treatment at the hands of her husband and his family. In addition, there is a risk that the Claimant will be left destitute for an indefinite period.

4.3   The Claimant submits that when considering the risk that she will destitute for an indefinite period, it is important to recognise that she has legitimate reasons for wishing to remain in the United Kingdom. The Secretary of State's policy on the victims of domestic violence is evidence of that.

4.4   To the extent that there is any dispute regarding the facts of this case, the Claimant submits that this Court should consider the evidence and make findings of fact necessary to determine whether there will be violations of Arts 3 and 8 of the ECHR.

HUGH SOUTHEY QC
TOOKS CHAMBERS

## P3.19 APPLICATION FOR INTERIM RELIEF

This Precedent should be read with **Precedent 20**, which is the draft order to be supplied with this application.

### Application notice

For help in completing this form please read the notes for guidance form N244Notes.

| | |
|---|---|
| Name of court: High Court, Queen's Bench Division, Administrative Court | |
| Claim no. | C/100/2011 |
| Warrant no. (if applicable) | |
| Claimant's name (including ref.) | K |
| Defendant's name (including ref.) | Cambridgeshire County Council |
| Date | 10 August 2011 |

1. What is your name or, if you are a solicitor, the name of your firm?

   John Smith

2. Are you a ☐ Claimant ☐ Defendant ☒ Solicitor

   ☐ Other *(please specify)*

   If you are a solicitor whom do you represent? Claimant

3. What order are you asking the court to make and why?

   The Defendant be required to maintain interim support for the Claimant. That order is sought because the Defendant has decided to terminate support.

4. Have you attached a draft of the order you are applying for? ☒ Yes ☐ No

5. How do you want to have this application dealt with? ☐ at a hearing ☒ without a hearing

   ☐ at a telephone hearing

6. How long do you think the hearing will last? ☐ Hours ☐ Minutes

   Is this time estimate agreed by all parties? ☐ Yes ☐ No

7. Give details of any fixed trial date or period

8. What level of Judge does your hearing need? High Court Judge

9. Who should be served with this application? Defendant

10.   What information will you be relying on, in support of your application?

☐ the attached witness statement

☐ the statement of case

☒ the evidence set out in the box below

| |
|---|
| If necessary, please continue on a separate sheet.<br>1. The Claimant has previously been in receipt of accommodation and other support pending a final determination of her entitlement to benefit.<br>2. On 10 August 2011 the Claimant's solicitors were informed that support would terminate on 12 August 2011.<br>3. If support is terminated there is a real risk that serious harm will be done to the Claimant. As the grounds in support of the claim make clear, she will be at risk of destitution and also physical abuse from her husband.<br>4. In light of the matters above and the strength of this claim for judicial review, it is submitted that an interim order maintaining support is appropriate.<br><br><br>**Statement of Truth**<br><br>(I believe) (The applicant believes) that the facts stated in this section (and any continuation sheets) are true.<br><br>Signed _____    Dated _____<br> Applicant('s Solicitor)('s litigation friend)<br><br>Full name   John Smith _____<br><br>Name of applicant's solicitor's firm   Smith & Co _____<br><br>Position or office held   Partner _____<br>(if signing on behalf of firm or company) |

11.   Signature and address details

Signed _____    Dated _____
 Applicant('s Solicitor)('s litigation friend)

Position or office held   Solicitor _____
(if signing on behalf of firm or company)

Applicant's address to which documents about this application should be sent

| Smith & Co<br>1 The Crescent<br>London | | If applicable | |
|---|---|---|---|
| | | Phone no. | 020 7777 1111 |
| | | Fax no. | |
| Postcode | | DX no. | |
| E C 1 A   1 P P | | Ref no. | JS/1 |

| E-mail address | |
|---|---|

# Application Notice (Form N244) – Notes for Guidance

Court Staff cannot give legal advice. If you need information or advice on a legal problem you can contact Community Legal Service Direct on 0845 345 4 345 or www.clsdirect.org.uk, or a Citizens Advice Bureau. Details of your local offices and contact numbers are available via their website www.citizensadvice.org.uk

## Paying the court fee

A court fee is payable depending on the type of application you are making. For example:

- To apply for judgment to be set aside
- To apply to vary a judgment or suspend enforcement
- To apply for a summons or order for a witness to attend
- To apply by consent, or without service of the application notice, for a judgment or order.

No fee is payable for an application by consent for an adjournment of a hearing if it is received by the court at least 14 days before the date of the hearing.

## What if I cannot afford the fee?

If you show that a payment of a court fee would involve undue hardship to you, you may be eligible for a fee concession.

For further information, or to apply for a fee concession, ask court staff for a copy of the combined booklet and form EX160A - Court fees - Do I have to pay them? This is also available from any county court office, or a copy of the leaflet can be downloaded from our website www.hmcourts-service.gov.uk

## Completing the form

### Question 3

Set out what order you are applying for and why; e.g. to adjourn the hearing because..., to set aside a judgment against me because... etc.

### Question 5

Most applications will require a hearing and you will be expected to attend. The court will allocate a hearing date and time for the application. Please indicate in a covering letter any dates that you are unavailable within the next six weeks.
The court will only deal with the application 'without a hearing' in the following circumstances.

- Where all the parties agree to the terms of the order being asked for;
- Where all the parties agree that the court should deal with the application without a hearing, or
- Where the court does not consider that a hearing would be appropriate.

Telephone hearings are only available in applications where at least one of parties involved in the case is legally represented. Not all applications will be suitable for a telephone hearing and the court may refuse your request.

### Question 6

If you do not know how long the hearing will take do not guess but leave these boxes blank.

### Question 7

If your case has already been allocated a hearing date or trial period please insert details of those dates in the box.

### Question 8

If your case is being heard in the High Court or a District Registry please indicate whether it is to be dealt with by a Master, District Judge or Judge.

### Question 9

Please indicate in the box provided who you want the court to sent a copy of the application to.

### Question 10

In this section please set out the information you want the court to take account of in support of the application you are making.
If you wish to rely on:

- **a witness statement,** tick the first box and attach the statement to the application notice. A witness statement form is available on request from the court office.

- **a statement of case,** tick the second box if you intend to rely on your particulars of claim or defence in support of your application.

- **written evidence** on this form, tick the third box and enter details in the space provided. You must also complete the statement of truth.
  Proceedings for contempt of court may be brought against a person who signs a statement of truth without an honest belief in its truth.

### Question 11

The application must be signed and include your current address and contact details. If you agree that the court and the other parties may communicate with you by Document Exchange, telephone, facsimile or email, complete the details

## Before returning your form to the court

Have you:
- signed the form on page 2,
- enclosed the correct fee or an application for fee remission,
- made sufficient copies of your application and supporting documentation. You will need to submit one copy for each party to be served and one copy for the court.

## P3.20  DRAFT ORDER GRANTING INTERIM RELIEF

C/100/2002

IN THE HIGH COURT OF JUSTICE

QUEEN'S BENCH DIVISION

ADMINISTRATIVE COURT

IN THE MATTER OF A CLAIM FOR JUDICIAL REVIEW

THE QUEEN (on the application of K) -v- CAMBRIDGESHIRE COUNTY COUNCIL

Whereas K was previously in receipt of support that Cambridgeshire County Council wish to terminate

And whereas K has applied for judicial review

It is ordered that Cambridgeshire County Council continue to provide accommodation and support for K until further order or the determination of this claim for judicial review.

## P3.21 CERTIFICATE OF SUITABILITY OF LITIGATION FRIEND

### Certificate of suitability of litigation friend

| | |
|---|---|
| **In the** | High Court, Queen's Bench Division, Administrative Court |

If you are acting
- **for a child**, you must serve a copy of the completed form on a parent or guardian of the child, or if there is no parent or guardian, the carer or the person with whom the child lives
- **for a patient**, you must serve a copy of the completed form on the person authorised under Part VII of the Mental Health Act 1983 or, if no person is authorised, the carer or person with whom the patient lives unless you **are** that person. You must also complete a certificate of service (obtainable from the court office)

| | |
|---|---|
| **Claim No.** | c/100/2002 |
| **Claimant** (including ref.) | K |
| **Defendant** (including ref.) | OXFORDSHIRE COUNTY COUNCIL |

You should send the completed form to the court with the claim form (if acting for the claimant) or when you take the first step on the defendant's behalf in the claim together with the certificate of service (if applicable)

You do not need to complete this form if you do have an authorisation under Part VII of the Mental Health Act 1983 to conduct legal proceedings on the person's behalf.

I consent to act as litigation friend for K .................................................................................. (claimant)(defendant)

I believe that the above named person is a

[x] child      [ ] patient *(give your reasons overleaf and attach a copy of any medical evidence in support)*

I am able to conduct proceedings on behalf of the above named person competently and fairly and I have no interests adverse to those of the above named person.

*delete if you are acting for the defendant*

*I undertake to pay any costs which the above named claimant may be ordered to pay in these proceedings subject to any right I may have to be repaid from the assets of the claimant.

Please write your name in capital letters

| [x] Mr | [ ] Mrs | [ ] Miss | Surname SMITH |
|---|---|---|---|
| [ ] Ms | [ ] Other _____ | | Forenames JOHN |

Address to which documents in this case are to be sent.

1 The Crescent
London
EC1A 1PP

**I certify that the information given in this form is correct**

Signed ........................................... **Date** ..............

The court office at

is open between 10 am and 4 pm Monday to Friday. When corresponding with the court, please address forms or letters to the Court Manager and quote the claim number.

N235 - w3  Certificate of suitability of litigation friend (4.99)    *Printed on behalf of The Court Service*

| **Claim No.** | c/100/2002 |
|---|---|

My reasons for believing that the (claimant)(defendant) is a patient are:-

# PART IV

# LEGISLATION, GUIDANCE AND PROTOCOL

# SENIOR COURTS ACT 1981

## PART I
## CONSTITUTION OF SENIOR COURTS

\*\*\*\*

### 29 Mandatory, prohibiting and quashing orders

(1) Subject to subsection (3A), the orders of mandamus, prohibition and certiorari shall be known instead as mandatory, prohibiting and quashing orders respectively.

(1A) The High Court shall have jurisdiction to make mandatory, prohibiting and quashing orders in those classes of case in which, immediately before 1st May 2004, it had jurisdiction to make orders of mandamus, prohibition and certiorari respectively.

(2) Every such order shall be final, subject to any right of appeal therefrom.

(3) In relation to the jurisdiction of the Crown Court, other than its jurisdiction in matters relating to trial on indictment, the High Court shall have all such jurisdiction to make mandatory, prohibiting or quashing orders as the High Court possesses in relation to the jurisdiction of an inferior court.

(3A) The High Court shall have no jurisdiction to make mandatory, prohibiting or quashing orders in relation to the jurisdiction of the Court Martial in matters relating to –

 (a) trial by the Court Martial for an offence; or
 (b) appeals from the Service Civilian Court.

(4) The power of the High Court under any enactment to require justices of the peace or a judge or officer of a county court to do any act relating to the duties of their respective offices, or to require a magistrates' court to state a case for the opinion of the High Court, in any case where the High Court formerly had by virtue of any enactment jurisdiction to make a rule absolute, or an order, for any of those purposes, shall be exercisable by mandatory order.

(5) In any statutory provision –

 (a) references to mandamus or to a writ or order of mandamus shall be read as references to a mandatory order;
 (b) references to prohibition or to a writ or order of prohibition shall be read as references to a prohibiting order;
 (c) references to certiorari or to a writ or order of certiorari shall be read as references to a quashing order; and
 (d) references to the issue or award of a writ of mandamus, prohibition or certiorari shall be read as references to the making of the corresponding mandatory, prohibiting or quashing order.

(6) In subsection (3) the reference to the Crown Court's jurisdiction in matters relating to trial on indictment does not include its jurisdiction relating to orders under section 17 of the Access to Justice Act 1999.

---

**Amendments**—Armed Forces Act 2001, s 23(1), (2); SI 2004/1033; Armed Forces Act 2006, s 378(1), Sch 16, para 93.

### 31   Application for judicial review

(1)   An application to the High Court for one or more of the following forms of relief, namely –

(a)   a mandatory, prohibiting or quashing order;

(b)   a declaration or injunction under subsection (2); or

(c)   an injunction under section 30 restraining a person not entitled to do so from acting in an office to which that section applies,

shall be made in accordance with rules of court by a procedure to be known as an application for judicial review.

(2)   A declaration may be made or an injunction granted under this subsection in any case where an application for judicial review, seeking that relief, has been made and the High Court considers that, having regard to –

(a)   the nature of the matters in respect of which relief may be granted by mandatory, prohibiting or quashing orders;

(b)   the nature of the persons and bodies against whom relief may be granted by such orders; and

(c)   all the circumstances of the case,

it would be just and convenient for the declaration to be made or of the injunction to be granted, as the case may be.

(3)   No application for judicial review shall be made unless the leave of the High Court has been obtained in accordance with rules of court; and the court shall not grant leave to make such an application unless it considers that the applicant has a sufficient interest in the matter to which the application relates.

(4)   On an application for judicial review the High Court may award to the applicant damages, restitution or the recovery of a sum due if –

(a)   the application includes a claim for such an award arising from any matter to which the application relates; and

(b)   the court is satisfied that such an award would have been made if the claim had been made in an action begun by the applicant at the time of making the application.

(5)   If, on an application for judicial review, the High Court quashes the decision to which the applica-tion relates, it may in addition –

(a)   remit the matter to the court, tribunal or authority which made the decision, with a direction to reconsider the matter and reach a decision in accordance with the findings of the High Court, or

(b)   substitute its own decision for the decision in question.

(5A)   But the power conferred by subsection (5)(b) is exercisable only if –

(a)   the decision in question was made by a court or tribunal,

(b)   the decision is quashed on the ground that there has been an error of law, and

(c)   without the error, there would have been only one decision which the court or tribunal could have reached.

(5B)   Unless the High Court otherwise directs, a decision substituted by it under subsection (5)(b) has effect as if it were a decision of the relevant court or tribunal.

(6)  Where the High Court considers that there has been undue delay in making an application for judicial review, the court may refuse to grant –

(a)  leave for the making of the application; or
(b)  any relief sought on the application,

if it considers that the granting of the relief sought would be likely to cause substantial hardship to, or substantially prejudice the rights of, any person or would be detrimental to good administration.

(7)  Subsection (6) is without prejudice to any enactment or rule of court which has the effect of limiting the time within which an application for judicial review may be made.

**Amendments**—SI 2004/1033; Tribunals, Courts and Enforcement Act 2007, s 141.

### 31A  Transfer of judicial review applications to Upper Tribunal

(1)  This section applies where an application is made to the High Court –

(a)  for judicial review, or
(b)  for permission to apply for judicial review.

(2)  If Conditions 1, 2, 3 and 4 are met, the High Court must by order transfer the application to the Upper Tribunal.

(2A)  If Conditions 1, 2, 3 and 5 are met, but Condition 4 is not, the High Court must by order transfer the application to the Upper Tribunal.

(3)  If Conditions 1, 2 and 4 are met, but Condition 3 is not, the High Court may by order transfer the application to the Upper Tribunal if it appears to the High Court to be just and convenient to do so.

(4)  Condition 1 is that the application does not seek anything other than –

(a)  relief under section 31(1)(a) and (b);
(b)  permission to apply for relief under section 31(1)(a) and (b);
(c)  an award under section 31(4);
(d)  interest;
(e)  costs.

(5)  Condition 2 is that the application does not call into question anything done by the Crown Court.

(6)  Condition 3 is that the application falls within a class specified under section 18(6) of the Tribunals, Courts and Enforcement Act 2007.

(7)  Condition 4 is that the application does not call into question any decision made under –

(a)  the Immigration Acts,
(b)  the British Nationality Act 1981 (c 61),
(c)  any instrument having effect under an enactment within paragraph (a) or (b), or
(d)  any other provision of law for the time being in force which determines British citizenship, British overseas territories citizenship, the status of a British National (Overseas) or British Overseas citizenship.

(8)  Condition 5 is that the application calls into question a decision of the Secretary of State not to treat submissions as an asylum claim or a human rights

claim within the meaning of Part 5 of the Nationality, Immigration and Asylum Act 2002 wholly or partly on the basis that they are not significantly different from material that has previously been considered (whether or not it calls into question any other decision).

**Amendments**—Tribunals, Courts and Enforcement Act 2007, s 19(1); Borders, Citizenship and Immigration Act 2009, s 53.

\*\*\*\*

### 43 Power of High Court to vary sentence on application for quashing order

(1) Where a person who has been sentenced for an offence –

(a)   by a magistrates' court; or

(b)   by the Crown Court after being convicted of the offence by a magistrates' court and committed to the Crown Court for sentence; or

(c)   by the Crown Court on appeal against conviction or sentence,

applies to the High Court in accordance with section 31 for a quashing order to remove the proceedings of the magistrates' court or the Crown Court into the High Court, then, if the High Court determines that the magistrates' court or the Crown Court had no power to pass the sentence, the High Court may, instead of quashing the conviction, amend it by substituting for the sentence passed any sentence which the magistrates' court or, in a case within paragraph (b), the Crown Court had power to impose.

(2) Any sentence passed by the High Court by virtue of this section in substitution for the sentence passed in the proceedings of the magistrates' court or the Crown Court shall, unless the High Court otherwise directs, begin to run from the time when it would have begun to run if passed in those proceedings; but in computing the term of the sentence, any time during which the offender was released on bail in pursuance of section 37(1)(d) of the Criminal Justice Act 1948 shall be disregarded.

(3) Subsections (1) and (2) shall, with the necessary modifications, apply in relation to any order of a magistrates' court or the Crown Court which is made on, but does not form part of, the conviction of an offender as they apply in relation to a conviction and sentence.

**Amendments**—SI 2004/1033.

# COUNTY COURTS ACT 1984

*Certiorari and prohibition*

\*\*\*\*

### 83 Stay of proceedings in case of certiorari or prohibition

(1) The grant by the High Court of leave to make an application for an order of certiorari or prohibition to a county court shall, if the High Court so directs, operate as a stay of the proceedings in question until the determination of the application, or until the High Court otherwise orders.

(2) Where any proceedings are so stayed, the judge of the county court shall from time to time adjourn the hearing of the proceedings to such day as he thinks fit.

### 84 Prohibition

(1) Where an application is made to the High Court for an order of prohibition addressed to any county court, the matter shall be finally disposed of by order.

(2) Upon any such application, the judge of the county court shall not be served with notice of it, and shall not, except by the order of a judge of the High Court –

(a)    be required to appear or be heard; or
(b)    be liable to any order for the payment of the costs of the application;

but the application shall be proceeded with and heard in the same manner in all respects as an appeal duly brought from a decision of the judge, and notice of the application shall be given to or served upon the same parties as in the case of an order made or refused by a judge in a matter within his jurisdiction.

\*\*\*\*

# HUMAN RIGHTS ACT 1998

*Introduction*

## 1　The Convention Rights

(1)　In this Act, 'the Convention rights' means the rights and fundamental freedoms set out in –

    (a)　Articles 2 to 12 and 14 of the Convention, and

    (b)　Articles 1 to 3 of the First Protocol, and

    (c)　Article 1 of the Thirteenth Protocol,

as read with Articles 16 to 18 of the Convention.

(2)　Those Articles are to have effect for the purposes of this Act subject to any designated derogation or reservation (as to which see sections 14 and 15).

(3)　The Articles are set out in Schedule 1.

(4)　The Secretary of State may by order make such amendments to this Act as he considers appropriate to reflect the effect, in relation to the United Kingdom, of a protocol.

(5)　In subsection (4) 'protocol' means a protocol to the Convention –

    (a)　which the United Kingdom has ratified; or

    (b)　which the United Kingdom has signed with a view to ratification.

(6)　No amendment may be made by an order under subsection (4) so as to come into force before the protocol concerned is in force in relation to the United Kingdom.

**Amendments**—SI 2003/1887; SI 2004/1574.

## 2　Interpretation of Convention rights

(1)　A court or tribunal determining a question which has arisen under this Act in connection with a Convention right must take into account any –

    (a)　judgment, decision, declaration or advisory opinion of the European Court of Human Rights,

    (b)　opinion of the Commission given in a report adopted under Article 31 of the Convention,

    (c)　decision of the Commission in connection with Article 26 or 27(2) of the Convention, or

    (d)　decision of the Committee of Ministers taken under Article 46 of the Convention,

whenever made or given, so far as, in the opinion of the court or tribunal, it is relevant to the proceedings in which that question has arisen.

(2)　Evidence of any judgment, decision, declaration or opinion of which account may have to be taken under this section is to be given in proceedings before any court or tribunal in such manner as may be provided by rules.

(3)　In this section 'rules' means rules of court or, in the case of proceedings before a tribunal, rules made for the purposes of this section –

(a)    by the Lord Chancellor or the Secretary of State, in relation to any proceedings outside Scotland;

(b)    by the Secretary of State, in relation to proceedings in Scotland; or

(c)    by a Northern Ireland department, in relation to proceedings before a tribunal in Northern Ireland-

    (i)    which deals with transferred matters; and

    (ii)    for which no rules made under paragraph (a) are in force.

**Amendments**—SI 2003/1887; SI 2005/3429.

*Legislation*

## 3   Interpretation of legislation

(1)   So far as it is possible to do so, primary legislation and subordinate legislation must be read and given effect in a way which is compatible with the Convention rights.

(2)   This section –

(a)    applies to primary legislation and subordinate legislation whenever enacted;

(b)    does not affect the validity, continuing operation or enforcement of any incompatible primary legislation; and

(c)    does not affect the validity, continuing operation or enforcement of any incompatible subordinate legislation if (disregarding any possibility of revocation) primary legislation prevents removal of the incompatibility.

## 4   Declaration of incompatibility

(1)   Subsection (2) applies in any proceedings in which a court determines whether a provision of primary legislation is compatible with a Convention right.

(2)   If the court is satisfied that the provision is incompatible with a Convention right, it may make a declaration of that incompatibility.

(3)   Subsection (4) applies in any proceedings in which a court determines whether a provision of subordinate legislation, made in the exercise of a power conferred by primary legislation, is compatible with a Convention right.

(4)   If the court is satisfied –

(a)    that the provision is incompatible with a Convention right, and

(b)    that (disregarding any possibility of revocation) the primary legislation concerned prevents removal of the incompatibility,

it may make a declaration of that incompatibility.

(5)   In this section 'court' means –

(a)    the Supreme Court;

(b)    the Judicial Committee of the Privy Council;

(c)    the Court Martial Appeal Court;

(d)    in Scotland, the High Court of Justiciary sitting otherwise than as a trial court or the Court of Session;

(e)    in England and Wales or Northern Ireland, the High Court or the Court of Appeal.

(f)     the Court of Protection, in any matter being dealt with by the President of the Family Division, the Vice-Chancellor or a puisne judge of the High Court.

(6)   A declaration under this section ('a declaration of incompatibility') –

(a)     does not affect the validity, continuing operation or enforcement of the provision in respect of which it is given; and
(b)     is not binding on the parties to the proceedings in which it is made.

**Amendments**—Mental Capacity Act 2005, s 67(1), Sch 6, para 43; Constitutional Reform Act 2005, s 40(4), Sch 9, Pt 1, para 66(1), (2); Armed Forces Act 2006, s 378(1), Sch 16, para 156.

## 5   Right of Crown to intervene

(1)   Where a court is considering whether to make a declaration of incompatibility, the Crown is entitled to notice in accordance with rules of court.

(2)   In any case to which subsection (1) applies –

(a)     a Minister of the Crown, or
(b)     a member of the Scottish Executive,
(c)     a Northern Ireland Minister,
(d)     a Northern Ireland department,

is entitled, on an application made to the court in accordance with rules of court, to be joined as a party to the proceedings.

(3)   An application under subsection (2) may be made at any time during the proceedings.

(4)   A person who has been made a party to criminal proceedings (other than in Scotland) as the result of an application under subsection (2) may, with leave, appeal to the Supreme Court against any declaration of incompatibility made in the proceedings.

(5)   In subsection (4) –

'criminal proceedings' includes all proceedings before the Court Martial Appeal Court; and
'leave' means leave granted by the court making the declaration of incompatibility or by the Supreme Court.

**Amendments**—Constitutional Reform Act 2005, s 40(4), Sch 9, Pt 1, para 66(1), (3); Armed Forces Act 2006, s 378(1), Sch 16, para 157.

*Public authorities*

## 6   Acts of public authorities

(1)   It is unlawful for a public authority to act in a way which is incompatible with a Convention right.

(2)   Subsection (1) does not apply to an act if –

(a)     as the result of one or more provisions of primary legislation, the authority could not have acted differently; or
(b)     in the case of one or more provisions of, or made under, primary legislation which cannot be read or given effect in a way which is

compatible with the Convention rights, the authority was acting so as to give effect to or enforce those provisions.

(3)   In this section, 'public authority' includes –

(a)    a court or tribunal, and
(b)    any person certain of whose functions are functions of a public nature,

but does not include either House of Parliament or a person exercising functions in connection with proceedings in Parliament.

(4) (*repealed*)

(5)   In relation to a particular act, a person is not a public authority by virtue only of subsection (3)(b) if the nature of the act is private.

(6)   'An act' includes a failure to act but does not include a failure to –

(a)    introduce in, or lay before, Parliament a proposal for legislation; or
(b)    make any primary legislation or remedial order.

**Amendments**—Constitutional Reform Act 2005, ss 40(4), 146, Sch 9, Pt 1, para 66(1), (4), Sch 18, Pt 5.

## 7   Proceedings

(1)   A person who claims that a public authority has acted (or proposes to act) in a way which is made unlawful by section 6(1) may –

(a)    bring proceedings against the authority under this Act in the appropriate court or tribunal, or
(b)    rely on the Convention right or rights concerned in any legal proceedings,

but only if he is (or would be) a victim of the unlawful act.

(2)   In subsection (1)(a) 'appropriate court or tribunal' means such court or tribunal as may be determined in accordance with rules; and proceedings against an authority includes a counterclaim or similar proceeding.

(3)   If the proceedings are brought on an application for judicial review, the applicant is to be taken to have a sufficient interest in relation to the unlawful act only if he is, or would be, a victim of that act.

(4)   If the proceedings are made by way of a petition for judicial review in Scotland, the applicant shall be taken to have title and interest to sue in relation to the unlawful act only if he is, or would be, a victim of that act.

(5)   Proceedings under subsection (1)(a) must be brought before the end of –

(a)    the period of one year beginning with the date on which the act complained of took place; or
(b)    such longer period as the court or tribunal considers equitable having regard to all the circumstances,

but that is subject to any rule imposing a stricter time limit in relation to the procedure in question.

(6)   In subsection (1)(b) 'legal proceedings' includes –

(a)    proceedings brought by or at the instigation of a public authority; and
(b)    an appeal against the decision of a court or tribunal.

(7) For the purposes of this section, a person is a victim of an unlawful act only if he would be a victim for the purposes of Article 34 of the Convention if proceedings were brought in the European Court of Human Rights in respect of that act.

(8) Nothing in this Act creates a criminal offence.

(9) In this section 'rules' means –

    (a)    in relation to proceedings before a court or tribunal outside Scotland, rules made by the Lord Chancellor the Secretary of State for the purposes of this section or rules of court,

    (b)    in relation to proceedings before a court or tribunal in Scotland, rules made by the Secretary of State for those purposes,

    (c)    in relation to proceedings before a tribunal in Northern Ireland –

        (i)    which deals with transferred matters; and

        (ii)    for which no rules made under paragraph (a) are in force, rules made by a Northern Ireland department for those purposes, and

includes provision made by order under section 1 of the Courts and Legal Services Act 1990.

(10) In making rules regard must be had to section 9.

(11) The Minister who has power to make rules in relation to a particular tribunal may, to the extent he considers it necessary to ensure that the tribunal can provide an appropriate remedy in relation to an act (or proposed act) of a public authority which is (or would be) unlawful as a result of section 6(1), by order add to –

    (a)    the relief or remedies which the tribunal may grant; or

    (b)    the grounds on which it may grant any of them.

(12) An order made under subsection (11) may contain such incidental, supplemental, consequential or transitional provision as the Minister making it considers appropriate.

(13) 'The Minister' includes the Northern Ireland department concerned.

---

**Amendments**—SI 2003/1887; SI 2005/3429.

## 8 Judicial remedies

(1) In relation to any act (or proposed act) of a public authority which the court finds is (or would be) unlawful, it may grant such relief or remedy, or make such order, within its jurisdiction as it considers just and appropriate.

(2) But damages may be awarded only by a court which has power to award damages, or to order the payment of compensation, in civil proceedings.

(3) No award of damages is to be made unless, taking account of all the circumstances of the case, including –

    (a)    any other relief or remedy granted, or order made, in relation to the act in question (by that or any other court), and

    (b)    the consequences of any decision (of that or any other court) in respect of that act,

the court is satisfied that the award is necessary to afford just satisfaction to the person in whose favour it is made.

(4)   In determining –

   (a)    whether to award damages, or
   (b)    the amount of an award,

the court must take into account the principles applied by the European Court of Human Rights in relation to the award of compensation under Article 41 of the Convention.

(5)   A public authority against which damages are awarded is to be treated –

   (a)    in Scotland, for the purposes of section 3 of the Law Reform (Miscellaneous Provisions) (Scotland) Act 1940 as if the award were made in an action of damages in which the authority has been found liable in respect of loss or damage to the person to whom the award is made;
   (b)    for the purposes of the Civil Liability (Contribution) Act 1978 as liable in respect of damage suffered by the person to whom the award is made.

(6)   In this section –

   'court' includes a tribunal;
   'damages' means damages for an unlawful act of a public authority; and
   'unlawful' means unlawful under section 6(1).

## 9   Judicial acts

(1)   Proceedings under section 7(1)(a) in respect of a judicial act may be brought only –

   (a)    by exercising a right of appeal;
   (b)    on an application (in Scotland a petition) for judicial review; or
   (c)    in such other forum as may be prescribed by rules.

(2)   That does not affect any rule of law which prevents a court from being the subject of judicial review.

(3)   In proceedings under this Act in respect of a judicial act done in good faith, damages may not be awarded otherwise than to compensate a person to the extent required by Article 5(5) of the Convention.

(4)   An award of damages permitted by subsection (3) is to be made against the Crown; but no award may be made unless the appropriate person, if not a party to the proceedings, is joined.

(5)   In this section –

   'appropriate person' means the Minister responsible for the court concerned, or a person or government department nominated by him;
   'court' includes a tribunal;
   'judge' includes a member of a tribunal, a justice of the peace (or, in Northern Ireland, a lay magistrate) and a clerk or other officer entitled to exercise the jurisdiction of a court;
   'judicial act' means a judicial act of a court and includes an act done on the instructions, or on behalf, of a judge;
   'rules' has the same meaning as in section 7(9).

---

**Amendments**—Justice (Northern Ireland) Act 2002, s 10(6), Sch 4, para 39.

*Remedial action*

**10 Power to take remedial action**

(1) This section applies if –

   (a) a provision of legislation has been declared under section 4 to be incompatible with a Convention right and, if an appeal lies –

      (i) all persons who may appeal have stated that they do not intend to do so;

      (ii) the time for bringing an appeal has expired and no appeal has been brought within that time; or

      (iii) an appeal brought within that time has been determined or abandoned; or

   (b) it appears to a Minister of the Crown or Her Majesty in Council that, having regard to a finding of the European Court of Human Rights made after the coming into force of this section in proceedings against the United Kingdom, a provision of legislation is incompatible with an obligation of the United Kingdom arising from the Convention.

(2) If a Minister of the Crown considers that there are compelling reasons for proceeding under this section, he may by order make such amendments to the legislation as he considers necessary to remove the incompatibility.

(3) If, in the case of subordinate legislation, a Minister of the Crown considers –

   (a) that it is necessary to amend the primary legislation under which the subordinate legislation in question was made, in order to enable the incompatibility to be removed, and

   (b) that there are compelling reasons for proceeding under this section,

he may by order make such amendments to the primary legislation as he considers appropriate.

(4) This section also applies where the provision in question is in subordinate legislation and has been quashed, or declared invalid, by reason of incompatibility with a Convention right and the Minister proposes to proceed under paragraph 2(b) of Schedule 2.

(5) If the legislation is an Order in Council, the power conferred by subsection (2) or (3) is exercisable by Her Majesty in Council.

(6) In this section 'legislation' does not include a Measure of the Church Assembly or of the General Synod of the Church of England.

(7) Schedule 2 makes further provision about remedial orders.

*Other rights and proceedings*

**11 Safeguard for existing human rights**

A person's reliance on a Convention right does not restrict –

   (a) any other right or freedom conferred on him by or under any law having effect in any part of the United Kingdom, or

   (b) his right to make any claim or bring any proceedings which he could make or bring apart from sections 7 to 9.

**12  Freedom of expression**

(1)  This section applies if a court is considering whether to grant any relief which, if granted, might affect the exercise of the Convention right to freedom of expression.

(2)  If the person against whom the application for relief is made ('the respondent') is neither present nor represented, no such relief is to be granted unless the court is satisfied –

(a)  that the applicant has taken all practicable steps to notify the respondent; or

(b)  that there are compelling reasons why the respondent should not be notified.

(3)  No such relief is to be granted so as to restrain publication before trial unless the court is satisfied that the applicant is likely to establish that publication should not be allowed.

(4)  The court must have particular regard to the importance of the Convention right to freedom of expression and, where the proceedings relate to material which the respondent claims, or which appears to the court, to be journalistic, literary or artistic material (or to conduct connected with such material), to –

(a)  the extent to which –

(i)  the material has, or is about to, become available to the public; or

(ii)  it is, or would be, in the public interest for the material to be published;

(b)  any relevant privacy code.

(5)  In this section –

'court' includes a tribunal; and
'relief' includes any remedy or order (other than in criminal proceedings).

**13  Freedom of thought, conscience and religion**

(1)  If a court's determination of any question arising under this Act might affect the exercise by a religious organisation (itself or its members collectively) of the Convention right to freedom of thought, conscience and religion, it must have particular regard to the importance of that right.

(2)  In this section 'court' includes a tribunal.

*Derogations and reservations*

**14  Derogations**

(1)  In this Act, 'designated derogation' means –

any derogation by the United Kingdom from an Article of the Convention, or of any protocol to the Convention, which is designated for the purposes of this Act in an order made by the Secretary of State.

(2)  *(repealed)*

(3)  If a designated derogation is amended or replaced it ceases to be a designated derogation.

(4)   But subsection (3) does not prevent the Secretary of State from exercising his power under subsection (1) to make a fresh designation order in respect of the Article concerned.

(5)   The Secretary of State must by order make such amendments to Schedule 3 as he considers appropriate to reflect –

(a)   any designation order; or
(b)   the effect of subsection (3).

(6)   A designation order may be made in anticipation of the making by the United Kingdom of a proposed derogation.

Amendments—SI 2001/1216; SI 2003/1887.

## 15   Reservations

(1)   In this Act, 'designated reservation' means –

(a)   the United Kingdom's reservation to Article 2 of the First Protocol to the Convention; and
(b)   any other reservation by the United Kingdom to an Article of the Convention, or of any protocol to the Convention, which is designated for the purposes of this Act in an order made by the Secretary of State.

(2)   The text of the reservation referred to in subsection (1)(a) is set out in Part II of Schedule 3.

(3)   If a designated reservation is withdrawn wholly or in part it ceases to be a designated reservation.

(4)   But subsection (3) does not prevent the Secretary of State from exercising his power under subsection (1)(b) to make a fresh designation order in respect of the Article concerned.

(5)   The Secretary of State must by order make such amendments to this Act as he considers appropriate to reflect –

(a)   any designation order; or
(b)   the effect of subsection (3).

Amendments—SI 2003/1887.

## 16   Period for which designated derogations have effect

(1)   If it has not already been withdrawn by the United Kingdom, a designated derogation ceases to have effect for the purposes of this Act –

at the end of the period of five years beginning with the date on which the order designating it was made.

(2)   At any time before the period –

(a)   fixed by subsection (1), or
(b)   extended by an order under this subsection,

comes to an end, the Secretary of State may by order extend it by a further period of five years.

(3)    An order under section 14(1 ceases to have effect at the end of the period for consideration, unless a resolution has been passed by each House approving the order.

(4)    Subsection (3) does not affect –

(a)    anything done in reliance on the order; or
(b)    the power to make a fresh order under section 14(1.

(5)    In subsection (3) 'period for consideration' means the period of forty days beginning with the day on which the order was made.

(6)    In calculating the period for consideration, no account is to be taken of any time during which –

(a)    Parliament is dissolved or prorogued; or
(b)    both Houses are adjourned for more than four days.

(7)    If a designated derogation is withdrawn by the United Kingdom, the Secretary of State must by order make such amendments to this Act as he considers are required to reflect that withdrawal.

Amendments—SI 2001/1216; SI 2003/1887.

### 17    Periodic review of designated reservations

(1)    The appropriate Minister must review the designated reservation referred to in section 15(1)(a) –

(a)    before the end of the period of five years beginning with the date on which section 1(2) came into force; and
(b)    if that designation is still in force, before the end of the period of five years beginning with the date on which the last report relating to it was laid under subsection (3).

(2)    The appropriate Minister must review each of the other designated reservations (if any) –

(a)    before the end of the period of five years beginning with the date on which the order designating the reservation first came into force; and
(b)    if the designation is still in force, before the end of the period of five years beginning with the date on which the last report relating to it was laid under subsection (3).

(3)    The Minister conducting a review under this section must prepare a report on the result of the review and lay a copy of it before each House of Parliament.

*Judges of the European Court of Human Rights*

### 18    Appointment to European Court of Human Rights

(1)    In this section 'judicial office' means the office of –

(a)    Lord Justice of Appeal, Justice of the High Court or Circuit judge, in England and Wales;
(b)    judge of the Court of Session or sheriff, in Scotland;
(c)    Lord Justice of Appeal, judge of the High Court or county court judge, in Northern Ireland.

(2) The holder of a judicial office may become a judge of the European Court of Human Rights ('the Court') without being required to relinquish his office.

(3) But he is not required to perform the duties of his judicial office while he is a judge of the Court.

(4) In respect of any period during which he is a judge of the Court –

(a) a Lord Justice of Appeal or Justice of the High Court is not to count as a judge of the relevant court for the purposes of section 2(1) or 4(1) of the Senior Courts Act 1981 (maximum number of judges) nor as a judge of the Senior Courts for the purposes of section 12(1) to (6) of that Act (salaries etc);

(b) a judge of the Court of Session is not to count as a judge of that court for the purposes of section 1(1) of the Court of Session Act 1988 (maximum number of judges) or of section 9(1)(c) of the Administration of Justice Act 1973 ('the 1973 Act') (salaries etc);

(c) a Lord Justice of Appeal or a judge of the High Court in Northern Ireland is not to count as a judge of the relevant court for the purposes of section 2(1) or 3(1) of the Judicature (Northern Ireland) Act 1978 (maximum number of judges) nor as a judge of the Senior Courts of Northern Ireland for the purposes of section 9(1)(d) of the 1973 Act (salaries etc);

(d) a Circuit judge is not to count as such for the purposes of section 18 of the Courts Act 1971 (salaries etc);

(e) a sheriff is not to count as such for the purposes of section 14 of the Sheriff Courts (Scotland) Act 1907 (salaries etc);

(f) a county court judge of Northern Ireland is not to count as such for the purposes of section 106 of the County Courts Act (Northern Ireland) 1959 (salaries etc).

(5) If a sheriff principal is appointed a judge of the Court, section 11(1) of the Sheriff Courts (Scotland) Act 1971 (temporary appointment of sheriff principal) applies, while he holds that appointment, as if his office is vacant.

(6) Schedule 3 makes provision about judicial pensions in relation to the holder of a judicial office who serves as a judge of the Court.

(7) The Lord Chancellor or the Secretary of State may by order make such transitional provision (including, in particular, provision for a temporary increase in the maximum number of judges) as he considers appropriate in relation to any holder of a judicial office who has completed his service as a judge of the Court.

(7A) The following paragraphs apply to the making of an order under subsection (7) in relation to any holder of a judicial office listed in subsection (1)(a) –

(a) before deciding what transitional provision it is appropriate to make, the person making the order must consult the Lord Chief Justice of England and Wales;

(b) before making the order, that person must consult the Lord Chief Justice of England and Wales.

(7B) The following paragraphs apply to the making of an order under subsection (7) in relation to any holder of a judicial office listed in subsection (1)(c) –

(a) before deciding what transitional provision it is appropriate to make, the person making the order must consult the Lord Chief Justice of Northern Ireland;

(b) before making the order, that person must consult the Lord Chief Justice of Northern Ireland.

(7C) The Lord Chief Justice of England and Wales may nominate a judicial office holder (within the meaning of section 109(4) of the Constitutional Reform Act 2005) to exercise his functions under this section.

(7D) The Lord Chief Justice of Northern Ireland may nominate any of the following to exercise his functions under this section –

(a) the holder of one of the offices listed in Schedule 1 to the Justice (Northern Ireland) Act 2002;

(b) a Lord Justice of Appeal (as defined in section 88 of that Act).

**Amendments**—Constitutional Reform Act 2005, ss 15(1), 59(5), Sch 4, Pt 1, para 278, Sch 11, Pts 1-3, paras 1(2), 4(1), (3), 6(1), (3)

*Parliamentary procedure*

## 19 Statements of compatibility

(1) A Minister of the Crown in charge of a Bill in either House of Parliament must, before Second Reading of the Bill –

(a) make a statement to the effect that in his view the provisions of the Bill are compatible with the Convention rights ('a statement of compatibility'); or

(b) make a statement to the effect that although he is unable to make a statement of compatibility the government nevertheless wishes the House to proceed with the Bill.

(2) The statement must be in writing and be published in such manner as the Minister making it considers appropriate.

*Supplemental*

## 20 Orders etc under this Act

(1) Any power of a Minister of the Crown to make an order under this Act is exercisable by statutory instrument.

(2) The power of the Lord Chancellor or the Secretary of State to make rules (other than rules of court) under section 2(3) or 7(9) is exercisable by statutory instrument.

(3) Any statutory instrument made under section 14, 15 or 16(7) must be laid before Parliament.

(4) No order may be made by the Lord Chancellor or the Secretary of State under section 1(4), 7(11) or 16(2) unless a draft of the order has been laid before, and approved by, each House of Parliament.

(5) Any statutory instrument made under section 18(7) or Schedule 4, or to which subsection (2) applies, shall be subject to annulment in pursuance of a resolution of either House of Parliament.

(6)   The power of a Northern Ireland department to make –

(a)   rules under section 2(3)(c) or 7(9)(c), or
(b)   an order under section 7(11),

is exercisable by statutory rule for the purposes of the Statutory Rules (Northern Ireland) Order 1979.

(7)   Any rules made under section 2(3)(c) or 7(9)(c) shall be subject to negative resolution; and section 41(6) of the Interpretation Act Northern Ireland) 1954 (meaning of 'subject to negative resolution') shall apply as if the power to make the rules were conferred by an Act of the Northern Ireland Assembly.

(8)   No order may be made by a Northern Ireland department under section 7(11) unless a draft of the order has been laid before, and approved by, the Northern Ireland Assembly.

**Amendments**—SI 2003/1887, SI 2005/3429.

## 21   Interpretation, etc

(1)   In this Act –

'amend' includes repeal and apply (with or without modifications);
'the appropriate Minister' means the Minister of the Crown having charge of the appropriate authorised government department (within the meaning of the Crown Proceedings Act 1947);
'the Commission' means the European Commission of Human Rights;
'the Convention' means the Convention for the Protection of Human Rights and Fundamental Freedoms, agreed by the Council of Europe at Rome on 4th November 1950 as it has effect for the time being in relation to the United Kingdom;
'declaration of incompatibility' means a declaration under section 4;
'Minister of the Crown' has the same meaning as in the Ministers of the Crown Act 1975;
'Northern Ireland Minister' includes the First Minister and the deputy First Minister in Northern Ireland;
'primary legislation' means any –
  (a)   public general Act;
  (b)   local and personal Act;
  (c)   private Act;
  (d)   Measure of the Church Assembly;
  (e)   Measure of the General Synod of the Church of England;
  (f)   Order in Council –
    (i)    made in exercise of Her Majesty's Royal Prerogative;
    (ii)   made under section 38(1)(a) of the Northern Ireland Constitution Act 1973 or the corresponding provision of the Northern Ireland Act 1998; or
    (iii)  amending an Act of a kind mentioned in paragraph (a), (b) or (c);
and includes an order or other instrument made under primary legislation (otherwise than by Welsh Ministers, the First Minister for Wales, the Counsel General to the Welsh Assembly Government, a member of the Scottish Executive, a Northern Ireland Minister or a

Northern Ireland department) to the extent to which it operates to bring one or more provisions of that legislation into force or amends any primary legislation;

'the First Protocol' means the protocol to the Convention agreed at Paris on 20th March 1952;

'the Eleventh Protocol' means the protocol to the Convention (restructuring the control machinery established by the Convention) agreed at Strasbourg on 11th May 1994;

'the Thirteenth Protocol' means the protocol to the Convention (concerning the abolition of the death penalty in all circumstances) agreed at Vilnius on 3rd May 2002;

'remedial order' means an order under section 10;

'subordinate legislation' means any –

    (a)    Order in Council other than one –

        (i)    made in exercise of Her Majesty's Royal Prerogative;

        (ii)    made under section 38(1)(a) of the Northern Ireland Constitution Act 1973 or the corresponding provision of the Northern Ireland Act 1998; or

        (iii)    amending an Act of a kind mentioned in the definition of primary legislation;

    (b)    Act of the Scottish Parliament;

    (ba)    Measure of the National Assembly for Wales;

    (bb)    Act of the National Assembly for Wales;

    (c)    Act of the Parliament of Northern Ireland;

    (d)    Measure of the Assembly established under section 1 of the Northern Ireland Assembly Act 1973;

    (e)    Act of the Northern Ireland Assembly;

    (f)    order, rules, regulations, scheme, warrant, byelaw or other instrument made under primary legislation (except to the extent to which it operates to bring one or more provisions of that legislation into force or amends any primary legislation);

    (g)    order, rules, regulations, scheme, warrant, byelaw or other instrument made under legislation mentioned in paragraph (b), (c), (d) or (e) or made under an Order in Council applying only to Northern Ireland;

    (h)    order, rules, regulations, scheme, warrant, byelaw or other instrument made by a member of the Scottish Executive, Welsh Ministers, the First Minister for Wales, the Counsel General to the Welsh Assembly Government, a Northern Ireland Minister or a Northern Ireland department in exercise of prerogative or other executive functions of Her Majesty which are exercisable by such a person on behalf of Her Majesty;

'transferred matters' has the same meaning as in the Northern Ireland Act 1998; and

'tribunal' means any tribunal in which legal proceedings may be brought.

(2)  The references in paragraphs (b) and (c) of section 2(1) to Articles are to Articles of the Convention as they had effect immediately before the coming into force of the Eleventh Protocol.

(3)   The reference in paragraph (d) of section 2(1) to Article 46 includes a reference to Articles 32 and 54 of the Convention as they had effect immediately before the coming into force of the Eleventh Protocol.

(4)   The references in section 2(1) to a report or decision of the Commission or a decision of the Committee of Ministers include references to a report or decision made as provided by paragraphs 3, 4 and 6 of Article 5 of the Eleventh Protocol (transitional provisions).

(5)   *(repealed)*

**Amendments**—SI 2004/1574; Government of Wales Act 2006, s 160(1), Sch 10, para 56; Armed Forces Act 2006, s 378(2), Sch 17.

**22   Short title, commencement, application and extent**

(1)   This Act may be cited as the Human Rights Act 1998.

(2)   Sections 18, 20 and 21(5) and this section come into force on the passing of this Act.

(3)   The other provisions of this Act come into force on such day as the Secretary of State may by order appoint; and different days may be appointed for different purposes.

(4)   Paragraph (b) of subsection (1) of section 7 applies to proceedings brought by or at the instigation of a public authority whenever the act in question took place; but otherwise that subsection does not apply to an act committed before the coming into force of that section.

(5)   This Act binds the Crown.

(6)   This Act extends to Northern Ireland.

(7)   *(repealed)*

**Amendments**—Armed Forces Act 2006, s 378(2), Sch 17.

## Schedules

## Schedule 1
### The Articles

### PART I
### THE CONVENTION – RIGHTS AND FREEDOMS

*Article 2*
Right to life

**1**

Everyone's right to life shall be protected by law. No one shall be deprived of his life intentionally save in the execution of a sentence of a court following his conviction of a crime for which this penalty is provided by law.

**2**

Deprivation of life shall not be regarded as inflicted in contravention of this Article when it results from the use of force which is no more than absolutely necessary –

(a)  in defence of any person from unlawful violence;
(b)  in order to effect a lawful arrest or to prevent the escape of a person lawfully detained;
(c)  in action lawfully taken for the purpose of quelling a riot or insurrection.

*Article 3*
Prohibition of torture

No one shall be subjected to torture or to inhuman or degrading treatment or punishment.

*Article 4*
Prohibition of slavery and forced labour

**1**

No one shall be held in slavery or servitude.

**2**

No one shall be required to perform forced or compulsory labour.

**3**

For the purpose of this Article the term 'forced or compulsory labour' shall not include –

(a)  any work required to be done in the ordinary course of detention imposed according to the provisions of Article 5 of this Convention or during conditional release from such detention;
(b)  any service of a military character or, in case of conscientious objectors in countries where they are recognised, service exacted instead of compulsory military service;
(c)  any service exacted in case of an emergency or calamity threatening the life or well-being of the community;
(d)  any work or service which forms part of normal civic obligations.

*Article 5*
Right to liberty and security

**1**

Everyone has the right to liberty and security of person. No one shall be deprived of his liberty save in the following cases and in accordance with a procedure prescribed by law –

(a)  the lawful detention of a person after conviction by a competent court;
(b)  the lawful arrest or detention of a person for non-compliance with the lawful order of a court or in order to secure the fulfilment of any obligation prescribed by law;

(c)    the lawful arrest or detention of a person effected for the purpose of bringing him before the competent legal authority on reasonable suspicion of having committed an offence or when it is reasonably considered necessary to prevent his committing an offence or fleeing after having done so;

(d)    the detention of a minor by lawful order for the purpose of educational supervision or his lawful detention for the purpose of bringing him before the competent legal authority;

(e)    the lawful detention of persons for the prevention of the spreading of infectious diseases, of persons of unsound mind, alcoholics or drug addicts or vagrants;

(f)    the lawful arrest or detention of a person to prevent his effecting an unauthorised entry into the country or of a person against whom action is being taken with a view to deportation or extradition.

**2**

Everyone who is arrested shall be informed promptly, in a language which he understands, of the reasons for his arrest and of any charge against him.

**3**

Everyone arrested or detained in accordance with the provisions of paragraph 1(c) of this Article shall be brought promptly before a judge or other officer authorised by law to exercise judicial power and shall be entitled to trial within a reasonable time or to release pending trial. Release may be conditioned by guarantees to appear for trial.

**4**

Everyone who is deprived of his liberty by arrest or detention shall be entitled to take proceedings by which the lawfulness of his detention shall be decided speedily by a court and his release ordered if the detention is not lawful.

**5**

Everyone who has been the victim of arrest or detention in contravention of the provisions of this Article shall have an enforceable right to compensation.

### *Article 6*
### Right to a fair trial

**1**

In the determination of his civil rights and obligations or of any criminal charge against him, everyone is entitled to a fair and public hearing within a reasonable time by an independent and impartial tribunal established by law. Judgment shall be pronounced publicly but the press and public may be excluded from all or part of the trial in the interest of morals, public order or national security in a democratic society, where the interests of juveniles or the protection of the private life of the parties so require, or to the extent strictly necessary in the opinion of the court in special circumstances where publicity would prejudice the interests of justice.

**2**

Everyone charged with a criminal offence shall be presumed innocent until proved guilty according to law.

**3**

Everyone charged with a criminal offence has the following minimum rights –

(a)    to be informed promptly, in a language which he understands and in detail, of the nature and cause of the accusation against him;

(b)    to have adequate time and facilities for the preparation of his defence;

(c)    to defend himself in person or through legal assistance of his own choosing or, if he has not sufficient means to pay for legal assistance, to be given it free when the interests of justice so require;

(d)    to examine or have examined witnesses against him and to obtain the attendance and examination of witnesses on his behalf under the same conditions as witnesses against him;

(e)    to have the free assistance of an interpreter if he cannot understand or speak the language used in court.

*Article 7*
No punishment without law

**1**

No one shall be held guilty of any criminal offence on account of any act or omission which did not constitute a criminal offence under national or international law at the time when it was committed. Nor shall a heavier penalty be imposed than the one that was applicable at the time the criminal offence was committed.

**2**

This Article shall not prejudice the trial and punishment of any person for any act or omission which, at the time when it was committed, was criminal according to the general principles of law recognised by civilised nations.

*Article 8*
Right to respect for private and family life

**1**

Everyone has the right to respect for his private and family life, his home and his correspondence.

**2**

There shall be no interference by a public authority with the exercise of this right except such as is in accordance with the law and is necessary in a democratic society in the interests of national security, public safety or the economic well-being of the country, for the prevention of disorder or crime, for the protection of health or morals, or for the protection of the rights and freedoms of others.

## Article 9
### Freedom of thought, conscience and religion

**1**

Everyone has the right to freedom of thought, conscience and religion; this right includes freedom to change his religion or belief and freedom, either alone or in community with others and in public or private, to manifest his religion or belief, in worship, teaching, practice and observance.

**2**

Freedom to manifest one's religion or beliefs shall be subject only to such limitations as are prescribed by law and are necessary in a democratic society in the interests of public safety, for the protection of public order, health or morals, or for the protection of the rights and freedoms of others.

## Article 10
### Freedom of expression

**1**

Everyone has the right to freedom of expression. This right shall include freedom to hold opinions and to receive and impart information and ideas without interference by public authority and regardless of frontiers. This Article shall not prevent States from requiring the licensing of broadcasting, television or cinema enterprises.

**2**

The exercise of these freedoms, since it carries with it duties and responsibilities, may be subject to such formalities, conditions, restrictions or penalties as are prescribed by law and are necessary in a democratic society, in the interests of national security, territorial integrity or public safety, for the prevention of disorder or crime, for the protection of health or morals, for the protection of the reputation or rights of others, for preventing the disclosure of information received in confidence, or for maintaining the authority and impartiality of the judiciary.

## Article 11
### Freedom of assembly and association

**1**

Everyone has the right to freedom of peaceful assembly and to freedom of association with others, including the right to form and to join trade unions for the protection of his interests.

**2**

No restrictions shall be placed on the exercise of these rights other than such as are prescribed by law and are necessary in a democratic society in the interests of national security or public safety, for the prevention of disorder or crime, for the protection of health or morals or for the protection of the rights and freedoms of others. This Article shall not prevent the imposition of lawful restrictions on the exercise of these rights by members of the armed forces, of the police or of the administration of the State.

### Article 12
### Right to marry

Men and women of marriageable age have the right to marry and to found a family, according to the national laws governing the exercise of this right.

### Article 14
### Prohibition of discrimination

The enjoyment of the rights and freedoms set forth in this Convention shall be secured without discrimination on any ground such as sex, race, colour, language, religion, political or other opinion, national or social origin, association with a national minority, property, birth or other status.

### Article 16
### Restrictions on political activity of aliens

Nothing in Articles 10, 11 and 14 shall be regarded as preventing the High Contracting Parties from imposing restrictions on the political activity of aliens.

### Article 17
### Prohibition of abuse of rights

Nothing in this Convention may be interpreted as implying for any State, group or person any right to engage in any activity or perform any act aimed at the destruction of any of the rights and freedoms set forth herein or at their limitation to a greater extent than is provided for in the Convention.

### Article 18
### Limitation on use of restrictions on rights

The restrictions permitted under this Convention to the said rights and freedoms shall not be applied for any purpose other than those for which they have been prescribed.

## PART II
## THE FIRST PROTOCOL

### Article 1
### Protection of property

Every natural or legal person is entitled to the peaceful enjoyment of his possessions. No one shall be deprived of his possessions except in the public interest and subject to the conditions provided for by law and by the general principles of international law.

The preceding provisions shall not, however, in any way impair the right of a State to enforce such laws as it deems necessary to control the use of property in accordance with the general interest or to secure the payment of taxes or other contributions or penalties.

*Article 2*
Right to education

No person shall be denied the right to education. In the exercise of any functions which it assumes in relation to education and to teaching, the State shall respect the right of parents to ensure such education and teaching in conformity with their own religious and philosophical convictions.

*Article 3*
Right to free elections

The High Contracting Parties undertake to hold free elections at reasonable intervals by secret ballot, under conditions which will ensure the free expression of the opinion of the people in the choice of the legislature.

**PART III**
ARTICLE 1 OF THE THIRTEENTH PROTOCOL

*Article 1*
Abolition of the death penalty

The death penalty shall be abolished. No one shall be condemned to such penalty or executed.

***

**Amendments**—SI 2004/1574.

**Schedule 2**
**Remedial Orders**

*Orders*

**1**

(1)   A remedial order may –

  (a)   contain such incidental, supplemental, consequential or transitional provision as the person making it considers appropriate;

  (b)   be made so as to have effect from a date earlier than that on which it is made;

  (c)   make provision for the delegation of specific functions;

  (d)   make different provision for different cases.

(2)   The power conferred by sub-paragraph (1)(a) includes –

  (a)   power to amend primary legislation (including primary legislation other than that which contains the incompatible provision); and

  (b)   power to amend or revoke subordinate legislation (including subordinate legislation other than that which contains the incompatible provision).

(3)   A remedial order may be made so as to have the same extent as the legislation which it affects.

(4)   No person is to be guilty of an offence solely as a result of the retrospective effect of a remedial order.

*Procedure*

**2**

No remedial order may be made unless –

    (a)    a draft of the order has been approved by a resolution of each House of Parliament made after the end of the period of 60 days beginning with the day on which the draft was laid; or

    (b)    it is declared in the order that it appears to the person making it that, because of the urgency of the matter, it is necessary to make the order without a draft being so approved.

*Orders laid in draft*

**3**

(1)   No draft may be laid under paragraph 2(a) unless –

    (a)    the person proposing to make the order has laid before Parliament a document which contains a draft of the proposed order and the required information; and

    (b)    the period of 60 days, beginning with the day on which the document required by this sub-paragraph was laid, has ended.

(2)   If representations have been made during that period, the draft laid under paragraph 2(a) must be accompanied by a statement containing –

    (a)    a summary of the representations; and

    (b)    if, as a result of the representations, the proposed order has been changed, details of the changes.

*Urgent cases*

**4**

(1)   If a remedial order ('the original order') is made without being approved in draft, the person making it must lay it before Parliament, accompanied by the required information, after it is made.

(2)   If representations have been made during the period of 60 days beginning with the day on which the original order was made, the person making it must (after the end of that period) lay before Parliament a statement containing –

    (a)    a summary of the representations; and

    (b)    if, as a result of the representations, he considers it appropriate to make changes to the original order, details of the changes.

(3)   If sub-paragraph (2)(b) applies, the person making the statement must –

    (a)    make a further remedial order replacing the original order; and

    (b)    lay the replacement order before Parliament.

(4)   If, at the end of the period of 120 days beginning with the day on which the original order was made, a resolution has not been passed by each House approving the original or replacement order, the order ceases to have effect (but without that affecting anything previously done under either order or the power to make a fresh remedial order).

*Definitions*

**5**

In this Schedule –

'representations' means representations about a remedial order (or proposed remedial order) made to the person making (or proposing to make) it and includes any relevant Parliamentary report or resolution; and

'required information' means –

(a) an explanation of the incompatibility which the order (or proposed order) seeks to remove, including particulars of the relevant declaration, finding or order; and

(b) a statement of the reasons for proceeding under section 10 and for making an order in those terms.

*Calculating periods*

**6**

In calculating any period for the purposes of this Schedule, no account is to be taken of any time during which –

(a) Parliament is dissolved or prorogued; or

(b) both Houses are adjourned for more than four days.

**7**

(1) This paragraph applies in relation to –

(a) any remedial order made, and any draft of such an order proposed to be made, –

(i) by the Scottish Ministers; or

(ii) within devolved competence (within the meaning of the Scotland Act 1998) by Her Majesty in Council; and

(b) any document or statement to be laid in connection with such an order (or proposed order).

(2) This Schedule has effect in relation to any such order (or proposed order), document or statement subject to the following modifications.

(3) Any reference to Parliament, each House of Parliament or both Houses of Parliament shall be construed as a reference to the Scottish Parliament.

(4) Paragraph 6 does not apply and instead, in calculating any period for the purposes of this Schedule, no account is to be taken of any time during which the Scottish Parliament is dissolved or is in recess for more than four days.

**Amendments**—Inserted by SI 2000/2040.

\*\*\*\*

## Schedule 4
## Judicial Pensions

Section 18(6)

### 1 Duty to make orders about pensions

(1) The appropriate Minister must by order make provision with respect to pensions payable to or in respect of any holder of a judicial office who serves as an ECHR judge.

(2) A pensions order must include such provision as the Minister making it considers is necessary to secure that –

(a)     an ECHR judge who was, immediately before his appointment as an ECHR judge, a member of a judicial pension scheme is entitled to remain as a member of that scheme;

(b)     the terms on which he remains a member of the scheme are those which would have been applicable had he not been appointed as an ECHR judge; and

(c)     entitlement to benefits payable in accordance with the scheme continues to be determined as if, while serving as an ECHR judge, his salary was that which would (but for section 18(4)) have been payable to him in respect of his continuing service as the holder of his judicial office.

### 2 Contributions

A pensions order may, in particular, make provision –

(a)     for any contributions which are payable by a person who remains a member of a scheme as a result of the order, and which would otherwise be payable by deduction from his salary, to be made otherwise than by deduction from his salary as an ECHR judge; and

(b)     for such contributions to be collected in such manner as may be determined by the administrators of the scheme.

### 3 Amendments of other enactments

A pensions order may amend any provision of, or made under, a pensions Act in such manner and to such extent as the Minister making the order considers necessary or expedient to ensure the proper administration of any scheme to which it relates.

### 4 Definitions

In this Schedule –

'appropriate Minister' means –

(a)     in relation to any judicial office whose jurisdiction is exercisable exclusively in relation to Scotland, the Secretary of State; and

(b)     otherwise, the Lord Chancellor;

'ECHR judge' means the holder of a judicial office who is serving as a judge of the Court;

'judicial pension scheme' means a scheme established by and in accordance with a pensions Act;

'pensions Act' means –

(a) the County Courts Act (Northern Ireland) 1959;
(b) the Sheriffs' Pensions (Scotland) Act 1961;
(c) the Judicial Pensions Act 1981; or
(d) the Judicial Pensions and Retirement Act 1993; and

'pensions order' means an order made under paragraph 1.

# TRIBUNALS COURTS AND ENFORCEMENT ACT 2007

\*\*\*\*

*'Judicial review'*

### 15  Upper Tribunal's 'judicial review' jurisdiction

(1)  The Upper Tribunal has power, in cases arising under the law of England and Wales or under the law of Northern Ireland, to grant the following kinds of relief –

    (a)    a mandatory order;
    (b)    a prohibiting order;
    (c)    a quashing order;
    (d)    a declaration;
    (e)    an injunction.

(2)  The power under subsection (1) may be exercised by the Upper Tribunal if –

    (a)    certain conditions are met (see section 18), or
    (b)    the tribunal is authorised to proceed even though not all of those conditions are met (see section 19(3) and (4)).

(3)  Relief under subsection (1) granted by the Upper Tribunal –

    (a)    has the same effect as the corresponding relief granted by the High Court on an application for judicial review, and
    (b)    is enforceable as if it were relief granted by the High Court on an application for judicial review.

(4)  In deciding whether to grant relief under subsection (1)(a), (b) or (c), the Upper Tribunal must apply the principles that the High Court would apply in deciding whether to grant that relief on an application for judicial review.

(5)  In deciding whether to grant relief under subsection (1)(d) or (e), the Upper Tribunal must –

    (a)    in cases arising under the law of England and Wales apply the principles that the High Court would apply in deciding whether to grant that relief under section 31(2) of the Senior Courts Act 1981 (c 54) on an application for judicial review, and
    (b)    in cases arising under the law of Northern Ireland apply the principles that the High Court would apply in deciding whether to grant that relief on an application for judicial review.

(6)  For the purposes of the application of subsection (3)(a) in relation to cases arising under the law of Northern Ireland –

    (a)    a mandatory order under subsection (1)(a) shall be taken to correspond to an order of mandamus,
    (b)    a prohibiting order under subsection (1)(b) shall be taken to correspond to an order of prohibition, and
    (c)    a quashing order under subsection (1)(c) shall be taken to correspond to an order of certiorari.

**Amendments**—Constitutional Reform Act 2005, s 59(5), Sch 11, Pt 1, para 1(2).

## 16 Application for relief under section 15(1)

(1) This section applies in relation to an application to the Upper Tribunal for relief under section 15(1).

(2) The application may be made only if permission (or, in a case arising under the law of Northern Ireland, leave) to make it has been obtained from the tribunal.

(3) The tribunal may not grant permission (or leave) to make the application unless it considers that the applicant has a sufficient interest in the matter to which the application relates.

(4) Subsection (5) applies where the tribunal considers –

    (a)    that there has been undue delay in making the application, and

    (b)    that granting the relief sought on the application would be likely to cause substantial hardship to, or substantially prejudice the rights of, any person or would be detrimental to good administration.

(5) The tribunal may –

    (a)    refuse to grant permission (or leave) for the making of the application;

    (b)    refuse to grant any relief sought on the application.

(6) The tribunal may award to the applicant damages, restitution or the recovery of a sum due if –

    (a)    the application includes a claim for such an award arising from any matter to which the application relates, and

    (b)    the tribunal is satisfied that such an award would have been made by the High Court if the claim had been made in an action begun in the High Court by the applicant at the time of making the application.

(7) An award under subsection (6) may be enforced as if it were an award of the High Court.

(8) Where –

    (a)    the tribunal refuses to grant permission (or leave) to apply for relief under section 15(1),

    (b)    the applicant appeals against that refusal, and

    (c)    the Court of Appeal grants the permission (or leave), the Court of Appeal may go on to decide the application for relief under section 15(1).

(9) Subsections (4) and (5) do not prevent Tribunal Procedure Rules from limiting the time within which applications may be made.

## 17 Quashing orders under section 15(1): supplementary provision

(1) If the Upper Tribunal makes a quashing order under section 15(1)(c) in respect of a decision, it may in addition –

(a)     remit the matter concerned to the court, tribunal or authority that made the decision, with a direction to reconsider the matter and reach a decision in accordance with the findings of the Upper Tribunal, or

(b)     substitute its own decision for the decision in question.

(2)  The power conferred by subsection (1)(b) is exercisable only if –

(a)     the decision in question was made by a court or tribunal,

(b)     the decision is quashed on the ground that there has been an error of law, and

(c)     without the error, there would have been only one decision that the court or tribunal could have reached.

(3)  Unless the Upper Tribunal otherwise directs, a decision substituted by it under subsection (1)(b) has effect as if it were a decision of the relevant court or tribunal.

**18  Limits of jurisdiction under section 15(1)**

(1)  This section applies where an application made to the Upper Tribunal seeks (whether or not alone) –

(a)     relief under section 15(1), or

(b)     permission (or, in a case arising under the law of Northern Ireland, leave) to apply for relief under section 15(1).

(2)  If Conditions 1 to 4 are met, the tribunal has the function of deciding the application.

(3)  If the tribunal does not have the function of deciding the application, it must by order transfer the application to the High Court.

(4)  Condition 1 is that the application does not seek anything other than –

(a)     relief under section 15(1);

(b)     permission (or, in a case arising under the law of Northern Ireland, leave) to apply for relief under section 15(1);

(c)     an award under section 16(6);

(d)     interest;

(e)     costs.

(5)  Condition 2 is that the application does not call into question anything done by the Crown Court.

(6)  Condition 3 is that the application falls within a class specified for the purposes of this subsection in a direction given in accordance with Part 1 of Schedule 2 to the Constitutional Reform Act 2005 (c 4).

(7)  The power to give directions under subsection (6) includes –

(a)     power to vary or revoke directions made in exercise of the power, and

(b)     power to make different provision for different purposes.

(8)  Condition 4 is that the judge presiding at the hearing of the application is either –

(a)     a judge of the High Court or the Court of Appeal in England and Wales or Northern Ireland, or a judge of the Court of Session, or

(b)     such other persons as may be agreed from time to time between the Lord Chief Justice, the Lord President, or the Lord Chief Justice of Northern Ireland, as the case may be, and the Senior President of Tribunals.

(9)  Where the application is transferred to the High Court under subsection (3) –

(a)     the application is to be treated for all purposes as if it –
   (i)     had been made to the High Court, and
   (ii)    sought things corresponding to those sought from the tribunal, and

(b)     any steps taken, permission (or leave) given or orders made by the tribunal in relation to the application are to be treated as taken, given or made by the High Court.

(10) Rules of court may make provision for the purpose of supplementing subsection (9).

(11) The provision that may be made by Tribunal Procedure Rules about amendment of an application for relief under section 15(1) includes, in particular, provision about amendments that would cause the application to become transferrable under subsection (3).

(12) For the purposes of subsection (9)(a)(ii), in relation to an application transferred to the High Court in Northern Ireland –

(a)     an order of mandamus shall be taken to correspond to a mandatory order under section 15(1)(a),
(b)     an order of prohibition shall be taken to correspond to a prohibiting order under section 15(1)(b), and
(c)     an order of certiorari shall be taken to correspond to a quashing order under section 15(1)(c).

**19  Transfer of judicial review applications from High Court**

(1) In the Senior Courts Act 1981 (c 54), after section 31 insert –

**'31A  Transfer of judicial review applications to Upper Tribunal**

(1) This section applies where an application is made to the High Court –

(a)     for judicial review, or
(b)     for permission to apply for judicial review.

(2) If Conditions 1, 2, 3 and 4 are met, the High Court must by order transfer the application to the Upper Tribunal.

(3) if Conditions 1, 2 and 4 are met, but Condition 3 is not, the High Court may by order transfer the application to the Upper Tribunal if it appears to the High Court to be just and convenient to do so.

(4)  Condition 1 is that the application does not seek anything other than –

(a)     relief under section 31(1)(a) and (b);
(b)     permission to apply for relief under section 31(1)(a) and (b);
(c)     an award under section 31(4);
(d)     interest;
(e)     costs.

(5) Condition 2 is that the application does not call into question anything done by the Crown Court.

(6) Condition 3 is that the application falls within a class specified under section 18(6) of the Tribunals, Courts and Enforcement Act 2007.

(7) Condition 4 is that the application does not call into question any decision made under –

    (a)    the Immigration Acts,

    (b)    the British Nationality Act 1981 (c 61),

    (c)    any instrument having effect under an enactment within paragraph (a) or (b), or

    (d)    any other provision of law for the time being in force which determines British citizenship, British overseas territories citizenship, the status of a British National (Overseas) or British Overseas citizenship.'

(2) In the Judicature (Northern Ireland) Act 1978 (c 23), after section 25 insert –

**'25A Transfer of judicial review applications to Upper Tribunal**

(1) This section applies where an application is made to the High Court –

    (a)    for judicial review, or

    (b)    for leave to apply for judicial review.

(2) If Conditions 1, 2, 3 and 4 are met, the High Court must by order transfer the application to the Upper Tribunal.

(3) If Conditions 1, 2 and 4 are met, but Condition 3 is not, the High Court may by order transfer the application to the Upper Tribunal if it appears to the High Court to be just and convenient to do so.

(4) Condition 1 is that the application does not seek anything other than –

    (a)    relief under section 18(1)(a) to (e);

    (b)    leave to apply for relief under section 18(1)(a) to (e);

    (c)    an award under section 20;

    (d)    interest;

    (e)    costs.

(5) Condition 2 is that the application does not call into question anything done by the Crown Court.

(6) Condition 3 is that the application falls within a class specified under section 18(6) of the Tribunals, Courts and Enforcement Act 2007.

(7) Condition 4 is that the application does not call into question any decision made under –

    (a)    the Immigration Acts,

    (b)    the British Nationality Act 1981,

    (c)    any instrument having effect under an enactment within paragraph (a) or (b), or

    (d)    any other provision of law for the time being in force which determines British citizenship, British overseas territories citizenship, the status of a British National (Overseas) or British Overseas citizenship.'

(3) Where an application is transferred to the Upper Tribunal under 31A of the Senior Courts Act 1981 (c 54) or section 25A of the Judicature (Northern Ireland) Act 1978 (transfer from the High Court of judicial review applications) –

    (a)    the application is to be treated for all purposes as if it –

        (i)    had been made to the tribunal, and

      (ii)    sought things corresponding to those sought from the High Court,

  (b)    the tribunal has the function of deciding the application, even if it does not fall within a class specified under section 18(6), and

  (c)    any steps taken, permission given, leave given or orders made by the High Court in relation to the application are to be treated as taken, given or made by the tribunal.

(4) Where –

  (a)    an application for permission is transferred to the Upper Tribunal under section 31A of the Senior Courts Act 1981 (c 54) and the tribunal grants permission, or

  (b)    an application for leave is transferred to the Upper Tribunal under section 25A of the Judicature (Northern Ireland) Act 1978 (c 23) and the tribunal grants leave, the tribunal has the function of deciding any subsequent application brought under the permission or leave, even if the subsequent application does not fall within a class specified under section 18(6).

(5) Tribunal Procedure Rules may make further provision for the purposes of supplementing subsections (3) and (4).

(6) For the purposes of subsection (3)(a)(ii), in relation to an application transferred to the Upper Tribunal under section 25A of the Judicature (Northern Ireland) Act 1978 –

  (a)    a mandatory order under section 15(1)(a) shall be taken to correspond to an order of mandamus,

  (b)    a prohibiting order under section 15(1)(b) shall be taken to correspond to an order of prohibition, and

  (c)    a quashing order under section 15(1)(c) shall be taken to correspond to an order of certiorari.

---

**Amendments**—Constitutional Reform Act 2005, s 59(5), Sch 11, Pt 1, para 1(2).

## 20 Transfer of judicial review applications from the Court of Session

(1) Where an application is made to the supervisory jurisdiction of the Court of Session, the Court –

  (a)    must, if Conditions 1, 2 and 4 are met, and

  (b)    may, if Conditions 1, 3 and 4 are met, but Condition 2 is not, by order transfer the application to the Upper Tribunal.

(2) Condition 1 is that the application does not seek anything other than an exercise of the supervisory jurisdiction of the Court of Session.

(3) Condition 2 is that the application falls within a class specified for the purposes of this subsection by act of sederunt made with the consent of the Lord Chancellor.

(4) Condition 3 is that the subject matter of the application is not a devolved Scottish matter.

(5) Condition 4 is that the application does not call into question any decision made under –

  (a)    the Immigration Acts,

(b) the British Nationality Act 1981 (c 61),

(c) any instrument having effect under an enactment within paragraph (a) or (b), or

(d) any other provision of law for the time being in force which determines British citizenship, British overseas territories citizenship, the status of a British National (Overseas) or British Overseas citizenship.

(6) There may not be specified under subsection (3) any class of application which includes an application the subject matter of which is a devolved Scottish matter.

(7) For the purposes of this section, the subject matter of an application is a devolved Scottish matter if it –

(a) concerns the exercise of functions in or as regards Scotland, and

(b) does not relate to a reserved matter within the meaning of the Scotland Act 1998 (c 46).

(8) In subsection (2), the reference to the exercise of the supervisory jurisdiction of the Court of Session includes a reference to the making of any order in connection with or in consequence of the exercise of that jurisdiction.

### 21 Upper Tribunal's 'judicial review' jurisdiction: Scotland

(1) The Upper Tribunal has the function of deciding applications transferred to it from the Court of Session under section 20(1).

(2) The powers of review of the Upper Tribunal in relation to such applications are the same as the powers of review of the Court of Session in an application to the supervisory jurisdiction of that Court.

(3) In deciding an application by virtue of subsection (1), the Upper Tribunal must apply principles that the Court of Session would apply in deciding an application to the supervisory jurisdiction of that Court.

(4) An order of the Upper Tribunal by virtue of subsection (1) –

(a) has the same effect as the corresponding order granted by the Court of Session on an application to the supervisory jurisdiction of that Court, and

(b) is enforceable as if it were an order so granted by that Court.

(5) Where an application is transferred to the Upper Tribunal by virtue of section 20(1), any steps taken or orders made by the Court of Session in relation to the application (other than the order to transfer the application under section 20(1)) are to be treated as taken or made by the tribunal.

(6) Tribunal Procedure Rules may make further provision for the purposes of supplementing subsection (5).

\*\*\*\*

# Civil Procedure Rules 1998

# SI 1998/3132

\*\*\*\*

## Practice Direction 32 – Evidence

### Evidence in General

1.1  Rule 32.2 sets out how evidence is to be given and facts are to be proved.

1.2  Evidence at a hearing other than the trial should normally be given by witness statement (see paragraph 17 onwards). However a witness may give evidence by affidavit if he wishes to do so (and see paragraph 1.4 below).

1.3  Statements of case (see paragraph 26 onwards) and application notices may also be used as evidence provided that their contents have been verified by a statement of truth.

(For information regarding evidence by deposition see Part 34 and Practice Direction 34A)

1.4  Affidavits must be used as evidence in the following instances:

(1)  where sworn evidence is required by an enactment ,rule, order or practice direction,

(2)  in any application for a search order, a freezing injunction, or an order requiring an occupier to permit another to enter his land, and

(3)  in any application for an order against anyone for alleged contempt of court.

1.5  If a party believes that sworn evidence is required by a court in another jurisdiction for any purpose connected with the proceedings, he may apply to the court for a direction that evidence shall be given only by affidavit on any pre-trial applications.

1.6  The court may give a direction under rule 32.15 that evidence shall be given by affidavit instead of or in addition to a witness statement or statement of case:

(1)  on its own initiative, or

(2)  after any party has applied to the court for such a direction.

1.7  An affidavit, where referred to in the Civil Procedure Rules or a practice direction, also means an affirmation unless the context requires otherwise.

### Affidavits

*Deponent*

2  A deponent is a person who gives evidence by affidavit or affirmation.

## Heading

3.1 The affidavit should be headed with the title of the proceedings (see paragraph 4 of Practice Direction 7A and paragraph 7 of Practice Direction 20); where the proceedings are between several parties with the same status it is sufficient to identify the parties as follows:

|  | Number: |
|---|---|
| A.B. (and others) | Claimants/Applicants |
| C.D. (and others) | Defendants/Respondents |
|  | (as appropriate) |

3.2 At the top right hand corner of the first page (and on the backsheet) there should be clearly written:

(1) the party on whose behalf it is made,
(2) the initials and surname of the deponent,
(3) the number of the affidavit in relation to that deponent,
(4) the identifying initials and number of each exhibit referred to, and
(5) the date sworn.

## Body of affidavit

4.1 The affidavit must, if practicable, be in the deponent's own words, the affidavit should be expressed in the first person and the deponent should:

(1) commence 'I (*full name*) of (*address*) state on oath ___ ',
(2) if giving evidence in his professional, business or other occupational capacity, give the address at which he works in (1) above, the position he holds and the name of his firm or employer,
(3) give his occupation or, if he has none, his description, and
(4) state if he is a party to the proceedings or employed by a party to the proceedings, if it be the case.

4.2 An affidavit must indicate:

(1) which of the statements in it are made from the deponent's own knowledge and which are matters of information or belief, and
(2) the source for any matters of information or belief.

4.3 Where a deponent:

(1) refers to an exhibit or exhibits, he should state 'there is now shown to me marked "___" the (*description of exhibit*)', and
(2) makes more than one affidavit (to which there are exhibits) in the same proceedings, the numbering of the exhibits should run consecutively throughout and not start again with each affidavit.

## Jurat

5.1 The jurat of an affidavit is a statement set out at the end of the document which authenticates the affidavit.

5.2 It must:

(1)    be signed by all deponents,

(2)    be completed and signed by the person before whom the affidavit was sworn whose name and qualification must be printed beneath his signature,

(3)    contain the full address of the person before whom the affidavit was sworn, and

(4)    follow immediately on from the text and not be put on a separate page.

## Format of affidavits

6.1 An affidavit should:

(1)    be produced on durable quality A4 paper with a 3.5 cm margin,

(2)    be fully legible and should normally be typed on one side of the paper only,

(3)    where possible, be bound securely in a manner which would not hamper filing, or otherwise each page should be endorsed with the case number and should bear the initials of the deponent and of the person before whom it was sworn,

(4)    have the pages numbered consecutively as a separate document (or as one of several documents contained in a file),

(5)    be divided into numbered paragraphs,

(6)    have all numbers, including dates, expressed in figures, and

(7)    give the reference to any document or documents mentioned either in the margin or in bold text in the body of the affidavit.

6.2 It is usually convenient for an affidavit to follow the chronological sequence of events or matters dealt with; each paragraph of an affidavit should as far as possible be confined to a distinct portion of the subject.

## Inability of deponent to read or sign affidavit

7.1 Where an affidavit is sworn by a person who is unable to read or sign it, the person before whom the affidavit is sworn must certify in the jurat that:

(1)    he read the affidavit to the deponent,

(2)    the deponent appeared to understand it, and

(3)    the deponent signed or made his mark, in his presence.

7.2 If that certificate is not included in the jurat, the affidavit may not be used in evidence unless the court is satisfied that it was read to the deponent and that he appeared to understand it. Two versions of the form of jurat with the certificate are set out at Annex 1 to this practice direction.

## Alterations to affidavits

8.1 Any alteration to an affidavit must be initialled by both the deponent and the person before whom the affidavit was sworn.

8.2 An affidavit which contains an alteration that has not been initialled may be filed or used in evidence only with the permission of the court.

## *Who may administer oaths and take affidavits*

9.1 Only the following may administer oaths and take affidavits –

(1) a commissioner for oaths,
(2) ...,
(3) other persons specified by statute;
(4) certain officials of the Senior Courts;
(5) a circuit judge or district judge;
(6) any justice of the peace; and
(7) certain officials of any county court appointed by the judge of that court for the purpose.

9.2 An affidavit must be sworn before a person independent of the parties or their representatives.

## *Filing of affidavits*

10.1 If the court directs that an affidavit is to be filed, it must be filed in the court or Division, or Office or Registry of the court or Division where the action in which it was or is to be used, is proceeding or will proceed.

10.2 Where an affidavit is in a foreign language:

(1) the party wishing to rely on it –
 (a) must have it translated, and
 (b) must file the foreign language affidavit with the court, and

(2) the translator must make and file with the court an affidavit verifying the translation and exhibiting both the translation and a copy of the foreign language affidavit.

## Exhibits

### *Manner of exhibiting documents*

11.1 A document used in conjunction with an affidavit should be:

(1) produced to and verified by the deponent, and remain separate from the affidavit, and
(2) identified by a declaration of the person before whom the affidavit was sworn.

11.2 The declaration should be headed with the name of the proceedings in the same way as the affidavit.

11.3 The first page of each exhibit should be marked:

(1) as in paragraph 3.2 above, and
(2) with the exhibit mark referred to in the affidavit.

### *Letters*

12.1 Copies of individual letters should be collected together and exhibited in a bundle or bundles. They should be arranged in chronological order with the earliest at the top, and firmly secured.

12.2 When a bundle of correspondence is exhibited, the exhibit should have a front page attached stating that the bundle consists of original letters and copies. They should be arranged and secured as above and numbered consecutively.

## Other documents

13.1 Photocopies instead of original documents may be exhibited provided the originals are made available for inspection by the other parties before the hearing and by the judge at the hearing.

13.2 Court documents must not be exhibited (official copies of such documents prove themselves).

13.3 Where an exhibit contains more than one document, a front page should be attached setting out a list of the documents contained in the exhibit; the list should contain the dates of the documents.

## Exhibits other than documents

14.1 Items other than documents should be clearly marked with an exhibit number or letter in such a manner that the mark cannot become detached from the exhibit.

14.2 Small items may be placed in a container and the container appropriately marked.

## General provisions

15.1 Where an exhibit contains more than one document:

    (1)    the bundle should not be stapled but should be securely fastened in a way that does not hinder the reading of the documents, and

    (2)    the pages should be numbered consecutively at bottom centre.

15.2 Every page of an exhibit should be clearly legible; typed copies of illegible documents should be included, paginated with 'a' numbers.

15.3 Where affidavits and exhibits have become numerous, they should be put into separate bundles and the pages numbered consecutively throughout.

15.4 Where on account of their bulk the service of exhibits or copies of exhibits on the other parties would be difficult or impracticable, the directions of the court should be sought as to arrangements for bringing the exhibits to the attention of the other parties and as to their custody pending trial.

## Affirmations

16 All provisions in this or any other practice direction relating to affidavits apply to affirmations with the following exceptions:

    (1)    the deponent should commence 'I (*name*) of (*address*) do solemnly and sincerely affirm ___', and

    (2)    in the jurat the word 'sworn' is replaced by the word 'affirmed'.

## Witness Statements

### Heading

17.1 The witness statement should be headed with the title of the proceedings (see paragraph 4 of Practice Direction 7A and paragraph 7 of Practice Direction 20); where the proceedings are between several parties with the same status it is sufficient to identify the parties as follows:

|  | Number: |
| --- | --- |
| A.B. (and others) | Claimants/Applicants |
| C.D. (and others) | Defendants/Respondents |
|  | (as appropriate) |

17.2 At the top right hand corner of the first page there should be clearly written:

(1)     the party on whose behalf it is made,
(2)     the initials and surname of the witness,
(3)     the number of the statement in relation to that witness,
(4)     the identifying initials and number of each exhibit referred to, and
(5)     the date the statement was made.

### Body of witness statement

18.1 The witness statement must, if practicable, be in the intended witness's own words, the statement should be expressed in the first person and should also state:

(1)     the full name of the witness,
(2)     his place of residence or, if he is making the statement in his professional, business or other occupational capacity, the address at which he works, the position he holds and the name of his firm or employer,
(3)     his occupation, or if he has none, his description, and
(4)     the fact that he is a party to the proceedings or is the employee of such a party if it be the case.

18.2 A witness statement must indicate:

(1)     which of the statements in it are made from the witness's own knowledge and which are matters of information or belief, and
(2)     the source for any matters of information or belief.

18.3 An exhibit used in conjunction with a witness statement should be verified and identified by the witness and remain separate from the witness statement.

18.4 Where a witness refers to an exhibit or exhibits, he should state 'I refer to the (*description of exhibit*) marked "___" '.

18.5 The provisions of paragraphs 11.3 to 15.4 (exhibits) apply similarly to witness statements as they do to affidavits.

18.6 Where a witness makes more than one witness statement to which there are exhibits, in the same proceedings, the numbering of the exhibits should run consecutively throughout and not start again with each witness statement.

## Format of witness statement

19.1 A witness statement should:

(1)    be produced on durable quality A4 paper with a 3.5 cm margin,

(2)    be fully legible and should normally be typed on one side of the paper only,

(3)    where possible, be bound securely in a manner which would not hamper filing, or otherwise each page should be endorsed with the case number and should bear the initials of the witness,

(4)    have the pages numbered consecutively as a separate statement (or as one of several statements contained in a file),

(5)    be divided into numbered paragraphs,

(6)    have all numbers, including dates, expressed in figures, and

(7)    give the reference to any document or documents mentioned either in the margin or in bold text in the body of the statement.

19.2 It is usually convenient for a witness statement to follow the chronological sequence of the events or matters dealt with, each paragraph of a witness statement should as far as possible be confined to a distinct portion of the subject.

## Statement of truth

20.1 A witness statement is the equivalent of the oral evidence which that witness would, if called, give in evidence; it must include a statement by the intended witness that he believes the facts in it are true.

20.2 To verify a witness statement the statement of truth is as follows:

'I believe that the facts stated in this witness statement are true'

20.3 Attention is drawn to rule 32.14 which sets out the consequences of verifying a witness statement containing a false statement without an honest belief in its truth.

(Paragraph 3A of Practice Direction 22 sets out the procedure to be followed where the person who should sign a document which is verified by a statement of truth is unable to read or sign the document)

## Alterations to witness statements

22.1 Any alteration to a witness statement must be initialled by the person making the statement or by the authorised person where appropriate (see paragraph 21).

22.2 A witness statement which contains an alteration that has not been initialled may be used in evidence only with the permission of the court.

## Filing of witness statements

23.1 If the court directs that a witness statement is to be filed, it must be filed in the court or Division, or Office or Registry of the court or Division where the action in which it was or is to be used, is proceeding or will proceed.

23.2 Where the court has directed that a witness statement in a foreign language is to be filed:

    (1)    the party wishing to rely on it must –
        (a)    have it translated, and
        (b)    file the foreign language witness statement with the court, and

    (2)    the translator must make and file with the court an affidavit verifying the translation and exhibiting both the translation and a copy of the foreign language witness statement.

## Certificate of court officer

24.1 Where the court has ordered that a witness statement is not to be open to inspection by the public or that words or passages in the statement are not to be open to inspection the court officer will so certify on the statement and make any deletions directed by the court under rule 32.13(4).

## Defects in affidavits, witness statements and exhibits

25.1 Where:

    (1)    an affidavit,
    (2)    a witness statement, or
    (3)    an exhibit to either an affidavit or a witness statement,

does not comply with Part 32 or this practice direction in relation to its form, the court may refuse to admit it as evidence and may refuse to allow the costs arising from its preparation.

25.2 Permission to file a defective affidavit or witness statement or to use a defective exhibit may be obtained from a judge in the court where the case is proceeding.

## Statements of Case

26.1 A statement of case may be used as evidence in an interim application provided it is verified by a statement of truth.

26.2 To verify a statement of case the statement of truth should be set out as follows:

> 'I believe the (*party on whose behalf the statement of case is being signed*) believes that the facts stated in the statement of case are true'.

26.3 Attention is drawn to rule 32.14 which sets out the consequences of verifying a witness statement containing a false statement without an honest belief in its truth.

(For information regarding statements of truth see Part 22 and Practice Direction 22)

(Practice Directions 7A and 17 provide further information concerning statements of case)

## Agreed Bundles for Hearings

27.1 The court may give directions requiring the parties to use their best endeavours to agree a bundle or bundles of documents for use at any hearing.

27.2 All documents contained in bundles which have been agreed for use at a hearing shall be admissible at that hearing as evidence of their contents, unless –

   (1)    the court orders otherwise; or

   (2)    a party gives written notice of objection to the admissibility of particular documents.

## Penalty

28.1

   (1)    Where a party alleges that a statement of truth or a disclosure statement is false the party must refer that allegation to the court dealing with the claim in which the statement of truth or disclosure statement has been made.

   (2)    The court may –

       (a)    exercise any of its powers under the rules;

       (b)    initiate steps to consider if there is a contempt of court and, where there is, to punish it;

       (Practice Direction RSC 52 and CCR 29 makes provision where committal to prison is a possibility if contempt is proved)

       (c)    direct the party making the allegation to refer the matter to the Attorney General with a request that the Attorney General consider whether to bring proceedings for contempt of court.

28.2

   (1)    A request to the Attorney General must be made in writing and sent to the Attorney General's Office at 20 Victoria Street, London, SW1H 0NF. The request must be accompanied by a copy of the order directing that the matter be referred to the Attorney General and must –

   (a)    identify the statement said to be false;

   (b)    explain –

       (i)    why it is false; and

       (ii)    why the maker knew the statement to be false at the time it was made; and

   (c)    explain why contempt proceedings would be appropriate in the light of the overriding objective in Part 1.

(2) The Attorney General prefers a request that comes from the court to one made direct by a party to the claim in which the alleged contempt occurred without prior consideration by the court. A request to the Attorney General is not a way of appealing against, or reviewing the decision of the judge.

28.3 Where a party makes an application to the court for permission to commence proceedings for contempt of court, it must be supported by written evidence of the facts and matters specified in paragraph 28.2(1) and the result of the request to the Attorney General made by the applicant.

28.4 The rules do not change the law of contempt or introduce new categories of contempt. A person applying to commence such proceedings should consider whether the incident complained of does amount to contempt of court and whether such proceedings would further the overriding objective in Part 1 of the Civil Procedure Rules.

## Video Conferencing

29.1 Guidance on the use of video conferencing in the civil courts is set out at Annex 3 to this practice direction.

A list of the sites which are available for video conferencing can be found on Her Majesty's Courts Service website at www.hmcourts-service.gov.uk.

## Annex 1

## Certificate to be used Where a Deponent to an Affidavit is Unable to Read or Sign it

Sworn at   this   day of   Before me, I having first read over the contents of this affidavit to the deponent *if there are exhibits, add* 'and explained the nature and effect of the exhibits referred to in it' who appeared to understand it and approved its content as accurate, and made his mark on the affidavit in my presence.

*Or,* (after, *Before me*) the witness to the mark of the deponent having been first sworn that he had read over etc (*as above*) and that he saw him make his mark on the affidavit. (*Witness must sign*).

## Certificate to be Used Where a Deponent to an Affirmation is Unable to Read or Sign it

Affirmed at   this   day of   Before me, I having first read over the contents of this affirmation to the deponent *if there are exhibits, add* 'and explained the nature and effect of the exhibits referred to in it' who appeared to understand it and approved its content as accurate, and made his mark on the affirmation in my presence.

*Or,* (after, *Before me*) the witness to the mark of the deponent having been first sworn that he had read over etc (*as above*) and that he saw him make his mark on the affirmation. (*Witness must sign*).

## Annex 3

## Video Conferencing Guidance

This guidance is for the use of video conferencing (VCF) in civil proceedings. It is in part based, with permission, upon the protocol of the Federal Court of Australia. It is intended to provide a guide to all persons involved in the use of VCF, although it does not attempt to cover all the practical questions which might arise.

## Video conferencing generally

1 The guidance covers the use of VCF equipment both (a) in a courtroom, whether via equipment which is permanently placed there or via a mobile unit, and (b) in a separate studio or conference room. In either case, the location at which the judge sits is referred to as the 'local site'. The other site or sites to and from which transmission is made are referred to as 'the remote site' and in any particular case any such site may be another courtroom. The guidance applies to cases where VCF is used for the taking of evidence and also to its use for other parts of any legal proceedings (for example, interim applications, case management conferences, pre-trial reviews).

2 VCF may be a convenient way of dealing with any part of proceedings: it can involve considerable savings in time and cost. Its use for the taking of evidence from overseas witnesses will, in particular, be likely to achieve a material saving of costs, and such savings may also be achieved by its use for taking domestic evidence. It is, however, inevitably not as ideal as having the witness physically present in court. Its convenience should not therefore be allowed to dictate its use. A judgment must be made in every case in which the use of VCF is being considered not only as to whether it will achieve an overall cost saving but as to whether its use will be likely to be beneficial to the efficient, fair and economic disposal of the litigation. In particular, it needs to be recognised that the degree of control a court can exercise over a witness at the remote site is or may be more limited than it can exercise over a witness physically before it.

3 When used for the taking of evidence, the objective should be to make the VCF session as close as possible to the usual practice in a trial court where evidence is taken in open court. To gain the maximum benefit, several differences have to be taken into account. Some matters, which are taken for granted when evidence is taken in the conventional way, take on a different dimension when it is taken by VCF: for example, the administration of the oath, ensuring that the witness understands who is at the local site and what their various roles are, the raising of any objections to the evidence and the use of documents.

4 It should not be presumed that all foreign governments are willing to allow their nationals or others within their jurisdiction to be examined before a court in England or Wales by means of VCF. If there is any doubt about this, enquiries should be directed to the Foreign and Commonwealth Office (International Legal Matters Unit, Consular Division) with a view to ensuring that the country from which the evidence is to be taken raises no objection to it at diplomatic level. The party who is directed to be responsible for arranging the VCF (see paragraph 8 below) will be required to make all necessary inquiries about this well in advance of the VCF and must be able to inform the court what those inquiries were and of their outcome.

5 Time zone differences need to be considered when a witness abroad is to be examined in England or Wales by VCF. The convenience of the witness, the parties, their representatives and the court must all be taken into account. The cost of the use of a commercial studio is usually greater outside normal business hours.

6 Those involved with VCF need to be aware that, even with the most advanced systems currently available, there are the briefest of delays between the receipt of the picture and that of the accompanying sound. If due allowance is not made for

this, there will be a tendency to 'speak over' the witness, whose voice will continue to be heard for a millisecond or so after he or she appears on the screen to have finished speaking.

7 With current technology, picture quality is good, but not as good as a television picture. The quality of the picture is enhanced if those appearing on VCF monitors keep their movements to a minimum.

## Preliminary arrangements

8 The court's permission is required for any part of any proceedings to be dealt with by means of VCF. Before seeking a direction, the applicant should notify the listing officer, diary manager or other appropriate court officer of the intention to seek it, and should enquire as to the availability of court VCF equipment for the day or days of the proposed VCF. The application for a direction should be made to the master, district judge or judge, as may be appropriate. If all parties consent to a direction, permission can be sought by letter, fax or e-mail, although the court may still require an oral hearing. All parties are entitled to be heard on whether or not such a direction should be given and as to its terms. If a witness at a remote site is to give evidence by an interpreter, consideration should be given at this stage as to whether the interpreter should be at the local site or the remote site. If a VCF direction is given, arrangements for the transmission will then need to be made. The court will ordinarily direct that the party seeking permission to use VCF is to be responsible for this. That party is hereafter referred to as 'the VCF arranging party'.

9 Subject to any order to the contrary, all costs of the transmission, including the costs of hiring equipment and technical personnel to operate it, will initially be the responsibility of, and must be met by, the VCF arranging party. All reasonable efforts should be made to keep the transmission to a minimum and so keep the costs down. All such costs will be considered to be part of the costs of the proceedings and the court will determine at such subsequent time as is convenient or appropriate who, as between the parties, should be responsible for them and (if appropriate) in what proportions.

10 The local site will, if practicable, be a courtroom but it may instead be an appropriate studio or conference room. The VCF arranging party must contact the listing officer, diary manager or other appropriate officer of the court which made the VCF direction and make arrangements for the VCF transmission. Details of the remote site, and of the equipment to be used both at the local site (if not being supplied by the court) and the remote site (including the number of ISDN lines and connection speed), together with all necessary contact names and telephone numbers, will have to be provided to the listing officer, diary manager or other court officer. The court will need to be satisfied that any equipment provided by the parties for use at the local site and also that at the remote site is of sufficient quality for a satisfactory transmission. The VCF arranging party must ensure that an appropriate person will be present at the local site to supervise the operation of the VCF throughout the transmission in order to deal with any technical problems. That party must also arrange for a technical assistant to be similarly present at the remote site for like purposes.

11 It is recommended that the judge, practitioners and witness should arrive at their respective VCF sites about 20 minutes prior to the scheduled commencement of the transmission.

12 If the local site is not a courtroom, but a conference room or studio, the judge will need to determine who is to sit where. The VCF arranging party must take care to ensure that the number of microphones is adequate for the speakers and that the panning of the camera for the practitioners' table encompasses all legal representatives so that the viewer can see everyone seated there.

13 The proceedings, wherever they may take place, form part of a trial to which the public is entitled to have access (unless the court has determined that they should be heard in private). If the local site is to be a studio or conference room, the VCF arranging party must ensure that it provides sufficient accommodation to enable a reasonable number of members of the public to attend.

14 In cases where the local site is a studio or conference room, the VCF arranging party should make arrangements, if practicable, for the royal coat of arms to be placed above the judge's seat.

15 In cases in which the VCF is to be used for the taking of evidence, the VCF arranging party must arrange for recording equipment to be provided by the court which made the VCF direction so that the evidence can be recorded. An associate will normally be present to operate the recording equipment when the local site is a courtroom. The VCF arranging party should take steps to ensure that an associate is present to do likewise when it is a studio or conference room. The equipment should be set up and tested before the VCF transmission. It will often be a valuable safeguard for the VCF arranging party also to arrange for the provision of recording equipment at the remote site. This will provide a useful back-up if there is any reduction in sound quality during the transmission. A direction from the court for the making of such a back-up recording must, however, be obtained first. This is because the proceedings are court proceedings and, save as directed by the court, no other recording of them must be made. The court will direct what is to happen to the back-up recording.

16 Some countries may require that any oath or affirmation to be taken by a witness accord with local custom rather than the usual form of oath or affirmation used in England and Wales. The VCF arranging party must make all appropriate prior inquiries and put in place all arrangements necessary to enable the oath or affirmation to be taken in accordance with any local custom. That party must be in a position to inform the court what those inquiries were, what their outcome was and what arrangements have been made. If the oath or affirmation can be administered in the manner normal in England and Wales, the VCF arranging party must arrange in advance to have the appropriate holy book at the remote site. The associate will normally administer the oath.

17 Consideration will need to be given in advance to the documents to which the witness is likely to be referred. The parties should endeavour to agree on this. It will usually be most convenient for a bundle of the copy documents to be prepared in advance, which the VCF arranging party should then send to the remote site.

18 Additional documents are sometimes quite properly introduced during the course of a witness's evidence. To cater for this, the VCF arranging party should ensure that equipment is available to enable documents to be transmitted between sites during the course of the VCF transmission. Consideration should be given to whether to use a document camera. If it is decided to use one, arrangements for its use will need to be established in advance. The panel operator will need to know the number and size of documents or objects if their images are to be sent by

document camera. In many cases, a simpler and sufficient alternative will be to ensure that there are fax transmission and reception facilities at the participating sites.

## The hearing

19 The procedure for conducting the transmission will be determined by the judge. He will determine who is to control the cameras. In cases where the VCF is being used for an application in the course of the proceedings, the judge will ordinarily not enter the local site until both sites are on line. Similarly, at the conclusion of the hearing, he will ordinarily leave the local site while both sites are still on line. The following paragraphs apply primarily to cases where the VCF is being used for the taking of the evidence of a witness at a remote site. In all cases, the judge will need to decide whether court dress is appropriate when using VCF facilities. It might be appropriate when transmitting from courtroom to courtroom. It might not be when a commercial facility is being used.

20 At the beginning of the transmission, the judge will probably wish to introduce himself and the advocates to the witness. He will probably want to know who is at the remote site and will invite the witness to introduce himself and anyone else who is with him. He may wish to give directions as to the seating arrangements at the remote site so that those present are visible at the local site during the taking of the evidence. He will probably wish to explain to the witness the method of taking the oath or of affirming, the manner in which the evidence will be taken, and who will be conducting the examination and cross-examination. He will probably also wish to inform the witness of the matters referred to in paragraphs 6 and 7 above (co-ordination of picture with sound, and picture quality).

21 The examination of the witness at the remote site should follow as closely as possible the practice adopted when a witness is in the courtroom. During examination, cross-examination and re-examination, the witness must be able to see the legal representative asking the question and also any other person (whether another legal representative or the judge) making any statements in regard to the witness's evidence. It will in practice be most convenient if everyone remains seated throughout the transmission.

****

# Part 44 – General Rules about Costs

**Contents of this Part**

**44.1 Scope of this Part**

This Part contains general rules about costs, entitlement to costs and orders in respect of pro bono representation.

---

**Amendments**—SI 2008/2178.

**44.2 Solicitor's duty to notify client**

Where –

(a)     the court makes a costs order against a legally represented party; and
(b)     the party is not present when the order is made,

the party's solicitor must notify his client in writing of the costs order no later than 7 days after the solicitor receives notice of the order.

**44.3 Court's discretion and circumstances to be taken into account when exercising its discretion as to costs**

(1) The court has discretion as to –

(a)     whether costs are payable by one party to another;
(b)     the amount of those costs; and
(c)     when they are to be paid.

(2) If the court decides to make an order about costs –

(a)     the general rule is that the unsuccessful party will be ordered to pay the costs of the successful party; but
(b)     the court may make a different order.

(3) The general rule does not apply to the following proceedings –

(a)     proceedings in the Court of Appeal on an application or appeal made in connection with proceedings in the Family Division; or
(b)     proceedings in the Court of Appeal from a judgment, direction, decision or order given or made in probate proceedings or family proceedings.

(4) In deciding what order (if any) to make about costs, the court must have regard to all the circumstances, including –

(a)     the conduct of all the parties;
(b)     whether a party has succeeded on part of his case, even if he has not been wholly successful; and
(c)     any payment into court or admissible offer to settle made by a party which is drawn to the court's attention, and which is not an offer to which costs consequences under Part 36 apply.

(5) The conduct of the parties includes –

(a)     conduct before, as well as during, the proceedings and in particular the extent to which the parties followed the Practice Direction (Pre-Action Conduct) or;any relevant pre-action protocol;
(b)     whether it was reasonable for a party to raise, pursue or contest a particular allegation or issue;
(c)     the manner in which a party has pursued or defended his case or a particular allegation or issue; and
(d)     whether a claimant who has succeeded in his claim, in whole or in part, exaggerated his claim.

(6) The orders which the court may make under this rule include an order that a party must pay –

(a)     a proportion of another party's costs;
(b)     a stated amount in respect of another party's costs;

- (c)   costs from or until a certain date only;
- (d)   costs incurred before proceedings have begun;
- (e)   costs relating to particular steps taken in the proceedings;
- (f)   costs relating only to a distinct part of the proceedings; and
- (g)   interest on costs from or until a certain date, including a date before judgment.

(7) Where the court would otherwise consider making an order under paragraph (6)(f), it must instead, if practicable, make an order under paragraph (6)(a) or (c).

(8) Where the court has ordered a party to pay costs, it may order an amount to be paid on account before the costs are assessed.

(9) Where a party entitled to costs is also liable to pay costs the court may assess the costs which that party is liable to pay and either –

- (a)   set off the amount assessed against the amount the party is entitled to be paid and direct him to pay any balance; or
- (b)   delay the issue of a certificate for the costs to which the party is entitled until he has paid the amount which he is liable to pay.

**Amendments**—SI 2006/3435.

### 44.3A  Costs orders relating to funding arrangements

(1) The court will not assess any additional liability until the conclusion of the proceedings, or the part of the proceedings, to which the funding arrangement relates.

('Funding arrangement' and 'additional liability' are defined in rule 43.2)

(2) At the conclusion of the proceedings, or the part of the proceedings, to which the funding arrangement relates the court may –

- (a)   make a summary assessment of all the costs, including any additional liability;
- (b)   make an order for detailed assessment of the additional liability but make a summary assessment of the other costs; or
- (c)   make an order for detailed assessment of all the costs.

(Part 47 sets out the procedure for the detailed assessment of costs)

**Amendments**—Inserted by SI 2000/1317.

### 44.3B  Limits on recovery under funding arrangements

(1) Unless the court orders otherwise, a party may not recover as an additional liability –

- (a)   any proportion of the percentage increase relating to the cost to the legal representative of the postponement of the payment of his fees and expenses;
- (b)   any provision made by a membership organisation which exceeds the likely cost to that party of the premium of an insurance policy against the risk of incurring a liability to pay the costs of other parties to the proceedings;

(c)     any additional liability for any period during which that party failed to provide information about a funding arrangement in accordance with a rule, practice direction or court order;

(d)     any percentage increase where a party has failed to comply with –

     (i)     a requirement in the Costs Practice Direction; or

     (ii)    a court order,

to disclose in any assessment proceedings, the reasons for setting the percentage increase at the level stated in the conditional fee agreement.

(e)     any insurance premium where that party has failed to provide information about the insurance policy in question by the time required by a rule, practice direction or court order. (Paragraph 9.3 of the Practice Direction (Pre-Action Conduct) provides that a party must inform any other party as soon as possible about a funding arrangement entered into before the start of proceedings.);

(2) This rule does not apply in any assessment under rule 48.9 (assessment of a solicitor's bill to his client).

(Rule 3.9 sets out the circumstances the court will consider on an application for the relief from a sanction for the failure to comply with any rule, practice direction or court order)

---

**Amendments**—SI 2000/1317; SI 2009/2092; SI 2009/3390.

### 44.3C Orders in respect of pro bono representation

(1) In this rule, 'the 2007 Act' means the Legal Services Act 2007.

(2) Where the court makes an order under section 194(3) of the 2007 Act –

(a)     the court may order the payment to the prescribed charity of a sum no greater than the costs specified in Part 45 to which the party with pro bono representation would have been entitled in accordance with that Part and in respect of that representation had it not been provided free of charge; or

(b)     where Part 45 does not apply, the court may determine the amount of the payment (other than a sum equivalent to fixed costs) to be made by the paying party to the prescribed charity by –

     (i)     making a summary assessment; or

     (ii)    making an order for detailed assessment,

of a sum equivalent to all or part of the costs the paying party would have been ordered to pay to the party with pro bono representation in respect of that representation had it not been provided free of charge.

(3) Where the court makes an order under section 194(3) of the 2007 Act, the order must specify that the payment by the paying party must be made to the prescribed charity.

(4) The receiving party must send a copy of the order to the prescribed charity within 7 days of receipt of the order.

(5) Where the court considers making or makes an order under section 194(3) of the 2007 Act, Parts 43 to 48 apply, where appropriate, with the following modifications –

(a)     references to 'costs orders', 'orders about costs' or 'orders for the payment of costs' are to be read, unless otherwise stated, as if they refer to an order under section 194(3);

(b)     references to 'costs' are to be read, as if they referred to a sum equivalent to the costs that would have been claimed by, incurred by or awarded to the party with pro bono representation in respect of that representation had it not been provided free of charge; and

(c)     references to 'receiving party' are to be read, as meaning a party who has pro bono representation and who would have been entitled to be paid costs in respect of that representation had it not been provided free of charge.

**Amendments**—Inserted by SI 2008/2178.

## 44.4 Basis of assessment

(1) Where the court is to assess the amount of costs (whether by summary or detailed assessment) it will assess those costs –

(a)     on the standard basis; or
(b)     on the indemnity basis,

but the court will not in either case allow costs which have been unreasonably incurred or are unreasonable in amount.

(Rule 48.3 sets out how the court decides the amount of costs payable under a contract)

(2) Where the amount of costs is to be assessed on the standard basis, the court will –

(a)     only allow costs which are proportionate to the matters in issue; and
(b)     resolve any doubt which it may have as to whether costs were reasonably incurred or reasonable and proportionate in amount in favour of the paying party.

(Factors which the court may take into account are set out in rule 44.5)

(3) Where the amount of costs is to be assessed on the indemnity basis, the court will resolve any doubt which it may have as to whether costs were reasonably incurred or were reasonable in amount in favour of the receiving party.

(4) Where –

(a)     the court makes an order about costs without indicating the basis on which the costs are to be assessed; or
(b)     the court makes an order for costs to be assessed on a basis other than the standard basis or the indemnity basis,

the costs will be assessed on the standard basis.

(5) (*revoked*)

(6) Where the amount of a solicitor's remuneration in respect of non-contentious business is regulated by any general orders made under the Solicitors Act 1974, the amount of the costs to be allowed in respect of any such business which falls to be assessed by the court will be decided in accordance with those general orders rather than this rule and rule 44.5.

Amendments—SI 2000/1317.

### 44.5 Factors to be taken into account in deciding the amount of costs

(1) The court is to have regard to all the circumstances in deciding whether costs were –

  (a) if it is assessing costs on the standard basis –
      (i) proportionately and reasonably incurred; or
      (ii) were proportionate and reasonable in amount, or

  (b) if it is assessing costs on the indemnity basis –
      (i) unreasonably incurred; or
      (ii) unreasonable in amount.

(2) In particular the court must give effect to any orders which have already been made.

(3) The court must also have regard to –

  (a) the conduct of all the parties, including in particular –
      (i) conduct before, as well as during, the proceedings; and
      (ii) the efforts made, if any, before and during the proceedings in order to try to resolve the dispute;

  (b) the amount or value of any money or property involved;
  (c) the importance of the matter to all the parties;
  (d) the particular complexity of the matter or the difficulty or novelty of the questions raised;
  (e) the skill, effort, specialised knowledge and responsibility involved;
  (f) the time spent on the case; and
  (g) the place where and the circumstances in which work or any part of it was done.

  (Rule 35.4(4) gives the court power to limit the amount that a party may recover with regard to the fees and expenses of an expert)

### 44.6 Fixed costs

A party may recover the fixed costs specified in Part 45 in accordance with that Part.

### 44.7 Procedure for assessing costs

Where the court orders a party to pay costs to another party (other than fixed costs) it may either –

  (a) make a summary assessment of the costs; or
  (b) order detailed assessment of the costs by a costs officer,

unless any rule, practice direction or other enactment provides otherwise.

(The Costs Practice Direction sets out the factors which will affect the court's decision under this rule)

Amendments—SI 2009/3390.

**44.8 Time for complying with an order for costs**

A party must comply with an order for the payment of costs within 14 days of –

(a) the date of the judgment or order if it states the amount of those costs,

(b) if the amount of those costs (or part of them) is decided later in accordance with Part 47, the date of the certificate which states the amount; or

(c) in either case, such later date as the court may specify.

(Part 47 sets out the procedure for detailed assessment of costs)

Amendments—SI 2000/1317.

**44.9 Costs on the small claims track and fast track**

(1) Part 27 (small claims) and Part 46 (fast track trial costs) contain special rules about –

(a) liability for costs;

(b) the amount of costs which the court may award; and

(c) the procedure for assessing costs.

(2) Once a claim is allocated to a particular track, those special rules shall apply to the period before, as well as after, allocation except where the court or a practice direction provides otherwise.

Amendments—SI 1999/1008.

**44.10 Limitation on amount court may allow where a claim allocated to the fast track settles before trial**

(1) Where the court –

(a) assesses costs in relation to a claim which –

(i) has been allocated to the fast track; and

(ii) settles before the start of the trial; and

(b) is considering the amount of costs to be allowed in respect of a party's advocate for preparing for the trial,

it may not allow in respect of those advocate's costs, an amount that exceeds the amount of fast track trial costs which would have been payable in relation to the claim had the trial taken place.

(2) When deciding the amount to be allowed in respect of the advocate's costs, the court shall have regard to –

(a) when the claim was settled; and

(b) when the court was notified that the claim had settled.

(3) In this rule, 'advocate' and 'fast track trial costs' have the meanings given to them by Part 46.

(Part 46 sets out the amount of fast track trial costs which may be awarded)

**44.11 Costs following allocation and re-allocation**

(1) Any costs orders made before a claim is allocated will not be affected by allocation.

(2) Where –

    (a)    a claim is allocated to a track; and

    (b)    the court subsequently re-allocates that claim to a different track;

then unless the court orders otherwise, any special rules about costs applying –

        (i)    to the first track, will apply to the claim up to the date of re-allocation; and

        (ii)    to the second track, will apply from the date of re-allocation.

(Part 26 deals with the allocation and re-allocation of claims between tracks)

### 44.12 Cases where costs orders deemed to have been made

(1) Where a right to costs arises under –

    (a)    rule 3.7 (defendant's right to costs where claim struck out for non-payment of fees);

    (b)    rule 36.10(1) or (2) (claimant's entitlement to costs where a Part 36 offer is accepted);

    (c)    (*revoked*)

    (d)    rule 38.6 (defendant's right to costs where claimant discontinues),

a costs order will be deemed to have been made on the standard basis.

(1A) Where such an order is deemed to be made in favour of a party with pro bono representation, that party may apply for an order under section 194(3) of the Legal Services Act 2007.

(2) Interest payable pursuant to section 17 of the Judgments Act 1838 or section 74 of the County Courts Act 1984 on the costs deemed to have been ordered under paragraph (1) shall begin to run from the date on which the event which gave rise to the entitlement to costs occurred.

Amendments—SI 2006/3435; SI 2008/2178.

### 44.12A Costs-only proceedings

(1) This rule sets out a procedure which may be followed where –

    (a)    the parties to a dispute have reached an agreement on all issues (including which party is to pay the costs) which is made or confirmed in writing; but

    (b)    they have failed to agree the amount of those costs; and

    (c)    no proceedings have been started.

(1A) (*revoked*)

(2) Either party to the agreement may start proceedings under this rule by issuing a claim form in accordance with Part 8.

(3) The claim form must contain or be accompanied by the agreement or confirmation.

(4) Except as provided in paragraph (4A), in proceedings to which this rule applies the court –

    (a)    may –

        (i)    make an order for costs to be determined by detailed assessment; or

      (ii)    dismiss the claim; and

  (b)    must dismiss the claim if it is opposed.

(4A) In proceedings to which Section II or Section VI of Part 45 applies, the court shall assess the costs in the manner set out in that Section and subject to rule 44.12B.

(5) Rule 48.3 (amount of costs where costs are payable pursuant to a contract) does not apply to claims started under the procedure in this rule.

(Rule 7.2 provides that proceedings are started when the court issues a claim form at the request of the claimant)

(Rule 8.1(6) provides that a practice direction may modify the Part 8 procedure)

---

**Amendments**—SI 2000/1317; SI 2002/2058; SI 2003/2113; SI 2004/3419; SI 2009/2092; SI 2010/621.

## 44.12B Costs-only proceedings – costs in respect of insurance premium in publication cases

(1) If in proceedings to which rule 44.12A applies it appears to the court that –

  (a)    if proceedings had been started, they would have been publication proceedings;

  (b)    one party admitted liability and made an offer of settlement on the basis of that admission;

  (c)    agreement was reached after that admission of liability and offer of settlement; and

  (d)    either –

      (i)    the party making the admission of liability and offer of settlement was not provided by the other party with the information about an insurance policy as required by the Practice Direction (Pre-Action Conduct); or

      (ii)    that party made the admission of liability and offer of settlement before, or within 42 days of, being provided by the other party with that information,

no costs may be recovered by the other party in respect of the insurance premium.

(2) In this rule, 'publication proceedings' means proceedings for –

  (a)    defamation;

  (b)    malicious falsehood; or

  (c)    breach of confidence involving publication to the public at large.

---

**Amendments**—Inserted by SI 2009/2092.

## 44.12C Costs-only application after a claim is started under Part 8 in accordance with Practice Direction 8B

(1) This rule sets out the procedure where –

  (a)    the parties to a dispute have reached an agreement on all issues (including which party is to pay the costs) which is made or confirmed in writing; but

  (b)    they have failed to agree the amount of those costs; and

  (c)    proceedings have been started under Part 8 in accordance with Practice Direction 8B.

(2) Either party may make an application for the court to determine the costs.

(3) Where an application is made under this rule the court will assess the costs in accordance with rule 45.34 or rule 45.37.

(4) Rule 48.3 (amount of costs where costs are payable pursuant to a contract) does not apply to an application under this rule.

(Practice Direction 8B sets out the procedure for a claim where the parties have followed the Pre-Action Protocol for Low Value Personal Injury Claims in Road Traffic Accidents.)

Amendments—SI 2010/621.

### 44.13 Special situations

(1) Where the court makes an order which does not mention costs –

    (a)    subject to paragraphs (1A) and (1B), the general rule is that no party is entitled –
        (i)    to costs; or
        (ii)    to seek an order under section 194(3) of the Legal Services Act 2007,

in relation to that order; but

    (b)    this does not affect any entitlement of a party to recover costs out of a fund held by that party as trustee or personal representative, or pursuant to any lease, mortgage or other security.

(1A) Where the court makes –

    (a)    an order granting permission to appeal;
    (b)    an order granting permission to apply for judicial review; or
    (c)    any other order or direction sought by a party on an application without notice,

and its order does not mention costs, it will be deemed to include an order for applicant's costs in the case.

(1B) Any party affected by a deemed order for costs under paragraph (1A) may apply at any time to vary the order.

(2) The court hearing an appeal may, unless it dismisses the appeal, make orders about the costs of the proceedings giving rise to the appeal as well as the costs of the appeal.

(3) Where proceedings are transferred from one court to another, the court to which they are transferred may deal with all the costs, including the costs before the transfer.

(4) Paragraph (3) is subject to any order of the court which ordered the transfer.

Amendments—SI 2001/4015; SI 2005/2292; SI 2008/2178.

**44.14 Court's powers in relation to misconduct**

(1) The court may make an order under this rule where –

    (a)    a party or his legal representative, in connection with a summary or detailed assessment, fails to comply with a rule, practice direction or court order; or

    (b)    it appears to the court that the conduct of a party or his legal representative, before or during the proceedings which gave rise to the assessment proceedings, was unreasonable or improper.

(2) Where paragraph (1) applies, the court may –

    (a)    disallow all or part of the costs which are being assessed; or

    (b)    order the party at fault or his legal representative to pay costs which he has caused any other party to incur.

(3) Where –

    (a)    the court makes an order under paragraph (2) against a legally represented party; and

    (b)    the party is not present when the order is made,

the party's solicitor must notify his client in writing of the order no later than 7 days after the solicitor receives notice of the order.

---

**Amendments**—SI 2000/1317.

**44.15 Providing information about funding arrangements**

(1) A party who seeks to recover an additional liability must provide information about the funding arrangement to the court and to other parties as required by a rule, practice direction or court order.

(2) Where the funding arrangement has changed, and the information a party has previously provided in accordance with paragraph (1) is no longer accurate, that party must file notice of the change and serve it on all other parties within 7 days.

(3) Where paragraph (2) applies, and a party has already filed –

    (a)    an allocation questionnaire; or

    (b)    a pre-trial check list (listing questionnaire),

he must file and serve a new estimate of the costs with the notice.

(The Costs Practice Direction sets out –

    –    the information to be provided when a party issues or responds to a claim form, files an allocation questionnaire, a pre-trial check list, and a claim for costs;

    –    the meaning of estimate of costs and the information required in it)

(Rule 44.3B sets out situations where the party will not recover a sum representing any additional liability)

---

**Amendments**—SI 2000/1317; SI 2002/2058; SI 2009/3390.

**44.16**

(1) This rule applies where the Conditional Fee Agreements Regulations 2000 or the Collective Conditional Fee Agreements Regulations 2000 continues to apply to an agreement which provides for a success fee.

(2) Where –

    (a)    the court disallows any amount of a legal representative's percentage increase in summary or detailed assessment proceedings; and

    (b)    the legal representative applies for an order that the disallowed amount should continue to be payable by his client,

the court may adjourn the hearing to allow the client to be –

    (i)    notified of the order sought; and

    (ii)    separately represented.

(Regulation 3(2)(b) of the Conditional Fee Agreements Regulations 2000, which applies to Conditional Fee Agreements entered into before 1 November 2005, provides that a conditional fee agreement which provides for a success fee must state that any amount of a percentage increase disallowed on assessment ceases to be payable unless the court is satisfied that it should continue to be so payable. Regulation 5(2)(b) of the Collective Conditional Fee Agreements Regulations 2000, which applies to Collective Conditional Fee Agreements entered into before 1 November 2005, makes similar provision in relation to collective conditional fee agreements)

**Amendments**—SI 2000/1317; SI 2001/256; SI 2002/2058; SI 2005/3515.

**44.17 Application of costs rules**

This Part and Part 45 (fixed costs), Part 46 (fast track trial costs, Part 47 (procedure for detailed assessment of costs and default provisions) and Part 48 (special cases), do not apply to the assessment of costs in proceedings to the extent that –

    (a)    section 11 of the Access to Justice Act 1999, and the provisions made under that Act; or

    (b)    regulations made under the Legal Aid Act 1988;

make different provision.

(The Costs Practice Direction sets out the procedure to be followed where a party was wholly or partially funded by the Legal Services Commission)

**Amendments**—Inserted by SI 2000/1317; SI 2009/3390.

**44.18 Costs capping orders – General**

(1) A costs capping order is an order limiting the amount of future costs (including disbursements) which a party may recover pursuant to an order for costs subsequently made.

(2) In this rule, "future costs" means costs incurred in respect of work done after the date of the costs capping order but excluding the amount of any additional liability.

(3) This rule does not apply to protective costs orders.

(4) A costs capping order may be in respect of –

    (a)    the whole litigation; or

    (b)    any issues which are ordered to be tried separately.

(5) The court may at any stage of proceedings make a costs capping order against all or

any of the parties, if –

    (a)    it is in the interests of justice to do so;

    (b)    there is a substantial risk that without such an order costs will be disproportionately incurred; and

    (c)    it is not satisfied that the risk in sub-paragraph (b) can be adequately controlled by –

        (i)    case management directions or orders made under Part 3; and

        (ii)    detailed assessment of costs.

(6) In considering whether to exercise its discretion under this rule, the court will consider all the circumstances of the case, including –

    (a)    whether there is a substantial imbalance between the financial position of the parties;

    (b)    whether the costs of determining the amount of the cap are likely to be proportionate to the overall costs of the litigation;

    (c)    the stage which the proceedings have reached; and

    (d)    the costs which have been incurred to date and the future costs.

(7) A costs capping order, once made, will limit the costs recoverable by the party subject to the order unless a party successfully applies to vary the order. No such variation will be made unless –

    (a)    there has been a material and substantial change of circumstances since the date when the order was made; or

    (b)    there is some other compelling reason why a variation should be made.

### 44.19 Application for a costs capping order

(1) An application for a costs capping order must be made on notice in accordance with Part 23.

(2) The application notice must –

    (a)    set out –

        (i)    whether the costs capping order is in respect of the whole of the litigation or a particular issue which is ordered to be tried separately; and

        (ii)    why a costs capping order should be made; and

    (b)    be accompanied by an estimate of costs setting out –

        (i)    the costs (and disbursements) incurred by the applicant to date; and

        (ii)    the costs (and disbursements) which the applicant is likely to incur in the future conduct of the proceedings.

(3) The court may give directions for the determination of the application and such directions may –

    (a)    direct any party to the proceedings –

        (i)     to file a schedule of costs in the form set out in the Costs Practice Direction;

        (ii)    to file written submissions on all or any part of the issues arising;

  (b)    fix the date and time estimate of the hearing of the application;

  (c)    indicate whether the judge hearing the application will sit with an assessor at the hearing of the application; and

  (d)    include any further directions as the court sees fit.

**Amendments**—SI 2009/3390.

### 44.20 Application to vary a costs capping order

An application to vary a costs capping order must be made by application notice pursuant to

\*\*\*\*

# The Costs Practice Direction

## Directions Relating to Part 44 – General Rules About Costs

### Section 7 – Solicitor's Duty to Notify Client: Rule 44.2

7.1 For the purposes of rule 44.2 'client' includes a party for whom a solicitor is acting and any other person (for example, an insurer, a trade union or the LSC) who has instructed the solicitor to act or who is liable to pay his fees.

7.2 Where a solicitor notifies a client of an order under that rule, he must also explain why the order came to be made.

7.3 Although rule 44.2 does not specify any sanction for breach of the rule the court may, either in the order for costs itself or in a subsequent order, require the solicitor to produce to the court evidence showing that he took reasonable steps to comply with the rule.

### Section 8 – Court's Discretion and Circumstances to Be Taken into Account When Exercising its Discretion as to Costs: Rule 44.3

8.1 Attention is drawn to the factors set out in this rule which may lead the court to depart from the general rule stated in rule 44.3(2) and to make a different order about costs.

8.2 In a probate claim where a defendant has in his defence given notice that he requires the will to be proved in solemn form (see paragraph 8.3 of the Practice Direction 57), the court will not make an order for costs against the defendant unless it appears that there was no reasonable ground for opposing the will. The term 'probate claim' is defined in rule 57.1(2).

8.3

    (1)    The court may make an order about costs at any stage in a case.

    (2)    In particular the court may make an order about costs when it deals with any application, makes any order or holds any hearing and that order about costs may relate to the costs of that application, order or hearing.

    (3)    Rule 44.3A(1) provides that the court will not assess any additional liability until the conclusion of the proceedings or the part of the proceedings to which the funding arrangement relates. (Paras 2.4 and 2.5 above explain when proceedings are concluded. As to the time when detailed assessment may be carried out see paragraphs 28.1, below.)

8.4 In deciding what order to make about costs the court is required to have regard to all the circumstances including any payment into court or admissible offer to settle made by a party which is drawn to the court's attention, and which is not an offer to which costs consequences under Part 36 apply.

8.5 There are certain costs orders which the court will commonly make in proceedings before trial. The following table sets out the general effect of these orders. The table is not an exhaustive list of the orders which the court may make.

| Term | Effect |
| --- | --- |
| Costs<br>Costs in any event | The party in whose favour the order is made is entitled to the costs in respect of the part of the proceedings to which the order relates, whatever other costs orders are made in the proceedings. |
| Costs in the case<br>Costs in the application | The party in whose favour the court makes an order for costs at the end of the proceedings is entitled to his costs of the part of the proceedings to which the order relates. |
| Costs reserved | The decision about costs is deferred to a later occasion, but if no later order is made the costs will be costs in the case. |
| Claimant's/defendant's costs in the case/application | If the party in whose favour the costs order is made is awarded costs at the end of the proceedings, that party is entitled to his costs of the part of the proceedings to which the order relates. If any other party is awarded costs at the end of the proceedings, the party in whose favour the final costs order is made is not liable to pay the costs of any other party in respect of the part of the proceedings to which the order relates. |
| Costs thrown away | Where, for example, a judgment or order is set aside, the party in whose favour the costs order is made is entitled to the costs which have been incurred as a consequence. This includes the costs of –<br><br>(a)   preparing for and attending any hearing at which the judgment or order which has been set aside was made;<br><br>(b)   preparing for and attending any hearing to set aside the judgment or order in question;<br><br>(c)   preparing for and attending any hearing at which the court orders the proceedings or the part in question to be adjourned;<br><br>(d)   any steps taken to enforce a judgment or order which has subsequently been set aside. |

| Term | Effect |
|---|---|
| Costs of and caused by | Where, for example, the court makes this order on an application to amend a statement of case, the party in whose favour the costs order is made is entitled to the costs of preparing for and attending the application and the costs of any consequential Amendment to his own statement of case. |
| Costs here and below | The party in whose favour the costs order is made is entitled not only to his costs in respect of the proceedings in which the court makes the order but also to his costs of the proceedings in any lower court. In the case of an appeal from a Divisional Court the party is not entitled to any costs incurred in any court below the Divisional Court. |
| No order as to costs<br>Each party to pay his own costs | Each party is to bear his own costs of the part of the proceedings to which the order relates whatever costs order the court makes at the end of the proceedings. |

8.6 Where, under rule 44.3(8), the court orders an amount to be paid before costs are assessed –

(1) the order will state that amount, and
(2) if no other date for payment is specified in the order rule 44.8 (Time for complying with an order for costs) will apply.

## Fees of counsel

8.7

(1) This paragraph applies where the court orders the detailed assessment of the costs of a hearing at which one or more counsel appeared for a party.
(2) Where an order for costs states the opinion of the court as to whether or not the hearing was fit for the attendance of one or more counsel, a costs officer conducting a detailed assessment of costs to which that order relates will have regard to the opinion stated.
(3) The court will generally express an opinion only where –
    (a) the paying party asks it to do so;
    (b) more than one counsel appeared for the party or,
    (c) the court wishes to record its opinion that the case was not fit for the attendance of counsel.

*Fees payable to conveyancing counsel appointed by the court to assist it*

8.8

(1)    Where the court refers any matter to the conveyancing counsel of the court the fees payable to counsel in respect of the work done or to be done will be assessed by the court in accordance with rule 44.3.

(2)    An appeal from a decision of the court in respect of the fees of such counsel will be dealt with under the general rules as to appeals set out in Part 52. If the appeal is against the decision of an authorised court officer, it will be dealt with in accordance with rules 47.20 to 47.23.

## Section 9 – Costs Orders Relating to Funding Arrangements: Rule 44.3a

9.1 Under an order for payment of 'costs', the costs payable will include an additional liability incurred under a funding arrangement.

9.2

(1)    If before the conclusion of the proceedings the court carries out a summary assessment of the base costs it may identify separately the amount allowed in respect of: solicitor's charges; counsels' fees; other disbursements; and any value added tax (VAT). Sections (13 and 14 of this practice direction deal with summary assessment.)

(2)    If an order for the base costs of a previous application or hearing did not identify separately the amounts allowed for solicitor's charges, counsel's fees and other disbursements, a court which later makes an assessment of an additional liability may apportion the base costs previously ordered.

## Section 10 – Limits on Recovery Under Funding Arrangements: Rule 44.3b

10.1 In a case to which rule 44.3(B)(1)(c) or (d) applies the party in default may apply for relief from the sanction. He should do so as quickly as possible after he becomes aware of the default. An application, supported by evidence, should be made under Part 23 to a costs judge or district judge of the court which is dealing with the case. (Attention is drawn to rules 3.8 and 3.9 which deal with sanctions and relief from sanctions).

10.2 Where the amount of any percentage increase recoverable by counsel may be affected by the outcome of the application, the solicitor issuing the application must serve on counsel a copy of the application notice and notice of the hearing as soon as practicable and in any event at least 2 days before the hearing. Counsel may make written submissions or may attend and make oral submissions at the hearing. (Paragraph 1.4 contains definitions of the terms 'counsel' and 'solicitor'.)

## Section 10A Orders in Respect of Pro Bono Representation: Rule 44.3c

10A.1 Rule 44.3C(2) sets out how the court may determine the amount of payment when making an order under section 194(3) of the Legal Services Act 2007. Paragraph 13.2 of this Practice Direction provides that the general rule is that the court will make a summary assessment of costs in the circumstances outlined in that paragraph unless there is good reason not to do so. This will apply to rule 44.3C(2)(b) with the modification that the summary assessment of the costs is to be read as meaning the summary assessment of the sum equivalent to the costs that would have been claimed by the party with pro bono representation in respect of that representation had it not been provided free of charge.

10A.2 Where an order under section 194(3) of the Legal Services Act 2007 is sought, to assist the court in making a summary assessment of the amount payable to the prescribed charity, the party who has pro bono representation must prepare, file and serve in accordance with paragraph 13.5(2) a written statement of the sum equivalent to the costs that party would have claimed for that legal representation had it not been provided free of charge.

## Section 11 – Factors to be Taken into Account in Deciding the Amount of Costs: Rule 44.5

11.1 In applying the test of proportionality the court will have regard to rule 1.1(2)(c). The relationship between the total of the costs incurred and the financial value of the claim may not be a reliable guide. A fixed percentage cannot be applied in all cases to the value of the claim in order to ascertain whether or not the costs are proportionate.

11.2 In any proceedings there will be costs which will inevitably be incurred and which are necessary for the successful conduct of the case. Solicitors are not required to conduct litigation at rates which are uneconomic. Thus in a modest claim the proportion of costs is likely to be higher than in a large claim, and may even equal or possibly exceed the amount in dispute.

11.3 Where a trial takes place, the time taken by the court in dealing with a particular issue may not be an accurate guide to the amount of time properly spent by the legal or other representatives in preparation for the trial of that issue.

11.4 Where a party has entered into a funding arrangement the costs claimed may, subject to rule 44.3B include an additional liability.

11.5 In deciding whether the costs claimed are reasonable and (on a standard basis assessment) proportionate, the court will consider the amount of any additional liability separately from the base costs.

11.6 In deciding whether the base costs are reasonable and (if relevant) proportionate the court will consider the factors set out in rule 44.5.

11.7 When the court is considering the factors to be taken into account in assessing an additional liability, it will have regard to the facts and circumstances as they reasonably appeared to the solicitor or counsel when the funding arrangement was entered into and at the time of any variation of the arrangement.

11.8

 (1) In deciding whether a percentage increase is reasonable relevant factors to be taken into account may include –
  (a) the risk that the circumstances in which the costs, fees or expenses would be payable might or might not occur;
  (b) the legal representative's liability for any disbursements;
  (c) what other methods of financing the costs were available to the receiving party.

11.9 A percentage increase will not be reduced simply on the ground that, when added to base costs which are reasonable and (where relevant) proportionate, the total appears disproportionate.

11.10 In deciding whether the cost of insurance cover is reasonable, relevant factors to be taken into account include:

 (1) where the insurance cover is not purchased in support of a conditional fee agreement with a success fee, how its cost compares with the likely cost of funding the case with a conditional fee agreement with a success fee and supporting insurance cover;
 (2) the level and extent of the cover provided;
 (3) the availability of any pre-existing insurance cover;
 (4) whether any part of the premium would be rebated in the event of early settlement;
 (5) the amount of commission payable to the receiving party or his legal representatives or other agents.

11.11 Where the court is considering a provision made by a membership organisation, rule 44.3B(1)(b) provides that any such provision which exceeds the likely cost to the receiving party of the premium of an insurance policy against the risk of incurring a liability to pay the costs of other parties to the proceedings is not recoverable. In such circumstances the court will, when assessing the additional liability, have regard to the factors set out in paragraph 11.10 above, in addition to the factors set out in rule 44.5.

## Section 12 – Procedure for Assessing Costs: Rule 44.7

12.1 Where the court does not order fixed costs (or no fixed costs are provided for) the amount of costs payable will be assessed by the court. This rule allows the court making an order about costs either –

 (a) to make a summary assessment of the amount of the costs, or
 (b) to order the amount to be decided in accordance with Part 47 (a detailed assessment).

12.2 An order for costs will be treated as an order for the amount of costs to be decided by a detailed assessment unless the order otherwise provides.

12.3 Whenever the court awards costs to be assessed by way of detailed assessment it should consider whether to exercise the power in rule 44.3(8) (Courts Discretion as to Costs) to order the paying party to pay such sum of money as it thinks just on account of those costs.

# Section 13 – Summary Assessment: General Provisions

13.1 Whenever a court makes an order about costs which does not provide for fixed costs to be paid the court should consider whether to make a summary assessment of costs.

13.2 The general rule is that the court should make a summary assessment of the costs –

(1)    at the conclusion of the trial of a case which has been dealt with on the fast track, in which case the order will deal with the costs of the whole claim, and

(2)    at the conclusion of any other hearing, which has lasted not more than one day, in which case the order will deal with the costs of the application or matter to which the hearing related. If this hearing disposes of the claim, the order may deal with the costs of the whole claim;

(3)    in hearings in the Court of Appeal to which paragraph 14 of Practice Direction 52 applies

unless there is good reason not to do so, e g where the paying party shows substantial grounds for disputing the sum claimed for costs that cannot be dealt with summarily or there is insufficient time to carry out a summary assessment.

13.3 The general rule in paragraph 13.2 does not apply to a mortgagee's costs incurred in mortgage possession proceedings or other proceedings relating to a mortgage unless the mortgagee asks the court to make an order for his costs to be paid by another party. Paragraphs 50.3 and 50.4 deal in more detail with costs relating to mortgages.

13.4 Where an application has been made and the parties to the application agree an order by consent without any party attending, the parties should agree a figure for costs to be inserted in the consent order or agree that there should be no order for costs. If the parties cannot agree the costs position, attendance on the appointment will be necessary but, unless good reason can be shown for the failure to deal with costs as set out above, no costs will be allowed for that attendance.

13.5

(1)    It is the duty of the parties and their legal representatives to assist the judge in making a summary assessment of costs in any case to which paragraph 13.2 above applies, in accordance with the following paragraphs.

(2)    Each party who intends to claim costs must prepare a written statement of those costs showing separately in the form of a schedule –

(a)    the number of hours to be claimed,

(b)    the hourly rate to be claimed,

(c)    the grade of fee earner;

(d)    the amount and nature of any disbursement to be claimed, other than counsel's fee for appearing at the hearing,

(e)    the amount of solicitor's costs to be claimed for attending or appearing at the hearing,

(f)    the fees of counsel to be claimed in respect of the hearing, and

(g)    any value added tax (VAT) to be claimed on these amounts.

(3)   The statement of costs should follow as closely as possible Form N260 and must be signed by the party or the party's legal representative. Where a litigant is an assisted person or is a LSC funded client or is represented by a solicitor in the litigant's employment the statement of costs need not include the certificate appended at the end of Form N260.

(4)   The statement of costs must be filed at court and copies of it must be served on any party against whom an order for payment of those costs is intended to be sought. The statement of costs must be filed and the copies of it must be served as soon as possible and in any event –
   (a)   for a fast track trial, not less than 2 days before the trial; and
   (b)   for all other hearings, not less than 24 hours before the time fixed for the hearing.

(5)   Where the litigant is or may be entitled to claim an additional liability the statement filed and served need not reveal the amount of that liability.

13.6 The failure by a party, without reasonable excuse, to comply with the foregoing paragraphs will be taken into account by the court in deciding what order to make about the costs of the claim, hearing or application, and about the costs of any further hearing or detailed assessment hearing that may be necessary as a result of that failure.

13.7 If the court makes a summary assessment of costs at the conclusion of proceedings the court will specify separately –

(a)   the base costs, and if appropriate, the additional liability allowed as solicitor's charges, counsel's fees, other disbursements and any VAT; and
(b)   the amount which is awarded under Part 46 (Fast Track Trial Costs).

13.8 The court awarding costs cannot make an order for a summary assessment of costs by a costs officer. If a summary assessment of costs is appropriate but the court awarding costs is unable to do so on the day, the court must give directions as to a further hearing before the same judge.

13.9 The court will not make a summary assessment of the costs of a receiving party who is an assisted person or LSC funded client.

13.10 A summary assessment of costs payable by an assisted person or LSC funded client is not by itself a determination of that person's liability to pay those costs (as to which see rule 44.17 and paragraphs 21.1 to 23.17 of this practice direction).

13.11

(1)   The court will not make a summary assessment of the costs of a receiving party who is a child or protected party within the meaning of Part 21 unless the solicitor acting for the child or protected party has waived the right to further costs (see paragraph 51.1 below).
(2)   The court may make a summary assessment of costs payable by a child or protected party.

13.12

(1)   Attention is drawn to rule 44.3A(1) which prevents the court from making a summary assessment of an additional liability before the conclusion of the proceedings or the part of the proceedings to which the funding arrangement relates. Where this applies, the court should

nonetheless make a summary assessment of the base costs of the hearing or application unless there is a good reason not to do so.

(2)  Where the court makes a summary assessment of the base costs all statements of costs and costs estimates put before the judge must be retained on the court file.

13.13  The court will not give its approval to disproportionate and unreasonable costs. Accordingly –

(a)  When the amount of the costs to be paid has been agreed between the parties the order for costs must state that the order is by consent.

(b)  If the judge is to make an order which is not by consent, the judge will, so far as possible, ensure that the final figure is not disproportionate and/or unreasonable having regard to Part 1 of the CPR. The judge will retain this responsibility notwithstanding the absence of challenge to individual items in the make-up of the figure sought. The fact that the paying party is not disputing the amount of costs can however be taken as some indication that the amount is proportionate and reasonable. The judge will therefore intervene only if satisfied that the costs are so disproportionate that it is right to do so.

## Section 14 – Summary Assessment Where Costs Claimed Include an Additional Liability

### *Orders made before the conclusion of the proceedings*

14.1  The existence of a conditional fee agreement or other funding arrangement within the meaning of rule 43.2 is not by itself a sufficient reason for not carrying out a summary assessment.

14.2  Where a legal representative acting for the receiving party has entered into a conditional fee agreement the court may summarily assess all the costs (other than any additional liability).

14.3  Where costs have been summarily assessed an order for payment will not be made unless the court has been satisfied that in respect of the costs claimed, the receiving party is at the time liable to pay to his legal representative an amount equal to or greater than the costs claimed. A statement in the form of the certificate appended at the end of Form N260 may be sufficient proof of liability. The giving of information under rule 44.15 (where that rule applies) is not sufficient.

14.4  The court may direct that any costs, for which the receiving party may not in the event be liable, shall be paid into court to await the outcome of the case, or shall not be enforceable until further order, or it may postpone the receiving party's right to receive payment in some other way.

### *Orders made at the conclusion of the proceedings*

14.5  Where there has been a split trial, (ie the trial of one or more issues separately from other issues), the court will not normally order detailed assessment of the additional liability until all issues have been tried unless the parties agree.

14.6 Rule 44.3A(1)(2) sets out the ways in which the court may deal with the assessment of the costs where there is a funding arrangement. Where the court orders detailed assessment of an additional liability but makes a summary assessment of the base costs –

(1)     The order will state separately the base costs allowed as solicitor's charges, counsel's fees, any other disbursements and any VAT.
(2)     the statements of costs upon which the judge based his summary assessment must be retained on the court file.

14.7 Where the court makes a summary assessment of an additional liability at the conclusion of proceedings, that assessment must relate to the whole of the proceedings; this will include any additional liability relating to base costs allowed by the court when making a summary assessment on a previous application or hearing.

14.8 Paragraph 13.13 applies where the parties are agreed about the total amount to be paid by way of costs, or are agreed about the amount of the base costs that will be paid. Where they disagree about the additional liability the court may summarily assess that liability or make an order for a detailed assessment.

14.9 In order to facilitate the court in making a summary assessment of any additional liability at the conclusion of the proceedings the party seeking such costs must prepare and have available for the court a bundle of documents which must include –

(1)     a copy of every notice of funding arrangement (Form N251) which has been filed by him;
(2)     a copy of every estimate and statement of costs filed by him;
(3)     a copy of the risk assessment prepared at the time any relevant funding arrangement was entered into and on the basis of which the amount of the additional liability was fixed.

## Section 15 – Costs on the Small Claims Track and Fast Track: Rule 44.9

15.1

(1)     Before a claim is allocated to one of those tracks the court is not restricted by any of the special rules that apply to that track.
(2)     Where a claim has been allocated to one of those tracks, the special rules which relate to that track will apply to work done before as well as after allocation save to the extent (if any) that an order for costs in respect of that work was made before allocation.
(3)     (i)     This paragraph applies where a claim, issued for a sum in excess of the normal financial scope of the small claims track, is allocated to that track only because an admission of part of the claim by the defendant reduces the amount in dispute to a sum within the normal scope of that track.
         (See also paragraph 7.4 of Practice Direction 26)
         (ii)    On entering judgment for the admitted part before allocation of the balance of the claim the court may allow costs in respect of the proceedings down to that date.

## Section 16 – Costs Following Allocation and Re-Allocation: Rule 44.11

16.1 This paragraph applies where the court is about to make an order to re-allocate a claim from the small claims track to another track.

16.2 Before making the order to re-allocate the claim, the court must decide whether any party is to pay costs to any other party down to the date of the order to re-allocate in accordance with the rules about costs contained in Part 27 (The Small Claims Track).

16.3 If it decides to make such an order about costs, the court will make a summary assessment of those costs in accordance with that Part.

## Section 17 – Costs-Only Proceedings: Rule 44.12a

17.1 ... A claim form under this rule should not be issued in the High Court unless the dispute to which the agreement relates was of such a value or type that had proceedings been begun they would have been commenced in the High Court.

17.2 A claim form which is to be issued in the High Court at the Royal Courts of Justice will be issued in the Costs Office.

17.3 Attention is drawn to rule 8.2 (in particular to paragraph (b)(ii)) and to rule 44.12A(3). The claim form must –

    (1)    identify the claim or dispute to which the agreement to pay costs relates;

    (2)    state the date and terms of the agreement on which the claimant relies;

    (3)    set out or have attached to it a draft of the order which the claimant seeks;

    (4)    state the amount of the costs claimed; and,

    (5)    state whether the costs are claimed on the standard or indemnity basis. If no basis is specified the costs will be treated as being on the standard basis.

17.4 The evidence to be filed and served with the claim form under Rule 8.5 must include copies of the documents on which the claimant relies to prove the defendant's agreement to pay costs.

17.5 A costs judge or a district judge has jurisdiction to hear and decide any issue which may arise in a claim issued under this rule irrespective of the amount of the costs claimed or of the value of the claim to which the agreement to pay costs relates. A costs officer may make an order by consent under paragraph 17.7, or an order dismissing a claim under paragraph 17.9 below.

17.6 When the time for filing the defendant's acknowledgment of service has expired, the claimant may by letter request the court to make an order in the terms of his claim, unless the defendant has filed an acknowledgment of service stating that he intends to contest the claim or to seek a different order.

17.7 Rule 40.6 applies where an order is to be made by consent. An order may be made by consent in terms which differ from those set out in the claim form.

17.8

    (1)    An order for costs made under this rule will be treated as an order for the amount of costs to be decided by a detailed assessment to which Part 47

and the practice directions relating to it apply. Rule 44.4(4) (determination of basis of assessment) also applies to the order.

(2)  ...

17.9

(1)  For the purposes of rule 44.12A(4)(b) –

(a)  a claim will be treated as opposed if the defendant files an acknowledgment of service stating that he intends to contest the making of an order for costs or to seek a different remedy; and

(b)  a claim will not be treated as opposed if the defendant files an acknowledgment of service stating that he disputes the amount of the claim for costs.

(2)  An order dismissing the claim will be made as soon as an acknowledgment of service opposing the claim is filed. The dismissal of a claim under rule 44.12A(4) does not prevent the claimant from issuing another claim form under Part 7 or Part 8 based on the agreement or alleged agreement to which the proceedings under this rule related.

17.10

(1)  Rule 8.9 (which provides that claims issued under Part 8 shall be treated as allocated to the multi-track) shall not apply to claims issued under this rule. A claim issued under this rule may be dealt with without being allocated to a track.

(2)  Rule 8.1(3) and Part 24 do not apply to proceedings brought under rule 44.12(A).

17.11 Nothing in this rule prevents a person from issuing a claim form under Part 7 or Part 8 to sue on an agreement made in settlement of a dispute where that agreement makes provision for costs, nor from claiming in that case an order for costs or a specified sum in respect of costs.

## Section 18 – Court's Powers in Relation to Misconduct: Rule 44.14

18.1 Before making an order under rule 44.14 the court must give the party or legal representative in question a reasonable opportunity to attend a hearing to give reasons why it should not make such an order.

18.2 Conduct before or during the proceedings which gave rise to the assessment which is unreasonable or improper includes steps which are calculated to prevent or inhibit the court from furthering the overriding objective.

18.3 Although rule 44.14(3) does not specify any sanction for breach of the obligation imposed by the rule the court may, either in the order under paragraph (2) or in a subsequent order, require the solicitor to produce to the court evidence that he took reasonable steps to comply with the obligation.

## Section 19 – Providing Information about Funding Arrangements: Rule 44.15

19.1

(1)  A party who wishes to claim an additional liability in respect of a funding arrangement must give any other party information about that

claim if he is to recover the additional liability. There is no requirement to specify the amount of the additional liability separately nor to state how it is calculated until it falls to be assessed. That principle is reflected in rules 44.3A(1) and rule 44.15, in the following paragraphs and in Sections 6, 13, 14 and 31 of this Practice Direction. Section 6 deals with estimates of costs, Sections 13 and 14 deal with summary assessment and Section 31 deals with detailed assessment.

(2)　In the following paragraphs a party who has entered into a funding arrangement is treated as a person who intends to recover a sum representing an additional liability by way of costs.

(3)　Attention is drawn to paragraph 57.9 of this Practice Direction which sets out time limits for the provision of information where a funding arrangement is entered into between 31 March and 2 July 2000 and proceedings relevant to that arrangement are commenced before 3 July 2000.

## *Method of giving information*

19.2

(1)　In this paragraph, 'claim form' includes petition and application notice, and the notice of funding to be filed or served is a notice containing the information set out in Form N251.

(2)　(a)　A claimant who has entered into a funding arrangement before starting the proceedings to which it relates must provide information to the court by filing the notice when he issues the claim form.

　　(b)　He must provide information to every other party by serving the notice. If he serves the claim form himself he must serve the notice with the claim form. If the court is to serve the claim form, the court will also serve the notice if the claimant provides it with sufficient copies for service.

(3)　A defendant who has entered into a funding arrangement before filing any document

　　(a)　must provide information to the court by filing notice with his first document. A 'first document' may be an acknowledgment of service, a defence, or any other document, such as an application to set aside a default judgment.

　　(b)　must provide information to every party by serving notice. If he serves his first document himself he must serve the notice with that document. If the court is to serve his first document the court will also serve the notice if the defendant provides it with sufficient copies for service.

(4)　In all other circumstances a party must file and serve notice within 7 days of entering into the funding arrangement concerned.

(Practice Direction (Pre-Action Conduct) provides that a party must inform any other party as soon as possible about a funding arrangement entered into prior to the start of proceedings.)

## Notice of change of information

19.3

(1) Rule 44.15 imposes a duty on a party to give notice of change if the information he has previously provided is no longer accurate. To comply he must file and serve notice containing the information set out in Form N251. Rule 44.15(3) may impose other duties in relation to new estimates of costs.

(2) Further notification need not be provided where a party has already given notice:

    (a) that he has entered into a conditional fee agreement with a legal representative and during the currency of that agreement either of them enters into another such agreement with an additional legal representative; or

    (b) of some insurance cover, unless that cover is cancelled or unless new cover is taken out with a different insurer.

(3) Part 6 applies to the service of notices.

(4) The notice must be signed by the party or by his legal representative.

## Information which must be provided

19.4

(1) Unless the court otherwise orders, a party who is required to supply information about a funding arrangement must state whether he has –

entered into a conditional fee agreement which provides for a success fee within the meaning of section 58(2) of the Courts and Legal Services Act 1990;

taken out an insurance policy to which section 29 of the Access to Justice Act 1999 applies;

made an arrangement with a body which is prescribed for the purpose of section 30 of that Act;

or more than one of these.

(2) Where the funding arrangement is a conditional fee agreement, the party must state the date of the agreement and identify the claim or claims to which it relates (including Part 20 claims if any).

(3) Where the funding arrangement is an insurance policy, the party must –

    (a) state the name and address of the insurer, the policy number and the date of the policy and identify the claim or claims to which it relates (including Part 20 claims if any);

    (b) state the level of cover provided by the insurance; and

    (c) state whether the insurance premiums are staged and, if so, the points at which an increased premium is payable.

(4) Where the funding arrangement is by way of an arrangement with a relevant body the party must state the name of the body and set out the date and terms of the undertaking it has given and must identify the claim or claims to which it relates (including Part 20 claims if any).

(5) Where a party has entered into more than one funding arrangement in respect of a claim, for example a conditional fee agreement and an

insurance policy, a single notice containing the information set out in Form N251 may contain the required information about both or all of them.

19.5 Where the court makes a Group Litigation Order, the court may give directions as to the extent to which individual parties should provide information in accordance with rule 44.15. (Part 19 deals with Group Litigation Orders.)

## *Transitional Provision*

19.6 The amendments to the parenthesis below paragraph 19.2 and to paragraph 19.4(3) do not apply where the funding arrangement was entered into before 1st October 2009 and the parenthesis below paragraph 19.2 and paragraph 19.4(3) in force immediately before that date will continue to apply to that funding arrangement as if those amendments had not been made.

## Section 20 – Procedure Where Legal Representative Wishes to Recover from his Client an Agreed Percentage Increase Which has been Disallowed or Reduced on Assessment: Rule 44.16

20.1

(1) Attention is drawn to regulation 3(2)(b) of the Conditional Fee Agreements Regulations 2000 and to regulation 5(2)(b) of the Collective Conditional Fee Agreements Regulations 2000, which provide that some or all of a success fee ceases to be payable in certain circumstances (Both sets of regulations were revoked by the Conditional Fee Agreements (Revocation) Regulations 2005 but continue to have effect in relation to conditional fee agreements and collective conditional fee agreements entered into before 1 November 2005).

(2) Rule 44.16 allows the court to adjourn a hearing at which the legal representative acting for the receiving party applies for an order that a disallowed amount should continue to be payable under the agreement.

20.2 In the following paragraphs 'counsel' means counsel who has acted in the case under a conditional fee agreement which provides for a success fee. A reference to counsel includes a reference to any person who appeared as an advocate in the case and who is not a partner or employee of the solicitor or firm which is conducting the claim or defence (as the case may be) on behalf of the receiving party.

## *Procedure following Summary Assessment*

20.3

(1) If the court disallows any amount of a legal representative's percentage increase, the court will, unless sub-paragraph (2) applies, give directions to enable an application to be made by the legal representative for the disallowed amount to be payable by his client, including, if appropriate, a direction that the application will be determined by a costs judge or district judge of the court dealing with the case.

(2)     The court that has made the summary assessment may then and there decide the issue whether the disallowed amount should continue to be payable, if:

    (a)     the receiving party and all parties to the relevant agreement consent to the court doing so;

    (b)     the receiving party (or, if corporate, an officer) is present in court; and

    (c)     the court is satisfied that the issue can be fairly decided then and there.

## Procedure following Detailed Assessment

20.4

(1)     Where detailed assessment proceedings have been commenced, and the paying party serves points of dispute (as to which see Section 34 of this Practice Direction), which show that he is seeking a reduction in any percentage increase charged by counsel on his fees, the solicitor acting for the receiving party must within 3 days of service deliver to counsel a copy of the relevant points of dispute and the bill of costs or the relevant parts of the bill.

(2)     Counsel must within 10 days thereafter inform the solicitor in writing whether or not he will accept the reduction sought or some other reduction. Counsel may state any points he wishes to have made in a reply to the points of dispute, and the solicitor must serve them on the paying party as or as part of a reply.

(3)     Counsel who fails to inform the solicitor within the time limits set out above will be taken to accept the reduction unless the court otherwise orders.

20.5 Where the paying party serves points of dispute seeking a reduction in any percentage increase charged by a legal representative acting for the receiving party, and that legal representative intends, if necessary, to apply for an order that any amount of the percentage disallowed as against the paying party shall continue to be payable by his client, the solicitor acting for the receiving party must, within 14 days of service of the points of dispute, give to his client a clear written explanation of the nature of the relevant point of dispute and the effect it will have if it is upheld in whole or in part by the court, and of the client's right to attend any subsequent hearings at court when the matter is raised.

20.6 Where the solicitor acting for a receiving party files a request for a detailed assessment hearing it must if appropriate, be accompanied by a certificate signed by him stating:

(1)     that the amount of the percentage increase in respect of counsel's fees or solicitor's charges is disputed;

(2)     whether an application will be made for an order that any amount of that increase which is disallowed should continue to be payable by his client;

(3)     that he has given his client an explanation in accordance with paragraph 20.5; and,

(4)     whether his client wishes to attend court when the amount of any relevant percentage increase may be decided.

20.7

(1)   The solicitor acting for the receiving party must within 7 days of receiving from the court notice of the date of the assessment hearing, notify his client, and if appropriate, counsel in writing of the date, time and place of the hearing.

(2)   Counsel may attend or be represented at the detailed assessment hearing and may make oral or written submissions.

20.8

(1)   At the detailed assessment hearing, the court will deal with the assessment of the costs payable by one party to another, including the amount of the percentage increase, and give a certificate accordingly.

(2)   The court may decide the issue whether the disallowed amount should continue to be payable under the relevant conditional fee agreement without an adjournment if:

(a)   the receiving party and all parties to the relevant agreement consent to the court deciding the issue without an adjournment,

(b)   the receiving party (or, if corporate, an officer or employee who has authority to consent on behalf of the receiving party) is present in court, and

(c)   the court is satisfied that the issue can be fairly decided without an adjournment.

(3)   In any other case the court will give directions and fix a date for the hearing of the application.

## Section 21 – Application of Costs Rules: Rule 44.17

21.1 Rule 44.17(b) excludes the costs rules to the extent that regulations under the Legal Aid Act 1988 make different provision. The primary examples of such regulations are the regulations providing prescribed rates (with or without enhancement).

21.2 Rule 44.17(a) provides that the procedure for detailed assessment does not apply to the extent that section 11 of the Access to Justice Act 1999 and provisions made under that Act make different provision.

21.3 Section 11 of the Access to Justice Act 1999 provides special protection against liability for costs for litigants who receive funding by the LSC (Legal Services Commission) as part of the Community Legal Service. Any costs ordered to be paid by a LSC funded client must not exceed the amount which is reasonable to pay having regard to all the circumstances including –

(a)   the financial resources of all the parties to the proceedings, and

(b)   their conduct in connection with the dispute to which the proceedings relate.

21.4 In this Practice Direction

'cost protection' means the limit on costs awarded against a LSC funded client set out in Section 11(1) of the Access to Justice Act 1999.

'partner' has the meaning given by the Community Legal Service (Costs) Regulations 2000.

21.5 Whether or not cost protection applies depends upon the 'level of service' for which funding was provided by the LSC in accordance with the Funding Code approved under section 9 of the Access to Justice Act 1999. The levels of service referred to are:

(1)     Legal Help – advice and assistance about a legal problem, not including representation or advocacy in proceedings.

(2)     Help at Court – advocacy at a specific hearing, where the advocate is not formally representing the client in the proceedings.

(3)     Family Mediation.

(4)     Legal Representation – representation in actual or contemplated proceedings. Legal Representation can take the form of Investigative Help (limited to investigating the merits of a potential claim) or Full Representation.

(5)     General Family Help and Help with Mediation.

21.6 Levels of service (4) and (5) are provided under a certificate (similar to a legal aid certificate). The certificate will state which level of service is covered. Where there are proceedings, a copy of the certificate will be lodged with the court.

21.7 Cost protection does not apply where –

(1)     The LSC funded client receives Help at Court;

(2)     The LSC funded client receives Legal Help only, i e where the solicitor is advising, but not representing a litigant in person. However, where the LSC funded client receives Legal Help, e g to write a letter before action, but later receives Legal Representation or General Family Help or Help with Mediation in respect of the same dispute, other than in family proceedings, cost protection does apply to all costs incurred by the receiving party in the funded proceedings or prospective proceedings;

(3)     The LSC funded client receives Genral Family help or Help with Mediation in family proceedings;

(4)     The LSC funded client receives Legal Representation in family proceedings.

21.8 Where cost protection does not apply, the court may award costs in the normal way …

21.9 Where work is done before the issue of a certificate, cost protection does not apply to those costs, except where –

(1)     pre-action Legal Help is given and the LSC funded client subsequently receives Legal Representation or General Family Help or Help with Mediation in respect of the same dispute, other than family proceedings; or

(2)     where urgent work is undertaken immediately before the grant of an emergency certificate, other than in family proceedings when no emergency application could be made as the LSC's offices were closed, provided that the solicitor seeks an emergency certificate at the first available opportunity and the certificate is granted.

21.10 If a LSC funded client's certificate is revoked, cost protection does not apply to work done before or after revocation.

21.11 If a LSC funded client's certificate is discharged, cost protection only applies to costs incurred before the date on which funded services ceased to be provided under the certificate. This may be a date before the date on which the certificate is formally discharged by the LSC (*Burridge v Stafford: Khan v Ali* 2000 1 WLR 927, 1999 4 All ER 660, CA).

21.11A Where an LSC funded clients has cost protection, the procedure described in Sections 22 and 23 of this Practice Direction applies. However that procedure does not apply in relation to costs claimed during any periods in the proceedings when the LSC funded client did not have cost protection, and the procedure set out in CPR Part 45 to 47 will apply (as appropriate) in relation to those periods.

## Assessing a LSC Funded Client's Resources

21.12 The first £100,000 of the value of the LSC funded client's interest in the main or only home is disregarded when assessing his or her financial resources for the purposes of S.11 and cannot be the subject of any enforcement process by the receiving party. The receiving party cannot apply for an order to sell the LSC funded client's home, but could secure the debt against any value exceeding £100,000 by way of a charging order.

21.13 The court may only take into account the value of the LSC funded client's clothes, household furniture, tools and implements of trade to the extent that it considers that having regard to the quantity or value of the items, the circumstances are exceptional.

21.14 The LSC funded client's resources include the resources of his or her partner, unless the partner has a contrary interest in the dispute in respect of which funded services are provided.

## Party acting in a Representative, Fiduciary or Official Capacity

21.15

(1) Where a LSC funded client is acting in a representative, fiduciary or official capacity, the court shall not take the personal resources of the party into account for the purposes of either a Section 11 order or costs against the Commission, but shall have regard to the value of any property or estate or the amount of any fund out of which the party is entitled to be indemnified, and may also have regard to the resources of any persons who are beneficially interested in the property, estate or fund.

(2) Similarly, where a party is acting as a litigation friend to a client who is a child or a protected party, the court shall not take the personal resources of the litigation friend into account in assessing the resources of the client.

(3) The purpose of this provision is to ensure that any liability is determined with reference to the value of the property or fund being used to pay for the litigation, and the financial position of those who may benefit from or rely on it.

## Costs against the LSC

21.16 Regulation 5 of the Community Legal Service (Cost Protection) Regulations 2000 governs when costs can be awarded against the LSC. This provision only applies where cost protection applies and the costs ordered to be paid by the LSC funded client do not fully meet the costs that would have been ordered to be paid by him or her if cost protection did not apply.

21.17 In this section and the following two sections of this practice direction 'non-funded party' means a party to proceedings who has not received LSC funded services in relation to these proceedings under a legal aid certificate or a certificate issued under the LSC Funding Code other than a certificate which has been revoked.

21.18 The following criteria set out in Regulation 5 must be satisfied before the LSC can be ordered to pay the whole or any part of the costs incurred by a non-funded party –

    (1)    the proceedings are finally decided in favour of a non-funded party;

    (2)    unless there is good reason for delay ... the non-funded party provides written notice of intention to seek an order against the LSC within 3 months of the making of the Section 11(1) costs order;

    (3)    the court is satisfied that it is just and equitable in the circumstances that provision for the costs should be made out of public funds; and

    (4)    where costs are incurred in a court of first instance, the following additional criteria must also be met –

        (i)    the proceedings were instituted by the LSC funded client;

        (ii)    the non-funded party is an individual; and

        (iii)    the non-funded party will suffer financial hardship unless the order is made.

    ('Section 11(1) costs order' is defined in paragraph 22.1, below)

21.19 In determining whether conditions (3) and (4) are satisfied, the court shall take into account the resources of the non-funded party and his partner (unless the partner has a contrary interest).

21.19A An order made under Regulation 5 may be made in relation to proceedings in the Court of Appeal, High Court or a county court, by a costs judge or a district judge.

## Effect of Appeals

21.20

    (1)    An order for costs can only be made against the LSC when the proceedings (including any appeal) are finally decided. Therefore, where a court of first instance decides in favour of a non-funded party and an appeal lies, any order made against the LSC shall not take effect until –

        (a)    where permission to appeal is required, the time limit for permission to appeal expires, without permission being granted;

        (b)    where permission to appeal is granted or is not required, the time limit for appeal expires without an appeal being brought.

    (2)    This means that, if the LSC funded client appeals, any earlier order against the LSC can never take effect. If the appeal is unsuccessful, the court can make a fresh order.

## Section 22 – Orders for Costs to which Section 11 of the Access to Justice Act 1999 Applies

22.1 In this Practice Direction:

'order for costs to be determined' means an order for costs to which Section 11 of the Access to Justice Act 1999 applies under which the amount of costs payable by the LSC funded client is to be determined by a costs judge or district judge under Section 23 of this Practice Direction.

'order specifying the costs payable' means an order for costs to which Section 11 of the Act applies and which specifies the amount which the LSC funded client is to pay.

'full costs' means, where an order to which Section 11 of the Act applies is made against a LSC funded client, the amount of costs which that person would, had cost protection not applied, have been ordered to pay.

'determination proceedings' means proceedings to which paragraphs 22.1 to 22.10 apply.

'Section 11(1) costs order' means an order for costs to be determined or an order specifying the costs payable other than an order specifying the costs payable which was made in determination proceedings.

'statement of resources' means

(1)     a statement, verified by a statement of truth, made by a party to proceedings setting out:

    (a)     his income and capital and financial commitments during the previous year and, if applicable, those of his partner;

    (b)     his estimated future financial resources and expectations and, if applicable, those of his partner ('partner' is defined in paragraph 21.4, above);

    (c)     a declaration that he and, if applicable, his partner, has not deliberately foregone or deprived himself of any resources or expectations;

    (d)     particulars of any application for funding made by him in connection with the proceedings; and,

    (e)     any other facts relevant to the determination of his resources; or

(2)     a statement, verified by a statement of truth, made by a client receiving funded services, setting out the information provided by the client under Regulation 6 of the Community Legal Service (Financial) Regulations 2000, and stating that there has been no significant change in the client's financial circumstances since the date on which the information was provided or, as the case may be, details of any such change.

'Regional Director' means any Regional Director appointed by the LSC and any member of his staff authorised to act on his behalf.

22.2 Regulations 8 to 13 of the Community Legal Service (Costs) Regulations 2000 as amended set out the procedure for seeking costs against a funded client and the LSC. The effect of these Regulations is set out in this section and the next section of this Practice Direction.

22.3 As from 5 June 2000, Regulations 9 to 13 of the Community Legal Service (Costs) Regulations 2000 as amended also apply to certificates issued under the Legal Aid Act 1988 where costs against the assisted person fall to be assessed under Regulation 124 of the Civil Legal Aid (General) Regulations 1989. In this section and the next section of this Practice Direction the expression 'LSC funded client' includes an assisted person (defined in rule 43.2).

22.4 Regulation 8 of the Community Legal Service (Costs) Regulations 2000 as amended provides that a party intending to seek an order for costs against a LSC funded client may at any time file and serve on the LSC funded client a statement of resources. If that statement is served 7 or more days before a date fixed for a hearing at which an order for costs may be made, the LSC funded client must also make a statement of resources and produce it at the hearing.

22.5 If the court decides to make an order for costs against a LSC funded client to whom cost protection applies it may either:

(1)    make an order for costs to be determined, or
(2)    make an order specifying the costs payable.

22.6 If the court makes an order for costs to be determined it may also

(1)    state the amount of full costs, or
(2)    make findings of facts, eg, concerning the conduct of all the parties which are to be taken into account by the court in the subsequent determination proceedings.

22.7 The court will not make order specifying the costs payable unless:

(1)    it considers that it has sufficient information before it to decide what amount is a reasonable amount for the LSC funded client to pay in accordance with Section 11 of the Act, and
(2)    either
       (a)    the order also states the amount of full costs, or
       (b)    the court considers that it has sufficient information before it to decide what amount is a reasonable amount for the LSC funded client to pay in accordance with Section 11 of the Act and is satisfied that, if it were to determine the full costs at that time, they would exceed the amounts specified in the order.

22.8 Where an order specifying the costs payable is made and the LSC funded client does not have cost protection in respect of all of the costs awarded in that order, the order must identify the sum payable (if any) in respect of which the LSC funded client has cost protection and the sum payable (if any) in respect of which he does not have cost protection.

22.9 The court cannot make an order under Regulations 8 to 13 of the Community Legal Service (Costs) Regulations 2000 as amended except in proceedings to which the next section of this Practice Direction applies.

## Section 23 – Determination Proceedings and Similar Proceedings under the Community Legal Service (Costs) Regulations 2000

23.1 This section of this Practice Direction deals with:

(1)    proceedings subsequent to the making of an order for costs to be determined,
(2)    variations in the amount stated in an order specifying the amount of costs payable and

(3)    the late determination of costs under an order for costs to be determined;

(4)    appeals in respect of determination.

23.2  In this section of this Practice Direction 'appropriate court office' means:

(1)    the district registry or county court in which the case was being dealt with when the Section 11(1) order was made, or to which it has subsequently been transferred; or

(2)    in all other cases, the Costs Office.

23.2A

(1)    This paragraph applies where the appropriate office is any of the following county courts:
Barnet, Bow, Brentford, Bromley, Central London, Clerkenwell and Shoreditch, Croydon, Edmonton, Ilford, Kingston, Lambeth, Mayors and City of Londohjkhjkhjkn, Romford, Uxbridge, Wandsworth, West London, Willesden and Woolwich.

(2)    Where this paragraph applies:–

    (i)    a receiving party seeking an order specifying costs payable by an LSC funded client and/or by the Legal Services Commission under this section must file his application in the Costs Office and, for all purposes relating to that application, the Costs Office will be treated as the appropriate office in that case; and

    (ii)   unless an order is made transferring the application to the Costs Office as part of the High Court, an appeal from any decision made by a costs judge shall lie to the Designated Civil Judge for the London Group of County Courts or such judge as he shall nominate. The appeal notice and any other relevant papers should be lodged at the Central London Civil Justice Centre.

23.3

(1)    A receiving party seeking an order specifying costs payable by an LSC funded client and/or by the LSC may within 3 months of an order for costs to be determined, file in the appropriate court office an application in Form N244 accompanied by

    (a)   the receiving party's bill of costs (unless the full costs have already been determined);

    (b)   the receiving party's statement of resources (unless the court is determining an application against a costs order against the LSC and the costs were not incurred in the court of first instance); and

    (c)   if the receiving party intends to seek costs against the LSC, written notice to that effect.

(2)    If the LSC funded client's liability has already been determined and is less than the full costs, the application will be for costs against the LSC only. If the LSC funded client's liability has not yet been determined, the receiving party must indicate if costs will be sought against the LSC if the funded client's liability is determined as less than the full costs.

(The LSC funded client's certificate will contain the addresses of the LSC funded client, his solicitor, and the relevant Regional Office of the LSC)

23.4  The receiving party must file the above documents in the appropriate court office and (where relevant) serve copies on the LSC funded client and the Regional

Director. In respect of applications for funded services made before 3 December 2001 a failure to file a request within the 3 months time limit specified in Regulation 10(2) is an absolute bar to the making of a costs order against the LSC. Where the application for funded services was made on or after 3 December 2001 the court does have power to extend the 3 months time limit, but only if the applicant can show good reason for the delay.

23.5  On being served with the application, the LSC funded client must respond by filing a statement of resources and serving a copy of it on the receiving party (and the Regional Director where relevant) within 21 days. The LSC funded client may also file and serve written points disputing the bill within the same time limit. (Under rule 3.1 the court may extend or shorten this time limit.)

23.6  If the LSC funded client fails to file a statement of resources without good reason, the court will determine his liability (and the amount of full costs if relevant) and need not hold an oral hearing for such determination.

23.7  When the LSC funded client files a statement or the 21 day period for doing so expires, the court will fix a hearing date and give the relevant parties at least 14 days notice. The court may fix a hearing without waiting for the expiry of the 21 day period if the application is made only against the LSC.

23.8  Determination proceedings will be listed for hearing before a costs judge or district judge. The determination of the liability on the LSC funded client will be listed as a private hearing.

23.9  Where the LSC funded client does not have cost protection in respect of all of the costs awarded, the order made by the costs judge or district judge must in addition to specifying the costs payable, identify the full costs in respect of which cost protection applies and the full costs in respect of which cost protection does not apply.

23.10  The Regional Director may appear at any hearing at which a costs order may be made against the LSC. Instead of appearing, he may file a written statement at court and serve a copy on the receiving party. The written statement should be filed and a copy served, not less than 7 days before the hearing.

## *Variation of an order specifying the costs payable*

23.11

    (1)   This paragraph applies where the amount stated in an order specifying the costs payable plus the amount ordered to be paid by the LSC is less than the full costs to which cost protection applies.

    (2)   The receiving party may apply to the court for a variation of the amount which the LSC funded client is required to pay on the ground that there has been a significant change in the client's circumstances since the date of the order.

23.12  On an application under paragraph 23.11, where the order specifying the costs payable does not state the full costs.

    (1)   the receiving party must file with his application the receiving party's statement of resources and bill of costs and copies of these documents should be served with the application.

(2) The LSC funded client must respond to the application by making a statement of resources which must be filed at court and served on the receiving party within 21 days thereafter. The LSC funded client may also file and serve written points disputing the bill within the same time limit.

(3) The court will, when determining the application assess the full costs identifying any part of them to which cost protection does apply and any part of them to which cost protection does not apply.

23.13 On an application under paragraph 23.11 the order specifying the costs payable may be varied as the court thinks fit. That variation must not increase:

(1) the amount of any costs ordered to be paid by the LSC, and
(2) the amount payable by the LSC funded client,

to a sum which is greater than the amount of the full costs plus the costs of the application.

23.14

(1) Where an order for costs to be determined has been made but the receiving party has not applied, within the three month time limit under paragraph 23.2, the receiving party may apply on any of the following grounds for a determination of the amount which the funded client is required to pay:

    (a) there has been a significant change in the funded client's circumstances since the date of the order for costs to be determined; or

    (b) material additional information about the funded client's financial resources is available which could not with reasonable diligence have been obtained by the receiving party at the relevant time; or

    (c) there were other good reasons for the failure by the receiving party to make an application within the time limit.

(2) An application for costs payable by the LSC cannot be made under this paragraph.

23.15

(1) Where the receiving party has received funded services in relation to the proceedings, the LSC may make an application under paragraphs 23.11 and 23.14 above.

(2) In respect of an application under paragraph 23.11 made by the LSC, the LSC must file and serve copies of the documents described in paragraph 23.12(1).

23.16 An application under paragraph 23.11, 23.14 and 23.15 must be commenced before the expiration of 6 years from the date on which the court made the order specifying the costs payable, or (as the case may be) the order for costs to be determined.

23.17 Applications under paragraphs 23.11, 23.14 and 23.15 should be made in the appropriate court office and should be made in Form N244 to be listed for a hearing before a costs judge or district judge.

23.18

(1) Save as mentioned above any determination made under Regulation 9 or 10 of the Costs Regulations is final (Regulation 11(1)). Any party with a

financial interest in the assessment of the full costs, other than a funded party, may appeal against that assessment in accordance with CPR Part 52 (Regulation 11(2) and CPR rule 47.20).

(2)     The receiving party or the Commission may appeal on a point of law against the making of a costs order against the Commission, against the amount of costs the Commission is required to pay or against the court's refusal to make such an order (Regulation 11(4)).

## Section 23A – Costs Capping Orders

### *When to make an application*

23A.1 The court will make a costs capping order only in exceptional circumstances.

23A.2 An application for a costs capping order must be made as soon as possible, preferably before or at the first case management hearing or shortly afterwards. The stage which the proceedings have reached at the time of the application will be one of the factors the court will consider when deciding whether to make a costs capping order.

### *Estimate of costs*

23A.3 The estimate of costs required by rule 44.19 must be in the form illustrated in Precedent H in the Schedule of Costs Precedents annexed to this Practice Direction.

### *Schedule of costs*

23A.4 The schedule of costs referred to in rule 44.19(3) –

(a)     must set out –
  (i)      each sub-heading as it appears in the applicant's estimate of costs (column 1);
  (ii)     alongside each sub-heading, the amount claimed by the applicant in the applicant's estimate of costs (column 2); and
  (iii)    alongside the figures referred to in sub-paragraph (ii) the amount that the respondent proposes should be allowed under each sub-heading (column 3); and

(b)     must be supported by a statement of truth.

### *Assessing the quantum of the costs cap*

23A.5 When assessing the quantum of a costs cap, the court will take into account the factors detailed in rule 44.5 and the relevant provisions supporting that rule in this Practice Direction. The court may also take into account when considering a party's estimate of the costs they are likely to incur in the future conduct of the proceedings a reasonable allowance on costs for contingencies.

23B.1 In this Section "trust fund" means property which is the subject of a trust, and includes the estate of a deceased person.

23B.2 This Section contains additional provisions to enable –

(a)    the parties to consider whether to apply for; and
(b)    the court to consider whether to make of its own initiative,

a costs capping order in proceedings relating to trust funds.

It supplements rules 44.17–20 and Section 23A of this Practice Direction.

23B.3 Any party to such proceedings who intends to apply for an order for the payment of costs out of the trust fund must file and serve on all other parties written notice of that intention together with an estimate of the costs likely to be incurred by that party.

23B.4 The documents mentioned in paragraph 23B.3 must be filed and served –

(a)    in a Part 7 claim, with the first statement of case; and
(b)    in a Part 8 claim, with the evidence (or, if a defendant does not intend to serve and file evidence, with the acknowledgement of service).

23B.5 When proceedings first come before the court for directions the court may make a costs capping order of its own initiative whether or not any party has applied for such an order.

****

# Part 52 – Appeals

**Contents of this Part**

*I General Rules about Appeals*

**52.1 Scope and interpretation**

(1) The rules in this Part apply to appeals to –

    (a)    the civil division of the Court of Appeal;
    (b)    the High Court; and
    (c)    a county court.

(2) This Part does not apply to an appeal in detailed assessment proceedings against a decision of an authorised court officer.

(Rules 47.20 to 47.23 deal with appeals against a decision of an authorised court officer in detailed assessment proceedings)

(3) In this Part –

 (a) 'appeal' includes an appeal by way of case stated;

 (b) 'appeal court' means the court to which an appeal is made;

 (c) 'lower court' means the court, tribunal or other person or body from whose decision an appeal is brought;

 (d) 'appellant' means a person who brings or seeks to bring an appeal;

 (e) 'respondent' means –

  (i) a person other than the appellant who was a party to the proceedings in the lower court and who is affected by the appeal; and

  (ii) a person who is permitted by the appeal court to be a party to the appeal; and

 (f) 'appeal notice' means an appellant's or respondent's notice.

(4) This Part is subject to any rule, enactment or practice direction which sets out special provisions with regard to any particular category of appeal.

**Amendments**—SI 2000/221; SI 2000/2092; SI 2005/3515.

## 52.2 Parties to comply with the Practice Direction 52

All parties to an appeal must comply with Practice Direction 52.

**Amendments**—SI 2000/221; SI 2009/3390.

## 52.3 Permission

(1) An appellant or respondent requires permission to appeal –

 (a) where the appeal is from a decision of a judge in a county court or the High Court, except where the appeal is against –

  (i) a committal order;

  (ii) a refusal to grant habeas corpus; or

  (iii) a secure accommodation order made under section 25 of the Children Act 1989; or

 (b) as provided by Practice Direction 52.

(Other enactments may provide that permission is required for particular appeals)

(2) An application for permission to appeal may be made –

 (a) to the lower court at the hearing at which the decision to be appealed was made; or

 (b) to the appeal court in an appeal notice.

(Rule 52.4 sets out the time limits for filing an appellant's notice at the appeal court. Rule 52.5 sets out the time limits for filing a respondent's notice at the appeal court. Any application for permission to appeal to the appeal court must be made in the appeal notice (see rules 52.4(1) and 52.5(3))

(Rule 52.13(1) provides that permission is required from the Court of Appeal for all appeals to that court from a decision of a county court or the High Court which was itself made on appeal)

(3) Where the lower court refuses an application for permission to appeal, a further application for permission to appeal may be made to the appeal court.

(4) Subject to paragraph (4A), where the appeal court, without a hearing, refuses permission to appeal, the person seeking permission may request the decision to be reconsidered at a hearing.

(4A) Where the Court of Appeal refuses permission to appeal without a hearing, it may, if it considers that the application is totally without merit, make an order that the person seeking permission may not request the decision to be reconsidered at a hearing ...

...

(4B) Rule 3.3(5) will not apply to an order that the person seeking permission may not request the decision to be reconsidered at a hearing made under paragraph (4A).

(5) A request under paragraph (4) must be filed within 7 days after service of the notice that permission has been refused.

(6) Permission to appeal may be given only where –

(a)     the court considers that the appeal would have a real prospect of success; or

(b)     there is some other compelling reason why the appeal should be heard.

(7) An order giving permission may –

(a)     limit the issues to be heard; and
(b)     be made subject to conditions.

(Rule 3.1(3) also provides that the court may make an order subject to conditions)

(Rule 25.15 provides for the court to order security for costs of an appeal)

**Amendments**—SI 2000/221; SI 2005/3515; SI 2006/1689; SI 2008/2178; SI 2009/3390.

### 52.4 Appellant's notice

(1) Where the appellant seeks permission from the appeal court it must be requested in the appellant's notice.

(2) The appellant must file the appellant's notice at the appeal court within –

(a)     such period as may be directed by the lower court (which may be longer or shorter than the period referred to in sub-paragraph (b)); or

(b)     where the court makes no such direction, 21 days after the date of the decision of the lower court that the appellant wishes to appeal.

(3) Subject to paragraph (4) and unless the appeal court orders otherwise, an appellant's notice must be served on each respondent –

(a)     as soon as practicable; and
(b)     in any event not later than 7 days,

after it is filed.

(4) Where an appellant seeks permission to appeal against a decision to refuse to grant an interim injunction under section 41 of the Policing and Crime Act 2009 the appellant is not required to serve the appellant's notice on the respondent.

**Amendments**—SI 2000/221; SI 2005/3515; SI 2010/1953.

## 52.5 Respondent's notice

(1) A respondent may file and serve a respondent's notice.

(2) A respondent who –

    (a)    is seeking permission to appeal from the appeal court; or

    (b)    wishes to ask the appeal court to uphold the order of the lower court for reasons different from or additional to those given by the lower court,

must file a respondent's notice.

(3) Where the respondent seeks permission from the appeal court it must be requested in the respondent's notice.

(4) A respondent's notice must be filed within –

    (a)    such period as may be directed by the lower court; or

    (b)    where the court makes no such direction, 14 days, after the date in paragraph (5).

(5) The date referred to in paragraph (4) is –

    (a)    the date the respondent is served with the appellant's notice where –

        (i)    permission to appeal was given by the lower court; or

        (ii)    permission to appeal is not required;

    (b)    the date the respondent is served with notification that the appeal court has given the appellant permission to appeal; or

    (c)    the date the respondent is served with notification that the application for permission to appeal and the appeal itself are to be heard together.

(6) Unless the appeal court orders otherwise a respondent's notice must be served on the appellant and any other respondent –

    (a)    as soon as practicable; and

    (b)    in any event not later than 7 days,

after it is filed.

(7) This rule does not apply where rules 53.4(4) applies.

**Amendments**—SI 2000/221; SI 2010/1953.

## 52.6 Variation of time

(1) An application to vary the time limit for filing an appeal notice must be made to the appeal court.

(2) The parties may not agree to extend any date or time limit set by –

    (a)    these Rules;

    (b)    the Practice Direction 52; or

    (c)    an order of the appeal court or the lower court.

(Rule 3.1(2)(a) provides that the court may extend or shorten the time for compliance with any rule, practice direction or court order (even if an application for extension is made after the time for compliance has expired))

(Rule 3.1(2)(b) provides that the court may adjourn or bring forward a hearing)

---

Amendments—SI 2000/221; SI 2009/3390.

### 52.7 Stay[GL]

Unless –

- (a)    the appeal court or the lower court orders otherwise; or
- (b)    the appeal is from the Immigration and Asylum Chamber of the Upper Tribunal,

an appeal shall not operate as a stay of any order or decision of the lower court.

---

Amendments—SI 2000/221; amended by SI 2006/1689; SI 2009/3390.

### 52.8 Amendment of appeal notice

An appeal notice may not be amended without the permission of the appeal court.

---

Amendments—SI 2000/221.

### 52.9 Striking out[GL] appeal notices and setting aside or imposing conditions on permission to appeal

(1) The appeal court may –

- (a)    strike out the whole or part of an appeal notice;
- (b)    set aside[GL] permission to appeal in whole or in part;
- (c)    impose or vary conditions upon which an appeal may be brought.

(2) The court will only exercise its powers under paragraph (1) where there is a compelling reason for doing so.

(3) Where a party was present at the hearing at which permission was given he may not subsequently apply for an order that the court exercise its powers under sub-paragraphs (1)(b) or (1)(c).

---

Amendments—SI 2000/221.

### 52.10 Appeal court's powers

(1) In relation to an appeal the appeal court has all the powers of the lower court.

(Rule 52.1(4) provides that this Part is subject to any enactment that sets out special provisions with regard to any particular category of appeal – where such an enactment gives a statutory power to a tribunal, person or other body it may be the case that the appeal court may not exercise that power on an appeal)

(2) The appeal court has power to –

- (a)    affirm, set aside or vary any order or judgment made or given by the lower court;
- (b)    refer any claim or issue for determination by the lower court;
- (c)    order a new trial or hearing;
- (d)    make orders for the payment of interest;
- (e)    make a costs order.

(3) In an appeal from a claim tried with a jury the Court of Appeal may, instead of ordering a new trial –

    (a)    make an order for damages$^{(GL)}$; or

    (b)    vary an award of damages made by the jury.

(4) The appeal court may exercise its powers in relation to the whole or part of an order of the lower court.

(Part 3 contains general rules about the court's case management powers)

(5) If the appeal court –

    (a)    refuses an application for permission to appeal;

    (b)    strikes out an appellant's notice; or

    (c)    dismisses an appeal,

and it considers that the application, the appellant's notice or the appeal is totally without merit, the provisions of paragraph (6) must be complied with.

(6) Where paragraph (5) applies –

    (a)    the court's order must record the fact that it considers the application, the appellant's notice or the appeal to be totally without merit; and

    (b)    the court must at the same time consider whether it is appropriate to make a civil restraint order.

**Amendments**—SI 2000/221; SI 2004/2072.

## 52.11 Hearing of appeals

(1) Every appeal will be limited to a review of the decision of the lower court unless –

    (a)    a practice direction makes different provision for a particular category of appeal; or

    (b)    the court considers that in the circumstances of an individual appeal it would be in the interests of justice to hold a re-hearing.

(2) Unless it orders otherwise, the appeal court will not receive –

    (a)    oral evidence; or

    (b)    evidence which was not before the lower court.

(3) The appeal court will allow an appeal where the decision of the lower court was –

    (a)    wrong; or

    (b)    unjust because of a serious procedural or other irregularity in the proceedings in the lower court.

(4) The appeal court may draw any inference of fact which it considers justified on the evidence.

(5) At the hearing of the appeal a party may not rely on a matter not contained in his appeal notice unless the appeal court gives permission.

**Amendments**—SI 2000/221.

## 52.12 Non-disclosure of Part 36 offers and payments

(1) The fact that a Part 36 offer or payment into court has been made must not be disclosed to any judge of the appeal court who is to hear or determine –

(a)    an application for permission to appeal; or
(b)    an appeal,

until all questions (other than costs) have been determined.

(2) Paragraph (1) does not apply if the Part 36 offer or payment into court is relevant to the substance of the appeal.

(3) Paragraph (1) does not prevent disclosure in any application in the appeal proceedings if disclosure of the fact that a Part 36 offer or payment into court has been made is properly relevant to the matter to be decided.

(Rule 36.3 has the effect that a Part 36 offer made in proceedings at first instance will not have consequences in any appeal proceedings. Therefore, a fresh Part 36 offer needs to be made in appeal proceedings. However, rule 52.12 applies to a Part 36 offer whether made in the original proceedings or in the appeal.)

Amendments—Inserted by SI 2000/221; amended by SI 2003/3361; SI 2006/3435.

## 52.12A Statutory appeals – court's power to hear any person

(1) In a statutory appeal, any person may apply for permission –

(a)    to file evidence; or
(b)    to make representations at the appeal hearing.

(2) An application under paragraph (1) must be made promptly.

Amendments—SI 2007/2204.

*II  Special Provisions applying to the Court of Appeal*

## 52.13 Second appeals to the court

(1) Permission is required from the Court of Appeal for any appeal to that court from a decision of a county court or the High Court which was itself made on appeal.

(2) The Court of Appeal will not give permission unless it considers that –

(a)    the appeal would raise an important point of principle or practice; or
(b)    there is some other compelling reason for the Court of Appeal to hear it.

Amendments—SI 2000/221.

## 52.14 Assignment of appeals to the Court of Appeal

(1) Where the court from or to which an appeal is made or from which permission to appeal is sought ('the relevant court') considers that –

(a)    an appeal which is to be heard by a county court or the High Court would raise an important point of principle or practice; or
(b)    there is some other compelling reason for the Court of Appeal to hear it,

the relevant court may order the appeal to be transferred to the Court of Appeal.

(The Master of the Rolls has the power to direct that an appeal which would be heard by a county court or the High Court should be heard instead by the Court of Appeal – see section 57 of the Access to Justice Act 1999)

(2) The Master of the Rolls or the Court of Appeal may remit an appeal to the court in which the original appeal was or would have been brought.

Amendments—SI 2000/221.

## 52.15 Judicial review appeals

(1) Where permission to apply for judicial review has been refused at a hearing in the High Court, the person seeking that permission may apply to the Court of Appeal for permission to appeal.

(2) An application in accordance with paragraph (1) must be made within 7 days of the decision of the High Court to refuse to give permission to apply for judicial review.

(3) On an application under paragraph (1), the Court of Appeal may, instead of giving permission to appeal, give permission to apply for judicial review.

(4) Where the Court of Appeal gives permission to apply for judicial review in accordance with paragraph (3), the case will proceed in the High Court unless the Court of Appeal orders otherwise.

Amendments—SI 2000/221.

## 52.16 Who may exercise the powers of the Court of Appeal

(1) A court officer assigned to the Civil Appeals Office who is –

    (a)    a barrister; or
    (b)    a solicitor

may exercise the jurisdiction of the Court of Appeal with regard to the matters set out in paragraph (2) with the consent of the Master of the Rolls.

(2) The matters referred to in paragraph (1) are –

    (a)    any matter incidental to any proceedings in the Court of Appeal;
    (b)    any other matter where there is no substantial dispute between the parties; and
    (c)    the dismissal of an appeal or application where a party has failed to comply with any order, rule or practice direction.

(3) A court officer may not decide an application for –

    (a)    permission to appeal;
    (b)    bail pending an appeal;
    (c)    an injunction(GL);
    (d)    a stay(GL) of any proceedings, other than a temporary stay of any order or decision of the lower court over a period when the Court of Appeal is not sitting or cannot conveniently be convened.

(4) Decisions of a court officer may be made without a hearing.

(5) A party may request any decision of a court officer to be reviewed by the Court of Appeal.

(6) At the request of a party, a hearing will be held to reconsider a decision of –

(a)     a single judge; or
(b)     a court officer,

made without a hearing.

(6A) A request under paragraph (5) or (6) must be filed within 7 days after the party is served with the notice of the decision.

(7) A single judge may refer any matter for a decision by a court consisting of two or more judges.

> (Section 54(6) of the Senior Courts Act 1981; provides that there is no appeal from the decision of a single judge on an application for permission to appeal) (Section 58(2) of the Senior Courts Act 1981 provides that there is no appeal to the House of Lords from decisions of the Court of Appeal that –
>
> (a)     are taken by a single judge or any officer or member of staff of that court in proceedings incidental to any cause or matter pending before the civil division of that court; and
> (b)     do not involve the determination of an appeal or of an application for permission to appeal,
>
> and which may be called into question by rules of court. Rules 52.16(5) and (6) provide the procedure for the calling into question of such decisions)

**Amendments**—SI 2000/221; SI 2003/3361; Constitutional Reform Act 2005, Sch 11, para 1(2).

*III Provisions about Reopening Appeals*

**52.17 Reopening of final appeals**

(1) The Court of Appeal or the High Court will not reopen a final determination of any appeal unless –

(a)     it is necessary to do so in order to avoid real injustice;
(b)     the circumstances are exceptional and make it appropriate to reopen the appeal; and
(c)     there is no alternative effective remedy.

(2) In paragraphs (1), (3), (4) and (6), 'appeal' includes an application for permission to appeal.

(3) This rule does not apply to appeals to a county court.

(4) Permission is needed to make an application under this rule to reopen a final determination of an appeal even in cases where under rule 52.3(1) permission was not needed for the original appeal.

(5) There is no right to an oral hearing of an application for permission unless, exceptionally, the judge so directs.

(6) The judge will not grant permission without directing the application to be served on the other party to the original appeal and giving him an opportunity to make representations.

(7) There is no right of appeal or review from the decision of the judge on the application for permission, which is final.

(8) The procedure for making an application for permission is set out in the Practice Direction 52.

Amendments—SI 2003/2113; SI 2009/3390.

*IV Statutory Rights of Appeal*

### 52.18 Appeals under the Law of Property Act 1922

An appeal lies to the High Court against a decision of the Secretary of State under paragraph 16 of Schedule 15 to the Law of Property Act 1922.

Amendments—SI 2007/2204; SI 2007/3543.

### 52.19 Appeals from certain tribunals

(1) A person who was a party to proceedings before a tribunal referred to in section 11(1) of the Tribunals and Inquiries Act 1992 and is dissatisfied in point of law with the decision of the tribunal may appeal to the High Court.

(2) The tribunal may, of its own initiative or at the request of a party to the proceedings before it, state, in the form of a special case for the decision of the High Court, a question of law arising in the course of the proceedings.

Amendments—SI 2007/2204.

### 52.20 Appeals under certain planning legislation

(1) Where the Secretary of State has given a decision in proceedings on an appeal under Part VII of the Town and Country Planning Act 1990 against an enforcement notice –

    (a)    the appellant;
    (b)    the local planning authority; or
    (c)    another person having an interest in the land to which the notice relates,

may appeal to the High Court against the decision on a point of law.

(2) Where the Secretary of State has given a decision in proceedings on an appeal under Part VIII of that Act against a notice under section 207 of that Act –

    (a)    the appellant;
    (b)    the local planning authority; or
    (c)    any person (other than the appellant) on whom the notice was served,

may appeal to the High Court against the decision on a point of law.

(3) Where the Secretary of State has given a decision in proceedings on an appeal under section 39 of the Planning (Listed Buildings and Conservation Areas) Act 1990 against a listed building enforcement notice –

    (a)    the appellant;
    (b)    the local planning authority; or
    (c)    any other person having an interest in the land to which the notice relates,

may appeal to the High Court against the decision on a point of law.

Amendments—SI 2007/2204.

# Practice Direction 52 – Appeals

## Appeals

## Contents of this Practice Direction

1.1 This Practice Direction is divided into five sections –

- Section I – General provisions about appeals
- Section II – General provisions about statutory appeals and appeals by way of case stated
- Section III – Provisions about specific appeals
- Section IV – Provisions about reopening appeals
- Section V – Transitional provisions relating to the abolition of the Asylum and Immigration Tribunal.

## Section I – General Provisions about Appeals

2.1 This practice direction applies to all appeals to which Part 52 applies except where specific provision is made for appeals to the Court of Appeal.

2.2 For the purpose only of appeals to the Court of Appeal from cases in family proceedings this Practice Direction will apply with such modifications as may be required.

## Routes of Appeal

2A.1 The court or judge to which an appeal is to be made (subject to obtaining any necessary permission) is set out in the tables below:

- Table 1 addresses appeals in cases other than insolvency proceedings and those cases to which Table 3 applies;
- Table 2 addresses insolvency proceedings; and
- Table 3 addresses certain family cases to which CPR Part 52 may apply.

The tables do not include so-called 'leap frog' appeals either to the Court of Appeal pursuant to s 57 of the Access to Justice Act 1999 or to the House of Lords pursuant to s 13 of the Administration of Justice Act 1969.

(An interactive routes of appeal guide can be found on the Court of Appeal's website at http://www.hmcourts-service.gov.uk/infoabout/coa_civil/ routes_app/ index.htm)

## Table 1

In this Table, reference to –

- (a) a 'Circuit judge' includes a recorder or a district judge who is exercising the jurisdiction of a circuit judge with the permission of the designated civil judge in respect of that case (see Practice Direction 2B (Allocation of cases to levels of judiciary), paragraph 11.1(d));
- (b) 'the Destinations of Appeal Order" means the Access to Justice Act 1999 (Destination of Appeals) Order 2000; and

(c)    'final decision' has the meaning for the purposes of this table as set out in paragraphs 2A.2 and 2A.3.

| COURT | TRACK/ NATURE OF CLAIM | JUDGE WHO MADE DECISION | NATURE OF DECISION UNDER APPEAL | APPEAL COURT |
|---|---|---|---|---|
| County | Part 7 claim | District judge | Interim decision | Circuit judge in county court |
| County | Part 7 claim, other than a claim allocated to the multi-track | District judge | Final decision | Circuit judge in the county court |
| County | Part 7 claim, allocated to the multi-track | District judge | Final decision | Court of Appeal |
| County | Part 8 claim | District judge | Any decision | Circuit judge in the county court |
| County | Claims or originating or pre-action applications started otherwise than by a Part 7 or Part 8 claim (for example an application under Part 23) | District judge | Any decision | Circuit judge in the county court |
| County | Specialist proceedings (under the Companies Act 1985 or the Companies Act 1989 or to which Sections I or II of Part 57 or any of Parts 60, 62 or 63 apply) | District judge | Interim decision | Circuit judge in the county court |

| COURT | TRACK/ NATURE OF CLAIM | JUDGE WHO MADE DECISION | NATURE OF DECISION UNDER APPEAL | APPEAL COURT |
|---|---|---|---|---|
| County | Specialist proceedings (under the Companies Act 1985 or the Companies Act 1989 or to which Sections I or II, of Part 57 or any of Parts 60, 62 or 63 apply) | District judge | Final decision | Court of Appeal |
| County | Part 7 claim | Circuit judge | Interim decision | Single judge of the High Court |
| County | Part 7 claim, other than a claim allocated to the multi-track | Circuit judge | Final decision | Single judge of the High Court |
| County | Part 7 claim, allocated to the multi-track | Circuit judge | Final decision | Court of Appeal |
| County | Part 8 claim | Circuit judge | Any decision | Single judge of the High Court |
| County | Claims or originating or pre-action applications started otherwise than by a Part 7 or Part 8 claim (for example an application under Part 23) | Circuit judge | Any decision | Single judge of the High Court |

| COURT | TRACK/ NATURE OF CLAIM | JUDGE WHO MADE DECISION | NATURE OF DECISION UNDER APPEAL | APPEAL COURT |
|---|---|---|---|---|
| County | Specialist proceedings (under the Companies Act 1985 or the Companies Act 1989 or to which Sections I or II of Part 57 or any of Parts 60, 62 or 63 apply) | Circuit judge | Interim decision | Single judge of the High Court |
| County | Specialist proceedings (under the Companies Act 1985 or the Companies Act 1989 or to which Sections I or II of Part 57 or any of Parts 60, 62 or 63 apply) | Circuit judge | Final decision | Court of Appeal |
| High | Part 7 claim | Master, district judge sitting in a district registry or any other judge referred to in article 2 of the Destination of Appeals Order (where appropriate) | Interim decision | Single judge of the High Court |

| COURT | TRACK/ NATURE OF CLAIM | JUDGE WHO MADE DECISION | NATURE OF DECISION UNDER APPEAL | APPEAL COURT |
|---|---|---|---|---|
| High | Part 7 claim, other than a claim allocated to the multi-track | Master, district judge sitting in a district registry or any other judge referred to in article 2 of the Destination of Appeals Order (where appropriate) | Final decision | Single judge of the High Court |
| High | Part 7 claim, allocated to the multi-track | Master, district judge sitting in a district registry or any other judge referred to in article 2 of the Destination of Appeals Order (where appropriate) | Final decision | Court of Appeal |
| High | Part 8 claim | Master, district judge sitting in a district registry or any other judge referred to in article 2 of the Destination of Appeals Order (where appropriate) | Any decision | Single judge of the High Court |

| COURT | TRACK/ NATURE OF CLAIM | JUDGE WHO MADE DECISION | NATURE OF DECISION UNDER APPEAL | APPEAL COURT |
|---|---|---|---|---|
| High | Claims or originating or pre-action applications started otherwise than by a Part 7 or Part 8 claim (for example an application under Part 23) | Master, district judge sitting in a district registry or any other judge referred to in article 2 of the Destination of Appeals Order (where appropriate) | Any decision | Single judge of the High Court |
| High | Specialist proceedings (under the Companies Act 1985 or the Companies Act 1989 or to which Sections I, II, or III of Part 57 or any of Parts 58 to 63 apply) | Master, district judge sitting in a district registry or any other judge referred to in article 2 of the Destination of Appeals Order (where appropriate) | Interim decision | Single judge of the High Court |
| High | Specialist proceedings (under the Companies Act 1985 or the Companies Act 1989 or to which Sections I, II or III of Part 57 or any of Parts 58 to 63 apply) | Master, district judge sitting in a district registry or any other judge referred to in article 2 of the Destination of Appeals Order (where appropriate) | Final decision | Court of Appeal |
| High | Any | High Court judge | Any decision | Court of Appeal |

## Table 2: Insolvency Proceedings

In this Table references to a 'Circuit judge' include a recorder or a district judge who is exercising the jurisdiction of a circuit judge with the permission of the designated civil judge in respect of that case (see: Practice Direction 2B, paragraph 11.1(d)).

| COURT | TRACK/ NATURE OF CLAIM | JUDGE WHO MADE DECISION | NATURE OF DECISION UNDER APPEAL | APPEAL COURT |
|---|---|---|---|---|
| County | Insolvency | District judge or circuit judge | Any | Single judge of the High Court |
| High Court | Insolvency | Registrar | Any | Single judge of the High Court |
| High Court | Insolvency | High Court judge | Any | Court of Appeal |

## Table 3: Proceedings which may be heard in the Family Division of the High Court and to which the CPR may apply.

The proceedings to which this table will apply include proceedings under the Inheritance (Provision for Family and Dependants) Act 1975 and proceedings under the Trusts of Land and Appointment of Trustees Act 1996.

For the meaning of 'final decision' for the purposes of this table see paragraphs 2A.2 and 2A.3 below.

| COURT | JUDGE WHO MADE DECISION | TRACK/ NATURE OF CLAIM | NATURE OF DECISION UNDER APPEAL | APPEAL COURT |
|---|---|---|---|---|
| High Court Principal Registry of the Family Division | District judge | Proceedings under CPR Pt 8 (if not allocated to any track or if simply treated as allocated to the multi-track under CPR 8.9(c)) | Any decision | High Court judge of the Family Division |

| COURT | JUDGE WHO MADE DECISION | TRACK/ NATURE OF CLAIM | NATURE OF DECISION UNDER APPEAL | APPEAL COURT |
|---|---|---|---|---|
| High Court Principal Registry of the Family Division | District judge | Proceedings under CPR Pt 8 specifically allocated to the multi-track by an order of the court. | Any decision | High Court judge of the Family Division |
| High Court Principal Registry of the Family Division | District judge | Proceedings under CPR Part 7 | Any decision other than a final decision | High Court judge of the Family Division |
| High Court Principal Registry of the Family Division | District judge | Proceedings under CPR Part 7 and allocated to the multi-track | Final decision | Court of Appeal |
| High Court Family Division | High Court judge | Proceedings under CPR Part 7 or 8 | Any | Court of Appeal |

2A.2 A 'final decision' is a decision of a court that would finally determine (subject to any possible appeal or detailed assessment of costs) the entire proceedings whichever way the court decided the issues before it. Decisions made on an application to strike-out or for summary judgment are not final decisions for the purpose of determining the appropriate route of appeal (Art. 1 Access to Justice Act 1999 (Destination of Appeals) Order 2000). Accordingly:

(1) a case management decision;
(2) the grant or refusal of interim relief;
(3) a summary judgment;
(4) a striking out,

are not final decisions for this purpose.

2A.3 A decision of a court is to be treated as a final decision for routes of appeal purposes where it:

(1) is made at the conclusion of part of a hearing or trial which has been split into parts; and
(2) would, if it had been made at the conclusion of that hearing or trial, have been a final decision.

Accordingly, a judgment on liability at the end of a split trial is a 'final decision' for this purpose and the judgment at the conclusion of the assessment of damages following a judgment on liability is also a "final decision" for this purpose.

2A.4 An order made:

(1)     on a summary or detailed assessment of costs; or

(2)     on an application to enforce a final decision,

is not a 'final decision' and any appeal from such an order will follow the routes of appeal set out in the tables above.

(Section 16(1) of the Supreme Court Act 1981 (as amended); section 77(1) of the County Courts Act 1984 (as amended); and the Access to Justice Act 1999 (Destination of Appeals) Order 2000 set out the provisions governing routes of appeal)

2A.5

(1)     Where an applicant attempts to file an appellant's notice and the appeal court does not have jurisdiction to issue the notice, a court officer may notify the applicant in writing that the appeal court does not have jurisdiction in respect of the notice.

(2)     Before notifying a person under paragraph (1) the court officer must confer –

(a)     with a judge of the appeal court; or

(b)     where the Court of Appeal, Civil Division is the appeal court, with a court officer who exercises the jurisdiction of that court under rule 52.16.

(3)     Where a court officer in the Court of Appeal, Civil Division notifies a person under paragraph (1), rule 52.16(5) shall not apply.

## Grounds for Appeal

3.1 Rule 52.11(3)(a) and (b) sets out the circumstances in which the appeal court will allow an appeal.

3.2 The grounds of appeal should –

(1)     set out clearly the reasons why rule 52.11(3)(a) or (b) is said to apply; and

(2)     specify, in respect of each ground, whether the ground raises an appeal on a point of law or is an appeal against a finding of fact.

## Permission to Appeal

4.1 Rule 52.3 sets out the circumstances when permission to appeal is required.

4.2 The permission of –

(a)     the Court of Appeal; or

(b)     where the lower court's rules allow, the lower court,

is required for all appeals to the Court of Appeal except as provided for by statute or rule 52.3.

(The requirement of permission to appeal may be imposed by a practice direction – see rule 52.3(b))

4.3 Where the lower court is not required to give permission to appeal, it may give an indication of its opinion as to whether permission should be given.

(Rule 52.1(3)(c) defines 'lower court')

4.3A

    (1)    This paragraph applies where a party applies for permission to appeal against a decision at the hearing at which the decision was made.

    (2)    Where this paragraph applies, the judge making the decision shall state –
        (a)    whether or not the judgment or order is final;
        (b)    whether an appeal lies from the judgment or order and, if so, to which appeal court;
        (c)    whether the court gives permission to appeal; and
        (d)    if not, the appropriate appeal court to which any further application for permission may be made.

(Rule 40.2(4) contains requirements as to the contents of the judgment or order in these circumstances)

4.3B Where no application for permission to appeal has been made in accordance with rule 52.3(2)(a) but a party requests further time to make such an application, the court may adjourn the hearing to give that party the opportunity to do so.

## Appeals from case management decisions

4.4 Case management decisions include decisions made under rule 3.1(2) and decisions about –

    (1)    disclosure
    (2)    filing of witness statements or experts reports
    (3)    directions about the timetable of the claim
    (4)    adding a party to a claim
    (5)    security for costs.

4.5 Where the application is for permission to appeal from a case management decision, the court dealing with the application may take into account whether –

    (1)    the issue is of sufficient significance to justify the costs of an appeal;
    (2)    the procedural consequences of an appeal (eg loss of trial date) outweigh the significance of the case management decision;
    (3)    it would be more convenient to determine the issue at or after trial.

## Court to which permission to appeal application should be made

4.6 An application for permission should be made orally at the hearing at which the decision to be appealed against is made.

4.7 Where:

    (a)    no application for permission to appeal is made at the hearing; or
    (b)    the lower court refuses permission to appeal,

an application for permission to appeal may be made to the appeal court in accordance with rules 52.3(2) and (3).

4.8 There is no appeal from the decision of the appeal court to allow or refuse permission to appeal to that court (although where the appeal court, without a hearing, refuses permission to appeal, the person seeking permission may request that decision to be reconsidered at a hearing). See section 54(4) of the Access to Justice Act and rule 52.3(2), (3), (4) and (5).

## Second appeals

4.9 An application for permission to appeal from a decision of the High Court or a county court which was itself made on appeal must be made to the Court of Appeal.

4.10 If permission to appeal is granted the appeal will be heard by the Court of Appeal.

## Consideration of Permission without a hearing

4.11 Applications for permission to appeal may be considered by the appeal court without a hearing.

4.12 If permission is granted without a hearing the parties will be notified of that decision and the procedure in paragraphs 6.1 to 6.6 will then apply.

4.13 If permission is refused without a hearing the parties will be notified of that decision with the reasons for it. The decision is subject to the appellant's right to have it reconsidered at an oral hearing. This may be before the same judge.

4.14 A request for the decision to be reconsidered at an oral hearing must be filed at the appeal court within 7 days after service of the notice that permission has been refused. A copy of the request must be served by the appellant on the respondent at the same time.

## Permission hearing

4.14A

(1)    This paragraph applies where an appellant, who is represented, makes a request for a decision to be reconsidered at an oral hearing.

(2)    The appellant's advocate must, at least 4 days before the hearing, in a brief written statement –

(a)    inform the court and the respondent of the points which he proposes to raise at the hearing;

(b)    set out his reasons why permission should be granted notwithstanding the reasons given for the refusal of permission; and

(c)    confirm, where applicable, that the requirements of paragraph 4.17 have been complied with (appellant in receipt of services funded by the Legal Services Commission).

4.15 Notice of a permission hearing will be given to the respondent but he is not required to attend unless the court requests him to do so.

4.16 If the court requests the respondent's attendance at the permission hearing, the appellant must supply the respondent with a copy of the appeal bundle (see paragraph 5.6A) within 7 days of being notified of the request, or such other period as the court may direct. The costs of providing that bundle shall be borne by the appellant initially, but will form part of the costs of the permission application.

## Appellants in receipt of services funded by the Legal Services Commission applying for permission to appeal

4.17 Where the appellant is in receipt of services funded by the Legal Services Commission (or legally aided) and permission to appeal has been refused by the appeal court without a hearing, the appellant must send a copy of the reasons the appeal court gave for refusing permission to the relevant office of the Legal Services Commission as soon as it has been received from the court. The court will require confirmation that this has been done if a hearing is requested to re-consider the question of permission.

### Limited permission

4.18 Where a court under rule 52.3(7) gives permission to appeal on some issues only, it will –

(1)    refuse permission on any remaining issues; or
(2)    reserve the question of permission to appeal on any remaining issues to the court hearing the appeal.

4.19 If the court reserves the question of permission under paragraph 4.18(2), the appellant must, within 14 days after service of the court's order, inform the appeal court and the respondent in writing whether he intends to pursue the reserved issues. If the appellant does intend to pursue the reserved issues, the parties must include in any time estimate for the appeal hearing, their time estimate for the reserved issues.

4.20 If the appeal court refuses permission to appeal on the remaining issues without a hearing and the applicant wishes to have that decision reconsidered at an oral hearing, the time limit in rule 52.3(5) shall apply. Any application for an extension of this time limit should be made promptly. The court hearing the appeal on the issues for which permission has been granted will not normally grant, at the appeal hearing, an application to extend the time limit in rule 52.3(5) for the remaining issues.

4.21 If the appeal court refuses permission to appeal on remaining issues at or after an oral hearing, the application for permission to appeal on those issues cannot be renewed at the appeal hearing. See section 54(4) of the Access to Justice Act 1999.

### Respondents' costs of permission applications

4.22 In most cases, applications for permission to appeal will be determined without the court requiring –

(1)    submissions from, or
(2)    if there is an oral hearing, attendance by

the respondent.

4.23 Where the court does not request submissions from or attendance by the respondent, costs will not normally be allowed to a respondent who volunteers submissions or attendance.

4.24 Where the court does request –

(1)    submissions from or attendance by the respondent; or
(2)    attendance by the respondent with the appeal to follow if permission is granted,

the court will normally allow the respondent his costs if permission is refused.

## Appellant's Notice

5.1 An appellant's notice must be filed and served in all cases except in an appeal against a decision to refuse to grant an interim injunction under section 41 of the Policing and Crime Act 2009. Where an application for permission to appeal is made to the appeal court it must be applied for in the appellant's notice.

## *Human Rights*

5.1A

(1)    This paragraph applies where the appellant seeks –
        (a)    to rely on any issue under the Human Rights Act 1998; or
        (b)    a remedy available under that Act,
for    the first time in an appeal.
(2)    The appellant must include in his appeal notice the information required by paragraph 15.1 of Practice Direction 16.
(3)    Paragraph 15.2 of Practice Direction 16 applies as if references to a statement of case were to the appeal notice.

5.1B CPR rule 19.4A and Practice Direction 16 shall apply as if references to the case management conference were to the application for permission to appeal.

(Practice Direction 19A provides for notice to be given and parties joined in certain circumstances to which this paragraph applies)

## *Extension of time for filing appellant's notice*

5.2 Where the time for filing an appellant's notice has expired, the appellant must –

(a)    file the appellant's notice; and
(b)    include in that appellant's notice an application for an extension of time.

The appellant's notice should state the reason for the delay and the steps taken prior to the application being made.

5.3 Where the appellant's notice includes an application for an extension of time and permission to appeal has been given or is not required the respondent has the right to be heard on that application. He must be served with a copy of the appeal bundle (see paragraph 5.6A). However, a respondent who unreasonably opposes an extension of time runs the risk of being ordered to pay the appellant's costs of that application.

5.4 If an extension of time is given following such an application the procedure at paragraphs 6.1 to 6.6 applies.

## Applications

5.5 Notice of an application to be made to the appeal court for a remedy incidental to the appeal (e g an interim remedy under rule 25.1 or an order for security for costs) may be included in the appeal notice or in a Part 23 application notice.

(Rule 25.15 deals with security for costs of an appeal)

(Paragraph 11 of this practice direction contains other provisions relating to applications)

## Documents

5.6

    (1)    This paragraph applies to every case except where the appeal –
        (a)    relates to a claim allocated to the small claims track; and
        (b)    is being heard in a county court or the High Court.
        (Paragraph 5.8 applies where this paragraph does not apply)

    (2)    The appellant must file the following documents together with an appeal bundle (see paragraph 5.6A) with his appellant's notice –
        (a)    two additional copies of the appellant's notice for the appeal court; and
        (b)    one copy of the appellant's notice for each of the respondents;
        (c)    one copy of his skeleton argument for each copy of the appellant's notice that is filed (see paragraph 5.9);
        (d)    a sealed copy of the order being appealed;
        (e)    a copy of any order giving or refusing permission to appeal, together with a copy of the judge's reasons for allowing or refusing permission to appeal;
        (f)    any witness statements or affidavits in support of any application included in the appellant's notice;
        (g)    a copy of the order allocating a case to a track (if any).

5.6A

    (1)    An appellant must include in his appeal bundle the following documents:
        (a)    a sealed copy of the appellant's notice;
        (b)    a sealed copy of the order being appealed;
        (c)    a copy of any order giving or refusing permission to appeal, together with a copy of the judge's reasons for allowing or refusing permission to appeal;
        (d)    any affidavit or witness statement filed in support of any application included in the appellant's notice;
        (e)    a copy of his skeleton argument;

(f)    except where sub-paragraph (1A) applies a transcript or note of judgment (see paragraph 5.12), and in cases where permission to appeal was given by the lower court or is not required those parts of any transcript of evidence which are directly relevant to any question at issue on the appeal;

(g)    the claim form and statements of case (where relevant to the subject of the appeal);

(h)    any application notice (or case management documentation) relevant to the subject of the appeal;

(i)    in cases where the decision appealed was itself made on appeal (eg from district judge to circuit judge), the first order, the reasons given and the appellant's notice used to appeal from that order;

(j)    in the case of judicial review or a statutory appeal, the original decision which was the subject of the application to the lower court;

(k)    in cases where the appeal is from a Tribunal, a copy of the Tribunal's reasons for the decision, a copy of the decision reviewed by the Tribunal and the reasons for the original decision and any document filed with the Tribunal setting out the grounds of appeal from that decision;

(l)    any other documents which the appellant reasonably considers necessary to enable the appeal court to reach its decision on the hearing of the application or appeal; and

(m)    such other documents as the court may direct.

(1A)    Where the appeal relates to a judgment following a determination on the papers under Part 8 in accordance with Practice Direction 8B, the appellant must include in the appeal bundle the order made by the court containing the reasons for the award of damages. A transcript of the judgment is not required.

(2)    All documents that are extraneous to the issues to be considered on the application or the appeal must be excluded. The appeal bundle may include affidavits, witness statements, summaries, experts' reports and exhibits but only where these are directly relevant to the subject matter of the appeal.

(3)    Where the appellant is represented, the appeal bundle must contain a certificate signed by his solicitor, counsel or other representative to the effect that he has read and understood paragraph (2) above and that the composition of the appeal bundle complies with it.

5.7 Where it is not possible to file all the above documents, the appellant must indicate which documents have not yet been filed and the reasons why they are not currently available. The appellant must then provide a reasonable estimate of when the missing document or documents can be filed and file them as soon as reasonably practicable.

## Small claims

5.8

(1)    This paragraph applies where –
   (a)    the appeal relates to a claim allocated to the small claims track; and
   (b)    the appeal is being heard in a county court or the High Court.

(1A)   An appellant's notice must be filed and served in Form N164.

(2)   The appellant must file the following documents with his appellant's notice –

   (a)   a sealed copy of the order being appealed; and

   (b)   any order giving or refusing permission to appeal, together with a copy of the reasons for that decision.

(3)   The appellant may, if relevant to the issues to be determined on the appeal, file any other document listed in paragraph 5.6 or 5.6A in addition to the documents referred to in sub-paragraph (2).

(4)   The appellant need not file a record of the reasons for judgment of the lower court with his appellant's notice unless sub-paragraph (5) applies.

(5)   The court may order a suitable record of the reasons for judgment of the lower court (see paragraph 5.12) to be filed –

   (a)   to enable it to decide if permission should be granted; or

   (b)   if permission is granted to enable it to decide the appeal.

## Skeleton arguments

5.9

(1)   The appellant's notice must, subject to (2) , (2A) and (3) below, be accompanied by a skeleton argument. Alternatively the skeleton argument may be included in the appellant's notice. Where the skeleton argument is so included it will not form part of the notice for the purposes of rule 52.8.

(2)   Where it is impracticable for the appellant's skeleton argument to accompany the appellant's notice it must be filed and served subject to (2A) below on all respondents within 14 days of filing the notice.

(2A)   The appellant's skeleton argument need not be served on any respondents in an appeal against a decision to refuse to grant an interim injunction under section 41 of the Policing and Crime Act 2009.

(3)   An appellant who is not represented need not file a skeleton argument but is encouraged to do so since this will be helpful to the court.

## Content of skeleton arguments

5.10

(1)   A skeleton argument must contain a numbered list of the points which the party wishes to make. These should both define and confine the areas of controversy. Each point should be stated as concisely as the nature of the case allows.

(2)   A numbered point must be followed by a reference to any document on which the party wishes to rely.

(3)   A skeleton argument must state, in respect of each authority cited –

   (a)   the proposition of law that the authority demonstrates; and

   (b)   the parts of the authority (identified by page or paragraph references) that support the proposition.

(4)   If more than one authority is cited in support of a given proposition, the skeleton argument must briefly state the reason for taking that course.

(5)    The statement referred to in sub-paragraph (4) should not materially add
       to the length of the skeleton argument but should be sufficient to
       demonstrate, in the context of the argument –
       (a)    the relevance of the authority or authorities to that argument; and
       (b)    that the citation is necessary for a proper presentation of that
              argument.

(6)    The cost of preparing a skeleton argument which –
       (a)    does not comply with the requirements set out in this paragraph;
              or
       (b)    was not filed within the time limits provided by this Practice
              Direction (or any further time granted by the court),

(7)    A skeleton argument filed in the Court of Appeal, Civil Division on
       behalf of the appellant should contain in paragraph 1 the advocate's
       time estimate for the hearing of the appeal.
will not be allowed on assessment except to the extent that the court otherwise
directs.

5.11 The appellant should consider what other information the appeal court will
need. This may include a list of persons who feature in the case or glossaries of
technical terms. A chronology of relevant events will be necessary in most appeals.

## Suitable record of the judgment

5.12 Where the judgment to be appealed has been officially recorded by the court,
an approved transcript of that record should accompany the appellant's notice.
Photocopies will not be accepted for this purpose. However, where there is no
officially recorded judgment, the following documents will be acceptable –

### WRITTEN JUDGMENTS

(1)    Where the judgment was made in writing a copy of that judgment
       endorsed with the judge's signature.

### NOTE OF JUDGMENT

(2)    When judgment was not officially recorded or made in writing a note of
       the judgment (agreed between the appellant's and respondent's
       advocates) should be submitted for approval to the judge whose decision
       is being appealed. If the parties cannot agree on a single note of the
       judgment, both versions should be provided to that judge with an
       explanatory letter. For the purpose of an application for permission to
       appeal the note need not be approved by the respondent or the lower
       court judge.

### ADVOCATES' NOTES OF JUDGMENTS WHERE THE APPELLANT IS
### UNREPRESENTED

(3)    When the appellant was unrepresented in the lower court it is the duty of
       any advocate for the respondent to make his/her note of judgment
       promptly available, free of charge to the appellant where there is no

officially recorded judgment or if the court so directs. Where the appellant was represented in the lower court it is the duty of his/her own former advocate to make his/her note available in these circumstances. The appellant should submit the note of judgment to the appeal court.

## REASONS FOR JUDGMENT IN TRIBUNAL CASES

(4)     A sealed copy of the tribunal's reasons for the decision.

5.13 An appellant may not be able to obtain an official transcript or other suitable record of the lower court's decision within the time within which the appellant's notice must be filed. In such cases the appellant's notice must still be completed to the best of the appellant's ability on the basis of the documentation available. However, it may be amended subsequently with the permission of the appeal court.

## *Advocates' notes of judgments*

5.14 Advocates' brief (or, where appropriate, refresher) fee includes –

(1)     remuneration for taking a note of the judgment of the court;
(2)     having the note transcribed accurately;
(3)     attempting to agree the note with the other side if represented;
(4)     submitting the note to the judge for approval where appropriate;
(5)     revising it if so requested by the judge;
(6)     providing any copies required for the appeal court, instructing solicitors and lay client; and
(7)     providing a copy of his note to an unrepresented appellant.

## *Transcripts or Notes of Evidence*

5.15 When the evidence is relevant to the appeal an official transcript of the relevant evidence must be obtained. Transcripts or notes of evidence are generally not needed for the purpose of determining an application for permission to appeal.

## *Notes of evidence*

5.16 If evidence relevant to the appeal was not officially recorded, a typed version of the judge's notes of evidence must be obtained.

## *Transcripts at public expense*

5.17 Where the lower court or the appeal court is satisfied that: –

(1)     an unrepresented appellant; or
(2)     an appellant whose legal representation is provided free of charge to the appellant and not funded by the Community Legal Service;

is in such poor financial circumstances that the cost of a transcript would be an excessive burden the court may certify that the cost of obtaining one official transcript should be borne at public expense.

5.18  In the case of a request for an official transcript of evidence or proceedings to be paid for at public expense, the court must also be satisfied that there are reasonable grounds for appeal. Whenever possible a request for a transcript at public expense should be made to the lower court when asking for permission to appeal.

## Filing and service of appellant's notice

5.19  Rule 52.4 sets out the procedure and time limits for filing and serving an appellant's notice. The appellant must file the appellant's notice at the appeal court within such period as may be directed by the lower court which should not normally exceed 35 days or, where the lower court directs no such period, within 21 days of the date of the decision that the appellant wishes to appeal.

(Rule 52.15 sets out the time limit for filing an application for permission to appeal against the refusal of the High Court to grant permission to apply for judicial review)

5.20  Where the lower court judge announces his decision and reserves the reasons for his judgment or order until a later date, he should, in the exercise of powers under rule 52.4(2)(a), fix a period for filing the appellant's notice at the appeal court that takes this into account.

5.21

(1)   Except where the appeal court orders otherwise a sealed copy of the appellant's notice, including any skeleton arguments must be served on all respondents in accordance with the timetable prescribed by rule 52.4(3) except where this requirement is modified by para-graph 5.9(2) in which case the skeleton argument should be served as soon as it is filed.

(2)   The appellant must, as soon as practicable, file a certificate of service of the documents referred to in paragraph (1).

5.22  Unless the court otherwise directs a respondent need not take any action when served with an appellant's notice until such time as notification is given to him that permission to appeal has been given.

5.23  The court may dispense with the requirement for service of the notice on a respondent. Any application notice seeking an order under rule 6.28 to dispense with service should set out the reasons relied on and be verified by a statement of truth.

5.24

(1)   Where the appellant is applying for permission to appeal in his appellant's notice, he must serve on the respondents his appellant's notice and skeleton argument (but not the appeal bundle), unless the appeal court directs otherwise.

(2)   Where permission to appeal –
      (a)   has been given by the lower court; or
      (b)   is not required,

the appellant must serve the appeal bundle on the respondents with the appellant's notice.

## *Amendment of Appeal Notice*

5.25 An appeal notice may be amended with permission. Such an application to amend and any application in opposition will normally be dealt with at the hearing unless that course would cause unnecessary expense or delay in which case a request should be made for the application to amend to be heard in advance.

## **Procedure after Permission is Obtained**

6.1 This paragraph sets out the procedure where –

    (1)    permission to appeal is given by the appeal court; or
    (2)    the appellant's notice is filed in the appeal court and –
        (a)    permission was given by the lower court; or
        (b)    permission is not required.

6.2 If the appeal court gives permission to appeal, the appeal bundle must be served on each of the respondents within 7 days of receiving the order giving permission to appeal.

(Part 6 (service of documents) provides rules on service)

6.3 The appeal court will send the parties –

    (1)    notification of –
        (a)    the date of the hearing or the period of time (the 'listing window') during which the appeal is likely to be heard; and
        (b)    in the Court of Appeal, the date by which the appeal will be heard (the 'hear by date');

    (2)    where permission is granted by the appeal court a copy of the order giving permission to appeal; and
    (3)    any other directions given by the court.

6.3A

    (1)    Where the appeal court grants permission to appeal, the appellant must add the following documents to the appeal bundle –
        (a)    the respondent's notice and skeleton argument (if any);
        (b)    those parts of the transcripts of evidence which are directly relevant to any question at issue on the appeal;
        (c)    the order granting permission to appeal and, where permission to appeal was granted at an oral hearing, the transcript (or note) of any judgment which was given; and
        (d)    any document which the appellant and respondent have agreed to add to the appeal bundle in accordance with paragraph 7.11.

    (2)    Where permission to appeal has been refused on a particular issue, the appellant must remove from the appeal bundle all documents that are relevant only to that issue.

## *Appeal Questionnaire in the Court of Appeal*

6.4 The Court of Appeal will send an Appeal Questionnaire to the appellant when it notifies him of the matters referred to in paragraph 6.3.

6.5 The appellant must complete and file the Appeal Questionnaire within 14 days of the date of the letter of notification of the matters in paragraph 6.3. The Appeal Questionnaire must contain:

(1)    if the appellant is legally represented, the advocate's time estimate for the hearing of the appeal;

(2)    where a transcript of evidence is relevant to the appeal, confirmation as to what parts of a transcript of evidence have been ordered where this is not already in the bundle of documents;

(3)    confirmation that copies of the appeal bundle are being prepared and will be held ready for the use of the Court of Appeal and an undertaking that they will be supplied to the court on request. For the purpose of these bundles photocopies of the transcripts will be accepted;

(4)    confirmation that copies of the Appeal Questionnaire and the appeal bundle have been served on the respondents and the date of that service.

## TIME ESTIMATES

6.6 The time estimate included in an Appeal Questionnaire must be that of the advocate who will argue the appeal. It should exclude the time required by the court to give judgment. If the respondent disagrees with the time estimate, the respondent must inform the court within 7 days of receipt of the Appeal Questionnaire. In the absence of such notification the respondent will be deemed to have accepted the estimate proposed on behalf of the appellant.

## Respondent

7.1 A respondent who wishes to ask the appeal court to vary the order of the lower court in any way must appeal and permission will be required on the same basis as for an appellant.

(Paragraph 3.2 applies to grounds of appeal by a respondent)

7.2 A respondent who wishes only to request that the appeal court upholds the judgment or order of the lower court whether for the reasons given in the lower court or otherwise does not make an appeal and does not therefore require permission to appeal in accordance with rule 52.3(1).

(Paragraph 7.6 requires a respondent to file a skeleton argument where he wishes to address the appeal court)

7.3

(1)    A respondent who wishes to appeal or who wishes to ask the appeal court to uphold the order of the lower court for reasons different from or additional to those given by the lower court must file a respondent's notice.

(2)    If the respondent does not file a respondent's notice, he will not be entitled, except with the permission of the court, to rely on any reason not relied on in the lower court.

7.3A Paragraphs 5.1A, 5.1B and 5.2 of this practice direction (Human Rights and extension for time for filing appellant's notice) also apply to a respondent and a respondent's notice.

## Time limits

7.4 The time limits for filing a respondent's notice are set out in rule 52.5 (4) and (5).

7.5 Where an extension of time is required the extension must be requested in the respondent's notice and the reasons why the respondent failed to act within the specified time must be included.

7.6 Except where paragraph 7.7A applies, the respondent must file a skeleton argument for the court in all cases where he proposes to address arguments to the court. The respondent's skeleton argument may be included within a respondent's notice. Where a skeleton argument is included within a respondent's notice it will not form part of the notice for the purposes of rule 52.8.

7.7

(1)    A respondent who –
    (a)    files a respondent's notice; but
    (b)    does not include his skeleton argument within that notice,

must file and serve his skeleton argument within 14 days of filing the notice.
(2)    A respondent who does not file a respondent's notice but who files a skeleton argument must file and serve that skeleton argument at least 7 days before the appeal hearing.
(Rule 52.5(4) sets out the period for filing and serving a respondent's notice)

7.7A

(1)    Where the appeal relates to a claim allocated to the small claims track and is being heard in a county court or the High Court, the respondent may file a skeleton argument but is not required to do so.
(2)    A respondent who is not represented need not file a skeleton argument but is encouraged to do so in order to assist the court.

7.7B The respondent must –

(1)    serve his skeleton argument on –
    (a)    the appellant; and
    (b)    any other respondent,

at the same time as he files it at the court; and
(2)    file a certificate of service.

## Content of skeleton arguments

7.8 A respondent's skeleton argument must conform to the directions at paragraphs 5.10 and 5.11 with any necessary modifications. It should, where appropriate, answer the arguments set out in the appellant's skeleton argument.

## Applications within respondent's notices

7.9 A respondent may include an application within a respondent's notice in accordance with paragraph 5.5 above.

## *Filing respondent's notices and skeleton arguments*

7.10

(1)     The respondent must file the following documents with his respondent's notice in every case:
    (a)     two additional copies of the respondent's notice for the appeal court; and
    (b)     one copy each for the appellant and any other respondents.

(2)     The respondent may file a skeleton argument with his respondent's notice and –
    (a)     where he does so he must file two copies; and
    (b)     where he does not do so he must comply with paragraph 7.7.

7.11 If the respondent wishes to rely on any documents which he reasonably considers necessary to enable the appeal court to reach its decision on the appeal in addition to those filed by the appellant, he must make every effort to agree amendments to the appeal bundle with the appellant.

7.12

(1)     If the representatives for the parties are unable to reach agreement, the respondent may prepare a supplemental bundle.
(2)     If the respondent prepares a supplemental bundle he must file it, together with the requisite number of copies for the appeal court, at the appeal court –
    (a)     with the respondent's notice; or
    (b)     if a respondent's notice is not filed, within 21 days after he is served with the appeal bundle.

7.13 The respondent must serve –

(1)     the respondent's notice;
(2)     his skeleton argument (if any); and
(3)     the supplemental bundle (if any),
on –
    (a)     the appellant; and
    (b)     any other respondent,
at the same time as he files them at the court.

## Appeals to the High Court

### *Application*

8.1 This paragraph applies where an appeal lies to a High Court judge from the decision of a county court or a district judge of the High Court.

8.2 The following table sets out the following venues for each circuit –

(a)     Appeal centres – court centres where appeals to which this paragraph applies may be filed, managed and heard. Paragraphs 8.6 to 8.8 provide for special arrangements in relation to the South Eastern Circuit.
(b)     Hearing only centres – court centres where appeals to which this paragraph applies may be heard by order made at an appeal centre (see paragraph 8.10).

| Circuit | Appeal Centres | Hearing Only Centres |
|---------|----------------|----------------------|
| **Midland Circuit** | Birmingham | Lincoln |
| | Nottingham | Leicester |
| | | Northampton |
| | | Stafford |
| **North Eastern Circuit** | Leeds | Teesside |
| | Newcastle | |
| | Sheffield | |
| **Northern Circuit** | Manchester | Carlisle |
| | Liverpool | |
| | Preston | |
| | Chester | |
| **Wales Circuit** | Cardiff | Caernarfon |
| | Swansea | |
| | Mold | |
| | ... | |
| **Western Circuit** | Bristol | Truro |
| | Exeter | Plymouth |
| | Winchester | |
| **South Eastern Circuit** | Royal Courts of Justice | |
| | Lewes | |
| | Luton | |
| | Norwich | |
| | Reading | |
| | Chelmsford | |
| | St Albans | |
| | Maidstone | |
| | Oxford | |

## *Venue for appeals and filing of notices on circuits other than the South Eastern Circuit*

8.3 Paragraphs 8.4 and 8.5 apply where the lower court is situated on a circuit other than the South Eastern Circuit.

8.4 The appellant's notice must be filed at an appeal centre on the circuit in which the lower court is situated. The appeal will be managed and heard at that appeal centre unless the appeal court orders otherwise.

8.5 A respondent's notice must be filed at the appeal centre where the appellant's notice was filed unless the appeal has been transferred to another appeal centre, in which case it must be filed at that appeal centre.

## *Venue for appeals and filing of notices on the South Eastern Circuit*

8.6 Paragraphs 8.7 and 8.8 apply where the lower court is situated on the South Eastern Circuit.

8.7 The appellant's notice must be filed at an appeal centre on the South Eastern Circuit. The appeal will be managed and heard at the Royal Courts of Justice unless the appeal court orders otherwise. An order that an appeal is to be managed or heard at another appeal centre may not be made unless the consent of the Presiding Judge of the circuit in charge of civil matters has been obtained.

8.8 A respondent's notice must be filed at the Royal Courts of Justice unless the appeal has been transferred to another appeal centre, in which case it must be filed at that appeal centre.

## *General provisions*

8.9 The appeal court may transfer an appeal to another appeal centre (whether or not on the same circuit). In deciding whether to do so the court will have regard to the criteria in rule 30.3 (criteria for a transfer order). The appeal court may do so either on application by a party or of its own initiative. Where an appeal is transferred under this paragraph, notice of transfer must be served on every person on whom the appellant's notice has been served. An appeal may not be transferred to an appeal centre on another circuit, either for management or hearing, unless the consent of the Presiding Judge of that circuit in charge of civil matters has been obtained.

8.10 Directions may be given for –

(a)　an appeal to be heard at a hearing only centre; or

(b)　an application in an appeal to be heard at any other venue,

instead of at the appeal centre managing the appeal.

8.11 Unless a direction has been made under 8.10, any application in the appeal must be made at the appeal centre where the appeal is being managed.

8.12 The appeal court may adopt all or any part of the procedure set out in paragraphs 6.4 to 6.6.

8.13 Where the lower court is a county court:

(1)　subject to paragraph (1A), appeals and applications for permission to appeal will be heard by a High Court Judge or by a person authorised under paragraphs (1), (2) or (4) of the Table in section 9(1) of the Supreme Court Act 1981 to act as a judge of the High Court;

(1A)　an appeal or application for permission to appeal from the decision of a Recorder in the county court may be heard by a Designated Civil Judge who is authorised under paragraph (5) of the Table in section 9(1) of the Supreme Court Act 1981 to act as a judge of the High Court; and

(2)    other applications in the appeal may be heard and directions in the appeal may be given either by a High Court Judge or by any person authorised under section 9 of the Supreme Court Act 1981 to act as a judge of the High Court.

8.14 In the case of appeals from Masters or district judges of the High Court, appeals, applications for permission and any other applications in the appeal may be heard and directions in the appeal may be given by a High Court Judge or by any person authorised under section 9 of the Supreme Court Act 1981 to act as a judge of the High Court.

## Appeals to a Judge of a County Court from a District Judge

8A.1 The Designated Civil Judge in consultation with his Presiding Judges has responsibility for allocating appeals from decisions of district judges to circuit judges.

## Re-Hearings

9.1 The hearing of an appeal will be a re-hearing (as opposed to a review of the decision of the lower court) if the appeal is from the decision of a minister, person or other body and the minister, person or other body –

(1)    did not hold a hearing to come to that decision; or
(2)    held a hearing to come to that decision, but the procedure adopted did not provide for the consideration of evidence.

## Appeals Transferred to the Court of Appeal

10.1 Where an appeal is transferred to the Court of Appeal under rule 52.14 the Court of Appeal may give such additional directions as are considered appropriate.

## Applications

11.1 Where a party to an appeal makes an application whether in an appeal notice or by Part 23 application notice, the provisions of Part 23 will apply.

11.2 The applicant must file the following documents with the notice

(1)    one additional copy of the application notice for the appeal court and one copy for each of the respondents;
(2)    where applicable a sealed copy of the order which is the subject of the main appeal;
(3)    a bundle of documents in support which should include:
    (a)    the Part 23 application notice; and
    (b)    any witness statements and affidavits filed in support of the application notice.

## Disposing of Applications or Appeals by Consent

*Dismissal of applications or appeals by consent*

12.1 These paragraphs do not apply where –

(1)    any party to the proceedings is a child or protected party; or
(2)    the appeal or application is to the Court of Appeal from a decision of the Court of Protection.

12.2 Where an appellant does not wish to pursue an application or an appeal, he may request the appeal court for an order that his application or appeal be dismissed. Such a request must contain a statement that the appellant is not a child or protected party and that the appeal or application is not from a decision of the Court of Protection. If such a request is granted it will usually be on the basis that the appellant pays the costs of the application or appeal.

12.3 If the appellant wishes to have the application or appeal dismissed without costs, his request must be accompanied by a consent signed by the respondent or his legal representative stating –

(1)    that the respondent is not a child or protected party and that the appeal or application is not from a decision of the Court of Protection; and
(2)    that he consents to the dismissal of the application or appeal without costs.

12.4 Where a settlement has been reached disposing of the application or appeal, the parties may make a joint request to the court stating that –

(1)    none of them is a child or protected party; and
(2)    the appeal or application is not from a decision of the Court of Protection,

and asking that the application or appeal be dismissed by consent. If the request is granted the application or appeal will be dismissed.

('Child' and 'protected party' have the same meaning as in rule 21.1(2).)

*Allowing unopposed appeals or applications on paper*

13.1 The appeal court will not normally make an order allowing an appeal unless satisfied that the decision of the lower court was wrong, but the appeal court may set aside or vary the order of the lower court with consent and without determining the merits of the appeal, if it is satisfied that there are good and sufficient reasons for doing so. Where the appeal court is requested by all parties to allow an application or an appeal the court may consider the request on the papers. The request should state that none of the parties is a child or protected party and that the application or appeal is not from a decision of the Court of Protection and set out the relevant history of the proceedings and the matters relied on as justifying the proposed order and be accompanied by a copy of the proposed order.

## Procedure for consent orders and agreements to pay periodical payments involving a child or protected party or in applications or appeals to the Court of Appeal from a decision of the Court of Protection

13.2 Where one of the parties is a child or protected party or the application or appeal is to the Court of Appeal from a decision of the Court of Protection –

(1)   a settlement relating to an appeal or application;...

(2)   in a personal injury claim for damages for future pecuniary loss, an agreement reached at the appeal stage to pay periodical payments; or

(3)   a request by an appellant for an order that his application or appeal be dismissed with or without the consent of the respondent,

requires the court's approval.

### Child

13.3 In cases involving a child a copy of the proposed order signed by the parties' solicitors should be sent to the appeal court, together with an opinion from the advocate acting on behalf of the child.

### Protected party

13.4 Where a party is a protected party the same procedure will be adopted, but the documents filed should also include any relevant reports prepared for the Court of Protection ...

('Child' and 'protected party' have the same meaning as in rule 21.1(2).)

### Periodical payments

13.5 Where periodical payments for future pecuniary loss have been negotiated in a personal injury case which is under appeal, the documents filed should include those which would be required in the case of a personal injury claim for damages for future pecuniary loss dealt with at first instance. Details can be found in Practice Direction 21.

## Summary Assessment of Costs

14.1 Costs are likely to be assessed by way of summary assessment at the following hearings:

(1)   contested directions hearings;

(2)   applications for permission to appeal at which the respondent is present;

(3)   dismissal list hearings in the Court of Appeal at which the respondent is present;

(4)   appeals from case management decisions; and

(5)   appeals listed for one day or less.

14.2 Parties attending any of the hearings referred to in paragraph 14.1 should be prepared to deal with the summary assessment.

## Other Special Provisions Regarding the Court of Appeal

### *Filing of Documents*

15.1

(1)     The documents relevant to proceedings in the Court of Appeal, Civil Division must be filed in the Civil Appeals Office Registry, Room E307, Royal Courts of Justice, Strand, London, WC2A 2LL.

(2)     The Civil Appeals Office will not serve documents and where service is required by the CPR or this practice direction it must be effected by the parties.

15.1A

(1)     A party may file by e-mail –
   (a)     an appellant's notice;
   (b)     a respondent's notice;
   (c)     an application notice,

In the Court of Appeal, Civil Division, using the e-mail account specified in the 'Guidelines for filing by E-mail' which appear on the Court of Appeal, Civil Division website at www.civilappeals.gov.uk.

(2)     A party may only file a notice in accordance with paragraph (1) where he is permitted to do so by the 'Guidelines for filing by E-mail'.

15.1B

(1)     A party to an appeal in the Court of Appeal, Civil Division may file –
   (a)     an appellant's notice;
   (b)     a respondent's notice; or
   (c)     an application notice,

electronically using the online forms service on the Court of Appeal, Civil Division website at *www.civilappeals.gov.uk*.

(2)     A party may only file a notice in accordance with paragraph (1) where he is permitted to so do by the 'Guidelines for filing electronically'. The Guidelines for filing electronically may be found on the Court of Appeal, Civil Division website.

(3)     The online forms service will assist the user in completing a document accurately but the user is responsible for ensuring that the rules and practice directions relating to the document have been complied with. Transmission by the service does not guarantee that the document will be accepted by the Court of Appeal, Civil Division.

(4)     A party using the online forms service in accordance with this paragraph is responsible for ensuring that the transmission or any document attached to it is filed within any relevant time limits.

(5)     Parties are advised not to transmit electronically any correspondence or documents of a confidential or sensitive nature, as security cannot be guaranteed.

(6)     Where a party wishes to file a document containing a statement of truth electronically, that party should retain the document containing the original signature and file with the court a version of the document on which the name of the person who has signed the statement of truth is typed underneath the statement.

## Core Bundles

15.2 In cases where the appeal bundle comprises more than 500 pages, exclusive of transcripts, the appellant's solicitors must, after consultation with the respondent's solicitors, also prepare and file with the court, in addition to copies of the appeal bundle (as amended in accordance with paragraph 7.11) the requisite number of copies of a core bundle.

15.3

    (1)    The core bundle must be filed within 28 days of receipt of the order giving permission to appeal or, where permission to appeal was granted by the lower court or is not required, within 28 days of the date of service of the appellant's notice on the respondent.

    (2)    The core bundle –
        (a)    must contain the documents which are central to the appeal; and
        (b)    must not exceed 150 pages.

## Preparation of bundles

15.4 The provisions of this paragraph apply to the preparation of appeal bundles, supplemental respondents' bundles where the parties are unable to agree amendments to the appeal bundle, and core bundles.

    (1)    **Rejection of bundles**. Where documents are copied unnecessarily or bundled incompletely, costs may be disallowed. Where the provisions of this Practice Direction as to the preparation or delivery of bundles are not followed the bundle may be rejected by the court or be made the subject of a special costs order.

    (2)    **Avoidance of duplication**. No more than one copy of any document should be included unless there is a good reason for doing otherwise (such as the use of a separate core bundle – see paragraph 15.2).

    (3)    **Pagination**
        (a)    Bundles must be paginated, each page being numbered individually and consecutively. The pagination used at trial must also be indicated. Letters and other documents should normally be included in chronological order. (An exception to consecutive page numbering arises in the case of core bundles where it may be preferable to retain the original numbering).
        (b)    Page numbers should be inserted in bold figures at the bottom of the page and in a form that can be clearly distinguished from any other pagination on the document.

    (4)    **Format and presentation**
        (a)    Where possible the documents should be in A4 format. Where a document has to be read across rather than down the page, it should be so placed in the bundle as to ensure that the text starts nearest the spine.
        (b)    Where any marking or writing in colour on a document is important, the document must be copied in colour or marked up correctly in colour.
        (c)    Documents which are not easily legible should be transcribed and the transcription marked and placed adjacent to the document transcribed.

(d)     Documents in a foreign language should be translated and the translation marked and placed adjacent to the document translated. The translation should be agreed or, if it cannot be agreed, each party's proposed translation should be included.

(e)     The size of any bundle should be tailored to its contents. A large lever arch file should not be used for just a few pages nor should files of whatever size be overloaded.

(f)     Where it will assist the Court of Appeal, different sections of the file may be separated by cardboard or other tabbed dividers so long as these are clearly indexed. Where, for example, a document is awaited when the appeal bundle is filed, a single sheet of paper can be inserted after a divider, indicating the nature of the document awaited. For example, 'Transcript of evidence of Mr J Smith (to follow)'.

(5)   **Binding**

(a)     All documents, with the exception of transcripts, must be bound together. This may be in a lever arch file, ring binder or plastic folder. Plastic sleeves containing loose documents must not be used. Binders and files must be strong enough to withstand heavy use.

(b)     Large documents such as plans should be placed in an easily accessible file. Large documents which will need to be opened up frequently should be inserted in a file larger than A4 size.

(6)   **Indices and labels**

(a)     An index must be included at the front of the bundle listing all the documents and providing the page references for each. In the case of documents such as letters, invoices or bank statements, they may be given a general description.

(b)     Where the bundles consist of more than one file, an index to all the files should be included in the first file and an index included for each file. Indices should, if possible, be on a single sheet. The full name of the case should not be inserted on the index if this would waste space. Documents should be identified briefly but properly.

(7)   **Identification**

(a)     Every bundle must be clearly identified, on the spine and on the front cover, with the name of the case and the Court of Appeal's reference. Where the bundle consists of more than one file, each file must be numbered on the spine, the front cover and the inside of the front cover.

(b)     Outer labels should use large lettering eg ' Appeal Bundle A' or 'Core Bundle'. The full title of the appeal and solicitors' names and addresses should be omitted. A label should be used on the front as well as on the spine.

(8)   **Staples etc**. All staples, heavy metal clips etc, must be removed.

(9)   **Statements of case**

(a)     Statements of case should be assembled in 'chapter' form – ie claim followed by particulars of claim, followed by further information, irrespective of date.

(b)     Redundant documents, eg particulars of claim overtaken by amendments, requests for further information recited in the answers given, should generally be excluded.

(10)   **New Documents**
    (a)     Before a new document is introduced into bundles which have already been delivered to the court, steps should be taken to ensure that it carries an appropriate bundle/page number so that it can be added to the court documents. It should not be stapled and it should be prepared with punch holes for immediate inclusion in the binders in use.
    (b)     If it is expected that a large number of miscellaneous new documents will from time to time be introduced, there should be a special tabbed empty loose-leaf file for that purpose. An index should be produced for this file, updated as necessary.

(11)   **Inter-solicitor correspondence**. Since inter-solicitor correspondence is unlikely to be required for the purposes of an appeal, only those letters which will need to be referred to should be copied.

(12)   **Sanctions for non-compliance**. If the appellant fails to comply with the requirements as to the provision of bundles of documents, the application or appeal will be referred for consideration to be given as to why it should not be dismissed for failure to so comply.

## Master in the Court of Appeal, Civil Division

15.5 The Master of the Rolls may designate an eligible officer to exercise judicial authority under rule 52.16 as Master. Other eligible officers may also be designated by the Master of the Rolls to exercise judicial authority under rule 52.16 and shall then be known as Deputy Masters.

## Respondent to notify Civil Appeals Office whether he intends to file respondent's notice

15.6 A respondent must, no later than 21 days after the date he is served with notification that –

(1)     permission to appeal has been granted; or
(2)     the application for permission to appeal and the appeal are to be heard together,
inform the Civil Appeals Office and the appellant in writing whether –
    (a)     he proposes to file a respondent's notice appealing the order or seeking to uphold the order for reasons different from, or additional to, those given by the lower court; or
    (b)     he proposes to rely on the reasons given by the lower court for its decision.

(Paragraph 15.11B requires all documents needed for an appeal hearing, including a respondent's skeleton argument, to be filed at least 7 days before the hearing)

## Listing and hear-by dates

15.7  The management of the list will be dealt with by the listing officer under the direction of the Master.

15.8  The Civil Appeals List of the Court of Appeal is divided as follows:

- *The applications list* – applications for permission to appeal and other applications.
- *The appeals list* – appeals where permission to appeal has been given or where an appeal lies without permission being required where a hearing date is fixed in advance. (Appeals in this list which require special listing arrangements will be assigned to the special fixtures list)
- *The expedited list* – appeals or applications where the Court of Appeal has directed an expedited hearing. The current practice of the Court of Appeal is summarised in *Unilever plc v Chefaro Proprietaries Ltd* (Practice Note) 1995 1 WLR 243.
- *The stand-out list* – Appeals or applications which, for good reason, are not at present ready to proceed and have been stood out by judicial direction.
- *The second fixtures list* – see paragraph 15.9A(1) below.
- *The second fixtures list* – if an appeal is designated as a 'second fixture' it means that a hearing date is arranged in advance on the express basis that the list is fully booked for the period in question and therefore the case will be heard only if a suitable gap occurs in the list.
- *The short-warned list* – appeals which the court considers may be prepared for the hearing by an advocate other than the one originally instructed with a half day's notice, or such other period as the court may direct.

## Special provisions relating to the short-warned list

15.9

(1)  Where an appeal is assigned to the short-warned list, the Civil Appeals Office will notify the parties' solicitors in writing. The court may abridge the time for filing any outstanding bundles in an appeal assigned to this list.

(2)  The solicitors for the parties must notify their advocate and their client as soon as the Civil Appeals Office notifies them that the appeal has been assigned to the short-warned list.

(3)  The appellant may apply in writing for the appeal to be removed from the short-warned list within 14 days of notification of its assignment. The application will be decided by a Lord Justice, or the Master, and will only be granted for the most compelling reasons.

(4)  The Civil Appeals Listing Officer may place an appeal from the short-warned list 'on call' from a given date and will inform the parties' advocates accordingly.

(5)  An appeal which is 'on call' may be listed for hearing on half a day's notice or such longer period as the court may direct.

(6)  Once an appeal is listed for hearing from the short warned list it becomes the immediate professional duty of the advocate instructed in the appeal, if he is unable to appear at the hearing, to take all practicable measures

to ensure that his lay client is represented at the hearing by an advocate who is fully instructed and able to argue the appeal.

## Special provisions relating to the special fixtures list

15.9A

(1)     The special fixtures list is a sub-division of the appeals list and is used to deal with appeals that may require special listing arrangements, such as the need to list a number of cases before the same constitution, in a particular order, during a particular period or at a given location.

(2)     The Civil Appeals Office will notify the parties' representatives, or the parties if acting in person, of the particular arrangements that will apply. The notice –

   (a)     will give details of the specific period during which a case is scheduled to be heard; and

   (b)     may give directions in relation to the filing of any outstanding documents.

(3)     The listing officer will notify the parties' representatives of the precise hearing date as soon as practicable. While every effort will be made to accommodate the availability of counsel, the requirements of the court will prevail.

## Requests for directions

15.10 To ensure that all requests for directions are centrally monitored and correctly allocated, all requests for directions or rulings (whether relating to listing or any other matters) should be made to the Civil Appeals Office. Those seeking directions or rulings must not approach the supervising Lord Justice either directly, or via his or her clerk.

## Bundles of authorities

15.11

(1)     Once the parties have been notified of the date fixed for the hearing, the appellant's advocate must, after consultation with his opponent, file a bundle containing photocopies of the authorities upon which each side will rely at the hearing.

(2)     The bundle of authorities should, in general –

   (a)     have the relevant passages of the authorities marked;

   (b)     not include authorities for propositions not in dispute; and

   (c)     not contain more than 10 authorities unless the scale of the appeal warrants more extensive citation.

(3)     The bundle of authorities must be filed –

   (a)     at least 7 days before the hearing; or

   (b)     where the period of notice of the hearing is less than 7 days, immediately.

(4)     If, through some oversight, a party intends, during the hearing, to refer to other authorities the parties may agree a second agreed bundle. The appellant's advocate must file this bundle at least 48 hours before the hearing commences.

(5)     A bundle of authorities must bear a certification by the advocates responsible for arguing the case that the requirements of sub-paragraphs (3) to (5) of paragraph 5.10 have been complied with in respect of each authority included.

## Supplementary skeleton arguments

15.11A

(1)     A supplementary skeleton argument on which the appellant wishes to rely must be filed at least 14 days before the hearing.

(2)     A supplementary skeleton argument on which the respondent wishes to rely must be filed at least 7 days before the hearing.

(3)     All supplementary skeleton arguments must comply with the requirements set out in paragraph 5.10.

(4)     At the hearing the court may refuse to hear argument from a party not contained in a skeleton argument filed within the relevant time limit set out in this paragraph.

## Papers for the appeal hearing

15.11B

(1)     All the documents which are needed for the appeal hearing must be filed at least 7 days before the hearing. Where a document has not been filed 10 days before the hearing a reminder will be sent by the Civil Appeals Office.

(2)     Any party who fails to comply with the provisions of paragraph (1) may be required to attend before the Presiding Lord Justice to seek permission to proceed with, or to oppose, the appeal.

## Disposal of bundles of documents

15.11C

(1)     Where the court has determined a case, the official transcriber will retain one set of papers. The Civil Appeals Office will destroy any remaining sets of papers not collected within 21 days of –
    (a)     where one or more parties attend the hearing, the date of the court's decision;
    (b)     where there is no attendance, the date of the notification of court's decision.

(2)     The parties should ensure that bundles of papers supplied to the court do not contain original documents (other than transcripts). The parties must ensure that they –
    (a)     bring any necessary original documents to the hearing; and
    (b)     retrieve any original documents handed up to the court before leaving the court.

(3)    The court will retain application bundles where permission to appeal has been granted. Where permission is refused the arrangements in sub-paragraph (1) will apply.

(4)    Where a single Lord Justice has refused permission to appeal on paper, application bundles will not be destroyed until after the time limit for seeking a hearing has expired.

## Reserved Judgments

15.12  Practice Direction 40E contains provisions relating to reserved judgments.

15.13–15.21  (*Paragraphs omitted*)

## Section II – General Provisions About Statutory Appeals and Appeals by way of Case Stated

16.1  This section contains general provisions about statutory appeals (paragraphs 17.1–17.11) and appeals by way of case stated (paragraphs 18.1–18.20).

16.2  Where any of the provisions in this Section provide for documents to be filed at the appeal court, these documents are in addition to any documents required under Part 52 or section 1 of this Practice Direction.

## Statutory Appeals

17.1  This part of this section –

(1)    applies where under any enactment an appeal (other than by way of case stated) lies to the court from a Minister of State, government department, tribunal or other person ('statutory appeals'); and

(2)    is subject to any provision about a specific category of appeal in any enactment or Section III of this practice direction.

## Part 52

17.2  Part 52 applies to statutory appeals with the following amendments –

## Filing of appellant's notice

17.3  Subject to paragraph 17.4AThe appellant must file the appellant's notice at the appeal court within 28 days after the date of the decision of the lower court being appealed.

17.4  Where a statement of the reasons for a decision is given later than the notice of that decision, the period for filing the appellant's notice is calculated from the date on which the statement is received by the appellant.

17.4A

(1)    Where the appellant wishes to appeal against a decision of the Administrative Appeals Chamber of the Upper Tribunal, the appellant's

notice must be filed within 42 days of the date on which the Upper Tribunal's decision on permission to appeal to the Court of Appeal is given.

(2) Where the appellant wishes to appeal against a decision of any other Chamber of the Upper Tribunal, the appellant's notice must be filed within 28 days of the date on which the Upper Tribunal's decision on permission to appeal to the Court of Appeal is given.

## *Service of appellant's notice*

17.5

(1) Subject to sub-paragraph (1A), in addition to the respondents to the appeal, the appellant must serve the appellant's notice in accordance with rule 52.4(3) on the chairman of the tribunal, Minister of State, government department or other person from whose decision the appeal is brought.

(1A) Sub-paragraph (1) does not apply to an appeal against a decision of the Upper Tribunal.

(2) In the case of an appeal from the decision of a tribunal that has no chairman or member who acts as a chairman, the appellant's notice must be served on the member or members of the tribunal.

## *Right of Minister etc to be heard on the appeal*

17.6 Where the appeal is from an order or decision of a Minister of State or government department, the Minister or department, as the case may be, is entitled to attend the hearing and to make representations to the court.

## *Rule 52.12A Statutory appeals – court's power to hear any person*

17.7 Where all the parties consent, the court may deal with an application under rule 52.12A without a hearing.

17.8 Where the court gives permission for a person to file evidence or to make representations at the appeal hearing, it may do so on conditions and may give case management directions.

17.9 An application for permission must be made by letter to the relevant court office, identifying the appeal, explaining who the applicant is and indicating why and in what form the applicant wants to participate in the hearing.

17.10 If the applicant is seeking a prospective order as to costs, the letter must say what kind of order and on what grounds.

17.11 Applications to intervene must be made at the earliest reasonable opportunity, since it will usually be essential not to delay the hearing.

## Appeals by way of Case Stated

18.1 This part of this section –

(1) applies where under any enactment –
(a) an appeal lies to the court by way of case stated; or

      (b)    a question of law may be referred to the court by way of case stated; and

  (2)    is subject to any provision about to a specific category of appeal in any enactment or Section III of this practice direction.

## *Part 52*

18.2 Part 52 applies to appeals by way of case stated subject to the following amendments.

## *Case stated by Crown Court or Magistrates' Court*

### APPLICATION TO STATE A CASE

18.3 The procedure for applying to the Crown Court or a magistrates' court to have a case stated for the opinion of the High Court is set out in the Crown Court Rules 1982 and the Magistrates' Courts Rules 1981 respectively.

### FILING OF APPELLANT'S NOTICE

18.4 The appellant must file the appellant's notice at the appeal court within 10 days after he receives the stated case.

### DOCUMENTS TO BE LODGED

18.5 The appellant must lodge the following documents with his appellant's notice –

  (1)    the stated case;
  (2)    a copy of the judgment, order or decision in respect of which the case has been stated; and
  (3)    where the judgment, order or decision in respect of which the case has been stated was itself given or made on appeal, a copy of the judgment, order or decision appealed from.

### SERVICE OF APPELLANT'S NOTICE

18.6 The appellant must serve the appellant's notice and accompanying documents on all respondents within 4 days after they are filed or lodged at the appeal court.

## *Case stated by Minister, government department, tribunal or other person*

### APPLICATION TO STATE A CASE

18.7 The procedure for applying to a Minister, government department, tribunal or other person ('Minister or tribunal etc') to have a case stated for the opinion of the court may be set out in –

  (1)    the enactment which provides for the right of appeal; or

(2)    any rules of procedure relating to the Minister or tribunal etc.

## Signing of stated case by Minister or tribunal etc

18.8

(1)    A case stated by a tribunal must be signed by –
    (a)    the chairman;
    (b)    the president; or
    (c)    in the case where the tribunal has neither person in sub-paragraph (a) or (b) nor any member who acts as its chairman or president, by the member or members of the tribunal.

(2)    A case stated by any other person must be signed by that person or by a person authorised to do so.

## Service of stated case by Minister or tribunal etc

18.9  The Minister or tribunal etc must serve the stated case on –

(1)    the party who requests the case to be stated; or
(2)    the party as a result of whose application to the court, the case was stated.

18.10  Where an enactment provides that a Minister or tribunal etc may state a case or refer a question of law to the court by way of case stated without a request being made, the Minister or tribunal etc must –

(1)    serve the stated case on those parties that the Minister or tribunal etc considers appropriate; and
(2)    give notice to every other party to the proceedings that the stated case has been served on the party named and on the date specified in the notice.

## Filing and service of appellant's notice

18.11  The party on whom the stated case was served must file the appellant's notice and the stated case at the appeal court and serve copies of the notice and stated case on –

(1)    the Minister or tribunal etc who stated the case; and
(2)    every party to the proceedings to which the stated case relates,

within 14 days after the stated case was served on him.

18.12  Where paragraph 18.10 applies the Minister or tribunal etc must –

(1)    file an appellant's notice and the stated case at the appeal court; and
(2)    serve copies of those documents on the persons served under paragraph 18.10,

within 14 days after stating the case.

18.13  Where –

(1)    a stated case has been served by the Minister or tribunal etc in accordance with paragraph 18.9; and

(2)    the party on whom the stated case was served does not file an appellant's notice in accordance with paragraph 18.11, any other party may file an appellant's notice with the stated case at the appeal court and serve a copy of the notice and the case on the persons listed in paragraph 18.11 within the period of time set out in paragraph 18.14.

18.14 The period of time referred to in paragraph 18.13 is 14 days from the last day on which the party on whom the stated case was served may file an appellant's notice in accordance with paragraph 18.11.

## AMENDMENT OF STATED CASE

18.15 The court may amend the stated case or order it to be returned to the Minister or tribunal etc for amendment and may draw inferences of fact from the facts stated in the case.

## RIGHT OF MINISTER ETC TO BE HEARD ON THE APPEAL

18.16 Where the case is stated by a Minister or government department, that Minister or department, as the case may be, is entitled to appear on the appeal and to make representations to the court.

## APPLICATION FOR ORDER TO STATE A CASE

18.17 An application to the court for an order requiring a minister or tribunal etc to state a case for the decision of the court, or to refer a question of law to the court by way of case stated must be made to the court which would be the appeal court if the case were stated.

18.18 An application to the court for an order directing a Minister or tribunal etc to –

(1)    state a case for determination by the court; or
(2)    refer a question of law to the court by way of case stated, must be made in accordance with CPR Part 23.

18.19 The application notice must contain –

(1)    the grounds of the application;
(2)    the question of law on which it is sought to have the case stated; and
(3)    any reasons given by the minister or tribunal etc for his or its refusal to state a case.

18.20 The application notice must be filed at the appeal court and served on –

(1)    the minister, department, secretary of the tribunal or other person as the case may be; and
(2)    every party to the proceedings to which the application relates, within 14 days after the appellant receives notice of the refusal of his request to state a case.

HEARING OF APPEAL BY WAY OF CASE STATED AND APPLICATION
FOR ORDER TO STATE A CASE

18.20A  The court may give directions requiring the proceedings to be heard by a
Divisional Court.

## Section III – Provisions about Specific Appeals

20.1  This section of this practice direction provides special provisions about the
appeals to which the following table refers. This Section is not exhaustive and does
not create, amend or remove any right of appeal.

20.2  Part 52 applies to all appeals to which this section applies subject to any
special provisions set out in this section.

20.3  Where any of the provisions in this section provide for documents to be filed
at the appeal court, these documents are in addition to any documents required
under Part 52 or Sections I or II of this practice direction.

| APPEALS TO THE COURT OF APPEAL | Paragraph |
| --- | --- |
| Articles 81 and 82 of the EC Treaty and Chapters I and II of Part I of the Competition Act 1998 | 21.10A |
| Asylum and Immigration Appeals | 21.7 |
| Civil Partnership – conditional order for dissolution or nullity | 21.1 |
| Competition Appeal Tribunal | 21.10 |
| Contempt of Court | 21.4 |
| Court of Protection | 21.12 |
| Decree nisi of divorce | 21.1 |
| Lands Tribunal | 21.9 |
| Nullity of marriage | 21.1 |
| Patents Court on appeal from Comptroller | 21.3 |
| Proscribed Organisations Appeal Commission | 21.11 |
| Revocation of patent | 21.2 |
| Special Commissioner (where the appeal is direct to the Court of Appeal) | 21.8 |
| Value Added Tax and Duties Tribunals (where the appeal is direct to the Court of Appeal) | 21.6 |

| APPEALS TO THE HIGH COURT | Paragraph |
|---|---|
| Agricultural Land Tribunal | 22.7 |
| Architects Act 1997, s 22 | 22.3 |
| Charities Act 1993 | 23.8A |
| Chiropractors Act 1994, s 31 | 22.3 |
| Clergy Pensions Measure 1961, s 38(3) | 23.2 |
| Commons Registration Act 1965 | 23.9 |
| Consumer Credit Act 1974 | 22.4 |
| Dentists Act 1984, s 20 or s 44 | 22.3 |
| Employment Tribunals Act 1996 | 22.6E |
| Extradition Act 2003 | 22.6A |
| Friendly Societies Act 1974 | 23.7 |
| Friendly Societies Act 1992 | 23.7 |
| Health Professions Order 2001, art 38 | 22.3 |
| Industrial and Provident Societies Act 1965 | 23.2, 23.7 |
| Industrial Assurance Act 1923 | 23.2, 23.7 |
| Industrial Assurance Act 1923, s 17 | 23.6 |
| Inheritance Tax Act 1984, s 222 | 23.3 |
| Inheritance Tax Act 1984, s 225 | 23.5 |
| Inheritance Tax Act 1984, ss 249(3) and 251 | 23.4 |
| Land Registration Act 1925 | 23.2 |
| Land Registration Act 2002 | 23.2, 23.8B |
| Law of Property Act 1922, para 16 of Sch 15 | 23.2 |
| Medical Act 1983, s 40 | 22.3 |
| Medicines Act 1968, ss 82(3) and 83(2) | 22.3 |
| Mental Health Review Tribunal | 22.8 |
| Merchant Shipping Act 1995 | 22.2 |
| National Health Service Act 1977 | 22.6D |

## Appeals to the Court of Appeal

### *Appeal against decree nisi of divorce or nullity of marriage or conditional dissolution or nullity order in relation to civil partnership*

21.1

(1) The appellant must file the appellant's notice at the Court of Appeal within 28 days after the date on which the decree was pronounced or conditional order made.

(2) The appellant must file the following documents with the appellant's notice –
    (a) the decree or conditional order; and
    (b) a certificate of service of the appellant's notice.

(3) The appellant's notice must be served on the appropriate district judge (see sub-paragraph (6)) in addition to the persons to be served under rule 52.4(3) and in accordance with that rule.

(4) The lower court may not alter the time limits for filing of the appeal notices.

(5) Where an appellant intends to apply to the Court of Appeal for an extension of time for serving or filing the appellant's notice he must give notice of that intention to the appropriate district judge (see sub-paragraph 6) before the application is made.

(6) In this paragraph 'the appropriate district judge' means, where the lower court is –
    (a) a county court, the district judge of that court;
    (b) a district registry, the district judge of that registry;
    (c) the Principal Registry of the Family Division, the senior district judge of that division.

### *Appeal against order for revocation of patent*

21.2

(1) This paragraph applies where an appeal lies to the Court of Appeal from an order for the revocation of a patent.

(2) The appellant must serve the appellant's notice on the Comptroller-General of Patents, Designs and Trade Marks (the 'Comptroller') in addition to the persons to be served under rule 52.4(3) and in accordance with that rule.

(3) Where, before the appeal hearing, the respondent decides not to oppose the appeal or not to attend the appeal hearing, he must immediately serve notice of that decision on –
    (a) the Comptroller; and
    (b) the appellant

(4) Where the respondent serves a notice in accordance with paragraph (3), he must also serve copies of the following documents on the Comptroller with that notice –
    (a) the petition;
    (b) any statements of claim;
    (c) any written evidence filed in the claim.

(5) Within 14 days after receiving the notice in accordance with paragraph (3), the Comptroller must serve on the appellant a notice stating whether or not he intends to attend the appeal hearing.

(6) The Comptroller may attend the appeal hearing and oppose the appeal –

    (a) in any case where he has given notice under paragraph (5) of his intention to attend; and

    (b) in any other case (including, in particular, a case where the respondent withdraws his opposition to the appeal during the hearing) if the Court of Appeal so directs or permits.

## *Appeal from Patents Court on appeal from Comptroller*

21.3 Where the appeal is from a decision of the Patents Court which was itself made on an appeal from a decision of the Comptroller-General of Patents, Designs and Trade Marks, the appellant must serve the appellant's notice on the Comptroller in addition to the persons to be served under rule 52.4(3) and in accordance with that rule.

## *Appeals in cases of contempt of court*

21.4 In an appeal under section 13 of the Administration of Justice Act 1960 (appeals in cases of contempt of court), the appellant must serve the appellant's notice on the court or the Upper Tribunal from whose order or decision the appeal is brought in addition to the persons to be served under rule 52.4(3) and in accordance with that rule.

...

## *Appeals from Value Added Tax and Duties Tribunals*

21.6

(1) An application to the Court of Appeal for permission to appeal from a value added tax and duties tribunal direct to that court must be made within 28 days after the date on which the tribunal certifies that its decision involves a point of law relating wholly or mainly to the construction of –

    (a) an enactment or of a statutory instrument; or

    (b) any of the Community Treaties or any Community Instrument,

which has been fully argued before and fully considered by it.

(2) The application must be made by the parties jointly filing at the Court of Appeal an appellant's notice that –

    (a) contains a statement of the grounds for the application; and

    (b) is accompanied by a copy of the decision to be appealed, endorsed with the certificate of the tribunal.

(3) The court will notify the appellant of its decision and –

    (a) where permission to appeal to the Court of Appeal is given, the appellant must serve the appellant's notice on the chairman of the tribunal in addition to the persons to be served under rule 52.4(3) within 14 days after that notification.

(b)     where permission to appeal to the Court of Appeal is refused, the period for appealing to the High Court is to be calculated from the date of the notification of that refusal.

## *Asylum and Immigration Appeals*

21.7

(1)     This paragraph applies to appeals from the Immigration and Asylum Chamber of the Upper Tribunal under section 13 of the Tribunals, Courts and Enforcement Act 2007.

(2)     The appellant is not required to file an appeal bundle in accordance with paragraph 5.6A of this practice direction, but must file the documents specified in paragraphs 5.6(2)(a) to (f) together with a copy of the Tribunal's determination.

(3)     The appellant's notice must be filed at the Court of Appeal within 14 days after the appellant is served with written notice of the decision of the Tribunal to grant or refuse permission to appeal.

(4)     The appellant must serve the appellant's notice in accordance with rule 52.4(3) on –
(a)     the persons to be served under that rule; and
(b)     the Immigration and Asylum Chamber of the Upper Tribunal.

(5)     On being served with the appellant's notice, the Immigration and Asylum Chamber of the Upper Tribunal must send to the Court of Appeal copies of the documents which were before the relevant Tribunal when it considered the appeal.

21.7A *(omitted)*

21.7B

(1)     This paragraph applies to appeals from the Immigration and Asylum Chamber of the Upper Tribunal which –
(a)     would otherwise be treated as abandoned under section 104(4A) of the Nationality, Immigration and Asylum Act 2002 (the '2002 Act'); but
(b)     meet the conditions set out in section 104(4B) or section 104(4C) of the 2002 Act.

(2)     Where section 104(4A) of the 2002 Act applies and the appellant wishes to pursue his appeal, the appellant must file a notice at the Court of Appeal –
(a)     where section 104(4B) of the 2002 Act applies, within 28 days of the date on which the appellant received notice of the grant of leave to enter or remain in the United Kingdom for a period exceeding 12 months; or
(b)     where section 104(4C) of the 2002 Act applies, within 28 days of the date on which the appellant received notice of the grant of leave to enter or remain in the United Kingdom.

(3)     Where the appellant does not comply with the time limits specified in paragraph (2) the appeal will be treated as abandoned in accordance with section 104(4) of the 2002 Act.

(4)     The appellant must serve the notice filed under paragraph (2) on the respondent.

(5)     Where section 104(4B) of the 2002 Act applies, the notice filed under paragraph (2) must state –

   (a)    the appellant's full name and date of birth;

   (b)    the Court of Appeal reference number;

   (c)    the Home Office reference number, if applicable;

   (d)    the date on which the appellant was granted leave to enter or remain in the United Kingdom for a period exceeding 12 months; and

   (e)    that the appellant wishes to pursue the appeal in so far as it is brought on the ground relating to the Refugee Convention specified in section 84(1)(g) of the 2002 Act.

(6)     Where section 104(4C) of the 2002 Act applies, the notice filed under paragraph (2) must state –

   (a)    the appellant's full name and date of birth;

   (b)    the Court of Appeal reference number;

   (c)    the Home Office reference number, if applicable;

   (d)    the date on which the appellant was granted leave to enter or remain in the United Kingdom; and

   (e)    that the appellant wishes to pursue the appeal in so far as it is brought on the ground relating to section 19B of the Race Relations Act 1976 specified in section 84(1)(b) of the 2002 Act.

(7)     Where an appellant has filed a notice under paragraph (2) the Court of Appeal will notify the appellant of the date on which it received the notice.

(8)     The Court of Appeal will send a copy of the notice issued under paragraph (7) to the respondent.

## *Appeal from Special Commissioners*

21.8

(1)     An application to the Court of Appeal for permission to appeal from the Special Commissioners direct to that court under section 56A of the Taxes Management Act 1970 must be made within 28 days after the date on which the Special Commissioners certify that their decision involves a point of law relating wholly or mainly to the construction of an enactment which has been fully argued before and fully considered before them.

(2)     The application must be made by the parties jointly filing at the Court of Appeal an appellant's notice that –

   (a)    contains a statement of the grounds for the application; and

   (b)    is accompanied by a copy of the decision to be appealed, endorsed with the certificate of the tribunal.

(3)     The court will notify the parties of its decision and –

   (a)    where permission to appeal to the Court of Appeal is given, the appellant must serve the appellant's notice on the Clerk to the Special Commissioners in addition to the persons to be served under rule 52.4(3) within 14 days after that notification.

(b)     where permission to appeal to the Court of Appeal is refused, the period for appealing to the High Court is to be calculated from the date of the notification of that refusal.

## Appeal from Lands Tribunal

21.9  The appellant must file the appellant's notice at the Court of Appeal within 28 days after the date of the decision of the tribunal.

## Appeal from Competition Appeal Tribunal

21.10

(1)     Where the appellant applies for permission to appeal at the hearing at which the decision is delivered by the tribunal and –
    (a)     permission is given; or
    (b)     permission is refused and the appellant wishes to make an application to the Court of Appeal for permission to appeal,

the appellant's notice must be filed at the Court of Appeal within 14 days after the date of that hearing.

(2)     Where the appellant applies in writing to the Registrar of the tribunal for permission to appeal and –
    (a)     permission is given; or
    (b)     permission is refused and the appellant wishes to make an application to the Court of Appeal for permission to appeal,

the appellant's notice must be filed at the Court of Appeal within 14 days after the date of receipt of the tribunal's decision on permission.

(3)     Where the appellant does not make an application to the tribunal for permission to appeal, but wishes to make an application to the Court of Appeal for permission, the appellant's notice must be filed at the Court of Appeal within 14 days after the end of the period within which he may make a written application to the Registrar of the tribunal.

## Appeals relating to the application of Articles 81 and 82 of the EC Treaty and Chapters I and II of Part I of the Competition Act 1998

21.10A

(1)     This paragraph applies to any appeal to the Court of Appeal relating to the application of –
    (a)     Article 81 or Article 82 of the Treaty establishing the European Community; or
    (b)     Chapter I or Chapter II of Part I of the Competition Act 1998.

(2)     In this paragraph –
    (a)     'the Act' means the Competition Act 1998;
    (b)     'the Commission' means the European Commission;
    (c)     'the Competition Regulation' means Council Regulation (EC) No 1/2003 of 16 December 2002 on the implementation of the rules on competition laid down in Articles 81 and 82 of the Treaty;

    (d)  'national competition authority' means –
        (i)    the Office of Fair Trading; and
        (ii)   any other person or body designated pursuant to Article 35 of the Competition Regulation as a national competition authority of the United Kingdom;
    (e)  'the Treaty' means the Treaty establishing the European Community.

(3)    Any party whose appeal notice raises an issue relating to the application of Article 81 or 82 of the Treaty, or Chapter I or II of Part I of the Act, must –
    (a)  state that fact in his appeal notice; and
    (b)  serve a copy of the appeal notice on the Office of Fair Trading at the same time as it is served on the other party to the appeal (addressed to the Director of Competition Policy Co-ordination, Office of Fair Trading, Fleetbank House, 2-6 Salisbury Square, London EC4Y 8JX).

(4)    Attention is drawn to the provisions of article 15.3 of the Competition Regulation, which entitles competition authorities and the Commission to submit written observations to national courts on issues relating to the application of Article 81 or 82 and, with the permission of the court in question, to submit oral observations to the court.

(5)    A national competition authority may also make written observations to the Court of Appeal, or apply for permission to make oral observations, on issues relating to the application of Chapter I or II.

(6)    If a national competition authority or the Commission intends to make written observations to the Court of Appeal, it must give notice of its intention to do so by letter to the Civil Appeals Office at the earliest opportunity.

(7)    An application by a national competition authority or the Commission for permission to make oral representations at the hearing of an appeal must be made by letter to the Civil Appeals Office at the earliest opportunity, identifying the appeal and indicating why the applicant wishes to make oral representations.

(8)    If a national competition authority or the Commission files a notice under sub-paragraph (6) or an application under sub-paragraph (7), it must at the same time serve a copy of the notice or application on every party to the appeal.

(9)    Any request by a national competition authority or the Commission for the court to send it any documents relating to an appeal should be made at the same time as filing a notice under sub-paragraph (6) or an application under sub-paragraph (7).

(10)  When the Court of Appeal receives a notice under sub-paragraph (6) it may give case management directions to the national competition authority or the Commission, including directions about the date by which any written observations are to be filed.

(11)  The Court of Appeal will serve on every party to the appeal a copy of any directions given or order made –
    (a)  on an application under sub-paragraph (7); or
    (b)  under sub-paragraph (10).

(12)  Every party to an appeal which raises an issue relating to the application of Article 81 or 82, and any national competition authority which has

been served with a copy of a party's appeal notice, is under a duty to notify the Court of Appeal at any stage of the appeal if they are aware that –

    (a)    the Commission has adopted, or is contemplating adopting, a decision in relation to proceedings which it has initiated; and

    (b)    the decision referred to in (a) above has or would have legal effects in relation to the particular agreement, decision or practice in issue before the court.

(13)    Where the Court of Appeal is aware that the Commission is contemplating adopting a decision as mentioned in sub-paragraph (12)(a), it shall consider whether to stay the appeal pending the Commission's decision.

(14)    Where any judgment is given which decides on the application of Article 81 or 82, the court shall direct that a copy of the transcript of the judgment shall be sent to the Commission.

Judgments may be sent to the Commission electronically to comp-amicus@cec.eu.int or by post to the European Commission – DG Competition, B–1049, Brussels.

## Appeal from Proscribed Organisations Appeal Commission

21.11

(1)    The appellant's notice must be filed at the Court of Appeal within 14 days after the date when the Proscribed Organisations Appeal Commission –

    (a)    granted; or

    (b)    where section 6(2)(b) of the Terrorism Act 2000 applies, refused permission to appeal.

## Appeal from the Court of Protection

21.12

(1)    In this paragraph –

    (a)    'P' means a person who lacks, or who is alleged to lack, capacity within the meaning of the Mental Capacity Act 2005 to make a decision or decisions in relation to any matter that is subject to an order of the Court of Protection;

    (b)    'the person effecting notification' means –

        (i)    the appellant;

        (ii)    an agent duly appointed by the appellant; or

        (iii)    such other person as the Court of Protection may direct,

who is required to notify P in accordance with this paragraph; and

    (c)    'final order' means a decision of the Court of Appeal that finally determines the appeal proceedings before it.

(2)    Where P is not a party to the proceedings, unless the Court of Appeal directs otherwise, the person effecting notification must notify P –

    (a)    that an appellant's notice has been filed with the Court of Appeal and –

        (i)    who the appellant is;

        (ii)    what final order the appellant is seeking;

   (iii) what will happen if the Court of Appeal makes the final order sought by the appellant; and

   (iv) that P may apply under rule 52.12A by letter for permission to file evidence or make representations at the appeal hearing;

  (b) of the final order, the effect of the final order and what steps P can take in relation to it; and

  (c) of such other events and documents as the Court of Appeal may direct.

(Paragraphs 17.7 to 17.11 of this practice direction contain provisions on how a third party can apply for permission to file evidence or make representations at an appeal hearing.)

(3) The person effecting notification must provide P with the information specified in sub-paragraph (2) –

  (a) within 14 days of the date on which the appellant's notice was filed with the Court of Appeal;

  (b) within 14 days of the date on which the final order was made; or

  (c) within such time as the Court of Appeal may direct,

as the case may be.

(4) The person effecting notification must provide P in person with the information specified in sub-paragraph (2) in a way that is appropriate to P's circumstances (for example, using simple language, visual aids or any other appropriate means).

(5) Where P is to be notified as to –

  (a) the existence or effect of a document other than the appellant's notice or final order; or

  (b) the taking place of an event,

the person effecting notification must explain to P –

   (i) in the case of a document, what the document is and what effect, if any, it has; or

   (ii) in the case of an event, what the event is and its relevance to P.

(6) The person effecting notification must, within 7 days of notifying P, file a certificate of notification (form N165) which certifies –

  (a) the date on which P was notified; and

  (b) that P was notified in accordance with this paragraph.

(7) Where the person effecting notification has not notified P in accordance with this paragraph, he must file with the Court of Appeal a certificate of non-notification (form N165) stating the reason why notification has not been effected.

(8) Where the person effecting notification must file a certificate of non-notification with the Court of Appeal, he must file the certificate within the following time limits –

  (a) where P is to be notified in accordance with sub-paragraph (2)(a) (appellant's notice), within 21 days of the appellant's notice being filed with the Court of Appeal;

  (b) where P is to be notified in accordance with sub-paragraph (2)(b) (final order), within 21 days of the final order being made by the Court of Appeal; or

    (c)    where P is to be notified of such other events and documents as may be directed by the Court of Appeal, within such time as the Court of Appeal directs.

(9)    The appellant or such other person as the Court of Appeal may direct may apply to the Court of Appeal seeking an order –

    (a)    dispensing with the requirement to comply with the provisions of this paragraph; or

    (b)    requiring some other person to comply with the provisions of this paragraph.

(10)    An application made under sub-paragraph (9) may be made in the appellant's notice or by Part 23 application notice.

(Paragraph 12 contains provisions about the dismissal of applications or appeals by consent. Paragraph 13 contains provisions about allowing unopposed appeals or applications on paper and procedures for consent orders and agreements to pay periodical payments involving a child or protected party or in appeals to the Court of Appeal from a decision of the Court of Protection.)

## Appeals in relation to serious crime prevention orders

21.13

(1)    This paragraph applies where the appeal is in relation to a serious crime prevention order and is made under section 23(1) of the Serious Crime Act 2007 or section 16 of the Supreme Court Act 1981.

(2)    The appellant must serve the appellant's notice on any person who made representations in the proceedings by virtue of section 9(1), (2) or (3) of the Serious Crime Act 2007 in addition to the persons to be served under rule 52.4(3) and in accordance with that rule.

## Appeals to the High Court – Queen's Bench Division

22.1 The following appeals are to be heard in the Queen's Bench Division.

## Statutory Appeals

## *Appeals under the Merchant Shipping Act 1995*

22.2

(1)    This paragraph applies to appeals under the Merchant Shipping Act 1995 and for this purpose a re-hearing and an application under section 61 of the Merchant Shipping Act 1995 are treated as appeals.

(2)    The appellant must file any report to the Secretary of State containing the decision from which the appeal is brought with the appellant's notice.

(3)    Where a re-hearing by the High Court is ordered under sections 64 or 269 of the Merchant Shipping Act 1995, the Secretary of State must give reasonable notice to the parties whom he considers to be affected by the re-hearing.

## Appeals against decisions affecting the registration of architects and health care professionals

22.3

(1)   This paragraph applies to an appeal to the High Court under –
      (a)   section 22 of the Architects Act 1997;
      (b)   section 82(3) and 83(2) of the Medicines Act 1968;
      (c)   section 12 of the Nurses, Midwives and Health Visitors Act 1997;
      (cc)  article 38 of the Nursing and Midwifery Order 2001;
      (d)   section 10 of the Pharmacy Act 1954;
      (e)   section 40 of the Medical Act 1983;
      (f)   section 29 or section 40 of the Dentists Act 1984;
      (g)   section 23 of the Opticians Act 1989;
      (h)   section 31 of the Osteopaths Act 1993;
      (i)   section 31 of the Chiropractors Act 1994;
      (j)   article 38 of the Health Professions Order 2011; and
      (k)   article 58 of the Pharmacy Order 2010.

(2)   Every appeal to which this paragraph applies must be supported by written evidence and, if the court so orders, oral evidence and will be by way of re-hearing.

(3)   The appellant must file the appellant's notice within 28 days after the decision that the appellant wishes to appeal.

(4)   In the case of an appeal under an enactment specified in column 1 of the following table, the persons to be made respondents are the persons specified in relation to that enactment in column 2 of the table and the person to be served with the appellant's notice is the person so specified in column 3.

| 1 Enactment | 2 Respondents | 3 Person to be served |
|---|---|---|
| Architects Act 1997, s 22 | The Architects' Registration Council of the United Kingdom | The registrar of the Council |
| Medicines Act 1968, s 82(3) and s 83(2) | The Pharmaceutical Society of Great Britain | The registrar of the Society |
| Nurses, Midwives and Health Visitors Act 1997, s 12 | The United Kingdom Central Council for Nursing, Midwifery and Health Visiting | The registrar of the Council |
| Pharmacy Act 1954, s 10 | The Pharmaceutical Society of Great Britain | The registrar of the Society |
| Medical Act 1983, s 40 | The General Medical Council | The Registrar of the Council |
| Dentists Act 1984, s 29 or s 44 | The General Dental Council | The Registrar of the Council |

| 1 Enactment | 2 Respondents | 3 Person to be served |
| --- | --- | --- |
| Opticians Act 1989, s 23 | The General Optical Council | The Registrar of the Council |
| Osteopaths Act 1993, s 31 | The General Osteopathic Council | The Registrar of the Council |
| Chiropractors Act 1994, s 31 | The General Chiropractic Council | The Registrar of the Council |
| Health Professions Order 2001, art 38 | The Health Professions Council | The Registrar of the Council |
| Pharmacy Order 2010, art 58 | The General Pharmaceutical Council | The Registrar of the Council |

## Consumer Credit Act 1974: appeal from Secretary of State

22.4

(1) A person dissatisfied in point of law with a decision of the Secretary of State on an appeal under section 41 of the Consumer Credit Act 1974 from a determination of the Office of Fair Trading who had a right to appeal to the Secretary of State, whether or not he exercised that right, may appeal to the High Court.

(2) The appellant must serve the appellant's notice on –
   (a) the Secretary of State;
   (b) the original applicant, if any, where the appeal is by a licensee under a group licence against compulsory variation, suspension or revocation of that licence; and
   (c) any other person as directed by the court.

(3) The appeal court may remit the matter to the Secretary of State to the extent necessary to enable him to provide the court with such further information as the court may direct.

(4) If the appeal court allows the appeal, it shall not set aside or vary the decision but shall remit the matter to the Secretary of State with the opinion of the court for hearing and determination by him.

## The Social Security Administration Act 1992

22.6

(1) Any person who by virtue of section 18 or 58(8) of the Social Security Administration Act 1992 ('the Act') is entitled and wishes to appeal against a decision of the Secretary of State on a question of law must, within the prescribed period, or within such further time as the Secretary of State may allow, serve on the Secretary of State a notice requiring him to state a case setting out –
   (a) his decision; and
   (b) the facts on which his decision was based.

(2)     Unless paragraph (3) applies the prescribed period is 28 days after receipt of the notice of the decision.

(3)     Where, within 28 days after receipt of notice of the decision, a request is made to the Secretary of State in accordance with regulations made under the Act to furnish a statement of the grounds of the decision, the prescribed period is 28 days after receipt of that statement.

(4)     Where under section 18 or section 58(8) of the Act, the Secretary of State refers a question of law to the court, he must state that question together with the relevant facts in a case.

(5)     The appellant's notice and the case stated must be filed at the appeal court and a copy of the notice and the case stated served on –

    (a)     the Secretary of State; and

    (b)     every person as between whom and the Secretary of State the question has arisen,

within 28 days after the case stated was served on the party at whose request, or as a result of whose application to the court, the case was stated.

(6)     Unless the appeal court otherwise orders, the appeal or reference shall not be heard sooner than 28 days after service of the appellant's notice.

(7)     The appeal court may order the case stated by the Secretary of State to be returned to the Secretary of State for him to hear further evidence.

## Appeals under the Extradition Act 2003

22.6A

(1) In this paragraph, 'the Act' means the Extradition Act 2003.

(2)     Appeals to the High Court under the Act must be brought in the Administrative Court of the Queen's Bench Division.

(2A)   The court may give directions requiring the proceedings to be heard by a Divisional Court.

(3)     Where an appeal is brought under section 26 or 28 of the Act –

    (a)     the appellant's notice must be filed and served before the expiry of 7 days, starting with the day on which the order is made;

    (b)     the appellant must endorse the appellant's notice with the date of the person's arrest;

    (c)     the High Court must begin to hear the substantive appeal within 40 days of the person's arrest; and

    (d)     the appellant must serve a copy of the appellant's notice on the Crown Prosecution Service, if they are not a party to the appeal, in addition to the persons to be served under rule 52.4(3) and in accordance with that rule.

(4)     The High Court may extend the period of 40 days under paragraph (3)(c) if it believes it to be in the interests of justice to do so.

(5)     Where an appeal is brought under section 103 of the Act, the appellant's notice must be filed and served before the expiry of 14 days, starting with the day on which the Secretary of State informs the person under section 100(1) or (4) of the Act of the order he has made in respect of the person.

(6)     Where an appeal is brought under section 105 of the Act, the appellant's notice must be filed and served before the expiry of 14 days, starting with the day on which the order for discharge is made.

(7)     Where an appeal is brought under section 108 of the Act the appellant's notice must be filed and served before the expiry of 14 days, starting with the day on which the Secretary of State informs the person that he has ordered his extradition.

(8)     Where an appeal is brought under section 110 of the Act the appellant's notice must be filed and served before the expiry of 14 days, starting with the day on which the Secretary of State informs the person acting on behalf of a category 2 territory, as defined in section 69 of the Act, of the order for discharge.

(Section 69 of the Act provides that a category 2 territory is that designated for the purposes of Part 2 of the Act).

(9)     Subject to paragraph (10), where an appeal is brought under section 103, 105, 108 or 110 of the Act, the High Court must begin to hear the substantive appeal within 76 days of the appellant's notice being filed.

(10)    Where an appeal is brought under section 103 of the Act before the Secretary of State has decided whether the person is to be extradited –
   (a)    the period of 76 days does not start until the day on which the Secretary of State informs the person of his decision; and
   (b)    the Secretary of State must, as soon as practicable after he informs the person of his decision, inform the High Court –
      (i)     of his decision; and
      (ii)    of the date on which he informs the person of his decision.

(11)    The High Court may extend the period of 76 days if it believes it to be in the interests of justice to do so.

(12)    Where an appeal is brought under section 103, 105, 108 or 110 of the Act, the appellant must serve a copy of the appellant's notice on –
   (a)    the Crown Prosecution Service; and
   (b)    the Home Office,

if they are not a party to the appeal, in addition to the persons to be served under rule 52.4(3) and in accordance with that rule.

## Appeals from decisions of the Law Society or the Solicitors Disciplinary Tribunal to the High Court

22.6B

(1)     This paragraph applies to appeals from the Law Society or the Solicitors Disciplinary Tribunal ("the Tribunal") to the High Court under the Solicitors Act 1974, the Administration of Justice Act 1985, the Courts and Legal Services Act 1990, the European Communities (Lawyer's Practice) Regulations 2000 or the European Communities (Recognition of Professional Qualifications) Regulations 2007.

(2)     The appellant must file the appellant's notice in the Administrative Court.

(3)     The appellant must, unless the court orders otherwise, serve the appellant's notice on –
   (a)    every party to the proceedings before the Tribunal; and;
   (b)    the Law Society.

(4)     The court may give directions requiring the proceedings to be heard by a Divisional Court.

*Appeals under s 289(6) of the Town and Country Planning
Act 1990 and s 65(5) of the Planning (Listed Buildings and
Conservation Areas) Act 1990*

22.6C

(1) An application for permission to appeal to the High Court under section 289 of the Town and Country Planning Act 1990 ('the TCP Act') or section 65 of the Planning (Listed Buildings and Conservation Areas) Act 1990 ('the PLBCA Act') must be made within 28 days after notice of the decision is given to the applicant.

(2) The application –
   (a) must be in writing and must set out the reasons why permission should be granted; and
   (b) if the time for applying has expired, must include an application to extend the time for applying, and must set out the reasons why the application was not made within that time.

(3) The applicant must, before filing the application, serve a copy of it on the persons referred to in sub-paragraph (11) with the draft appellant's notice and a copy of the witness statement or affidavit to be filed with the application.

(4) The applicant must file the application in the Administrative Court Office with –
   (i) a copy of the decision being appealed;
   (ii) a draft appellant's notice;
   (iii) a witness statement or affidavit verifying any facts relied on; and
   (iv) a witness statement or affidavit giving the name and address of, and the place and date of service on, each person who has been served with the application. If any person who ought to be served has not been served, the witness statement or affidavit must state that fact and the reason why the person was not served.

(5) An application will be heard –
   (a) by a single judge; and
   (b) unless the court otherwise orders, not less than 21 days after it was filed at the Administrative Court Office.

(6) Any person served with the application is entitled to appear and be heard.

(7) Any respondent who intends to use a witness statement or affidavit at the hearing –
   (a) must file it in the Administrative Court Office; and
   (b) must serve a copy on the applicant as soon as is practicable and in any event, unless the court otherwise allows, at least 2 days before the hearing.

(8) The court may allow the applicant to use a further witness statement or affidavit.

(9) Where on the hearing of an application the court is of the opinion that a person who ought to have been served has not been served, the court may adjourn the hearing, on such terms as it directs, in order that the application may be served on that person.

(10) Where the court grants permission –
   (a) it may impose terms as to costs and as to giving security;

     (b)    it may give directions; and

     (c)    the relevant appellant's notice must be served and filed within 7 days of the grant.

(11)    The persons to be served with the appellant's notice are –

     (a)    the Secretary of State;

     (b)    the local planning authority who served the notice or gave the decision, as the case may be, or, where the appeal is brought by that authority, the appellant or applicant in the proceedings in which the decision appealed against was given;

     (c)    in the case of an appeal brought by virtue of section 289(1) of the TCP Act or section 65(1) of the PLBCA Act, any other person having an interest in the land to which the notice relates; and

     (d)    in the case of an appeal brought by virtue of section 289(2) of the TCP Act, any other person on whom the notice to which those proceedings related was served.

(12)    The appeal will be heard and determined by a single judge unless the court directs that the matter be heard and determined by a Divisional Court.

(13)    The court may remit the matter to the Secretary of State to the extent necessary to enable him to provide the court with such further information in connection with the matter as the court may direct.

(14)    Where the court is of the opinion that the decision appealed against was erroneous in point of law, it will not set aside or vary that decision but will remit the matter to the Secretary of State for re-hearing and determination in accordance with the opinion of the court.

(15)    The court may give directions as to the exercise, until an appeal brought by virtue of section 289(1) of the TCP Act is finally concluded and any re-hearing and determination by the Secretary of State has taken place, of the power to serve, and institute proceedings (including criminal proceedings) concerning –

     (a)    a stop notice under section 183 of that Act; and

     (b)    a breach of condition notice under section 187A of that Act.

## *National Health Service Act 1977: appeal from tribunal*

22.6D

(1)    This paragraph applies to an appeal from a tribunal constituted under section 46 of the National Health Service Act 1977.

(2)    The appellant must file the appellant's notice at the High Court within 14 days after the date of the decision of the tribunal.

## *Employment Tribunals Act 1996: appeal from tribunal*

22.6E

(1)    This paragraph applies to an appeal from a tribunal constituted under section 1 of the Employment Tribunals Act 1996.

(2)    The appellant must file the appellant's notice at the High Court within 42 days after the date of the decision of the tribunal.

(3)    The appellant must serve the appellant's notice on the secretary of the tribunal.

## Appeals by way of case stated

### *Reference of question of law by Agriculture Land Tribunal*

22.7

    (1)    A question of law referred to the High Court by an Agricultural Land Tribunal under section 6 of the Agriculture (Miscellaneous Provisions) Act 1954 shall be referred by way of case stated by the Tribunal.

    (2)    Where the proceedings before the tribunal arose on an application under section 11 of the Agricultural Holdings Act 1986, an –

        (a)    application notice for an order under section 6 that the tribunal refers a question of law to the court; and

        (b)    appellant's notice by which an appellant seeks the court's determination on a question of law,

must be served on the authority having power to enforce the statutory requirement specified in the notice in addition to every other party to those proceedings and on the secretary of the tribunal.

    (3)    Where, in accordance with paragraph (2), a notice is served on the authority mentioned in that paragraph, that authority may attend the appeal hearing and make representations to the court.

### *Case stated by Mental Health Review Tribunal*

22.8

    (1)    In this paragraph 'the Act' means the Mental Health Act 1983 and 'party to proceedings' means –

        (a)    the person who initiated the proceedings; and

        (b)    any person to whom, in accordance with rules made under section 78 of the Act, the tribunal sent notice of the application or reference or a request instead notice of reference.

    (2)    A party to proceedings shall not be entitled to apply to the High Court for an order under section 78(8) of the Act directing the tribunal to state a case for determination by court unless –

        (a)    within 21 days after the decision of the tribunal was communicated to him in accordance with rules made under section 78 of the Act he made a written request to the tribunal to state a case; and

        (b)    either the tribunal

            (i)    failed to comply with that request within 21 days after it was made; or

            (ii)    refused to comply with it.

    (3)    The period for filing the application notice for an order under section 78(8) of the Act is –

        (a)    where the tribunal failed to comply with the applicant's request to state a case within the period mentioned in paragraph (2)(b)(i), 14 days after the expiration of that period;

        (b)    where the tribunal refused that request, 14 days after receipt by the applicant of notice of the refusal of his request.

(4)     A Mental Health Review Tribunal by whom a case is stated shall be entitled to attend the proceedings for the determination of the case and make representations to the court.

(5)     If the court allows the appeal, it may give any direction which the tribunal ought to have given under Part V of the Act.

## Case stated under section 289 of the Town and Country Planning Act 1990 or section 65 of the Planning (Listed Buildings and Conservation Areas) Act 1990

22.8A  A case stated under section 289(3) of the Town and Country Planning Act 1990 or section 65(2) of the Planning (Listed Buildings and Conservation Areas) Act 1990 will be heard and determined by a single judge unless the court directs that the matter be heard and determined by a Divisional Court.

### Appeals to the High Court – Chancery Division

23.1  The following appeals are to be heard in the Chancery Division

## Determination of appeal or case stated under various Acts

23.2  Any appeal to the High Court, and any case stated or question referred for the opinion of that court under any of the following enactments shall be heard in the Chancery Division –

(1)     paragraph 16 of Schedule 15 to the Law of Property Act 1922;
(2)     the Industrial Assurance Act 1923;
(3)     the Land Registration Act 1925;
(4)     section 205(4) of the Water Resources Act 1991;
(5)     section 38(3) of the Clergy Pensions Measure 1961;
(6)     the Industrial and Provident Societies Act 1965;
(7)     section 151 of the Pension Schemes Act 1993;
(8)     section 173 of the Pension Schemes Act 1993; and
(9)     section 97 of the Pensions Act 1995;...
(10)    the Charities Act 1993;
(11)    section 13 and 13B of Stamp Act 1891;
(12)    section 705A of the Income and Corporation Taxes Act 1988;
(13)    regulation 22 of the General Commissioners (Jurisdiction and Procedure) Regulations 1994;
(14)    section 53, 56A or 100C(4) of the Taxes Management Act 1970;
(15)    section 222(3), 225, 249(3) or 251 of the Inheritance Tax Act 1984;
(16)    regulation 8(3) or 10 of the Stamp Duty Reserve Tax Regulations 1986;
(17)    the Land Registration Act 2002;
(18)    regulation 74 of the European Public Limited-Liability Company Regulations 2004.

(This list is not exhaustive)

*Statutory appeals*

## APPEAL UNDER SECTION 222 OF THE INHERITANCE TAX ACT 1984

23.3

(1)  This paragraph applies to appeals to the High Court under section 222(3) of the Inheritance Tax Act 1984 (the '1984 Act') and regulation 8(3) of the Stamp Duty Reserve Tax Regulations 1986 (the '1986 Regulations').

(2)  The appellant's notice must –

    (a)    state the date on which the Commissioners for HM Revenue and Customs (the 'Board') gave notice to the appellant under section 221 of the 1984 Act or regulation 6 of the 1986 Regulations of the determination that is the subject of the appeal;

    (b)    state the date on which the appellant gave to the Board notice of appeal under section 222(1) of the 1984 Act or regulation 8(1) of the 1986 Regulations and, if notice was not given within the time permitted, whether the Board or the Special Commissioners have given their consent to the appeal being brought out of time, and, if they have, the date they gave their consent; and

    (c)    either state that the appellant and the Board have agreed that the appeal may be to the High Court or contain an application for permission to appeal to the High Court.

(3)  The appellant must file the following documents with the appellant's notice –

    (a)    Two copies of the notice referred to in paragraph 2(a);

    (b)    Two copies of the notice of appeal (under section 222(1) of the 1984 Act or regulation 8(1) of the 1986 Regulations) referred to in paragraph 2(b); and

    (c)    where the appellant's notice contains an application for permission to appeal, written evidence setting out the grounds on which it is alleged that the matters to be decided on the appeal are likely to be substantially confined to questions of law.

(4)  The appellant must –

    (a)    file the appellant's notice at the court; and

    (b)    serve the appellant's notice on the Board,

within 30 days of the date on which the appellant gave to the Board notice of appeal under section 222(1) of the 1984 Act or regulation 8(1) of the 1986 Regulations or, if the Board or the Special Commissioners have given consent to the appeal being brought out of time, within 30 days of the date on which such consent was given.

(5)  The court will set a date for the hearing of not less than 40 days from the date that the appellant's notice was filed.

(6)  Where the appellant's notice contains an application for permission to appeal –

    (a)    a copy of the written evidence filed in accordance with paragraph (3)(c) must be served on the Board with the appellant's notice; and

    (b)    the Board –

        (i)    may file written evidence; and

(ii) if it does so, must serve a copy of that evidence on the appellant,

within 30 days after service of the written evidence under paragraph (6)(a).

(7) The appellant may not rely on any grounds of appeal not specified in the notice referred to in paragraph (2)(b) on the hearing of the appeal without the permission of the court.

## APPEALS UNDER SECTION 53 AND 100C(4) OF THE TAXES MANAGEMENT ACT 1970 AND SECTION 249(3) OR 251 OF THE INHERITANCE TAX ACT 1984

23.4

(1) The appellant must serve the appellant's notice on –
    (a) the General or Special Commissioners against whose decision, award or determination the appeal is brought; and
    (b) (i) in the case of an appeal brought under section 100C(4) of the Taxes Management Act 1970 or section 249(3) of the Inheritance Tax Act 1984 by any party other than the defendant in the proceedings before the Commissioners, that defendant; or
        (ii) in any other case, the Commissioners for HM Revenue and Customs.

(2) The appellant must file the appellant's notice at the court within 30 days after the date of the decision, award or determination against which the appeal is brought.

(3) Within 30 days of the service on them of the appellant's notice, the General or Special Commissioners, as the case may be, must –
    (a) file two copies of a note of their findings and of the reasons for their decision, award or determination at the court; and
    (b) serve a copy of the note on every other party to the appeal.

(4) Any document to be served on the General or Special Commissioners may be served by delivering or sending it to their clerk.

...

## APPEALS UNDER SECTION 56A OF THE TAXES MANAGEMENT ACT 1970, SECTION 225 OF THE INHERITANCE TAX ACT 1984 AND REGULATION 10 OF THE STAMP DUTY RESERVE TAX REGULATIONS 1986

23.5

(1) The appellant must file the appellant's notice –
    (a) where the appeal is made following the refusal of the Special Commissioners to issue a certificate under section 56A(2)(b) of the Taxes Management Act 1970, within 28 days from the date of the release of the decision of the Special Commissioners containing the refusal;

(b)   where the appeal is made following the refusal of permission to appeal to the Court of Appeal under section 56A(2)(c) of that Act, within 28 days from the date when permission is refused; or

(c)   in all other cases within 56 days after the date of the decision or determination that the appellant wishes to appeal.

## APPEAL UNDER SECTION 17 OF THE INDUSTRIAL ASSURANCE ACT 1923

23.6   The appellant must file the appellant's notice within 21 days after the date of the Commissioner's refusal or direction under section 17(3) of the Industrial Assurance Act 1923.

## APPEALS AFFECTING INDUSTRIAL AND PROVIDENT SOCIETIES ETC

23.7

(1)   This paragraph applies to all appeals under –
   (a)   the Friendly Societies Act 1974;
   (b)   the Friendly Societies Act 1992;
   (c)   the Industrial Assurance Act 1923; and
   (d)   the Industrial and Provident Societies Act 1965.

(2)   At any stage on an appeal, the court may –
   (a)   direct that the appellant's notice be served on any person;
   (b)   direct that notice be given by advertisement or otherwise of –
      (i)    the bringing of the appeal;
      (ii)   the nature of the appeal; and
      (iii)  the time when the appeal will or is likely to be heard; or
   (c)   give such other directions as it thinks proper to enable any person interested in –
      (i)    the society, trade union, alleged trade union or industrial assurance company; or
      (ii)   the subject matter of the appeal,
   to appear and be heard at the appeal hearing.

## APPEAL FROM VALUE ADDED TAX AND DUTIES TRIBUNAL

23.8

(1)   A party to proceedings before a Value Added Tax and Duties Tribunal who is dissatisfied in point of law with a decision of the tribunal may appeal under section 11(1) of the Tribunals and Inquiries Act 1992 to the High Court.

(2)   The appellant must file the appellant's notice –
   (a)   where the appeal is made following the refusal of the Value Added Tax and Duties Tribunal to grant a certificate under article 2(b) of the Value Added Tax and Duties Tribunal Appeals Order 1986, within 28 days from the date of the release of the decision containing the refusal;

(b)     in all other cases within 56 days after the date of the decision or determination that the appellant wishes to appeal.

## APPEAL AGAINST AN ORDER OR DECISION OF THE CHARITY COMMISSIONERS

23.8A

(1)     In this paragraph –
'the Act' means the Charities Act 1993; and
'the Commissioners' means the Charity Commissioners for England and Wales.

(2)     The Attorney-General, unless he is the appellant, must be made a respondent to the appeal.

(3)     The appellant's notice must state the grounds of the appeal, and the appellant may not rely on any other grounds without the permission of the court.

(4)     Sub-paragraphs (5) and (6) apply, in addition to the above provisions, where the appeal is made under section 16(12) of the Act.

(5)     If the Commissioners have granted a certificate that it is a proper case for an appeal, a copy of the certificate must be filed with the appellant's notice.

(6)     If the appellant applies in the appellant's notice for permission to appeal under section 16(13) of the Act –

(a)     the appellant's notice must state –

(i)     that the appellant has requested the Commissioners to grant a certificate that it is a proper case for an appeal, and they have refused to do so;

(ii)     the date of such refusal;

(iii)     the grounds on which the appellant alleges that it is a proper case for an appeal; and

(iv)     if the application for permission to appeal is made with the consent of any other party to the proposed appeal, that fact;

(b)     if the Commissioners have given reasons for refusing a certificate, a copy of the reasons must be attached to the appellant's notice;

(c)     the court may, before determining the application, direct the Commissioners to file a written statement of their reasons for refusing a certificate;

(d)     the court will serve on the appellant a copy of any statement filed under sub-paragraph (c).

## APPEAL AGAINST A DECISION OF THE ADJUDICATOR UNDER SECTION 111 OF THE LAND REGISTRATION ACT 2002

23.8B

(1)     A person who is aggrieved by a decision of the adjudicator and who wishes to appeal that decision must obtain permission to appeal.

(2) The appellant must serve on the adjudicator a copy of the appeal court's decision on a request for permission to appeal as soon as reasonably practicable and in any event within 14 days of receipt by the appellant of the decision on permission.

(3) The appellant must serve on the adjudicator and the Chief Land Registrar a copy of any order by the appeal court to stay a decision of the adjudicator pending the outcome of the appeal as soon as reasonably practicable and in any event within 14 days of receipt by the appellant of the appeal court's order to stay.

(4) The appellant must serve on the adjudicator and the Chief Land Registrar a copy of the appeal court's decision on the appeal as soon as reasonably practicable and in any event within 14 days of receipt by the appellant of the appeal court's decision.

## APPEALS UNDER REGULATION 74 OF THE EUROPEAN PUBLIC LIMITED-LIABILITY COMPANY REGULATIONS 2004

23.8C

(1) In this paragraph –
    (a) 'the 2004 Regulations' means the European Public Limited-Liability Company Regulations 2004;
    (b) 'the EC Regulation' means Council Regulation (EC) No 2157/2001 of 8 October 2001 on the Statute for a European company (SE);
    (c) 'SE' means a European public limited-liability company (Societas Europaea) within the meaning of Article 1 of the EC Regulation.

(2) This paragraph applies to appeals under regulation 74 of the 2004 Regulations against the opposition –
    (a) of the Secretary of State or national financial supervisory authority to the transfer of the registered office of an SE under Article 8(14) of the EC Regulation; and
    (b) of the Secretary of State to the participation by a company in the formation of an SE by merger under Article 19 of the EC Regulation.

(3) Where an SE seeks to appeal against the opposition of the national financial supervisory authority to the transfer of its registered office under Article 8(14) of the EC Regulation, it must serve the appellant's notice on both the national financial supervisory authority and the Secretary of State.

(4) The appellant's notice must contain an application for permission to appeal.

(5) The appeal will be a review of the decision of the Secretary of State and not a re-hearing. The grounds of review are set out in regulation 74(2) of the 2004 Regulations.

(6) The appeal will be heard by a High Court judge.

## *Appeals by way of case stated*

### PROCEEDINGS UNDER THE COMMONS REGISTRATION ACT 1965

23.9

  (1)    A person aggrieved by the decision of a Commons Commissioner who requires the Commissioner to state a case for the opinion of the High Court under section 18 of the Commons Registration Act 1965 must file the appellant's notice within 42 days from the date on which notice of the decision was sent to the aggrieved person.

  (2)    Proceedings under that section are assigned to the Chancery Division.

### Appeals to a County Court

### *Local Government (Miscellaneous Provisions) Act 1976*

24.1 Where one of the grounds upon which an appeal against a notice under sections 21, 23 or 35 of the Local Government (Miscellaneous Provisions) Act 1976 is brought is that –

  (a)    it would have been fairer to serve the notice on another person; or

  (b)    that it would be reasonable for the whole or part of the expenses to which the appeal relates to be paid by some other person,

that person must be made a respondent to the appeal, unless the court, on application of the appellant made without notice, otherwise directs.

### *Appeals under sections 204 and 204A of the Housing Act 1996*

24.2

  (1)    An appellant should include appeals under section 204 and section 204A of the Housing Act 1996 in one appellant's notice.

  (2)    If it is not possible to do so (for example because an urgent application under section 204A is required) the appeals may be included in separate appellant's notices.

  (3)    An appeal under section 204A may include an application for an order under section 204A(4)(a) requiring the authority to secure that accommodation is available for the applicant's occupation.

  (4)    If, exceptionally, the court makes an order under section 204A(4)(a) without notice, the appellant's notice must be served on the authority together with the order. Such an order will normally require the authority to secure that accommodation is available until a hearing date when the authority can make representations as to whether the order under section 204A(4)(a) should be continued.

### *Appeal under Part II of the Immigration and Asylum Act 1999 (carriers' liability)*

24.3

  (1)    A person appealing to a county court under section 35A or section 40B of the Immigration and Asylum Act 1999 ('the Act') against a decision

by the Secretary of State to impose a penalty under section 32 or a charge under section 40 of the Act must, subject to paragraph (2), file the appellant's notice within 28 days after receiving the penalty notice or charge notice.

(2)     Where the appellant has given notice of objection to the Secretary of State under section 35(4) or section 40A(3) of the Act within the time prescribed for doing so, he must file the appellant's notice within 28 days after receiving notice of the Secretary of State's decision in response to the notice of objection.

(3)     Sections 35A and 40B of the Act provide that any appeal under those sections shall be a re-hearing of the Secretary of State's decision to impose a penalty or charge, and therefore rule 52.11(1) does not apply.

## *Representation of the People Act 1983—appeals against decisions of registration officers*

24.4

(1)     This paragraph applies in relation to an appeal against a decision of a registration officer, being a decision referred to in section 56(1) of the Representation of the People Act 1983 ('the Act').

(2)     Where a person ('the appellant') has given notice of such an appeal in accordance with the relevant requirements of section 56, and of the regulations made under section 53 ('the Regulations'), of the Act, the registration officer must, within 7 days after he receives the notice, forward –
(a)     the notice; and
(b)     the statement required by the Regulations,

by post to the county court.

(3)     The respondents to the appeal will be –
(a)     the registration officer; and
(b)     if the decision of the registration officer was given in favour of any other person than the appellant, that other person.

(4)     On the hearing of the appeal –
(a)     the statement forwarded to the court by the registration officer, and any document containing information submitted to the court by the registration officer pursuant to the Regulations, are admissible as evidence of the facts stated in them; and
(b)     the court –
(i)     may draw any inference of fact that the registration officer might have drawn; and
(ii)    may give any decision and make any order that the registration officer ought to have given or made.

(5)     A respondent to an appeal (other than the registration officer) is not liable for nor entitled to costs, unless he appears before the court in support of the registration officer's decision.

(6)     Rule 52.4, and paragraphs 5, 6 and 7 of this practice direction, do not apply to an appeal to which this paragraph applies.

## Representation of the People Act 1983—special provision in relation to anonymous entries in the register

24.5

(1)    In this paragraph –
'anonymous entry' has the meaning given by section 9B(4) of the Representation of the People Act 1983;
'appeal notice' means the notice required by regulation 32 of the Representation of the People (England and Wales) Regulations 2001.

(2)    This paragraph applies to an appeal to a county court to which paragraph 24.4 applies if a party to the appeal is a person –
(a)    whose entry in the register is an anonymous entry; or
(b)    who has applied for such an entry.

(3)    This paragraph also applies to an appeal to the Court of Appeal from a decision of a county court in an appeal to which paragraph 24.4 applies.

(4)    The appellant may indicate in his appeal notice that he has applied for an anonymous entry, or that his entry in the register is an anonymous entry.

(5)    The respondent or any other person who applies to become a party to the proceedings may indicate in a respondent's notice or an application to join the proceedings that his entry in the register is an anonymous entry, or that he has applied for an anonymous entry.

(6)    Where the appellant gives such an indication in his appeal notice, the court will refer the matter to a district judge for directions about the further conduct of the proceedings, and, in particular, directions about how the matter should be listed in the court list.

(7)    Where the court otherwise becomes aware that a party to the appeal is a person referred to in sub-paragraph (2), the court will give notice to the parties that no further step is to be taken until the court has given any necessary directions for the further conduct of the matter.

(8)    In the case of proceedings in a county court, the hearing will be in private unless the court orders otherwise.

(9)    In the case of proceedings in the Court of Appeal, the hearing may be in private if the court so orders.

## Representation of the People Act 1983—appeals selected as test cases

24.6

(1)    Where two or more appeals to which paragraph 24.4 applies involve the same point of law, the court may direct that one appeal ('the test-case appeal') is to be heard first as a test case.

(2)    The court will send a notice of the direction to each party to all of those appeals.

(3)    Where any party to an appeal other than the test-case appeal gives notice to the court, within 7 days after the notice is served on him, that he desires the appeal to which he is a party to be heard –
(a)    the court will hear that appeal after the test-case appeal is disposed of;
(b)    the court will give the parties to that appeal notice of the day on which it will be heard; and

    (c)    the party who gave the notice is not entitled to receive any costs of the separate hearing of that appeal unless the judge otherwise orders.

(4)    Where no notice is given under sub-paragraph (3) within the period limited by that paragraph –

    (a)    the decision on the test-case appeal binds the parties to each of the other appeals;

    (b)    without further hearing, the court will make, in each other appeal, an order similar to the order in the test-case appeal; and

    (c)    the party to each other appeal who is in the same interest as the unsuccessful party to the selected appeal is liable for the costs of the test-case appeal in the same manner and to the same extent as the unsuccessful party to that appeal and an order directing him to pay such costs may be made and enforced accordingly.

(5)    Sub-paragraph (4)(a) does not affect the right to appeal to the Court of Appeal of any party to an appeal other than the test-case appeal.

## *Appeals under section 11 of the UK Borders Act 2007*

24.7

(1)    A person appealing to a county court under section 11 of the UK Borders Act 2007 ('the Act') against a decision by the Secretary of State to impose a penalty under section 9(1) of the Act, must, subject to paragraph (2), file the appellant's notice within 28 days after receiving the penalty notice.

(2)    Where the appellant has given notice of objection to the Secretary of State under section 10 of the Act within the time prescribed for doing so, the appellant's notice must be filed within 28 days after receiving notice of the Secretary of State's decision in response to the notice of objection.

## Section IV – Provisions about Reopening Appeals

### *Reopening of Final Appeals*

25.1 This paragraph applies to applications under rule 52.17 for permission to reopen a final determination of an appeal.

25.2 In this paragraph, 'appeal' includes an application for permission to appeal.

25.3 Permission must be sought from the court whose decision the applicant wishes to reopen.

25.4 The application for permission must be made by application notice and supported by written evidence, verified by a statement of truth.

25.5 A copy of the application for permission must not be served on any other party to the original appeal unless the court so directs.

25.6 Where the court directs that the application for permission is to be served on another party, that party may within 14 days of the service on him of the copy of the application file and serve a written statement either supporting or opposing the application.

25.7 The application for permission, and any written statements supporting or opposing it, will be considered on paper by a single judge, and will be allowed to proceed only if the judge so directs.

## Section V

*Transitional Provisions relating to the abolition of the Asylum and Immigration Tribunal*

(1) Rules 52.7 and 54.28 to 54.36, paragraphs, paragraphs 21.7, 21.7A and 21.7B of Practice Direction 52 and the whole of Practice Direction 54B in force immediately before the 15 February 2010 will continue to apply to the applications, references, orders and cases, as appropriate, set out in paragraphs 5, 7, 9,10, 11 and 13(1) (c) of Schedule 4 to the Transfer of Functions of the Asylum and Immigration Tribunal Order 2009 as if –

(i) rule 52.7 and paragraphs 21.7 and 21.7B of Practice Direction 52 had not been amended; and

(ii) paragraph 21.7A of Practice Direction 52, rules 54.28 to 54.36 and Practice Direction 54B had not been revoked.

(2) For the purpose of service of any claim form issued before 15 February 2010 paragraph 6.2 of Practice Direction 54A shall apply with modification so that the reference in that paragraph to the Immigration and Asylum Chamber of the First-tier Tribunal shall be treated as a reference to the Asylum and Immigration Tribunal.

(3) For ease of reference, the amended and revoked provisions are reproduced below in italics:

### *52.7 Stay*

*Unless –*

*(a) the appeal court or the lower court orders otherwise; or*
*(b) the appeal is from the Asylum and Immigration Tribunal,*

*an appeal shall not operate as a stay of any order or decision of the lower court.*

*Applications for Statutory Review under Section 103A of the Nationality, Immigration and Asylum Act 2002*

### *54.28 Scope and Interpretation*

*(1) This Section of this Part contains rules about applications to the High Court under section 103A of the Nationality, Immigration and Asylum Act 2002 for an order requiring the Asylum and Immigration Tribunal to reconsider its decision on an appeal.*

*(2) In this Section –*

*(a) 'the 2002 Act' means the Nationality, Immigration and Asylum Act 2002;*

*(b* 'the 2004 Act' means the Asylum and Immigration (Treatment of Claimants, etc.) Act 2004;

*(c)* 'appellant' means the appellant in the proceedings before the Tribunal;

*(d)* 'applicant' means a person applying to the High Court under section 103A;

*(e)* 'asylum claim' has the meaning given in section 113(1) of the 2002 Act;

*(ea)* 'fast track case' means any case in relation to which an order made under section 26(8) of the 2004 Act provides that the time period for making an application under section 103A(1) of the 2002 Act or giving notification under paragraph 30(5) of Schedule 2 to the 2004 Act is less than 5 days;

*(f)* 'filter provision' means paragraph 30 of Schedule 2 to the 2004 Act;

*(g)* 'order for reconsideration' means an order under section 103A(1) requiring the Tribunal to reconsider its decision on an appeal;

*(h)* 'section 103A' means section 103A of the 2002 Act;

*(i)* 'Tribunal' means the Asylum and Immigration Tribunal.

*(3) Any reference in this Section to a period of time specified in –*

*(a)* section 103A(3) for making an application for an order under section 103A(1); or

*(b)* paragraph 30(5)(b) of Schedule 2 to the 2004 Act for giving notice under that paragraph, includes a reference to that period as varied by any order under section 26(8) of the 2004 Act.

*(4) Rule 2.8 applies to the calculation of the periods of time specified in –*

*(a)* section 103A(3); and

*(b)* paragraph 30(5)(b) of Schedule 2 to the 2004 Act.

*(5) Save as provided otherwise, the provisions of this Section apply to an application under section 103A regardless of whether the filter provision has effect in relation to that application.*

### 54.28A  Representation of applicants while filter provision has effect

*(1) This rule applies during any period in which the filter provision has effect.*

*(2) An applicant may, for the purpose of taking any step under rule 54.29 or 54.30, be represented by any person permitted to provide him with immigration advice or immigration services under section 84 of the Immigration and Asylum Act 1999.*

*(3) A representative acting for an applicant under paragraph (2) shall be regarded as the applicant's legal representative for the purpose of rule 22.1 (Documents to be verified by a statement of truth) regardless of whether he would otherwise be so regarded.*

### 54.28B  Service of documents on appellants within the jurisdiction

*(1) In proceedings under this Section, rules 6.7 and 6.23(2)(a) do not apply to the service of documents on an appellant who is within the jurisdiction.*

*(2) Where a representative is acting for an appellant who is within the jurisdiction, a document must be served on the appellant by –*

*(a)* serving it on the appellant's representative; or

*(b)* serving it on the appellant personally or sending it to the appellant's address by first class post (or an alternative service which provides for delivery on the next business day),

*but if the document is served on the appellant under sub-paragraph (b), a copy must also at the same time be sent to the appellant's representative.*

### 54.29 *Application for review*

*(1) Subject to paragraph (5), an application for an order for reconsideration must be made by filing an application notice –*

(a)    *during a period in which the filter provision has effect, with the Tribunal at the address specified in the relevant practice direction; and*

(b)    *at any other time, at the Administrative Court Office.*

*(2) During any period in which the filter provision does not have effect, the applicant must file with the application notice –*

(a)    *the notice of the immigration, asylum or nationality decision to which the appeal related;*

(b)    *any other document which was served on the appellant giving reasons for that decision;*

(c)    *the grounds of appeal to the Tribunal;*

(d)    *the Tribunal's determination on the appeal; and*

(e)    *any other documents material to the application which were before the Tribunal.*

*(2A) During any period in which the filter provision has effect, the applicant must file with the application notice a list of the documents referred to in paragraph (2)(a) to (e).*

*(3) The applicant must also file with the application notice written submissions setting out –*

(a)    *the grounds upon which it is contended that the Tribunal made an error of law which may have affected its decision; and*

(b)    *reasons in support of those grounds.*

*(4) Where the applicant –*

(a)    *was the respondent to the appeal; and*

(b)    *was required to serve the Tribunal's determination on the appellant,*

*the application notice must contain a statement of the date on which, and the means by which, the determination was served.*

*(5) Where the applicant is in detention under the Immigration Acts, the application may be made either –*

(a)    *in accordance with paragraphs (1) to (3); or*

(b)    *by serving the documents specified in paragraphs (1) to (3) on the person having custody of him.*

*(6) Where an application is made in accordance with paragraph (5)(b), the person on whom the application notice is served must –*

(a)    *endorse on the notice the date that it is served on him;*

(b)    *give the applicant an acknowledgment in writing of receipt of the notice; and*

(c)    *forward the notice and documents within 2 days*

(i)    *during a period in which the filter provision has effect, to the Tribunal; and*

(ii)    *at any other time, to the Administrative Court Office.*

### 54.30 *Application to extend time limit*

*An application to extend the time limit for making an application under section 103A(1) must –*

(a)    *be made in the application notice;*

*(b)*    set out the grounds on which it is contended that the application notice could not reasonably practicably have been filed within the time limit; and

*(c)*    be supported by written evidence verified by a statement of truth.

### 54.31 Procedure while filter provision has effect

*(1)* This rule applies during any period in which the filter provision has effect.

*(2)* Where the applicant receives notice from the Tribunal that it –

*(a)*    does not propose to make an order for reconsideration; or

*(b)*    does not propose to grant permission for the application to be made outside the relevant time limit,

and the applicant wishes the court to consider the application, the applicant must file a notice in writing at the Administrative Court Office in accordance with paragraph 30(5)(b) of Schedule 2 to the 2004 Act.

*(2A)* The applicant must file with the notice –

*(a)*    a copy of the Tribunal's notification that it does not propose to make an order for reconsideration or does not propose to grant permission for the application to be made outside the relevant time limit (referred to in CPR rule 54.31(2));

*(b)*    any other document which was served on the applicant by the Tribunal giving reasons for its decision in paragraph (a);

*(c)*    written evidence in support of any application by the applicant seeking permission to make the application outside the relevant time limit, if applicable;

*(d)*    a copy of the application for reconsideration under section 103A of the 2002 Act (Form AIT/103A), as submitted to the Tribunal (referred to in Rule 54.29(1)(a).

*(3)* Where the applicant –

*(a)*    was the respondent to the appeal; and

*(b)*    was required to serve the notice from the Tribunal mentioned in paragraph (2) on the appellant,

the notice filed in accordance with paragraph 30(5)(b) of Schedule 2 to the 2004 Act must contain a statement of the date on which, and the means by which, the notice from the Tribunal was served.

*(4)* A notice which is filed outside the period specified in paragraph 30(5)(b) must –

*(a)*    set out the grounds on which it is contended that the notice could not reasonably practicably have been filed within that period; and

*(b)*    be supported by written evidence verified by a statement of truth.

*(5)* If the applicant wishes to respond to the reasons given by the Tribunal for its decision that it –

*(a)*    does not propose to make an order for reconsideration; or

*(b)*    does not propose to grant permission for the application to be made outside the relevant time limit,

the notice filed in accordance with paragraph 30(5)(b) of Schedule 2 to the 2004 Act must be accompanied by written submissions setting out the grounds upon which the applicant disputes any of the reasons given by the Tribunal and giving reasons in support of those grounds.

**54.32  Procedure in fast track cases while filter provision does not have effect**

*(1)  This rule applies only during a period in which the filter provision does not have effect.*

*(2)  Where a party applies for an order for reconsideration in a fast track case –*

   *(a)   the court will serve copies of the application notice and written submissions on the other party to the appeal; and*

   *(b)   the other party to the appeal may file submissions in response to the application not later than 2 days after being served with the application.*

**54.33  Determination of the application by the Administrative Court**

*(1)  This rule, and rules 54.34 and 54.35, apply to applications under section 103A which are determined by the Administrative Court.*

*(2)  The application will be considered by a single judge without a hearing.*

*(3)  Unless it orders otherwise, the court will not receive evidence which was not submitted to the Tribunal.*

*(4)  Subject to paragraph (5), where the court determines an application for an order for reconsideration, it may –*

   *(a)   dismiss the application;*

   *(b)   make an order requiring the Tribunal to reconsider its decision on the appeal under section 103A(1) of the 2002 Act; or*

   *(c)   refer the appeal to the Court of Appeal under section 103C of the 2002 Act.*

*(5)  The court will only make an order requiring the Tribunal to reconsider its decision on an appeal if it thinks that –*

   *(a)   the Tribunal may have made an error of law; and*

   *(b)   there is a real possibility that the Tribunal would make a different decision on reconsidering the appeal (which may include making a different direction under section 87 of the 2002 Act).*

*(6)  Where the Court of Appeal has restored the application to the court under section 103C(2)(g) of the 2002 Act, the court may not refer the appeal to the Court of Appeal.*

*(7)  The court's decision shall be final and there shall be no appeal from that decision or renewal of the application.*

**54.34  Service of order**

*(1)  The court will send copies of its order to –*

   *(a)   the applicant and the other party to the appeal, except where paragraph (2) applies; and*

   *(b)   the Tribunal.*

*(2)  Where the appellant is within the jurisdiction and the application relates, in whole or in part, to an asylum claim, the court will send a copy of its order to the Secretary of State.*

*(2A)  Paragraph (2) does not apply in a fast track case.*

*(3)  Where the court sends an order to the Secretary of State under paragraph (2), the Secretary of State must –*

   *(a)   serve the order on the appellant; and*

   *(b)   immediately after serving the order, notify –*

      *(i)   the court; and*

(ii)     where the order requires the Tribunal to reconsider its decision on the appeal, the Tribunal,

on what date and by what method the order was served.

*(4) The Secretary of State must provide the notification required by paragraph (3)(b) no later than 28 days after the date on which the court sends him a copy of its order.*

*(5) If, 28 days after the date on which the court sends a copy of its order to the Secretary of State in accordance with paragraph (2), the Secretary of State has not provided the notification required by paragraph (3)(b)(i), the court may serve the order on the appellant.*

*(5A) Where the court serves an order for reconsideration under paragraph (5), it will notify the Tribunal of the date on which the order was served.*

*(6) If the court makes an order under section 103D(1) of the 2002 Act, it will send copies of that order to –*

(a)     the appellant's legal representative; and
(b)     the Legal Services Commission.

*(7) Where paragraph (2) applies, the court will not serve copies of an order under section 103D(1) of the 2002 Act until either –*

(a)     the Secretary of State has provided the notification required by paragraph (3)(b); or
(b)     28 days after the date on which the court sent a copy of its order to the Secretary of State,

whichever is the earlier.

### 54.35  Costs

*The court shall make no order as to the costs of an application under this Section except, where appropriate, an order under section 103D(1) of the 2002 Act.*

### 54.36  Continuing an application in circumstances in which it would otherwise be treated as abandoned

*(1) This rule applies to an application under section 103A of the 2002 Act which –*

(a)     would otherwise be treated as abandoned under section 104(4A) of the 2002 Act; but
(b)     meets the conditions set out in section 104(4B) or section 104(4C) of the 2002 Act.

*(2) Where section 104(4A) of the 2002 Act applies and the applicant wishes to pursue the application, the applicant must file a notice at the Administrative Court Office –*

(a)     where section 104(4B) of the 2002 Act applies, within 28 days of the date on which the applicant received notice of the grant of leave to enter or remain in the United Kingdom for a period exceeding 12 months; or
(b)     where section 104(4C) of the 2002 Act applies, within 28 days of the date on which the applicant received notice of the grant of leave to enter or remain in the United Kingdom.

*(3) Where the applicant does not comply with the time limits specified in paragraph (2), the application will be treated as abandoned in accordance with section 104(4) of the 2002 Act.*

*(4) The applicant must serve the notice filed under paragraph (2) on the other party to the appeal.*

*(5) Where section 104(4B) of the 2002 Act applies, the notice filed under paragraph (2) must state –*

 (a) the applicant's full name and date of birth;

 (b) the Administrative Court reference number;

 (c) the Home Office reference number, if applicable;

 (d) the date on which the applicant was granted leave to enter or remain in the United Kingdom for a period exceeding 12 months; and

 (e) that the applicant wishes to pursue the application insofar as it is brought on grounds relating to the Refugee Convention specified in section 84(1)(g) of the 2002 Act.

*(6) Where section 104(4C) of the 2002 Act applies, the notice filed under paragraph (2) must state –*

 (a) the applicant's full name and date of birth;

 (b) the Administrative Court reference number;

 (c) the Home Office reference number, if applicable;

 (d) the date on which the applicant was granted leave to enter or remain in the United Kingdom; and

 (e) that the applicant wishes to pursue the application insofar as it is brought on grounds relating to section 19B of the Race Relations Act 1976 specified in section 84(1)(b) of the 2002 Act.

*(7) Where an applicant has filed a notice under paragraph (2) the court will notify the applicant of the date on which it received the notice.*

*(8) The court will send a copy of the notice issued under paragraph (7) to the other party to the appeal.*

### PRACTICE DIRECTION 52 – APPEALS

## Asylum and Immigration Appeals

*21.7*

*(1) This paragraph applies to appeals –*

 (a) from the Immigration Appeal Tribunal under section 103 of the Nationality, Immigration and Asylum Act 2002 ('the 2002 Act'); and

 (b) from the Asylum and Immigration Tribunal under the following provisions of the 2002 Act –

  (i) section 103B (appeal from the Tribunal following reconsideration); and

  (ii) section 103E (appeal from the Tribunal sitting as a panel).

*(2) The appellant is not required to file an appeal bundle in accordance with paragraph 5.6A of this practice direction, but must file the documents specified in paragraphs 5.6(2)(a) to (f) together with a copy of the Tribunal's determination.*

*(3) The appellant's notice must be filed at the Court of Appeal within 14 days after the appellant is served with written notice of the decision of the Tribunal to grant or refuse permission to appeal.*

*(4) The appellant must serve the appellant's notice in accordance with rule 52.4(3) on –*

 (a) the persons to be served under that rule; and

 (b) the Asylum and Immigration Tribunal.

*(5) On being served with the appellant's notice, the Asylum and Immigration Tribunal must send to the Court of Appeal copies of the documents which were before the relevant Tribunal when it considered the appeal.*

**21.7A**

*(1) This paragraph applies to appeals from the Asylum and Immigration Tribunal referred to the Court of Appeal under section 103C of the Nationality, Immigration and Asylum Act 2002.*

*(2) On making an order referring an appeal to the Court of Appeal, the High Court shall send to the Court of Appeal copies of –*

> *(a)  that order and any other order made in relation to the application for reconsideration; and*
> *(b)  the application notice, written submissions and other documents filed under rule 54.29*

*(3) Unless the court directs otherwise, the application notice filed under rule 54.29 shall be treated as the appellant's notice.*

*(4) The respondent may file a respondent's notice within 14 days after the date on which the respondent is served with the order of the High Court referring the appeal to the Court of Appeal.*

*(5) The Court of Appeal may give such additional directions as are appropriate.*

**21.7B**

*(1) This paragraph applies to appeals from the Asylum and Immigration Tribunal which –*

> *(a)  would otherwise be treated as abandoned under section 104(4A) of the Nationality, Immigration and Asylum Act 2002 (the '2002 Act'); but*
> *(b)  meet the conditions set out in section 104(4B) or section 104(4C) of the 2002 Act.*

*(2) Where section 104(4A) of the 2002 Act applies and the appellant wishes to pursue his appeal, the appellant must file a notice at the Court of Appeal –*

> *(a)  where section 104(4B) of the 2002 Act applies, within 28 days of the date on which the appellant received notice of the grant of leave to enter or remain in the United Kingdom for a period exceeding 12 months; or*
> *(b)  where section 104(4C) of the 2002 Act applies, within 28 days of the date on which the appellant received notice of the grant of leave to enter or remain in the United Kingdom.*

*(3) Where the appellant does not comply with the time limits specified in paragraph (2) the appeal will be treated as abandoned in accordance with section 104(4) of the 2002 Act.*

*(4) The appellant must serve the notice filed under paragraph (2) on the respondent.*

*(5) Where section 104(4B) of the 2002 Act applies, the notice filed under paragraph (2) must state –*

> *(a)  the appellant's full name and date of birth;*
> *(b)  the Court of Appeal reference number;*
> *(c)  the Home Office reference number, if applicable;*
> *(d)  the date on which the appellant was granted leave to enter or remain in the United Kingdom for a period exceeding 12 months; and*
> *(e)  that the appellant wishes to pursue the appeal in so far as it is brought on the ground relating to the Refugee Convention specified in section 84(1)(g) of the 2002 Act.*

*(6) Where section 104(4C) of the 2002 Act applies, the notice filed under paragraph (2) must state –*

*(a) the appellant's full name and date of birth;*

*(b) the Court of Appeal reference number;*

*(c) the Home Office reference number, if applicable;*

*(d) the date on which the appellant was granted leave to enter or remain in the United Kingdom; and*

*(e) that the appellant wishes to pursue the appeal in so far as it is brought on the ground relating to section 19B of the Race Relations Act 1976 specified in section 84(1)(b) of the 2002 Act.*

*(7) Where an appellant has filed a notice under paragraph (2) the Court of Appeal will notify the appellant of the date on which it received the notice.*

*(8) The Court of Appeal will send a copy of the notice issued under paragraph (7) to the respondent.*

## PRACTICE DIRECTION 54A – RULE 54.7 – SERVICE OF CLAIM FORM

6.2

*Where the defendant or interested party to the claim for judicial review is –*

   *(a)   the Asylum and Immigration Tribunal, the address for service of the claim form is the Asylum and Immigration Tribunal, Official Correspondence Unit, PO Box 6987, Leicester, LE1 6ZX or fax number 0116 249 4131;*

   *(b)   the Crown, service of the claim form must be effected on the solicitor acting for the relevant government department as if the proceedings were civil proceedings as defined in the Crown Proceedings Act 1947.*

*(The practice direction supplementing Part 66 gives the list published under section 17 of the Crown Proceedings Act 1947 of the solicitors acting in civil proceedings (as defined in that Act) for the different government departments on whom service is to be effected, and of their addresses.)*

*(Part 6 contains provisions about the service of claim forms.)*

## PRACTICE DIRECTION 54B – APPLICATIONS FOR STAUTUTORY REVIEW UNDER SECTION 103A OF THE NATIONALITY, IMMIGRATION AND ASYLUM ACT 2002

*This Practice Direction supplements Section III of CPR Part 54*

*1 Attention is drawn to:*

   *(1)   Sections 103A, 103C and 103D of the Nationality, Immigration and Asylum Act 2002 (inserted by section 26(6) of the Asylum and Immigration (Treatment of Claimants, etc.) Act 2004); and*

   *(2)   Paragraph 30 of Schedule 2 to the 2004 Act.*

## The Court

*2.1 Applications for review under section 103A(1) of the 2002 Act are dealt with in the Administrative Court, subject to the transitional filter provision in paragraph 30 of Schedule 2 of the 2004 Act which provides that they shall initially be considered by a member of the Tribunal.*

*2.2 During any period in which the filter provision has effect, the address for filing section 103A applications shall be the Asylum and Immigration Tribunal, P.O. Box 6987, Leicester LE1 6ZX.*

*2.3 Where a fast track order within the meaning of Rule 54.32(3) applies to a section 103A application, paragraph 2.2 shall not apply and the address for filing the application shall be the address specified in the Tribunal's determination of the appeal.*

## Access to court orders served on the appellant by the Secretary of State

*3.1 Where the court sends a copy of its order on a section 103A application to the Secretary of State but not the appellant in accordance with Rule 54.34(2), then Rules 5.4(3)(b) and 5.4(5)(a)(ii) are modified as follows.*

*3.2 Neither the appellant nor any other person may obtain from the records of the court a copy of the court's order on the section 103A application, or of any order made under section 103D(1) of the 2002 Act in relation to that application, until either the Secretary of State has given the court the notification required by Rule 54.34(3)(b) or 28 days after the date on which the court sent a copy of the order to the Secretary of State, whichever is the earlier.*

## Referral to Court of Appeal

*4.1 Where the court refers an appeal to the Court of Appeal, its order will set out the question of law raised by the appeal which is of such importance that it should be decided by the Court of Appeal.*

*4.2 Paragraph 21.7A of the practice direction supplementing Part 52 makes provision about appeals which are referred to the Court of Appeal.*

\*\*\*\*

# Part 54 – Judicial Review and Statutory Review

**Contents of this Part**

*Section I – Judicial Review*

**54.1 Scope and interpretation**

(1) This Section of this Part contains rules about judicial review.

(2) In this Section –

    (a)    a 'claim for judicial review' means a claim to review the lawfulness of –
        (i)    an enactment; or
        (ii)    a decision, action or failure to act in relation to the exercise of a public function.

    (b)–(d) …
    (e)    'the judicial review procedure' means the Part 8 procedure as modified by this Section;
    (f)    'interested party' means any person (other than the claimant and defendant) who is directly affected by the claim; and

(g)    'court' means the High Court, unless otherwise stated.

(Rule 8.1(6)(b) provides that a rule or practice direction may, in relation to a specified type of proceedings, disapply or modify any of these rules set out in Part 8 as they apply to those proceedings)

Amendments—SI 2000/2092; SI 2003/364; SI 2003/3361.

### 54.2  When this Section must be used

The judicial review procedure must be used in a claim for judicial review where the claimant is seeking –

(a)    a mandatory order;
(b)    a prohibiting order;
(c)    a quashing order; or
(d)    an injunction under section 30 of the Senior Courts Act 1981 (restraining a person from acting in any office in which he is not entitled to act).

Amendments—SI 2000/2092; SI 2003/364.

### 54.3  When this Section may be used

(1)  The judicial review procedure may be used in a claim for judicial review where the claimant is seeking –

(a)    a declaration; or
(b)    an injunction(GL).

(Section 31(2) of the Senior Courts Act 1981 sets out the circumstances in which the court may grant a declaration or injunction in a claim for judicial review)

(Where the claimant is seeking a declaration or injunction in addition to one of the remedies listed in rule 54.2, the judicial review procedure must be used)

(2)  A claim for judicial review may include a claim for damages, restitution or the recovery of a sum due but may not seek such a remedy alone.

(Section 31(4) of the Senior Courts Act 1981 sets out the circumstances in which the court may award damages, restitution or the recovery of a sum due on a claim for judicial review)

Amendments—SI 2000/2092; SI 2003/364; SI 2003/3361; Constitutional Reform Act 2005, Sch 11, para 1(2).

### 54.4  Permission required

The court's permission to proceed is required in a claim for judicial review whether started under this Section or transferred to the Administrative Court.

Amendments—SI 2000/2092; SI 2003/364.

### 54.5  Time limit for filing claim form

(1)  The claim form must be filed –

(a)    promptly; and

    (b)    in any event not later than 3 months after the grounds to make the claim first arose.

(2) The time limit in this rule may not be extended by agreement between the parties.

(3) This rule does not apply when any other enactment specifies a shorter time limit for making the claim for judicial review.

---

**Amendments**—SI 2000/2092.

## 54.6 Claim form

(1) In addition to the matters set out in rule 8.2 (contents of the claim form) the claimant must also state –

    (a)    the name and address of any person he considers to be an interested party;

    (b)    that he is requesting permission to proceed with a claim for judicial review; and

    (c)    any remedy (including any interim remedy) he is claiming.

(Part 25 sets out how to apply for an interim remedy)

(2) The claim form must be accompanied by the documents required by Practice Direction 54A.

---

**Amendments**—SI 2000/2092; SI 2009/3309.

## 54.7 Service of claim form

The claim form must be served on –

    (a)    the defendant; and

    (b)    unless the court otherwise directs, any person the claimant considers to be an interested party, within 7 days after the date of issue.

---

**Amendments**—SI 2000/2092.

## 54.8 Acknowledgment of service

(1) Any person served with the claim form who wishes to take part in the judicial review must file an acknowledgment of service in the relevant practice form in accordance with the following provisions of this rule.

(2) Any acknowledgment of service must be –

    (a)    filed not more than 21 days after service of the claim form; and

    (b)    served on –

        (i)    the claimant; and

        (ii)    subject to any direction under rule 54.7(b), any other person named in the claim form, as soon as practicable and, in any event, not later than 7 days after it is filed.

(3) The time limits under this rule may not be extended by agreement between the parties.

(4) The acknowledgment of service –

    (a)    must –

   (i)    where the person filing it intends to contest the claim, set out a
          summary of his grounds for doing so; and

   (ii)   state the name and address of any person the person filing it
          considers to be an interested party; and

   (b)    may include or be accompanied by an application for directions.

(5) Rule 10.3(2) does not apply.

---

Amendments—SI 2000/2092.

### 54.9 Failure to file acknowledgment of service

(1) Where a person served with the claim form has failed to file an
acknowledgment of service in accordance with rule 54.8, he –

   (a)    may not take part in a hearing to decide whether permission should be
          given unless the court allows him to do so; but

   (b)    provided he complies with rule 54.14 or any other direction of the court
          regarding the filing and service of –
          (i)    detailed grounds for contesting the claim or supporting it on
                 additional grounds; and
          (ii)   any written evidence,

   may take part in the hearing of the judicial review.

(2) Where that person takes part in the hearing of the judicial review, the court
may take his failure to file an acknowledgment of service into account when
deciding what order to make about costs.

(3) Rule 8.4 does not apply.

---

Amendments—SI 2000/2092.

### 54.10 Permission given

(1) Where permission to proceed is given the court may also give directions.

(2) Directions under paragraph (1) may include —

   (a)    a stay$^{(GL)}$ of proceedings to which the claim relates;
   (b)    directions requiring the proceedings to be heard by a Divisional Court.

(Rule 3.7 provides a sanction for the non-payment of the fee payable when
permission to proceed has been given)

---

Amendments—SI 2000/2092; SI 2010/2577.

### 54.11 Service of order giving or refusing permission

The court will serve –

   (a)    the order giving or refusing permission; and
   (b)    any directions,

on –

          (i)    the claimant;
          (ii)   the defendant; and
          (iii)  any other person who filed an acknowledgment of service.

Amendments—SI 2000/2092.

### 54.12 Permission decision without a hearing

(1) This rule applies where the court, without a hearing –

(a)   refuses permission to proceed; or
(b)   gives permission to proceed –
    (i)    subject to conditions; or
    (ii)   on certain grounds only.

(2) The court will serve its reasons for making the decision when it serves the order giving or refusing permission in accordance with rule 54.11.

(3) The claimant may not appeal but may request the decision to be reconsidered at a hearing.

(4) A request under paragraph (3) must be filed within 7 days after service of the reasons under paragraph (2).

(5) The claimant, defendant and any other person who has filed an acknowledgment of service will be given at least 2 days' notice of the hearing date.

(6) The court may give directions requiring the proceedings to be heard by a Divisional Court.

Amendments—SI 2000/2092; SI 2010/2577.

### 54.13 Defendant etc may not apply to set aside[(GL)]

Neither the defendant nor any other person served with the claim form may apply to set aside[(GL)] an order giving permission to proceed.

Amendments—Inserted by SI 2000/2092.

### 54.14 Response

(1) A defendant and any other person saved with the claim form who wishes to contest the claim or support it on additional grounds must file and serve –

(a)   detailed grounds for contesting the claim or supporting it on additional grounds; and
(b)   any written evidence,

within 35 days after service of the order giving permission.

(2) The following rules do not apply –

(a)   rule 8.5(3) and 8.5(4) (defendant to file and serve written evidence at the same time as acknowledgment of service); and
(b)   rule 8.5(5) and 8.5(6) (claimant to file and serve reply within 14 days).

Amendments—Inserted by SI 2000/2092.

### 54.15 Where claimant seeks to rely on additional grounds

The court's permission is required if a claimant seeks to rely on grounds other than those for which he has been given permission to proceed.

Amendments—SI 2000/2092.

### 54.16 Evidence

(1) Rule 8.6(1) does not apply.

(2) No written evidence may be relied on unless –

    (a)    it has been served in accordance with any –
        (i)    rule under this Section; or
        (ii)   direction of the court; or

    (b)    the court gives permission.

Amendments—SI 2000/2092; SI 2002/2058; SI 2003/364.

### 54.17 Court's powers to hear any person

(1) Any person may apply for permission –

    (a)    to file evidence; or
    (b)    make representations at the hearing of the judicial review.

(2) An application under paragraph (1) should be made promptly.

Amendments—SI 2000/2092.

### 54.18 Judicial review may be decided without a hearing

The court may decide the claim for judicial review without a hearing where all the parties agree.

Amendments—SI 2000/2092.

### 54.19 Court's powers in respect of quashing orders

(1) This rule applies where the court makes a quashing order in respect of the decision to which the claim relates.

(2) The court may –

    (a)    (i)    remit the matter to the decision-maker; and
    (ii)   direct it to reconsider the matter and reach a decision in accordance with the judgment of the court; or
    (b)    in so far as any enactment permits, substitute its own decision for the decision to which the claim relates.

    (Section 31 of the Senior Courts Act 1981 enables the High Court, subject to certain conditions, to substitute its own decision for the decision in question.)

Amendments—SI 2000/2092; SI 2007/3543; Constitutional Reform Act 2005, Sch 11, para 1(2).

### 54.20 Transfer

The court may –

    (a)    order a claim to continue as if it had not been started under this Section; and

(b)     where it does so, give directions about the future management of the claim.

(Part 30 (transfer) applies to transfers to and from the Administrative Court)

---

**Amendments**—SI 2000/2092; SI 2003/364.

**54.21–54.27**

(*Revoked*)

**54.28–54.35**

(*Revoked*)

# Practice Direction 54A – Judicial Review

## Judicial Review

1.1 In addition to Part 54 and this practice direction attention is drawn to –

- section 31 of the Senior Courts Act 1981; and
- the Human Rights Act 1998.

## The Court

2.1 Part 54 claims for judicial review are dealt with in the Administrative Court.

(Practice Direction 54D contains provisions about where a claim for judicial review may be started, administered and heard.)

## Rule 54.5 – Time Limit for Filing Claim Form

4.1 Where the claim is for a quashing order in respect of a judgment, order or conviction, the date when the grounds to make the claim first arose, for the purposes of rule 54.5(1)(b), is the date of that judgment, order or conviction.

## Rule 54.6 – Claim Form

*Interested parties*

5.1 Where the claim for judicial review relates to proceedings in a court or tribunal, any other parties to those proceedings must be named in the claim form as interested parties under rule 54.6(1)(a) (and therefore served with the claim form under rule 54.7(b)).

5.2 For example, in a claim by a defendant in a criminal case in the Magistrates' or Crown Court for judicial review of a decision in that case, the prosecution must always be named as an interested party.

*Human rights*

5.3 Where the claimant is seeking to raise any issue under the Human Rights Act 1998, or seeks a remedy available under that Act, the claim form must include the information required by paragraph 15 of Practice Direction 16.

*Devolution issues*

5.4 Where the claimant intends to raise a devolution issue, the claim form must –

(1) specify that the applicant wishes to raise a devolution issue and identify the relevant provisions of the Government of Wales Act 2006, the Northern Ireland Act 1998 or the Scotland Act 1998; and
(2) contain a summary of the facts, circumstances and points of law on the basis of which it is alleged that a devolution issue arises.

5.5 In this practice direction 'devolution issue' has the same meaning as in paragraph 1, Schedule 9 to the Government of Wales Act 2006, paragraph 1, Schedule 10 to the Northern Ireland Act 1998; and paragraph 1, Schedule 6 to the Scotland Act 1998.

## Claim form

5.6 The claim form must include or be accompanied by –

    (1)    a detailed statement of the claimant's grounds for bringing the claim for judicial review;

    (2)    a statement of the facts relied on;

    (3)    any application to extend the time limit for filing the claim form;

    (4)    any application for directions ...

    ...

5.7 In addition, the claim form must be accompanied by –

    (1)    any written evidence in support of the claim or application to extend time;

    (2)    a copy of any order that the claimant seeks to have quashed;

    (3)    where the claim for judicial review relates to a decision of a court or tribunal, an approved copy of the reasons for reaching that decision;

    (4)    copies of any documents on which the claimant proposes to rely;

    (5)    copies of any relevant statutory material;

    (6)    a list of essential documents for advance reading by the court (with page references to the passages relied on); and

5.8 Where it is not possible to file all the above documents, the claimant must indicate which documents have not been filed and the reasons why they are not currently available.

## Bundle of documents

5.9 The claimant must file two copies of a paginated and indexed bundle containing all the documents referred to in paragraphs 5.6 and 5.7.

5.10 Attention is drawn to rules 8.5(1) and 8.5(7).

## Rule 54.7 – Service of Claim Form

6.1 Except as required by rules 54.11 or 54.12(2), the Administrative Court will not serve documents and service must be effected by the parties.

6.2 Where the defendant or interested party to the claim for judicial review is –

    (a)    the Immigration and Asylum Chamber of the First-tier Tribunal, the address for service of the claim form is Official Correspondence Unit, PO Box 6987, Leicester, LE1 6ZX or fax number 0116 249 4240;

    (b)    the Crown, service of the claim form must be effected on the solicitor acting for the relevant government department as if the proceedings were civil proceedings as defined in the Crown Proceedings Act 1947.

(Practice Direction 66 gives the list published under section 17 of the Crown Proceedings Act 1947 of the solicitors acting in civil proceedings (as defined in that Act) for the different government departments on whom service is to be effected, and of their addresses.)

(Part 6 contains provisions about the service of claim forms.)

## Rule 54.8 – Acknowledgment of Service

7.1 Attention is drawn to rule 8.3(2) and the relevant practice direction and to rule 10.5.

## Rule 54.10 – Permission Given

### Directions

8.1 Case management directions under rule 54.10(1) may include directions about serving the claim form and any evidence on other persons.

8.2 Where a claim is made under the Human Rights Act 1998, a direction may be made for giving notice to the Crown or joining the Crown as a party. Attention is drawn to rule 19.4A and paragraph 6 of Practice Direction 19A.

### Permission without a hearing

8.4 The court will generally, in the first instance, consider the question of permission without a hearing.

### Permission hearing

8.5 Neither the defendant nor any other interested party need attend a hearing on the question of permission unless the court directs otherwise.

8.6 Where the defendant or any party does attend a hearing, the court will not generally make an order for costs against the claimant.

## Rule 54.11 – Service of Order Giving or Refusing Permission

9.1 An order refusing permission or giving it subject to conditions or on certain grounds only must set out or be accompanied by the court's reasons for coming to that decision.

## Rule 54.14 – Response

10.1 Where the party filing the detailed grounds intends to rely on documents not already filed, he must file a paginated bundle of those documents when he files the detailed grounds.

# Rule 54.15 – Where Claimant Seeks to Rely on Additional Grounds

11.1 Where the claimant intends to apply to rely on additional grounds at the hearing of the claim for judicial review, he must give notice to the court and to any other person served with the claim form no later than 7 clear days before the hearing (or the warned date where appropriate).

# Rule 54.16 – Evidence

12.1 Disclosure is not required unless the court orders otherwise.

# Rule 54.17 – Court's Powers to Hear any Person

13.1 Where all the parties consent, the court may deal with an application under rule 54.17 without a hearing.

13.2 Where the court gives permission for a person to file evidence or make representations at the hearing of the claim for judicial review, it may do so on conditions and may give case management directions.

13.3 An application for permission should be made by letter to the Administrative Court office, identifying the claim, explaining who the applicant is and indicating why and in what form the applicant wants to participate in the hearing.

13.4 If the applicant is seeking a prospective order as to costs, the letter should say what kind of order and on what grounds.

13.5 Applications to intervene must be made at the earliest reasonable opportunity, since it will usually be essential not to delay the hearing.

# Rule 54.20 – Transfer

14.1 Attention is drawn to rule 30.5.

14.2 In deciding whether a claim is suitable for transfer to the Administrative Court, the court will consider whether it raises issues of public law to which Part 54 should apply.

## *Skeleton arguments*

15.1 The claimant must file and serve a skeleton argument not less than 21 working days before the date of the hearing of the judicial review (or the warned date).

15.2 The defendant and any other party wishing to make representations at the hearing of the judicial review must file and serve a skeleton argument not less than 14 working days before the date of the hearing of the judicial review (or the warned date).

15.3 Skeleton arguments must contain –

(1)   a time estimate for the complete hearing, including delivery of judgment;
(2)   a list of issues;

(3) a list of the legal points to be taken (together with any relevant authorities with page references to the passages relied on);

(4) a chronology of events (with page references to the bundle of documents (see paragraph 16.1);

(5) a list of essential documents for the advance reading of the court (with page references to the passages relied on) (if different from that filed with the claim form) and a time estimate for that reading; and

(6) a list of persons referred to.

## Bundle of documents to be filed

16.1 The claimant must file a paginated and indexed bundle of all relevant documents required for the hearing of the judicial review when he files his skeleton argument.

16.2 The bundle must also include those documents required by the defendant and any other party who is to make representations at the hearing.

## Agreed final order

17.1 If the parties agree about the final order to be made in a claim for judicial review, the claimant must file at the court a document (with 2 copies) signed by all the parties setting out the terms of the proposed agreed order together with a short statement of the matters relied on as justifying the proposed agreed order and copies of any authorities or statutory provisions relied on.

17.2 The court will consider the documents referred to in paragraph 17.1 and will make the order if satisfied that the order should be made.

17.3 If the court is not satisfied that the order should be made, a hearing date will be set.

17.4 Where the agreement relates to an order for costs only, the parties need only file a document signed by all the parties setting out the terms of the proposed order.

## Section II – Applications for Permission to Apply for Judicial Review in Immigration and Asylum Cases – Challenging Removal

18.1

(1) This Section applies where –

(a) a person has been served with a copy of directions for his removal from the United Kingdom by the UK Border Agency of the Home Office and notified that this Section applies; and

(b) that person makes an application for permission to apply for judicial review before his removal takes effect.

(2) This Section does not prevent a person from applying for judicial review after he has been removed.

(3) The requirements contained in this Section of this Practice Direction are additional to those contained elsewhere in the Practice Direction.

18.2

(1) A person who makes an application for permission to apply for judicial review must file a claim form and a copy at court, and the claim form must –

(a) indicate on its face that this Section of the Practice Direction applies; and

(b) be accompanied by –
  (i) a copy of the removal directions and the decision to which the application relates; and
  (ii) any document served with the removal directions including any document which contains the UK Border Agency's factual summary of the case; and

(c) contain or be accompanied by the detailed statement of the claimant's grounds for bringing the claim for judicial review; or

(d) if the claimant is unable to comply with paragraph (b) or (c), contain or be accompanied by a statement of the reasons why.

(2) The claimant must, immediately upon issue of the claim, send copies of the issued claim form and accompanying documents to the address specified by the UK Border Agency.

(Rule 54.7 also requires the defendant to be served with the claim form within 7 days of the date of issue. Rule 6.10 provides that service on a Government Department must be effected on the solicitor acting for that Department, which in the case of the UK Border Agency is the Treasury Solicitor. The address for the Treasury Solicitor may be found in the Annex to Part 66 of these Rules.)

18.3 Where the claimant has not complied with paragraph 18.2(1)(b) or (c) and has provided reasons why he is unable to comply, and the court has issued the claim form, the Administrative Court –

(a) will refer the matter to a Judge for consideration as soon as practicable; and

(b) will notify the parties that it has done so.

18.4 If, upon a refusal to grant permission to apply for judicial review, the Court indicates that the application is clearly without merit, that indication will be included in the order refusing permission.

****

# Practice Direction 54D – Administrative Court (Venue)

## Administrative Court (Venue)

### Scope and purpose

1.1 This Practice Direction concerns the place in which a claim before the Administrative Court should be started and administered and the venue at which it will be determined.

1.2 This Practice Direction is intended to facilitate access to justice by enabling cases to be administered and determined in the most appropriate location. To achieve this purpose it provides flexibility in relation to where claims are to be administered and enables claims to be transferred to different venues.

### Venue – general provisions

2.1 The claim form in proceedings in the Administrative Court may be issued at the Administrative Court Office of the High Court at –

(1)  the Royal Courts of Justice in London; or
(2)  at the District Registry of the High Court at Birmingham, Cardiff, Leeds, or Manchester unless the claim is one of the excepted classes of claim set out in paragraph 3 of this Practice Direction which may only be started and determined at the Royal Courts of Justice in London.

2.2 Any claim started in Birmingham will normally be determined at a court in the Midland region (geographically covering the area of the Midland Circuit); in Cardiff in Wales; in Leeds in the North-Eastern Region (geographically covering the area of the North Eastern Circuit); in London at the Royal Courts of Justice; and in Manchester, in the North-Western Region (geographically covering the Northern Circuit).

### Excepted classes of claim

3.1 The excepted classes of claim referred to in paragraph 2.1(2) are –

(1)  proceedings to which Part 76 or Part 79 applies, and for the avoidance of doubt –
    (a)  proceedings relating to control orders (within the meaning of Part 76);
    (b)  financial restrictions proceedings (within the meaning of Part 79);
    (c)  proceedings relating to terrorism or alleged terrorists (where that is a relevant feature of the claim); and
    (d)  proceedings in which a special advocate is or is to be instructed;

(2)  proceedings to which RSC Order 115 applies;
(3)  proceedings under the Proceeds of Crime Act 2002;
(4)  appeals to the Administrative Court under the Extradition Act 2003;
(5)  proceedings which must be heard by a Divisional Court; and
(6)  proceedings relating to the discipline of solicitors.

3.2 If a claim form is issued at an Administrative Court office other than in London and includes one of the excepted classes of claim, the proceedings will be transferred to London.

## Urgent applications

4.1 During the hours when the court is open, where an urgent application needs to be made to the Administrative Court outside London, the application must be made to the judge designated to deal with such applications in the relevant District Registry.

4.2 Any urgent application to the Administrative Court during the hours when the court is closed, must be made to the duty out of hours High Court judge by telephoning 020 7947 6000.

## Assignment to another venue

5.1 The proceedings may be transferred from the office at which the claim form was issued to another office. Such transfer is a judicial act.

5.2 The general expectation is that proceedings will be administered and determined in the region with which the claimant has the closest connection, subject to the following considerations as applicable –

(1)  any reason expressed by any party for preferring a particular venue;
(2)  the region in which the defendant, or any relevant office or department of the defendant, is based;
(3)  the region in which the claimant's legal representatives are based;
(4)  the ease and cost of travel to a hearing;
(5)  the availability and suitability of alternative means of attending a hearing (for example, by videolink);
(6)  the extent and nature of media interest in the proceedings in any particular locality;
(7)  the time within which it is appropriate for the proceedings to be determined;
(8)  whether it is desirable to administer or determine the claim in another region in the light of the volume of claims issued at, and the capacity, resources and workload of, the court at which it is issued;
(9)  whether the claim raises issues sufficiently similar to those in another outstanding claim to make it desirable that it should be determined together with, or immediately following, that other claim; and
(10)  whether the claim raises devolution issues and for that reason whether it should more appropriately be determined in London or Cardiff.

5.3

(1)  When an urgent application is made under paragraph 4.1 or 4.2, this will not by itself decide the venue for the further administration or determination of the claim.
(2)  The court dealing with the urgent application may direct that the case be assigned to a particular venue.

(3)     When an urgent application is made under paragraph 4.2, and the court does not make a direction under sub-paragraph (2), the claim will be assigned in the first place to London but may be reassigned to another venue at a later date.

5.4 The court may on an application by a party or of its own initiative direct that the claim be determined in a region other than that of the venue in which the claim is currently assigned. The considerations in paragraph 5.2 apply.

5.5 Once assigned to a venue, the proceedings will be both administered from that venue and determined by a judge of the Administrative Court at a suitable court within that region, or, if the venue is in London, at the Royal Courts of Justice. The choice of which court (of those within the region which are identified by the Presiding Judge of the circuit suitable for such hearing) will be decided, subject to availability, by the considerations in paragraph 5.2.

5.6 When giving directions under rule 54.10, the court may direct that proceedings be reassigned to another region for hearing (applying the considerations in paragraph 5.2). If no such direction is given, the claim will be heard in the same region as that in which the permission application was determined (whether on paper or at a hearing).

\*\*\*\*

# Pre-Action Protocol for Judicial Review

## Introduction

**This protocol applies to proceedings <u>within England and Wales only</u>. It does not affect the time-limit specified by Rule 54.5(1) of the Civil Procedure Rules which requires that any claim form in an application for judicial review must be filed promptly and in any event not later than 3 months after the grounds to make the claim first arose.**[1]

1 Judicial review allows people with a sufficient interest in a decision or action by a public body to ask a judge to review the lawfulness of:

- an enactment; or
- a decision, action or failure to act in relation to the exercise of a public function.

2 Judicial review may be used where there is no right of appeal or where all avenues of appeal have been exhausted.

> 1      While the court does have the discretion under Rule 3.1(2)(a) of the Civil Procedure Rules to allow a late claim, this is only used in exceptional circumstances. **Compliance with the protocol alone is unlikely to be sufficient to persuade the court to allow a late claim**

## Alternative Dispute Resolution

3.1 The parties should consider whether some form of alternative dispute resolution procedure would be more suitable than litigation, and if so, endeavour to agree which form to adopt. Both the Claimant and Defendant may be required by the Court to provide evidence that alternative means of resolving their dispute were considered. The Courts take the view that litigation should be a last resort, and that claims should not be issued prematurely when a settlement is still actively being explored. Parties are warned that if the protocol is not followed (including this paragraph) then the Court must have regard to such conduct when determining costs. However, parties should also note that a claim for judicial review 'must be filed promptly and in any event not later than 3 months after the grounds to make the claim first arose'.

3.2 It is not practicable in this protocol to address in detail how the parties might decide which method to adopt to resolve their particular dispute. However, summarised below are some of the options for resolving disputes without litigation:

- Discussion and negotiation.
- Ombudsmen – the Parliamentary and Health Service and the Local Government Ombudsmen have discretion to deal with complaints relating to maladministration. The British and Irish Ombudsman Association provide information about Ombudsman schemes and other complaint handling bodies and this is available from their website at *www.bioa.org.uk*. Parties may wish to note that the Ombudsmen are not able to look into a complaint once court action has been commenced.
- Early neutral evaluation by an independent third party (for example, a lawyer experienced in the field of administrative law or an individual experienced in the subject matter of the claim).
- Mediation – a form of facilitated negotiation assisted by an independent neutral party.

3.3 The Legal Services Commission has published a booklet on 'Alternatives to Court', CLS Direct Information Leaflet 23 (*www.clsdirect.org.uk*), which lists a number of organisations that provide alternative dispute resolution services.

*3.4 It is expressly recognised that no party can or should be forced to mediate or enter into any form of ADR.*

**4 Judicial review may not be appropriate in every instance.**

**Claimants are strongly advised to seek appropriate legal advice when considering such proceedings and, in particular, before adopting this protocol or making a claim. Although the Legal Services Commission will not normally grant full representation before a letter before claim has been sent and the proposed defendant given a reasonable time to respond, initial funding may be available, for eligible claimants, to cover the work necessary to write this. (See Annex C for more information).**

5 This protocol sets out a code of good practice and contains the steps which parties should generally follow before making a claim for judicial review.

6 This protocol does not impose a greater obligation on a public body to disclose documents or give reasons for its decision than that already provided for in statute or common law. However, where the court considers that a public body should have provided **relevant** documents and/or information, particularly where this failure is a breach of a statutory or common law requirement, it may impose sanctions.

**This protocol will not be appropriate where the defendant does not have the legal power to change the decision being challenged, for example decisions issued by tribunals such as the Asylum and Immigration Tribunal.**

**This protocol will not be appropriate in urgent cases, for example, when directions have been set, or are in force, for the claimant's removal from the UK, or where there is an urgent need for an interim order to compel a public body to act where it has unlawfully refused to do so (for example, the failure of a local housing authority to secure interim accommodation for a homeless claimant) a claim should be made immediately. A letter before claim will not stop the implementation of a disputed decision in all instances.**

7 All claimants will need to satisfy themselves whether they should follow the protocol, depending upon the circumstances of his or her case. Where the use of the protocol is appropriate, the court will normally expect all parties to have complied with it and will take into account compliance or non-compliance when giving directions for case management of proceedings or when making orders for costs. However, even in emergency cases, it is good practice to fax to the defendant the draft claim form which the claimant intends to issue. A claimant is also normally required to notify a defendant when an interim mandatory order is being sought.

## The Letter before Claim

8 Before making a claim, the claimant should send a letter to the defendant. The purpose of this letter is to identify the issues in dispute and establish whether litigation can be avoided.

9 Claimants should normally use the suggested **standard format** for the letter outlined at Annex A.

10 The letter should contain **the date and details of the decision, act or omission being challenged and a clear summary of the facts** on which the claim is based. It should also contain the **details of any relevant information** that the claimant is seeking and an explanation of why this is considered relevant.

11 The letter should normally contain the **details of any interested parties** known to the claimant. They should be sent a **copy** of the letter before claim **for information. Claimants are strongly advised to seek appropriate legal advice when considering such proceedings and, in particular, before sending the letter before claim to other interested parties or making a claim.**

12 A claim should not normally be made until the proposed reply date given in the letter before claim has passed, unless the circumstances of the case require more immediate action to be taken.

## The Letter of Response

13 Defendants should normally respond within 14 days using the **standard format** at Annex B. Failure to do so will be taken into account by the court and sanctions may be imposed unless there are good reasons.

14 Where it is not possible to reply within the proposed time-limit the defendant should send an interim reply and propose a reasonable extension. Where an extension is sought, reasons should be given and, where required, additional information requested. **This will not affect the time-limit for making a claim for judicial review** nor will it bind the claimant where he or she considers this to be unreasonable. However, where the court considers that a subsequent claim is made prematurely it may impose sanctions.

15 If the **claim is being conceded in full**, the reply should say so in clear and unambiguous terms.

16 If the **claim is being conceded in part or not being conceded at all**, the reply should say so in clear and unambiguous terms, and:

- (a) where appropriate, contain a new decision, clearly identifying what aspects of the claim are being conceded and what are not, or, give a clear timescale within which the new decision will be issued;
- (b) provide a fuller explanation for the decision, if considered appropriate to do so;
- (c) address any points of dispute, or explain why they cannot be addressed;
- (d) enclose any **relevant** documentation requested by the claimant, or explain why the documents are not being enclosed; and
- (e) where appropriate, confirm whether or not they will oppose any application for an interim remedy.

17 The response should be sent to **all interested parties** identified by the claimant and contain details of any other parties who the defendant considers also have an interest.

# Annex A
# Letter before Claim

## Section 1 – Information Required in a Letter Before Claim

**Proposed Claim for Judicial Review**

1  **To**

(*Insert the name and address of the proposed defendant – see details in section 2*)

2  **The claimant**

(*Insert the title, first and last name and the address of the claimant*)

3  **Reference details**

(*When dealing with large organisations it is important to understand that the information relating to any particular individual's previous dealings with it may not be immediately available, therefore it is important to set out the relevant reference numbers for the matter in dispute and/or the identity of those within the public body who have been handling the particular matter in dispute – see details in section 3*)

4  **The details of the matter being challenged**

(*Set out clearly the matter being challenged, particularly if there has been more than one decision*)

5  **The issue**

(*Set out the date and details of the decision, or act or omission being challenged, a brief summary of the facts and why it is contented to be wrong*)

6  **The details of the action that the defendant is expected to take**

(*Set out the details of the remedy sought, including whether a review or any interim remedy are being requested*)

7  **The details of the legal advisers, if any, dealing with this claim**

(*Set out the name, address and reference details of any legal advisers dealing with the claim*)

8  **The details of any interested parties**

(*Set out the details of any interested parties and confirm that they have been sent a copy of this letter*)

9  **The details of any information sought**

(*Set out the details of any information that is sought. This may include a request for a fuller explanation of the reasons for the decision that is being challenged*)

10  **The details of any documents that are considered relevant and necessary**

(*Set out the details of any documentation or policy in respect of which the disclosure is sought and explain why these are relevant. If you rely on a statutory duty to disclose, this should be specified*)

11  **The address for reply and service of court documents**

(*Insert the address for the reply*)

12 **Proposed reply date**

(*The precise time will depend upon the circumstances of the individual case. However, although a shorter or longer time may be appropriate in a particular case, 14 days is a reasonable time to allow in most circumstances*)

## Section 2 – Address for Sending the Letter Before Claim

Public bodies have requested that, for certain types of cases, in order to ensure a prompt response, letters before claim should be sent to specific addresses.

- **Where the claim concerns a decision in an Immigration, Asylum or Nationality case:**
  - The Judicial Review Management Unit
    UK Border Agency
    1st Floor
    Green Park House
    29 Wellesley Road
    Croydon CR0 2AJ

- **Where the claim concerns a decision by the Legal Services Commission:**
  - The address on the decision letter/notification; and
  - Legal Director
    Corporate Legal Team
    Legal Services Commission
    4 Abbey Orchard Street
    London SW1P 2BS.

- Where the claim concerns a decision by a local authority:
  - The address on the decision letter/notification; and
  - Their legal department

- **Where the claim concerns a decision by a department or body for whom Treasury Solicitor acts** *and Treasury Solicitor has already been involved in the case* a copy should also be sent, quoting the Treasury Solicitor's reference, to:
  - The Treasury Solicitor,
    One Kemble Street,
    London,
    WC2B 4TS

- In all other circumstances, the letter should be sent to the address on the letter notifying the decision.

## Section 3 – Specific Reference Details Required

Public bodies have requested that the following information should be provided in order to ensure prompt response.

- **Where the claim concerns an Immigration, Asylum or Nationality case, dependent upon the nature of the case:**
  - The Home Office reference number
  - The Port reference number
  - The Asylum and Immigration Tribunal reference number
  - The National Asylum Support Service reference number

Or, if these are unavailable:
  – The full name, nationality and date of birth of the claimant.

- **Where the claim concerns a decision by the Legal Services Commission:**
  – The certificate reference number.

## Annex B
## Response to a Letter before Claim

### Information Required in a Response to a Letter Before Claim

#### Proposed Claim for Judicial Review

#### 1 The claimant

(*Insert the title, first and last names and the address to which any reply should be sent*)

#### 2 From

(*Insert the name and address of the defendant*)

#### 3 Reference details

(*Set out the relevant reference numbers for the matter in dispute and the identity of those within the public body who have been handling the issue*)

#### 4 The details of the matter being challenged

(*Set out details of the matter being challenged, providing a fuller explanation of the decision, where this is considered appropriate*)

#### 5 Response to the proposed claim

(*Set out whether the issue in question is conceded in part, or in full, or will be contested. Where it is not proposed to disclose any information that has been requested, explain the reason for this. Where an interim reply is being sent and there is a realistic prospect of settlement, details should be included*)

#### 6 Details of any other interested parties

(*Identify any other parties who you consider have an interest who have not already been sent a letter by the claimant*)

#### 7 Address for further correspondence and service of court documents

(*Set out the address for any future correspondence on this matter*)

## Annex C
## Notes on Public Funding for Legal Costs in Judicial Review

Public funding for legal costs in judicial review is available from legal professionals and advice agencies which have contracts with the Legal Services Commission as part of the Community Legal Service. Funding may be provided for:

- *Legal Help* to provide initial advice and assistance with any legal problem; or

- *Legal Representation* to allow you to be represented in court if you are taking or defending court proceedings. This is available in two forms:
- *Investigative Help* is limited to funding to investigate the strength of the proposed claim. It includes the issue and conduct of proceedings only so far as is necessary to obtain disclosure of relevant information or to protect the client's position in relation to any urgent hearing or time-limit for the issue of proceedings. This includes the work necessary to write a **letter before claim** to the body potentially under challenge, setting out the grounds of challenge, and giving that body a reasonable opportunity, typically 14 days, in which to respond.
- *Full Representation* is provided to represent you in legal proceedings and includes litigation services, advocacy services, and all such help as is usually given by a person providing representation in proceedings, including steps preliminary or incidental to proceedings, and/or arriving at or giving affect to a compromise to avoid or bring to an end any proceedings. Except in emergency cases, a proper **letter before claim** must be sent and the other side must be given an opportunity to respond before *Full Representation* is granted.

Further information on the type(s) of help available and the criteria for receiving that help may be found in the Legal Service Manual Volume 3: '*The Funding Code*'. This may be found on the Legal Services Commission website at: www.legalservices.co.uk

A list of contracted firms and Advice Agencies may be found on the Community Legal Services website at: www.justask.org.uk

# The Tribunal Procedure (Upper Tribunal) Rules 2008

# SI 2008/2698

\*\*\*\*

## PART 4
### JUDICIAL REVIEW PROCEEDINGS IN THE UPPER TRIBUNAL

**27 Application of this Part to judicial review proceedings transferred to the Upper Tribunal**

(1) When a court transfers judicial review proceedings to the Upper Tribunal, the Upper Tribunal –

    (a)    must notify each party in writing that the proceedings have been transferred to the Upper Tribunal; and

    (b)    must give directions as to the future conduct of the proceedings.

(2) The directions given under paragraph (1)(b) may modify or disapply for the purposes of the proceedings any of the provisions of the following rules in this Part.

(3) In proceedings transferred from the Court of Session under section 20(1) of the 2007 Act, the directions given under paragraph (1)(b) must –

    (a)    if the Court of Session did not make a first order specifying the required intimation, service and advertisement of the petition, state the Upper Tribunal's requirements in relation to those matters;

    (b)    state whether the Upper Tribunal will consider summary dismissal of the proceedings; and

    (c)    where necessary, modify or disapply provisions relating to permission in the following rules in this Part.

**28 Applications for permission to bring judicial review proceedings**

(1) A person seeking permission to bring judicial review proceedings before the Upper Tribunal under section 16 of the 2007 Act must make a written application to the Upper Tribunal for such permission.

(2) Subject to paragraph (3), an application under paragraph (1) must be made promptly and, unless any other enactment specifies a shorter time limit, must be sent or delivered to the Upper Tribunal so that it is received no later than 3 months after the date of the decision, action or omission to which the application relates.

(3) An application for permission to bring judicial review proceedings challenging a decision of the First-tier Tribunal may be made later than the time required by paragraph (2) if it is made within 1 month after the date on which the First-tier Tribunal sent –

    (a)    written reasons for the decision; or

    (b)    notification that an application for the decision to be set aside has been unsuccessful, provided that that application was made in time.

(4) The application must state –

(a)    the name and address of the applicant, the respondent and any other person whom the applicant considers to be an interested party;

(b)    the name and address of the applicant's representative (if any);

(c)    an address where documents for the applicant may be sent or delivered;

(d)    details of the decision challenged (including the date, the full reference and the identity of the decision maker);

(e)    that the application is for permission to bring judicial review proceedings;

(f)    the outcome that the applicant is seeking; and

(g)    the facts and grounds on which the applicant relies.

(5) If the application relates to proceedings in a court or tribunal, the application must name as an interested party each party to those proceedings who is not the applicant or a respondent.

(6) The applicant must send with the application –

(a)    a copy of any written record of the decision in the applicant's possession or control; and

(b)    copies of any other documents in the applicant's possession or control on which the applicant intends to rely.

(7) If the applicant provides the application to the Upper Tribunal later than the time required by paragraph (2) or (3) or by an extension of time allowed under rule 5(3)(a) (power to extend time) –

(a)    the application must include a request for an extension of time and the reason why the application was not provided in time; and

(b)    unless the Upper Tribunal extends time for the application under rule 5(3)(a) (power to extend time) the Upper Tribunal must not admit the application.

(8) Except where rule 28A(2)(a) (special provisions for fresh claim proceedings) applies, when the Upper Tribunal receives the application it must send a copy of the application and any accompanying documents to each person named in the application as a respondent or interested party.

Amendments—SI 2009/274; SI 2011/2343.

### 28A  Special provisions for fresh claim proceedings

(1) The Upper Tribunal must not accept an application for permission to bring fresh claim proceedings unless it is either accompanied by any required fee or the Upper Tribunal accepts an undertaking that the fee will be paid.

(2) Within 9 days of making an application referred to in paragraph (1), an applicant must provide –

(a)    a copy of the application and any accompanying documents to each person named in the application as a respondent or an interested party; and

(b)    the Upper Tribunal with a written statement of when and how this was done.

Amendments—Inserted by SI 2011/2343.

**29 Acknowledgment of service**

(1) A person who is sent or provided with a copy of an application for permission under rule 28(8) (application for permission to bring judicial review proceedings) or rule 28A(2) (a) (special provision for fresh claim proceedings) and wishes to take part in the proceedings must provide to the Upper Tribunal an acknowledgment of service so that it is received no later than 21 days after the date on which the Upper Tribunal sent, or in fresh claim proceedings the applicant provided a copy of the application to that person.

(2) An acknowledgment of service under paragraph (1) must be in writing and state –

    (a)    whether the person intends to support or oppose the application for permission;

    (b)    their grounds for any support or opposition under sub-paragraph (a), or any other submission or information which it considers may assist the Upper Tribunal; and

    (c)    the name and address of any other person not named in the application as a respondent or interested party whom the person providing the acknowledgment considers to be an interested party.

(2A) In fresh claim proceedings, a person who provides an acknowledgement of service under paragraph (1) must also provide a copy to –

    (a)    the applicant; and

    (b)    any other person named in the application under rule 28(4)(a) or acknowledgement of service under paragraph (2)(c)

no later than the time specified in paragraph (1).

(3) A person who is provided with a copy of an application for permission under rule 28(8) or (2) (a) but does not provide an acknowledgment of service to the Upper Tribunalmay not take part in the application for permission unless allowed to do so by the Upper Tribunal, but may take part in the subsequent proceedings if the application is successful.

---

Amendments—SI 2009/274; SI 2011/651; SI 2011/2343.

**30 Decision on permission or summary dismissal, and reconsideration of permission or summary dismissal at a hearing**

(1) The Upper Tribunal must send to the applicant, each respondent and any other person who provided an acknowledgment of service to the Upper Tribunal, and may send to any other person who may have an interest in the proceedings, written notice of –

    (a)    its decision in relation to the application for permission; and

    (b)    the reasons for any refusal of the application, or any limitations or conditions on permission.

(2) In proceedings transferred from the Court of Session under section 20(1) of the 2007 Act, where the Upper Tribunal has considered whether summarily to dismiss of the proceedings, the Upper Tribunal must send to the applicant and each respondent, and may send to any other person who may have an interest in the proceedings, written notice of –

    (a)    its decision in relation to the summary dismissal of proceedings; and

(b)     the reasons for any decision summarily to dismiss part or all of the proceedings, or any limitations or conditions on the continuation of such proceedings.

(3) Paragraph (4) applies where the Upper Tribunal, without a hearing –

(a)     determines an application for permission to bring judicial review proceedings and either refuses permission, or gives permission on limited grounds or subject to conditions; or

(b)     in proceedings transferred from the Court of Session, summarily dismisses part or all of the proceedings, or imposes any limitations or conditions on the continuation of such proceedings.

(4) In the circumstances specified in paragraph (3) the applicant may apply for the decision to be reconsidered at a hearing.

(5) An application under paragraph (4) must be made in writing and must be sent or delivered to the Upper Tribunal so that it is received within 14 days, or in fresh claim proceedings 9 days, after the date on which the Upper Tribunal sent written notice of its decision regarding the application to the applicant.

**Amendments**—SI 2011/2343.

### 31 Responses

(1) Any person to whom the Upper Tribunal has sent notice of the grant of permission under rule 30(1) (notification of decision on permission), and who wishes to contest the application or support it on additional grounds, must provide detailed grounds for contesting or supporting the application to the Upper Tribunal.

(2) Any detailed grounds must be provided in writing and must be sent or delivered to the Upper Tribunal so that they are received not more than 35 days after the Upper Tribunal sent notice of the grant of permission under rule 30(1).

### 32 Applicant seeking to rely on additional grounds

The applicant may not rely on any grounds, other than those grounds on which the applicant obtained permission for the judicial review proceedings, without the consent of the Upper Tribunal.

### 33 Right to make representations

Each party and, with the permission of the Upper Tribunal, any other person, may –

(a)     submit evidence, except at the hearing of an application for permission;

(b)     make representations at any hearing which they are entitled to attend; and

(c)     make written representations in relation to a decision to be made without a hearing.

### 33A Amendments and additional grounds resulting in transfer of proceedings to the High Court in England and Wales

(1) This rule applies only to judicial review proceedings arising under the law of England and Wales.

(2) In relation to such proceedings –

(a)   the powers of the Upper Tribunal to permit or require amendments under rule 5(3)(c) extend to amendments which would, once in place, give rise to an obligation or power to transfer the proceedings to the High Court in England and Wales under section 18(3) of the 2007 Act or paragraph (3);

(b)   except with the permission of the Upper Tribunal, additional grounds may not be advanced, whether by an applicant or otherwise, if they would give rise to an obligation or power to transfer the proceedings to the High Court in England and Wales under section 18(3) of the 2007 Act or paragraph (3).

(3) Where the High Court in England and Wales has transferred judicial review proceedings to the Upper Tribunal under any power or duty and subsequently the proceedings are amended or any party advances additional grounds –

(a)   if the proceedings in their present form could not have been transferred to the Upper Tribunal under the relevant power or duty had they been in that form at the time of the transfer, the Upper Tribunal must transfer the proceedings back to the High Court in England and Wales;

(b)   subject to sub-paragraph (a), where the proceedings were transferred to the Upper Tribunal under section 31A(3) of the Senior Courts Act 1981(power to transfer judicial review proceedings to the Upper Tribunal), the Upper Tribunal may transfer proceedings back to the High Court in England and Wales if it appears just and convenient to do so.

**Amendments**—Inserted by SI 2011/2343.

\*\*\*\*

## 40 Decisions

(1) The Upper Tribunal may give a decision orally at a hearing.

(2) Except where rule 40A (special procedure for providing notice of a decision relating to an asylum case) applies, the Upper Tribunal must provide to each party as soon as reasonably practicable after making a decision which finally disposes of all issues in the proceedings (except a decision under Part 7) –

(a)   a decision notice stating the Tribunal's decision; and

(b)   notification of any rights of review or appeal against the decision and the time and manner in which such rights of review or appeal may be exercised.

(3) Subject to rule 14(11) (prevention of disclosure or publication of documents and information), the Upper Tribunal must provide written reasons for its decision with a decision notice provided under paragraph (2)(a) unless –

(a)   the decision was made with the consent of the parties; or

(b)   the parties have consented to the Upper Tribunal not giving written reasons.

(4) The Upper Tribunal may provide written reasons for any decision to which paragraph (2) does not apply.

(5) In a national security certificate appeal, when the Upper Tribunal provides a notice or reasons to the parties under this rule, it must also provide the notice or reasons to the relevant Minister and the Information Commissioner, if they are not parties.

**Amendments**—SI 2009/274; SI 2009/1975; SI 2010/43; SI 2010/44.

\*\*\*\*

## PART 7
### CORRECTING, SETTING ASIDE, REVIEWING AND APPEALING DECISIONS OF THE UPPER TRIBUNAL

### 44 Application for permission to appeal

(1) A person seeking permission to appeal must make a written application to the Upper Tribunal for permission to appeal.

(2) Paragraph (3) applies to an application under paragraph (1) in respect of a decision –

    (a)    on an appeal against a decision in a social security and child support case (as defined in the Tribunal Procedure (First-tier Tribunal) (Social Entitlement Chamber) Rules 2008);

    (b)    on an appeal against a decision in proceedings in the War Pensions and Armed Forces Compensation Chamber of the First-tier Tribunal;

    (ba)    on an appeal against a decision of a Pensions Appeal Tribunal for Scotland or Northern Ireland; or

    (c)    in proceedings under the Forfeiture Act 1982.

(3) Where this paragraph applies, the application must be sent or delivered to the Upper Tribunal so that it is received within 3 months after the date on which the Upper Tribunal sent to the person making the application –

    (a)    written notice of the decision;

    (b)    notification of amended reasons for, or correction of, the decision following a review; or

    (c)    notification that an application for the decision to be set aside has been unsuccessful.

(3A) An application under paragraph (1) in respect of a decision in an asylum case or an immigration case must be sent or delivered to the Upper Tribunal so that it is received within the appropriate period after the Upper Tribunal or, as the case may be in an asylum case, the Secretary of State for the Home Department, sent any of the documents in paragraph (3) to the party making the application.

(3B) The appropriate period referred to in paragraph (3A) is as follows –

    (a)    where the person who appealed to the First-tier Tribunal is in the United Kingdom at the time that the application is made –
        (i)    twelve working days; or
        (ii)    if the party making the application is in detention under the Immigration Acts, seven working days; and

    (b)    where the person who appealed to the First-tier Tribunal is outside the United Kingdom at the time that the application is made, thirty eight days.

(3C) Where a notice of decision is sent electronically or delivered personally, the time limits in paragraph (3B) are –

    (a)    in sub-paragraph (a)(i), ten working days;

    (b)    in sub-paragraph (a)(ii), five working days; and

    (c)    in sub-paragraph (b), ten working days.

(3D) An application under paragraph (1) in respect of a decision in a financial services case must be sent or delivered to the Upper Tribunal so that it is received within 14 days after the date on which the Upper Tribunal sent to the person making the application –

    (a)    written notice of the decision;

    (b)    notification of amended reasons for, or correction of, the decision following a review; or

    (c)    notification that an application for the decision to be set aside has been unsuccessful.

(4) Where paragraph (3), (3A) or (3D) does not apply, an application under paragraph (1) must be sent or delivered to the Upper Tribunal so that it is received within 1 month after the latest of the dates on which the Upper Tribunal sent to the person making the application –

    (a)    written reasons for the decision;

    (b)    notification of amended reasons for, or correction of, the decision following a review; or

    (c)    notification that an application for the decision to be set aside has been unsuccessful.

(5) The date in paragraph (3)(c) or (4)(c) applies only if the application for the decision to be set aside was made within the time stipulated in rule 43 (setting aside a decision which disposes of proceedings) or any extension of that time granted by the Upper Tribunal.

(6) If the person seeking permission to appeal provides the application to the Upper Tribunal later than the time required by paragraph (3), (3A), (3D) or (4), or by any extension of time under rule 5(3)(a) (power to extend time) –

    (a)    the application must include a request for an extension of time and the reason why the application notice was not provided in time; and

    (b)    unless the Upper Tribunal extends time for the application under rule 5(3)(a) (power to extend time) the Upper Tribunal must refuse the application.

(7) An application under paragraph (1) must –

    (a)    identify the decision of the Tribunal to which it relates;

    (b)    identify the alleged error or errors of law in the decision; and

    (c)    state the result the party making the application is seeking.

**Amendments**—SI 2009/274; SI 2010/44; SI 2010/747; SI 2011/651.

### 45 Upper Tribunal's consideration of application for permission to appeal

(1) On receiving an application for permission to appeal the Upper Tribunal may review the decision in accordance with rule 46 (review of a decision), but may only do so if –

(a)    when making the decision the Upper Tribunal overlooked a legislative provision or binding authority which could have had a material effect on the decision; or

(b)    since the Upper Tribunal's decision, a court has made a decision which is binding on the Upper Tribunal and which, had it been made before the Upper Tribunal's decision, could have had a material effect on the decision.

(2) If the Upper Tribunal decides not to review the decision, or reviews the decision and decides to take no action in relation to the decision or part of it, the Upper Tribunal must consider whether to give permission to appeal in relation to the decision or that part of it.

(3) The Upper Tribunal must send a record of its decision to the parties as soon as practicable.

(4) If the Upper Tribunal refuses permission to appeal it must send with the record of its decision –

(a)    a statement of its reasons for such refusal; and

(b)    notification of the right to make an application to the relevant appellate court for permission to appeal and the time within which, and the method by which, such application must be made.

(5) The Upper Tribunal may give permission to appeal on limited grounds, but must comply with paragraph (4) in relation to any grounds on which it has refused permission.

****

# Practice Direction – Fresh Claim Judicial Review in the Immigration and Asylum Chamber of the Upper Tribunal

17 October 2011

## Part 1
## Preliminary

### *1 Interpretation*

1.1 In these Practice Directions:-

'applicant' has the same meaning as in the UT Rules;
'the application' means the written application under rule 28 for permission to bring judicial review proceedings;
'fresh claim proceedings' has the same meaning as in the UT Rules;
'party' has the same meaning as in the UT Rules;
'respondent' has the same meaning as in the UT Rules;
'the Tribunal' means the Immigration and Asylum Chamber of the Upper Tribunal;
'UKBA' means the UK Border Agency of the Home Office;
'UT Rules' means the Tribunal Procedure (Upper Tribunal) Rules 2008 and 'rule', followed by a number, means the rule bearing that number in the UT Rules.

## Part 2
## Scope

### *2 Scope*

2.1 Parts 3 and 4 of these Practice Directions apply to fresh claim proceedings.

2.2 Part 5 of these Practice Directions applies to proceedings to which Part 3 applies, where:-

(a)    a person has been served with a copy of directions for that person's removal from the United Kingdom by UKBA and notified that Part 5 applies; and

(b)    that person makes an application to the Tribunal or a court for permission to bring judicial review proceedings or to apply for judicial review, before the removal takes effect.

2.3 In the case of proceedings transferred to the Tribunal by a court, the Tribunal will expect the applicant to have complied with all relevant Practice Directions of that court that applied up to the point of transfer.

In the event of non-compliance, the Tribunal will make such directions pursuant to rule 27(1)(b) as are necessary and which may, in particular, include applying provisions of these Practice Directions.

## Part 3
## General Provisions

The application to bring judicial review proceedings

### 3 Form of application

3.1 The application must be made using the form displayed on the Upper Tribunal's website at the time the application is made.

### 4 Additional materials to be filed with the application

4.1 Without prejudice to rule 28, the application must be accompanied by:-

   (a)   any written evidence on which it is intended to rely (but see paragraph 4.2 below);

   (b)   copies of any relevant statutory material; and

   (c)   a list of essential documents for advance reading by the Tribunal (with page references to the passages relied on).

4.2 The applicant may rely on the matters set out in the application as evidence under this Practice Direction if the application is verified by a statement of truth.

### 5 Bundle of documents to be sent etc. with the application

5.1 The applicant must file two copies of a paginated and indexed bundle containing all the documents required by rule 28 and these Practice Directions to be sent or delivered with the application.

### 6 Permission without a hearing

6.1 The Tribunal will generally, in the first instance, consider the question of permission without a hearing.

THE SUBSTANTIVE HEARING

### 7 Additional grounds at the substantive hearing

7.1 Where an applicant who has been given permission to bring judicial review proceedings intends to apply under rule 32 to rely on additional grounds at the substantive hearing, the applicant must give written notice to the Tribunal and to any other person served with the application, not later than 7 working days before that hearing.

### 8 Skeleton arguments for the substantive hearing

8.1 The applicant must serve a skeleton argument on the Tribunal and on any other person served with the application, not later than 21 days before the substantive hearing.

8.2 The respondent and any other party wishing to make representations at the hearing must serve a skeleton argument on the Tribunal and on the applicant, not later than 14 days before the hearing.

8.3 Skeleton arguments must contain:-

(a)   a time estimate for the complete hearing, including the giving of the decision by the Tribunal;

(b)   a list of issues;

(c)   a list of the legal points to be taken (together with any relevant authorities with page references to the passages relied on);

(d)   a chronology of events (with page references to the bundle of documents (see Practice Direction 9 below);

(e)   a list of essential documents for the advance reading of the Tribunal (with page references to the passages relied on) (if different from that served with the application) and a time estimate for that reading; and

(f)   a list of persons referred to.

## 9  Bundle of documents for the substantive hearing

9.1 The applicant must serve on the Tribunal and any other person served with the application a paginated and indexed bundle of all relevant documents required for the substantive hearing, when the applicant's skeleton argument is served.

9.2 The bundle must also include those documents required by the respondent and any other person who is expected to make representations at the hearing.

## 10  Agreed final order

10.1 If the parties agree about the final order to be made, the applicant must file at the Tribunal a document (with 2 copies) signed by all the parties setting out the terms of the proposed agreed order, together with a short statement of the matters relied on as justifying the proposed agreed order and copies of any authorities or statutory provisions relied on.

10.2 The Tribunal will consider the documents referred to in paragraph 10.1 above and will make the order if satisfied that the order should be made.

10.3 If the Tribunal is not satisfied that the order should be made, a hearing date will be set.

## Part 4
## Urgent Applications For Permission To Bring Judicial Review Proceedings

## 11  Request for Urgent Consideration

11.1 Where it is intended to request the Tribunal to deal urgently with the application or where an interim injunction is sought, the applicant must serve with the application a written 'Request for Urgent Consideration', in the form displayed on the Upper Tribunal's website at the time the application is made, which states:

(a)   the need for urgency;

(b)    the timescale sought for the consideration of the application (eg. within 72 hours or sooner if necessary); and

(c)    the date by which the substantive hearing should take place.

11.2 Where an interim injunction is sought, the applicant must, in addition, provide:

(a)    the draft order; and

(b)    the grounds for the injunction.

## 12 Notifying the other parties

12.1 The applicant must serve (by fax and post) the application form and the Request for Urgent Consideration on the respondent and interested parties, advising them of the application and that they may make representations.

12.2 Where an interim injunction is sought, the applicant must serve (by fax and post) the draft order and grounds for the injunction on the respondent and interested parties, advising them of the application and that they may make representations.

## 13 Consideration by Tribunal

13.1 The Tribunal will consider the application within the time requested and may make such order as it considers appropriate.

13.2 If the Tribunal specifies that a hearing shall take place within a specified time, the representatives of the parties must liaise with the Tribunal and each other to fix a hearing of the application within that time.

## Part 5
## Applications Which Challenge Removal

## 14 General

14.1 The requirements contained in this Part are additional to those contained in Part 3 and (where applicable) Part 4 of these Practice Directions.

14.2 Nothing in these Practice Directions prevents a person from making the application after that person has been removed from the United Kingdom.

## 15 Special requirements regarding the application

15.1 Without prejudice to rule 28, the application must:-

(a)    indicate on its face that this Part of these Practice Directions applies; and

(b)    be accompanied by:

    (i)    a copy of the removal directions and the decisions to which the application relates; and

    (ii)    any document served with the removal directions including any document which contains UKBA's factual summary of the case; and

(c)    contain or be accompanied by the detailed statement of the applicant's grounds for making the application.

15.2 If the applicant is unable to comply with paragraph 15.1(b) or (c) above, the application must contain or be accompanied by a statement of the reasons why.

15.3 Notwithstanding rule 28A, immediately upon issue of the application, the applicant must send copies of the issued application form and accompanying documents to the address specified by the United Kingdom Border Agency.

## 16 Referral in case of non- compliance

16.1 Where the applicant has not complied with Practice Direction 15.1(b) or (c) above and has provided reasons for not complying, and the Tribunal has issued the application form, the Tribunal's staff will:-

(a)    refer the matter to a Judge for consideration as soon as practicable; and
(b)    notify the parties that they have done so.

## 17 Application clearly without merit

17.1 If, upon a refusal to grant permission to bring judicial review proceedings, the Tribunal indicates that the application is clearly without merit, that indication will be included in the order refusing permission.

These Practice Directions are made by the Senior President of Tribunals with the agreement of the Lord Chancellor. They are made in the exercise of powers conferred by the Tribunals, Courts and Enforcement Act 2007.

**Lord Justice Carnwath**

*Senior President Of Tribunals*

# Administrative Court Guidance
# Notes for Guidance on Applying for Judicial Review

## Section 1
## General Introduction

1. These notes are not intended to be exhaustive but are designed to offer an outline of the procedure to be followed when seeking to make an application for judicial review in the Administrative Court. For further details of the procedure to be followed you and your epresentatives/legal advisers should consult Part 54 of the Civil Procedure Rules (CPR) and the Practice Directions accompanying Part 54.

## Section 2
## What is judicial review?

2.1 Judicial review is the procedure by which you can seek to challenge the decision, action or failure to act of a public body such as a government department or a local authority or other body exercising a public law function. If you are challenging the decision of a court, the jurisdiction of judicial review extends only to decisions of inferior courts. It does not extend to decisions of the High Court or Court of Appeal. Judicial review must be used where you are seeking:

- a mandatory order (i.e. an order requiring the public body to do something and formerly known as an order of mandamus);
- a prohibiting order (i.e. an order preventing the public body from doing something and formerly known as an order of prohibition); or
- a quashing order (i.e. an order quashing the public body's decision and formerly known as an order of certiorari)
- a declaration
- HRA Damages

2.2 Claims can either be heard by a single Judge or a Divisional Court (a court of two judges). The Administrative Court sits at the following locations, although in appropriate cases arrangements may be made for sittings at alternative locations:

- **The Royal Courts of Justice in London** – (address for correspondence: Room C315, Royal Courts of Justice, Strand, London, WC2A 2LL);
- **Birmingham Civil Justice Centre** – (address for correspondence: Priory Courts, 33 Bull Street, Birmingham, B4 6DS);
- **Cardiff Civil Justice Centre** – (address for correspondence:2 Park Street, Cardiff, CF10 1ET);
- **Leeds Combined Court Centre** – (address for correspondence:1 Oxford Row, Leeds, LS1 3BG);
- **Manchester Civil Justice Centre** – (address for correspondence:1 Bridge Street West, Manchester, M3 3FX)

## Section 3
## What is the pre-action protocol?

3.1 The protocol sets out a code of good practice and contains the steps which parties should generally follow before making a claim for judicial review. The objective of the pre-action protocol is to avoid unnecessary litigation.

3.2 Before making your claim for judicial review, you should send a letter to the defendant. The purpose of this letter is to identify the issues in dispute and establish whether litigation can be avoided. The letter should contain the date and details of the decision, act or omission being challenged and a clear summary of the facts on which the claim is based. It should also contain the details of any relevant information that the claimant is seeking and an explanation of why this is considered relevant. A claim should not normally be made until the proposed reply date given in the letter before claim has passed, unless the circumstances of the case require more immediate action to be taken.

3.3 Defendants should normally respond to that letter within 14 days and sanctions may be imposed unless there are good reasons for not responding within that period.

NB – The protocol does not affect the time limit specified by CPR Part 54.5(1) namely that an application for permission to apply for judicial review must be made promptly and in any event not later than 3 months after the grounds upon which the claim is based first arose.

NB – You should seek advice as to whether the protocol is appropriate in the circumstances of your case. Use of the protocol will not be appropriate where the defendant does not have the legal power to change the decision being challenged. It also may not be appropriate in circumstances where the application is urgent.

NB – A letter before claim will not automatically stop the implementation of a disputed decision.

NB – Even in emergency cases, it is good practice to fax the draft claim form that you are intending to issue to the defendant. You will also normally be required to notify a defendant when you are seeking an interim order; i.e. an order giving some form of relief pending the final determination of the claim.

3.4 Any claim for judicial review must indicate whether or not the protocol has been complied with. If the protocol has not been complied with, the reasons for failing to do so should be set out in the claim form.

## Section 4
## Where should I commence proceedings?

4.1 Claims for judicial review under CPR Part 54 are dealt with in the Administrative Court.

4.2 Claims may be issued at the District Registry of the High Court at Birmingham, Cardiff, Leeds or Manchester as well as at the Royal Courts of Justice in London. Cases started in Birmingham will normally be determined at a court in the Midland region; in Cardiff in Wales; in Leeds in the North-Eastern Region; in London at the Royal Courts of Justice and in Manchester, in the North-Western Region.

4.3 The general expectation is that proceedings will be administered and determined in the region with which the claimant has the closest connection, subject to the following considerations as applicable –

(1)   any reason expressed by any party for preferring a particular venue;
(2)   the region in which the defendant, or any relevant office or department of the defendant, is based;
(3)   the region in which the claimant's legal representatives are based;
(4)   the ease and cost of travel to a hearing;
(5)   the availability and suitability of alternative means of attending a hearing (for example, by videolink);
(6)   the extent and nature of media interest in the proceedings in any particular locality;
(7)   the time within which it is appropriate for the proceedings to be determined;
(8)   whether it is desirable to administer or determine the claim in another region in the light of the volume of claims issued at, and the capacity, resources and workload of, the court at which it is issued;
(9)   whether the claim raises issues sufficiently similar to those in another outstanding claim to make it desirable that it should be determined together with, or immediately following, that other claim; and
(10)  whether the claim raises devolution issues and for that reason whether it should more appropriately be determined in London or Cardiff.

## Can I get Legal Services Commission funding (Legal Aid) for my application?

4.4 Neither the Court nor the Administrative Court Offices have power to grant funding (previously legal aid). The responsibility for the provision of public funding is held by the Legal Services Commission.

4.5 Further information on the type(s) of help available and the criteria for receiving that help may be found on the Legal Services Commission website at http://www.legalservices.gov.uk/.

4.6 A list of contracted firms and Advice Agencies may be found on the Community Legal Services website at http://www.communitylegaladvice.org.uk/. Community Legal Advice can also provide you with a list of solicitors in your area if you telephone them on 0845 345 4 345.

## Section 5
## When should I lodge my application for permission to apply for judicial review?

5.1 The claim form must be filed promptly and in any event not later than three months after the grounds upon which the claim is based first arose (CPR Part 54.5).

5.2 The court has the power to extend the period for the lodging of an application for permission to apply for judicial review but will only do so where it is satisfied there are very good reasons for doing so.

NB – The time for the lodging of the application may not be extended by agreement between the parties.

NB – If you are seeking an extension of time for the lodging of your application, you must make the application in the claim form, setting out the grounds in support of that application to extend time (CPR Part 54.5).

## Section 6
## Is there a fee to pay and if so, when should I pay it?

6.1 A fee of £60.00 is payable when you lodge your application for permission to apply for Judicial Review. A further £215.00 is payable if you wish to pursue the claim if permission is granted (Civil Proceedings Fees (Amendment) Order 2011).

NB – If you are in receipt of certain types of benefits you may be entitled to remission of any fee due as part of judicial review proceedings. If you believe you may be entitled to fee remission you should apply to the relevant Administrative Court Office using Form

EX160 (Application for a Fee Remission) and lodge the application with your claim form.

NB – Cheques should be made payable to HMCTS. If you lodge your claim form at the court office in person, personal cheques must be supported by a cheque guarantee card presented at the time the claim form is lodged.

Fees may be paid by credit or debit card in London when presented in person to the Royal Courts of Justice Fees Office. The Administrative Court Office in Cardiff will accept payment by debit card **only** when presented in person at their office, and the Birmingham and Manchester offices accept payment by both credit and debit cards at their counters and over the telephone.

At the present time, the Administrative Court Office in Leeds does not accept payment of fees by credit or debit card.

## Section 7
## How do I apply for judicial review?

7.1 An application for permission to apply for judicial review must be made by claim form (Form N461).

7.2 The claim form must include or be accompanied by —

- a detailed statement of the claimant's grounds for bringing the claim for judicial review;
- a statement of the facts relied on;
- any application to extend the time limit for filing the claim form; and
- any application for directions.

7.3 Where you are seeking to raise any issue under the Human Rights Act 1998, or a remedy available under that Act, the claim form must include the information required by paragraph 16 of the Practice Direction supplementing Part 16 of the Civil Procedure Rules.

7.4 Where you intend to raise a devolution issue, the claim form must specify that you (a) wish to raise a devolution issue (b) identify the relevant provisions of the Government of Wales Act 1998, and (c) contain a summary of the facts, circumstances and points of law on the basis of which it is alleged that a devolution issue arises. Cases involving Welsh devolution issues are expected to be lodged at the Administrative Court Office in Wales.

7.5 The claim form must also be accompanied by

- any written evidence in support of the claim or application to extend time;
- a copy of any order that you are seeking to have quashed;
- where the claim for judicial review relates to a decision of a court or tribunal, an approved copy of the reasons for reaching that decision;
- copies of any documents upon which you propose to rely;
- copies of any relevant statutory material;
- a list of essential documents for advance reading by the court (with page references to the passages relied upon). Where only part of a page needs to be read, that part should be indicated, by side-lining or in some other way, but not by highlighting.

NB – Where it is not possible for you to file all the above documents, you must indicate which documents have not been filed and the reasons why they are not currently available. The defendant and/or the interested party may seek an extension of time for the lodging of its acknowledgement of service pending receipt of the missing documents.

## *What documents do I need to lodge?*

7.6 You must file the original claim form and witness statement, together with a set of paginated and indexed copy documents for the courts use containing the documents referred to in paragraph 7.5 above (CPR Part 54.6 and Practice Direction 54). You should also file a complete set of copy documents (including a copy claim form and witness statement) in a paginated and indexed set for the courts use. Please ensure you paginate in consecutive page number order throughout your bundle. Also ensure that each page has a page number on it and provide an index, which lists the description of documents contained in your bundle together with their page reference numbers.

7.7 Please note that if your case is of a criminal nature then the Court will require you to lodge two paginated and indexed bundles of copy documents.

7.8 You must also lodge sufficient additional copies of the claim form for the court to seal them (i.e. stamp them with the court seal) so that you can serve them on the defendant and any interested parties. The sealed copies will be returned to you so that you can serve them on the defendant and any interested parties.

7.9 If you are represented by solicitors they must also provide a paginated, indexed bundle of the relevant legislative provisions and statutory instruments required for the proper consideration of the application. If you are acting in person you should comply with this requirement if possible.

NB – Applications that do not comply with the requirements of CPR Part 54 and Practice Direction 54 will not be accepted, save in exceptional circumstances. In this context a matter will be regarded as exceptional where a decision is sought from the Court within 14 days of the lodging of the application. In such circumstances an undertaking will be required to provide compliance with the requirements of the CPR within a specified period.

NB – If the only reason given in support of urgency is the imminent expiry of the three month time limit for lodging an application, the papers will nonetheless be returned for compliance with Part 54 and Practice Direction 54. In those circumstances you must seek an extension of time and provide reasons for the delay in lodging the papers in proper form.

## *Whom should I serve my application on?*

7.10 The sealed copy claim form (and accompanying documents) must be served on the defendant and any person that you consider to be an interested party (unless the court directs otherwise) within 7 days of the date of issue (i.e. the date shown on the court seal). The Administrative Court Office will not serve your claim on the defendant or any interested party.

NB – An interested party is a person who is likely to be directly affected by your judicial review application.

NB – Please note that under the provisions of the Crown Proceedings Act 1947 service must be upon the Department responsible for the Defendant.

NB – Where the claim for judicial review relates to proceedings in a court or tribunal, any other parties to those proceedings must be named in the claim form as interested parties and served with the claim form (CPR 54 PD.5). For example, in a claim by a defendant in a criminal case in the Magistrates' or Crown Court for judicial review of a decision in that case, the prosecution must always be named as an interested party.

7.11 You should lodge a Certificate of Service in Form N215 in the relevant Administrative Court Office within 7 days of serving the defendant and other interested parties.

7.12 The date of deemed service is calculated in accordance with CPR part 6.14 (see methods of service below).

| **Method** – First class post, Document Exchange (DX) or other service which provides for delivery on the next business day. | **Deemed date of service** – The second business day after it was posted, left with, delivered to or collected by the relevant service provider provided that day is a business day; or if not, the next business day after that.;- |
|---|---|
| | Posted — Deemed served<br>Monday — Wednesday<br>Tuesday — Thursday<br>Wednesday — Friday<br>Thursday — Monday<br>Friday — Monday |
| | **Please note:** If the service date falls on a Public Holiday the deemed service date is the first working day following the Public Holiday. |
| Method – Delivering the document to or leaving it at the relevant place. | Deemed date of service – Where it is delivered to or left at the relevant place before 12.00 midnight, on the second business day after that day. |
| Method – Fax | Deemed date of service – The second business day after the transmission of the fax (e.g. if the fax is sent at 10.30pm on Monday, it will be deemed served on Wednesday. |
| Method – Other electronic method e.g. e-mail | Deemed date of service – The second business day after sending the email or other electronic transmission. |
| Method – Personal Service | Deemed date of service – The second business day after completing the relevant step required by CPR 6.5 (3). |

NB – The time for a Defendant and any Interested Party to lodge an acknowledgement of service (21 days) commences from the date that the claim is deemed served upon them.

## Section 8
## What do I do if my application is urgent?

8.1 If you want to make an application for your application for permission to be heard/considered by a Judge as a matter of urgency and/or to seek an interim injunction, you must complete a Request for Urgent Consideration, Form N463, which can be obtained from the HMCS website or the relevant Administrative Court Office. The form sets out the reasons for urgency and the timescale sought for the consideration of the permission application, e.g. within 72 hours or sooner if necessary, and the date by which the substantive hearing should take place.

8.2 Where you are seeking an interim injunction, you must, in addition, provide a draft order; and the grounds for the injunction. You must serve the claim form, the draft order and the application for urgency on the defendant and interested parties (by FAX and by post), advising them of the application and informing them that they may make representations directly to the Court in respect of your application.

8.3 A judge will consider the application within the time requested and may make such order as he/she considers appropriate.

NB – The judge may refuse your application for permission at this stage if he/she considers it appropriate, in the circumstances, to do so.

8.4 If the Judge directs that an oral hearing must take place within a specified time the Administrative Court Office will liaise with you and the representatives of the other parties to fix a permission hearing within the time period directed.

8.5 Where a manifestly inappropriate urgency application is made, consideration may, in appropriate cases, be given to making a wasted costs order.

## Section 9
## What is an acknowledgement of service?

9.1 Any person who has been served with the claim form and who wishes to take part in the judicial review should file an acknowledgment of service (Form N462) in the Administrative Court Office, within 21 days of the proceedings being served upon them.

NB – Whilst there is no requirement upon you to serve the defendant and any interested party with a Form N462 for completion by them, it is good practice to do so.

9.2 The acknowledgement of service must set out the summary of grounds for contesting the claim and the name and address of any person considered to be an interested party (who has not previously been identified and served as an interested party).

9.3 The acknowledgement of service must be served upon you and the interested parties no later than 7 days after it is filed with the court.

NB – Failure to file an acknowledgement of service renders it necessary for the party concerned to obtain the permission of the court to take part in any oral hearing of the application for permission.

## Section 10
## What happens after the defendant and/or the interested party has lodged an acknowledgement of service, or the time for lodging such has expired?

10.1 Applications for permission to proceed with the claim for judicial review are considered by a single judge on the papers. The purpose of this procedure is to ensure that applications are dealt with speedily and without unnecessary expense.

10.2 The papers will be forwarded to the judge by the Administrative Court Office upon receipt of the Acknowledgement of Service or at the expiry of the time limit for lodging such acknowledgement – whichever is earlier.

10.3 The judge's decision and the reasons for it (Form JRJ) will be served upon you, the defendant and any other person served with the claim form.

10.4 If the judge grants permission and you wish to pursue the claim, you must lodge a further fee of £215.00 (or a further Application for Remission of Fee (Form EX160) with the relevant Administrative Court Office within 7 days of service of the judge's decision upon you.

NB – If you do not lodge the additional fee, your file will be closed.

## Section 11
## What happens if my application for permission is refused, or if permission is granted subject to conditions or in part only?

11.1 If permission is refused, or is granted subject to conditions or on certain grounds only, you may request a reconsideration of that decision at an oral hearing.

11.2 Request for an oral hearing must be made on the Notice of Renewal, Form 86b, (a copy of which will be sent to you at the same time as the judge's decision) and must be filed within 7 days after service of the notification of the judge's decision upon you (CPR Part 54.11 & 54.12).

11.3 Where the judge directs an oral hearing or you renew your application after refusal following consideration on paper, you may appear in person or be represented by an advocate (if you are legally represented). If you are not legally represented you may seek the court's permission to have someone speak on your behalf at the hearing.

NB – Any application for permission to have someone speak on your behalf should be made to the judge hearing the application who will make such decision as he considers appropriate in all of the circumstances.

11.4 Notice of the hearing is given to you, the defendant and any interested party by the Administrative Court List Office. An oral hearing is allocated a total of 30 minutes of court time. If it is considered that 30 minutes of court time is insufficient, you may provide a written estimate of the time required for the hearing and request a special fixture.

11.5 Neither the defendant nor any other interested party need attend a hearing on the question of permission unless the court directs otherwise.

## Section 12
## What happens if my application for permission is granted?

12.1 On granting permission the court may make case management directions under CPR 54.10(1) for the progression of the case. Case management directions may include directions as to venue, as to the service of the claim form and any evidence on other persons and as to expedition.

12.2 Where a claim is made under the Human Rights Act 1998, a direction may be made for the giving of notice to the Crown or joining the Crown as a party. In that regard you attention is drawn to the requirements of Civil Procedure rule 19.4A and paragraph 6 of the Practice Direction supplementing Section I of Part 19.

### *When should the defendant/interested party lodge its evidence following the grant of permission?*

12.3 A party upon whom a claim form has been served and who wishes to contest the claim (or support it on additional grounds) must, within 35 days of service of the order granting permission, file and serve on the Court and all of the other parties

- Detailed grounds for contesting the claim or supporting it on additional grounds and
- Any written evidence relied upon.

12.4 Any party who has done so may be represented at the hearing.

12.5 Where the party filing the detailed grounds intends to rely on documents not already filed, a paginated bundle of those documents must be filed at the Court when the detailed grounds are filed.

12.6 The Court has power to extend or abridge the time for lodging evidence.

## Section 13
## What happens when my case is ready for hearing?

13.1 When the time for lodging of evidence by the parties has expired, the case enters a warned list and all parties are informed of this by letter.

13.2 Where a direction has been given for expedition, the case will take priority over other cases waiting to be fixed and enters an expedited warned list.

### *What is the procedure for the listing of a case for hearing?*

NB – The procedure is the same whether you act in person or are legally represented.

13.3 Where advocate's details have been placed on the court record, the parties will be contacted by the relevant Administrative Court List Office in order to seek to agree a date for the hearing. You and advocate's clerks will be offered a range of dates and will have 48 hours to take up one of the dates offered. If the parties fail to contact the List Office within 48 hours, the List Office will fix the hearing on one of the dates offered without further notice and the parties will be notified of that fixture by letter. Where a hearing is listed in this way the hearing will only be vacated by the Administrative Court Office if both parties consent and good reason is provided for the need to vacate the fixture, using the adjournment form available from Administrative Court Listing Offices.

13.4 There may be circumstances where you are unable to attend at court on the date fixed to hear your application, i.e. as a result of illness or accident. If you are unlikely to be able to attend court on the hearing date you must notify the relevant List Office immediately. You should contact the other parties to seek their consent to the adjournment using the adjournment form. If illness is the cause of your inability to attend, a medical certificate should also be provided. Your application for an adjournment will be considered by the Appropriate Officer of the relevant Administrative Court Office.

Please note there is a fee payable for any application to adjourn **unless** the application is made with the consent of all parties and lodged with the court no later than 14 days before the date of the hearing. If you are entitled to fee remission, you must lodge an Application for a Fee Remission (Form Ex160) with your adjournment form.

13.5 Where agreement to an adjournment cannot be reached, a formal application for adjournment must be made to the Court (on notice to all parties) using Form PF244 – Administrative Court Office. Please note that there is a fee payable (£80.00) for any application to adjourn made without the consent of all parties, notwithstanding when it is lodged, unless you are entitled to fee remission, in which case you must lodge an Application for a Fee Remission (Form Ex160) with your application. Where all parties consent to an adjournment within 14 days of the date of the hearing, a fee of £45.00 is payable.

13.6 There are occasions when circumstances, outside the control of the List Office, may necessitate them having to vacate a hearing at very short notice. Sometimes this can be as late as 4.30pm the day before the case is listed. This could be as a result of a case unexpectedly overrunning, a judge becoming unavailable, or other reasons. The List Office will endeavour to re-fix the case on the next available date convenient to the parties.

## What is the short warned list?

13.7 Whilst the Administrative Court usually gives fixed dates for hearings, there is also a need to short warn a number of cases to cover the large number of settlements that occur in the list. Parties in cases that are selected to be short warned will be notified that their case is likely to be listed from a specified date, and that they may be called into the list at less than a day's notice from that date. If the case does not get on during that period, a date as soon as possible after that period will be fixed in consultation with the parties.

## What is a Skeleton Argument and do I need to lodge one?

13.8 A skeleton argument is a document lodged with the court by a party prior to the substantive hearing of any application for judicial review.

13.9 Whilst there is no requirement for a litigant in person to lodge a skeleton argument there is nothing to prevent you from doing so if you wish and if you consider that it would assist the Court.

13.10 If you wish to lodge a skeleton argument you must file it with the Court and serve it on the other parties not less than 21 working days before the date of the hearing of the judicial review or the short warned date, where a case has been "short warned".

13.11 The defendant and any other party wishing to make representations at the hearing of the judicial review must file and serve a skeleton argument not less than 14 working days before the date of the hearing of the judicial review (or the short warned date).

13.12 The skeleton argument must contain:

- A time estimate for the complete hearing, including delivery of judgment;
- A list of issues;
- A list of the legal points to be taken (together with any relevant authorities with page references to the passages relied on);
- A chronology of events (with page references to the bundle of documents);
- A list of essential documents for the advance reading of the court (with page references to the passages relied on) (if different from that filed with the claim form) and a time estimate for that reading; and
- A list of persons referred to.

### *What is a trial bundle and when should I lodge it?*

13.13 You must file a paginated and indexed bundle of all relevant documents required for the hearing of the judicial review whether or not you file a skeleton argument. The bundle must be filed with the court and served on the other parties not less than 21 working days before the hearing.

NB – Two copies of the bundle are required by the Court when the application is to be heard by a Divisional Court.

NB – The bundle must also include those documents required by the defendant and any other party who is to make representations at the hearing.

## Section 14
## What if I need to make an application to the court for further orders/directions after the grant of permission?

14.1 Where case management decisions or directions are sought after permission has been granted, application should be made by way of an application under CPR Part 23, using Form PF244 – Administrative Court Office. You will be required to pay a fee for such application (currently £80.00, or £45.00 if all parties provide their written consent to the order being made), unless you are entitled to fee remission (in which case you should complete and submit a form EX160 with you application).

## Section 15
## Can my substantive application be determined without the need for a hearing?

15.1 The court may decide a claim for judicial review without a hearing where all parties agree (CPR Part 54.18).

## Section 16
## What do I need to do if the proceedings settle by consent prior to the substantive hearing of the application?

16.1 If you reach agreement with the other parties as to the terms of the final order to be made in your claim, you must file at the court a document (with 2 copies) signed by all the parties setting out the terms of the proposed agreed order.

NB – There is a fee of £45.00 payable on lodging the consent order, unless you are entitled to fee remission, in which case you must complete and submit a Form EX 160 (Application for a Fee Remission) with your application.

NB – If you agree with the other parties that a mandatory order etc. is required, the draft order should be accompanied by a statement of reasons (i.e. a short statement of the matters relied on as justifying the proposed agreed order) and copies of any authorities or statutory provisions relied on. If settlement is reached before permission is considered, the draft consent order must include provision for permission to be granted.

NB – Such a statement is not required where the agreement as to disposal (usually by way of withdrawal of the application) requires an order for costs or a detailed assessment of the Claimant's Legal Services Commission costs – in those circumstances the parties should file a draft consent order setting out the terms of settlement signed by all parties.

16.2 The court will consider the documents submitted and will make the order if it is satisfied that the order should be made. If the court is not satisfied that the order should be made, the court will give directions and may direct that a hearing date be set for the matter to be considered further. Section 17

## *What if I want to discontinue the proceedings at any stage?*

Before service of the claim form etc. on the other parties,

17.1 If you have not yet served any of the parties with the sealed claim form and accompanying documents you may discontinue the proceedings by notifying the Court in writing of your intention to do so. The Court will accept a letter of withdrawal provided that you confirm in writing that you have not effected service on the parties.

After service of the claim form etc. on the other parties,

17.2 Discontinuance of a claim is governed by CPR Part 38. Discontinuance renders you liable for the costs incurred by the other parties until the date of discontinuance.

17.3 There is a right to discontinue a claim at any time, except where:

- An interim injunction has been granted or an undertaking has been given – in those circumstances the permission of the court is required to discontinue the proceedings (an example of this would be where bail had been granted pending determination of the application for judicial review)
- Interim payment has been made by defendant – in those circumstances the consent of the defendant or the permission of the court is required to discontinue the proceedings
- There is more than one claimant – in those circumstances the consent of every other claimant or the permission of the court is required to discontinue the proceedings.

17.4 If you wish to discontinue the proceedings at any stage after the service of those proceedings upon the other parties you must file a Notice of Discontinuance in the requisite form (N279) at the relevant Administrative Court Office and serve a copy on every other party.

17.5 A defendant may apply to set aside the Notice of Discontinuance, within 28 days of being served with it (CPR Part 38.4).

NB – If the parties require any order for costs, then a draft order setting out the terms of the order sought is required. A Notice of Discontinuance would not be appropriate in those circumstances.

## Section 18
## Will I be responsible for the costs of the defendant and/or the interested parties if my application is unsuccessful?

18.1 The general rule is that the party losing a substantive claim for judicial review will be ordered to pay the costs of the other parties. However, the Judge considering the matter has discretion to deal with the issue of costs as he/she considers appropriate in all of the circumstances.

NB – Costs may be awarded in respect of an unsuccessful paper application. Any application by the defendant/interested party for costs will normally be made in the Acknowledgment of Service.

## Section 19
## What can I do if I am unhappy with the Judge's decision?

*Civil matters*

### APPEAL AFTER REFUSAL OF PERMISSION

19.1 If you are unhappy with the Court's decision in a civil matter you can appeal to the Court of Appeal Civil Division (with permission of the Court of Appeal (CPR Part 52.15)). Application to the Court of Appeal for permission to Appeal must be made within 7 days of the refusal by the Administrative Court of permission to apply for judicial review.

## APPEAL AFTER SUBSTANTIVE HEARING

19.2 In substantive applications, permission to appeal may be sought from the Administrative Court when it determines the claim for judicial review. If an application for permission to appeal is not made at the conclusion of the case, the application for permission to appeal must be made to the Court of Appeal Civil Division within 21 days (CPR Part 52.3 & 52.4).

19.3 Guidance as to procedure should be sought from the Civil Appeals Office, Royal Courts of Justice, Strand, London, WC2A 2LL.

## *Criminal matters*

## APPEAL AFTER REFUSAL OF PERMISSION

19.4 There is no further remedy in the domestic courts after a refusal of permission by the Administrative Court.

## APPEAL AFTER SUBSTANTIVE HEARING

19.5 If you are unhappy with the Court's decision in a substantive claim for judicial review in a criminal matter, you can appeal to the Supreme Court but only with the leave of the Administrative Court or the Supreme Court and such leave may only be granted if:

(a) The Administrative Court certifies that a point of law of general public importance is involved in its decision; and

(b) It appears to the Administrative Court or the Supreme Court that the point is one which ought to be considered by the Supreme Court. (see The Administration of Justice Act 1960 s.1) .

## Section 20
## Where can I get advice about procedural matters?

20.1 If in doubt about any procedural matter you can contact the relevant Administrative Court Office, telephone numbers below. Court staff cannot give legal advice as to the merits of a case.

- Birmingham Civil Justice Centre – 0121 250 6319;
- Cardiff Civil Justice Centre – 029 2037 6460;
- Leeds Combined Court Centre – 0113 306 2578;
- Manchester Civil Justice Centre – 0161 240 5313;
- The Royal Courts of Justice in London – 020 7947 6655.

20.2 The forms referred to in this guidance can be downloaded from the Justice website

(www.justice.gov.uk).

Updated 1 April 2011

# Administrative Court Listing Policy

## *Listing cases in the Administrative Court*

The following cases are currently awaiting listing in the Administrative Court. The following lists include all cases that entered the warned list and expedited warned lists prior to 10.30am on Monday which are still awaiting substantive hearings, and those cases currently awaiting oral and renewed permission hearings.

## *Lists*

These lists are updated every Monday. Any cases that are entered into lists after 10.30 am on a Monday will appear in next week's lists, subject to any priority listing.

## *Agreeing dates with counsel*

Where counsel has been placed on the court record, their chambers will be contacted by the Administrative Court list office in order to agree a convenient date for the hearing. Counsel's clerks will be offered a range of dates and be given 48 hours to take up one of the dates offered. If counsel's clerks fail to confirm an agreed date with the List Office within 48 hours the court will fix the hearing on one of the dates offered **without further notice.**

Where a hearing is listed in this way, a request to adjourn is unlikely to be granted unless all parties consent to the adjournment. If such request is refused, a formal application for adjournment must be made to the court on notice to the other parties. Please note that there is a fee payable for any request for adjournment unless the request is made by consent **and** lodged with the court no later than 14 days before the date of the hearing. The same procedure is followed where a claimant is in person.

## *Warned and Expedited Warned Lists*

Whilst the Administrative Court usually gives fixed dates for hearings, there is also a need to short warn a number of cases to cover the large number of settlements that occur in the list. Parties in cases that are selected to be short warned will be notified that their case is likely to be listed from a specified date and that they may be listed at less than a day's notice from that date.

Approximately 6 cases are short warned in any specified week. If the case is not listed during that period, a date will be fixed for the hearing in consultation with the parties.
Please note: expedited cases will usually receive a fixed date.

## *Settlement*

If there is good reason why your case should not be listed for hearing at the present time (e.g. a possible settlement is being negotiated; further directions are required etc), please notify the list office immediately on 020 7947 6655, selecting option 1.

# Practice Direction (Judgments: Form and Citation)

**[2001] 1 WLR 194, [2001] 1 All ER 19**

LORD CHIEF JUSTICE
Published 16 January, 2001

Changes intended to make it easier to distribute, store and search judgments, and less expensive and time-consuming to reproduce them for use in court, have been introduced.

In order to facilitate publication of judgments on the World Wide Web, and their subsequent use by those with access to the Web, all judgments in every division of the High Court and the Court of Appeal would be issued with paragraph numbering.

A form of neutral citation of judgments, by means of an official number attributed to the judgment by the court, would apply immediately in all divisions of the Court of Appeal and in the administrative court and would be introduced in other parts of the High Court as soon as practicable.

A reported judgment could be cited by means of a copy of a reproduction of the judgment in electronic form authorised by the publisher of the relevant series of reports, provided that the report was presented to the court in an easily legible form and the advocate presenting it was satisfied that it had not been reproduced in a garbled form from the data source.

Lord Woolf, Lord Chief Justice, sitting in the Court of the Lord Chief Justice, so stated in a practice direction issued and coming into force on January 11, 2001.

**THE LORD CHIEF JUSTICE**

said that the practice direction was made with the concurrence of the Master of the Rolls, the Vice-Chancellor and the President of the Family Division.

It represented the next stage in the process of modernising the arrangements for the preparation, distribution and citation of judgments given in every division of the High Court, whether in London or in courts outside London.

*Form of judgments*

1.1 With effect from January 11, 2001, all judgments in every division of the High Court and the Court of Appeal would be prepared for delivery, or issued as approved judgments, with single spacing, paragraph numbering (in the margins) but no page numbers.

In courts with more than one judge, the paragraph numbering would continue sequentially through each judgment, and would not start again at the beginning of the second judgment. Indented paragraphs would not be given a number.

1.2 The main reason of these changes was to facilitate the publication of judgments on the World Wide Web and their subsequent use by the increasing numbers of those who had access to the Web. The changes should also assist those who used and wished to search judgments stored on electronic databases.

1.3 It was desirable in the interests of consistency that all judgments prepared for delivery, or issued as approved judgments, in county courts, should also contain paragraph numbering (in the margins).

*Neutral citation of judgments*

2.1 With effect from January 11, 2001 a form of neutral citation would be introduced in both divisions of the Court of Appeal and in the administrative court. A unique number would be given by the official shorthand writers to each approved judgment issued out of those courts.

The judgments would be numbered in the following way:

Court of Appeal (Civil Division) ([2000] EWCA Civ 1, 2, 3 etc.

Court of Appeal (Criminal Division) ([2000] EWCA Crim 1, 2, 3 etc.

High Court (Administrative Court) ([2000] EWHC Admin 1, 2, 3 etc.

2.2 Under the new arrangements, paragraph 59 in *Smith v Jones*, the tenth numbered judgment of the year in the Civil Division of the Court of Appeal, would be cited: *Smith v Jones* ([2001] EWCA Civ 10 at [59].

2.3 The neutral citation would be the official number attributed to the judgment by the court and must always be used on at least one occasion when the judgment was cited in a later judgment.

Once the judgment was reported, the neutral citation would appear in front of the familiar citation from the law report series: thus *Smith v Jones* ([2001] EWCA Civ 10 at [30]; [2001] QB 124; [2001] 2 All ER 364, etc).

The paragraph number must be the number allotted by the court in all future versions of the judgment.

2.4 If a judgment was cited on more than one occasion in a later judgment, it would be of the greatest assistance if only one abbreviation, if desired, was used. Thus *Smith v Jones* ([2001] EWCA Civ 10) could be abbreviated on subsequent occasions to *Smith v Jones*, or *Smith's* case, but preferably not both in the same judgment.

2.5 If it was desired to cite more than one paragraph of a judgment each numbered paragraph should be enclosed with a square bracket: thus *Smith v Jones* ([2001] EWCA Civ 10 at [30]-[35], or *Smith v Jones* ([2001] EWCA Civ 10 at [30], [35], and [40]-[43].

2.6 The neutral citation arrangements would be extended to include other parts of the High Court as soon as the necessary administrative arrangements could be made.

2.7 The administrative court citation would be given to all judgments in the administrative court, whether they were delivered by a divisional court or by a single judge.

*Citation of judgments in court*

3.1 For the avoidance of doubt, it should be emphasised that both the High Court and the Court of Appeal required that where a case had been reported in the official *Law Reports* published by the Incorporated Council of Law reporting for England and Wales it had to be cited from that source. Other series of reports could only be used when a case was not reported in the *Law Reports*.

3.2 It would in future be permissible to cite a judgment reported in a series of reports, including those of the Incorporated Council of Law reporting, by means of a copy of a reproduction of the judgment in electronic form that had been authorised by the publisher of the relevant series, provided that:

(i)  the report was presented to the court in an easily legible form (a 12 point font was preferred but a 10 or 11-point font was acceptable)

(ii)  the advocate presenting the report was satisfied that it had not been reproduced in a garbled form from the data source.

In any case of doubt the court would rely on the printed text of the report, unless the editor of the report had certified that an electronic version was more accurate because it corrected an error contained in an earlier printed text of the report.

*Concluding comments*

4.1 The changes described in this practice direction followed what was becoming accepted international practice.

They were intended to make it easier to distribute, store and search judgments, and less expensive and time-consuming to reproduce them for use in court.

Lord Justice Brooke was still responsible for advising the Judges' Council on those matters, and any comments on the new arrangements, or suggestions about ways in which they could be improved still further, should be addressed to him at the Royal Courts of Justice, WC2A 2LL.

# Practice Direction: Upper Tribunal Applications for Judicial Review

**IN THE SUPREME COURT OF ENGLAND AND WALES**

**DIRECTION – CLASSES OF CASES SPECIFIED UNDER SECTION 18(6) OF THE TRIBUNALS, COURTS AND ENFORCEMENT ACT 2007**

It is ordered as follows

1 The following direction takes effect in relation to an application made to the High Court or Upper Tribunal on or after 3 November 2008 that seeks relief of a kind mentioned in section 15(1) of the Tribunals, Courts and Enforcement Act 2007 ("the 2007" Act").

2 The Lord Chief Justice hereby directs that the following classes of case are specified for the purposes of section 18(6) of the 2007 Act –

    a    Any decision of the First-Tier Tribunal on an appeal made in exercise of a right conferred by the Criminal Injuries Compensation Scheme in compliance with section 5(1) of the Criminal Injuries Compensation Act 1996 (appeals against decisions on review); and

    b    Any decision of the First-Tier Tribunal made under Tribunal Procedure Rules or section 9 of the 2007 Act where there is no right of appeal to the Upper Tribunal and that decision is not an excluded decision within paragraph (b), (c) or (f) of section 11(5) of the 2007 Act.

3 This Direction does not have effect where an application seeks (whether or not alone) a declaration of incompatibility under section 4 of the Human Rights Act 1998.

4 This Direction is made by the Lord Chief Justice with the agreement of the Lord Chancellor. It is made in the exercise of powers conferred by section 18(6) of the 2007 Act and in accordance with Part 1 of Schedule 2 to the Constitutional Reform Act 2005.

**The Right Honourable Lord Judge**
**Lord Chief Justice of England and Wales**

# Practice Direction: Upper Tribunal Fresh Claims for Judicial Review

**IN THE SENIOR COURTS OF ENGLAND AND WALES**

**DIRECTION – CLASS OF CASES SPECIFIED FOR THE PURPOSES OF SECTION 18(6) OF THE TRIBUNALS, COURTS AND ENFORCEMENT ACT 2007**

1 The Lord Chief Justice hereby specifies the following classes of case for the purposes of section 18)6) of the Tribunals, Court and Enforcement Act ("the 2007 Act "):

> applications calling into question a decision of the Secretary of State not to treat submissions as an asylum claim or a human rights claim within the meaning of Part 5 of the Nationality, Immigration and Asylum Act 2002 wholly or partly on the basis that they are not significantly different from material that has been previously considered.

2 An application also falls within the class specified in paragraph 1 if, in addition to calling into question a decision of the sort there described, it challenges

(i)     a decision or decisions or remove (or direct the removal of) the applicant from the United Kingdom; or

(ii)    a failure or failures by the Secretary of State to make a decision on submissions said to support an asylum or human rights claim;

both (i) and (ii); but not if it challenges any other decision.

3 This direction takes effect on 17/10/11 in relation to applications made on or after that date to the High Court or Upper Tribunal for judicial review or for permission to apply for judicial review that seek relief of a kind mentioned in section 15(1) of the 2007 Act.

4 For the avoidance of doubt,

(i)     a case which has been transferred under this direction continues to fall within the specified class of case and the Upper Tribunal has the function of deciding the application, where, after transfer, additional material is submitted to the Secretary of State for decision but no decision has been made upon that material;

(ii)    this direction does not have effect where an application seeks a declaration of incompatibility under section 4 of the Human Rights Act 1998, or where the applicant seeks to challenge detention.

5 This direction is made by the Lord Chief Justice with the agreement of the Lord Chancellor. It is made in the exercise of powers conferred by section 18(6) and (7) of the 2007 Act and in accordance with Part 1 of Schedule 2 of the Constitutional Reform Act 2005.

**The Right Honourable Lord Judge**
**Lord Chief Justice of England and Wales**

# INDEX

References are to paragraph numbers.